MW00655622

# Lotto Winning Wheels For POWERBALL & MEGA MILLIONS

Also for...

- California Super Lotto
- Hot Lotto
- Kansas Super Cash
- Wild Card 2
- Trinidad/Tobago Lotto Plus
- Australia Powerball
- England Thunderball
- Greek Tzoker
- India Sikkim Thunderball
- Turkey Sans Topu

Gail Howard

Printed and bound in the United States of America.

Howard, Gail
Lotto Winning Wheels for Powerball & Mega Millions

First Edition Printing 2003
Second Edition 2006

Published by:
Smart Luck Publishers
P.O. Box 81770
Las Vegas, Nevada 89180-1770.
Web Address: www.smartluck.com

ISBN-10: 0-945760-41-8
ISBN-13: 978-0-945760-41-2

# TABLE OF CONTENTS

**Powerball Balanced Wheels – Win 4 with 5 Right**



**Powerball Balanced Wheels – Win 4 with 4 Right**



**Powerball Balanced Wheels – Win 5 with 5 Right**

# POWERBALL & POWERBALL CLONES

Powerball is America's favorite lottery game. Tantalizing jackpots upwards of $100 million have attracted ticket buyers from every segment of the population. Even $200 million jackpots are not uncommon. A record-breaking Powerball jackpot of $365 million was recently won on February 18, 2006.

Lotto began as a game in which all six winning numbers were drawn from one number field. Powerball revolutionized the lotto game by changing the format to two drawings in one – with five numbers drawn from one set of numbers and the sixth number drawn from a separate set of numbers.

This structural enhancement gave lotto players everything they demanded in one game: A super large jackpot, a hefty second prize and more ways to win. The ingenious Powerball innovation was created by Steve Caputo who, at the time, was finance director of the Oregon Lottery. Powerball was introduced to the playing public by the Multi-State Lottery Corporation in April 1992.

Because of its huge success, the Powerball format is widely imitated and has spawned many Powerball wannabes including Mega Millions, Hot Lotto and Wild Card 2. The Powerball format has been copied in Australia, Canada, England, Greece, India, Trinidad/Tobago and Turkey.

As new record-breaking Powerball jackpots generated enviable media coverage, a few individual states replaced lotto with their own Powerball-type games: California Super Lotto, Kansas Super Cash, Lotto Texas and Washington Lotto Plus.

However, after just 150 drawings, Washington's 5/43 + 1/23 Lotto Plus was canceled on October 4, 2003, and replaced with the old 6/49 Lotto game. It took Texas lottery officials 310 drawings to realize that a state even as large as Texas couldn't succeed with its own Powerball-type game. On April 22, 2006, they admitted defeat, cancelled the 5/44 + 1/44 Powerball-type game and reverted to the old 6/54 Lotto game, thereby reducing the odds by half. Canada's 5/39 + 1/5 Wild 5 was terminated on February 5, 2004 after just 175 drawings.

Powerball-type games are better suited to a larger multi-state player base because of the huge odds.

When the odds against winning the jackpot are astronomical, jackpots are seldom won, causing many rollovers to occur. Jackpots of $100 million or more get the attention of the media which in turn promote jackpot fever. Jackpots upwards of $300 million get everyone's attention. The second highest Powerball jackpot was $314.9 million. The winner collected his prize in a cash lump sum of $113 million rather than having it doled out over a period of thirty years. Mega Millions' top prize of $363 million was won in May 2000, when it was called The Big Game.

**Powerball-type games are any lottery games in which the player chooses five numbers from one large set of numbers and also chooses one number from an entirely different set of numbers. To collect the jackpot millions, you must match all six winning numbers.**

In the Multi-State Powerball game you choose five numbers from 1 to 55 and one number from 1 to 42 (5/55 + 1/42). Below are the Powerball-type games being played in the world at the time this book was published in 2006.

| | |
|---|---|
| **5/55 + 1/42** | **Powerball** |
| **5/56 + 1/46** | **Mega Millions** |

| | |
|---|---|
| **5/47 + 1/27** | **California SuperLotto Plus** |
| **5/45 + 1/45** | **Australia Powerball** |
| **5/45 + 1/20** | **Greek Tzoker** |
| **5/42 + 1/15** | **India Thunderball** |
| **5/39 + 1/19** | **Hot Lotto** |
| **5/36 + 1/10** | **Trinidad Lotto Plus** |
| **5/34 + 1/14** | **England Thunderball** |
| **5/34 + 1/14** | **Turkey Sans Topu** |
| **5/32 + 1/25** | **Kansas Super Cash** |
| **5/31 + 1/16** | **Wild Card 2** |

The 5/55 + 1/42 Powerball game is played in 31 jurisdictions: Arizona, Colorado, Connecticut, District of Columbia, Delaware, Idaho, Indiana, Iowa, Kansas, Kentucky, Louisiana, Maine, Minnesota, Missouri, Montana, Nebraska, New Hampshire, New Mexico, North Carolina, North Dakota, Oklahoma, Oregon, Pennsylvania, Rhode Island, South Carolina, South Dakota, Tennessee, Vermont, West Virginia, Wisconsin and the Virgin Islands.

The 5/56 + 1/46 Mega Millions game is played in 12 states: California, Georgia, Illinois, Maryland, Massachusetts, Michigan, New Jersey, New York, Ohio, Texas, Virginia, and Washington State.

The 5/39 + 1/19 Hot Lotto is played in 8 jurisdictions: District of Columbia, Iowa, Kansas, Minnesota, Montana, New Hampshire, South Dakota and West Virginia.

The 5/31 + 1/16 (16 cards) Wild Card 2 is played in four states: Idaho, Montana, North Dakota and South Dakota.

A Powerball-type game is played in 43 states and 7 countries including the Virgin Islands.

Changes in lotteries take place periodically. For the latest updates, visit my web site at **www.smartluck.com**.

**The systems in this book remain the same no matter how many numbers are added to the game, as long as five numbers are chosen from one group of numbers and one additional number is chosen from a separate group of numbers.**

In Mega Millions, the player chooses five numbers from 1 to 56 and one number from an additional set of 46 numbers.

Mega Millions has the highest number of numbers from which the single ball is chosen, which gives it the distinction of having the highest odds against winning of all the Powerball-type games.

In a straight pick-5 (5/55) game, the odds of getting the five winning numbers are one in 3,478,761. In a straight pick-6 (6/55) game, the odds of getting the six winning numbers are less than one in 29 million. But when you have to pick five numbers from one group of 55 numbers and one number from a separate group of 42 numbers, the odds multiply to one in 146 million!

The quantity of Powerball balls in the game makes a huge difference. If the Powerball ball were chosen from 55 balls instead of 42 balls, the odds of winning the jackpot would increase by 45 million to one in 191 million, up from one in 146 million.

Keep in mind that jackpots grow to lotto fever size only when no one wins them for a long time. Lottery officials love that because the higher the jackpot, the more tickets they sell.

If the first prize jackpot were the only prize offered, I would advise you to pass on these games. The odds are just too high to offer more than a glimmer of hope. But since most Powerball-type games have nine prize categories and a worthwhile second prize, they are worth playing. And for a few days between drawings, you can dream dreams, make plans and promises and feel filthy rich.

## PUBLISHED ODDS CHARTS

The PUBLISHED ODDS CHARTS show the actual odds of winning each of the prize categories in each of the Powerball-type games currently in existence. Read the odds in this chart as "your chances are one in ... (whatever the number)".

Or place a dollar sign in front of the odds and you will know the average amount of money you would have to spend on tickets to win each of the prize categories in the various Powerball-type games – if you don't use a Balanced Wheeling System. Although Wild Card 2 gives two plays for a dollar, I gave the odds straight for one play.

Notice that in every game, the odds against winning 2 + 1 are much greater than winning a prize with 3 numbers. The Powerball ball increases the odds in every prize category where it is required.

| 5/56 + 1/46 Mega Millions | |
|---|---|
| 5 + 1 | 175,711,536 |
| 5 | 3,904,701 |
| 4 + 1 | 689,065 |
| 4 | 15,313 |
| 3 + 1 | 13,781 |
| 3 | 306 |
| 2 + 1 | 844 |
| 1 + 1 | 141 |
| 0 + 1 | 75 |

| 5/47 + 1/27 California SuperLotto Plus | |
|---|---|
| 5 + 1 | 41,416,353 |
| 5 | 1,592,937 |
| 4 + 1 | 197,221 |
| 4 | 7,585 |
| 3 + 1 | 4,810 |
| 3 | 185 |
| 2 + 1 | 361 |
| 1 + 1 | 74 |
| 0 + 1 | 49 |

| 5/55 + 1/42 Powerball | |
|---|---|
| 5 + 1 | 146,107,962 |
| 5 | 3,563,609 |
| 4 + 1 | 584,432 |
| 4 | 14,254 |
| 3 + 1 | 11,927 |
| 3 | 291 |
| 2 + 1 | 745 |
| 1 + 1 | 127 |
| 0 + 1 | 69 |

| 5/45 + 1/45 Australia Powerball | |
|---|---|
| 5 + 1 | 9,163,193 |
| 5 | 208,254 |
| 4 + 1 | 45,816 |
| 4 | 1,041 |
| 3 + 1 | 1,175 |
| 3 | 27 |
| 2 + 1 | 93 |

| 5/45 + 1/20<br>Greece Tzoker | |
|---|---|
| 5 + 1 | 24,435,180 |
| 5 | 1,286,062 |
| 4 + 1 | 122,176 |
| 4 | 64,303 |
| 3 + 1 | 3,133 |
| 3 | 165 |
| 2 + 1 | 247 |
| 1 + 1 | 53 |
| 0 + 1 | 19 |

| 5/36 + 1/10<br>Trinidad/Tobago Lotto Plus | |
|---|---|
| 5 + 1 | 3,769,920 |
| 5 | 418,880 |
| 4 + 1 | 24,322 |
| 4 | 2,702 |
| 3 + 1 | 811 |
| 3 | 90 |
| 2 + 1 | 83 |
| 1 + 1 | 26 |
| 0 + 1 | 9 |

| 5/42 + 1/15<br>India Thunderball | |
|---|---|
| 5 + 1 | 12,760,020 |
| 5 | 911,430 |
| 4 + 1 | 68,973 |
| 4 | 4,927 |
| 3 + 1 | 1,916 |
| 3 | 137 |
| 2 + 1 | 164 |
| 1 + 1 | 39 |
| 0 + 1 | 14 |

| 5/34 + 1/14<br>England Thunderball | |
|---|---|
| 5 + 1 | 3,895,584 |
| 5 | 299,660 |
| 4 + 1 | 26,866 |
| 4 | 2,067 |
| 3 + 1 | 960 |
| 3 | 74 |
| 2 + 1 | 107 |
| 1 + 1 | 33 |

| 5/39 + 1/19<br>Hot Lotto | |
|---|---|
| 5 + 1 | 10,939,383 |
| 5 | 607,744 |
| 4 + 1 | 64,349 |
| 4 | 3,575 |
| 3 + 1 | 1,950 |
| 3 | 108 |
| 2 + 1 | 183 |
| 1 + 1 | 47 |
| 0 + 1 | 39 |

| 5/34 + 1/14<br>Turkey Sans Topu | |
|---|---|
| 5 + 1 | 3,895,584 |
| 5 | 299,660 |
| 4 + 1 | 26,866 |
| 4 | 2,067 |
| 3 + 1 | 960 |
| 3 | 74 |
| 2 + 1 | 107 |
| 1 + 1 | 33 |
| 0 + 1 | 13 |

| 5/32 + 1/25 Kansas Super Cash | |
|---|---|
| 5 + 1 | 2,517,200 |
| 5 | 104,883 |
| 4 + 1 | 18,646 |
| 4 | 777 |
| 3 + 1 | 717 |
| 3 | 30 |
| 2 + 1 | 86 |
| 1 + 1 | 29 |

| 5/31 + 1/16 Wild Card 2 | |
|---|---|
| 5 + 1 | 2,718,576 |
| 5 | 181,238 |
| 4 + 1 | 20,912 |
| 4 | 1,394 |
| 3 + 1 | 836 |
| 3 | 56 |
| 2 + 1 | 16 |
| 1 + 1 | 16 |
| 0 + 1 | 16 |

# A FEW WORDS ON PLAYING SMARTER

Before we get into the Powerball-type Balanced Wheeling Systems – which is the purpose of this book – let me give you a few of my basic rules to help you play the game smarter. (All my number selection methods from the simplest to the most complex are covered in great detail in the book, *Lottery Master Guide*.)

Treat the five numbers you mark on one game panel as you would any pick-5 game. The same number selection methods apply. And the five numbers can be wheeled using any of my pick-5 wheeling systems. The main difference is the Minimum and Maximum Prizes you can win with the Powerball Balanced Wheels® in this book.

Lottery numbers are randomly drawn. But randomly drawn numbers form patterns that can be tracked and used to our advantage. Having carefully analyzed the drawing results of more than 160 different lotto games worldwide, with histories going back as far as 1955, I have verified the following incredibly simple rule.

**That which is MOST POSSIBLE happens MOST OFTEN.
That which is LEAST POSSIBLE happens LEAST OFTEN.**

The key to my successful number selection methods is playing the probabilities. If you play a pattern that occurs only five percent of the time, you can expect that pattern to lose 95 percent of the time, giving you no chance to win 95 percent of the time. So, don't buck the probabilities.

## ODD-EVEN TIPS

When you select your numbers, try to have a relatively even mix of odd and even numbers. All odd or all even numbers are rarely drawn, occurring less than three percent of the time. The best mix is to have 3/2 or 2/3 which means three odd and two even, or two odd and three even. One of these two patterns will occur in two-thirds of the drawings.

## HIGH-LOW TIPS

Winning numbers are usually spread across the entire number field. If we take a number field and cut it in half, we have the low half and the high half. In a 55-number game, numbers 1 to 27 would be in the low half, and numbers 28 to 55 would be in the high half. All high or all low numbers are rarely drawn, occurring only three percent of the time.

The best mix is to have 3/2 or 2/3 which means three high and two low, or two high and three low. One of these two patterns will occur in two-thirds of the drawings.

## NUMBER GROUP TIPS

Look at a list of past winning numbers for the game you play and you'll see, more often than not, that one or more of the number groups is not represented. For example, in the combination 5-17-32-49-55, there are no 20's. Tracking and studying Number Groups can help you decide which group to omit and which group to give extra heavy play.

## GAMES SKIPPED TIPS

List the number of games skipped (games out) since the last hit (win) for each of the winning numbers during the last five games. Then mark the number of times each skip occurred. If any skip from 0 to 5 did not occur, play one or more of the numbers that are out that many games.

## REPEAT HITS TIPS

In Powerball-type games, on average, one number will repeat from the last drawing about every other drawing or 40 percent of the time.

## HOT NUMBER TIPS

Numbers that have been out for six losing games *or less* account for about half of the winning numbers. Numbers that have been out for nine losing games or less account for about two-thirds of all the winning numbers. Numbers that have been out for twelve losing games or less account for about three-quarters of all the winning numbers. This tells us that hot numbers are more likely to hit, but don't forget to include at least one long shot in your group of five.

## COLD NUMBER TIPS

It is difficult to know when a number will end a long losing streak. If you play a number every drawing because you think it is "due," you could be chasing it for many months. (Number 45 in New York Lotto sat out 100 drawings before it finally hit.)

Although, when a number has been out for 60 or 70 games, it might be worth chasing.

## POOL YOUR WAY TO RICHES

Several of the 74 lotto jackpots won with my systems were won by groups of people who pooled their money. Sharing the ticket cost with others stretches your lottery budget. By playing with a group you can afford to buy more lottery tickets – and play larger wheeling systems – than you could (or should) by yourself. Draw up an agreement and have the members of your pool sign it.

## CASH IN ON THE LUCK OF OTHERS

When you form a lotto pool or syndicate, your group is also pooling its aggregate luck. A jackpot could happen because of the luck just one member brings to your pool. Select your partners carefully. Share your luck with winners, not with losers. Avoid negative people. Not only are they unlucky, but they dampen enthusiasm and drain energy from others. You want to enhance your own luck, not dilute its strength. One quick way to tell winners from losers is to simply ask them: "Do you think you are a lucky person?" Many people quickly admit, "I'm unlucky. I never win anything."

They won't bring good luck to your group either.

## CASH IN ON A POSITIVE ATTITUDE

No one should play games of chance out of desperation because they need the winnings. The needy have a greater fear of losing the hard-earned money they gamble with. It is just one of life's dirty tricks that the very fear of losing blocks the winning forces. Thoughts are charged with energy, especially when triggered by emotion. Fear attracts exactly that which one fears. A strong desire for a goal that is charged with positive energy, attracts a positive response, especially when every effort is made to attain that goal.

## AVOID COMBINATIONS PREVIOUSLY DRAWN

Many players like to bet the numbers that have won someone else a big jackpot, and by doing so, they are almost guaranteed NOT to win one themselves. In Powerball with two drawings a week, a set of five numbers plus the Powerball Ball has a chance of being drawn once every 1,404,884 years!!! And Mega Millions has a chance of being drawn once every 1,689,534 years!!! This should also answer the question I am so often asked, "Shouldn't I keep playing the same set of numbers every week because they are due to hit sometime?"

## AVOID BETTING FIVE CONSECUTIVE NUMBERS

In nearly 1,500 Powerball drawings, not only have five consecutive numbers never been drawn, but neither have four consecutive numbers. Even three consecutive numbers have been drawn only nine times. Though entirely possible, four consecutive numbers out of five would be a very rare occurrence.

## AVOID BETTING ONE NUMBER GROUP

Never choose all five numbers from one number group, such as all single digits, or all teens, or all 20's, etc.

All five winning numbers drawn from one group is highly unlikely - if not impossible.

## AVOID THE COMBINATION 1-2-3-4-5

The most popular set of numbers most often played is: 1-2-3-4-5 with 6 as the Powerball ball. According to Charles Strutt, executive director of the Multi-State Lottery Association, "Ten thousand people play them in each drawing." If Jack Whitaker had won with the numbers 1-2-3-4-5-6, his record-breaking cash lump sum of $113 million would have been split with 10,000 other tickets. Each Powerball jackpot winner would have collected a lump sum of $11,300. HOW SMART IS THAT - to buck the odds of one in 146 million to have a chance of winning, at *most*, an $11,300 jackpot? Don't worry. You wouldn't win it anyway because the selection is too far out of balance to come up in a random drawing.

## AVOID PATTERN BETTING

Pattern betting is the second most popular method of marking bet slips. Patterns of numbers marked in a row to make a straight line, either across the bet slip or vertically or diagonally get heavy play – which means sharing the prize with many others if the numbers are drawn as winners. Other designs such as patterns of initials or numbers also get heavy play.

## AVOID NUMBER MULTIPLES

Other popular combinations that get heavy play are the number multiples, especially 5-10-15-20-25 and 7-14-21-28-35.

## AVOID ALL SAME LAST DIGITS

Many people like to play same last digits, such as 3-13-23-33-43, or all digits that end in seven, or some other favorite lucky number. Even four same last digits occur in less than one tenth of one percent of all drawings. Winning sets of numbers with three same last digits occur in less than two percent of all drawings. Winning sets of numbers with two last digits the same occur in about 16 percent of all drawings. Winning sets of numbers with no last digit repeated happens most often – in more than 83 percent of all drawings.

## AVOID LOW NUMBER COMBINATIONS

The majority of lotto players like to play the calendar numbers, such as birth dates and anniversaries – and their children's ages. This means that the most heavily played numbers are 1 through 31. Powerball has 55 numbers. If you play only the calendar numbers, you might be sharing your jackpot with dozens of other winners. I'm not saying that you shouldn't play your personal numbers if you feel they are lucky for you. But I would recommend that you include a couple of high numbers so that just in case your numbers do hit, you win a prize that's worth something.

## NIX QUICK PICKS

Quick Picks are used by lazy people who want to be in the action without putting any effort into winning. When you read articles about jackpot winners, it appears as though they all used either Quick Picks, birth dates or their children's ages. The vast majority of people do play that way. If the majority of tickets sold are Quick Picks, then it makes sense that the majority of jackpots won should be won with Quick Picks. However, when I saw the actual figures, I found that you have a better chance of winning by picking numbers randomly out of a hat than by using Quick Picks.

# THE BALANCED GAME®

Randomly drawn numbers tend to be more or less evenly distributed across the entire number field of any lottery game. So it is important to select the five numbers and place them on your bet slips closest to the way they are actually drawn.

When you add the five winning numbers together, you get a sum. A typical sum in a 5/55 drawing could be: **6 + 18 + 20 + 41 + 55 = a sum of 140.**

If you study a list of the past winning numbers for any lottery game, you'll see that randomly drawn numbers tend to be evenly distributed over the entire number field. Add up the five winning numbers for several of the drawings and you will find that most of the winning sets fall within the same range of sums.

After analyzing most lottery games in existence, I discovered that more than 70 percent of the past sets of winning numbers are produced by only 27 or 28 percent of all the possible sums.

If you want to give your odds more leverage, that is, 0play with the probabilities more in your favor, then be sure that the sum of your five-number bet falls within the Most Probable Range of Sums® for the game you are playing.

**For Powerball-type games, a Balanced Game® is a five-number combination that falls within the Most Probable Range® of sums.**

**MOST PROBABLE RANGE OF SUMS®**

| Game | Range | Lottery Name |
|---|---|---|
| 5/56 | 106 - 179 | Mega Millions |
| 5/55 | 104 - 176 | Powerball |
| 5/47 | 89 - 151 | California SuperLotto Plus |
| 5/45 | 86 - 144 | Australia Powerball |
| 5/45 | 86 - 144 | Greece Tzoker |
| 5/42 | 80 - 135 | India Thunderball |
| 5/39 | 75 - 125 | Hot Lotto |
| 5/36 | 69 - 116 | Trinidad/Tobago Lotto Plus |
| 5/34 | 66 - 109 | U.K. Thunderball |
| 5/34 | 66 - 109 | Turkey Sans Topu |
| 5/32 | 62 - 103 | Kansas Super Cash |
| 5/31 | 60 - 100 | Wild Card 2 |

Use the 70 percent Most Probable Range of Sums® for the game YOU play.

## BALANCED WHEELS®

You don't have to be a math genius to know that if you bet half the numbers in your game, your chances of trapping the winning numbers are greatly improved.

There are two distinct but equally important methods to help you win: Number Selection and Wheeling. The key to winning more lottery prizes is to use both Balanced Wheeling Systems and number selection strategies to lower the odds against you. Scientific number selection and wheeling are equally important. But, Powerball Balanced Wheels® is what this book is all about. Number selection strategies are explained in depth in my book, *Lottery Master Guide.*

Read the next two important paragraphs twice or until you are sure you understand the meaning:

**Wheeling is a method of mixing (combining) many numbers. Balanced Wheels allow you to choose large groups of numbers, then arranges those numbers in special patterns to give a specific minimum win guarantee – if some or all of the winning numbers are in your wheeled group.**

**Balanced Wheels *force* all the winning numbers that are in your group to *come together* to give you at least one specific prize.**

First you choose your group of numbers. Wheeling does NOT choose the numbers for you. You choose your own numbers. Wheeling simply combines the group of numbers you have already chosen.

If you were to take a group of numbers and create your own sets of five numbers in the same amount of combinations as one of my wheels, you would not be covering all possible combinations of the required prize category and you would not have a win guarantee. **To cover the most numbers in the fewest sets and get a specific minimum win guarantee, you must use my mathematically correct Balanced Wheels.**

A Balanced Wheel® is merely a guide – but an absolutely essential guide – to show the order in which to place your own chosen numbers when filling in your bet slips. The wheel itself arranges your numbers.

Each Balanced Wheel® guarantees at least one specific prize if the five (four, three or two) winning numbers (with and without the Powerball ball) are in the group of numbers you have chosen. If you are lucky, you may win several prizes. Winning several prizes all at once makes these wheels exciting and fun to use.

If you are very lucky, you could win a first prize jackpot. In addition to the guaranteed minimum prize, this book also tells you the maximum number of multiple prizes that are possible to win with each Powerball Balanced Wheel.

You will be amazed to see just how many prizes you can win all at once! The minimum and maximum prizes appear in chart form above each wheel. See page 26 for a full explanation of these charts.

Balanced Wheels are shortened or abbreviated versions of Full Wheels. They cover just enough combinations to give the desired win guarantee. This makes wheeling many numbers affordable. And the more numbers you wheel, the greater are your chances of trapping the winning numbers.

If you were to play every possible five-number combination (the Full System Wheel) of 24 numbers, you would have to play 42,504 games for just one drawing. But by using my abbreviated Balanced Wheel, you can cover 24 numbers in just 54 games – and still have a minimum win guarantee.

The lower the win guarantee, the fewer combinations that are covered which means the lower the ticket cost and more numbers that can be wheeled for the money.

American lottery players first learned about wheeling in 1983 when I introduced "The Dimitrov Wheeling Systems" and wrote about them extensively in *Gambling Times* magazine and various lottery magazines. The first wheeling book I sold was *How to Win at Lotto & Pick 6* written by Ivan Dimitrov. His book had only 65 wheeling systems in it. I popularized "The Dimitrov Wheeling Systems" and made the name famous.

It was entirely through my efforts – my books, newsletters, articles in national magazines, television appearances and especially my 30-minute television infomercial – that wheeling systems became known.

Those early primitive Dimitrov wheeling systems have been plagiarized by copy-cat authors who sell them in their books and software. Real experts do not resort to stealing the work of others. I am the only person who has a legal contract to sell the Dimitrov Wheeling systems. No one else has been authorized to publish or sell them. Ivan Dimitrov is a personal friend and I know for a fact that he has never authorized anyone since me to publish his wheels or to use his name commercially.

Ivan Dimitrov was never a mathematics professor, nor was he a mathematician, nor did he ever live in Austria – as those who steal his wheels without his permission proclaim. Ivan Dimitrov is a Bulgarian. You can read the entire story, "The Real Facts Behind The Dimitrov Wheeling Systems," by visiting my web site: **www.smartluck.com/dimitrov.htm**.

In 1987, I improved on the wheeling concept by creating totally different wheeling systems. I combined my Balanced Game® system with wheeling to produce the most Balanced Games possible within each wheel itself. This eliminated the unbalanced, wasted combinations that appear at the beginning and end of Dimitrov's and all other wheeling systems.

The combinations that result from the built-in Balanced Game® feature are patterned closest to the way the winning numbers are actually drawn. This unique feature refined wheeling to a state-of-the-art science. It is no wonder my Balanced Wheels have produced dozens of first prize lotto jackpot winners!

My unique copyrighted and trademarked Balanced Wheels®, which I introduced in the May 1987 issue of my *Lottery Buster* newsletter, were published in the January 1988 edition of my book, *Lotto How to Wheel a Fortune.* And they immediately became recognized as mathematically valid systems. In a July 24, 1988 article, the New York *Daily News* reported: "Wheeling systems like [Gail] Howard's have the most respectability among critics since they concede that the wheels offer a systematic way of reducing the odds."

These secret formulas were created to produce the most Balanced Games possible within each wheel itself. It's not surprising that my wheels have won 74 first prize lotto jackpots worth $97 million dollars. Balanced Wheels® are not sold legally by anyone else anywhere in the world. Anyone selling Balanced Wheels® is in violation of Federal Trademark and Copyright Law.

Before I created my unique Balanced Wheeling Systems, it was very difficult to both wheel the numbers *and* have Balanced Games®. All other wheeling systems sold in this country and elsewhere grouped the low numbers together in the first part of the system and grouped the high numbers together at the end of the system, leaving very few combinations with balanced games in the middle of the system.

The question of where to place one's chosen numbers in order to get Balanced Games was one my readers in the early 1980's asked most often. To clear up the confusion, I came up with a solution that structured wheeling systems internally to give the most balanced games possible *within* the wheel itself.

When using my Balanced Wheels®, you can place your chosen numbers in any order and it will not affect the win guarantee. You can place them in ascending order from low to high, or in descending order from high to low, or you can mix them all up.

With Balanced Wheels®, a much smaller percentage of combinations falls outside the Balanced Game® parameters. Given the nature of wheeling, this is not always possible to totally avoid. Do not eliminate those combinations. You must play every combination in a system or you will destroy the win guarantee. Besides, even an unbalanced combination is capable of winning a small prize – which may be your guaranteed minimum win.

## HOW TO WHEEL

It's remarkable that such powerful systems can be so simple and easy to use. **You simply exchange the system letters for your chosen numbers.** There is no faster, easier, yet effective way to get immediate odds improvement. And these wheels will work for any Powerball-type game in the world. The size of the two number fields is not significant.

**For convenience, I will refer to all the systems in this book as Powerball systems. And the sixth number that is chosen from the second number field, I will refer to as "PB" or the "Powerball Ball."**

Once you understand how to use one system, you will know how to use all of them. They all work the same easy way. You won't believe how simple it is to wheel your numbers until you try. **It's merely a matter of exchanging the system letters for the numbers you have chosen.**

I'll use Powerball Balanced Wheel 54108PB to show you how to do it. This system wheels eight numbers plus the Powerball number (PB). So, you are playing the various combinations that can be made from eight numbers plus the PB (Powerball Ball) number.

First choose eight *different* numbers plus a PB number. You can't use the same number more than once in the first group. However, a number used in the group from which the five are chosen *can* be repeated as the PB.

Look closely at the chart. You'll see room for your eight numbers in the eight boxes below the letters A through H. Write your eight chosen numbers in the boxes under the letters **A** through **H**, below **"Your 8 Numbers + PB to Wheel."** Your numbers can be entered in any order, or from low to high. Write the number you have chosen from the second group of numbers in the PB box.

## POWERBALL BALANCED WHEEL® 54108PB

**Wheel 8 Numbers + PB in 5 Games for a 4 of 5 Win**

With Powerball

| Numbers Matched | Maximum Wins | | | | | | Minimum Wins | | | | | |
|---|---|---|---|---|---|---|---|---|---|---|---|---|
| | 5 + 1 | 4 + 1 | 3 + 1 | 2 + 1 | 1 + 1 | 0 + 1 | 5 + | 4 + 1 | 3 + 1 | 2 + 1 | 1 + 1 | 0 + 1 |
| 5 + 1 | 1 | 2 | 1 | 1 | 0 | 0 | 0 | 1 | 2 | 2 | 0 | 0 |
| 4 + 1 | - | 2 | 2 | 0 | 1 | 0 | - | 0 | 2 | 2 | 1 | 0 |
| 3 + 1 | - | - | 4 | 0 | 0 | 1 | - | - | 0 | 4 | 1 | 0 |
| 2 + 1 | - | - | - | 4 | 0 | 1 | - | - | - | 1 | 3 | 1 |
| 1 + 1 | - | - | - | - | 4 | 1 | - | - | - | - | 2 | 3 |
| 0 + 1 | - | - | - | - | - | 5 | - | - | - | - | - | 5 |

Without Powerball

| Numbers Matched | Maximum Wins | | | | | Minimum Wins | | | | |
|---|---|---|---|---|---|---|---|---|---|---|
| | 5 + 0 | 4 + 0 | 3 + 0 | 2 + 0 | 1 + 0 | 5 + 0 | 4 + 0 | 3 + 0 | 2 + 0 | 1 + 0 |
| 5 + 0 | 1 | 2 | 1 | 1 | 0 | 0 | 1 | 2 | 2 | 0 |
| 4 + 0 | - | 2 | 2 | 0 | 1 | - | 0 | 2 | 2 | 1 |
| 3 + 0 | - | - | 4 | 0 | 0 | - | - | 0 | 4 | 1 |
| 2 + 0 | - | - | - | 4 | 0 | - | - | - | 1 | 3 |
| 1 + 0 | - | - | - | - | 4 | - | - | - | - | 2 |

**Your 8 Numbers + PB to Wheel**

| A | B | C | D | E | F | G | H | PB |
|---|---|---|---|---|---|---|---|---|
| 6 (4) | 18 (2) | 20 (3) | 41 (4) | 55 (3) | 37 (3) | 27 (2) | 48 (4) | 34 (5) |

**The 5 Games to Play**

| | | | | | | |
|---|---|---|---|---|---|---|
| 1. | A 6 | B 18 | D 41 | G 27 | H 48 | PB 34 |
| 2. | A 6 | C 20 | D 41 | E 55 | H 48 | PB 34 |
| 3. | A 6 | C 20 | D 41 | F 37 | H 48 | PB 34 |
| 4. | A 6 | D 41 | E 55 | F 37 | H 48 | PB 23 |
| 5. | B 18 | C 20 | E 55 | F 37 | G 27 | PB 34 |



Under **"The 5 Games to Play,"** notice there is a tiny letter in the upper left hand corner of each box. Write the number you have placed under the letter **'A'** in each box in the system where you see a little **A**. Next, write the number you have placed in box **B** in all the boxes that have little **B**'s in them. Continue with the rest of the numbers until you have filled in every box in the system. **The letters tell which of your chosen numbers should be placed in which lettered box to make the right combinations.**

Now write the number you have chosen from the second group of numbers in each of the separate **'PB'** boxes at the end on the far right.

When you have finished, your eight number picks plus the PB will be perfectly wheeled into the five correct

## POWERBALL BALANCED WHEEL® 54108PB

### Wheel 8 Numbers + PB in 5 Games for a 4 of 5 Win

With Powerball

| Numbers Matched | Maximum Wins 5 + 1 | 4 + 1 | 3 + 1 | 2 + 1 | 1 + 1 | 0 + 1 | Minimum Wins 5 + 1 | 4 + 1 | 3 + 1 | 2 + 1 | 1 + 1 | 0 + 1 |
|---|---|---|---|---|---|---|---|---|---|---|---|---|
| 5 + 1 | 1 | 2 | 1 | 1 | 0 | 0 | 0 | 1 | 2 | 2 | 0 | 0 |
| 4 + 1 | - | 2 | 2 | 0 | 1 | 0 | - | 0 | 2 | 2 | 1 | 0 |
| 3 + 1 | - | - | 4 | 0 | 0 | 1 | - | - | 0 | 4 | 1 | 0 |
| 2 + 1 | - | - | - | 4 | 0 | 1 | - | - | - | 1 | 3 | 1 |
| 1 + 1 | - | - | - | - | 4 | 1 | - | - | - | - | 2 | 3 |
| 0 + 1 | - | - | - | - | - | 5 | - | - | - | - | - | 5 |

Without Powerball

| Numbers Matched | Maximum Wins 5 + 0 | 4 + 0 | 3 + 0 | 2 + 0 | 1 + 0 | Minimum Wins 5 + 0 | 4 + 0 | 3 + 0 | 2 + 0 | 1 + 0 |
|---|---|---|---|---|---|---|---|---|---|---|
| 5 + 0 | 1 | 2 | 1 | 1 | 0 | 0 | 1 | 2 | 2 | 0 |
| 4 + 0 | - | 2 | 2 | 0 | 1 | - | 0 | 2 | 2 | 1 |
| 3 + 0 | - | - | 4 | 0 | 0 | - | - | 0 | 4 | 1 |
| 2 + 0 | - | - | - | 4 | 0 | - | - | - | 1 | 3 |
| 1 + 0 | - | - | - | - | 4 | - | - | - | - | 2 |

**Your 8 Numbers + PB to Wheel**

| A | B | C | D | E | F | G | H | PB |
|---|---|---|---|---|---|---|---|---|
| 3 | 14 | 18 | 26 | 29 | 35 | 38 | 47 | 23 |

**The 5 Games to Play**

| | | | | | | |
|---|---|---|---|---|---|---|
| 1. | A 3 | B 14 | D 26 | G 38 | H 47 | PB 23 |
| 2. | A 3 | C 18 | D 26 | E 29 | H 47 | PB 23 |
| 3. | A 3 | C 18 | D 26 | F 35 | H 47 | PB 23 |
| 4. | A 3 | D 26 | E 29 | F 35 | H 47 | PB 23 |
| 5. | B 14 | C 18 | E 29 | F 35 | G 38 | PB 23 |



combinations ready to be transferred to your bet slips so you can buy your tickets. That is all there is to it. My wheeling systems are as easy to use as A-B-C! So simple, even a child can do it.

Let's try one sample system before you go off on your own. The eight numbers I've chosen for this example are:

3, 14, 18, 26, 29, 35, 38, 47, plus 23 as the PB number. Notice that number 3 is in all the boxes with little A's in them; number 14 is written in all the little B boxes; number 18 is in all the C boxes; and 26 is in all the D boxes, etc.

I entered the numbers from low to high because my wheels are Balanced, but the numbers could have been placed in any order and it would not affect the win guarantee.

This is what the bet slip would look like after we have filled in all five games with the numbers used in the example.

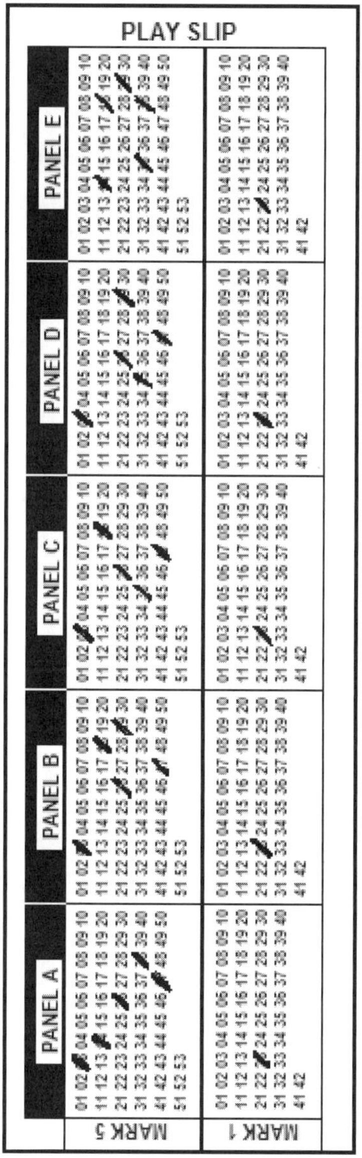


For the minimum win guarantee to be valid, you must play every game in the system – and be careful not to make any mistakes when filling in your bet slips. One mistake could cost you your win guarantee. It's always possible that you may win much more than the guaranteed minimum. The maximum number of prizes you could hope to win are shown above each system in the book. See page 26 to understand how to read the Minimum and Maximum Prize Charts.

## WIN GUARANTEES EXPLAINED

With Balanced Wheeling Systems you can choose your own win guarantee. The minimum win guarantee you select determines the ticket cost and the number of combinations in the system. Every wheeling system in this book has a valid win guarantee for a specific prize. However, **let me make this perfectly clear:**

**If the required number of winning numbers are NOT in the group you have chosen, THERE IS NO WIN GUARANTEE! If all the numbers you choose are losers, the wheel cannot help you.**

If you had 11 favorite numbers you wanted to wheel, you could spend as little as $2 or as much as $462 to wheel those 11 numbers, depending on the win guarantee you choose.

First I will explain the win guarantees for the five numbers you select from the first group of numbers in a Powerball-type of game. Then in the next chapter, I will incorporate the PB number in the Minimum and Maximum prizes and show you how to read those charts.

The ten types of wheeling systems are categorized by their minimum win guarantees, meaning the least you could expect to win – if you meet the conditions of the wheel. The systems in this book are grouped together as separate chapters according to their minimum win guarantees. The lower the win guarantee, the lower the ticket cost and the fewer combinations covered.

Each Balanced Wheel has a minimum win guarantee that requires having a specific number of winning numbers in the chosen group–either two, three, four or five, depending on the win guarantee.

The minimum prize guaranteed is the prize most easily won. But you could get lucky and win up to the maximum number of multiple prizes possible, or you could get very lucky and win the first prize jackpot with any system in this book.

Besides the 5 out of 5 Full System Wheels, there are nine categories of abbreviated Balanced Wheels. They are distinguished by their minimum win guarantee, which is the smallest prize the wheel guarantees.

There are 4 out of 4, 4 out of 5, 3 out of 3, 3 out of 4, and 3 out of 5, 2 out of 2, 2 out of 3, 2 out of 4 and 2 out of 5 Balanced Wheels. Those numbers describe the various minimum win guarantees for the first set of five numbers you choose in a Powerball-type game.

The first number of the system category (on the left) tells the minimum prize it guarantees to win. The second number (on the right), tells how many winning numbers in the wheeled group must match the winning numbers drawn to win the minimum prize.

The **4** out of **4** Balanced Wheels® guarantee at least one four-number prize if just four of the five winning numbers are in your wheeled group.

The **4** out of **5** Balanced Wheels® guarantee at least one four-number prize if all five winning numbers are in your wheeled group.

The **3** out of **3** Balanced Wheels® guarantee at least one three-number prize if just three of the five winning numbers are in your wheeled group.

The **3** out of **4** Balanced Wheels® guarantee at least one three-number prize if just four of the five winning numbers are in your wheeled group.

The **3** out of **5** Balanced Wheels® guarantee at least one three-number prize if all five winning numbers are in your wheeled group.

The **2** out of **2** Balanced Wheels® guarantee at least one two-number prize if just two of the five winning numbers are in your wheeled group.

The **2** out of **3** Balanced Wheels® guarantee at least one two-number prize if just three of the five winning numbers are in your wheeled group.

The **2** out of **4** Balanced Wheels® guarantee at least one two-number prize if four of the five winning numbers are in your wheeled group.

The **2** out of **5** Balanced Wheels® guarantee at least one two-number prize if all five winning numbers are in your wheeled group.

The lower the win guarantee, the more numbers that can be wheeled for the money. The 2 out of 5 systems cost the *least* to play for the amount of numbers wheeled, and give the *greatest* odds improvement because of the leverage. A word of caution: **Because the 2 out of 5 wheels cover so many numbers in very few combinations, don't expect to win many multiple prizes as you would with systems with higher win guarantees**. The 5 out of 5 Full Wheels cost the most to use and have the worst odds improvement.

## MINIMUM AND MAXIMUM WINS

Shown above each of the wheeling systems in this book are the maximum number of multiple prizes it is possible to win, as well as the minimum number of prizes the system guarantees. **Maximum Prizes are possible but not guaranteed. Only Minimum Prizes are guaranteed.**

Pay close attention while I explain how to read the Minimum and Maximum Prize listings. Once you understand how to read one listing, you can read all of them the same way. It's a simple, easy, convenient and practical way to see all the win information at a glance.

Each Powerball Balanced Wheel has above it four types of prize categories:

1) Maximum number of wins possible if you guessed the Powerball ball correctly.

2) Minimum number of wins guaranteed if you guessed the Powerball ball correctly.

3) Maximum wins possible if you did NOT guess the Powerball ball correctly.

4) Minimum wins guaranteed if you did NOT guess the Powerball ball correctly.

I'll use system #54108PB as the example again to show you how to read the Minimum and Maximum Prizes. This is a 4 out of 5 Balanced Wheel, which means it guarantees one four-number prize if all five of the winning numbers are in the wheeled group. But, there is more to it than that when we incorporate the Powerball ball.

## Maximum & Minimum Prize Table

With Powerball

| Numbers Matched | Maximum Wins | | | | | | Minimum Wins | | | | | |
|---|---|---|---|---|---|---|---|---|---|---|---|---|
| | 5 + 1 | 4 + 1 | 3 + 1 | 2 + 1 | 1 + 1 | 0 + 1 | 5 + 1 | 4 + 1 | 3 + 1 | 2 + 1 | 1 + 1 | 0 + 1 |
| 5 + 1 | 1 | 2 | 1 | 1 | 0 | 0 | 0 | 1 | 2 | 2 | 0 | 0 |
| 4 + 1 | - | 2 | 2 | 0 | 1 | 0 | - | 0 | 2 | 2 | 1 | 0 |
| 3 + 1 | - | - | 4 | 0 | 0 | 1 | - | - | 0 | 4 | 1 | 0 |
| 2 + 1 | - | - | - | 4 | 0 | 1 | - | - | - | 1 | 3 | 1 |
| 1 + 1 | - | - | - | - | 4 | 1 | - | - | - | - | 2 | 3 |
| 0 + 1 | - | - | - | - | - | 5 | - | - | - | - | - | 5 |

Without Powerball

| Numbers Matched | Maximum Wins | | | | | Minimum Wins | | | | |
|---|---|---|---|---|---|---|---|---|---|---|
| | 5 + 0 | 4 + 0 | 3 + 0 | 2 + 0 | 1 + 0 | 5 + 0 | 4 + 0 | 3 + 0 | 2 + 0 | 1 + 0 |
| 5 + 0 | 1 | 2 | 1 | 1 | 0 | 0 | 1 | 2 | 2 | 0 |
| 4 + 0 | - | 2 | 2 | 0 | 1 | - | 0 | 2 | 2 | 1 |
| 3 + 0 | - | - | 4 | 0 | 0 | - | - | 0 | 4 | 1 |
| 2 + 0 | - | - | - | 4 | 0 | - | - | - | 1 | 3 |
| 1 + 0 | - | - | - | - | 4 | - | - | - | - | 2 |

The top set of charts show the Maximum Wins and Minimum Wins WITH Powerball, which applies if the number you placed in the PB box is a PB winner.

Prize categories are listed in the column on the far left, and again across the top of the chart. The numbers within the chart are the number of prizes you could win. Reading the first line of prizes under the Maximum Wins, you see that if you trap all five winning numbers in your chosen group of eight numbers and the number you placed in the PB box is also a winner (5+1), you could win one 5+1 jackpot plus two 4+1 prizes plus one each of 3+1 and 2+1 prizes.

Continuing across under the Minimum Wins, you see that if you trap all five winning numbers plus the PB number (5+1), you are guaranteed to win one 4+1 plus two 3+1 and two 2+1 prizes.

Reading the second line, if you get just four of the five winning numbers plus the PB number, you could win two 4+1 and two 3+1 prizes. Continuing across with the second line under the Minimum Wins, you see that you would be guaranteed to win two 3+1 and two 2+1 prizes.

The third line shows that if you had only three of the five winning numbers, but you also matched the PB number, you could win four 3+1 prizes plus one 0+1 prize but, continuing across under the Minimum Wins, you are guaranteed to win four 2+1 prizes plus one 1+1 prize. I think you get the picture.

What happens if you *miss* the PB number – if you get the five winning numbers but NOT the Powerball number? The bottom set of charts shows the Maximum Wins and Minimum Wins WITHOUT the Powerball, which means if the number you placed in the PB box is a loser.

As before, prize categories are listed in the column on the far left, and again across the top of the chart. The numbers within the chart are the number of prizes you could win if you have trapped some or all of the winning numbers in your chosen group of eight.

Reading the first line of prizes under the Maximum Wins, you see that if you have all five winning numbers in your chosen group of eight numbers but NOT the PB number (5+0), you could win a 5-number prize plus two 4-number prizes and one 3-number prize and one 2-number prize. But you are guaranteed to win one 4-number prize plus two 3-number prizes and two 2-number prizes.

Continuing across under the Minimum Wins, you see that if you trap all five winning numbers but not the PB number (5+0), you are guaranteed to win one 4-number plus two 3-number and two 2-number prizes.

Reading the second line, if you get just four of the five winning numbers in your group numbers but not the PB number (4+0), you could win two each of 4-number prizes and 3-number prizes (plus one 1-number prize if applicable). Continuing across with the second line under the Minimum Wins, you see that you would be guaranteed to win two 3-number prizes and two 2-number prizes.

The third line shows that if you have only three of the five winning numbers and no PB number, you could win four 3-number prizes but, continuing across under the Minimum Wins, you are guaranteed to win four 2-number prizes plus one 1-number prize (where applicable). The fourth line shows that with two of the five winning numbers, you could win four 2-number prizes but you are guaranteed to win one, and so on.

The win guarantees stated in all the charts are valid only if you play all the games in the system and if you do not make any errors when filling in your bet slips. For prizes that include the PB, the same PB number must be used consistently throughout the entire wheel.

Every Balanced Wheel in this book is guaranteed 100 percent accurate – no holes. The wheels are printed directly from the software. No typesetting is involved so no human errors are possible. If a wheel fails its win guarantee, look to see where you made the error. It would not be the fault of the wheel.

Having said that–and at the risk of being misunderstood–my advice would be NOT TO USE the same PB number in every combination in the wheel. You will increase your chances of winning by using several different PB numbers throughout the wheel. Of course, Minimum and Maximum Wins With Powerball in the Prize Table will NOT apply, but the Minimum and Maximum Wins Without Powerball will still be valid.

## CHOOSING THE POWERBALL BALL

The Powerball Ball number (PB) is extremely hard to choose. And in most of these games it is more difficult to guess than a direct hit in roulette. In Powerball, the average number of games skipped between wins for the PB is 39, so choosing a PB number is equivalent to choosing a long shot number in pick-5 or pick-6 games. The average number of skips for the other five numbers is only 8. So, you can see how much easier it is to pick one of the five numbers than to pick the PB number.

The average number of skips between wins for the PB varies between 69 for the coldest number and 20 for the very hottest number. It doesn't pay to chase long shots since the longest skip was 324 games. Two PB numbers sat out for more than 200 games; and 25 other numbers were out more than 100 games each. Even 20, the hottest PB number to date, sat out 76 games without a win (from March to December 2000.)

Even with thousands of drawings, Long Term Trend Charts will never fill in with enough history to be of value in choosing a PB. The Short Term Bias Trackers® which work extremely well for the five-number picks, are almost useless for choosing a best PB pick.

There are no discernible patterns and no way to predict if an Odd Number or an Even Number will come up in the next drawing. The PB has been drawn as an Odd Number nine times in a row; and eight times in a row as an Even Number. Such long series have happened several times, which makes choosing Odd or Even Numbers unpredictable.

The High Low Bias Tracker® has produced a Low PB Number 14 drawings in a row. Several other times, 10, 12 and 13 drawings in a row had a series of all High or all Low Numbers.

Tracking the PB of other Powerball-type games shows the same lack of pattern. Even the Canada Wild 5 (5/39 + 1/5), in which the PB is chosen from just five numbers, the same lack of pattern exists. In this relatively new game, there have been instances of Odd Number PBs being drawn 13 games in a row.

I wish I cold tell you a secret formula for picking the PB number, but after thoroughly researching it and testing it, I found that no earthly means can improve the odds of choosing a PB number. Sad to say, a winning PB number can be chosen only by Dumb Luck.

One way to increase your chances of trapping the PB number in your wheel is to use a variety of PB numbers in the PB boxes. Of course, the Minimum and Maximum

Wins With Powerball Ball will no longer be valid. However, the Minimum and Maximum Wins Without Powerball Ball will still be valid.

Wheels with win guarantees that incorporate a variety of PB numbers would be much more expensive for the player to use.

## TIMES IN THE WHEEL™ HANDICAPPING FEATURE

The TIMES IN THE WHEEL™ all-important handicapping feature enables you to give extra heavy play to your strongest numbers. It tells how many times each number position is in the wheel, so you can place your best numbers in the system positions that appear most often in the wheel.

Players who use my scientific tools to analyze the numbers know that certain numbers in any given drawing are far more likely to win than others. Some numbers are best, second best, and so on, in varying degrees. You can give extra heavy play to your strongest number picks by placing them under the letters that appear more often in the wheel you are using.

Some Balanced Wheels® have an equal distribution of the letters (number positions) within the wheel. In that case, each of your chosen numbers gets equal play. But in those wheels that have unequal distribution of the number positions, you can place your strongest numbers where they will appear most often, and your weakest numbers in the positions that appear least often.

Naturally, when you use this feature, your numbers will not appear in order from low to high. You can place your chosen numbers in any order you wish. Win guarantees can be destroyed only if you make an error when filling in your bet slips, or if you don't play every combination in the system.

Notice the tiny numbers in the bottom right-hand corner under each letter under "Your 8 Numbers + PB to Wheel." These tiny numbers tell you how many times each of those lettered system positions are in the wheel.

Notice that in Balanced Wheel #54108PB, the system positions **A** and **D** and **H** are in the wheel four times. But system positions **B** and **G** are in the wheel only two times. So, you would place your strongest numbers in positions **A-D-H**, your second best numbers in positions **C-E-F**, and your weakest numbers in positions **B-G**.

## WHEELING GUIDELINES

**RULE #1. It is more important to wheel MORE numbers than to choose a higher win guarantee.** Unless you use my number selection strategies before each drawing to find the best possible choices, you need to include as many numbers as your lottery budget can afford. To win prizes, you must trap some winning numbers in your wheeled group. The more numbers you wheel, the easier it is to trap the winning numbers.

**RULE #2. The optimum number of numbers to wheel is about HALF the numbers in your game—*not* to exceed 4 or 5 numbers *over* that.** Otherwise you will be spending MORE money chasing a *smaller* guaranteed prize. It's true that the more numbers you wheel, the easier it is to trap the winning numbers in your chosen group — but only up to a certain point is it worth the cost. When wheeling most or all of the numbers in a game with an *affordable* wheel, the numbers will be too spread out, so that even when the minimum prize is won, it may not cover the cost of the wheel. Multiple prize wins are rare with such wheels.

**RULE #3. Do NOT try to include ALL the numbers in your game in one wheel.** There are many smarter ways to play all the numbers. When all the numbers in the game are played using SEVERAL wheels, your money does not lose leverage. On the contrary, by using several wheels at once, you have several minimum win guarantees, as opposed to using one large system that wheels ALL the numbers in the game and guarantees ONE minimum prize. Always keep in mind, you will have the most success if you do not wheel more than 4 or 5 numbers more than half the numbers in your game.

**RULE #4. When using multiple wheels, do NOT give all the numbers equal play.** When wheeling all the numbers in the game, it's still important to carefully select a group of numbers, and wheel your strongest numbers with other groups of numbers. Placing numbers in multiple wheels an equal number of times will not bring the best results. You *must give a bias* to favored groups of numbers which appear in more wheels than other less favored numbers do.

**RULE #5. Do not make many SMALL wheels just for the sake of using multiple wheels.** It's a bad risk for a large investment of cash. When many small wheels are used, the winning numbers are less likely to come together in one wheel, resulting in a costly disappointment. Spending $6 on one 12-number wheel is not a big risk. But risking $60 on TEN 12-number wheels is a waste of money that could be put to better use with wheeling strategy. A $60 budget would be better spent on two 20-number wheels.

**RULE #6. Players with small budgets should use Balanced Wheels® with the lowest win guarantees.** To have the best chance of trapping the winning numbers, try to include as many numbers as your lottery budget allows. Most of the jackpot winners who won with my wheeling systems used Balanced Wheels® with the lower win guarantees – which allowed them to wheel more numbers at an affordable ticket cost.

**RULE #7. You do not have to be in every drawing.** Buy tickets only when you feel you have some good numbers.

**RULE #8. Cash in on Good Old Fashioned Dumb Luck.** Luck does come in streaks. If you're on a losing streak, cut back on the amount you spend on tickets. You don't have to spend a fortune to wheel a fortune. For as little as $2 you can wheel 10 numbers plus the PB number and get a 3 out of 5 win guarantee. When you start winning, you can afford to spend more because you may be on a roll! – and because you would be playing with "their" money.

## QUICK WHEEL FINDER TABLES

To help you decide faster which wheel you want to use, there are four types of listings of the 189 wheels in this book.

### INSTANT WHEEL INDEX

Using the INSTANT WHEEL INDEX on Page 273, you can quickly see all the wheels in this book, in rows by numbers wheeled and columns by win guarantee. This shows at a glance (within the chart), how many combinations are required for each wheel.

## INSTANT WHEEL FINDER

The INSTANT WHEEL FINDER™ chart, on page 274, makes it a snap to locate the page number of your chosen wheel. The win guarantees (2/5, 2/4, 2/3, 2/2, 3/5, 3/4, 3/3, 4/5, 4/4, 5/5) are at the top of the Wheel Finder and the numbers to wheel are listed down the left side of the chart. The numbers within the chart (where the win guarantee meets the number of numbers to wheel) show the page number on which you will find that wheel.

## BUDGET WHEEL FINDER® BY COST

How much do you want to spend on tickets? The Budget Wheel Finder BY COST on page 275, makes it fast and easy to choose a wheel that matches the dollar amount you want to spend on tickets. The first column on the left (Cost) shows the ticket cost (at $1 per game) by the number of combinations or game panels to play. The second column (##'s) shows the number of numbers in the wheel. The third column (Win) shows the win guarantee, and the fourth column (Page) tells you the page number in this book where the wheel is located. For example, the first line tells you that the wheel has 2 combinations ($2 cost); and that 10 numbers are wheeled; it has a Win 3 with 5 win guarantee, and shows that you will find the wheel on page 167.

## BUDGET WHEEL FINDER® By NUMBERS TO WHEEL

How many numbers do you want to wheel? The Budget Wheel Finder BY NUMBERS on page 277 makes it fast and easy to choose a wheel that matches the number of numbers you want to wheel. The first column on the left (##'s.) shows the number of numbers to wheel;

the next column shows the ticket cost or number of combinations to be played; the third column shows the win guarantee; and the fourth column shows the page on which to find the wheel. Let's say you have 10 numbers you want to wheel. When you come down to 10 in the first column, you see you have a choice of six systems that wheel 10 numbers. Next decide how much money you want to invest (ticket cost) in those 10 numbers based on the number of games to be played. Then go right to the page of the wheel of your choice!

## A FINAL WORD TO FUTURE JACKPOT WINNERS

When jackpots are won with my systems, it gives me enormous pleasure to hear from my winners – and makes my work immensely more meaningful. In fact, the success of my jackpot winners is the force that drives me to create new and better ways to help us win.

I never accept money or gifts from my winners. On the contrary, my first prize jackpot winners get my latest books and software FREE. After all, it is THEY who inspire me with their success.

I appreciate it immensely when jackpot winners publicly acknowledge (to the lottery officials and to the press) that they used the Gail Howard system to win. Not only is it ethical, appropriate and fair to give credit where credit is due, but it establishes a personal life-long bond, a link of friendship, between us.

When you win your first prize jackpot with my Balanced Wheels and/or number selections strategies, tell ME the happy news right after you tell your family! I love to hear from my winners no matter how small the jackpot. I won't publicize your name if you ask me not to. But I must have complete verifiable documentation about your win for my own personal files so I can claim another documented jackpot won with my systems. Your success is my success.

When you write to me, tell me: 1) The amount of the prize you won. 2) The country in which you won and the game you played. 3) The date you won. 4) Which Balanced Wheel you used. 5) Which of my books or software programs you used to win. 6) Permission to use your name or tell me that you want it kept private. 7) Include your telephone number and/or e-mail address so I can personally congratulate you.

In your letter, tell anything you want me to know about yourself because we are going to be life-long friends. Are you married? Have children? Are you going to continue working? What is or was your occupation? How do you plan to use the windfall? How did you feel when you realized you had won the first prize jackpot? Where did you first hear about my systems? Tell me if you use a computer so I can send you a complimentary copy of my software, which is in English only. Write to me in English if possible, but if it is not possible, write to me in your language and I will have it translated if I don't speak your language.

I hope you win a first prize soon. I'd love to share your joy and welcome another very special person to the exclusive Club of Gail Howard Lottery Jackpot Winners.

# LOTTERY PRODUCTS TO HELP YOU WIN!

Smart people don't wait for Dumb Luck. Whether it's big jackpots you are after, or winning smaller prizes consistently, you can improve your "luck" by using knowledge and skill to zero in on winning lotto numbers.

Wheeling is very important because it allows you to play with large groups of numbers. However, wheeling is only half the battle. Being armed with powerful number selection strategies, and knowing how to target numbers most likely to hit is equally important. Your best bet to beat the lottery is to use both weapons TOGETHER!

The following pages describe the lottery products currently available. I'll begin with books and charts which can be used by anyone without a computer. Keep in mind that this book was printed in 2006. In the future, prices are subject to change, and new products will be added. I am continually developing and testing new ideas and enhancing and improving my old original published methods. I have working ideas for several new books and software.

To read the latest and most complete information about my products, visit my web site at: www.gailhoward.com. Or to be notified by email, sign up on my website at: http://smartluck.com/signup.htm.

Or send a self-addressed, stamped envelop to the address near the bottom of the order form at the end of this book. If you are not on my current mailing list, or if you have moved since placing your last order, send us a change of address form so you won't miss out on exciting new products as they become available.

Whether you use a computer or not, *Lottery Master Guide* is an absolute MUST read for EVERY serious lotto player. It is the most complete book on lottery strategy ever written.

If you DO NOT use a computer, you can order a printed set of Lottery Advantage® Charts to scientifically select the best numbers for the lotto game YOU play.

If you DO use a computer, for best results you should order at least TWO Smart Luck® programs: ADVANTAGE PLUS™ to scientifically select the numbers, and a Smart Luck® WHEEL program to wheel the numbers.

Advantage Plus™ programs contain no wheels. Wheel programs contain no game histories nor number selection methods.

## LOTTERY BOOKS AND CHARTS

- **LOTTERY MASTER GUIDE** - the complete book on how to select numbers most likely to win pick-5, pick-6, pick-10, Powerball, and Mega Millions. A must read for everyone who plays lotto.
- **LOTTO HOW TO WHEEL A FORTUNE** - wheeling systems for all pick-6 lotto games.
- **LOTTO WHEEL FIVE TO WIN** - wheeling systems for all pick-5 lotto games.

- **LOTTO WINNING WHEELS FOR POWERBALL & MEGA MILLIONS** - wheeling systems for all Powerball-type games.
- **LOTTERY ADVANTAGE® CHARTS** - printed set of charts helps pick the best numbers for any specific lotto game of your choice.

## LOTTERY SOFTWARE (for PCs)

**ADVANTAGE PLUS** is the software you need for choosing the best numbers to play. Advantage Plus has all the original, unique, Gail Howard proven number selection methods for choosing lotto numbers that have the greatest probability of winning.

For one low price of $79.95 plus shipping, you get all the game histories that we track, including all pick 4, pick-5, pick-6, pick-7, pick-8, pick-9 and pick-10 games played in the USA, Australia, Canada and also most European, Asian and Latin American countries around the world. Check our web site for our most current list to see if your country is included: www.smartluck.com/slhfiles.htm.

**SMART LUCK WHEELING PROGRAMS** are available for pick-4 through pick-10 lotto games.

- **WHEEL SIX PLUS**™ has 1,650 wheeling systems: 844 for pick-6 lotto, and 792 wheels for pick-7 Lotto games.
- **WHEEL FIVE PLUS**™ has 475 wheeling systems for pick-5 lotto games.
- **WHEEL FOUR PLUS**™ has 651 wheeling systems for pick-4 lotto games. (NOT for 0000-9999 4-digit type games.)
- **FULL WHEEL GENERATOR**™ has Full Wheels for all pick-4, pick-5, pick-6, pick-7, pick-8, pick-9, and pick-10 lotto or keno games. Want to buy a guaranteed jackpot? This program will make ALL combinations for you. But these wheels can be very expensive to use for more than just a few numbers.
- **KENO WHEEL**™ has 527 wheeling systems for pick-10 keno. Can also be used for Pick-9 and Pick-8 keno and lottery games.

# POWERBALL BALANCED WHEEL® 52320PB

## Wheel 20 Numbers + PB in 4 Games for a 2 of 5 Win

With Powerball

| Numbers | Maximum Wins | | | | | | Minimum Wins | | | | | |
|---|---|---|---|---|---|---|---|---|---|---|---|---|
| Matched | 5 + 1 | 4 + 1 | 3 + 1 | 2 + 1 | 1 + 1 | 0 + 1 | 5 + 1 | 4 + 1 | 3 + 1 | 2 + 1 | 1 + 1 | 0 + 1 |
| 5 + 1 | 1 | 0 | 0 | 0 | 0 | 3 | 0 | 0 | 0 | 1 | 3 | 0 |
| 4 + 1 | - | 1 | 0 | 0 | 0 | 3 | - | 0 | 0 | 0 | 4 | 0 |
| 3 + 1 | - | - | 1 | 0 | 0 | 3 | - | - | 0 | 0 | 3 | 1 |
| 2 + 1 | - | - | - | 1 | 0 | 3 | - | - | - | 0 | 2 | 2 |
| 1 + 1 | - | - | - | - | 1 | 3 | - | - | - | - | 1 | 3 |
| 0 + 1 | - | - | - | - | - | 4 | - | - | - | - | - | 4 |

Without Powerball

| Numbers | Maximum Wins | | | | | Minimum Wins | | | | |
|---|---|---|---|---|---|---|---|---|---|---|
| Matched | 5 + 0 | 4 + 0 | 3 + 0 | 2 + 0 | 1 + 0 | 5 + 0 | 4 + 0 | 3 + 0 | 2 + 0 | 1 + 0 |
| 5 + 0 | 1 | 0 | 0 | 0 | 0 | 0 | 0 | 0 | 1 | 3 |
| 4 + 0 | - | 1 | 0 | 0 | 0 | - | 0 | 0 | 0 | 4 |
| 3 + 0 | - | - | 1 | 0 | 0 | - | - | 0 | 0 | 3 |
| 2 + 0 | - | - | - | 1 | 0 | - | - | - | 0 | 2 |
| 1 + 0 | - | - | - | - | 1 | - | - | - | - | 1 |

## Your 20 Numbers + PB to Wheel

| A | B | C | D | E | F | G | H | I | J | K |
|---|---|---|---|---|---|---|---|---|---|---|
| 1 | 1 | 1 | 1 | 1 | 1 | 1 | 1 | 1 | 1 | 1 |

| L | M | N | O | P | Q | R | S | T | PB |
|---|---|---|---|---|---|---|---|---|---|
| 1 | 1 | 1 | 1 | 1 | 1 | 1 | 1 | 1 | 4 |

## The 4 Games to Play

| | | | | | | |
|---|---|---|---|---|---|---|
| 1. | A | E | M | O | S | PB |
| 2. | B | F | G | Q | T | PB |
| 3. | C | I | J | N | P | PB |
| 4. | D | H | K | L | R | PB |



# POWERBALL BALANCED WHEEL® 52321PB

## Wheel 21 Numbers + PB in 6 Games for a 2 of 5 Win

With Powerball

| Numbers | Maximum Wins | | | | | | Minimum Wins | | | | | |
|---|---|---|---|---|---|---|---|---|---|---|---|---|
| Matched | 5 + 1 | 4 + 1 | 3 + 1 | 2 + 1 | 1 + 1 | 0 + 1 | 5 + 1 | 4 + 1 | 3 + 1 | 2 + 1 | 1 + 1 | 0 + 1 |
| 5 + 1 | 1 | 1 | 0 | 0 | 1 | 3 | 0 | 0 | 0 | 1 | 4 | 1 |
| 4 + 1 | - | 2 | 0 | 0 | 0 | 4 | - | 0 | 0 | 0 | 5 | 1 |
| 3 + 1 | - | - | 2 | 0 | 0 | 4 | - | - | 0 | 0 | 3 | 3 |
| 2 + 1 | - | - | - | 2 | 0 | 4 | - | - | - | 0 | 2 | 4 |
| 1 + 1 | - | - | - | - | 2 | 4 | - | - | - | - | 1 | 5 |
| 0 + 1 | - | - | - | - | - | 6 | - | - | - | - | - | 6 |

Without Powerball

| Numbers | Maximum Wins | | | | | Minimum Wins | | | | |
|---|---|---|---|---|---|---|---|---|---|---|
| Matched | 5 + 0 | 4 + 0 | 3 + 0 | 2 + 0 | 1 + 0 | 5 + 0 | 4 + 0 | 3 + 0 | 2 + 0 | 1 + 0 |
| 5 + 0 | 1 | 1 | 0 | 0 | 1 | 0 | 0 | 0 | 1 | 4 |
| 4 + 0 | - | 2 | 0 | 0 | 0 | - | 0 | 0 | 0 | 5 |
| 3 + 0 | - | - | 2 | 0 | 0 | - | - | 0 | 0 | 3 |
| 2 + 0 | - | - | - | 2 | 0 | - | - | - | 0 | 2 |
| 1 + 0 | - | - | - | - | 2 | - | - | - | - | 1 |

(Continued Next Page)

**POWERBALL BALANCED WHEEL® 52321PB** (Continued from previous page)

## Your 21 Numbers + PB to Wheel

| A | B | C | D | E | F | G | H | I | J | K |
|---|---|---|---|---|---|---|---|---|---|---|
| 1 | 1 | 1 | 1 | 1 | 2 | 2 | 2 | 2 | 2 | 2 |
| **L** | **M** | **N** | **O** | **P** | **Q** | **R** | **S** | **T** | **U** | **PB** |
| 2 | 2 | 2 | 1 | 1 | 1 | 1 | 1 | 1 | 1 | 6 |

## The 6 Games to Play

| | | | | | | | | | | | | | |
|---|---|---|---|---|---|---|---|---|---|---|---|---|---|
| 1. | A | D | P | Q | S | PB | 4. | F | J | K | L | M | PB |
| 2. | B | C | O | R | T | PB | 5. | G | H | I | J | N | PB |
| 3. | E | F | K | M | U | PB | 6. | G | H | I | L | N | PB |



# POWERBALL BALANCED WHEEL® 52322PB

## Wheel 22 Numbers + PB in 6 Games for a 2 of 5 Win

With Powerball

| Numbers Matched | Maximum Wins | | | | | | Minimum Wins | | | | | |
|---|---|---|---|---|---|---|---|---|---|---|---|---|
| | 5 + 1 | 4 + 1 | 3 + 1 | 2 + 1 | 1 + 1 | 0 + 1 | 5 + 1 | 4 + 1 | 3 + 1 | 2 + 1 | 1 + 1 | 0 + 1 |
| 5 + 1 | 1 | 0 | 1 | 1 | 0 | 3 | 0 | 0 | 0 | 1 | 4 | 1 |
| 4 + 1 | - | 1 | 1 | 0 | 1 | 3 | - | 0 | 0 | 0 | 5 | 1 |
| 3 + 1 | - | - | 2 | 0 | 0 | 4 | - | - | 0 | 0 | 3 | 3 |
| 2 + 1 | - | - | - | 2 | 0 | 4 | - | - | - | 0 | 2 | 4 |
| 1 + 1 | - | - | - | - | 2 | 4 | - | - | - | - | 1 | 5 |
| 0 + 1 | - | - | - | - | - | 6 | - | - | - | - | - | 6 |

Without Powerball

| Numbers Matched | Maximum Wins | | | | | Minimum Wins | | | | |
|---|---|---|---|---|---|---|---|---|---|---|
| | 5 + 0 | 4 + 0 | 3 + 0 | 2 + 0 | 1 + 0 | 5 + 0 | 4 + 0 | 3 + 0 | 2 + 0 | 1 + 0 |
| 5 + 0 | 1 | 0 | 1 | 1 | 0 | 0 | 0 | 0 | 1 | 4 |
| 4 + 0 | - | 1 | 1 | 0 | 1 | - | 0 | 0 | 0 | 5 |
| 3 + 0 | - | - | 2 | 0 | 0 | - | - | 0 | 0 | 3 |
| 2 + 0 | - | - | - | 2 | 0 | - | - | - | 0 | 2 |
| 1 + 0 | - | - | - | - | 2 | - | - | - | - | 1 |

## Your 22 Numbers + PB to Wheel

| A | B | C | D | E | F | G | H |
|---|---|---|---|---|---|---|---|
| 1 | 2 | 1 | 2 | 2 | 2 | 1 | 1 |
| **I** | **J** | **K** | **L** | **M** | **N** | **O** | **P** |
| 1 | 1 | 1 | 1 | 1 | 1 | 2 | 1 |
| **Q** | **R** | **S** | **T** | **U** | **V** | **PB** | |
| 1 | 1 | 2 | 2 | 1 | 2 | 6 | |

## The 6 Games to Play

| | | | | | | | | | | | | | |
|---|---|---|---|---|---|---|---|---|---|---|---|---|---|
| 1. | A | G | M | N | U | PB | 4. | C | J | K | O | R | PB |
| 2. | B | D | E | S | V | PB | 5. | D | E | F | T | V | PB |
| 3. | B | F | O | S | T | PB | 6. | H | I | L | P | Q | PB |

# POWERBALL BALANCED WHEEL® 52323PB

## Wheel 23 Numbers + PB in 7 Games for a 2 of 5 Win

With Powerball

| Numbers Matched | Maximum Wins 5 + 1 | 4 + 1 | 3 + 1 | 2 + 1 | 1 + 1 | 0 + 1 | Minimum Wins 5 + 1 | 4 + 1 | 3 + 1 | 2 + 1 | 1 + 1 | 0 + 1 |
|---|---|---|---|---|---|---|---|---|---|---|---|---|
| 5 + 1 | 1 | 1 | 1 | 1 | 0 | 3 | 0 | 0 | 0 | 1 | 4 | 2 |
| 4 + 1 | - | 2 | 1 | 0 | 1 | 3 | - | 0 | 0 | 0 | 5 | 2 |
| 3 + 1 | - | - | 3 | 0 | 0 | 4 | - | - | 0 | 0 | 3 | 4 |
| 2 + 1 | - | - | - | 3 | 0 | 4 | - | - | - | 0 | 2 | 5 |
| 1 + 1 | - | - | - | - | 3 | 4 | - | - | - | - | 1 | 6 |
| 0 + 1 | - | - | - | - | - | 7 | - | - | - | - | - | 7 |

Without Powerball

| Numbers Matched | Maximum Wins 5 + 0 | 4 + 0 | 3 + 0 | 2 + 0 | 1 + 0 | Minimum Wins 5 + 0 | 4 + 0 | 3 + 0 | 2 + 0 | 1 + 0 |
|---|---|---|---|---|---|---|---|---|---|---|
| 5 + 0 | 1 | 1 | 1 | 1 | 0 | 0 | 0 | 0 | 1 | 4 |
| 4 + 0 | - | 2 | 1 | 0 | 1 | - | 0 | 0 | 0 | 5 |
| 3 + 0 | - | - | 3 | 0 | 0 | - | - | 0 | 0 | 3 |
| 2 + 0 | - | - | - | 3 | 0 | - | - | - | 0 | 2 |
| 1 + 0 | - | - | - | - | 3 | - | - | - | - | 1 |

## Your 23 Numbers + PB to Wheel

| A | B | C | D | E | F | G | H |
|---|---|---|---|---|---|---|---|
| 1 | 3 | 1 | 1 | 1 | 1 | 1 | 1 |
| **I** | **J** | **K** | **L** | **M** | **N** | **O** | **P** |
| 2 | 3 | 3 | 1 | 2 | 2 | 1 | 1 |
| **Q** | **R** | **S** | **T** | **U** | **V** | **W** | **PB** |
| 1 | 1 | 2 | 3 | 1 | 1 | 1 | 7 |

## The 7 Games to Play

| | | | | | | |
|---|---|---|---|---|---|---|
| 1. | A | E | Q | R | V | PB |
| 2. | B | I | K | N | T | PB |
| 3. | B | J | K | M | T | PB |
| 4. | B | J | K | S | T | PB |
| 5. | C | G | H | O | W | PB |
| 6. | D | F | L | P | U | PB |
| 7. | I | J | M | N | S | PB |



# POWERBALL BALANCED WHEEL® 52324PB

## Wheel 24 Numbers + PB in 8 Games for a 2 of 5 Win

With Powerball

| Numbers Matched | Maximum Wins 5 + 1 | 4 + 1 | 3 + 1 | 2 + 1 | 1 + 1 | 0 + 1 | Minimum Wins 5 + 1 | 4 + 1 | 3 + 1 | 2 + 1 | 1 + 1 | 0 + 1 |
|---|---|---|---|---|---|---|---|---|---|---|---|---|
| 5 + 1 | 1 | 0 | 2 | 0 | 0 | 5 | 0 | 0 | 0 | 1 | 5 | 2 |
| 4 + 1 | - | 1 | 1 | 1 | 0 | 5 | - | 0 | 0 | 0 | 6 | 2 |
| 3 + 1 | - | - | 2 | 0 | 1 | 5 | - | - | 0 | 0 | 4 | 4 |
| 2 + 1 | - | - | - | 2 | 1 | 5 | - | - | - | 0 | 2 | 6 |
| 1 + 1 | - | - | - | - | 3 | 5 | - | - | - | - | 1 | 7 |
| 0 + 1 | - | - | - | - | - | 8 | - | - | - | - | - | 8 |

(Continued Next Page)

## POWERBALL BALANCED WHEEL® 52324PB (Continued from previous page)

Without Powerball

| Numbers Matched | Maximum Wins 5 + 0 | 4 + 0 | 3 + 0 | 2 + 0 | 1 + 0 | Minimum Wins 5 + 0 | 4 + 0 | 3 + 0 | 2 + 0 | 1 + 0 |
|---|---|---|---|---|---|---|---|---|---|---|
| 5 + 0 | 1 | 0 | 2 | 0 | 0 | 0 | 0 | 0 | 1 | 5 |
| 4 + 0 | - | 1 | 1 | 1 | 0 | - | 0 | 0 | 0 | 6 |
| 3 + 0 | - | - | 2 | 0 | 1 | - | - | 0 | 0 | 4 |
| 2 + 0 | - | - | - | 2 | 1 | - | - | - | 0 | 2 |
| 1 + 0 | - | - | - | - | 3 | - | - | - | - | 1 |

## Your 24 Numbers + PB to Wheel

| A | B | C | D | E | F | G | H | I |
|---|---|---|---|---|---|---|---|---|
| 1 | 1 | 1 | 1 | 2 | 2 | 2 | 2 | 2 |
| **J** | **K** | **L** | **M** | **N** | **O** | **P** | **Q** | **R** |
| 2 | 2 | 2 | 2 | 2 | 2 | 2 | 3 | 3 |
| **S** | **T** | **U** | **V** | **W** | **X** | **PB** | | |
| 1 | 1 | 1 | 1 | 1 | 1 | 8 | | |

## The 8 Games to Play

| | | | | | | |
|---|---|---|---|---|---|---|
| 1. | A | C | S | W | X | PB |
| 2. | B | D | T | U | V | PB |
| 3. | E | G | J | M | Q | PB |
| 4. | E | M | N | P | Q | PB |
| 5. | F | H | K | O | R | PB |
| 6. | F | I | K | L | R | PB |
| 7. | G | J | N | P | Q | PB |
| 8. | H | I | L | O | R | PB |



# POWERBALL BALANCED WHEEL® 52325PB

### Wheel 25 Numbers + PB in 9 Games for a 2 of 5 Win

With Powerball

| Numbers Matched | Maximum Wins 5 + 1 | 4 + 1 | 3 + 1 | 2 + 1 | 1 + 1 | 0 + 1 | Minimum Wins 5 + 1 | 4 + 1 | 3 + 1 | 2 + 1 | 1 + 1 | 0 + 1 |
|---|---|---|---|---|---|---|---|---|---|---|---|---|
| 5 + 1 | 1 | 1 | 1 | 1 | 0 | 5 | 0 | 0 | 0 | 1 | 5 | 3 |
| 4 + 1 | - | 2 | 1 | 0 | 1 | 5 | - | 0 | 0 | 0 | 6 | 3 |
| 3 + 1 | - | - | 3 | 0 | 0 | 6 | - | - | 0 | 0 | 4 | 5 |
| 2 + 1 | - | - | - | 3 | 0 | 6 | - | - | - | 0 | 2 | 7 |
| 1 + 1 | - | - | - | - | 3 | 6 | - | - | - | - | 1 | 8 |
| 0 + 1 | - | - | - | - | - | 9 | - | - | - | - | - | 9 |

Without Powerball

| Numbers Matched | Maximum Wins 5 + 0 | 4 + 0 | 3 + 0 | 2 + 0 | 1 + 0 | Minimum Wins 5 + 0 | 4 + 0 | 3 + 0 | 2 + 0 | 1 + 0 |
|---|---|---|---|---|---|---|---|---|---|---|
| 5 + 0 | 1 | 1 | 1 | 1 | 0 | 0 | 0 | 0 | 1 | 5 |
| 4 + 0 | - | 2 | 1 | 0 | 1 | - | 0 | 0 | 0 | 6 |
| 3 + 0 | - | - | 3 | 0 | 0 | - | - | 0 | 0 | 4 |
| 2 + 0 | - | - | - | 3 | 0 | - | - | - | 0 | 2 |
| 1 + 0 | - | - | - | - | 3 | - | - | - | - | 1 |

(Continued Next Page)

**POWERBALL BALANCED WHEEL® 52325PB** (Continued from previous page)

## Your 25 Numbers + PB to Wheel

| A | B | C | D | E | F | G | H | I |
|---|---|---|---|---|---|---|---|---|
| 2 | 1 | 1 | 2 | 1 | 3 | 3 | 2 | 1 |
| **J** | **K** | **L** | **M** | **N** | **O** | **P** | **Q** | **R** |
| 3 | 2 | 1 | 2 | 2 | 3 | 2 | 1 | 2 |
| **S** | **T** | **U** | **V** | **W** | **X** | **Y** | **PB** | |
| 2 | 1 | 2 | 1 | 1 | 1 | 3 | 9 | |

## The 9 Games to Play

| | | | | | | |
|---|---|---|---|---|---|---|
| 1. | A | G | J | O | Y | PB |
| 2. | A | H | P | U | Y | PB |
| 3. | B | C | L | W | X | PB |
| 4. | D | F | K | N | S | PB |
| 5. | D | F | M | N | R | PB |
| 6. | E | I | Q | T | V | PB |
| 7. | F | K | M | R | S | PB |
| 8. | G | H | J | O | Y | PB |
| 9. | G | J | O | P | U | PB |



# POWERBALL BALANCED WHEEL® 52326PB

## Wheel 26 Numbers + PB in 10 Games for a 2 of 5 Win

With Powerball

| Numbers Matched | Maximum Wins 5 + 1 | 4 + 1 | 3 + 1 | 2 + 1 | 1 + 1 | 0 + 1 | Minimum Wins 5 + 1 | 4 + 1 | 3 + 1 | 2 + 1 | 1 + 1 | 0 + 1 |
|---|---|---|---|---|---|---|---|---|---|---|---|---|
| 5 + 1 | 1 | 1 | 1 | 1 | 0 | 6 | 0 | 0 | 0 | 1 | 5 | 4 |
| 4 + 1 | - | 2 | 1 | 0 | 1 | 6 | - | 0 | 0 | 0 | 6 | 4 |
| 3 + 1 | - | - | 3 | 0 | 0 | 7 | - | - | 0 | 0 | 4 | 6 |
| 2 + 1 | - | - | - | 3 | 0 | 7 | - | - | - | 0 | 2 | 8 |
| 1 + 1 | - | - | - | - | 3 | 7 | - | - | - | - | 1 | 9 |
| 0 + 1 | - | - | - | - | - | 10 | - | - | - | - | - | 10 |

Without Powerball

| Numbers Matched | Maximum Wins 5 + 0 | 4 + 0 | 3 + 0 | 2 + 0 | 1 + 0 | Minimum Wins 5 + 0 | 4 + 0 | 3 + 0 | 2 + 0 | 1 + 0 |
|---|---|---|---|---|---|---|---|---|---|---|
| 5 + 0 | 1 | 1 | 1 | 1 | 0 | 0 | 0 | 0 | 1 | 5 |
| 4 + 0 | - | 2 | 1 | 0 | 1 | - | 0 | 0 | 0 | 6 |
| 3 + 0 | - | - | 3 | 0 | 0 | - | - | 0 | 0 | 4 |
| 2 + 0 | - | - | - | 3 | 0 | - | - | - | 0 | 2 |
| 1 + 0 | - | - | - | - | 3 | - | - | - | - | 1 |

## Your 26 Numbers + PB to Wheel

| A | B | C | D | E | F | G | H | I |
|---|---|---|---|---|---|---|---|---|
| 1 | 3 | 2 | 3 | 3 | 1 | 3 | 2 | 2 |
| **J** | **K** | **L** | **M** | **N** | **O** | **P** | **Q** | **R** |
| 1 | 1 | 1 | 2 | 2 | 1 | 2 | 1 | 1 |
| **S** | **T** | **U** | **V** | **W** | **X** | **Y** | **Z** | **PB** |
| 2 | 2 | 3 | 3 | 3 | 3 | 1 | 1 | 10 |

## The 10 Games to Play

| | | | | | | |
|---|---|---|---|---|---|---|
| 1. | A | L | Q | R | Z | PB |
| 2. | B | D | I | U | X | PB |
| 3. | B | D | S | U | X | PB |
| 4. | B | M | N | U | X | PB |



(Continued Next Page)

**POWERBALL BALANCED WHEEL® 52326PB** (Continued from previous page)

| | | | | | | |
|---|---|---|---|---|---|---|
| 5. | C | E | G | T | W | PB |
| 6. | C | H | P | T | V | PB |
| 7. | D | I | M | N | S | PB |
| 8. | E | G | H | V | W | PB |
| 9. | E | G | P | V | W | PB |
| 10. | F | J | K | O | Y | PB |



# POWERBALL BALANCED WHEEL® 52327PB

## Wheel 27 Numbers + PB in 11 Games for a 2 of 5 Win

With Powerball

| Numbers Matched | Maximum Wins 5 + 1 | 4 + 1 | 3 + 1 | 2 + 1 | 1 + 1 | 0 + 1 | Minimum Wins 5 + 1 | 4 + 1 | 3 + 1 | 2 + 1 | 1 + 1 | 0 + 1 |
|---|---|---|---|---|---|---|---|---|---|---|---|---|
| 5 + 1 | 1 | 1 | 1 | 1 | 0 | 7 | 0 | 0 | 0 | 1 | 6 | 4 |
| 4 + 1 | - | 2 | 1 | 0 | 1 | 7 | - | 0 | 0 | 0 | 7 | 4 |
| 3 + 1 | - | - | 3 | 0 | 0 | 8 | - | - | 0 | 0 | 5 | 6 |
| 2 + 1 | - | - | - | 3 | 0 | 8 | - | - | - | 0 | 3 | 8 |
| 1 + 1 | - | - | - | - | 3 | 8 | - | - | - | - | 1 | 10 |
| 0 + 1 | - | - | - | - | - | 11 | - | - | - | - | - | 11 |

Without Powerball

| Numbers Matched | Maximum Wins 5 + 0 | 4 + 0 | 3 + 0 | 2 + 0 | 1 + 0 | Minimum Wins 5 + 0 | 4 + 0 | 3 + 0 | 2 + 0 | 1 + 0 |
|---|---|---|---|---|---|---|---|---|---|---|
| 5 + 0 | 1 | 1 | 1 | 1 | 0 | 0 | 0 | 0 | 1 | 6 |
| 4 + 0 | - | 2 | 1 | 0 | 1 | - | 0 | 0 | 0 | 7 |
| 3 + 0 | - | - | 3 | 0 | 0 | - | - | 0 | 0 | 5 |
| 2 + 0 | - | - | - | 3 | 0 | - | - | - | 0 | 3 |
| 1 + 0 | - | - | - | - | 3 | - | - | - | - | 1 |

## Your 27 Numbers + PB to Wheel

| A | B | C | D | E | F | G | H | I | J |
|---|---|---|---|---|---|---|---|---|---|
| 3 | 1 | 2 | 3 | 2 | 2 | 2 | 2 | 2 | 2 |
| **K** | **L** | **M** | **N** | **O** | **P** | **Q** | **R** | **S** | **T** |
| 2 | 1 | 2 | 2 | 2 | 1 | 2 | 3 | 1 | 3 |
| **U** | **V** | **W** | **X** | **Y** | **Z** | **aa** | **PB** | | |
| 2 | 3 | 2 | 2 | 1 | 3 | 2 | 11 | | |

## The 11 Games to Play

| | | | | | | |
|---|---|---|---|---|---|---|
| 1. | A | D | Q | T | Z | PB |
| 2. | A | D | T | Z | aa | PB |
| 3. | A | E | M | T | Z | PB |
| 4. | B | L | P | S | Y | PB |
| 5. | C | I | O | V | X | PB |
| 6. | C | J | N | R | V | PB |
| 7. | D | E | M | Q | aa | PB |
| 8. | F | G | H | U | V | PB |
| 9. | F | K | R | U | W | PB |
| 10. | G | H | K | R | W | PB |
| 11. | I | J | N | O | X | PB |

# POWERBALL BALANCED WHEEL® 52328PB

## Wheel 28 Numbers + PB in 12 Games for a 2 of 5 Win

With Powerball

| Numbers Matched | Maximum Wins | | | | | | Minimum Wins | | | | | |
|---|---|---|---|---|---|---|---|---|---|---|---|---|
| | 5 + 1 | 4 + 1 | 3 + 1 | 2 + 1 | 1 + 1 | 0 + 1 | 5 + 1 | 4 + 1 | 3 + 1 | 2 + 1 | 1 + 1 | 0 + 1 |
| 5 + 1 | 1 | 0 | 1 | 1 | 1 | 8 | 0 | 0 | 0 | 1 | 8 | 3 |
| 4 + 1 | - | 1 | 1 | 0 | 2 | 8 | - | 0 | 0 | 0 | 8 | 4 |
| 3 + 1 | - | - | 2 | 0 | 1 | 9 | - | - | 0 | 0 | 6 | 6 |
| 2 + 1 | - | - | - | 2 | 1 | 9 | - | - | - | 0 | 4 | 8 |
| 1 + 1 | - | - | - | - | 3 | 9 | - | - | - | - | 2 | 10 |
| 0 + 1 | - | - | - | - | - | 12 | - | - | - | - | - | 12 |

Without Powerball

| Numbers Matched | Maximum Wins | | | | | Minimum Wins | | | | |
|---|---|---|---|---|---|---|---|---|---|---|
| | 5 + 0 | 4 + 0 | 3 + 0 | 2 + 0 | 1 + 0 | 5 + 0 | 4 + 0 | 3 + 0 | 2 + 0 | 1 + 0 |
| 5 + 0 | 1 | 0 | 1 | 1 | 1 | 0 | 0 | 0 | 1 | 8 |
| 4 + 0 | - | 1 | 1 | 0 | 2 | - | 0 | 0 | 0 | 8 |
| 3 + 0 | - | - | 2 | 0 | 1 | - | - | 0 | 0 | 6 |
| 2 + 0 | - | - | - | 2 | 1 | - | - | - | 0 | 4 |
| 1 + 0 | - | - | - | - | 3 | - | - | - | - | 2 |

## Your 28 Numbers + PB to Wheel

| A | B | C | D | E | F | G | H | I | J |
|---|---|---|---|---|---|---|---|---|---|
| 2 | 2 | 3 | 2 | 2 | 2 | 2 | 2 | 2 | 2 |
| **K** | **L** | **M** | **N** | **O** | **P** | **Q** | **R** | **S** | **T** |
| 2 | 2 | 2 | 2 | 2 | 2 | 2 | 2 | 2 | 3 |
| **U** | **V** | **W** | **X** | **Y** | **Z** | **aa** | **bb** | **PB** | |
| 2 | 3 | 2 | 2 | 2 | 2 | 2 | 3 | 12 | |

## The 12 Games to Play

| | | | | | | |
|---|---|---|---|---|---|---|
| 1. | A | I | R | S | V | PB |
| 2. | A | O | S | V | aa | PB |
| 3. | B | E | Q | T | bb | PB |
| 4. | B | F | P | Q | Z | PB |
| 5. | C | G | L | W | X | PB |
| 6. | C | I | O | R | aa | PB |
| 7. | C | N | U | V | W | PB |
| 8. | D | H | J | K | bb | PB |
| 9. | D | H | M | T | Y | PB |
| 10. | E | F | P | Z | bb | PB |
| 11. | G | L | N | U | X | PB |
| 12. | J | K | M | T | Y | PB |



# POWERBALL BALANCED WHEEL® 52329PB

## Wheel 29 Numbers + PB in 13 Games for a 2 of 5 Win

With Powerball

| Numbers Matched | Maximum Wins | | | | | | Minimum Wins | | | | | |
|---|---|---|---|---|---|---|---|---|---|---|---|---|
| | 5 + 1 | 4 + 1 | 3 + 1 | 2 + 1 | 1 + 1 | 0 + 1 | 5 + 1 | 4 + 1 | 3 + 1 | 2 + 1 | 1 + 1 | 0 + 1 |
| 5 + 1 | 1 | 1 | 1 | 1 | 0 | 9 | 0 | 0 | 0 | 1 | 8 | 4 |
| 4 + 1 | - | 2 | 1 | 0 | 1 | 9 | - | 0 | 0 | 0 | 8 | 5 |
| 3 + 1 | - | - | 3 | 0 | 0 | 10 | - | - | 0 | 0 | 6 | 7 |
| 2 + 1 | - | - | - | 3 | 0 | 10 | - | - | - | 0 | 4 | 9 |
| 1 + 1 | - | - | - | - | 3 | 10 | - | - | - | - | 2 | 11 |
| 0 + 1 | - | - | - | - | - | 13 | - | - | - | - | - | 13 |

(Continued Next Page)

## POWERBALL BALANCED WHEEL® 52329PB (Continued from previous page)

Without Powerball

| Numbers Matched | Maximum Wins | | | | | Minimum Wins | | | | |
|---|---|---|---|---|---|---|---|---|---|---|
| | 5 + 0 | 4 + 0 | 3 + 0 | 2 + 0 | 1 + 0 | 5 + 0 | 4 + 0 | 3 + 0 | 2 + 0 | 1 + 0 |
| 5 + 0 | 1 | 1 | 1 | 1 | 0 | 0 | 0 | 0 | 1 | 8 |
| 4 + 0 | - | 2 | 1 | 0 | 1 | - | 0 | 0 | 0 | 8 |
| 3 + 0 | - | - | 3 | 0 | 0 | - | - | 0 | 0 | 6 |
| 2 + 0 | - | - | - | 3 | 0 | - | - | - | 0 | 4 |
| 1 + 0 | - | - | - | - | 3 | - | - | - | - | 2 |

## Your 29 Numbers + PB to Wheel

| A | B | C | D | E | F | G | H | I | J |
|---|---|---|---|---|---|---|---|---|---|
| 2 | 2 | 2 | 2 | 2 | 3 | 2 | 2 | 2 | 2 |
| **K** | **L** | **M** | **N** | **O** | **P** | **Q** | **R** | **S** | **T** |
| 2 | 3 | 2 | 3 | 2 | 2 | 3 | 2 | 3 | 3 |
| **U** | **V** | **W** | **X** | **Y** | **Z** | **aa** | **bb** | **cc** | **PB** |
| 2 | 2 | 2 | 2 | 2 | 2 | 2 | 2 | 3 | 13 |

## The 13 Games to Play

| | | | | | | |
|---|---|---|---|---|---|---|
| 1. | A | K | S | T | Y | PB |
| 2. | A | M | R | W | Y | PB |
| 3. | B | H | T | V | Z | PB |
| 4. | B | I | S | X | Z | PB |
| 5. | C | F | L | P | cc | PB |
| 6. | C | G | P | Q | U | PB |
| 7. | D | E | N | aa | bb | PB |
| 8. | D | J | N | O | aa | PB |
| 9. | E | J | N | O | bb | PB |
| 10. | F | G | L | Q | cc | PB |
| 11. | F | L | Q | U | cc | PB |
| 12. | H | I | T | V | X | PB |
| 13. | K | M | R | S | W | PB |



# POWERBALL BALANCED WHEEL® 52330PB

## Wheel 30 Numbers + PB in 14 Games for a 2 of 5 Win

With Powerball

| Numbers Matched | Maximum Wins | | | | | | Minimum Wins | | | | | |
|---|---|---|---|---|---|---|---|---|---|---|---|---|
| | 5 + 1 | 4 + 1 | 3 + 1 | 2 + 1 | 1 + 1 | 0 + 1 | 5 + 1 | 4 + 1 | 3 + 1 | 2 + 1 | 1 + 1 | 0 + 1 |
| 5 + 1 | 1 | 1 | 1 | 1 | 0 | 10 | 0 | 0 | 0 | 1 | 8 | 5 |
| 4 + 1 | - | 2 | 1 | 0 | 1 | 10 | - | 0 | 0 | 0 | 8 | 6 |
| 3 + 1 | - | - | 3 | 0 | 0 | 11 | - | - | 0 | 0 | 6 | 8 |
| 2 + 1 | - | - | - | 3 | 0 | 11 | - | - | - | 0 | 4 | 10 |
| 1 + 1 | - | - | - | - | 3 | 11 | - | - | - | - | 2 | 12 |
| 0 + 1 | - | - | - | - | - | 14 | - | - | - | - | - | 14 |

Without Powerball

| Numbers Matched | Maximum Wins | | | | | Minimum Wins | | | | |
|---|---|---|---|---|---|---|---|---|---|---|
| | 5 + 0 | 4 + 0 | 3 + 0 | 2 + 0 | 1 + 0 | 5 + 0 | 4 + 0 | 3 + 0 | 2 + 0 | 1 + 0 |
| 5 + 0 | 1 | 1 | 1 | 1 | 0 | 0 | 0 | 0 | 1 | 8 |
| 4 + 0 | - | 2 | 1 | 0 | 1 | - | 0 | 0 | 0 | 8 |
| 3 + 0 | - | - | 3 | 0 | 0 | - | - | 0 | 0 | 6 |
| 2 + 0 | - | - | - | 3 | 0 | - | - | - | 0 | 4 |
| 1 + 0 | - | - | - | - | 3 | - | - | - | - | 2 |

(Continued Next Page)

**POWERBALL BALANCED WHEEL® 52330PB** (Continued from previous page)

## Your 30 Numbers + PB to Wheel

| A | B | C | D | E | F | G | H | I | J | K |
|---|---|---|---|---|---|---|---|---|---|---|
| 3 | 2 | 2 | 3 | 2 | 2 | 2 | 2 | 3 | 2 | 2 |

| L | M | N | O | P | Q | R | S | T | U | V |
|---|---|---|---|---|---|---|---|---|---|---|
| 2 | 3 | 3 | 3 | 3 | 2 | 2 | 2 | 3 | 2 | 2 |

| W | X | Y | Z | aa | bb | cc | dd | PB |
|---|---|---|---|---|---|---|---|---|
| 3 | 2 | 2 | 3 | 2 | 2 | 2 | 2 | 14 |

## The 14 Games to Play

| | | | | | | |
|---|---|---|---|---|---|---|
| 1. | A | D | T | Z | aa | PB |
| 2. | A | D | T | Z | dd | PB |
| 3. | A | J | L | aa | dd | PB |
| 4. | B | E | I | X | bb | PB |
| 5. | B | H | I | X | cc | PB |
| 6. | C | K | O | R | Y | PB |
| 7. | C | O | Q | V | Y | PB |
| 8. | D | J | L | T | Z | PB |
| 9. | E | H | I | bb | cc | PB |
| 10. | F | G | S | U | W | PB |
| 11. | F | M | N | P | S | PB |
| 12. | G | M | N | P | W | PB |
| 13. | K | O | Q | R | V | PB |
| 14. | M | N | P | U | W | PB |



# POWERBALL BALANCED WHEEL® 52331PB

## Wheel 31 Numbers + PB in 15 Games for a 2 of 5 Win

With Powerball

| Numbers Matched | Maximum Wins 5 + 1 | 4 + 1 | 3 + 1 | 2 + 1 | 1 + 1 | 0 + 1 | Minimum Wins 5 + 1 | 4 + 1 | 3 + 1 | 2 + 1 | 1 + 1 | 0 + 1 |
|---|---|---|---|---|---|---|---|---|---|---|---|---|
| 5 + 1 | 1 | 1 | 1 | 1 | 0 | 11 | 0 | 0 | 0 | 1 | 8 | 6 |
| 4 + 1 | - | 2 | 1 | 0 | 1 | 11 | - | 0 | 0 | 0 | 8 | 7 |
| 3 + 1 | - | - | 3 | 0 | 0 | 12 | - | - | 0 | 0 | 6 | 9 |
| 2 + 1 | - | - | - | 3 | 0 | 12 | - | - | - | 0 | 4 | 11 |
| 1 + 1 | - | - | - | - | 3 | 12 | - | - | - | - | 2 | 13 |
| 0 + 1 | - | - | - | - | - | 15 | - | - | - | - | - | 15 |

Without Powerball

| Numbers Matched | Maximum Wins 5 + 0 | 4 + 0 | 3 + 0 | 2 + 0 | 1 + 0 | Minimum Wins 5 + 0 | 4 + 0 | 3 + 0 | 2 + 0 | 1 + 0 |
|---|---|---|---|---|---|---|---|---|---|---|
| 5 + 0 | 1 | 1 | 1 | 1 | 0 | 0 | 0 | 0 | 1 | 8 |
| 4 + 0 | - | 2 | 1 | 0 | 1 | - | 0 | 0 | 0 | 8 |
| 3 + 0 | - | - | 3 | 0 | 0 | - | - | 0 | 0 | 6 |
| 2 + 0 | - | - | - | 3 | 0 | - | - | - | 0 | 4 |
| 1 + 0 | - | - | - | - | 3 | - | - | - | - | 2 |

## Your 31 Numbers + PB to Wheel

| A | B | C | D | E | F | G | H | I | J | K |
|---|---|---|---|---|---|---|---|---|---|---|
| 3 | 3 | 2 | 2 | 2 | 3 | 2 | 2 | 2 | 2 | 3 |

| L | M | N | O | P | Q | R | S | T | U | V |
|---|---|---|---|---|---|---|---|---|---|---|
| 2 | 3 | 2 | 3 | 2 | 3 | 2 | 2 | 3 | 2 | 2 |

| W | X | Y | Z | aa | bb | cc | dd | ee | PB |
|---|---|---|---|---|---|---|---|---|---|
| 3 | 3 | 2 | 3 | 2 | 3 | 2 | 3 | 2 | 15 |

(Continued Next Page)

**POWERBALL BALANCED WHEEL® 52331PB** (Continued from previous page)

## The 15 Games to Play

| | | | | | | |
|---|---|---|---|---|---|---|
| 1. | A | B | V | X | Z | PB |
| 2. | A | B | X | Z | ee | PB |
| 3. | A | P | V | aa | ee | PB |
| 4. | B | P | X | Z | aa | PB |
| 5. | C | F | M | bb | dd | PB |
| 6. | C | G | N | S | bb | PB |
| 7. | D | I | J | O | Y | PB |
| 8. | D | I | K | T | W | PB |
| 9. | E | H | Q | U | cc | PB |
| 10. | E | L | Q | R | U | PB |
| 11. | F | G | M | S | dd | PB |
| 12. | F | M | N | bb | dd | PB |
| 13. | H | L | Q | R | cc | PB |
| 14. | J | K | O | T | W | PB |
| 15. | K | O | T | W | Y | PB |



# POWERBALL BALANCED WHEEL® 52332PB

## Wheel 32 Numbers + PB in 16 Games for a 2 of 5 Win

With Powerball

| Numbers Matched | Maximum Wins | | | | | | Minimum Wins | | | | | |
|---|---|---|---|---|---|---|---|---|---|---|---|---|
| | 5 + 1 | 4 + 1 | 3 + 1 | 2 + 1 | 1 + 1 | 0 + 1 | 5 + 1 | 4 + 1 | 3 + 1 | 2 + 1 | 1 + 1 | 0 + 1 |
| 5 + 1 | 1 | 1 | 1 | 1 | 0 | 12 | 0 | 0 | 0 | 1 | 8 | 7 |
| 4 + 1 | - | 2 | 1 | 0 | 1 | 12 | - | 0 | 0 | 0 | 8 | 8 |
| 3 + 1 | - | - | 3 | 0 | 0 | 13 | - | - | 0 | 0 | 6 | 10 |
| 2 + 1 | - | - | - | 3 | 0 | 13 | - | - | - | 0 | 4 | 12 |
| 1 + 1 | - | - | - | - | 3 | 13 | - | - | - | - | 2 | 14 |
| 0 + 1 | - | - | - | - | - | 16 | - | - | - | - | - | 16 |

Without Powerball

| Numbers Matched | Maximum Wins | | | | | Minimum Wins | | | | |
|---|---|---|---|---|---|---|---|---|---|---|
| | 5 + 0 | 4 + 0 | 3 + 0 | 2 + 0 | 1 + 0 | 5 + 0 | 4 + 0 | 3 + 0 | 2 + 0 | 1 + 0 |
| 5 + 0 | 1 | 1 | 1 | 1 | 0 | 0 | 0 | 0 | 1 | 8 |
| 4 + 0 | - | 2 | 1 | 0 | 1 | - | 0 | 0 | 0 | 8 |
| 3 + 0 | - | - | 3 | 0 | 0 | - | - | 0 | 0 | 6 |
| 2 + 0 | - | - | - | 3 | 0 | - | - | - | 0 | 4 |
| 1 + 0 | - | - | - | - | 3 | - | - | - | - | 2 |

## Your 32 Numbers + PB to Wheel

| A | B | C | D | E | F | G | H | I | J | K |
|---|---|---|---|---|---|---|---|---|---|---|
| 2 | 2 | 3 | 3 | 3 | 2 | 2 | 3 | 2 | 2 | 2 |
| **L** | **M** | **N** | **O** | **P** | **Q** | **R** | **S** | **T** | **U** | **V** |
| 2 | 3 | 2 | 3 | 3 | 2 | 3 | 2 | 3 | 3 | 2 |
| **W** | **X** | **Y** | **Z** | **aa** | **bb** | **cc** | **dd** | **ee** | **ff** | **PB** |
| 3 | 2 | 2 | 2 | 3 | 3 | 3 | 2 | 3 | 3 | 16 |

## The 16 Games to Play

| | | | | | | |
|---|---|---|---|---|---|---|
| 1. | A | D | O | R | ff | PB |
| 2. | A | G | Y | Z | ff | PB |
| 3. | B | H | U | W | cc | PB |
| 4. | B | Q | S | V | W | PB |
| 5. | C | J | L | N | X | PB |
| 6. | C | J | M | T | aa | PB |
| 7. | C | M | T | X | aa | PB |
| 8. | D | G | O | R | ff | PB |
| 9. | D | O | R | Y | Z | PB |
| 10. | E | F | P | bb | dd | PB |



(Continued Next Page)

**POWERBALL BALANCED WHEEL® 52332PB** (Continued from previous page)

| | | | | | | |
|---|---|---|---|---|---|---|
| 11. | E | I | P | bb | ee | PB |
| 12. | E | K | P | bb | ee | PB |
| 13. | F | I | K | dd | ee | PB |
| 14. | H | Q | S | U | cc | PB |
| 15. | H | U | V | W | cc | PB |
| 16. | L | M | N | T | aa | PB |



# POWERBALL BALANCED WHEEL® 52334PB

## Wheel 34 Numbers + PB in 18 Games for a 2 of 5 Win

With Powerball

| Numbers Matched | Maximum Wins 5 + 1 | 4 + 1 | 3 + 1 | 2 + 1 | 1 + 1 | 0 + 1 | Minimum Wins 5 + 1 | 4 + 1 | 3 + 1 | 2 + 1 | 1 + 1 | 0 + 1 |
|---|---|---|---|---|---|---|---|---|---|---|---|---|
| 5 + 1 | 1 | 1 | 0 | 2 | 2 | 12 | 0 | 0 | 0 | 1 | 8 | 9 |
| 4 + 1 | - | 2 | 0 | 2 | 0 | 14 | - | 0 | 0 | 0 | 8 | 10 |
| 3 + 1 | - | - | 3 | 0 | 0 | 15 | - | - | 0 | 0 | 6 | 12 |
| 2 + 1 | - | - | - | 3 | 0 | 15 | - | - | - | 0 | 4 | 14 |
| 1 + 1 | - | - | - | - | 3 | 15 | - | - | - | - | 2 | 16 |
| 0 + 1 | - | - | - | - | - | 18 | - | - | - | - | - | 18 |

Without Powerball

| Numbers Matched | Maximum Wins 5 + 0 | 4 + 0 | 3 + 0 | 2 + 0 | 1 + 0 | Minimum Wins 5 + 0 | 4 + 0 | 3 + 0 | 2 + 0 | 1 + 0 |
|---|---|---|---|---|---|---|---|---|---|---|
| 5 + 0 | 1 | 1 | 0 | 2 | 2 | 0 | 0 | 0 | 1 | 8 |
| 4 + 0 | - | 2 | 0 | 2 | 0 | - | 0 | 0 | 0 | 8 |
| 3 + 0 | - | - | 3 | 0 | 0 | - | - | 0 | 0 | 6 |
| 2 + 0 | - | - | - | 3 | 0 | - | - | - | 0 | 4 |
| 1 + 0 | - | - | - | - | 3 | - | - | - | - | 2 |

## Your 34 Numbers + PB to Wheel

| A | B | C | D | E | F | G | H | I |
|---|---|---|---|---|---|---|---|---|
| 3 | 3 | 2 | 3 | 3 | 2 | 2 | 2 | 3 |
| **J** | **K** | **L** | **M** | **N** | **O** | **P** | **Q** | **R** |
| 3 | 3 | 3 | 2 | 3 | 2 | 3 | 3 | 2 |
| **S** | **T** | **U** | **V** | **W** | **X** | **Y** | **Z** | **aa** |
| 2 | 2 | 3 | 3 | 2 | 3 | 3 | 2 | 3 |
| **bb** | **cc** | **dd** | **ee** | **ff** | **gg** | **hh** | **PB** | |
| 3 | 3 | 3 | 3 | 2 | 3 | 3 | 18 | |

## The 18 Games to Play

| | | | | | | |
|---|---|---|---|---|---|---|
| 1. | A | F | U | V | X | PB |
| 2. | A | I | V | X | aa | PB |
| 3. | A | L | V | X | hh | PB |
| 4. | B | D | P | Y | bb | PB |
| 5. | B | K | Q | bb | dd | PB |
| 6. | B | P | T | Y | bb | PB |
| 7. | C | E | N | U | ee | PB |
| 8. | C | G | S | W | Z | PB |
| 9. | D | J | cc | ff | gg | PB |
| 10. | D | K | Q | T | dd | PB |
| 11. | E | G | N | Z | ee | PB |
| 12. | E | N | S | W | ee | PB |
| 13. | F | I | L | aa | hh | PB |
| 14. | H | J | M | cc | gg | PB |
| 15. | H | M | O | R | ff | PB |
| 16. | I | L | U | aa | hh | PB |
| 17. | J | O | R | cc | gg | PB |
| 18. | K | P | Q | Y | dd | PB |

# POWERBALL BALANCED WHEEL® 52336PB

## Wheel 36 Numbers + PB in 20 Games for a 2 of 5 Win

With Powerball

| Numbers Matched | Maximum Wins | | | | | | Minimum Wins | | | | | |
|---|---|---|---|---|---|---|---|---|---|---|---|---|
| | 5 + 1 | 4 + 1 | 3 + 1 | 2 + 1 | 1 + 1 | 0 + 1 | 5 + 1 | 4 + 1 | 3 + 1 | 2 + 1 | 1 + 1 | 0 + 1 |
| 5 + 1 | 1 | 1 | 0 | 2 | 1 | 15 | 0 | 0 | 0 | 1 | 8 | 11 |
| 4 + 1 | - | 2 | 0 | 2 | 0 | 16 | - | 0 | 0 | 0 | 8 | 12 |
| 3 + 1 | - | - | 3 | 0 | 0 | 17 | - | - | 0 | 0 | 6 | 14 |
| 2 + 1 | - | - | - | 3 | 0 | 17 | - | - | - | 0 | 4 | 16 |
| 1 + 1 | - | - | - | - | 3 | 17 | - | - | - | - | 2 | 18 |
| 0 + 1 | - | - | - | - | - | 20 | - | - | - | - | - | 20 |

Without Powerball

| Numbers Matched | Maximum Wins | | | | | Minimum Wins | | | | |
|---|---|---|---|---|---|---|---|---|---|---|
| | 5 + 0 | 4 + 0 | 3 + 0 | 2 + 0 | 1 + 0 | 5 + 0 | 4 + 0 | 3 + 0 | 2 + 0 | 1 + 0 |
| 5 + 0 | 1 | 1 | 0 | 2 | 1 | 0 | 0 | 0 | 1 | 8 |
| 4 + 0 | - | 2 | 0 | 2 | 0 | - | 0 | 0 | 0 | 8 |
| 3 + 0 | - | - | 3 | 0 | 0 | - | - | 0 | 0 | 6 |
| 2 + 0 | - | - | - | 3 | 0 | - | - | - | 0 | 4 |
| 1 + 0 | - | - | - | - | 3 | - | - | - | - | 2 |

## Your 36 Numbers + PB to Wheel

| A | B | C | D | E | F | G | H | I | J |
|---|---|---|---|---|---|---|---|---|---|
| 3 | 3 | 3 | 3 | 3 | 3 | 3 | 3 | 3 | 3 |
| **K** | **L** | **M** | **N** | **O** | **P** | **Q** | **R** | **S** | **T** |
| 3 | 3 | 3 | 2 | 2 | 2 | 2 | 2 | 2 | 2 |
| **U** | **V** | **W** | **X** | **Y** | **Z** | **aa** | **bb** | **cc** | **dd** |
| 2 | 3 | 3 | 3 | 3 | 3 | 3 | 3 | 3 | 3 |
| **ee** | **ff** | **gg** | **hh** | **ii** | **jj** | **PB** | | | |
| 3 | 3 | 3 | 3 | 3 | 3 | 20 | | | |

## The 20 Games to Play

| | | | | | | |
|---|---|---|---|---|---|---|
| 1. | A | E | W | aa | cc | PB |
| 2. | A | M | aa | cc | jj | PB |
| 3. | A | O | P | aa | cc | PB |
| 4. | B | D | ee | gg | ii | PB |
| 5. | B | I | Y | gg | ii | PB |
| 6. | B | N | U | gg | ii | PB |
| 7. | C | G | Z | ff | hh | PB |
| 8. | C | J | V | Z | ff | PB |
| 9. | C | S | T | Z | ff | PB |
| 10. | D | I | N | Y | ee | PB |
| 11. | D | I | U | Y | ee | PB |
| 12. | E | M | O | W | jj | PB |
| 13. | E | M | P | W | jj | PB |
| 14. | F | H | L | X | bb | PB |
| 15. | F | K | L | X | dd | PB |
| 16. | F | L | Q | R | X | PB |
| 17. | G | J | S | V | hh | PB |
| 18. | G | J | T | V | hh | PB |
| 19. | H | K | Q | bb | dd | PB |
| 20. | H | K | R | bb | dd | PB |

# POWERBALL BALANCED WHEEL® 52339PB

## Wheel 39 Numbers + PB in 23 Games for a 2 of 5 Win

With Powerball

| Numbers Matched | Maximum Wins | | | | | | Minimum Wins | | | | | |
|---|---|---|---|---|---|---|---|---|---|---|---|---|
| | 5 + 1 | 4 + 1 | 3 + 1 | 2 + 1 | 1 + 1 | 0 + 1 | 5 + 1 | 4 + 1 | 3 + 1 | 2 + 1 | 1 + 1 | 0 + 1 |
| 5 + 1 | 1 | 1 | 0 | 2 | 1 | 18 | 0 | 0 | 0 | 1 | 11 | 11 |
| 4 + 1 | - | 2 | 0 | 2 | 0 | 19 | - | 0 | 0 | 0 | 11 | 12 |
| 3 + 1 | - | - | 3 | 0 | 0 | 20 | - | - | 0 | 0 | 8 | 15 |
| 2 + 1 | - | - | - | 3 | 0 | 20 | - | - | - | 0 | 5 | 18 |
| 1 + 1 | - | - | - | - | 3 | 20 | - | - | - | - | 2 | 21 |
| 0 + 1 | - | - | - | - | - | 23 | - | - | - | - | - | 23 |

Without Powerball

| Numbers Matched | Maximum Wins | | | | | Minimum Wins | | | | |
|---|---|---|---|---|---|---|---|---|---|---|
| | 5 + 0 | 4 + 0 | 3 + 0 | 2 + 0 | 1 + 0 | 5 + 0 | 4 + 0 | 3 + 0 | 2 + 0 | 1 + 0 |
| 5 + 0 | 1 | 1 | 0 | 2 | 1 | 0 | 0 | 0 | 1 | 11 |
| 4 + 0 | - | 2 | 0 | 2 | 0 | - | 0 | 0 | 0 | 11 |
| 3 + 0 | - | - | 3 | 0 | 0 | - | - | 0 | 0 | 8 |
| 2 + 0 | - | - | - | 3 | 0 | - | - | - | 0 | 5 |
| 1 + 0 | - | - | - | - | 3 | - | - | - | - | 2 |

## Your 39 Numbers + PB to Wheel

| A | B | C | D | E | F | G | H | I | J |
|---|---|---|---|---|---|---|---|---|---|
| 3 | 3 | 3 | 3 | 3 | 3 | 3 | 3 | 3 | 3 |
| **K** | **L** | **M** | **N** | **O** | **P** | **Q** | **R** | **S** | **T** |
| 3 | 3 | 3 | 3 | 3 | 3 | 3 | 3 | 3 | 3 |
| **U** | **V** | **W** | **X** | **Y** | **Z** | **aa** | **bb** | **cc** | **dd** |
| 3 | 3 | 3 | 3 | 3 | 3 | 2 | 3 | 2 | 3 |
| **ee** | **ff** | **gg** | **hh** | **ii** | **jj** | **kk** | ***ll*** | **mm** | **PB** |
| 3 | 3 | 3 | 3 | 3 | 3 | 3 | 3 | 3 | 23 |

## The 23 Games to Play

| | | | | | | |
|---|---|---|---|---|---|---|
| 1. | A | E | Z | dd | mm | PB |
| 2. | A | K | bb | kk | mm | PB |
| 3. | A | N | P | Z | mm | PB |
| 4. | B | G | *Q* | ff | jj | PB |
| 5. | B | J | S | gg | jj | PB |
| 6. | B | O | ff | ii | jj | PB |
| 7. | C | F | L | U | W | PB |
| 8. | C | T | U | V | *ll* | PB |
| 9. | C | V | X | hh | *ll* | PB |
| 10. | D | H | Y | aa | ee | PB |
| 11. | D | H | Y | cc | ee | PB |
| 12. | D | I | M | R | Y | PB |
| 13. | E | K | N | dd | kk | PB |
| 14. | E | N | P | bb | dd | PB |
| 15. | F | L | V | W | *ll* | PB |
| 16. | F | T | W | X | hh | PB |
| 17. | G | J | O | gg | ii | PB |
| 18. | G | O | *Q* | S | ii | PB |
| 19. | H | I | M | R | ee | PB |
| 20. | I | M | R | aa | cc | PB |
| 21. | J | *Q* | S | ff | gg | PB |
| 22. | K | P | Z | bb | kk | PB |
| 23. | L | T | U | X | hh | PB |

# POWERBALL BALANCED WHEEL® 52342PB

## Wheel 42 Numbers + PB in 26 Games for a 2 of 5 Win

With Powerball

| Numbers Matched | Maximum Wins 5 + 1 | 4 + 1 | 3 + 1 | 2 + 1 | 1 + 1 | 0 + 1 | Minimum Wins 5 + 1 | 4 + 1 | 3 + 1 | 2 + 1 | 1 + 1 | 0 + 1 |
|---|---|---|---|---|---|---|---|---|---|---|---|---|
| 5 + 1 | 1 | 0 | 3 | 0 | 3 | 19 | 0 | 0 | 0 | 1 | 13 | 12 |
| 4 + 1 | - | 1 | 2 | 1 | 2 | 20 | - | 0 | 0 | 0 | 12 | 14 |
| 3 + 1 | - | - | 2 | 2 | 1 | 21 | - | - | 0 | 0 | 9 | 17 |
| 2 + 1 | - | - | - | 4 | 0 | 22 | - | - | - | 0 | 6 | 20 |
| 1 + 1 | - | - | - | - | 4 | 22 | - | - | - | - | 3 | 23 |
| 0 + 1 | - | - | - | - | - | 26 | - | - | - | - | - | 26 |

Without Powerball

| Numbers Matched | Maximum Wins 5 + 0 | 4 + 0 | 3 + 0 | 2 + 0 | 1 + 0 | Minimum Wins 5 + 0 | 4 + 0 | 3 + 0 | 2 + 0 | 1 + 0 |
|---|---|---|---|---|---|---|---|---|---|---|
| 5 + 0 | 1 | 0 | 3 | 0 | 3 | 0 | 0 | 0 | 1 | 13 |
| 4 + 0 | - | 1 | 2 | 1 | 2 | - | 0 | 0 | 0 | 12 |
| 3 + 0 | - | - | 2 | 2 | 1 | - | - | 0 | 0 | 9 |
| 2 + 0 | - | - | - | 4 | 0 | - | - | - | 0 | 6 |
| 1 + 0 | - | - | - | - | 4 | - | - | - | - | 3 |

## Your 42 Numbers + PB to Wheel

| A | B | C | D | E | F | G | H | I | J | K |
|---|---|---|---|---|---|---|---|---|---|---|
| 3 | 4 | 3 | 3 | 4 | 3 | 3 | 3 | 3 | 3 | 3 |
| **L** | **M** | **N** | **O** | **P** | **Q** | **R** | **S** | **T** | **U** | **V** |
| 3 | 3 | 3 | 3 | 3 | 3 | 3 | 3 | 3 | 3 | 3 |
| **W** | **X** | **Y** | **Z** | **aa** | **bb** | **cc** | **dd** | **ee** | **ff** | **gg** |
| 3 | 3 | 3 | 3 | 4 | 3 | 3 | 3 | 3 | 3 | 3 |
| **hh** | **ii** | **jj** | **kk** | ***ll*** | **mm** | **nn** | **oo** | **pp** | **PB** | |
| 3 | 3 | 3 | 4 | 3 | 3 | 3 | 3 | 3 | 26 | |

## The 26 Games to Play

| | | | | | | | | | | | | | |
|---|---|---|---|---|---|---|---|---|---|---|---|---|---|
| 1. | A | D | U | hh | pp | PB | 14. | E | M | aa | dd | jj | PB |
| 2. | A | G | Z | nn | pp | PB | 15. | E | R | W | aa | dd | PB |
| 3. | A | N | V | hh | pp | PB | 16. | E | S | X | aa | jj | PB |
| 4. | B | F | P | ii | kk | PB | 17. | F | J | ff | ii | mm | PB |
| 5. | B | J | O | kk | mm | PB | 18. | F | L | O | ii | oo | PB |
| 6. | B | L | ff | kk | oo | PB | 19. | G | V | Z | hh | nn | PB |
| 7. | B | O | P | ff | kk | PB | 20. | H | I | K | cc | gg | PB |
| 8. | C | H | I | bb | ee | PB | 21. | H | I | *Q* | cc | *ll* | PB |
| 9. | C | K | ee | gg | *ll* | PB | 22. | J | L | P | mm | oo | PB |
| 10. | C | *Q* | bb | cc | ee | PB | 23. | K | *Q* | bb | gg | *ll* | PB |
| 11. | D | G | N | U | nn | PB | 24. | M | R | S | W | X | PB |
| 12. | D | N | U | V | Z | PB | 25. | R | T | W | Y | jj | PB |
| 13. | E | M | T | Y | aa | PB | 26. | S | T | X | Y | dd | PB |

# POWERBALL BALANCED WHEEL® 52345PB

## Wheel 45 Numbers + PB in 30 Games for a 2 of 5 Win

With Powerball

| Numbers Matched | Maximum Wins 5 + 1 | 4 + 1 | 3 + 1 | 2 + 1 | 1 + 1 | 0 + 1 | Minimum Wins 5 + 1 | 4 + 1 | 3 + 1 | 2 + 1 | 1 + 1 | 0 + 1 |
|---|---|---|---|---|---|---|---|---|---|---|---|---|
| 5 + 1 | 1 | 0 | 3 | 0 | 3 | 23 | 0 | 0 | 0 | 1 | 13 | 16 |
| 4 + 1 | - | 1 | 2 | 1 | 2 | 24 | - | 0 | 0 | 0 | 12 | 18 |
| 3 + 1 | - | - | 2 | 2 | 3 | 23 | - | - | 0 | 0 | 9 | 21 |
| 2 + 1 | - | - | - | 4 | 0 | 26 | - | - | - | 0 | 6 | 24 |
| 1 + 1 | - | - | - | - | 5 | 25 | - | - | - | - | 3 | 27 |
| 0 + 1 | - | - | - | - | - | 30 | - | - | - | - | - | 30 |

Without Powerball

| Numbers Matched | Maximum Wins 5 + 0 | 4 + 0 | 3 + 0 | 2 + 0 | 1 + 0 | Minimum Wins 5 + 0 | 4 + 0 | 3 + 0 | 2 + 0 | 1 + 0 |
|---|---|---|---|---|---|---|---|---|---|---|
| 5 + 0 | 1 | 0 | 3 | 0 | 3 | 0 | 0 | 0 | 1 | 13 |
| 4 + 0 | - | 1 | 2 | 1 | 2 | - | 0 | 0 | 0 | 12 |
| 3 + 0 | - | - | 2 | 2 | 3 | - | - | 0 | 0 | 9 |
| 2 + 0 | - | - | - | 4 | 0 | - | - | - | 0 | 6 |
| 1 + 0 | - | - | - | - | 5 | - | - | - | - | 3 |

## Your 45 Numbers + PB to Wheel

| A | B | C | D | E | F | G | H | I | J |
|---|---|---|---|---|---|---|---|---|---|
| 3 | 4 | 4 | 3 | 4 | 3 | 3 | 3 | 3 | 4 |
| **K** | **L** | **M** | **N** | **O** | **P** | **Q** | **R** | **S** | **T** |
| 4 | 3 | 3 | 3 | 3 | 4 | 3 | 4 | 3 | 3 |
| **U** | **V** | **W** | **X** | **Y** | **Z** | **aa** | **bb** | **cc** | **dd** |
| 3 | 3 | 3 | 3 | 3 | 3 | 5 | 4 | 3 | 3 |
| **ee** | **ff** | **gg** | **hh** | **ii** | **jj** | **kk** | ***ll*** | **mm** | **nn** |
| 3 | 3 | 4 | 3 | 4 | 4 | 3 | 3 | 3 | 3 |
| **oo** | **pp** | **qq** | **rr** | **ss** | **PB** | | | | |
| 3 | 4 | 3 | 4 | 3 | 30 | | | | |

## The 30 Games to Play

| | | | | | | |
|---|---|---|---|---|---|---|
| 1. | A | E | T | qq | rr | PB |
| 2. | A | H | ee | hh | qq | PB |
| 3. | A | *Q* | W | kk | qq | PB |
| 4. | B | C | J | ii | jj | PB |
| 5. | B | K | bb | ii | mm | PB |
| 6. | B | R | U | aa | ii | PB |
| 7. | B | Z | aa | ii | pp | PB |
| 8. | C | K | aa | jj | pp | PB |
| 9. | C | R | aa | bb | jj | PB |
| 10. | C | U | Z | jj | mm | PB |
| 11. | D | M | S | ff | ss | PB |
| 12. | D | O | P | ff | gg | PB |
| 13. | D | V | X | Y | ff | PB |
| 14. | E | H | *Q* | T | rr | PB |
| 15. | E | H | W | kk | rr | PB |
| 16. | E | *Q* | ee | hh | rr | PB |
| 17. | F | G | I | dd | oo | PB |
| 18. | F | I | L | N | *ll* | PB |
| 19. | F | I | cc | nn | oo | PB |
| 20. | G | L | N | cc | dd | PB |
| 21. | G | cc | dd | *ll* | nn | PB |
| 22. | J | K | R | Z | bb | PB |
| 23. | J | K | U | bb | pp | PB |
| 24. | J | R | aa | mm | pp | PB |



(Continued Next Page)

**POWERBALL BALANCED WHEEL® 52345PB** (Continued from previous page)

| | | | | | | |
|---|---|---|---|---|---|---|
| 25. | L | N | ll | nn | oo | PB |
| 26. | M | O | X | Y | ss | PB |
| 27. | M | P | V | gg | ss | PB |
| 28. | O | P | S | V | gg | PB |
| 29. | P | S | X | Y | gg | PB |
| 30. | T | W | ee | hh | kk | PB |



# POWERBALL BALANCED WHEEL® 52347PB

## Wheel 47 Numbers + PB in 33 Games for a 2 of 5 Win

With Powerball

| Numbers Matched | Maximum Wins 5 + 1 | 4 + 1 | 3 + 1 | 2 + 1 | 1 + 1 | 0 + 1 | Minimum Wins 5 + 1 | 4 + 1 | 3 + 1 | 2 + 1 | 1 + 1 | 0 + 1 |
|---|---|---|---|---|---|---|---|---|---|---|---|---|
| 5 + 1 | 1 | 0 | 2 | 2 | 3 | 25 | 0 | 0 | 0 | 1 | 13 | 19 |
| 4 + 1 | - | 1 | 2 | 1 | 3 | 26 | - | 0 | 0 | 0 | 12 | 21 |
| 3 + 1 | - | - | 2 | 2 | 3 | 26 | - | - | 0 | 0 | 9 | 24 |
| 2 + 1 | - | - | - | 4 | 0 | 29 | - | - | - | 0 | 6 | 27 |
| 1 + 1 | - | - | - | - | 5 | 28 | - | - | - | - | 3 | 30 |
| 0 + 1 | - | - | - | - | - | 33 | - | - | - | - | - | 33 |

Without Powerball

| Numbers Matched | Maximum Wins 5 + 0 | 4 + 0 | 3 + 0 | 2 + 0 | 1 + 0 | Minimum Wins 5 + 0 | 4 + 0 | 3 + 0 | 2 + 0 | 1 + 0 |
|---|---|---|---|---|---|---|---|---|---|---|
| 5 + 0 | 1 | 0 | 2 | 2 | 3 | 0 | 0 | 0 | 1 | 13 |
| 4 + 0 | - | 1 | 2 | 1 | 3 | - | 0 | 0 | 0 | 12 |
| 3 + 0 | - | - | 2 | 2 | 3 | - | - | 0 | 0 | 9 |
| 2 + 0 | - | - | - | 4 | 0 | - | - | - | 0 | 6 |
| 1 + 0 | - | - | - | - | 5 | - | - | - | - | 3 |

## Your 47 Numbers + PB to Wheel

| A | B | C | D | E | F | G | H | I | J |
|---|---|---|---|---|---|---|---|---|---|
| 3 | 3 | 3 | 3 | 3 | 5 | 3 | 3 | 3 | 4 |
| **K** | **L** | **M** | **N** | **O** | **P** | **Q** | **R** | **S** | **T** |
| 3 | 3 | 4 | 3 | 3 | 4 | 3 | 4 | 3 | 3 |
| **U** | **V** | **W** | **X** | **Y** | **Z** | **aa** | **bb** | **cc** | **dd** |
| 4 | 4 | 4 | 4 | 4 | 4 | 3 | 4 | 4 | 4 |
| **ee** | **ff** | **gg** | **hh** | **ii** | **jj** | **kk** | **ll** | **mm** | **nn** |
| 3 | 4 | 4 | 4 | 4 | 3 | 4 | 4 | 3 | 3 |
| **oo** | **pp** | **qq** | **rr** | **ss** | **tt** | **uu** | **PB** | | |
| 4 | 4 | 3 | 3 | 3 | 3 | 4 | 33 | | |

## The 33 Games to Play

| | | | | | | |
|---|---|---|---|---|---|---|
| 1. | A | I | W | dd | pp | PB |
| 2. | A | J | O | ff | kk | PB |
| 3. | A | R | ll | oo | tt | PB |
| 4. | B | F | bb | cc | gg | PB |
| 5. | B | H | M | Z | ss | PB |
| 6. | B | P | U | hh | uu | PB |
| 7. | C | D | L | jj | nn | PB |
| 8. | C | E | ee | jj | rr | PB |
| 9. | C | Q | ee | mm | nn | PB |
| 10. | D | E | L | ee | rr | PB |
| 11. | D | L | Q | jj | mm | PB |
| 12. | E | Q | mm | nn | rr | PB |
| 13. | F | H | bb | gg | hh | PB |
| 14. | F | M | P | Z | cc | PB |
| 15. | F | M | U | Z | hh | PB |
| 16. | F | cc | hh | ss | uu | PB |



(Continued Next Page)

## POWERBALL BALANCED WHEEL® 52347PB (Continued from previous page)

| | | | | | | |
|---|---|---|---|---|---|---|
| 17. | G | K | N | X | qq | PB |
| 18. | G | N | S | T | aa | PB |
| 19. | G | N | V | Y | ii | PB |
| 20. | H | P | U | cc | uu | PB |
| 21. | I | J | ff | kk | tt | PB |
| 22. | I | O | R | *ll* | oo | PB |
| 23. | J | R | dd | ff | oo | PB |
| 24. | J | W | ff | *ll* | pp | PB |
| 25. | K | S | Y | aa | qq | PB |
| 26. | K | T | V | Y | ii | PB |
| 27. | M | Z | bb | gg | uu | PB |
| 28. | O | W | dd | pp | tt | PB |
| 29. | P | U | bb | gg | ss | PB |
| 30. | R | W | kk | oo | pp | PB |
| 31. | S | V | X | aa | ii | PB |
| 32. | T | V | X | ii | qq | PB |
| 33. | X | Y | dd | kk | *ll* | PB |



# POWERBALL BALANCED WHEEL® 52355PB

## Wheel 55 Numbers + PB in 45 Games for a 2 of 5 Win

With Powerball

| Numbers Matched | Maximum Wins 5 + 1 | 4 + 1 | 3 + 1 | 2 + 1 | 1 + 1 | 0 + 1 | Minimum Wins 5 + 1 | 4 + 1 | 3 + 1 | 2 + 1 | 1 + 1 | 0 + 1 |
|---|---|---|---|---|---|---|---|---|---|---|---|---|
| 5 + 1 | 1 | 1 | 1 | 3 | 5 | 34 | 0 | 0 | 0 | 1 | 15 | 29 |
| 4 + 1 | - | 2 | 0 | 3 | 5 | 35 | - | 0 | 0 | 0 | 14 | 31 |
| 3 + 1 | - | - | 2 | 3 | 3 | 37 | - | - | 0 | 0 | 10 | 35 |
| 2 + 1 | - | - | - | 5 | 0 | 40 | - | - | - | 0 | 6 | 39 |
| 1 + 1 | - | - | - | - | 5 | 40 | - | - | - | - | 3 | 42 |
| 0 + 1 | - | - | - | - | - | 45 | - | - | - | - | - | 45 |

Without Powerball

| Numbers Matched | Maximum Wins 5 + 0 | 4 + 0 | 3 + 0 | 2 + 0 | 1 + 0 | Minimum Wins 5 + 0 | 4 + 0 | 3 + 0 | 2 + 0 | 1 + 0 |
|---|---|---|---|---|---|---|---|---|---|---|
| 5 + 0 | 1 | 1 | 1 | 3 | 5 | 0 | 0 | 0 | 1 | 15 |
| 4 + 0 | - | 2 | 0 | 3 | 5 | - | 0 | 0 | 0 | 14 |
| 3 + 0 | - | - | 2 | 3 | 3 | - | - | 0 | 0 | 10 |
| 2 + 0 | - | - | - | 5 | 0 | - | - | - | 0 | 6 |
| 1 + 0 | - | - | - | - | 5 | - | - | - | - | 3 |

## Your 55 Numbers + PB to Wheel

| A | B | C | D | E | F | G | H | I | J |
|---|---|---|---|---|---|---|---|---|---|
| 4 | 4 | 4 | 5 | 4 | 5 | 4 | 5 | 4 | 5 |
| **K** | **L** | **M** | **N** | **O** | **P** | **Q** | **R** | **S** | **T** |
| 4 | 4 | 4 | 4 | 4 | 5 | 5 | 4 | 4 | 4 |
| **U** | **V** | **W** | **X** | **Y** | **Z** | **aa** | **bb** | **cc** | **dd** |
| 4 | 5 | 5 | 5 | 4 | 4 | 4 | 4 | 4 | 4 |
| **ee** | **ff** | **gg** | **hh** | **ii** | **jj** | **kk** | ***ll*** | **mm** | **nn** |
| 4 | 4 | 4 | 4 | 4 | 4 | 5 | 4 | 4 | 4 |
| **oo** | **pp** | **qq** | **rr** | **ss** | **tt** | **uu** | **vv** | **ww** | **xx** |
| 5 | 4 | 5 | 5 | 4 | 4 | 3 | 3 | 3 | 3 |
| **yy** | **zz** | **AA** | **BB** | **CC** | **PB** | | | | |
| 3 | 3 | 3 | 3 | 4 | 45 | | | | |

(Continued Next Page)

**POWERBALL BALANCED WHEEL® 52355PB** (Continued from previous page)

## The 45 Games to Play

| | | | | | | |
|---|---|---|---|---|---|---|
| 1. | A | B | H | J | ss | PB |
| 2. | A | G | W | qq | CC | PB |
| 3. | A | I | X | aa | hh | PB |
| 4. | A | O | R | ee | *ll* | PB |
| 5. | B | G | I | O | aa | PB |
| 6. | B | L | R | dd | pp | PB |
| 7. | B | X | ee | hh | *ll* | PB |
| 8. | C | N | U | bb | ff | PB |
| 9. | C | U | Y | Z | nn | PB |
| 10. | C | U | tt | uu | BB | PB |
| 11. | C | U | tt | vv | ww | PB |
| 12. | D | F | V | qq | rr | PB |
| 13. | D | P | jj | kk | qq | PB |
| 14. | D | P | kk | rr | CC | PB |
| 15. | D | *Q* | gg | oo | qq | PB |
| 16. | D | T | W | mm | qq | PB |
| 17. | E | K | cc | ii | pp | PB |
| 18. | E | L | ii | xx | AA | PB |
| 19. | E | L | ii | yy | zz | PB |
| 20. | E | M | S | dd | ii | PB |
| 21. | F | P | kk | mm | rr | PB |
| 22. | F | *Q* | T | oo | rr | PB |
| 23. | F | *Q* | V | oo | CC | PB |
| 24. | F | W | gg | jj | rr | PB |
| 25. | G | H | J | ee | *ll* | PB |
| 26. | G | R | X | hh | ss | PB |
| 27. | H | I | J | R | aa | PB |
| 28. | H | J | O | X | hh | PB |
| 29. | H | J | O | X | ss | PB |
| 30. | I | aa | ee | *ll* | ss | PB |
| 31. | K | L | M | S | cc | PB |
| 32. | K | cc | dd | xx | zz | PB |
| 33. | K | cc | dd | yy | AA | PB |
| 34. | M | S | pp | xx | yy | PB |
| 35. | M | S | pp | zz | AA | PB |
| 36. | N | Y | ff | uu | ww | PB |
| 37. | N | Y | ff | vv | BB | PB |
| 38. | N | Z | ff | nn | tt | PB |
| 39. | P | *Q* | W | kk | oo | PB |
| 40. | P | T | V | gg | kk | PB |
| 41. | *Q* | V | jj | mm | oo | PB |
| 42. | T | gg | jj | mm | CC | PB |
| 43. | V | W | Y | bb | tt | PB |
| 44. | Z | bb | nn | uu | vv | PB |
| 45. | Z | bb | nn | ww | BB | PB |



# POWERBALL BALANCED WHEEL® 52356PB

## Wheel 56 Numbers + PB in 48 Games for a 2 of 5 Win

With Powerball

| Numbers Matched | Maximum Wins | | | | | | Minimum Wins | | | | | |
|---|---|---|---|---|---|---|---|---|---|---|---|---|
| | 5 + 1 | 4 + 1 | 3 + 1 | 2 + 1 | 1 + 1 | 0 + 1 | 5 + 1 | 4 + 1 | 3 + 1 | 2 + 1 | 1 + 1 | 0 + 1 |
| 5 + 1 | 1 | 0 | 2 | 6 | 3 | 36 | 0 | 0 | 0 | 1 | 15 | 32 |
| 4 + 1 | - | 1 | 2 | 3 | 4 | 38 | - | 0 | 0 | 0 | 14 | 34 |
| 3 + 1 | - | - | 2 | 3 | 4 | 39 | - | - | 0 | 0 | 10 | 38 |
| 2 + 1 | - | - | - | 5 | 1 | 42 | - | - | - | 0 | 6 | 42 |
| 1 + 1 | - | - | - | - | 6 | 42 | - | - | - | - | 3 | 45 |
| 0 + 1 | - | - | - | - | - | 48 | - | - | - | - | - | 48 |

(Continued Next Page)

**POWERBALL BALANCED WHEEL® 52356PB** (Continued from previous page)

Without Powerball

| Numbers Matched | Maximum Wins | | | | | Minimum Wins | | | | |
|---|---|---|---|---|---|---|---|---|---|---|
| | 5 + 0 | 4 + 0 | 3 + 0 | 2 + 0 | 1 + 0 | 5 + 0 | 4 + 0 | 3 + 0 | 2 + 0 | 1 + 0 |
| 5 + 0 | 1 | 0 | 2 | 6 | 3 | 0 | 0 | 0 | 1 | 15 |
| 4 + 0 | - | 1 | 2 | 3 | 4 | - | 0 | 0 | 0 | 14 |
| 3 + 0 | - | - | 2 | 3 | 4 | - | - | 0 | 0 | 10 |
| 2 + 0 | - | - | - | 5 | 1 | - | - | - | 0 | 6 |
| 1 + 0 | - | - | - | - | 6 | - | - | - | - | 3 |

# Your 56 Numbers + PB to Wheel

| | | | | | | | | | |
|---|---|---|---|---|---|---|---|---|---|
| A | B | C | D | E | F | G | H | I | J |
| 5 | 6 | 5 | 5 | 5 | 5 | 5 | 5 | 5 | 5 |
| K | L | M | N | O | P | Q | R | S | T |
| 5 | 6 | 5 | 4 | 4 | 5 | 4 | 5 | 4 | 4 |
| U | V | W | X | Y | Z | aa | bb | cc | dd |
| 4 | 4 | 4 | 4 | 4 | 4 | 4 | 5 | 4 | 5 |
| ee | ff | gg | hh | ii | jj | kk | *ll* | mm | nn |
| 4 | 4 | 5 | 5 | 5 | 4 | 4 | 4 | 4 | 4 |
| oo | pp | qq | rr | ss | tt | uu | vv | ww | xx |
| 4 | 5 | 4 | 5 | 4 | 4 | 4 | 3 | 3 | 3 |
| yy | zz | AA | BB | CC | DD | PB | | | |
| 3 | 3 | 3 | 3 | 3 | 4 | 48 | | | |

# The 48 Games to Play

| | | | | | | |
|---|---|---|---|---|---|---|
| 1. | A | B | L | P | ss | PB |
| 2. | A | C | L | P | hh | PB |
| 3. | A | P | R | bb | DD | PB |
| 4. | A | P | T | gg | rr | PB |
| 5. | A | P | dd | ii | pp | PB |
| 6. | B | D | E | F | H | PB |
| 7. | B | G | W | nn | oo | PB |
| 8. | B | I | J | O | Y | PB |
| 9. | B | K | M | aa | tt | PB |
| 10. | B | M | V | gg | ii | PB |
| 11. | C | L | R | bb | gg | PB |
| 12. | C | L | T | hh | ii | PB |
| 13. | C | L | T | ss | DD | PB |
| 14. | C | L | dd | pp | rr | PB |
| 15. | D | F | G | I | V | PB |
| 16. | D | F | G | Y | aa | PB |
| 17. | D | F | I | J | tt | PB |
| 18. | D | F | K | M | O | PB |
| 19. | E | G | H | O | tt | PB |
| 20. | E | H | I | J | aa | PB |
| 21. | E | H | J | K | V | PB |
| 22. | E | H | K | M | Y | PB |
| 23. | G | I | J | K | M | PB |
| 24. | N | S | cc | vv | BB | PB |
| 25. | N | S | cc | ww | yy | PB |
| 26. | N | U | Z | cc | jj | PB |
| 27. | N | cc | ee | ff | uu | PB |
| 28. | O | V | Y | aa | tt | PB |
| 29. | Q | W | X | *ll* | mm | PB |
| 30. | Q | kk | *ll* | oo | qq | PB |
| 31. | Q | *ll* | nn | xx | zz | PB |
| 32. | Q | *ll* | nn | AA | CC | PB |
| 33. | R | T | bb | dd | pp | PB |
| 34. | R | bb | hh | rr | DD | PB |



(Continued Next Page)

## POWERBALL BALANCED WHEEL® 52356PB (Continued from previous page)

| | | | | | | |
|---|---|---|---|---|---|---|
| 35. | R | bb | ii | rr | ss | PB |
| 36. | S | U | ff | hh | rr | PB |
| 37. | S | Z | ee | jj | uu | PB |
| 38. | U | ee | uu | vv | ww | PB |
| 39. | U | ee | uu | yy | BB | PB |
| 40. | W | kk | qq | xx | AA | PB |
| 41. | W | kk | qq | zz | CC | PB |
| 42. | X | kk | mm | nn | qq | PB |
| 43. | X | mm | oo | xx | CC | PB |
| 44. | X | mm | oo | zz | AA | PB |
| 45. | Z | ff | jj | vv | yy | PB |
| 46. | Z | ff | jj | ww | BB | PB |
| 47. | dd | gg | hh | pp | ss | PB |
| 48. | dd | gg | ii | pp | DD | PB |



# POWERBALL BALANCED WHEEL® 52215PB

## Wheel 15 Numbers + PB in 3 Games for a 2 of 4 Win

With Powerball

| Numbers Matched | Maximum Wins | | | | | | Minimum Wins | | | | | |
|---|---|---|---|---|---|---|---|---|---|---|---|---|
| | 5 + 1 | 4 + 1 | 3 + 1 | 2 + 1 | 1 + 1 | 0 + 1 | 5 + 1 | 4 + 1 | 3 + 1 | 2 + 1 | 1 + 1 | 0 + 1 |
| 5 + 1 | 1 | 0 | 0 | 0 | 0 | 2 | 0 | 0 | 0 | 2 | 1 | 0 |
| 4 + 1 | - | 1 | 0 | 0 | 0 | 2 | - | 0 | 0 | 1 | 2 | 0 |
| 3 + 1 | - | - | 1 | 0 | 0 | 2 | - | - | 0 | 0 | 3 | 0 |
| 2 + 1 | - | - | - | 1 | 0 | 2 | - | - | - | 0 | 2 | 1 |
| 1 + 1 | - | - | - | - | 1 | 2 | - | - | - | - | 1 | 2 |
| 0 + 1 | - | - | - | - | - | 3 | - | - | - | - | - | 3 |

Without Powerball

| Numbers Matched | Maximum Wins | | | | | Minimum Wins | | | | |
|---|---|---|---|---|---|---|---|---|---|---|
| | 5 + 0 | 4 + 0 | 3 + 0 | 2 + 0 | 1 + 0 | 5 + 0 | 4 + 0 | 3 + 0 | 2 + 0 | 1 + 0 |
| 5 + 0 | 1 | 0 | 0 | 0 | 0 | 0 | 0 | 0 | 2 | 1 |
| 4 + 0 | - | 1 | 0 | 0 | 0 | - | 0 | 0 | 1 | 2 |
| 3 + 0 | - | - | 1 | 0 | 0 | - | - | 0 | 0 | 3 |
| 2 + 0 | - | - | - | 1 | 0 | - | - | - | 0 | 2 |
| 1 + 0 | - | - | - | - | 1 | - | - | - | - | 1 |

## Your 15 Numbers + PB to Wheel

| A | B | C | D | E | F | G | H |
|---|---|---|---|---|---|---|---|
| 1 | 1 | 1 | 1 | 1 | 1 | 1 | 1 |
| I | J | K | L | M | N | O | PB |
| 1 | 1 | 1 | 1 | 1 | 1 | 1 | 3 |

## The 3 Games to Play

| | | | | | | |
|---|---|---|---|---|---|---|
| 1. | A | B | L | M | N | PB |
| 2. | C | D | E | K | O | PB |
| 3. | F | G | H | I | J | PB |

# POWERBALL BALANCED WHEEL® 52216PB

## Wheel 16 Numbers + PB in 5 Games for a 2 of 4 Win

With Powerball

| Numbers Matched | Maximum Wins | | | | | | Minimum Wins | | | | | |
|---|---|---|---|---|---|---|---|---|---|---|---|---|
| | 5 + 1 | 4 + 1 | 3 + 1 | 2 + 1 | 1 + 1 | 0 + 1 | 5 + 1 | 4 + 1 | 3 + 1 | 2 + 1 | 1 + 1 | 0 + 1 |
| 5 + 1 | 1 | 1 | 1 | 0 | 0 | 2 | 0 | 0 | 0 | 2 | 2 | 1 |
| 4 + 1 | - | 2 | 0 | 1 | 0 | 2 | - | 0 | 0 | 1 | 3 | 1 |
| 3 + 1 | - | - | 2 | 1 | 0 | 2 | - | - | 0 | 0 | 4 | 1 |
| 2 + 1 | - | - | - | 3 | 0 | 2 | - | - | - | 0 | 2 | 3 |
| 1 + 1 | - | - | - | - | 3 | 2 | - | - | - | - | 1 | 4 |
| 0 + 1 | - | - | - | - | - | 5 | - | - | - | - | - | 5 |

Without Powerball

| Numbers Matched | Maximum Wins | | | | | Minimum Wins | | | | |
|---|---|---|---|---|---|---|---|---|---|---|
| | 5 + 0 | 4 + 0 | 3 + 0 | 2 + 0 | 1 + 0 | 5 + 0 | 4 + 0 | 3 + 0 | 2 + 0 | 1 + 0 |
| 5 + 0 | 1 | 1 | 1 | 0 | 0 | 0 | 0 | 0 | 2 | 2 |
| 4 + 0 | - | 2 | 0 | 1 | 0 | - | 0 | 0 | 1 | 3 |
| 3 + 0 | - | - | 2 | 1 | 0 | - | - | 0 | 0 | 4 |
| 2 + 0 | - | - | - | 3 | 0 | - | - | - | 0 | 2 |
| 1 + 0 | - | - | - | - | 3 | - | - | - | - | 1 |

## Your 16 Numbers + PB to Wheel

| A | B | C | D | E | F | G | H | I |
|---|---|---|---|---|---|---|---|---|
| 2 | 1 | 1 | 2 | 1 | 1 | 2 | 1 | 1 |

| J | K | L | M | N | O | P | PB |
|---|---|---|---|---|---|---|---|
| 2 | 1 | 3 | 1 | 3 | 1 | 2 | 5 |

## The 5 Games to Play

| | | | | | | |
|---|---|---|---|---|---|---|
| 1. | A | D | L | N | P | PB |
| 2. | A | G | J | L | N | PB |
| 3. | B | E | F | O | P | PB |
| 4. | C | H | I | K | M | PB |
| 5. | D | G | J | L | N | PB |



# POWERBALL BALANCED WHEEL® 52217PB

## Wheel 17 Numbers + PB in 5 Games for a 2 of 4 Win

With Powerball

| Numbers Matched | Maximum Wins | | | | | | Minimum Wins | | | | | |
|---|---|---|---|---|---|---|---|---|---|---|---|---|
| | 5 + 1 | 4 + 1 | 3 + 1 | 2 + 1 | 1 + 1 | 0 + 1 | 5 + 1 | 4 + 1 | 3 + 1 | 2 + 1 | 1 + 1 | 0 + 1 |
| 5 + 1 | 1 | 0 | 2 | 0 | 0 | 2 | 0 | 0 | 0 | 2 | 2 | 1 |
| 4 + 1 | - | 1 | 1 | 1 | 0 | 2 | - | 0 | 0 | 1 | 3 | 1 |
| 3 + 1 | - | - | 2 | 0 | 1 | 2 | - | - | 0 | 0 | 4 | 1 |
| 2 + 1 | - | - | - | 2 | 1 | 2 | - | - | - | 0 | 2 | 3 |
| 1 + 1 | - | - | - | - | 3 | 2 | - | - | - | - | 1 | 4 |
| 0 + 1 | - | - | - | - | - | 5 | - | - | - | - | - | 5 |

Without Powerball

| Numbers Matched | Maximum Wins | | | | | Minimum Wins | | | | |
|---|---|---|---|---|---|---|---|---|---|---|
| | 5 + 0 | 4 + 0 | 3 + 0 | 2 + 0 | 1 + 0 | 5 + 0 | 4 + 0 | 3 + 0 | 2 + 0 | 1 + 0 |
| 5 + 0 | 1 | 0 | 2 | 0 | 0 | 0 | 0 | 0 | 2 | 2 |
| 4 + 0 | - | 1 | 1 | 1 | 0 | - | 0 | 0 | 1 | 3 |
| 3 + 0 | - | - | 2 | 0 | 1 | - | - | 0 | 0 | 4 |
| 2 + 0 | - | - | - | 2 | 1 | - | - | - | 0 | 2 |
| 1 + 0 | - | - | - | - | 3 | - | - | - | - | 1 |

(Continued Next Page)

**POWERBALL BALANCED WHEEL® 52217PB** (Continued from previous page)

## Your 17 Numbers + PB to Wheel

| A | B | C | D | E | F | G | H | I |
|---|---|---|---|---|---|---|---|---|
| 1 | 2 | 1 | 2 | 1 | 1 | 2 | 1 | 1 |

| J | K | L | M | N | O | P | Q | PB |
|---|---|---|---|---|---|---|---|---|
| 2 | 2 | 2 | 1 | 1 | 1 | 3 | 1 | 5 |

## The 5 Games to Play

| | | | | | | |
|---|---|---|---|---|---|---|
| 1. | A | F | I | M | Q | PB |
| 2. | B | D | K | L | P | PB |
| 3. | B | G | J | L | P | PB |
| 4. | C | E | H | N | O | PB |
| 5. | D | G | J | K | P | PB |



# POWERBALL BALANCED WHEEL® 52218PB

## Wheel 18 Numbers + PB in 6 Games for a 2 of 4 Win

With Powerball

| Numbers Matched | Maximum Wins 5 + 1 | 4 + 1 | 3 + 1 | 2 + 1 | 1 + 1 | 0 + 1 | Minimum Wins 5 + 1 | 4 + 1 | 3 + 1 | 2 + 1 | 1 + 1 | 0 + 1 |
|---|---|---|---|---|---|---|---|---|---|---|---|---|
| 5 + 1 | 1 | 1 | 1 | 1 | 0 | 2 | 0 | 0 | 0 | 2 | 2 | 2 |
| 4 + 1 | - | 2 | 1 | 0 | 1 | 2 | - | 0 | 0 | 1 | 3 | 2 |
| 3 + 1 | - | - | 3 | 0 | 0 | 3 | - | - | 0 | 0 | 4 | 2 |
| 2 + 1 | - | - | - | 3 | 0 | 3 | - | - | - | 0 | 2 | 4 |
| 1 + 1 | - | - | - | - | 3 | 3 | - | - | - | - | 1 | 5 |
| 0 + 1 | - | - | - | - | - | 6 | - | - | - | - | - | 6 |

Without Powerball

| Numbers Matched | Maximum Wins 5 + 0 | 4 + 0 | 3 + 0 | 2 + 0 | 1 + 0 | Minimum Wins 5 + 0 | 4 + 0 | 3 + 0 | 2 + 0 | 1 + 0 |
|---|---|---|---|---|---|---|---|---|---|---|
| 5 + 0 | 1 | 1 | 1 | 1 | 0 | 0 | 0 | 0 | 2 | 2 |
| 4 + 0 | - | 2 | 1 | 0 | 1 | - | 0 | 0 | 1 | 3 |
| 3 + 0 | - | - | 3 | 0 | 0 | - | - | 0 | 0 | 4 |
| 2 + 0 | - | - | - | 3 | 0 | - | - | - | 0 | 2 |
| 1 + 0 | - | - | - | - | 3 | - | - | - | - | 1 |

## Your 18 Numbers + PB to Wheel

| A | B | C | D | E | F | G | H | I | J |
|---|---|---|---|---|---|---|---|---|---|
| 1 | 2 | 3 | 1 | 3 | 2 | 1 | 1 | 2 | 1 |

| K | L | M | N | O | P | Q | R | PB |
|---|---|---|---|---|---|---|---|---|
| 1 | 1 | 1 | 1 | 1 | 2 | 3 | 3 | 6 |

## The 6 Games to Play

| | | | | | | |
|---|---|---|---|---|---|---|
| 1. | A | G | K | L | N | PB |
| 2. | B | C | E | Q | R | PB |
| 3. | B | F | I | P | Q | PB |
| 4. | C | E | F | P | R | PB |
| 5. | C | E | I | Q | R | PB |
| 6. | D | H | J | M | O | PB |

# POWERBALL BALANCED WHEEL® 52219PB

## Wheel 19 Numbers + PB in 7 Games for a 2 of 4 Win

With Powerball

| Numbers Matched | Maximum Wins | | | | | | Minimum Wins | | | | | |
|---|---|---|---|---|---|---|---|---|---|---|---|---|
| | 5 + 1 | 4 + 1 | 3 + 1 | 2 + 1 | 1 + 1 | 0 + 1 | 5 + 1 | 4 + 1 | 3 + 1 | 2 + 1 | 1 + 1 | 0 + 1 |
| 5 + 1 | 1 | 0 | 2 | 0 | 0 | 4 | 0 | 0 | 0 | 2 | 4 | 1 |
| 4 + 1 | - | 1 | 1 | 1 | 0 | 4 | - | 0 | 0 | 1 | 4 | 2 |
| 3 + 1 | - | - | 2 | 0 | 1 | 4 | - | - | 0 | 0 | 5 | 2 |
| 2 + 1 | - | - | - | 2 | 1 | 4 | - | - | - | 0 | 3 | 4 |
| 1 + 1 | - | - | - | - | 3 | 4 | - | - | - | - | 1 | 6 |
| 0 + 1 | - | - | - | - | - | 7 | - | - | - | - | - | 7 |

Without Powerball

| Numbers Matched | Maximum Wins | | | | | Minimum Wins | | | | |
|---|---|---|---|---|---|---|---|---|---|---|
| | 5 + 0 | 4 + 0 | 3 + 0 | 2 + 0 | 1 + 0 | 5 + 0 | 4 + 0 | 3 + 0 | 2 + 0 | 1 + 0 |
| 5 + 0 | 1 | 0 | 2 | 0 | 0 | 0 | 0 | 0 | 2 | 4 |
| 4 + 0 | - | 1 | 1 | 1 | 0 | - | 0 | 0 | 1 | 4 |
| 3 + 0 | - | - | 2 | 0 | 1 | - | - | 0 | 0 | 5 |
| 2 + 0 | - | - | - | 2 | 1 | - | - | - | 0 | 3 |
| 1 + 0 | - | - | - | - | 3 | - | - | - | - | 1 |

## Your 19 Numbers + PB to Wheel

| A | B | C | D | E | F | G | H | I | J |
|---|---|---|---|---|---|---|---|---|---|
| 3 | 2 | 1 | 2 | 1 | 2 | 2 | 2 | 2 | 2 |
| **K** | **L** | **M** | **N** | **O** | **P** | **Q** | **R** | **S** | **PB** |
| 3 | 1 | 2 | 2 | 1 | 1 | 2 | 2 | 2 | 7 |

## The 7 Games to Play

| | | | | | | |
|---|---|---|---|---|---|---|
| 1. | A | F | H | R | S | PB |
| 2. | A | F | I | M | S | PB |
| 3. | A | H | I | M | R | PB |
| 4. | B | D | J | K | *Q* | PB |
| 5. | B | G | J | K | N | PB |
| 6. | C | E | L | O | P | PB |
| 7. | D | G | K | N | *Q* | PB |



# POWERBALL BALANCED WHEEL® 52220PB

## Wheel 20 Numbers + PB in 8 Games for a 2 of 4 Win

With Powerball

| Numbers Matched | Maximum Wins | | | | | | Minimum Wins | | | | | |
|---|---|---|---|---|---|---|---|---|---|---|---|---|
| | 5 + 1 | 4 + 1 | 3 + 1 | 2 + 1 | 1 + 1 | 0 + 1 | 5 + 1 | 4 + 1 | 3 + 1 | 2 + 1 | 1 + 1 | 0 + 1 |
| 5 + 1 | 1 | 1 | 1 | 1 | 0 | 4 | 0 | 0 | 0 | 2 | 4 | 2 |
| 4 + 1 | - | 2 | 1 | 0 | 1 | 4 | - | 0 | 0 | 1 | 4 | 3 |
| 3 + 1 | - | - | 3 | 0 | 0 | 5 | - | - | 0 | 0 | 5 | 3 |
| 2 + 1 | - | - | - | 3 | 0 | 5 | - | - | - | 0 | 3 | 5 |
| 1 + 1 | - | - | - | - | 3 | 5 | - | - | - | - | 1 | 7 |
| 0 + 1 | - | - | - | - | - | 8 | - | - | - | - | - | 8 |

Without Powerball

| Numbers Matched | Maximum Wins | | | | | Minimum Wins | | | | |
|---|---|---|---|---|---|---|---|---|---|---|
| | 5 + 0 | 4 + 0 | 3 + 0 | 2 + 0 | 1 + 0 | 5 + 0 | 4 + 0 | 3 + 0 | 2 + 0 | 1 + 0 |
| 5 + 0 | 1 | 1 | 1 | 1 | 0 | 0 | 0 | 0 | 2 | 4 |
| 4 + 0 | - | 2 | 1 | 0 | 1 | - | 0 | 0 | 1 | 4 |
| 3 + 0 | - | - | 3 | 0 | 0 | - | - | 0 | 0 | 5 |
| 2 + 0 | - | - | - | 3 | 0 | - | - | - | 0 | 3 |
| 1 + 0 | - | - | - | - | 3 | - | - | - | - | 1 |

(Continued Next Page)

**POWERBALL BALANCED WHEEL® 52220PB** (Continued from previous page)

## Your 20 Numbers + PB to Wheel

| A | B | C | D | E | F | G | H | I | J | K |
|---|---|---|---|---|---|---|---|---|---|---|
| 1 | 2 | 3 | 3 | 2 | 2 | 3 | 3 | 1 | 2 | 2 |

| L | M | N | O | P | Q | R | S | T | PB |
|---|---|---|---|---|---|---|---|---|---|
| 1 | 1 | 2 | 2 | 1 | 2 | 2 | 2 | 3 | 8 |

## The 8 Games to Play

| | | | | | | |
|---|---|---|---|---|---|---|
| 1. | A | I | L | M | P | PB |
| 2. | B | D | K | N | Q | PB |
| 3. | B | G | H | Q | T | PB |
| 4. | C | E | F | R | S | PB |
| 5. | C | E | J | O | R | PB |
| 6. | C | F | J | O | S | PB |
| 7. | D | G | H | K | T | PB |
| 8. | D | G | H | N | T | PB |



# POWERBALL BALANCED WHEEL® 52221PB

## Wheel 21 Numbers + PB in 9 Games for a 2 of 4 Win

With Powerball

| Numbers Matched | Maximum Wins 5 + 1 | 4 + 1 | 3 + 1 | 2 + 1 | 1 + 1 | 0 + 1 | Minimum Wins 5 + 1 | 4 + 1 | 3 + 1 | 2 + 1 | 1 + 1 | 0 + 1 |
|---|---|---|---|---|---|---|---|---|---|---|---|---|
| 5 + 1 | 1 | 1 | 0 | 2 | 1 | 4 | 0 | 0 | 0 | 2 | 4 | 3 |
| 4 + 1 | - | 2 | 0 | 2 | 0 | 5 | - | 0 | 0 | 1 | 4 | 4 |
| 3 + 1 | - | - | 3 | 0 | 0 | 6 | - | - | 0 | 0 | 5 | 4 |
| 2 + 1 | - | - | - | 3 | 0 | 6 | - | - | - | 0 | 3 | 6 |
| 1 + 1 | - | - | - | - | 3 | 6 | - | - | - | - | 1 | 8 |
| 0 + 1 | - | - | - | - | - | 9 | - | - | - | - | - | 9 |

Without Powerball

| Numbers Matched | Maximum Wins 5 + 0 | 4 + 0 | 3 + 0 | 2 + 0 | 1 + 0 | Minimum Wins 5 + 0 | 4 + 0 | 3 + 0 | 2 + 0 | 1 + 0 |
|---|---|---|---|---|---|---|---|---|---|---|
| 5 + 0 | 1 | 1 | 0 | 2 | 1 | 0 | 0 | 0 | 2 | 4 |
| 4 + 0 | - | 2 | 0 | 2 | 0 | - | 0 | 0 | 1 | 4 |
| 3 + 0 | - | - | 3 | 0 | 0 | - | - | 0 | 0 | 5 |
| 2 + 0 | - | - | - | 3 | 0 | - | - | - | 0 | 3 |
| 1 + 0 | - | - | - | - | 3 | - | - | - | - | 1 |

## Your 21 Numbers + PB to Wheel

| A | B | C | D | E | F | G | H | I | J | K |
|---|---|---|---|---|---|---|---|---|---|---|
| 1 | 2 | 1 | 2 | 3 | 2 | 3 | 3 | 3 | 2 | 3 |

| L | M | N | O | P | Q | R | S | T | U | PB |
|---|---|---|---|---|---|---|---|---|---|---|
| 3 | 2 | 2 | 2 | 3 | 1 | 2 | 1 | 3 | 1 | 9 |

## The 9 Games to Play

| | | | | | | |
|---|---|---|---|---|---|---|
| 1. | A | C | Q | S | U | PB |
| 2. | B | D | N | O | P | PB |
| 3. | B | J | M | N | P | PB |
| 4. | D | J | M | O | P | PB |
| 5. | E | F | G | R | T | PB |
| 6. | E | G | H | K | T | PB |
| 7. | E | G | I | L | T | PB |
| 8. | F | H | I | K | L | PB |
| 9. | H | I | K | L | R | PB |

# POWERBALL BALANCED WHEEL® 52222PB

## Wheel 22 Numbers + PB in 10 Games for a 2 of 4 Win

With Powerball

| Numbers Matched | Maximum Wins | | | | | | Minimum Wins | | | | | |
|---|---|---|---|---|---|---|---|---|---|---|---|---|
| | 5 + 1 | 4 + 1 | 3 + 1 | 2 + 1 | 1 + 1 | 0 + 1 | 5 + 1 | 4 + 1 | 3 + 1 | 2 + 1 | 1 + 1 | 0 + 1 |
| 5 + 1 | 1 | 0 | 2 | 0 | 0 | 7 | 0 | 0 | 0 | 2 | 5 | 3 |
| 4 + 1 | - | 1 | 1 | 1 | 0 | 7 | - | 0 | 0 | 1 | 5 | 4 |
| 3 + 1 | - | - | 2 | 0 | 1 | 7 | - | - | 0 | 0 | 6 | 4 |
| 2 + 1 | - | - | - | 2 | 2 | 6 | - | - | - | 0 | 3 | 7 |
| 1 + 1 | - | - | - | - | 3 | 7 | - | - | - | - | 1 | 9 |
| 0 + 1 | - | - | - | - | - | 10 | - | - | - | - | - | 10 |

Without Powerball

| Numbers Matched | Maximum Wins | | | | | Minimum Wins | | | | |
|---|---|---|---|---|---|---|---|---|---|---|
| | 5 + 0 | 4 + 0 | 3 + 0 | 2 + 0 | 1 + 0 | 5 + 0 | 4 + 0 | 3 + 0 | 2 + 0 | 1 + 0 |
| 5 + 0 | 1 | 0 | 2 | 0 | 0 | 0 | 0 | 0 | 2 | 5 |
| 4 + 0 | - | 1 | 1 | 1 | 0 | - | 0 | 0 | 1 | 5 |
| 3 + 0 | - | - | 2 | 0 | 1 | - | - | 0 | 0 | 6 |
| 2 + 0 | - | - | - | 2 | 2 | - | - | - | 0 | 3 |
| 1 + 0 | - | - | - | - | 3 | - | - | - | - | 1 |

## Your 22 Numbers + PB to Wheel

| A | B | C | D | E | F | G | H |
|---|---|---|---|---|---|---|---|
| 1 | 3 | 3 | 3 | 3 | 2 | 1 | 3 |
| **I** | **J** | **K** | **L** | **M** | **N** | **O** | **P** |
| 3 | 2 | 3 | 3 | 1 | 2 | 2 | 2 |
| **Q** | **R** | **S** | **T** | **U** | **V** | **PB** | |
| 3 | 1 | 2 | 3 | 3 | 1 | 10 | |

## The 10 Games to Play

| | | | | | | |
|---|---|---|---|---|---|---|
| 1. | A | G | M | R | V | PB |
| 2. | B | F | J | N | P | PB |
| 3. | B | F | N | O | S | PB |
| 4. | B | J | O | P | S | PB |
| 5. | C | D | K | T | U | PB |
| 6. | C | E | H | Q | U | PB |
| 7. | C | I | K | L | Q | PB |
| 8. | D | E | I | L | U | PB |
| 9. | D | H | L | Q | T | PB |
| 10. | E | H | I | K | T | PB |



# POWERBALL BALANCED WHEEL® 52223PB

## Wheel 23 Numbers + PB in 11 Games for a 2 of 4 Win

With Powerball

| Numbers Matched | Maximum Wins | | | | | | Minimum Wins | | | | | |
|---|---|---|---|---|---|---|---|---|---|---|---|---|
| | 5 + 1 | 4 + 1 | 3 + 1 | 2 + 1 | 1 + 1 | 0 + 1 | 5 + 1 | 4 + 1 | 3 + 1 | 2 + 1 | 1 + 1 | 0 + 1 |
| 5 + 1 | 1 | 1 | 1 | 1 | 0 | 7 | 0 | 0 | 0 | 2 | 5 | 4 |
| 4 + 1 | - | 2 | 1 | 0 | 1 | 7 | - | 0 | 0 | 1 | 5 | 5 |
| 3 + 1 | - | - | 3 | 0 | 0 | 8 | - | - | 0 | 0 | 6 | 5 |
| 2 + 1 | - | - | - | 3 | 0 | 8 | - | - | - | 0 | 3 | 8 |
| 1 + 1 | - | - | - | - | 3 | 8 | - | - | - | - | 1 | 10 |
| 0 + 1 | - | - | - | - | - | 11 | - | - | - | - | - | 11 |

(Continued Next Page)

## POWERBALL BALANCED WHEEL® 52223PB (Continued from previous page)

Without Powerball

| Numbers Matched | Maximum Wins 5 + 0 | 4 + 0 | 3 + 0 | 2 + 0 | 1 + 0 | Minimum Wins 5 + 0 | 4 + 0 | 3 + 0 | 2 + 0 | 1 + 0 |
|---|---|---|---|---|---|---|---|---|---|---|
| 5 + 0 | 1 | 1 | 1 | 1 | 0 | 0 | 0 | 0 | 2 | 5 |
| 4 + 0 | - | 2 | 1 | 0 | 1 | - | 0 | 0 | 1 | 5 |
| 3 + 0 | - | - | 3 | 0 | 0 | - | - | 0 | 0 | 6 |
| 2 + 0 | - | - | - | 3 | 0 | - | - | - | 0 | 3 |
| 1 + 0 | - | - | - | - | 3 | - | - | - | - | 1 |

## Your 23 Numbers + PB to Wheel

| A | B | C | D | E | F | G | H |
|---|---|---|---|---|---|---|---|
| 1 | 3 | 1 | 3 | 3 | 1 | 3 | 3 |
| **I** | **J** | **K** | **L** | **M** | **N** | **O** | **P** |
| 3 | 3 | 3 | 2 | 3 | 3 | 2 | 3 |
| **Q** | **R** | **S** | **T** | **U** | **V** | **W** | **PB** |
| 2 | 3 | 2 | 1 | 3 | 1 | 3 | 11 |

## The 11 Games to Play

| | | | | | | |
|---|---|---|---|---|---|---|
| 1. | A | C | F | T | V | PB |
| 2. | B | D | M | R | U | PB |
| 3. | B | E | I | M | W | PB |
| 4. | B | I | K | P | U | PB |
| 5. | D | E | K | U | W | PB |
| 6. | D | I | P | R | W | PB |
| 7. | E | K | M | P | R | PB |
| 8. | G | H | J | N | O | PB |
| 9. | G | H | J | N | S | PB |
| 10. | G | L | O | Q | S | PB |
| 11. | H | J | L | N | Q | PB |



# POWERBALL BALANCED WHEEL® 52224PB

## Wheel 24 Numbers + PB in 12 Games for a 2 of 4 Win

With Powerball

| Numbers Matched | Maximum Wins 5 + 1 | 4 + 1 | 3 + 1 | 2 + 1 | 1 + 1 | 0 + 1 | Minimum Wins 5 + 1 | 4 + 1 | 3 + 1 | 2 + 1 | 1 + 1 | 0 + 1 |
|---|---|---|---|---|---|---|---|---|---|---|---|---|
| 5 + 1 | 1 | 1 | 1 | 1 | 0 | 8 | 0 | 0 | 0 | 2 | 6 | 4 |
| 4 + 1 | - | 2 | 1 | 0 | 1 | 8 | - | 0 | 0 | 1 | 6 | 5 |
| 3 + 1 | - | - | 3 | 0 | 0 | 9 | - | - | 0 | 0 | 6 | 6 |
| 2 + 1 | - | - | - | 3 | 0 | 9 | - | - | - | 0 | 4 | 8 |
| 1 + 1 | - | - | - | - | 3 | 9 | - | - | - | - | 2 | 10 |
| 0 + 1 | - | - | - | - | - | 12 | - | - | - | - | - | 12 |

Without Powerball

| Numbers Matched | Maximum Wins 5 + 0 | 4 + 0 | 3 + 0 | 2 + 0 | 1 + 0 | Minimum Wins 5 + 0 | 4 + 0 | 3 + 0 | 2 + 0 | 1 + 0 |
|---|---|---|---|---|---|---|---|---|---|---|
| 5 + 0 | 1 | 1 | 1 | 1 | 0 | 0 | 0 | 0 | 2 | 6 |
| 4 + 0 | - | 2 | 1 | 0 | 1 | - | 0 | 0 | 1 | 6 |
| 3 + 0 | - | - | 3 | 0 | 0 | - | - | 0 | 0 | 6 |
| 2 + 0 | - | - | - | 3 | 0 | - | - | - | 0 | 4 |
| 1 + 0 | - | - | - | - | 3 | - | - | - | - | 2 |

(Continued Next Page)

**POWERBALL BALANCED WHEEL® 52224PB** (Continued from previous page)

## Your 24 Numbers + PB to Wheel

| A | B | C | D | E | F | G | H | I |
|---|---|---|---|---|---|---|---|---|
| 2 | 3 | 2 | 2 | 3 | 3 | 2 | 3 | 2 |
| **J** | **K** | **L** | **M** | **N** | **O** | **P** | **Q** | **R** |
| 2 | 3 | 3 | 3 | 3 | 2 | 2 | 2 | 2 |
| **S** | **T** | **U** | **V** | **W** | **X** | **PB** | | |
| 2 | 2 | 3 | 3 | 3 | 3 | 12 | | |

## The 12 Games to Play

| | | | | | | |
|---|---|---|---|---|---|---|
| 1. | A | B | H | W | X | PB |
| 2. | A | J | O | T | X | PB |
| 3. | B | H | J | T | W | PB |
| 4. | B | H | O | W | X | PB |
| 5. | C | D | N | Q | S | PB |
| 6. | C | F | L | N | V | PB |
| 7. | D | F | L | Q | V | PB |
| 8. | E | G | I | P | R | PB |
| 9. | E | I | K | M | U | PB |
| 10. | E | K | M | P | U | PB |
| 11. | F | L | N | S | V | PB |
| 12. | G | K | M | R | U | PB |



# POWERBALL BALANCED WHEEL® 52225PB

## Wheel 25 Numbers + PB in 13 Games for a 2 of 4 Win

With Powerball

| Numbers Matched | Maximum Wins 5 + 1 | 4 + 1 | 3 + 1 | 2 + 1 | 1 + 1 | 0 + 1 | Minimum Wins 5 + 1 | 4 + 1 | 3 + 1 | 2 + 1 | 1 + 1 | 0 + 1 |
|---|---|---|---|---|---|---|---|---|---|---|---|---|
| 5 + 1 | 1 | 1 | 1 | 1 | 0 | 9 | 0 | 0 | 0 | 2 | 6 | 5 |
| 4 + 1 | - | 2 | 1 | 0 | 1 | 9 | - | 0 | 0 | 1 | 6 | 6 |
| 3 + 1 | - | - | 3 | 0 | 0 | 10 | - | - | 0 | 0 | 6 | 7 |
| 2 + 1 | - | - | - | 3 | 0 | 10 | - | - | - | 0 | 4 | 9 |
| 1 + 1 | - | - | - | - | 3 | 10 | - | - | - | - | 2 | 11 |
| 0 + 1 | - | - | - | - | - | 13 | - | - | - | - | - | 13 |

Without Powerball

| Numbers Matched | Maximum Wins 5 + 0 | 4 + 0 | 3 + 0 | 2 + 0 | 1 + 0 | Minimum Wins 5 + 0 | 4 + 0 | 3 + 0 | 2 + 0 | 1 + 0 |
|---|---|---|---|---|---|---|---|---|---|---|
| 5 + 0 | 1 | 1 | 1 | 1 | 0 | 0 | 0 | 0 | 2 | 6 |
| 4 + 0 | - | 2 | 1 | 0 | 1 | - | 0 | 0 | 1 | 6 |
| 3 + 0 | - | - | 3 | 0 | 0 | - | - | 0 | 0 | 6 |
| 2 + 0 | - | - | - | 3 | 0 | - | - | - | 0 | 4 |
| 1 + 0 | - | - | - | - | 3 | - | - | - | - | 2 |

## Your 25 Numbers + PB to Wheel

| A | B | C | D | E | F | G | H | I |
|---|---|---|---|---|---|---|---|---|
| 3 | 3 | 2 | 2 | 3 | 3 | 3 | 3 | 2 |
| **J** | **K** | **L** | **M** | **N** | **O** | **P** | **Q** | **R** |
| 3 | 3 | 2 | 2 | 3 | 3 | 2 | 3 | 2 |
| **S** | **T** | **U** | **V** | **W** | **X** | **Y** | **PB** | |
| 2 | 3 | 2 | 3 | 3 | 3 | 2 | 13 | |

## The 13 Games to Play

| | | | | | | |
|---|---|---|---|---|---|---|
| 1. | A | I | O | P | V | PB |
| 2. | A | L | N | O | V | PB |


(Continued Next Page)

**POWERBALL BALANCED WHEEL® 52225PB** (Continued from previous page)

| | | | | | | |
|---|---|---|---|---|---|---|
| 3. | A | N | O | S | V | PB |
| 4. | B | C | G | U | W | PB |
| 5. | B | G | K | M | W | PB |
| 6. | B | G | K | W | Y | PB |
| 7. | C | K | M | U | Y | PB |
| 8. | D | E | J | *Q* | T | PB |
| 9. | D | F | H | R | X | PB |
| 10. | E | F | H | *Q* | X | PB |
| 11. | E | J | *Q* | R | T | PB |
| 12. | F | H | J | T | X | PB |
| 13. | I | L | N | P | S | PB |



# POWERBALL BALANCED WHEEL® 52226PB

## Wheel 26 Numbers + PB in 14 Games for a 2 of 4 Win

With Powerball

| Numbers Matched | Maximum Wins 5 + 1 | 4 + 1 | 3 + 1 | 2 + 1 | 1 + 1 | 0 + 1 | Minimum Wins 5 + 1 | 4 + 1 | 3 + 1 | 2 + 1 | 1 + 1 | 0 + 1 |
|---|---|---|---|---|---|---|---|---|---|---|---|---|
| 5 + 1 | 1 | 1 | 1 | 1 | 0 | 10 | 0 | 0 | 0 | 2 | 7 | 5 |
| 4 + 1 | - | 2 | 1 | 0 | 1 | 10 | - | 0 | 0 | 1 | 7 | 6 |
| 3 + 1 | - | - | 3 | 0 | 0 | 11 | - | - | 0 | 0 | 7 | 7 |
| 2 + 1 | - | - | - | 3 | 0 | 11 | - | - | - | 0 | 4 | 10 |
| 1 + 1 | - | - | - | - | 3 | 11 | - | - | - | - | 2 | 12 |
| 0 + 1 | - | - | - | - | - | 14 | - | - | - | - | - | 14 |

Without Powerball

| Numbers Matched | Maximum Wins 5 + 0 | 4 + 0 | 3 + 0 | 2 + 0 | 1 + 0 | Minimum Wins 5 + 0 | 4 + 0 | 3 + 0 | 2 + 0 | 1 + 0 |
|---|---|---|---|---|---|---|---|---|---|---|
| 5 + 0 | 1 | 1 | 1 | 1 | 0 | 0 | 0 | 0 | 2 | 7 |
| 4 + 0 | - | 2 | 1 | 0 | 1 | - | 0 | 0 | 1 | 7 |
| 3 + 0 | - | - | 3 | 0 | 0 | - | - | 0 | 0 | 7 |
| 2 + 0 | - | - | - | 3 | 0 | - | - | - | 0 | 4 |
| 1 + 0 | - | - | - | - | 3 | - | - | - | - | 2 |

## Your 26 Numbers + PB to Wheel

| A | B | C | D | E | F | G | H | I |
|---|---|---|---|---|---|---|---|---|
| 2 | 2 | 3 | 3 | 3 | 3 | 2 | 3 | 3 |
| **J** | **K** | **L** | **M** | **N** | **O** | **P** | **Q** | **R** |
| 3 | 3 | 3 | 3 | 3 | 3 | 2 | 2 | 3 |
| **S** | **T** | **U** | **V** | **W** | **X** | **Y** | **Z** | **PB** |
| 3 | 3 | 3 | 2 | 2 | 3 | 3 | 2 | 14 |

## The 14 Games to Play

| | | | | | | |
|---|---|---|---|---|---|---|
| 1. | A | D | I | S | W | PB |
| 2. | A | G | M | W | Z | PB |
| 3. | B | C | F | V | Y | PB |
| 4. | B | O | P | *Q* | V | PB |
| 5. | C | F | O | P | Y | PB |
| 6. | C | F | O | *Q* | Y | PB |
| 7. | D | G | I | M | S | PB |
| 8. | D | I | M | S | Z | PB |
| 9. | E | H | J | K | U | PB |
| 10. | E | H | R | T | X | PB |
| 11. | E | L | N | U | X | PB |
| 12. | H | J | L | N | T | PB |
| 13. | J | K | L | R | X | PB |
| 14. | K | N | R | T | U | PB |

# POWERBALL BALANCED WHEEL® 52227PB

## Wheel 27 Numbers + PB in 15 Games for a 2 of 4 Win

With Powerball

| Numbers Matched | Maximum Wins 5 + 1 | 4 + 1 | 3 + 1 | 2 + 1 | 1 + 1 | 0 + 1 | Minimum Wins 5 + 1 | 4 + 1 | 3 + 1 | 2 + 1 | 1 + 1 | 0 + 1 |
|---|---|---|---|---|---|---|---|---|---|---|---|---|
| 5 + 1 | 1 | 1 | 1 | 1 | 0 | 11 | 0 | 0 | 0 | 2 | 7 | 6 |
| 4 + 1 | - | 2 | 1 | 0 | 1 | 11 | - | 0 | 0 | 1 | 7 | 7 |
| 3 + 1 | - | - | 3 | 0 | 0 | 12 | - | - | 0 | 0 | 7 | 8 |
| 2 + 1 | - | - | - | 4 | 0 | 11 | - | - | - | 0 | 4 | 11 |
| 1 + 1 | - | - | - | - | 4 | 11 | - | - | - | - | 2 | 13 |
| 0 + 1 | - | - | - | - | - | 15 | - | - | - | - | - | 15 |

Without Powerball

| Numbers Matched | Maximum Wins 5 + 0 | 4 + 0 | 3 + 0 | 2 + 0 | 1 + 0 | Minimum Wins 5 + 0 | 4 + 0 | 3 + 0 | 2 + 0 | 1 + 0 |
|---|---|---|---|---|---|---|---|---|---|---|
| 5 + 0 | 1 | 1 | 1 | 1 | 0 | 0 | 0 | 0 | 2 | 7 |
| 4 + 0 | - | 2 | 1 | 0 | 1 | - | 0 | 0 | 1 | 7 |
| 3 + 0 | - | - | 3 | 0 | 0 | - | - | 0 | 0 | 7 |
| 2 + 0 | - | - | - | 4 | 0 | - | - | - | 0 | 4 |
| 1 + 0 | - | - | - | - | 4 | - | - | - | - | 2 |

## Your 27 Numbers + PB to Wheel

| A | B | C | D | E | F | G | H | I | J |
|---|---|---|---|---|---|---|---|---|---|
| 2 | 3 | 2 | 3 | 3 | 3 | 3 | 4 | 3 | 2 |
| **K** | **L** | **M** | **N** | **O** | **P** | **Q** | **R** | **S** | **T** |
| 3 | 3 | 2 | 2 | 3 | 3 | 2 | 4 | 2 | 3 |
| **U** | **V** | **W** | **X** | **Y** | **Z** | **aa** | **PB** | | |
| 3 | 3 | 3 | 3 | 2 | 3 | 3 | 15 | | |

## The 15 Games to Play

| | | | | | | |
|---|---|---|---|---|---|---|
| 1. | A | G | I | W | aa | PB |
| 2. | A | J | Q | W | Y | PB |
| 3. | B | E | L | P | X | PB |
| 4. | B | F | O | U | X | PB |
| 5. | B | H | R | X | Z | PB |
| 6. | C | D | K | T | V | PB |
| 7. | C | M | N | S | V | PB |
| 8. | D | K | M | T | V | PB |
| 9. | D | K | N | S | T | PB |
| 10. | E | F | H | R | U | PB |
| 11. | E | H | O | R | Z | PB |
| 12. | F | L | P | U | Z | PB |
| 13. | G | I | J | Y | aa | PB |
| 14. | G | I | Q | W | aa | PB |
| 15. | H | L | O | P | R | PB |



# POWERBALL BALANCED WHEEL® 52228PB

## Wheel 28 Numbers + PB in 16 Games for a 2 of 4 Win

With Powerball

| Numbers Matched | Maximum Wins 5 + 1 | 4 + 1 | 3 + 1 | 2 + 1 | 1 + 1 | 0 + 1 | Minimum Wins 5 + 1 | 4 + 1 | 3 + 1 | 2 + 1 | 1 + 1 | 0 + 1 |
|---|---|---|---|---|---|---|---|---|---|---|---|---|
| 5 + 1 | 1 | 1 | 0 | 2 | 2 | 10 | 0 | 0 | 0 | 2 | 8 | 6 |
| 4 + 1 | - | 2 | 0 | 2 | 0 | 12 | - | 0 | 0 | 1 | 7 | 8 |
| 3 + 1 | - | - | 3 | 0 | 0 | 13 | - | - | 0 | 0 | 7 | 9 |
| 2 + 1 | - | - | - | 4 | 0 | 12 | - | - | - | 0 | 4 | 12 |
| 1 + 1 | - | - | - | - | 4 | 12 | - | - | - | - | 2 | 14 |
| 0 + 1 | - | - | - | - | - | 16 | - | - | - | - | - | 16 |

(Continued Next Page)

## POWERBALL BALANCED WHEEL® 52228PB (Continued from previous page)

Without Powerball

| Numbers Matched | Maximum Wins 5 + 0 | 4 + 0 | 3 + 0 | 2 + 0 | 1 + 0 | Minimum Wins 5 + 0 | 4 + 0 | 3 + 0 | 2 + 0 | 1 + 0 |
|---|---|---|---|---|---|---|---|---|---|---|
| 5 + 0 | 1 | 1 | 0 | 2 | 2 | 0 | 0 | 0 | 2 | 8 |
| 4 + 0 | - | 2 | 0 | 2 | 0 | - | 0 | 0 | 1 | 7 |
| 3 + 0 | - | - | 3 | 0 | 0 | - | - | 0 | 0 | 7 |
| 2 + 0 | - | - | - | 4 | 0 | - | - | - | 0 | 4 |
| 1 + 0 | - | - | - | - | 4 | - | - | - | - | 2 |

# Your 28 Numbers + PB to Wheel

| A | B | C | D | E | F | G | H | I | J |
|---|---|---|---|---|---|---|---|---|---|
| 3 | 2 | 3 | 2 | 2 | 3 | 3 | 4 | 3 | 3 |
| **K** | **L** | **M** | **N** | **O** | **P** | **Q** | **R** | **S** | **T** |
| 3 | 3 | 3 | 2 | 3 | 3 | 3 | 3 | 3 | 4 |
| **U** | **V** | **W** | **X** | **Y** | **Z** | **aa** | **bb** | **PB** | |
| 3 | 3 | 3 | 2 | 3 | 3 | 3 | 2 | 16 | |

# The 16 Games to Play

| | | | | | | |
|---|---|---|---|---|---|---|
| 1. | A | L | M | R | S | PB |
| 2. | A | N | P | S | aa | PB |
| 3. | A | P | Q | S | aa | PB |
| 4. | B | D | E | X | bb | PB |
| 5. | B | K | O | V | X | PB |
| 6. | C | F | H | T | U | PB |
| 7. | C | G | U | W | Y | PB |
| 8. | C | I | J | U | Z | PB |
| 9. | D | K | O | Q | V | PB |
| 10. | E | K | O | V | bb | PB |
| 11. | F | G | I | W | Z | PB |
| 12. | F | H | J | T | Y | PB |
| 13. | G | H | J | T | W | PB |
| 14. | H | I | T | Y | Z | PB |
| 15. | L | M | N | Q | R | PB |
| 16. | L | M | P | R | aa | PB |



# POWERBALL BALANCED WHEEL® 52230PB

## Wheel 30 Numbers + PB in 18 Games for a 2 of 4 Win

With Powerball

| Numbers Matched | Maximum Wins 5 + 1 | 4 + 1 | 3 + 1 | 2 + 1 | 1 + 1 | 0 + 1 | Minimum Wins 5 + 1 | 4 + 1 | 3 + 1 | 2 + 1 | 1 + 1 | 0 + 1 |
|---|---|---|---|---|---|---|---|---|---|---|---|---|
| 5 + 1 | 1 | 1 | 0 | 2 | 1 | 13 | 0 | 0 | 0 | 2 | 9 | 7 |
| 4 + 1 | - | 2 | 0 | 2 | 0 | 14 | - | 0 | 0 | 1 | 8 | 9 |
| 3 + 1 | - | - | 3 | 0 | 0 | 15 | - | - | 0 | 0 | 8 | 10 |
| 2 + 1 | - | - | - | 4 | 0 | 14 | - | - | - | 0 | 5 | 13 |
| 1 + 1 | - | - | - | - | 4 | 14 | - | - | - | - | 2 | 16 |
| 0 + 1 | - | - | - | - | - | 18 | - | - | - | - | - | 18 |

Without Powerball

| Numbers Matched | Maximum Wins 5 + 0 | 4 + 0 | 3 + 0 | 2 + 0 | 1 + 0 | Minimum Wins 5 + 0 | 4 + 0 | 3 + 0 | 2 + 0 | 1 + 0 |
|---|---|---|---|---|---|---|---|---|---|---|
| 5 + 0 | 1 | 1 | 0 | 2 | 1 | 0 | 0 | 0 | 2 | 9 |
| 4 + 0 | - | 2 | 0 | 2 | 0 | - | 0 | 0 | 1 | 8 |
| 3 + 0 | - | - | 3 | 0 | 0 | - | - | 0 | 0 | 8 |
| 2 + 0 | - | - | - | 4 | 0 | - | - | - | 0 | 5 |
| 1 + 0 | - | - | - | - | 4 | - | - | - | - | 2 |

(Continued Next Page)

**POWERBALL BALANCED WHEEL® 52230PB** (Continued from previous page)

## Your 30 Numbers + PB to Wheel

| A | B | C | D | E | F | G | H | I | J | K |
|---|---|---|---|---|---|---|---|---|---|---|
| 3 | 3 | 3 | 3 | 3 | 3 | 3 | 3 | 3 | 2 | 3 |
| **L** | **M** | **N** | **O** | **P** | **Q** | **R** | **S** | **T** | **U** | **V** |
| 2 | 3 | 4 | 3 | 3 | 3 | 3 | 3 | 3 | 3 | 4 |
| **W** | **X** | **Y** | **Z** | **aa** | **bb** | **cc** | **dd** | **PB** | | |
| 3 | 3 | 3 | 3 | 3 | 3 | 3 | 3 | 18 | | |

## The 18 Games to Play

| | | | | | | |
|---|---|---|---|---|---|---|
| 1. | A | D | Q | T | cc | PB |
| 2. | A | F | P | Q | dd | PB |
| 3. | A | H | Q | W | cc | PB |
| 4. | B | I | M | N | V | PB |
| 5. | B | K | O | R | Y | PB |
| 6. | B | N | U | V | aa | PB |
| 7. | C | E | J | S | bb | PB |
| 8. | C | E | L | S | bb | PB |
| 9. | C | G | S | X | Z | PB |
| 10. | D | F | P | cc | dd | PB |
| 11. | D | H | P | T | W | PB |
| 12. | E | G | X | Z | bb | PB |
| 13. | F | H | T | W | dd | PB |
| 14. | G | J | L | X | Z | PB |
| 15. | I | K | M | Y | aa | PB |
| 16. | I | M | O | R | U | PB |
| 17. | K | N | U | V | Y | PB |
| 18. | N | O | R | V | aa | PB |



# POWERBALL BALANCED WHEEL® 52231PB

## Wheel 31 Numbers + PB in 19 Games for a 2 of 4 Win

With Powerball

| Numbers Matched | Maximum Wins 5 + 1 | 4 + 1 | 3 + 1 | 2 + 1 | 1 + 1 | 0 + 1 | Minimum Wins 5 + 1 | 4 + 1 | 3 + 1 | 2 + 1 | 1 + 1 | 0 + 1 |
|---|---|---|---|---|---|---|---|---|---|---|---|---|
| 5 + 1 | 1 | 0 | 3 | 0 | 3 | 12 | 0 | 0 | 0 | 2 | 11 | 6 |
| 4 + 1 | - | 1 | 2 | 1 | 2 | 13 | - | 0 | 0 | 1 | 10 | 8 |
| 3 + 1 | - | - | 2 | 2 | 1 | 14 | - | - | 0 | 0 | 9 | 10 |
| 2 + 1 | - | - | - | 4 | 0 | 15 | - | - | - | 0 | 6 | 13 |
| 1 + 1 | - | - | - | - | 4 | 15 | - | - | - | - | 3 | 16 |
| 0 + 1 | - | - | - | - | - | 19 | - | - | - | - | - | 19 |

Without Powerball

| Numbers Matched | Maximum Wins 5 + 0 | 4 + 0 | 3 + 0 | 2 + 0 | 1 + 0 | Minimum Wins 5 + 0 | 4 + 0 | 3 + 0 | 2 + 0 | 1 + 0 |
|---|---|---|---|---|---|---|---|---|---|---|
| 5 + 0 | 1 | 0 | 3 | 0 | 3 | 0 | 0 | 0 | 2 | 11 |
| 4 + 0 | - | 1 | 2 | 1 | 2 | - | 0 | 0 | 1 | 10 |
| 3 + 0 | - | - | 2 | 2 | 1 | - | - | 0 | 0 | 9 |
| 2 + 0 | - | - | - | 4 | 0 | - | - | - | 0 | 6 |
| 1 + 0 | - | - | - | - | 4 | - | - | - | - | 3 |

(Continued Next Page)

**POWERBALL BALANCED WHEEL® 52231PB** (Continued from previous page)

## Your 31 Numbers + PB to Wheel

| A | B | C | D | E | F | G | H | I | J | K |
|---|---|---|---|---|---|---|---|---|---|---|
| 3 | 3 | 3 | 3 | 3 | 3 | 3 | 3 | 3 | 4 | 3 |
| **L** | **M** | **N** | **O** | **P** | **Q** | **R** | **S** | **T** | **U** | **V** |
| 3 | 3 | 3 | 3 | 3 | 3 | 3 | 3 | 3 | 3 | 4 |
| **W** | **X** | **Y** | **Z** | **aa** | **bb** | **cc** | **dd** | **ee** | **PB** | |
| 3 | 3 | 3 | 3 | 3 | 3 | 3 | 3 | 3 | 19 | |

## The 19 Games to Play

| | | | | | | |
|---|---|---|---|---|---|---|
| 1. | A | I | K | Z | ee | PB |
| 2. | A | M | T | Z | ee | PB |
| 3. | A | N | O | W | ee | PB |
| 4. | B | D | U | aa | dd | PB |
| 5. | B | H | L | X | aa | PB |
| 6. | B | J | S | V | aa | PB |
| 7. | C | E | P | Y | cc | PB |
| 8. | C | F | P | *Q* | Y | PB |
| 9. | C | G | R | Y | bb | PB |
| 10. | D | H | S | X | dd | PB |
| 11. | D | J | L | V | dd | PB |
| 12. | E | F | G | *Q* | cc | PB |
| 13. | E | F | R | bb | cc | PB |
| 14. | G | P | *Q* | R | bb | PB |
| 15. | H | J | U | V | X | PB |
| 16. | I | K | M | O | T | PB |
| 17. | I | M | N | T | W | PB |
| 18. | J | L | S | U | V | PB |
| 19. | K | N | O | W | Z | PB |



# POWERBALL BALANCED WHEEL® 52232PB

## Wheel 32 Numbers + PB in 20 Games for a 2 of 4 Win

With Powerball

| Numbers Matched | Maximum Wins | | | | | | Minimum Wins | | | | | |
|---|---|---|---|---|---|---|---|---|---|---|---|---|
| | 5 + 1 | 4 + 1 | 3 + 1 | 2 + 1 | 1 + 1 | 0 + 1 | 5 + 1 | 4 + 1 | 3 + 1 | 2 + 1 | 1 + 1 | 0 + 1 |
| 5 + 1 | 1 | 0 | 3 | 0 | 3 | 13 | 0 | 0 | 0 | 2 | 11 | 7 |
| 4 + 1 | - | 1 | 2 | 1 | 2 | 14 | - | 0 | 0 | 1 | 10 | 9 |
| 3 + 1 | - | - | 2 | 2 | 1 | 15 | - | - | 0 | 0 | 9 | 11 |
| 2 + 1 | - | - | - | 4 | 0 | 16 | - | - | - | 0 | 6 | 14 |
| 1 + 1 | - | - | - | - | 4 | 16 | - | - | - | - | 3 | 17 |
| 0 + 1 | - | - | - | - | - | 20 | - | - | - | - | - | 20 |

Without Powerball

| Numbers Matched | Maximum Wins | | | | | Minimum Wins | | | | |
|---|---|---|---|---|---|---|---|---|---|---|
| | 5 + 0 | 4 + 0 | 3 + 0 | 2 + 0 | 1 + 0 | 5 + 0 | 4 + 0 | 3 + 0 | 2 + 0 | 1 + 0 |
| 5 + 0 | 1 | 0 | 3 | 0 | 3 | 0 | 0 | 0 | 2 | 11 |
| 4 + 0 | - | 1 | 2 | 1 | 2 | - | 0 | 0 | 1 | 10 |
| 3 + 0 | - | - | 2 | 2 | 1 | - | - | 0 | 0 | 9 |
| 2 + 0 | - | - | - | 4 | 0 | - | - | - | 0 | 6 |
| 1 + 0 | - | - | - | - | 4 | - | - | - | - | 3 |

(Continued Next Page)

**POWERBALL BALANCED WHEEL® 52232PB** (Continued from previous page)

## Your 32 Numbers + PB to Wheel

| A | B | C | D | E | F | G | H | I | J | K |
|---|---|---|---|---|---|---|---|---|---|---|
| 3 | 3 | 3 | 3 | 3 | 3 | 3 | 3 | 4 | 3 | 3 |
| **L** | **M** | **N** | **O** | **P** | **Q** | **R** | **S** | **T** | **U** | **V** |
| 3 | 4 | 3 | 3 | 3 | 3 | 3 | 3 | 3 | 3 | 4 |
| **W** | **X** | **Y** | **Z** | **aa** | **bb** | **cc** | **dd** | **ee** | **ff** | **PB** |
| 3 | 3 | 3 | 3 | 3 | 4 | 3 | 3 | 3 | 3 | 20 |

## The 20 Games to Play

| | | | | | | | | | | | | | |
|---|---|---|---|---|---|---|---|---|---|---|---|---|---|
| 1. | A | H | *Q* | S | W | PB | 11. | D | J | K | Z | aa | PB |
| 2. | A | M | S | Y | bb | PB | 12. | E | I | K | V | ee | PB |
| 3. | A | N | P | S | X | PB | 13. | F | G | R | U | ff | PB |
| 4. | B | F | O | R | dd | PB | 14. | F | L | R | T | ff | PB |
| 5. | B | G | O | dd | ff | PB | 15. | G | L | T | U | dd | PB |
| 6. | B | L | O | T | U | PB | 16. | H | M | N | W | bb | PB |
| 7. | C | D | I | V | aa | PB | 17. | H | P | W | X | Y | PB |
| 8. | C | E | J | Z | ee | PB | 18. | I | J | V | Z | cc | PB |
| 9. | C | I | K | V | cc | PB | 19. | M | N | *Q* | Y | bb | PB |
| 10. | D | E | aa | cc | ee | PB | 20. | M | P | *Q* | X | bb | PB |



# POWERBALL BALANCED WHEEL® 52234PB

## Wheel 34 Numbers + PB in 23 Games for a 2 of 4 Win

With Powerball

| Numbers Matched | Maximum Wins 5 + 1 | 4 + 1 | 3 + 1 | 2 + 1 | 1 + 1 | 0 + 1 | Minimum Wins 5 + 1 | 4 + 1 | 3 + 1 | 2 + 1 | 1 + 1 | 0 + 1 |
|---|---|---|---|---|---|---|---|---|---|---|---|---|
| 5 + 1 | 1 | 0 | 3 | 0 | 3 | 16 | 0 | 0 | 0 | 2 | 11 | 10 |
| 4 + 1 | - | 1 | 2 | 1 | 2 | 17 | - | 0 | 0 | 1 | 10 | 12 |
| 3 + 1 | - | - | 2 | 2 | 3 | 16 | - | - | 0 | 0 | 9 | 14 |
| 2 + 1 | - | - | - | 4 | 0 | 19 | - | - | - | 0 | 6 | 17 |
| 1 + 1 | - | - | - | - | 5 | 18 | - | - | - | - | 3 | 20 |
| 0 + 1 | - | - | - | - | - | 23 | - | - | - | - | - | 23 |

Without Powerball

| Numbers Matched | Maximum Wins 5 + 0 | 4 + 0 | 3 + 0 | 2 + 0 | 1 + 0 | Minimum Wins 5 + 0 | 4 + 0 | 3 + 0 | 2 + 0 | 1 + 0 |
|---|---|---|---|---|---|---|---|---|---|---|
| 5 + 0 | 1 | 0 | 3 | 0 | 3 | 0 | 0 | 0 | 2 | 11 |
| 4 + 0 | - | 1 | 2 | 1 | 2 | - | 0 | 0 | 1 | 10 |
| 3 + 0 | - | - | 2 | 2 | 3 | - | - | 0 | 0 | 9 |
| 2 + 0 | - | - | - | 4 | 0 | - | - | - | 0 | 6 |
| 1 + 0 | - | - | - | - | 5 | - | - | - | - | 3 |

(Continued Next Page)

**POWERBALL BALANCED WHEEL® 52234PB** (Continued from previous page)

## Your 34 Numbers + PB to Wheel

| A | B | C | D | E | F | G | H | I |
|---|---|---|---|---|---|---|---|---|
| 5 | 4 | 3 | 3 | 3 | 3 | 3 | 3 | 3 |
| **J** | **K** | **L** | **M** | **N** | **O** | **P** | **Q** | **R** |
| 4 | 3 | 3 | 3 | 4 | 3 | 4 | 4 | 3 |
| **S** | **T** | **U** | **V** | **W** | **X** | **Y** | **Z** | **aa** |
| 3 | 4 | 3 | 4 | 3 | 3 | 3 | 3 | 4 |
| **bb** | **cc** | **dd** | **ee** | **ff** | **gg** | **hh** | **PB** | |
| 3 | 3 | 3 | 4 | 4 | 4 | 3 | 23 | |

## The 23 Games to Play

| | | | | | | |
|---|---|---|---|---|---|---|
| 1. | A | B | J | N | gg | PB |
| 2. | A | C | P | ee | ff | PB |
| 3. | A | J | N | aa | ee | PB |
| 4. | A | M | V | ee | gg | PB |
| 5. | A | P | U | ff | gg | PB |
| 6. | B | C | V | aa | gg | PB |
| 7. | B | M | P | aa | ff | PB |
| 8. | B | U | V | aa | ee | PB |
| 9. | C | J | M | N | U | PB |
| 10. | D | E | O | R | hh | PB |
| 11. | D | F | X | Y | hh | PB |
| 12. | D | Q | T | cc | hh | PB |
| 13. | E | F | R | Y | cc | PB |
| 14. | E | Q | R | T | X | PB |
| 15. | F | O | Q | T | Y | PB |
| 16. | G | H | K | S | dd | PB |
| 17. | G | I | L | W | Z | PB |
| 18. | G | S | W | bb | dd | PB |
| 19. | H | I | K | L | bb | PB |
| 20. | H | K | W | Z | bb | PB |
| 21. | I | L | S | Z | dd | PB |
| 22. | J | N | P | V | ff | PB |
| 23. | O | Q | T | X | cc | PB |



# POWERBALL BALANCED WHEEL® 52236PB

## Wheel 36 Numbers + PB in 26 Games for a 2 of 4 Win

With Powerball

| Numbers Matched | Maximum Wins 5 + 1 | 4 + 1 | 3 + 1 | 2 + 1 | 1 + 1 | 0 + 1 | Minimum Wins 5 + 1 | 4 + 1 | 3 + 1 | 2 + 1 | 1 + 1 | 0 + 1 |
|---|---|---|---|---|---|---|---|---|---|---|---|---|
| 5 + 1 | 1 | 0 | 3 | 0 | 3 | 19 | 0 | 0 | 0 | 2 | 12 | 12 |
| 4 + 1 | - | 1 | 2 | 1 | 2 | 20 | - | 0 | 0 | 1 | 11 | 14 |
| 3 + 1 | - | - | 2 | 2 | 1 | 21 | - | - | 0 | 0 | 10 | 16 |
| 2 + 1 | - | - | - | 4 | 2 | 20 | - | - | - | 0 | 6 | 20 |
| 1 + 1 | - | - | - | - | 6 | 20 | - | - | - | - | 3 | 23 |
| 0 + 1 | - | - | - | - | - | 26 | - | - | - | - | - | 26 |

Without Powerball

| Numbers Matched | Maximum Wins 5 + 0 | 4 + 0 | 3 + 0 | 2 + 0 | 1 + 0 | Minimum Wins 5 + 0 | 4 + 0 | 3 + 0 | 2 + 0 | 1 + 0 |
|---|---|---|---|---|---|---|---|---|---|---|
| 5 + 0 | 1 | 0 | 3 | 0 | 3 | 0 | 0 | 0 | 2 | 12 |
| 4 + 0 | - | 1 | 2 | 1 | 2 | - | 0 | 0 | 1 | 11 |
| 3 + 0 | - | - | 2 | 2 | 1 | - | - | 0 | 0 | 10 |
| 2 + 0 | - | - | - | 4 | 2 | - | - | - | 0 | 6 |
| 1 + 0 | - | - | - | - | 6 | - | - | - | - | 3 |

(Continued Next Page)

**POWERBALL BALANCED WHEEL® 52236PB** (Continued from previous page)

## Your 36 Numbers + PB to Wheel

| A | B | C | D | E | F | G | H | I | J |
|---|---|---|---|---|---|---|---|---|---|
| 3 | 4 | 6 | 5 | 4 | 3 | 3 | 4 | 5 | 3 |
| **K** | **L** | **M** | **N** | **O** | **P** | **Q** | **R** | **S** | **T** |
| 3 | 3 | 3 | 3 | 3 | 3 | 4 | 4 | 3 | 4 |
| **U** | **V** | **W** | **X** | **Y** | **Z** | **aa** | **bb** | **cc** | **dd** |
| 4 | 3 | 3 | 3 | 4 | 5 | 4 | 4 | 3 | 4 |
| **ee** | **ff** | **gg** | **hh** | **ii** | **jj** | **PB** | | | |
| 3 | 4 | 3 | 3 | 4 | 3 | 26 | | | |

## The 26 Games to Play

| | | | | | | | | | | | | | |
|---|---|---|---|---|---|---|---|---|---|---|---|---|---|
| 1. | A | K | S | W | ee | PB | 14. | D | E | U | Z | ii | PB |
| 2. | A | L | M | S | jj | PB | 15. | D | H | Q | Y | Z | PB |
| 3. | A | O | cc | ee | jj | PB | 16. | D | I | Q | aa | ii | PB |
| 4. | B | F | G | dd | hh | PB | 17. | D | R | T | Z | aa | PB |
| 5. | B | G | X | dd | gg | PB | 18. | E | H | I | T | Z | PB |
| 6. | B | J | V | X | dd | PB | 19. | E | I | Q | R | bb | PB |
| 7. | B | N | P | dd | gg | PB | 20. | F | J | V | gg | hh | PB |
| 8. | C | D | Z | bb | ff | PB | 21. | F | N | P | X | hh | PB |
| 9. | C | E | Y | aa | ff | PB | 22. | G | J | N | P | V | PB |
| 10. | C | H | U | aa | bb | PB | 23. | H | I | R | ff | ii | PB |
| 11. | C | I | R | U | Y | PB | 24. | K | L | M | W | ee | PB |
| 12. | C | Q | T | U | ff | PB | 25. | K | O | W | cc | jj | PB |
| 13. | C | T | Y | bb | ii | PB | 26. | L | M | O | S | cc | PB |



# POWERBALL BALANCED WHEEL® 52239PB

## Wheel 39 Numbers + PB in 30 Games for a 2 of 4 Win

With Powerball

| Numbers Matched | Maximum Wins | | | | | | Minimum Wins | | | | | |
|---|---|---|---|---|---|---|---|---|---|---|---|---|
| | 5 + 1 | 4 + 1 | 3 + 1 | 2 + 1 | 1 + 1 | 0 + 1 | 5 + 1 | 4 + 1 | 3 + 1 | 2 + 1 | 1 + 1 | 0 + 1 |
| 5 + 1 | 1 | 0 | 2 | 2 | 3 | 22 | 0 | 0 | 0 | 2 | 12 | 16 |
| 4 + 1 | - | 1 | 2 | 1 | 3 | 23 | - | 0 | 0 | 1 | 11 | 18 |
| 3 + 1 | - | - | 2 | 2 | 2 | 24 | - | - | 0 | 0 | 10 | 20 |
| 2 + 1 | - | - | - | 4 | 2 | 24 | - | - | - | 0 | 6 | 24 |
| 1 + 1 | - | - | - | - | 6 | 24 | - | - | - | - | 3 | 27 |
| 0 + 1 | - | - | - | - | - | 30 | - | - | - | - | - | 30 |

(Continued Next Page)

## POWERBALL BALANCED WHEEL® 52239PB (Continued from previous page)

Without Powerball

| Numbers Matched | Maximum Wins | | | | | Minimum Wins | | | | |
|---|---|---|---|---|---|---|---|---|---|---|
| | 5 + 0 | 4 + 0 | 3 + 0 | 2 + 0 | 1 + 0 | 5 + 0 | 4 + 0 | 3 + 0 | 2 + 0 | 1 + 0 |
| 5 + 0 | 1 | 0 | 2 | 2 | 3 | 0 | 0 | 0 | 2 | 12 |
| 4 + 0 | - | 1 | 2 | 1 | 3 | - | 0 | 0 | 1 | 11 |
| 3 + 0 | - | - | 2 | 2 | 2 | - | - | 0 | 0 | 10 |
| 2 + 0 | - | - | - | 4 | 2 | - | - | - | 0 | 6 |
| 1 + 0 | - | - | - | - | 6 | - | - | - | - | 3 |

# Your 39 Numbers + PB to Wheel

| A | B | C | D | E | F | G | H | I | J |
|---|---|---|---|---|---|---|---|---|---|
| 4 | 4 | 4 | 6 | 4 | 4 | 3 | 3 | 3 | 4 |
| **K** | **L** | **M** | **N** | **O** | **P** | **Q** | **R** | **S** | **T** |
| 4 | 5 | 4 | 4 | 3 | 4 | 3 | 4 | 4 | 3 |
| **U** | **V** | **W** | **X** | **Y** | **Z** | **aa** | **bb** | **cc** | **dd** |
| 4 | 4 | 3 | 4 | 3 | 4 | 4 | 4 | 4 | 4 |
| **ee** | **ff** | **gg** | **hh** | **ii** | **jj** | **kk** | ***ll*** | **mm** | **PB** |
| 4 | 5 | 5 | 3 | 4 | 3 | 3 | 4 | 4 | 30 |

# The 30 Games to Play

| | | | | | | | | | | | | | |
|---|---|---|---|---|---|---|---|---|---|---|---|---|---|
| 1. | A | B | dd | ii | *ll* | PB | 16. | D | S | V | aa | mm | PB |
| 2. | A | I | O | Z | dd | PB | 17. | E | G | P | U | hh | PB |
| 3. | A | K | M | bb | dd | PB | 18. | E | H | T | U | cc | PB |
| 4. | A | W | Z | dd | jj | PB | 19. | E | P | T | U | Y | PB |
| 5. | B | I | M | W | *ll* | PB | 20. | E | *Q* | U | cc | kk | PB |
| 6. | B | K | Z | bb | *ll* | PB | 21. | F | L | ee | ff | mm | PB |
| 7. | B | M | O | jj | *ll* | PB | 22. | F | N | R | V | ff | PB |
| 8. | C | D | N | X | mm | PB | 23. | G | H | Y | cc | hh | PB |
| 9. | C | F | L | aa | gg | PB | 24. | G | *Q* | T | hh | kk | PB |
| 10. | C | J | V | ff | gg | PB | 25. | H | P | *Q* | Y | kk | PB |
| 11. | C | R | S | ee | ff | PB | 26. | I | K | bb | ii | jj | PB |
| 12. | D | F | J | S | X | PB | 27. | J | L | R | gg | mm | PB |
| 13. | D | J | N | aa | ee | PB | 28. | K | O | W | bb | ii | PB |
| 14. | D | L | N | S | gg | PB | 29. | L | V | X | ee | gg | PB |
| 15. | D | R | X | aa | ff | PB | 30. | M | P | Z | cc | ii | PB |

# POWERBALL BALANCED WHEEL® 52242PB

## Wheel 42 Numbers + PB in 34 Games for a 2 of 4 Win

With Powerball

| Numbers Matched | Maximum Wins 5 + 1 | 4 + 1 | 3 + 1 | 2 + 1 | 1 + 1 | 0 + 1 | Minimum Wins 5 + 1 | 4 + 1 | 3 + 1 | 2 + 1 | 1 + 1 | 0 + 1 |
|---|---|---|---|---|---|---|---|---|---|---|---|---|
| 5 + 1 | 1 | 0 | 3 | 0 | 3 | 27 | 0 | 0 | 0 | 2 | 13 | 19 |
| 4 + 1 | - | 1 | 2 | 1 | 2 | 28 | - | 0 | 0 | 1 | 12 | 21 |
| 3 + 1 | - | - | 2 | 2 | 1 | 29 | - | - | 0 | 0 | 11 | 23 |
| 2 + 1 | - | - | - | 4 | 0 | 30 | - | - | - | 0 | 6 | 28 |
| 1 + 1 | - | - | - | - | 5 | 29 | - | - | - | - | 3 | 31 |
| 0 + 1 | - | - | - | - | - | 34 | - | - | - | - | - | 34 |

Without Powerball

| Numbers Matched | Maximum Wins 5 + 0 | 4 + 0 | 3 + 0 | 2 + 0 | 1 + 0 | Minimum Wins 5 + 0 | 4 + 0 | 3 + 0 | 2 + 0 | 1 + 0 |
|---|---|---|---|---|---|---|---|---|---|---|
| 5 + 0 | 1 | 0 | 3 | 0 | 3 | 0 | 0 | 0 | 2 | 13 |
| 4 + 0 | - | 1 | 2 | 1 | 2 | - | 0 | 0 | 1 | 12 |
| 3 + 0 | - | - | 2 | 2 | 1 | - | - | 0 | 0 | 11 |
| 2 + 0 | - | - | - | 4 | 0 | - | - | - | 0 | 6 |
| 1 + 0 | - | - | - | - | 5 | - | - | - | - | 3 |

## Your 42 Numbers + PB to Wheel

| A | B | C | D | E | F | G | H | I | J | K |
|---|---|---|---|---|---|---|---|---|---|---|
| 3 | 4 | 5 | 5 | 5 | 3 | 5 | 3 | 3 | 3 | 5 |
| **L** | **M** | **N** | **O** | **P** | **Q** | **R** | **S** | **T** | **U** | **V** |
| 3 | 5 | 3 | 5 | 5 | 5 | 5 | 3 | 5 | 5 | 4 |
| **W** | **X** | **Y** | **Z** | **aa** | **bb** | **cc** | **dd** | **ee** | **ff** | **gg** |
| 5 | 3 | 3 | 3 | 5 | 3 | 5 | 5 | 3 | 5 | 5 |
| **hh** | **ii** | **jj** | **kk** | ***ll*** | **mm** | **nn** | **oo** | **pp** | **PB** | |
| 5 | 3 | 5 | 5 | 3 | 3 | 3 | 3 | 3 | 34 | |

## The 34 Games to Play

| | | | | | | | | | | | | | |
|---|---|---|---|---|---|---|---|---|---|---|---|---|---|
| 1. | A | F | X | ee | pp | PB | 15. | D | O | *Q* | ff | kk | PB |
| 2. | A | H | I | ee | oo | PB | 16. | D | R | cc | hh | jj | PB |
| 3. | A | bb | ee | *ll* | oo | PB | 17. | E | G | *Q* | aa | jj | PB |
| 4. | B | J | V | Z | ii | PB | 18. | E | K | cc | dd | ff | PB |
| 5. | B | L | S | V | nn | PB | 19. | E | R | U | gg | kk | PB |
| 6. | B | N | V | Y | mm | PB | 20. | F | H | I | bb | *ll* | PB |
| 7. | B | V | ii | mm | nn | PB | 21. | F | X | bb | oo | pp | PB |
| 8. | C | D | K | aa | gg | PB | 22. | G | K | W | hh | kk | PB |
| 9. | C | E | M | O | hh | PB | 23. | G | O | P | cc | gg | PB |
| 10. | C | G | R | T | ff | PB | 24. | H | I | X | *ll* | pp | PB |
| 11. | C | P | dd | jj | kk | PB | 25. | J | L | S | Z | mm | PB |
| 12. | C | *Q* | U | W | cc | PB | 26. | J | N | Y | Z | nn | PB |
| 13. | D | E | P | T | W | PB | 27. | K | M | P | *Q* | R | PB |
| 14. | D | G | M | U | dd | PB | 28. | K | O | T | U | jj | PB |



(Continued Next Page)

**POWERBALL BALANCED WHEEL® 52242PB** (Continued from previous page)

| | | | | | | |
|---|---|---|---|---|---|---|
| 29. | L | N | S | Y | ii | PB |
| 30. | M | T | aa | cc | kk | PB |
| 31. | M | W | ff | gg | jj | PB |
| 32. | O | R | W | aa | dd | PB |
| 33. | P | U | aa | ff | hh | PB |
| 34. | Q | T | dd | gg | hh | PB |



# POWERBALL BALANCED WHEEL® 52245PB

## Wheel 45 Numbers + PB in 38 Games for a 2 of 4 Win

With Powerball

| Numbers Matched | Maximum Wins | | | | | | Minimum Wins | | | | | |
|---|---|---|---|---|---|---|---|---|---|---|---|---|
| | 5 + 1 | 4 + 1 | 3 + 1 | 2 + 1 | 1 + 1 | 0 + 1 | 5 + 1 | 4 + 1 | 3 + 1 | 2 + 1 | 1 + 1 | 0 + 1 |
| 5 + 1 | 1 | 0 | 2 | 2 | 3 | 30 | 0 | 0 | 0 | 2 | 13 | 23 |
| 4 + 1 | - | 1 | 2 | 1 | 3 | 31 | - | 0 | 0 | 1 | 12 | 25 |
| 3 + 1 | - | - | 2 | 2 | 2 | 32 | - | - | 0 | 0 | 11 | 27 |
| 2 + 1 | - | - | - | 4 | 0 | 34 | - | - | - | 0 | 6 | 32 |
| 1 + 1 | - | - | - | - | 5 | 33 | - | - | - | - | 3 | 35 |
| 0 + 1 | - | - | - | - | - | 38 | - | - | - | - | - | 38 |

Without Powerball

| Numbers Matched | Maximum Wins | | | | | Minimum Wins | | | | |
|---|---|---|---|---|---|---|---|---|---|---|
| | 5 + 0 | 4 + 0 | 3 + 0 | 2 + 0 | 1 + 0 | 5 + 0 | 4 + 0 | 3 + 0 | 2 + 0 | 1 + 0 |
| 5 + 0 | 1 | 0 | 2 | 2 | 3 | 0 | 0 | 0 | 2 | 13 |
| 4 + 0 | - | 1 | 2 | 1 | 3 | - | 0 | 0 | 1 | 12 |
| 3 + 0 | - | - | 2 | 2 | 2 | - | - | 0 | 0 | 11 |
| 2 + 0 | - | - | - | 4 | 0 | - | - | - | 0 | 6 |
| 1 + 0 | - | - | - | - | 5 | - | - | - | - | 3 |

## Your 45 Numbers + PB to Wheel

| A | B | C | D | E | F | G | H | I | J |
|---|---|---|---|---|---|---|---|---|---|
| 3 | 4 | 5 | 4 | 3 | 5 | 5 | 3 | 4 | 3 |
| **K** | **L** | **M** | **N** | **O** | **P** | **Q** | **R** | **S** | **T** |
| 4 | 5 | 5 | 5 | 3 | 4 | 5 | 5 | 5 | 4 |
| **U** | **V** | **W** | **X** | **Y** | **Z** | **aa** | **bb** | **cc** | **dd** |
| 5 | 5 | 5 | 4 | 5 | 5 | 5 | 4 | 5 | 5 |
| **ee** | **ff** | **gg** | **hh** | **ii** | **jj** | **kk** | **ll** | **mm** | **nn** |
| 4 | 5 | 3 | 4 | 4 | 3 | 4 | 5 | 3 | 4 |
| **oo** | **pp** | **qq** | **rr** | **ss** | **PB** | | | | |
| 5 | 5 | 3 | 3 | 3 | 38 | | | | |

## The 38 Games to Play

| | | | | | | |
|---|---|---|---|---|---|---|
| 1. | A | H | jj | kk | rr | PB |
| 2. | A | I | gg | mm | rr | PB |
| 3. | A | K | O | ee | kk | PB |
| 4. | B | D | P | X | nn | PB |
| 5. | B | E | bb | nn | ss | PB |
| 6. | B | J | bb | nn | qq | PB |
| 7. | B | T | hh | ii | nn | PB |
| 8. | C | F | U | Y | Z | PB |
| 9. | C | G | R | V | cc | PB |
| 10. | C | L | Q | dd | pp | PB |
| 11. | C | M | N | S | ff | PB |
| 12. | C | W | aa | ll | oo | PB |
| 13. | D | E | J | T | ii | PB |
| 14. | D | I | bb | hh | kk | PB |
| 15. | D | T | ii | qq | ss | PB |
| 16. | E | P | X | hh | qq | PB |



(Continued Next Page)

**POWERBALL BALANCED WHEEL® 52245PB** (Continued from previous page)

| | | | | | | |
|---|---|---|---|---|---|---|
| 17. | F | G | N | aa | dd | PB |
| 18. | F | L | R | W | ff | PB |
| 19. | F | M | V | *ll* | pp | PB |
| 20. | F | *Q* | S | cc | oo | PB |
| 21. | G | L | M | U | oo | PB |
| 22. | G | *Q* | Y | ff | *ll* | PB |
| 23. | G | S | W | Z | pp | PB |
| 24. | H | I | K | ee | jj | PB |
| 25. | H | O | gg | jj | mm | PB |
| 26. | I | K | O | ee | rr | PB |
| 27. | J | P | X | hh | ss | PB |
| 28. | K | ee | gg | kk | mm | PB |
| 29. | L | N | Z | cc | *ll* | PB |
| 30. | L | S | V | Y | aa | PB |
| 31. | M | *Q* | R | Z | aa | PB |
| 32. | M | W | Y | cc | dd | PB |
| 33. | N | *Q* | U | V | W | PB |
| 34. | N | R | Y | oo | pp | PB |
| 35. | P | T | X | bb | ii | PB |
| 36. | R | S | U | dd | *ll* | PB |
| 37. | U | aa | cc | ff | pp | PB |
| 38. | V | Z | dd | ff | oo | PB |



# POWERBALL BALANCED WHEEL® 52247PB

## Wheel 47 Numbers + PB in 41 Games for a 2 of 4 Win

With Powerball

| Numbers Matched | Maximum Wins 5 + 1 | 4 + 1 | 3 + 1 | 2 + 1 | 1 + 1 | 0 + 1 | Minimum Wins 5 + 1 | 4 + 1 | 3 + 1 | 2 + 1 | 1 + 1 | 0 + 1 |
|---|---|---|---|---|---|---|---|---|---|---|---|---|
| 5 + 1 | 1 | 0 | 2 | 4 | 2 | 32 | 0 | 0 | 0 | 2 | 13 | 26 |
| 4 + 1 | - | 1 | 1 | 5 | 0 | 34 | - | 0 | 0 | 1 | 12 | 28 |
| 3 + 1 | - | - | 2 | 2 | 3 | 34 | - | - | 0 | 0 | 11 | 30 |
| 2 + 1 | - | - | - | 4 | 1 | 36 | - | - | - | 0 | 6 | 35 |
| 1 + 1 | - | - | - | - | 5 | 36 | - | - | - | - | 3 | 38 |
| 0 + 1 | - | - | - | - | - | 41 | - | - | - | - | - | 41 |

Without Powerball

| Numbers Matched | Maximum Wins 5 + 0 | 4 + 0 | 3 + 0 | 2 + 0 | 1 + 0 | Minimum Wins 5 + 0 | 4 + 0 | 3 + 0 | 2 + 0 | 1 + 0 |
|---|---|---|---|---|---|---|---|---|---|---|
| 5 + 0 | 1 | 0 | 2 | 4 | 2 | 0 | 0 | 0 | 2 | 13 |
| 4 + 0 | - | 1 | 1 | 5 | 0 | - | 0 | 0 | 1 | 12 |
| 3 + 0 | - | - | 2 | 2 | 3 | - | - | 0 | 0 | 11 |
| 2 + 0 | - | - | - | 4 | 1 | - | - | - | 0 | 6 |
| 1 + 0 | - | - | - | - | 5 | - | - | - | - | 3 |

## Your 47 Numbers + PB to Wheel

| A | B | C | D | E | F | G | H | I | J |
|---|---|---|---|---|---|---|---|---|---|
| 4 | 4 | 5 | 5 | 4 | 3 | 5 | 4 | 5 | 4 |
| **K** | **L** | **M** | **N** | **O** | **P** | **Q** | **R** | **S** | **T** |
| 4 | 3 | 5 | 5 | 5 | 4 | 5 | 4 | 4 | 4 |
| **U** | **V** | **W** | **X** | **Y** | **Z** | **aa** | **bb** | **cc** | **dd** |
| 5 | 4 | 5 | 4 | 5 | 5 | 5 | 3 | 5 | 5 |
| **ee** | **ff** | **gg** | **hh** | **ii** | **jj** | **kk** | ***ll*** | **mm** | **nn** |
| 5 | 4 | 5 | 3 | 5 | 3 | 4 | 5 | 4 | 5 |
| **oo** | **pp** | **qq** | **rr** | **ss** | **tt** | **uu** | **PB** | | |
| 3 | 5 | 4 | 4 | 4 | 5 | 5 | 41 | | |

(Continued Next Page)

**POWERBALL BALANCED WHEEL® 52247PB** (Continued from previous page)

## The 41 Games to Play

| # | | | | | | |
|---|---|---|---|---|---|---|
| 1. | A | E | K | ff | kk | PB |
| 2. | A | H | M | qq | tt | PB |
| 3. | A | T | X | jj | oo | PB |
| 4. | A | V | mm | ss | tt | PB |
| 5. | B | F | R | V | bb | PB |
| 6. | B | J | R | S | tt | PB |
| 7. | B | L | R | V | hh | PB |
| 8. | B | P | R | mm | rr | PB |
| 9. | C | D | ee | gg | nn | PB |
| 10. | C | G | N | U | pp | PB |
| 11. | C | I | O | W | ii | PB |
| 12. | C | *Q* | aa | cc | uu | PB |
| 13. | C | Y | Z | dd | *ll* | PB |
| 14. | D | G | W | Y | uu | PB |
| 15. | D | I | N | *Q* | Z | PB |
| 16. | D | O | U | aa | dd | PB |
| 17. | D | cc | ii | *ll* | pp | PB |
| 18. | E | H | ff | oo | ss | PB |
| 19. | E | M | T | X | ff | PB |
| 20. | E | M | ff | jj | qq | PB |
| 21. | F | J | L | S | mm | PB |
| 22. | F | P | hh | rr | tt | PB |
| 23. | G | I | aa | ee | *ll* | PB |
| 24. | G | O | Z | cc | gg | PB |
| 25. | G | *Q* | dd | ii | nn | PB |
| 26. | H | K | T | X | kk | PB |
| 27. | H | K | jj | kk | ss | PB |
| 28. | I | U | Y | cc | nn | PB |
| 29. | I | dd | gg | pp | uu | PB |
| 30. | J | P | S | V | rr | PB |
| 31. | J | S | bb | hh | mm | PB |
| 32. | K | M | kk | oo | qq | PB |
| 33. | L | P | bb | rr | tt | PB |
| 34. | M | T | X | qq | ss | PB |
| 35. | N | O | *ll* | nn | uu | PB |
| 36. | N | W | cc | dd | ee | PB |
| 37. | N | Y | aa | gg | ii | PB |
| 38. | O | *Q* | Y | ee | pp | PB |
| 39. | *Q* | U | W | gg | *ll* | PB |
| 40. | U | Z | ee | ii | uu | PB |
| 41. | W | Z | aa | nn | pp | PB |



# POWERBALL BALANCED WHEEL® 52255PB

## Wheel 55 Numbers + PB in 52 Games for a 2 of 4 Win

With Powerball

| Numbers Matched | Maximum Wins 5 + 1 | 4 + 1 | 3 + 1 | 2 + 1 | 1 + 1 | 0 + 1 | Minimum Wins 5 + 1 | 4 + 1 | 3 + 1 | 2 + 1 | 1 + 1 | 0 + 1 |
|---|---|---|---|---|---|---|---|---|---|---|---|---|
| 5 + 1 | 1 | 0 | 1 | 5 | 2 | 43 | 0 | 0 | 0 | 2 | 17 | 33 |
| 4 + 1 | - | 1 | 1 | 4 | 1 | 45 | - | 0 | 0 | 1 | 14 | 37 |
| 3 + 1 | - | - | 2 | 2 | 2 | 46 | - | - | 0 | 0 | 13 | 39 |
| 2 + 1 | - | - | - | 4 | 0 | 48 | - | - | - | 0 | 8 | 44 |
| 1 + 1 | - | - | - | - | 5 | 47 | - | - | - | - | 3 | 49 |
| 0 + 1 | - | - | - | - | - | 52 | - | - | - | - | - | 52 |

Without Powerball

| Numbers Matched | Maximum Wins 5 + 0 | 4 + 0 | 3 + 0 | 2 + 0 | 1 + 0 | Minimum Wins 5 + 0 | 4 + 0 | 3 + 0 | 2 + 0 | 1 + 0 |
|---|---|---|---|---|---|---|---|---|---|---|
| 5 + 0 | 1 | 0 | 1 | 5 | 2 | 0 | 0 | 0 | 2 | 17 |
| 4 + 0 | - | 1 | 1 | 4 | 1 | - | 0 | 0 | 1 | 14 |
| 3 + 0 | - | - | 2 | 2 | 2 | - | - | 0 | 0 | 13 |
| 2 + 0 | - | - | - | 4 | 0 | - | - | - | 0 | 8 |
| 1 + 0 | - | - | - | - | 5 | - | - | - | - | 3 |

(Continued Next Page)

**POWERBALL BALANCED WHEEL® 52255PB** (Continued from previous page)

## Your 55 Numbers + PB to Wheel

| A | B | C | D | E | F | G | H | I | J |
|---|---|---|---|---|---|---|---|---|---|
| 5 | 5 | 5 | 5 | 5 | 5 | 5 | 5 | 5 | 5 |
| **K** | **L** | **M** | **N** | **O** | **P** | **Q** | **R** | **S** | **T** |
| 5 | 5 | 5 | 5 | 5 | 5 | 5 | 5 | 5 | 5 |
| **U** | **V** | **W** | **X** | **Y** | **Z** | **aa** | **bb** | **cc** | **dd** |
| 5 | 5 | 5 | 5 | 5 | 5 | 5 | 5 | 5 | 5 |
| **ee** | **ff** | **gg** | **hh** | **ii** | **jj** | **kk** | ***ll*** | **mm** | **nn** |
| 5 | 5 | 5 | 5 | 5 | 5 | 5 | 5 | 5 | 5 |
| **oo** | **pp** | **qq** | **rr** | **ss** | **tt** | **uu** | **vv** | **ww** | **xx** |
| 5 | 5 | 4 | 4 | 4 | 4 | 4 | 4 | 3 | 4 |
| **yy** | **zz** | **AA** | **BB** | **CC** | **PB** | | | | |
| 4 | 4 | 4 | 3 | 4 | 52 | | | | |

## The 52 Games to Play

| | | | | | | | | | | | | | |
|---|---|---|---|---|---|---|---|---|---|---|---|---|---|
| 1. | A | D | M | U | nn | PB | 23. | F | L | M | ff | ii | PB |
| 2. | A | F | J | O | X | PB | 24. | F | P | aa | jj | nn | PB |
| 3. | A | H | L | jj | *ll* | PB | 25. | F | U | gg | *ll* | pp | PB |
| 4. | A | P | ff | gg | hh | PB | 26. | G | I | *Q* | dd | mm | PB |
| 5. | A | S | aa | ii | pp | PB | 27. | G | R | Y | cc | oo | PB |
| 6. | B | C | E | *Q* | oo | PB | 28. | H | J | gg | ii | nn | PB |
| 7. | B | G | K | N | kk | PB | 29. | H | M | O | P | pp | PB |
| 8. | B | I | T | Y | bb | PB | 30. | H | U | X | aa | ff | PB |
| 9. | B | R | V | Z | mm | PB | 31. | I | N | Z | ee | oo | PB |
| 10. | B | W | cc | dd | ee | PB | 32. | J | L | P | S | U | PB |
| 11. | C | G | T | V | ee | PB | 33. | J | M | aa | hh | *ll* | PB |
| 12. | C | I | R | W | kk | PB | 34. | K | *Q* | R | bb | ee | PB |
| 13. | C | K | Y | Z | dd | PB | 35. | K | T | W | mm | oo | PB |
| 14. | C | N | bb | cc | mm | PB | 36. | L | X | hh | nn | pp | PB |
| 15. | D | F | H | S | hh | PB | 37. | M | S | X | gg | jj | PB |
| 16. | D | J | ff | jj | pp | PB | 38. | N | *Q* | V | W | Y | PB |
| 17. | D | L | O | aa | gg | PB | 39. | O | S | ff | *ll* | nn | PB |
| 18. | D | P | X | ii | *ll* | PB | 40. | O | U | hh | ii | jj | PB |
| 19. | E | G | W | Z | bb | PB | 41. | *Q* | T | Z | cc | kk | PB |
| 20. | E | I | K | V | cc | PB | 42. | V | bb | dd | kk | oo | PB |
| 21. | E | N | R | T | dd | PB | 43. | qq | rr | ss | ww | CC | PB |
| 22. | E | Y | ee | kk | mm | PB | 44. | qq | tt | uu | vv | xx | PB |



(Continued Next Page)

**POWERBALL BALANCED WHEEL® 52255PB** (Continued from previous page)

| | | | | | | |
|---|---|---|---|---|---|---|
| 45. | qq | vv | xx | zz | CC | PB |
| 46. | qq | yy | AA | BB | CC | PB |
| 47. | rr | ss | tt | yy | AA | PB |
| 48. | rr | ss | vv | xx | BB | PB |
| 49. | rr | tt | uu | zz | CC | PB |
| 50. | ss | uu | yy | zz | AA | PB |
| 51. | tt | uu | ww | zz | BB | PB |
| 52. | vv | ww | xx | yy | AA | PB |



# POWERBALL BALANCED WHEEL® 52256PB

## Wheel 56 Numbers + PB in 54 Games for a 2 of 4 Win

With Powerball

| Numbers Matched | Maximum Wins 5 + 1 | 4 + 1 | 3 + 1 | 2 + 1 | 1 + 1 | 0 + 1 | Minimum Wins 5 + 1 | 4 + 1 | 3 + 1 | 2 + 1 | 1 + 1 | 0 + 1 |
|---|---|---|---|---|---|---|---|---|---|---|---|---|
| 5 + 1 | 1 | 1 | 0 | 3 | 7 | 42 | 0 | 0 | 0 | 2 | 19 | 33 |
| 4 + 1 | - | 2 | 0 | 0 | 10 | 42 | - | 0 | 0 | 1 | 16 | 37 |
| 3 + 1 | - | - | 2 | 0 | 8 | 44 | - | - | 0 | 0 | 14 | 40 |
| 2 + 1 | - | - | - | 4 | 1 | 49 | - | - | - | 0 | 9 | 45 |
| 1 + 1 | - | - | - | - | 5 | 49 | - | - | - | - | 4 | 50 |
| 0 + 1 | - | - | - | - | - | 54 | - | - | - | - | - | 54 |

Without Powerball

| Numbers Matched | Maximum Wins 5 + 0 | 4 + 0 | 3 + 0 | 2 + 0 | 1 + 0 | Minimum Wins 5 + 0 | 4 + 0 | 3 + 0 | 2 + 0 | 1 + 0 |
|---|---|---|---|---|---|---|---|---|---|---|
| 5 + 0 | 1 | 1 | 0 | 3 | 7 | 0 | 0 | 0 | 2 | 19 |
| 4 + 0 | - | 2 | 0 | 0 | 10 | - | 0 | 0 | 1 | 16 |
| 3 + 0 | - | - | 2 | 0 | 8 | - | - | 0 | 0 | 14 |
| 2 + 0 | - | - | - | 4 | 1 | - | - | - | 0 | 9 |
| 1 + 0 | - | - | - | - | 5 | - | - | - | - | 4 |

## Your 56 Numbers + PB to Wheel

| | | | | | | | | | |
|---|---|---|---|---|---|---|---|---|---|
| A | B | C | D | E | F | G | H | I | J |
| 5 | 5 | 5 | 5 | 5 | 5 | 5 | 5 | 5 | 5 |
| K | L | M | N | O | P | Q | R | S | T |
| 5 | 5 | 5 | 5 | 5 | 5 | 5 | 5 | 5 | 5 |
| U | V | W | X | Y | Z | aa | bb | cc | dd |
| 5 | 5 | 5 | 5 | 5 | 5 | 5 | 5 | 5 | 5 |
| ee | ff | gg | hh | ii | jj | kk | *ll* | mm | nn |
| 5 | 5 | 5 | 5 | 5 | 5 | 5 | 5 | 5 | 5 |
| oo | pp | qq | rr | ss | tt | uu | vv | ww | xx |
| 5 | 5 | 5 | 4 | 4 | 5 | 4 | 5 | 4 | 5 |
| yy | zz | AA | BB | CC | DD | PB | | | |
| 4 | 4 | 4 | 4 | 4 | 4 | 54 | | | |

## The 54 Games to Play

| | | | | | | |
|---|---|---|---|---|---|---|
| 1. | A | C | L | cc | nn | PB |
| 2. | A | D | ff | gg | hh | PB |
| 3. | A | E | G | P | T | PB |
| 4. | A | F | I | V | dd | PB |
| 5. | A | J | Z | aa | kk | PB |
| 6. | B | H | K | X | jj | PB |
| 7. | B | M | *Q* | Y | *ll* | PB |
| 8. | B | N | U | W | oo | PB |
| 9. | B | O | S | bb | ii | PB |
| 10. | B | R | ee | mm | pp | PB |



(Continued Next Page)

**POWERBALL BALANCED WHEEL® 52256PB** (Continued from previous page)

| | | | | | | |
|---|---|---|---|---|---|---|
| 11. | C | D | E | F | aa | PB |
| 12. | C | G | Z | dd | ff | PB |
| 13. | C | I | T | hh | kk | PB |
| 14. | C | J | P | V | gg | PB |
| 15. | D | G | V | cc | kk | PB |
| 16. | D | I | P | Z | nn | PB |
| 17. | D | J | L | T | dd | PB |
| 18. | E | I | J | cc | ff | PB |
| 19. | E | L | V | Z | hh | PB |
| 20. | E | dd | gg | kk | nn | PB |
| 21. | F | G | J | hh | nn | PB |
| 22. | F | L | P | ff | kk | PB |
| 23. | F | T | Z | cc | gg | PB |
| 24. | G | I | L | aa | gg | PB |
| 25. | H | M | S | ee | oo | PB |
| 26. | H | N | O | *Q* | mm | PB |
| 27. | H | R | U | ii | *ll* | PB |
| 28. | H | W | Y | bb | pp | PB |
| 29. | K | M | N | ii | pp | PB |
| 30. | K | O | U | Y | ee | PB |
| 31. | K | *Q* | R | bb | oo | PB |
| 32. | K | S | W | *ll* | mm | PB |
| 33. | M | O | R | W | jj | PB |
| 34. | M | U | X | bb | mm | PB |
| 35. | N | R | S | X | Y | PB |
| 36. | N | bb | ee | jj | *ll* | PB |
| 37. | O | X | *ll* | oo | pp | PB |
| 38. | P | aa | cc | dd | hh | PB |
| 39. | *Q* | S | U | jj | pp | PB |
| 40. | *Q* | W | X | ee | ii | PB |
| 41. | T | V | aa | ff | nn | PB |
| 42. | Y | ii | jj | mm | oo | PB |
| 43. | qq | rr | uu | vv | BB | PB |
| 44. | qq | ss | uu | ww | zz | PB |
| 45. | qq | tt | uu | yy | CC | PB |
| 46. | qq | tt | xx | zz | AA | PB |
| 47. | qq | zz | BB | CC | DD | PB |
| 48. | rr | ss | tt | vv | DD | PB |
| 49. | rr | vv | ww | xx | CC | PB |
| 50. | rr | vv | yy | zz | AA | PB |
| 51. | ss | tt | vv | yy | DD | PB |
| 52. | ss | xx | AA | BB | CC | PB |
| 53. | tt | ww | xx | yy | BB | PB |
| 54. | uu | ww | xx | AA | DD | PB |



# POWERBALL BALANCED WHEEL® 52112PB

## Wheel 12 Numbers + PB in 4 Games for a 2 of 3 Win

With Powerball

| Numbers Matched | Maximum Wins | | | | | | Minimum Wins | | | | | |
|---|---|---|---|---|---|---|---|---|---|---|---|---|
| | 5 + 1 | 4 + 1 | 3 + 1 | 2 + 1 | 1 + 1 | 0 + 1 | 5 + 1 | 4 + 1 | 3 + 1 | 2 + 1 | 1 + 1 | 0 + 1 |
| 5 + 1 | 1 | 0 | 2 | 0 | 0 | 1 | 0 | 0 | 0 | 4 | 0 | 0 |
| 4 + 1 | - | 1 | 1 | 1 | 0 | 1 | - | 0 | 0 | 2 | 2 | 0 |
| 3 + 1 | - | - | 2 | 0 | 1 | 1 | - | - | 0 | 1 | 2 | 1 |
| 2 + 1 | - | - | - | 2 | 1 | 1 | - | - | - | 0 | 3 | 1 |
| 1 + 1 | - | - | - | - | 3 | 1 | - | - | - | - | 1 | 3 |
| 0 + 1 | - | - | - | - | - | 4 | - | - | - | - | - | 4 |

(Continued Next Page)

## POWERBALL BALANCED WHEEL® 52112PB (Continued from previous page)

Without Powerball

| Numbers Matched | Maximum Wins 5 + 0 | 4 + 0 | 3 + 0 | 2 + 0 | 1 + 0 | Minimum Wins 5 + 0 | 4 + 0 | 3 + 0 | 2 + 0 | 1 + 0 |
|---|---|---|---|---|---|---|---|---|---|---|
| 5 + 0 | 1 | 0 | 2 | 0 | 0 | 0 | 0 | 0 | 4 | 0 |
| 4 + 0 | - | 1 | 1 | 1 | 0 | - | 0 | 0 | 2 | 2 |
| 3 + 0 | - | - | 2 | 0 | 1 | - | - | 0 | 1 | 2 |
| 2 + 0 | - | - | - | 2 | 1 | - | - | - | 0 | 3 |
| 1 + 0 | - | - | - | - | 3 | - | - | - | - | 1 |

## Your 12 Numbers + PB to Wheel

| A | B | C | D | E | F | G |
|---|---|---|---|---|---|---|
| 1 | 3 | 1 | 2 | 2 | 1 | 2 |

| H | I | J | K | L | PB |
|---|---|---|---|---|---|
| 2 | 1 | 2 | 2 | 1 | 4 |

## The 4 Games to Play

| | | | | | | |
|---|---|---|---|---|---|---|
| 1. | A | C | F | I | L | PB |
| 2. | B | D | E | J | K | PB |
| 3. | B | D | G | H | K | PB |
| 4. | B | E | G | H | J | PB |



# POWERBALL BALANCED WHEEL® 52113PB

## Wheel 13 Numbers + PB in 5 Games for a 2 of 3 Win

With Powerball

| Numbers Matched | Maximum Wins 5 + 1 | 4 + 1 | 3 + 1 | 2 + 1 | 1 + 1 | 0 + 1 | Minimum Wins 5 + 1 | 4 + 1 | 3 + 1 | 2 + 1 | 1 + 1 | 0 + 1 |
|---|---|---|---|---|---|---|---|---|---|---|---|---|
| 5 + 1 | 1 | 1 | 1 | 1 | 0 | 1 | 0 | 0 | 0 | 4 | 1 | 0 |
| 4 + 1 | - | 2 | 1 | 0 | 1 | 1 | - | 0 | 0 | 2 | 2 | 1 |
| 3 + 1 | - | - | 3 | 0 | 0 | 2 | - | - | 0 | 1 | 2 | 2 |
| 2 + 1 | - | - | - | 3 | 0 | 2 | - | - | - | 0 | 3 | 2 |
| 1 + 1 | - | - | - | - | 3 | 2 | - | - | - | - | 1 | 4 |
| 0 + 1 | - | - | - | - | - | 5 | - | - | - | - | - | 5 |

Without Powerball

| Numbers Matched | Maximum Wins 5 + 0 | 4 + 0 | 3 + 0 | 2 + 0 | 1 + 0 | Minimum Wins 5 + 0 | 4 + 0 | 3 + 0 | 2 + 0 | 1 + 0 |
|---|---|---|---|---|---|---|---|---|---|---|
| 5 + 0 | 1 | 1 | 1 | 1 | 0 | 0 | 0 | 0 | 4 | 1 |
| 4 + 0 | - | 2 | 1 | 0 | 1 | - | 0 | 0 | 2 | 2 |
| 3 + 0 | - | - | 3 | 0 | 0 | - | - | 0 | 1 | 2 |
| 2 + 0 | - | - | - | 3 | 0 | - | - | - | 0 | 3 |
| 1 + 0 | - | - | - | - | 3 | - | - | - | - | 1 |

## Your 13 Numbers + PB to Wheel

| A | B | C | D | E | F | G |
|---|---|---|---|---|---|---|
| 3 | 1 | 2 | 3 | 1 | 1 | 2 |

| H | I | J | K | L | M | PB |
|---|---|---|---|---|---|---|
| 1 | 2 | 3 | 3 | 1 | 2 | 5 |

## The 5 Games to Play

| | | | | | | |
|---|---|---|---|---|---|---|
| 1. | A | C | J | K | M | PB |
| 2. | A | D | G | J | K | PB |
| 3. | A | D | I | J | K | PB |
| 4. | B | E | F | H | L | PB |
| 5. | C | D | G | I | M | PB |

# POWERBALL BALANCED WHEEL® 52114PB

## Wheel 14 Numbers + PB in 6 Games for a 2 of 3 Win

With Powerball

| Numbers Matched | Maximum Wins 5 + 1 | 4 + 1 | 3 + 1 | 2 + 1 | 1 + 1 | 0 + 1 | Minimum Wins 5 + 1 | 4 + 1 | 3 + 1 | 2 + 1 | 1 + 1 | 0 + 1 |
|---|---|---|---|---|---|---|---|---|---|---|---|---|
| 5 + 1 | 1 | 0 | 1 | 1 | 1 | 2 | 0 | 0 | 0 | 4 | 2 | 0 |
| 4 + 1 | - | 1 | 1 | 0 | 2 | 2 | - | 0 | 0 | 2 | 4 | 0 |
| 3 + 1 | - | - | 2 | 0 | 1 | 3 | - | - | 0 | 1 | 4 | 1 |
| 2 + 1 | - | - | - | 2 | 1 | 3 | - | - | - | 0 | 4 | 2 |
| 1 + 1 | - | - | - | - | 3 | 3 | - | - | - | - | 2 | 4 |
| 0 + 1 | - | - | - | - | - | 6 | - | - | - | - | - | 6 |

Without Powerball

| Numbers Matched | Maximum Wins 5 + 0 | 4 + 0 | 3 + 0 | 2 + 0 | 1 + 0 | Minimum Wins 5 + 0 | 4 + 0 | 3 + 0 | 2 + 0 | 1 + 0 |
|---|---|---|---|---|---|---|---|---|---|---|
| 5 + 0 | 1 | 0 | 1 | 1 | 1 | 0 | 0 | 0 | 4 | 2 |
| 4 + 0 | - | 1 | 1 | 0 | 2 | - | 0 | 0 | 2 | 4 |
| 3 + 0 | - | - | 2 | 0 | 1 | - | - | 0 | 1 | 4 |
| 2 + 0 | - | - | - | 2 | 1 | - | - | - | 0 | 4 |
| 1 + 0 | - | - | - | - | 3 | - | - | - | - | 2 |

## Your 14 Numbers + PB to Wheel

| A | B | C | D | E | F | G | H |
|---|---|---|---|---|---|---|---|
| 2 | 2 | 3 | 3 | 2 | 2 | 2 | 2 |

| I | J | K | L | M | N | PB |
|---|---|---|---|---|---|---|
| 2 | 2 | 2 | 2 | 2 | 2 | 6 |

## The 6 Games to Play

| | | | | | | |
|---|---|---|---|---|---|---|
| 1. | A | B | H | M | N | PB |
| 2. | A | C | H | L | N | PB |
| 3. | B | C | D | L | M | PB |
| 4. | C | E | F | I | J | PB |
| 5. | D | E | G | I | K | PB |
| 6. | D | F | G | J | K | PB |



# POWERBALL BALANCED WHEEL® 52115PB

## Wheel 15 Numbers + PB in 7 Games for a 2 of 3 Win

With Powerball

| Numbers Matched | Maximum Wins 5 + 1 | 4 + 1 | 3 + 1 | 2 + 1 | 1 + 1 | 0 + 1 | Minimum Wins 5 + 1 | 4 + 1 | 3 + 1 | 2 + 1 | 1 + 1 | 0 + 1 |
|---|---|---|---|---|---|---|---|---|---|---|---|---|
| 5 + 1 | 1 | 1 | 1 | 1 | 0 | 3 | 0 | 0 | 0 | 4 | 2 | 1 |
| 4 + 1 | - | 2 | 1 | 0 | 1 | 3 | - | 0 | 0 | 2 | 4 | 1 |
| 3 + 1 | - | - | 3 | 0 | 0 | 4 | - | - | 0 | 1 | 4 | 2 |
| 2 + 1 | - | - | - | 3 | 0 | 4 | - | - | - | 0 | 4 | 3 |
| 1 + 1 | - | - | - | - | 3 | 4 | - | - | - | - | 2 | 5 |
| 0 + 1 | - | - | - | - | - | 7 | - | - | - | - | - | 7 |

Without Powerball

| Numbers Matched | Maximum Wins 5 + 0 | 4 + 0 | 3 + 0 | 2 + 0 | 1 + 0 | Minimum Wins 5 + 0 | 4 + 0 | 3 + 0 | 2 + 0 | 1 + 0 |
|---|---|---|---|---|---|---|---|---|---|---|
| 5 + 0 | 1 | 1 | 1 | 1 | 0 | 0 | 0 | 0 | 4 | 2 |
| 4 + 0 | - | 2 | 1 | 0 | 1 | - | 0 | 0 | 2 | 4 |
| 3 + 0 | - | - | 3 | 0 | 0 | - | - | 0 | 1 | 4 |
| 2 + 0 | - | - | - | 3 | 0 | - | - | - | 0 | 4 |
| 1 + 0 | - | - | - | - | 3 | - | - | - | - | 2 |

(Continued Next Page)

**POWERBALL BALANCED WHEEL® 52115PB** (Continued from previous page)

## Your 15 Numbers + PB to Wheel

| A | B | C | D | E | F | G | H |
|---|---|---|---|---|---|---|---|
| 2 | 3 | 3 | 2 | 2 | 2 | 3 | 2 |

| I | J | K | L | M | N | O | PB |
|---|---|---|---|---|---|---|---|
| 2 | 2 | 2 | 3 | 2 | 2 | 3 | 7 |

## The 7 Games to Play

| | | | | | | |
|---|---|---|---|---|---|---|
| 1. | A | B | G | M | O | PB |
| 2. | A | C | K | M | N | PB |
| 3. | B | C | G | K | O | PB |
| 4. | B | C | G | N | O | PB |
| 5. | D | E | H | J | L | PB |
| 6. | D | F | H | I | L | PB |
| 7. | E | F | I | J | L | PB |



# POWERBALL BALANCED WHEEL® 52116PB

## Wheel 16 Numbers + PB in 8 Games for a 2 of 3 Win

With Powerball

| Numbers | Maximum Wins | | | | | | Minimum Wins | | | | | |
|---|---|---|---|---|---|---|---|---|---|---|---|---|
| Matched | 5 + 1 | 4 + 1 | 3 + 1 | 2 + 1 | 1 + 1 | 0 + 1 | 5 + 1 | 4 + 1 | 3 + 1 | 2 + 1 | 1 + 1 | 0 + 1 |
| 5 + 1 | 1 | 1 | 1 | 1 | 0 | 4 | 0 | 0 | 0 | 4 | 3 | 1 |
| 4 + 1 | - | 2 | 1 | 0 | 1 | 4 | - | 0 | 0 | 2 | 4 | 2 |
| 3 + 1 | - | - | 3 | 0 | 0 | 5 | - | - | 0 | 1 | 4 | 3 |
| 2 + 1 | - | - | - | 3 | 0 | 5 | - | - | - | 0 | 4 | 4 |
| 1 + 1 | - | - | - | - | 3 | 5 | - | - | - | - | 2 | 6 |
| 0 + 1 | - | - | - | - | - | 8 | - | - | - | - | - | 8 |

Without Powerball

| Numbers | Maximum Wins | | | | | Minimum Wins | | | | |
|---|---|---|---|---|---|---|---|---|---|---|
| Matched | 5 + 0 | 4 + 0 | 3 + 0 | 2 + 0 | 1 + 0 | 5 + 0 | 4 + 0 | 3 + 0 | 2 + 0 | 1 + 0 |
| 5 + 0 | 1 | 1 | 1 | 1 | 0 | 0 | 0 | 0 | 4 | 3 |
| 4 + 0 | - | 2 | 1 | 0 | 1 | - | 0 | 0 | 2 | 4 |
| 3 + 0 | - | - | 3 | 0 | 0 | - | - | 0 | 1 | 4 |
| 2 + 0 | - | - | - | 3 | 0 | - | - | - | 0 | 4 |
| 1 + 0 | - | - | - | - | 3 | - | - | - | - | 2 |

## Your 16 Numbers + PB to Wheel

| A | B | C | D | E | F | G | H | I |
|---|---|---|---|---|---|---|---|---|
| 3 | 2 | 2 | 3 | 2 | 2 | 3 | 3 | 2 |

| J | K | L | M | N | O | P | PB |
|---|---|---|---|---|---|---|---|
| 3 | 3 | 2 | 2 | 2 | 3 | 3 | 8 |

## The 8 Games to Play

| | | | | | | |
|---|---|---|---|---|---|---|
| 1. | A | B | D | O | P | PB |
| 2. | A | C | D | N | P | PB |
| 3. | A | D | M | O | P | PB |
| 4. | B | C | M | N | O | PB |
| 5. | E | F | G | I | L | PB |
| 6. | E | G | H | J | K | PB |
| 7. | F | H | J | K | L | PB |
| 8. | G | H | I | J | K | PB |

# POWERBALL BALANCED WHEEL® 52117PB

## Wheel 17 Numbers + PB in 9 Games for a 2 of 3 Win

With Powerball

| Numbers Matched | Maximum Wins 5 + 1 | 4 + 1 | 3 + 1 | 2 + 1 | 1 + 1 | 0 + 1 | Minimum Wins 5 + 1 | 4 + 1 | 3 + 1 | 2 + 1 | 1 + 1 | 0 + 1 |
|---|---|---|---|---|---|---|---|---|---|---|---|---|
| 5 + 1 | 1 | 1 | 0 | 2 | 2 | 3 | 0 | 0 | 0 | 4 | 4 | 1 |
| 4 + 1 | - | 2 | 0 | 2 | 0 | 5 | - | 0 | 0 | 2 | 5 | 2 |
| 3 + 1 | - | - | 3 | 0 | 0 | 6 | - | - | 0 | 1 | 4 | 4 |
| 2 + 1 | - | - | - | 3 | 0 | 6 | - | - | - | 0 | 4 | 5 |
| 1 + 1 | - | - | - | - | 3 | 6 | - | - | - | - | 2 | 7 |
| 0 + 1 | - | - | - | - | - | 9 | - | - | - | - | - | 9 |

Without Powerball

| Numbers Matched | Maximum Wins 5 + 0 | 4 + 0 | 3 + 0 | 2 + 0 | 1 + 0 | Minimum Wins 5 + 0 | 4 + 0 | 3 + 0 | 2 + 0 | 1 + 0 |
|---|---|---|---|---|---|---|---|---|---|---|
| 5 + 0 | 1 | 1 | 0 | 2 | 2 | 0 | 0 | 0 | 4 | 4 |
| 4 + 0 | - | 2 | 0 | 2 | 0 | - | 0 | 0 | 2 | 5 |
| 3 + 0 | - | - | 3 | 0 | 0 | - | - | 0 | 1 | 4 |
| 2 + 0 | - | - | - | 3 | 0 | - | - | - | 0 | 4 |
| 1 + 0 | - | - | - | - | 3 | - | - | - | - | 2 |

## Your 17 Numbers + PB to Wheel

| A | B | C | D | E | F | G | H | I |
|---|---|---|---|---|---|---|---|---|
| 2 | 2 | 3 | 3 | 3 | 2 | 3 | 3 | 3 |

| J | K | L | M | N | O | P | Q | PB |
|---|---|---|---|---|---|---|---|---|
| 3 | 3 | 3 | 3 | 2 | 2 | 2 | 3 | 9 |

## The 9 Games to Play

| | | | | | | |
|---|---|---|---|---|---|---|
| 1. | A | B | N | O | P | PB |
| 2. | A | C | E | P | Q | PB |
| 3. | B | C | E | O | Q | PB |
| 4. | C | D | E | N | Q | PB |
| 5. | D | F | I | K | L | PB |
| 6. | D | G | H | J | M | PB |
| 7. | F | G | H | J | M | PB |
| 8. | G | I | K | L | M | PB |
| 9. | H | I | J | K | L | PB |



# POWERBALL BALANCED WHEEL® 52118PB

## Wheel 18 Numbers + PB in 10 Games for a 2 of 3 Win

With Powerball

| Numbers Matched | Maximum Wins 5 + 1 | 4 + 1 | 3 + 1 | 2 + 1 | 1 + 1 | 0 + 1 | Minimum Wins 5 + 1 | 4 + 1 | 3 + 1 | 2 + 1 | 1 + 1 | 0 + 1 |
|---|---|---|---|---|---|---|---|---|---|---|---|---|
| 5 + 1 | 1 | 1 | 0 | 2 | 1 | 5 | 0 | 0 | 0 | 4 | 3 | 3 |
| 4 + 1 | - | 2 | 0 | 2 | 0 | 6 | - | 0 | 0 | 2 | 4 | 4 |
| 3 + 1 | - | - | 3 | 0 | 0 | 7 | - | - | 0 | 1 | 4 | 5 |
| 2 + 1 | - | - | - | 3 | 0 | 7 | - | - | - | 0 | 4 | 6 |
| 1 + 1 | - | - | - | - | 3 | 7 | - | - | - | - | 2 | 8 |
| 0 + 1 | - | - | - | - | - | 10 | - | - | - | - | - | 10 |

(Continued Next Page)

## POWERBALL BALANCED WHEEL® 52118PB (Continued from previous page)

Without Powerball

| Numbers Matched | Maximum Wins 5 + 0 | 4 + 0 | 3 + 0 | 2 + 0 | 1 + 0 | Minimum Wins 5 + 0 | 4 + 0 | 3 + 0 | 2 + 0 | 1 + 0 |
|---|---|---|---|---|---|---|---|---|---|---|
| 5 + 0 | 1 | 1 | 0 | 2 | 1 | 0 | 0 | 0 | 4 | 3 |
| 4 + 0 | - | 2 | 0 | 2 | 0 | - | 0 | 0 | 2 | 4 |
| 3 + 0 | - | - | 3 | 0 | 0 | - | - | 0 | 1 | 4 |
| 2 + 0 | - | - | - | 3 | 0 | - | - | - | 0 | 4 |
| 1 + 0 | - | - | - | - | 3 | - | - | - | - | 2 |

### Your 18 Numbers + PB to Wheel

| A | B | C | D | E | F | G | H | I | J |
|---|---|---|---|---|---|---|---|---|---|
| (3) | (3) | (3) | (3) | (2) | (3) | (3) | (3) | (3) | (3) |

| K | L | M | N | O | P | Q | R | PB |
|---|---|---|---|---|---|---|---|---|
| (3) | (2) | (2) | (3) | (2) | (3) | (3) | (3) | (10) |

### The 10 Games to Play

| | | | | | | |
|---|---|---|---|---|---|---|
| 1. | A | B | D | Q | R | PB |
| 2. | A | C | L | P | Q | PB |
| 3. | A | C | O | P | Q | PB |
| 4. | B | C | D | P | R | PB |
| 5. | B | D | L | O | R | PB |
| 6. | E | F | G | J | K | PB |
| 7. | E | H | I | M | N | PB |
| 8. | F | G | J | K | M | PB |
| 9. | F | H | I | K | N | PB |
| 10. | G | H | I | J | N | PB |



## POWERBALL BALANCED WHEEL® 52119PB

### Wheel 19 Numbers + PB in 11 Games for a 2 of 3 Win

With Powerball

| Numbers Matched | Maximum Wins 5 + 1 | 4 + 1 | 3 + 1 | 2 + 1 | 1 + 1 | 0 + 1 | Minimum Wins 5 + 1 | 4 + 1 | 3 + 1 | 2 + 1 | 1 + 1 | 0 + 1 |
|---|---|---|---|---|---|---|---|---|---|---|---|---|
| 5 + 1 | 1 | 1 | 0 | 2 | 1 | 6 | 0 | 0 | 0 | 4 | 5 | 2 |
| 4 + 1 | - | 2 | 0 | 2 | 0 | 7 | - | 0 | 0 | 2 | 6 | 3 |
| 3 + 1 | - | - | 3 | 0 | 0 | 8 | - | - | 0 | 1 | 5 | 5 |
| 2 + 1 | - | - | - | 3 | 0 | 8 | - | - | - | 0 | 5 | 6 |
| 1 + 1 | - | - | - | - | 3 | 8 | - | - | - | - | 2 | 9 |
| 0 + 1 | - | - | - | - | - | 11 | - | - | - | - | - | 11 |

Without Powerball

| Numbers Matched | Maximum Wins 5 + 0 | 4 + 0 | 3 + 0 | 2 + 0 | 1 + 0 | Minimum Wins 5 + 0 | 4 + 0 | 3 + 0 | 2 + 0 | 1 + 0 |
|---|---|---|---|---|---|---|---|---|---|---|
| 5 + 0 | 1 | 1 | 0 | 2 | 1 | 0 | 0 | 0 | 4 | 5 |
| 4 + 0 | - | 2 | 0 | 2 | 0 | - | 0 | 0 | 2 | 6 |
| 3 + 0 | - | - | 3 | 0 | 0 | - | - | 0 | 1 | 5 |
| 2 + 0 | - | - | - | 3 | 0 | - | - | - | 0 | 5 |
| 1 + 0 | - | - | - | - | 3 | - | - | - | - | 2 |

### Your 19 Numbers + PB to Wheel

| A | B | C | D | E | F | G | H | I | J |
|---|---|---|---|---|---|---|---|---|---|
| (3) | (3) | (2) | (3) | (3) | (3) | (3) | (3) | (3) | (3) |

| K | L | M | N | O | P | Q | R | S | PB |
|---|---|---|---|---|---|---|---|---|---|
| (2) | (3) | (3) | (3) | (3) | (3) | (3) | (3) | (3) | (11) |

### The 11 Games to Play

| | | | | | | |
|---|---|---|---|---|---|---|
| 1. | A | C | L | M | O | PB |
| 2. | A | F | J | M | N | PB |



(Continued Next Page)

**POWERBALL BALANCED WHEEL® 52119PB** (Continued from previous page)

| | | | | | | |
|---|---|---|---|---|---|---|
| 3. | A | K | L | M | O | PB |
| 4. | B | D | E | Q | R | PB |
| 5. | B | E | G | P | R | PB |
| 6. | B | H | I | R | S | PB |
| 7. | C | F | J | K | N | PB |
| 8. | D | G | H | P | Q | PB |
| 9. | D | G | I | Q | S | PB |
| 10. | E | H | I | P | S | PB |
| 11. | F | J | L | N | O | PB |



# POWERBALL BALANCED WHEEL® 52120PB

## Wheel 20 Numbers + PB in 12 Games for a 2 of 3 Win

With Powerball

| Numbers Matched | Maximum Wins 5 + 1 | 4 + 1 | 3 + 1 | 2 + 1 | 1 + 1 | 0 + 1 | Minimum Wins 5 + 1 | 4 + 1 | 3 + 1 | 2 + 1 | 1 + 1 | 0 + 1 |
|---|---|---|---|---|---|---|---|---|---|---|---|---|
| 5 + 1 | 1 | 0 | 1 | 3 | 1 | 6 | 0 | 0 | 0 | 4 | 7 | 1 |
| 4 + 1 | - | 1 | 1 | 2 | 1 | 7 | - | 0 | 0 | 2 | 8 | 2 |
| 3 + 1 | - | - | 2 | 1 | 1 | 8 | - | - | 0 | 1 | 7 | 4 |
| 2 + 1 | - | - | - | 3 | 0 | 9 | - | - | - | 0 | 6 | 6 |
| 1 + 1 | - | - | - | - | 3 | 9 | - | - | - | - | 3 | 9 |
| 0 + 1 | - | - | - | - | - | 12 | - | - | - | - | - | 12 |

Without Powerball

| Numbers Matched | Maximum Wins 5 + 0 | 4 + 0 | 3 + 0 | 2 + 0 | 1 + 0 | Minimum Wins 5 + 0 | 4 + 0 | 3 + 0 | 2 + 0 | 1 + 0 |
|---|---|---|---|---|---|---|---|---|---|---|
| 5 + 0 | 1 | 0 | 1 | 3 | 1 | 0 | 0 | 0 | 4 | 7 |
| 4 + 0 | - | 1 | 1 | 2 | 1 | - | 0 | 0 | 2 | 8 |
| 3 + 0 | - | - | 2 | 1 | 1 | - | - | 0 | 1 | 7 |
| 2 + 0 | - | - | - | 3 | 0 | - | - | - | 0 | 6 |
| 1 + 0 | - | - | - | - | 3 | - | - | - | - | 3 |

## Your 20 Numbers + PB to Wheel

| A | B | C | D | E | F | G | H | I | J | K |
|---|---|---|---|---|---|---|---|---|---|---|
| 3 | 3 | 3 | 3 | 3 | 3 | 3 | 3 | 3 | 3 | 3 |

| L | M | N | O | P | Q | R | S | T | PB |
|---|---|---|---|---|---|---|---|---|---|
| 3 | 3 | 3 | 3 | 3 | 3 | 3 | 3 | 3 | 12 |

## The 12 Games to Play

| | | | | | | |
|---|---|---|---|---|---|---|
| 1. | A | B | E | Q | T | PB |
| 2. | A | C | E | P | T | PB |
| 3. | A | D | N | S | T | PB |
| 4. | B | C | N | P | Q | PB |
| 5. | B | D | P | Q | S | PB |
| 6. | C | D | E | N | S | PB |
| 7. | F | G | H | J | M | PB |
| 8. | F | I | J | L | O | PB |
| 9. | F | J | K | M | R | PB |
| 10. | G | H | K | O | R | PB |
| 11. | G | I | L | M | O | PB |
| 12. | H | I | K | L | R | PB |

# POWERBALL BALANCED WHEEL® 52121PB

## Wheel 21 Numbers + PB in 13 Games for a 2 of 3 Win

With Powerball

| Numbers Matched | Maximum Wins | | | | | | Minimum Wins | | | | | |
|---|---|---|---|---|---|---|---|---|---|---|---|---|
| | 5 + 1 | 4 + 1 | 3 + 1 | 2 + 1 | 1 + 1 | 0 + 1 | 5 + 1 | 4 + 1 | 3 + 1 | 2 + 1 | 1 + 1 | 0 + 1 |
| 5 + 1 | 1 | 0 | 3 | 0 | 3 | 6 | 0 | 0 | 0 | 4 | 7 | 2 |
| 4 + 1 | - | 1 | 2 | 1 | 2 | 7 | - | 0 | 0 | 2 | 8 | 3 |
| 3 + 1 | - | - | 2 | 2 | 1 | 8 | - | - | 0 | 1 | 7 | 5 |
| 2 + 1 | - | - | - | 4 | 0 | 9 | - | - | - | 0 | 6 | 7 |
| 1 + 1 | - | - | - | - | 4 | 9 | - | - | - | - | 3 | 10 |
| 0 + 1 | - | - | - | - | - | 13 | - | - | - | - | - | 13 |

Without Powerball

| Numbers Matched | Maximum Wins | | | | | Minimum Wins | | | | |
|---|---|---|---|---|---|---|---|---|---|---|
| | 5 + 0 | 4 + 0 | 3 + 0 | 2 + 0 | 1 + 0 | 5 + 0 | 4 + 0 | 3 + 0 | 2 + 0 | 1 + 0 |
| 5 + 0 | 1 | 0 | 3 | 0 | 3 | 0 | 0 | 0 | 4 | 7 |
| 4 + 0 | - | 1 | 2 | 1 | 2 | - | 0 | 0 | 2 | 8 |
| 3 + 0 | - | - | 2 | 2 | 1 | - | - | 0 | 1 | 7 |
| 2 + 0 | - | - | - | 4 | 0 | - | - | - | 0 | 6 |
| 1 + 0 | - | - | - | - | 4 | - | - | - | - | 3 |

## Your 21 Numbers + PB to Wheel

| A | B | C | D | E | F | G | H | I | J | K |
|---|---|---|---|---|---|---|---|---|---|---|
| 3 | 3 | 3 | 3 | 3 | 3 | 3 | 4 | 3 | 3 | 3 |
| **L** | **M** | **N** | **O** | **P** | **Q** | **R** | **S** | **T** | **U** | **PB** |
| 3 | 3 | 3 | 3 | 3 | 3 | 3 | 4 | 3 | 3 | 13 |

## The 13 Games to Play

| | | | | | | |
|---|---|---|---|---|---|---|
| 1. | A | D | L | Q | U | PB |
| 2. | A | E | K | M | Q | PB |
| 3. | A | G | P | Q | U | PB |
| 4. | B | C | O | R | T | PB |
| 5. | B | F | J | N | R | PB |
| 6. | B | H | I | R | S | PB |
| 7. | C | F | I | N | T | PB |
| 8. | C | H | J | S | T | PB |
| 9. | D | E | K | L | P | PB |
| 10. | D | G | L | M | P | PB |
| 11. | E | G | K | M | U | PB |
| 12. | F | H | N | O | S | PB |
| 13. | H | I | J | O | S | PB |



# POWERBALL BALANCED WHEEL® 52122PB

## Wheel 22 Numbers + PB in 14 Games for a 2 of 3 Win

With Powerball

| Numbers Matched | Maximum Wins | | | | | | Minimum Wins | | | | | |
|---|---|---|---|---|---|---|---|---|---|---|---|---|
| | 5 + 1 | 4 + 1 | 3 + 1 | 2 + 1 | 1 + 1 | 0 + 1 | 5 + 1 | 4 + 1 | 3 + 1 | 2 + 1 | 1 + 1 | 0 + 1 |
| 5 + 1 | 1 | 0 | 3 | 0 | 3 | 7 | 0 | 0 | 0 | 4 | 7 | 3 |
| 4 + 1 | - | 1 | 2 | 1 | 2 | 8 | - | 0 | 0 | 2 | 8 | 4 |
| 3 + 1 | - | - | 2 | 2 | 1 | 9 | - | - | 0 | 1 | 7 | 6 |
| 2 + 1 | - | - | - | 4 | 0 | 10 | - | - | - | 0 | 6 | 8 |
| 1 + 1 | - | - | - | - | 4 | 10 | - | - | - | - | 3 | 11 |
| 0 + 1 | - | - | - | - | - | 14 | - | - | - | - | - | 14 |

(Continued Next Page)

## POWERBALL BALANCED WHEEL® 52122PB (Continued from previous page)

Without Powerball

| Numbers Matched | Maximum Wins 5 + 0 | 4 + 0 | 3 + 0 | 2 + 0 | 1 + 0 | Minimum Wins 5 + 0 | 4 + 0 | 3 + 0 | 2 + 0 | 1 + 0 |
|---|---|---|---|---|---|---|---|---|---|---|
| 5 + 0 | 1 | 0 | 3 | 0 | 3 | 0 | 0 | 0 | 4 | 7 |
| 4 + 0 | - | 1 | 2 | 1 | 2 | - | 0 | 0 | 2 | 8 |
| 3 + 0 | - | - | 2 | 2 | 1 | - | - | 0 | 1 | 7 |
| 2 + 0 | - | - | - | 4 | 0 | - | - | - | 0 | 6 |
| 1 + 0 | - | - | - | - | 4 | - | - | - | - | 3 |

## Your 22 Numbers + PB to Wheel

| A | B | C | D | E | F | G | H |
|---|---|---|---|---|---|---|---|
| 3 | 3 | 3 | 3 | 3 | 3 | 3 | 3 |
| **I** | **J** | **K** | **L** | **M** | **N** | **O** | **P** |
| 3 | 3 | 3 | 4 | 4 | 4 | 4 | 3 |
| **Q** | **R** | **S** | **T** | **U** | **V** | **PB** | |
| 3 | 3 | 3 | 3 | 3 | 3 | 14 | |

## The 14 Games to Play

| | | | | | | |
|---|---|---|---|---|---|---|
| 1. | A | B | R | T | U | PB |
| 2. | A | C | Q | S | T | PB |
| 3. | A | D | N | O | T | PB |
| 4. | B | C | D | S | U | PB |
| 5. | B | N | O | Q | U | PB |
| 6. | C | N | O | R | S | PB |
| 7. | D | N | O | Q | R | PB |
| 8. | E | F | G | P | V | PB |
| 9. | E | H | K | L | M | PB |
| 10. | E | I | J | L | M | PB |
| 11. | F | H | I | K | V | PB |
| 12. | F | J | L | M | V | PB |
| 13. | G | H | J | K | P | PB |
| 14. | G | I | L | M | P | PB |



# POWERBALL BALANCED WHEEL® 52123PB

## Wheel 23 Numbers + PB in 16 Games for a 2 of 3 Win

With Powerball

| Numbers Matched | Maximum Wins 5 + 1 | 4 + 1 | 3 + 1 | 2 + 1 | 1 + 1 | 0 + 1 | Minimum Wins 5 + 1 | 4 + 1 | 3 + 1 | 2 + 1 | 1 + 1 | 0 + 1 |
|---|---|---|---|---|---|---|---|---|---|---|---|---|
| 5 + 1 | 1 | 0 | 1 | 5 | 3 | 6 | 0 | 0 | 0 | 4 | 7 | 5 |
| 4 + 1 | - | 1 | 1 | 4 | 2 | 8 | - | 0 | 0 | 2 | 8 | 6 |
| 3 + 1 | - | - | 2 | 2 | 3 | 9 | - | - | 0 | 1 | 7 | 8 |
| 2 + 1 | - | - | - | 4 | 0 | 12 | - | - | - | 0 | 6 | 10 |
| 1 + 1 | - | - | - | - | 5 | 11 | - | - | - | - | 3 | 13 |
| 0 + 1 | - | - | - | - | - | 16 | - | - | - | - | - | 16 |

Without Powerball

| Numbers Matched | Maximum Wins 5 + 0 | 4 + 0 | 3 + 0 | 2 + 0 | 1 + 0 | Minimum Wins 5 + 0 | 4 + 0 | 3 + 0 | 2 + 0 | 1 + 0 |
|---|---|---|---|---|---|---|---|---|---|---|
| 5 + 0 | 1 | 0 | 1 | 5 | 3 | 0 | 0 | 0 | 4 | 7 |
| 4 + 0 | - | 1 | 1 | 4 | 2 | - | 0 | 0 | 2 | 8 |
| 3 + 0 | - | - | 2 | 2 | 3 | - | - | 0 | 1 | 7 |
| 2 + 0 | - | - | - | 4 | 0 | - | - | - | 0 | 6 |
| 1 + 0 | - | - | - | - | 5 | - | - | - | - | 3 |

(Continued Next Page)

**POWERBALL BALANCED WHEEL® 52123PB** (Continued from previous page)

## Your 23 Numbers + PB to Wheel

| A | B | C | D | E | F | G | H |
|---|---|---|---|---|---|---|---|
| 4 | 3 | 3 | 3 | 4 | 4 | 4 | 3 |
| **I** | **J** | **K** | **L** | **M** | **N** | **O** | **P** |
| 3 | 3 | 3 | 4 | 5 | 3 | 3 | 3 |
| **Q** | **R** | **S** | **T** | **U** | **V** | **W** | **PB** |
| 3 | 4 | 3 | 4 | 3 | 4 | 4 | 16 |

## The 16 Games to Play

| | | | | | | |
|---|---|---|---|---|---|---|
| 1. | A | C | K | O | W | PB |
| 2. | A | E | L | M | W | PB |
| 3. | A | F | R | V | W | PB |
| 4. | A | G | M | T | W | PB |
| 5. | B | D | N | Q | U | PB |
| 6. | B | H | I | S | U | PB |
| 7. | B | J | P | S | U | PB |
| 8. | C | E | G | T | V | PB |
| 9. | C | F | L | M | R | PB |
| 10. | D | H | I | J | P | PB |
| 11. | D | I | N | Q | S | PB |
| 12. | E | F | O | R | T | PB |
| 13. | E | K | L | T | V | PB |
| 14. | F | G | K | M | R | PB |
| 15. | G | L | M | O | V | PB |
| 16. | H | J | N | P | Q | PB |



# POWERBALL BALANCED WHEEL® 52124PB

## Wheel 24 Numbers + PB in 17 Games for a 2 of 3 Win

With Powerball

| Numbers Matched | Maximum Wins 5 + 1 | 4 + 1 | 3 + 1 | 2 + 1 | 1 + 1 | 0 + 1 | Minimum Wins 5 + 1 | 4 + 1 | 3 + 1 | 2 + 1 | 1 + 1 | 0 + 1 |
|---|---|---|---|---|---|---|---|---|---|---|---|---|
| 5 + 1 | 1 | 0 | 2 | 2 | 3 | 9 | 0 | 0 | 0 | 4 | 7 | 6 |
| 4 + 1 | - | 1 | 2 | 1 | 3 | 10 | - | 0 | 0 | 2 | 8 | 7 |
| 3 + 1 | - | - | 2 | 2 | 2 | 11 | - | - | 0 | 1 | 7 | 9 |
| 2 + 1 | - | - | - | 4 | 0 | 13 | - | - | - | 0 | 6 | 11 |
| 1 + 1 | - | - | - | - | 4 | 13 | - | - | - | - | 3 | 14 |
| 0 + 1 | - | - | - | - | - | 17 | - | - | - | - | - | 17 |

Without Powerball

| Numbers Matched | Maximum Wins 5 + 0 | 4 + 0 | 3 + 0 | 2 + 0 | 1 + 0 | Minimum Wins 5 + 0 | 4 + 0 | 3 + 0 | 2 + 0 | 1 + 0 |
|---|---|---|---|---|---|---|---|---|---|---|
| 5 + 0 | 1 | 0 | 2 | 2 | 3 | 0 | 0 | 0 | 4 | 7 |
| 4 + 0 | - | 1 | 2 | 1 | 3 | - | 0 | 0 | 2 | 8 |
| 3 + 0 | - | - | 2 | 2 | 2 | - | - | 0 | 1 | 7 |
| 2 + 0 | - | - | - | 4 | 0 | - | - | - | 0 | 6 |
| 1 + 0 | - | - | - | - | 4 | - | - | - | - | 3 |

## Your 24 Numbers + PB to Wheel

| A | B | C | D | E | F | G | H | I |
|---|---|---|---|---|---|---|---|---|
| 4 | 4 | 3 | 3 | 3 | 4 | 3 | 4 | 4 |
| **J** | **K** | **L** | **M** | **N** | **O** | **P** | **Q** | **R** |
| 4 | 4 | 3 | 3 | 4 | 3 | 3 | 3 | 4 |
| **S** | **T** | **U** | **V** | **W** | **X** | **PB** | | |
| 4 | 4 | 3 | 3 | 4 | 4 | 17 | | |

(Continued Next Page)

**POWERBALL BALANCED WHEEL® 52124PB** (Continued from previous page)

## The 17 Games to Play

| | | | | | | |
|---|---|---|---|---|---|---|
| 1. | A | C | G | I | X | PB |
| 2. | A | C | O | W | X | PB |
| 3. | A | D | I | M | X | PB |
| 4. | A | E | V | W | X | PB |
| 5. | B | F | H | N | S | PB |
| 6. | B | J | K | N | T | PB |
| 7. | B | L | N | *Q* | R | PB |
| 8. | B | N | P | R | U | PB |
| 9. | C | D | E | M | V | PB |
| 10. | D | G | M | O | W | PB |
| 11. | E | G | I | O | V | PB |
| 12. | F | I | K | R | W | PB |
| 13. | F | J | L | P | T | PB |
| 14. | F | J | *Q* | T | U | PB |
| 15. | H | J | R | S | T | PB |
| 16. | H | K | L | S | U | PB |
| 17. | H | K | P | *Q* | S | PB |



# POWERBALL BALANCED WHEEL® 52125PB

## Wheel 25 Numbers + PB in 19 Games for a 2 of 3 Win

With Powerball

| Numbers Matched | Maximum Wins 5 + 1 | 4 + 1 | 3 + 1 | 2 + 1 | 1 + 1 | 0 + 1 | Minimum Wins 5 + 1 | 4 + 1 | 3 + 1 | 2 + 1 | 1 + 1 | 0 + 1 |
|---|---|---|---|---|---|---|---|---|---|---|---|---|
| 5 + 1 | 1 | 0 | 2 | 3 | 4 | 9 | 0 | 0 | 0 | 4 | 7 | 8 |
| 4 + 1 | - | 1 | 2 | 3 | 1 | 12 | - | 0 | 0 | 2 | 8 | 9 |
| 3 + 1 | - | - | 3 | 1 | 2 | 13 | - | - | 0 | 1 | 7 | 11 |
| 2 + 1 | - | - | - | 4 | 0 | 15 | - | - | - | 0 | 6 | 13 |
| 1 + 1 | - | - | - | - | 5 | 14 | - | - | - | - | 3 | 16 |
| 0 + 1 | - | - | - | - | - | 19 | - | - | - | - | - | 19 |

Without Powerball

| Numbers Matched | Maximum Wins 5 + 0 | 4 + 0 | 3 + 0 | 2 + 0 | 1 + 0 | Minimum Wins 5 + 0 | 4 + 0 | 3 + 0 | 2 + 0 | 1 + 0 |
|---|---|---|---|---|---|---|---|---|---|---|
| 5 + 0 | 1 | 0 | 2 | 3 | 4 | 0 | 0 | 0 | 4 | 7 |
| 4 + 0 | - | 1 | 2 | 3 | 1 | - | 0 | 0 | 2 | 8 |
| 3 + 0 | - | - | 3 | 1 | 2 | - | - | 0 | 1 | 7 |
| 2 + 0 | - | - | - | 4 | 0 | - | - | - | 0 | 6 |
| 1 + 0 | - | - | - | - | 5 | - | - | - | - | 3 |

## Your 25 Numbers + PB to Wheel

| A | B | C | D | E | F | G | H | I |
|---|---|---|---|---|---|---|---|---|
| 4 | 4 | 4 | 3 | 4 | 4 | 3 | 4 | 3 |
| **J** | **K** | **L** | **M** | **N** | **O** | **P** | **Q** | **R** |
| 4 | 4 | 4 | 3 | 4 | 4 | 5 | 4 | 4 |
| **S** | **T** | **U** | **V** | **W** | **X** | **Y** | **PB** | |
| 4 | 4 | 3 | 3 | 5 | 3 | 4 | 19 | |

## The 19 Games to Play

| | | | | | | |
|---|---|---|---|---|---|---|
| 1. | A | B | O | *Q* | Y | PB |
| 2. | A | C | S | T | Y | PB |
| 3. | A | D | W | X | Y | PB |
| 4. | A | G | U | W | Y | PB |
| 5. | B | C | *Q* | S | W | PB |
| 6. | B | D | *Q* | T | U | PB |
| 7. | B | G | *Q* | T | X | PB |
| 8. | C | D | G | O | S | PB |



(Continued Next Page)

## POWERBALL BALANCED WHEEL® 52125PB (Continued from previous page)

| | | | | | | |
|---|---|---|---|---|---|---|
| 9. | C | O | S | U | X | PB |
| 10. | E | F | H | N | P | PB |
| 11. | E | I | K | L | M | PB |
| 12. | E | J | K | L | V | PB |
| 13. | E | O | R | T | W | PB |
| 14. | F | H | I | P | V | PB |
| 15. | F | H | J | M | P | PB |
| 16. | F | H | K | L | R | PB |
| 17. | I | J | N | R | W | PB |
| 18. | J | K | L | N | P | PB |
| 19. | M | N | P | R | V | PB |



# POWERBALL BALANCED WHEEL® 52126PB

## Wheel 26 Numbers + PB in 20 Games for a 2 of 3 Win

With Powerball

| Numbers Matched | Maximum Wins 5 + 1 | 4 + 1 | 3 + 1 | 2 + 1 | 1 + 1 | 0 + 1 | Minimum Wins 5 + 1 | 4 + 1 | 3 + 1 | 2 + 1 | 1 + 1 | 0 + 1 |
|---|---|---|---|---|---|---|---|---|---|---|---|---|
| 5 + 1 | 1 | 0 | 2 | 4 | 2 | 11 | 0 | 0 | 0 | 4 | 7 | 9 |
| 4 + 1 | - | 1 | 1 | 5 | 0 | 13 | - | 0 | 0 | 2 | 8 | 10 |
| 3 + 1 | - | - | 2 | 2 | 3 | 13 | - | - | 0 | 1 | 7 | 12 |
| 2 + 1 | - | - | - | 4 | 1 | 15 | - | - | - | 0 | 6 | 14 |
| 1 + 1 | - | - | - | - | 5 | 15 | - | - | - | - | 3 | 17 |
| 0 + 1 | - | - | - | - | - | 20 | - | - | - | - | - | 20 |

Without Powerball

| Numbers Matched | Maximum Wins 5 + 0 | 4 + 0 | 3 + 0 | 2 + 0 | 1 + 0 | Minimum Wins 5 + 0 | 4 + 0 | 3 + 0 | 2 + 0 | 1 + 0 |
|---|---|---|---|---|---|---|---|---|---|---|
| 5 + 0 | 1 | 0 | 2 | 4 | 2 | 0 | 0 | 0 | 4 | 7 |
| 4 + 0 | - | 1 | 1 | 5 | 0 | - | 0 | 0 | 2 | 8 |
| 3 + 0 | - | - | 2 | 2 | 3 | - | - | 0 | 1 | 7 |
| 2 + 0 | - | - | - | 4 | 1 | - | - | - | 0 | 6 |
| 1 + 0 | - | - | - | - | 5 | - | - | - | - | 3 |

## Your 26 Numbers + PB to Wheel

| A | B | C | D | E | F | G | H | I |
|---|---|---|---|---|---|---|---|---|
| 4 | 3 | 3 | 4 | 4 | 4 | 5 | 4 | 4 |
| **J** | **K** | **L** | **M** | **N** | **O** | **P** | **Q** | **R** |
| 4 | 4 | 5 | 3 | 4 | 4 | 4 | 4 | 3 |
| **S** | **T** | **U** | **V** | **W** | **X** | **Y** | **Z** | **PB** |
| 4 | 4 | 3 | 4 | 4 | 4 | 4 | 3 | 20 |

## The 20 Games to Play

| | | | | | | |
|---|---|---|---|---|---|---|
| 1. | A | C | K | M | Y | PB |
| 2. | A | E | F | X | Y | PB |
| 3. | A | G | V | W | Y | PB |
| 4. | A | K | R | U | Y | PB |
| 5. | B | D | L | S | T | PB |
| 6. | B | H | P | Q | Z | PB |
| 7. | B | I | J | N | O | PB |
| 8. | C | E | G | R | X | PB |
| 9. | C | F | U | V | W | PB |
| 10. | D | G | I | L | Q | PB |
| 11. | D | H | J | L | P | PB |
| 12. | D | L | N | O | Z | PB |
| 13. | E | G | M | U | X | PB |
| 14. | E | K | V | W | X | PB |
| 15. | F | G | J | K | Q | PB |
| 16. | F | M | R | V | W | PB |



(Continued Next Page)

**POWERBALL BALANCED WHEEL® 52126PB** (Continued from previous page)

| | | | | | | |
|---|---|---|---|---|---|---|
| 17. | H | I | N | O | P | PB |
| 18. | H | L | P | S | T | PB |
| 19. | I | J | S | T | Z | PB |
| 20. | N | O | Q | S | T | PB |



# POWERBALL BALANCED WHEEL® 52127PB

## Wheel 27 Numbers + PB in 21 Games for a 2 of 3 Win

With Powerball

| Numbers Matched | Maximum Wins 5 + 1 | 4 + 1 | 3 + 1 | 2 + 1 | 1 + 1 | 0 + 1 | Minimum Wins 5 + 1 | 4 + 1 | 3 + 1 | 2 + 1 | 1 + 1 | 0 + 1 |
|---|---|---|---|---|---|---|---|---|---|---|---|---|
| 5 + 1 | 1 | 0 | 2 | 2 | 6 | 10 | 0 | 0 | 0 | 4 | 9 | 8 |
| 4 + 1 | - | 1 | 1 | 2 | 6 | 11 | - | 0 | 0 | 2 | 10 | 9 |
| 3 + 1 | - | - | 2 | 2 | 2 | 15 | - | - | 0 | 1 | 8 | 12 |
| 2 + 1 | - | - | - | 4 | 0 | 17 | - | - | - | 0 | 7 | 14 |
| 1 + 1 | - | - | - | - | 5 | 16 | - | - | - | - | 3 | 18 |
| 0 + 1 | - | - | - | - | - | 21 | - | - | - | - | - | 21 |

Without Powerball

| Numbers Matched | Maximum Wins 5 + 0 | 4 + 0 | 3 + 0 | 2 + 0 | 1 + 0 | Minimum Wins 5 + 0 | 4 + 0 | 3 + 0 | 2 + 0 | 1 + 0 |
|---|---|---|---|---|---|---|---|---|---|---|
| 5 + 0 | 1 | 0 | 2 | 2 | 6 | 0 | 0 | 0 | 4 | 9 |
| 4 + 0 | - | 1 | 1 | 2 | 6 | - | 0 | 0 | 2 | 10 |
| 3 + 0 | - | - | 2 | 2 | 2 | - | - | 0 | 1 | 8 |
| 2 + 0 | - | - | - | 4 | 0 | - | - | - | 0 | 7 |
| 1 + 0 | - | - | - | - | 5 | - | - | - | - | 3 |

## Your 27 Numbers + PB to Wheel

| A | B | C | D | E | F | G | H | I | J |
|---|---|---|---|---|---|---|---|---|---|
| 4 | 4 | 3 | 4 | 4 | 4 | 5 | 4 | 4 | 3 |
| **K** | **L** | **M** | **N** | **O** | **P** | **Q** | **R** | **S** | **T** |
| 4 | 4 | 4 | 3 | 4 | 4 | 4 | 4 | 4 | 4 |
| **U** | **V** | **W** | **X** | **Y** | **Z** | **aa** | **PB** | | |
| 4 | 4 | 4 | 4 | 3 | 4 | 4 | 21 | | |

## The 21 Games to Play

| | | | | | | |
|---|---|---|---|---|---|---|
| 1. | A | C | L | X | Y | PB |
| 2. | A | E | Q | X | Z | PB |
| 3. | A | J | L | N | X | PB |
| 4. | A | K | T | V | X | PB |
| 5. | B | D | M | R | W | PB |
| 6. | B | F | G | U | W | PB |
| 7. | B | G | O | P | U | PB |
| 8. | B | H | I | S | aa | PB |
| 9. | C | E | N | V | Z | PB |
| 10. | C | J | K | Q | T | PB |
| 11. | D | F | M | O | P | PB |
| 12. | D | G | H | M | S | PB |
| 13. | D | I | M | U | aa | PB |
| 14. | E | J | V | Y | Z | PB |
| 15. | E | K | L | T | Z | PB |
| 16. | F | G | I | W | aa | PB |
| 17. | F | H | R | S | U | PB |
| 18. | G | L | Q | R | V | PB |
| 19. | H | O | P | S | W | PB |
| 20. | I | O | P | R | aa | PB |
| 21. | K | N | Q | T | Y | PB |

# POWERBALL BALANCED WHEEL® 52128PB

## Wheel 28 Numbers + PB in 23 Games for a 2 of 3 Win

With Powerball

| Numbers Matched | Maximum Wins 5 + 1 | 4 + 1 | 3 + 1 | 2 + 1 | 1 + 1 | 0 + 1 | Minimum Wins 5 + 1 | 4 + 1 | 3 + 1 | 2 + 1 | 1 + 1 | 0 + 1 |
|---|---|---|---|---|---|---|---|---|---|---|---|---|
| 5 + 1 | 1 | 1 | 0 | 3 | 9 | 9 | 0 | 0 | 0 | 4 | 9 | 10 |
| 4 + 1 | - | 2 | 0 | 3 | 6 | 12 | - | 0 | 0 | 2 | 10 | 11 |
| 3 + 1 | - | - | 2 | 3 | 3 | 15 | - | - | 0 | 1 | 8 | 14 |
| 2 + 1 | - | - | - | 5 | 0 | 18 | - | - | - | 0 | 7 | 16 |
| 1 + 1 | - | - | - | - | 5 | 18 | - | - | - | - | 3 | 20 |
| 0 + 1 | - | - | - | - | - | 23 | - | - | - | - | - | 23 |

Without Powerball

| Numbers Matched | Maximum Wins 5 + 0 | 4 + 0 | 3 + 0 | 2 + 0 | 1 + 0 | Minimum Wins 5 + 0 | 4 + 0 | 3 + 0 | 2 + 0 | 1 + 0 |
|---|---|---|---|---|---|---|---|---|---|---|
| 5 + 0 | 1 | 1 | 0 | 3 | 9 | 0 | 0 | 0 | 4 | 9 |
| 4 + 0 | - | 2 | 0 | 3 | 6 | - | 0 | 0 | 2 | 10 |
| 3 + 0 | - | - | 2 | 3 | 3 | - | - | 0 | 1 | 8 |
| 2 + 0 | - | - | - | 5 | 0 | - | - | - | 0 | 7 |
| 1 + 0 | - | - | - | - | 5 | - | - | - | - | 3 |

## Your 28 Numbers + PB to Wheel

| A | B | C | D | E | F | G | H | I | J |
|---|---|---|---|---|---|---|---|---|---|
| 4 | 5 | 4 | 4 | 3 | 4 | 3 | 5 | 4 | 4 |
| **K** | **L** | **M** | **N** | **O** | **P** | **Q** | **R** | **S** | **T** |
| 5 | 4 | 4 | 3 | 4 | 4 | 3 | 4 | 4 | 5 |
| **U** | **V** | **W** | **X** | **Y** | **Z** | **aa** | **bb** | **PB** | |
| 5 | 4 | 4 | 5 | 5 | 4 | 4 | 4 | 23 | |

## The 23 Games to Play

| # | | | | | | |
|---|---|---|---|---|---|---|
| 1. | A | E | J | Q | bb | PB |
| 2. | A | F | P | V | aa | PB |
| 3. | A | G | J | N | bb | PB |
| 4. | A | I | R | T | Y | PB |
| 5. | B | C | U | W | Y | PB |
| 6. | B | D | H | T | U | PB |
| 7. | B | H | T | U | Z | PB |
| 8. | B | K | S | U | X | PB |
| 9. | B | L | M | O | U | PB |
| 10. | C | D | M | O | Z | PB |
| 11. | C | H | L | S | W | PB |
| 12. | C | K | L | T | X | PB |
| 13. | D | K | W | X | Z | PB |
| 14. | D | L | S | Y | Z | PB |
| 15. | E | F | G | I | aa | PB |
| 16. | E | N | P | R | V | PB |
| 17. | F | I | N | Q | aa | PB |
| 18. | F | J | R | aa | bb | PB |
| 19. | G | P | Q | R | V | PB |
| 20. | H | K | M | X | Y | PB |
| 21. | H | K | O | X | Y | PB |
| 22. | I | J | P | V | bb | PB |
| 23. | M | O | S | T | W | PB |

# POWERBALL BALANCED WHEEL® 52129PB

## Wheel 29 Numbers + PB in 25 Games for a 2 of 3 Win

With Powerball

| Numbers Matched | Maximum Wins 5 + 1 | 4 + 1 | 3 + 1 | 2 + 1 | 1 + 1 | 0 + 1 | Minimum Wins 5 + 1 | 4 + 1 | 3 + 1 | 2 + 1 | 1 + 1 | 0 + 1 |
|---|---|---|---|---|---|---|---|---|---|---|---|---|
| 5 + 1 | 1 | 1 | 0 | 4 | 6 | 13 | 0 | 0 | 0 | 4 | 12 | 9 |
| 4 + 1 | - | 2 | 0 | 2 | 7 | 14 | - | 0 | 0 | 2 | 12 | 11 |
| 3 + 1 | - | - | 2 | 2 | 5 | 16 | - | - | 0 | 1 | 10 | 14 |
| 2 + 1 | - | - | - | 4 | 2 | 19 | - | - | - | 0 | 8 | 17 |
| 1 + 1 | - | - | - | - | 6 | 19 | - | - | - | - | 4 | 21 |
| 0 + 1 | - | - | - | - | - | 25 | - | - | - | - | - | 25 |

Without Powerball

| Numbers Matched | Maximum Wins 5 + 0 | 4 + 0 | 3 + 0 | 2 + 0 | 1 + 0 | Minimum Wins 5 + 0 | 4 + 0 | 3 + 0 | 2 + 0 | 1 + 0 |
|---|---|---|---|---|---|---|---|---|---|---|
| 5 + 0 | 1 | 1 | 0 | 4 | 6 | 0 | 0 | 0 | 4 | 12 |
| 4 + 0 | - | 2 | 0 | 2 | 7 | - | 0 | 0 | 2 | 12 |
| 3 + 0 | - | - | 2 | 2 | 5 | - | - | 0 | 1 | 10 |
| 2 + 0 | - | - | - | 4 | 2 | - | - | - | 0 | 8 |
| 1 + 0 | - | - | - | - | 6 | - | - | - | - | 4 |

## Your 29 Numbers + PB to Wheel

| A | B | C | D | E | F | G | H | I | J |
|---|---|---|---|---|---|---|---|---|---|
| 6 | 4 | 5 | 4 | 4 | 4 | 5 | 4 | 4 | 5 |
| **K** | **L** | **M** | **N** | **O** | **P** | **Q** | **R** | **S** | **T** |
| 4 | 4 | 4 | 4 | 4 | 4 | 4 | 4 | 5 | 5 |
| **U** | **V** | **W** | **X** | **Y** | **Z** | **aa** | **bb** | **cc** | **PB** |
| 4 | 4 | 4 | 4 | 5 | 5 | 4 | 4 | 4 | 25 |

## The 25 Games to Play

| | | | | | | |
|---|---|---|---|---|---|---|
| 1. | A | C | L | S | aa | PB |
| 2. | A | D | L | Q | cc | PB |
| 3. | A | E | Z | bb | cc | PB |
| 4. | A | H | P | aa | cc | PB |
| 5. | A | K | Q | aa | bb | PB |
| 6. | A | L | P | V | bb | PB |
| 7. | B | F | J | U | X | PB |
| 8. | B | G | N | X | Y | PB |
| 9. | B | I | J | T | W | PB |
| 10. | B | M | N | O | R | PB |
| 11. | C | D | H | S | bb | PB |
| 12. | C | D | K | P | Z | PB |
| 13. | C | E | P | Q | S | PB |
| 14. | C | K | S | V | cc | PB |
| 15. | D | E | V | Z | aa | PB |
| 16. | E | H | K | L | Z | PB |
| 17. | F | G | J | R | Y | PB |
| 18. | F | I | O | W | Y | PB |
| 19. | F | J | M | N | T | PB |
| 20. | G | I | M | W | X | PB |
| 21. | G | M | T | U | Y | PB |
| 22. | G | O | T | U | Y | PB |
| 23. | H | Q | S | V | Z | PB |
| 24. | I | N | R | U | W | PB |
| 25. | J | O | R | T | X | PB |

# POWERBALL BALANCED WHEEL® 52130PB

## Wheel 30 Numbers + PB in 26 Games for a 2 of 3 Win

With Powerball

| Numbers Matched | Maximum Wins | | | | | | Minimum Wins | | | | | |
|---|---|---|---|---|---|---|---|---|---|---|---|---|
| | 5 + 1 | 4 + 1 | 3 + 1 | 2 + 1 | 1 + 1 | 0 + 1 | 5 + 1 | 4 + 1 | 3 + 1 | 2 + 1 | 1 + 1 | 0 + 1 |
| 5 + 1 | 1 | 0 | 0 | 7 | 5 | 13 | 0 | 0 | 0 | 4 | 12 | 10 |
| 4 + 1 | - | 1 | 0 | 5 | 6 | 14 | - | 0 | 0 | 2 | 12 | 12 |
| 3 + 1 | - | - | 1 | 4 | 3 | 18 | - | - | 0 | 1 | 10 | 15 |
| 2 + 1 | - | - | - | 4 | 2 | 20 | - | - | - | 0 | 8 | 18 |
| 1 + 1 | - | - | - | - | 6 | 20 | - | - | - | - | 4 | 22 |
| 0 + 1 | - | - | - | - | - | 26 | - | - | - | - | - | 26 |

Without Powerball

| Numbers Matched | Maximum Wins | | | | | Minimum Wins | | | | |
|---|---|---|---|---|---|---|---|---|---|---|
| | 5 + 0 | 4 + 0 | 3 + 0 | 2 + 0 | 1 + 0 | 5 + 0 | 4 + 0 | 3 + 0 | 2 + 0 | 1 + 0 |
| 5 + 0 | 1 | 0 | 0 | 7 | 5 | 0 | 0 | 0 | 4 | 12 |
| 4 + 0 | - | 1 | 0 | 5 | 6 | - | 0 | 0 | 2 | 12 |
| 3 + 0 | - | - | 1 | 4 | 3 | - | - | 0 | 1 | 10 |
| 2 + 0 | - | - | - | 4 | 2 | - | - | - | 0 | 8 |
| 1 + 0 | - | - | - | - | 6 | - | - | - | - | 4 |

## Your 30 Numbers + PB to Wheel

| A | B | C | D | E | F | G | H | I | J | K |
|---|---|---|---|---|---|---|---|---|---|---|
| 4 | 5 | 4 | 6 | 4 | 5 | 4 | 4 | 4 | 4 | 4 |
| **L** | **M** | **N** | **O** | **P** | **Q** | **R** | **S** | **T** | **U** | **V** |
| 5 | 4 | 4 | 4 | 5 | 4 | 4 | 4 | 4 | 4 | 5 |
| **W** | **X** | **Y** | **Z** | **aa** | **bb** | **cc** | **dd** | **PB** | | |
| 4 | 6 | 4 | 4 | 4 | 5 | 4 | 4 | 26 | | |

## The 26 Games to Play

| | | | | | | |
|---|---|---|---|---|---|---|
| 1. | A | B | U | Y | bb | PB |
| 2. | A | F | H | W | X | PB |
| 3. | A | G | I | K | X | PB |
| 4. | A | N | O | X | dd | PB |
| 5. | B | F | G | Y | dd | PB |
| 6. | B | G | H | O | bb | PB |
| 7. | B | I | N | X | bb | PB |
| 8. | B | K | W | bb | dd | PB |
| 9. | C | D | E | Z | cc | PB |
| 10. | C | J | Q | V | aa | PB |
| 11. | C | L | M | R | V | PB |
| 12. | C | L | P | S | T | PB |
| 13. | D | E | J | M | S | PB |
| 14. | D | E | L | P | aa | PB |
| 15. | D | M | T | Z | aa | PB |
| 16. | D | Q | S | V | Z | PB |
| 17. | D | R | S | aa | cc | PB |
| 18. | E | Q | R | T | V | PB |
| 19. | F | G | N | U | W | PB |
| 20. | F | I | O | W | Y | PB |
| 21. | F | K | O | U | bb | PB |
| 22. | H | I | U | X | dd | PB |
| 23. | H | K | N | X | Y | PB |
| 24. | J | L | P | R | Z | PB |
| 25. | J | P | T | V | cc | PB |
| 26. | L | M | P | Q | cc | PB |

# POWERBALL BALANCED WHEEL® 52131PB

## Wheel 31 Numbers + PB in 27 Games for a 2 of 3 Win

With Powerball

| Numbers Matched | Maximum Wins 5 + 1 | 4 + 1 | 3 + 1 | 2 + 1 | 1 + 1 | 0 + 1 | Minimum Wins 5 + 1 | 4 + 1 | 3 + 1 | 2 + 1 | 1 + 1 | 0 + 1 |
|---|---|---|---|---|---|---|---|---|---|---|---|---|
| 5 + 1 | 1 | 0 | 0 | 5 | 0 | 21 | 0 | 0 | 0 | 4 | 11 | 12 |
| 4 + 1 | - | 1 | 0 | 3 | 2 | 21 | - | 0 | 0 | 2 | 12 | 13 |
| 3 + 1 | - | - | 1 | 2 | 2 | 22 | - | - | 0 | 1 | 9 | 17 |
| 2 + 1 | - | - | - | 2 | 2 | 23 | - | - | - | 0 | 8 | 19 |
| 1 + 1 | - | - | - | - | 5 | 22 | - | - | - | - | 3 | 24 |
| 0 + 1 | - | - | - | - | - | 27 | - | - | - | - | - | 27 |

Without Powerball

| Numbers Matched | Maximum Wins 5 + 0 | 4 + 0 | 3 + 0 | 2 + 0 | 1 + 0 | Minimum Wins 5 + 0 | 4 + 0 | 3 + 0 | 2 + 0 | 1 + 0 |
|---|---|---|---|---|---|---|---|---|---|---|
| 5 + 0 | 1 | 0 | 0 | 5 | 0 | 0 | 0 | 0 | 4 | 11 |
| 4 + 0 | - | 1 | 0 | 3 | 2 | - | 0 | 0 | 2 | 12 |
| 3 + 0 | - | - | 1 | 2 | 2 | - | - | 0 | 1 | 9 |
| 2 + 0 | - | - | - | 2 | 2 | - | - | - | 0 | 8 |
| 1 + 0 | - | - | - | - | 5 | - | - | - | - | 3 |

## Your 31 Numbers + PB to Wheel

| A | B | C | D | E | F | G | H | I | J | K |
|---|---|---|---|---|---|---|---|---|---|---|
| 3 | 3 | 5 | 3 | 5 | 5 | 5 | 5 | 5 | 5 | 5 |
| **L** | **M** | **N** | **O** | **P** | **Q** | **R** | **S** | **T** | **U** | **V** |
| 5 | 5 | 5 | 3 | 3 | 5 | 5 | 5 | 5 | 3 | 5 |
| **W** | **X** | **Y** | **Z** | **aa** | **bb** | **cc** | **dd** | **ee** | **PB** | |
| 5 | 3 | 3 | 5 | 5 | 3 | 5 | 3 | 5 | 27 | |

## The 27 Games to Play

| | | | | | | |
|---|---|---|---|---|---|---|
| 1. | A | B | P | Y | dd | PB |
| 2. | A | D | O | P | U | PB |
| 3. | A | U | X | bb | dd | PB |
| 4. | B | D | P | X | bb | PB |
| 5. | B | O | U | Y | bb | PB |
| 6. | C | E | N | aa | ee | PB |
| 7. | C | F | H | K | Z | PB |
| 8. | C | G | L | R | V | PB |
| 9. | C | I | J | M | Q | PB |
| 10. | C | S | T | W | cc | PB |
| 11. | D | O | X | Y | dd | PB |
| 12. | E | F | M | V | cc | PB |
| 13. | E | G | J | K | T | PB |
| 14. | E | H | I | L | S | PB |
| 15. | E | Q | R | W | Z | PB |
| 16. | F | G | Q | S | ee | PB |
| 17. | F | I | R | T | aa | PB |
| 18. | F | J | L | N | W | PB |
| 19. | G | H | M | W | aa | PB |
| 20. | G | I | N | Z | cc | PB |
| 21. | H | J | R | cc | ee | PB |
| 22. | H | N | Q | T | V | PB |
| 23. | I | K | V | W | ee | PB |
| 24. | J | S | V | Z | aa | PB |
| 25. | K | L | Q | aa | cc | PB |
| 26. | K | M | N | R | S | PB |
| 27. | L | M | T | Z | ee | PB |

# POWERBALL BALANCED WHEEL® 52132PB

## Wheel 32 Numbers + PB in 28 Games for a 2 of 3 Win

With Powerball

| Numbers Matched | Maximum Wins 5 + 1 | 4 + 1 | 3 + 1 | 2 + 1 | 1 + 1 | 0 + 1 | Minimum Wins 5 + 1 | 4 + 1 | 3 + 1 | 2 + 1 | 1 + 1 | 0 + 1 |
|---|---|---|---|---|---|---|---|---|---|---|---|---|
| 5 + 1 | 1 | 0 | 3 | 0 | 3 | 21 | 0 | 0 | 0 | 4 | 11 | 13 |
| 4 + 1 | - | 1 | 2 | 1 | 2 | 22 | - | 0 | 0 | 2 | 12 | 14 |
| 3 + 1 | - | - | 2 | 2 | 1 | 23 | - | - | 0 | 1 | 9 | 18 |
| 2 + 1 | - | - | - | 4 | 0 | 24 | - | - | - | 0 | 8 | 20 |
| 1 + 1 | - | - | - | - | 5 | 23 | - | - | - | - | 3 | 25 |
| 0 + 1 | - | - | - | - | - | 28 | - | - | - | - | - | 28 |

Without Powerball

| Numbers Matched | Maximum Wins 5 + 0 | 4 + 0 | 3 + 0 | 2 + 0 | 1 + 0 | Minimum Wins 5 + 0 | 4 + 0 | 3 + 0 | 2 + 0 | 1 + 0 |
|---|---|---|---|---|---|---|---|---|---|---|
| 5 + 0 | 1 | 0 | 3 | 0 | 3 | 0 | 0 | 0 | 4 | 11 |
| 4 + 0 | - | 1 | 2 | 1 | 2 | - | 0 | 0 | 2 | 12 |
| 3 + 0 | - | - | 2 | 2 | 1 | - | - | 0 | 1 | 9 |
| 2 + 0 | - | - | - | 4 | 0 | - | - | - | 0 | 8 |
| 1 + 0 | - | - | - | - | 5 | - | - | - | - | 3 |

## Your 32 Numbers + PB to Wheel

| A | B | C | D | E | F | G | H | I | J | K |
|---|---|---|---|---|---|---|---|---|---|---|
| 3 | 3 | 3 | 3 | 5 | 5 | 5 | 5 | 5 | 5 | 5 |
| **L** | **M** | **N** | **O** | **P** | **Q** | **R** | **S** | **T** | **U** | **V** |
| 5 | 5 | 5 | 5 | 5 | 5 | 3 | 5 | 4 | 5 | 5 |
| **W** | **X** | **Y** | **Z** | **aa** | **bb** | **cc** | **dd** | **ee** | **ff** | **PB** |
| 5 | 5 | 5 | 5 | 3 | 3 | 4 | 3 | 3 | 5 | 28 |

## The 28 Games to Play

| | | | | | | |
|---|---|---|---|---|---|---|
| 1. | A | B | C | bb | ee | PB |
| 2. | A | D | T | cc | ee | PB |
| 3. | A | R | aa | dd | ee | PB |
| 4. | B | D | T | aa | cc | PB |
| 5. | B | R | T | cc | dd | PB |
| 6. | C | D | R | bb | dd | PB |
| 7. | C | T | aa | bb | cc | PB |
| 8. | E | F | L | N | W | PB |
| 9. | E | G | H | V | ff | PB |
| 10. | E | I | J | O | P | PB |
| 11. | E | K | Q | X | Z | PB |
| 12. | E | M | S | U | Y | PB |
| 13. | F | G | K | O | U | PB |
| 14. | F | H | P | Q | S | PB |
| 15. | F | I | Y | Z | ff | PB |
| 16. | F | J | M | V | X | PB |
| 17. | G | I | S | W | X | PB |
| 18. | G | J | L | Q | Y | PB |
| 19. | G | M | N | P | Z | PB |
| 20. | H | I | K | L | M | PB |
| 21. | H | J | U | W | Z | PB |
| 22. | H | N | O | X | Y | PB |
| 23. | I | N | Q | U | V | PB |
| 24. | J | K | N | S | ff | PB |
| 25. | K | P | V | W | Y | PB |
| 26. | L | O | S | V | Z | PB |
| 27. | L | P | U | X | ff | PB |
| 28. | M | O | Q | W | ff | PB |

# POWERBALL BALANCED WHEEL® 52134PB

## Wheel 34 Numbers + PB in 31 Games for a 2 of 3 Win

With Powerball

| Numbers Matched | Maximum Wins 5 + 1 | 4 + 1 | 3 + 1 | 2 + 1 | 1 + 1 | 0 + 1 | Minimum Wins 5 + 1 | 4 + 1 | 3 + 1 | 2 + 1 | 1 + 1 | 0 + 1 |
|---|---|---|---|---|---|---|---|---|---|---|---|---|
| 5 + 1 | 1 | 0 | 2 | 2 | 5 | 21 | 0 | 0 | 0 | 4 | 12 | 15 |
| 4 + 1 | - | 1 | 1 | 3 | 3 | 23 | - | 0 | 0 | 2 | 12 | 17 |
| 3 + 1 | - | - | 2 | 2 | 2 | 25 | - | - | 0 | 1 | 9 | 21 |
| 2 + 1 | - | - | - | 4 | 0 | 27 | - | - | - | 0 | 8 | 23 |
| 1 + 1 | - | - | - | - | 5 | 26 | - | - | - | - | 3 | 28 |
| 0 + 1 | - | - | - | - | - | 31 | - | - | - | - | - | 31 |

Without Powerball

| Numbers Matched | Maximum Wins 5 + 0 | 4 + 0 | 3 + 0 | 2 + 0 | 1 + 0 | Minimum Wins 5 + 0 | 4 + 0 | 3 + 0 | 2 + 0 | 1 + 0 |
|---|---|---|---|---|---|---|---|---|---|---|
| 5 + 0 | 1 | 0 | 2 | 2 | 5 | 0 | 0 | 0 | 4 | 12 |
| 4 + 0 | - | 1 | 1 | 3 | 3 | - | 0 | 0 | 2 | 12 |
| 3 + 0 | - | - | 2 | 2 | 2 | - | - | 0 | 1 | 9 |
| 2 + 0 | - | - | - | 4 | 0 | - | - | - | 0 | 8 |
| 1 + 0 | - | - | - | - | 5 | - | - | - | - | 3 |

## Your 34 Numbers + PB to Wheel

| A | B | C | D | E | F | G | H | I |
|---|---|---|---|---|---|---|---|---|
| 4 | 3 | 5 | 5 | 5 | 5 | 4 | 4 | 5 |
| **J** | **K** | **L** | **M** | **N** | **O** | **P** | **Q** | **R** |
| 5 | 5 | 5 | 5 | 4 | 4 | 5 | 3 | 4 |
| **S** | **T** | **U** | **V** | **W** | **X** | **Y** | **Z** | **aa** |
| 4 | 5 | 5 | 5 | 5 | 5 | 4 | 5 | 5 |
| **bb** | **cc** | **dd** | **ee** | **ff** | **gg** | **hh** | **PB** | |
| 4 | 4 | 5 | 4 | 5 | 5 | 5 | 31 | |

## The 31 Games to Play

| | | | | | | |
|---|---|---|---|---|---|---|
| 1. | A | B | O | *Q* | S | PB |
| 2. | A | G | R | S | bb | PB |
| 3. | A | H | O | S | ee | PB |
| 4. | A | N | S | Y | cc | PB |
| 5. | B | G | H | R | cc | PB |
| 6. | B | N | Y | bb | ee | PB |
| 7. | C | D | ff | gg | hh | PB |
| 8. | C | E | L | M | aa | PB |
| 9. | C | F | J | U | W | PB |
| 10. | C | I | K | T | X | PB |
| 11. | C | P | V | Z | dd | PB |
| 12. | D | E | T | U | dd | PB |
| 13. | D | F | I | M | V | PB |
| 14. | D | J | K | L | P | PB |
| 15. | D | W | X | Z | aa | PB |
| 16. | E | F | P | X | ff | PB |
| 17. | E | I | J | Z | gg | PB |
| 18. | E | K | V | W | hh | PB |
| 19. | F | K | aa | dd | gg | PB |
| 20. | F | L | T | Z | hh | PB |
| 21. | G | N | O | R | Y | PB |
| 22. | G | *Q* | R | cc | ee | PB |
| 23. | H | N | *Q* | Y | bb | PB |
| 24. | H | O | bb | cc | ee | PB |
| 25. | I | L | W | dd | ff | PB |
| 26. | I | P | U | aa | hh | PB |
| 27. | J | M | X | dd | hh | PB |
| 28. | J | T | V | aa | ff | PB |



(Continued Next Page)

**POWERBALL BALANCED WHEEL® 52134PB** (Continued from previous page)

| | | | | | | |
|---|---|---|---|---|---|---|
| 29. | K | M | U | Z | ff | PB |
| 30. | L | U | V | X | gg | PB |
| 31. | M | P | T | W | gg | PB |



# POWERBALL BALANCED WHEEL® 52136PB

## Wheel 36 Numbers + PB in 34 Games for a 2 of 3 Win

With Powerball

| Numbers Matched | Maximum Wins 5 + 1 | 4 + 1 | 3 + 1 | 2 + 1 | 1 + 1 | 0 + 1 | Minimum Wins 5 + 1 | 4 + 1 | 3 + 1 | 2 + 1 | 1 + 1 | 0 + 1 |
|---|---|---|---|---|---|---|---|---|---|---|---|---|
| 5 + 1 | 1 | 0 | 0 | 7 | 5 | 21 | 0 | 0 | 0 | 4 | 14 | 16 |
| 4 + 1 | - | 1 | 0 | 5 | 6 | 22 | - | 0 | 0 | 2 | 14 | 18 |
| 3 + 1 | - | - | 1 | 4 | 3 | 26 | - | - | 0 | 1 | 11 | 22 |
| 2 + 1 | - | - | - | 4 | 2 | 28 | - | - | - | 0 | 9 | 25 |
| 1 + 1 | - | - | - | - | 6 | 28 | - | - | - | - | 4 | 30 |
| 0 + 1 | - | - | - | - | - | 34 | - | - | - | - | - | 34 |

Without Powerball

| Numbers Matched | Maximum Wins 5 + 0 | 4 + 0 | 3 + 0 | 2 + 0 | 1 + 0 | Minimum Wins 5 + 0 | 4 + 0 | 3 + 0 | 2 + 0 | 1 + 0 |
|---|---|---|---|---|---|---|---|---|---|---|
| 5 + 0 | 1 | 0 | 0 | 7 | 5 | 0 | 0 | 0 | 4 | 14 |
| 4 + 0 | - | 1 | 0 | 5 | 6 | - | 0 | 0 | 2 | 14 |
| 3 + 0 | - | - | 1 | 4 | 3 | - | - | 0 | 1 | 11 |
| 2 + 0 | - | - | - | 4 | 2 | - | - | - | 0 | 9 |
| 1 + 0 | - | - | - | - | 6 | - | - | - | - | 4 |

## Your 36 Numbers + PB to Wheel

| A | B | C | D | E | F | G | H | I | J |
|---|---|---|---|---|---|---|---|---|---|
| 4 | 5 | 4 | 5 | 5 | 4 | 5 | 5 | 5 | 4 |
| **K** | **L** | **M** | **N** | **O** | **P** | **Q** | **R** | **S** | **T** |
| 5 | 5 | 5 | 5 | 4 | 5 | 5 | 5 | 6 | 4 |
| **U** | **V** | **W** | **X** | **Y** | **Z** | **aa** | **bb** | **cc** | **dd** |
| 4 | 5 | 5 | 5 | 5 | 5 | 5 | 5 | 5 | 4 |
| **ee** | **ff** | **gg** | **hh** | **ii** | **jj** | **PB** | | | |
| 4 | 5 | 4 | 5 | 4 | 5 | 34 | | | |

## The 34 Games to Play

| | | | | | | |
|---|---|---|---|---|---|---|
| 1. | A | C | F | S | ii | PB |
| 2. | A | I | O | S | gg | PB |
| 3. | A | J | S | T | dd | PB |
| 4. | A | N | U | ee | hh | PB |
| 5. | B | D | E | Y | cc | PB |
| 6. | B | G | aa | bb | jj | PB |
| 7. | B | H | M | Q | X | PB |
| 8. | B | K | W | Z | ff | PB |
| 9. | B | L | P | R | V | PB |
| 10. | C | I | U | dd | gg | PB |
| 11. | C | J | O | S | ee | PB |
| 12. | C | N | S | T | hh | PB |
| 13. | D | G | K | P | X | PB |
| 14. | D | H | R | Z | aa | PB |
| 15. | D | L | Q | ff | jj | PB |
| 16. | D | M | V | W | bb | PB |
| 17. | E | G | Q | R | W | PB |
| 18. | E | H | K | L | bb | PB |
| 19. | E | M | P | aa | ff | PB |
| 20. | E | V | X | Z | jj | PB |



(Continued Next Page)

**POWERBALL BALANCED WHEEL® 52136PB** (Continued from previous page)

| | | | | | | |
|---|---|---|---|---|---|---|
| 21. | F | I | J | U | hh | PB |
| 22. | F | I | T | ee | gg | PB |
| 23. | F | N | O | dd | hh | PB |
| 24. | G | H | V | cc | ff | PB |
| 25. | G | L | M | Y | Z | PB |
| 26. | H | P | W | Y | jj | PB |
| 27. | I | N | dd | ee | ii | PB |
| 28. | J | N | gg | hh | ii | PB |
| 29. | K | M | R | cc | jj | PB |
| 30. | K | *Q* | V | Y | aa | PB |
| 31. | L | W | X | aa | cc | PB |
| 32. | O | S | T | U | ii | PB |
| 33. | P | *Q* | Z | bb | cc | PB |
| 34. | R | X | Y | bb | ff | PB |



# POWERBALL BALANCED WHEEL® 52139PB

## Wheel 39 Numbers + PB in 40 Games for a 2 of 3 Win

With Powerball

| Numbers Matched | Maximum Wins 5 + 1 | 4 + 1 | 3 + 1 | 2 + 1 | 1 + 1 | 0 + 1 | Minimum Wins 5 + 1 | 4 + 1 | 3 + 1 | 2 + 1 | 1 + 1 | 0 + 1 |
|---|---|---|---|---|---|---|---|---|---|---|---|---|
| 5 + 1 | 1 | 0 | 1 | 6 | 9 | 23 | 0 | 0 | 0 | 4 | 17 | 19 |
| 4 + 1 | - | 1 | 1 | 4 | 8 | 26 | - | 0 | 0 | 2 | 16 | 22 |
| 3 + 1 | - | - | 2 | 1 | 10 | 27 | - | - | 0 | 1 | 13 | 26 |
| 2 + 1 | - | - | - | 4 | 4 | 32 | - | - | - | 0 | 10 | 30 |
| 1 + 1 | - | - | - | - | 7 | 33 | - | - | - | - | 5 | 35 |
| 0 + 1 | - | - | - | - | - | 40 | - | - | - | - | - | 40 |

Without Powerball

| Numbers Matched | Maximum Wins 5 + 0 | 4 + 0 | 3 + 0 | 2 + 0 | 1 + 0 | Minimum Wins 5 + 0 | 4 + 0 | 3 + 0 | 2 + 0 | 1 + 0 |
|---|---|---|---|---|---|---|---|---|---|---|
| 5 + 0 | 1 | 0 | 1 | 6 | 9 | 0 | 0 | 0 | 4 | 17 |
| 4 + 0 | - | 1 | 1 | 4 | 8 | - | 0 | 0 | 2 | 16 |
| 3 + 0 | - | - | 2 | 1 | 10 | - | - | 0 | 1 | 13 |
| 2 + 0 | - | - | - | 4 | 4 | - | - | - | 0 | 10 |
| 1 + 0 | - | - | - | - | 7 | - | - | - | - | 5 |

## Your 39 Numbers + PB to Wheel

| A | B | C | D | E | F | G | H | I | J |
|---|---|---|---|---|---|---|---|---|---|
| 5 | 5 | 7 | 5 | 6 | 5 | 5 | 5 | 5 | 5 |
| **K** | **L** | **M** | **N** | **O** | **P** | **Q** | **R** | **S** | **T** |
| 5 | 5 | 5 | 5 | 5 | 5 | 5 | 5 | 5 | 6 |
| **U** | **V** | **W** | **X** | **Y** | **Z** | **aa** | **bb** | **cc** | **dd** |
| 5 | 5 | 5 | 5 | 5 | 5 | 5 | 5 | 5 | 6 |
| **ee** | **ff** | **gg** | **hh** | **ii** | **jj** | **kk** | ***ll*** | **mm** | **PB** |
| 5 | 5 | 5 | 5 | 5 | 5 | 5 | 5 | 5 | 40 |

## The 40 Games to Play

| | | | | | | |
|---|---|---|---|---|---|---|
| 1. | A | C | L | kk | mm | PB |
| 2. | A | E | T | dd | ii | PB |
| 3. | A | F | I | X | Y | PB |
| 4. | A | J | X | ee | ff | PB |
| 5. | A | R | ee | ii | *ll* | PB |
| 6. | B | D | H | Z | bb | PB |
| 7. | B | G | N | P | aa | PB |
| 8. | B | K | *Q* | S | U | PB |
| 9. | B | M | W | gg | jj | PB |
| 10. | B | O | V | cc | hh | PB |



(Continued Next Page)

## POWERBALL BALANCED WHEEL® 52139PB (Continued from previous page)

| | | | | | | |
|---|---|---|---|---|---|---|
| 11. | C | E | F | T | ff | PB |
| 12. | C | E | J | *ll* | mm | PB |
| 13. | C | E | Y | ff | kk | PB |
| 14. | C | I | J | ii | kk | PB |
| 15. | C | R | X | dd | kk | PB |
| 16. | C | Y | dd | ee | mm | PB |
| 17. | D | G | K | W | hh | PB |
| 18. | D | M | O | P | *Q* | PB |
| 19. | D | N | U | cc | jj | PB |
| 20. | D | S | V | aa | gg | PB |
| 21. | E | I | L | R | ee | PB |
| 22. | E | I | T | X | mm | PB |
| 23. | F | J | L | T | dd | PB |
| 24. | F | R | ff | ii | mm | PB |
| 25. | F | T | ee | kk | *ll* | PB |
| 26. | G | H | M | U | V | PB |
| 27. | G | O | S | Z | jj | PB |
| 28. | G | *Q* | bb | cc | gg | PB |
| 29. | H | K | N | O | gg | PB |
| 30. | H | P | S | W | cc | PB |
| 31. | H | *Q* | aa | hh | jj | PB |
| 32. | I | L | dd | ff | *ll* | PB |
| 33. | J | R | T | Y | dd | PB |
| 34. | K | M | Z | aa | cc | PB |
| 35. | K | P | V | bb | jj | PB |
| 36. | L | X | Y | ii | *ll* | PB |
| 37. | M | N | S | bb | hh | PB |
| 38. | N | *Q* | V | W | Z | PB |
| 39. | O | U | W | aa | bb | PB |
| 40. | P | U | Z | gg | hh | PB |



# POWERBALL BALANCED WHEEL® 52142PB

## Wheel 42 Numbers + PB in 42 Games for a 2 of 3 Win

With Powerball

| Numbers Matched | Maximum Wins 5 + 1 | 4 + 1 | 3 + 1 | 2 + 1 | 1 + 1 | 0 + 1 | Minimum Wins 5 + 1 | 4 + 1 | 3 + 1 | 2 + 1 | 1 + 1 | 0 + 1 |
|---|---|---|---|---|---|---|---|---|---|---|---|---|
| 5 + 1 | 1 | 0 | 0 | 0 | 20 | 21 | 0 | 0 | 0 | 4 | 17 | 21 |
| 4 + 1 | - | 1 | 0 | 0 | 16 | 25 | - | 0 | 0 | 2 | 16 | 24 |
| 3 + 1 | - | - | 1 | 0 | 12 | 29 | - | - | 0 | 1 | 13 | 28 |
| 2 + 1 | - | - | - | 1 | 8 | 33 | - | - | - | 0 | 10 | 32 |
| 1 + 1 | - | - | - | - | 5 | 37 | - | - | - | - | 5 | 37 |
| 0 + 1 | - | - | - | - | - | 42 | - | - | - | - | - | 42 |

Without Powerball

| Numbers Matched | Maximum Wins 5 + 0 | 4 + 0 | 3 + 0 | 2 + 0 | 1 + 0 | Minimum Wins 5 + 0 | 4 + 0 | 3 + 0 | 2 + 0 | 1 + 0 |
|---|---|---|---|---|---|---|---|---|---|---|
| 5 + 0 | 1 | 0 | 0 | 0 | 20 | 0 | 0 | 0 | 4 | 17 |
| 4 + 0 | - | 1 | 0 | 0 | 16 | - | 0 | 0 | 2 | 16 |
| 3 + 0 | - | - | 1 | 0 | 12 | - | - | 0 | 1 | 13 |
| 2 + 0 | - | - | - | 1 | 8 | - | - | - | 0 | 10 |
| 1 + 0 | - | - | - | - | 5 | - | - | - | - | 5 |

(Continued Next Page)

**POWERBALL BALANCED WHEEL® 52142PB** (Continued from previous page)

## Your 42 Numbers + PB to Wheel

| A | B | C | D | E | F | G | H | I | J | K |
|---|---|---|---|---|---|---|---|---|---|---|
| 5 | 5 | 5 | 5 | 5 | 5 | 5 | 5 | 5 | 5 | 5 |
| L | M | N | O | P | Q | R | S | T | U | V |
| 5 | 5 | 5 | 5 | 5 | 5 | 5 | 5 | 5 | 5 | 5 |
| W | X | Y | Z | aa | bb | cc | dd | ee | ff | gg |
| 5 | 5 | 5 | 5 | 5 | 5 | 5 | 5 | 5 | 5 | 5 |
| hh | ii | jj | kk | *ll* | mm | nn | oo | pp | PB | |
| 5 | 5 | 5 | 5 | 5 | 5 | 5 | 5 | 5 | 42 | |

## The 42 Games to Play

| | | | | | | |
|---|---|---|---|---|---|---|
| 1. | A | B | V | ee | oo | PB |
| 2. | A | H | P | R | S | PB |
| 3. | A | I | K | W | *ll* | PB |
| 4. | A | L | N | X | Z | PB |
| 5. | A | gg | ii | jj | kk | PB |
| 6. | B | H | W | Z | kk | PB |
| 7. | B | I | L | P | ii | PB |
| 8. | B | K | S | X | gg | PB |
| 9. | B | N | R | jj | *ll* | PB |
| 10. | C | D | *Q* | aa | pp | PB |
| 11. | C | E | M | dd | mm | PB |
| 12. | C | F | J | O | bb | PB |
| 13. | C | G | T | U | Y | PB |
| 14. | C | cc | ff | hh | nn | PB |
| 15. | D | E | F | T | ff | PB |
| 16. | D | G | M | O | nn | PB |
| 17. | D | J | U | cc | dd | PB |
| 18. | D | Y | bb | hh | mm | PB |
| 19. | E | G | aa | bb | cc | PB |
| 20. | E | J | Y | nn | pp | PB |
| 21. | E | O | *Q* | U | hh | PB |
| 22. | F | G | dd | hh | pp | PB |
| 23. | F | M | *Q* | Y | cc | PB |
| 24. | F | U | aa | mm | nn | PB |
| 25. | G | J | *Q* | ff | mm | PB |
| 26. | H | I | N | gg | oo | PB |
| 27. | H | K | L | ee | jj | PB |
| 28. | H | V | X | ii | *ll* | PB |
| 29. | I | R | X | ee | kk | PB |
| 30. | I | S | V | Z | jj | PB |
| 31. | J | M | T | aa | hh | PB |
| 32. | K | N | P | V | kk | PB |
| 33. | K | R | Z | ii | oo | PB |
| 34. | L | R | V | W | gg | PB |
| 35. | L | S | kk | *ll* | oo | PB |
| 36. | M | U | bb | ff | pp | PB |
| 37. | N | S | W | ee | ii | PB |
| 38. | O | T | cc | mm | pp | PB |
| 39. | O | Y | aa | dd | ff | PB |
| 40. | P | W | X | jj | oo | PB |
| 41. | P | Z | ee | gg | *ll* | PB |
| 42. | *Q* | T | bb | dd | nn | PB |

# POWERBALL BALANCED WHEEL® 52145PB

## Wheel 45 Numbers + PB in 53 Games for a 2 of 3 Win

With Powerball

| Numbers Matched | Maximum Wins | | | | | | Minimum Wins | | | | | |
|---|---|---|---|---|---|---|---|---|---|---|---|---|
| | 5 + 1 | 4 + 1 | 3 + 1 | 2 + 1 | 1 + 1 | 0 + 1 | 5 + 1 | 4 + 1 | 3 + 1 | 2 + 1 | 1 + 1 | 0 + 1 |
| 5 + 1 | 1 | 0 | 1 | 8 | 13 | 30 | 0 | 0 | 0 | 4 | 19 | 30 |
| 4 + 1 | - | 1 | 1 | 7 | 10 | 34 | - | 0 | 0 | 2 | 18 | 33 |
| 3 + 1 | - | - | 2 | 7 | 5 | 39 | - | - | 0 | 1 | 14 | 38 |
| 2 + 1 | - | - | - | 5 | 7 | 41 | - | - | - | 0 | 11 | 42 |
| 1 + 1 | - | - | - | - | 9 | 44 | - | - | - | - | 5 | 48 |
| 0 + 1 | - | - | - | - | - | 53 | - | - | - | - | - | 53 |

Without Powerball

| Numbers Matched | Maximum Wins | | | | | Minimum Wins | | | | |
|---|---|---|---|---|---|---|---|---|---|---|
| | 5 + 0 | 4 + 0 | 3 + 0 | 2 + 0 | 1 + 0 | 5 + 0 | 4 + 0 | 3 + 0 | 2 + 0 | 1 + 0 |
| 5 + 0 | 1 | 0 | 1 | 8 | 13 | 0 | 0 | 0 | 4 | 19 |
| 4 + 0 | - | 1 | 1 | 7 | 10 | - | 0 | 0 | 2 | 18 |
| 3 + 0 | - | - | 2 | 7 | 5 | - | - | 0 | 1 | 14 |
| 2 + 0 | - | - | - | 5 | 7 | - | - | - | 0 | 11 |
| 1 + 0 | - | - | - | - | 9 | - | - | - | - | 5 |

## Your 45 Numbers + PB to Wheel

| A | B | C | D | E | F | G | H | I | J |
|---|---|---|---|---|---|---|---|---|---|
| 6 | 7 | 6 | 7 | 5 | 5 | 9 | 6 | 7 | 5 |
| **K** | **L** | **M** | **N** | **O** | **P** | **Q** | **R** | **S** | **T** |
| 5 | 5 | 5 | 5 | 6 | 5 | 6 | 8 | 7 | 6 |
| **U** | **V** | **W** | **X** | **Y** | **Z** | **aa** | **bb** | **cc** | **dd** |
| 5 | 5 | 7 | 5 | 5 | 5 | 6 | 5 | 8 | 5 |
| **ee** | **ff** | **gg** | **hh** | **ii** | **jj** | **kk** | ***ll*** | **mm** | **nn** |
| 6 | 6 | 5 | 7 | 6 | 5 | 5 | 5 | 6 | 7 |
| **oo** | **pp** | **qq** | **rr** | **ss** | **PB** | | | | |
| 8 | 5 | 6 | 6 | 5 | 53 | | | | |

## The 53 Games to Play

| | | | | | | |
|---|---|---|---|---|---|---|
| 1. | A | B | O | hh | ii | PB |
| 2. | A | C | H | T | mm | PB |
| 3. | A | D | *Q* | ee | qq | PB |
| 4. | A | G | R | aa | cc | PB |
| 5. | A | I | S | nn | oo | PB |
| 6. | A | W | aa | ff | rr | PB |
| 7. | B | C | G | *Q* | rr | PB |
| 8. | B | D | cc | ff | mm | PB |
| 9. | B | G | I | R | oo | PB |
| 10. | B | H | W | ee | oo | PB |
| 11. | B | I | T | aa | qq | PB |
| 12. | B | S | nn | oo | rr | PB |
| 13. | C | D | I | W | hh | PB |
| 14. | C | O | aa | ee | nn | PB |
| 15. | C | *Q* | R | S | cc | PB |
| 16. | C | ff | ii | oo | qq | PB |
| 17. | D | G | S | W | oo | PB |
| 18. | D | G | cc | hh | nn | PB |
| 19. | D | H | S | aa | ii | PB |
| 20. | D | O | R | T | rr | PB |
| 21. | E | F | K | P | gg | PB |
| 22. | E | J | N | U | Y | PB |
| 23. | E | L | V | kk | *ll* | PB |
| 24. | E | M | Z | jj | ss | PB |



(Continued Next Page)

## POWERBALL BALANCED WHEEL® 52145PB (Continued from previous page)

| | | | | | | |
|---|---|---|---|---|---|---|
| 25. | E | X | bb | dd | pp | PB |
| 26. | F | J | L | M | dd | PB |
| 27. | F | N | V | X | jj | PB |
| 28. | F | U | Z | bb | kk | PB |
| 29. | F | Y | *ll* | pp | ss | PB |
| 30. | G | H | R | nn | qq | PB |
| 31. | G | O | T | cc | oo | PB |
| 32. | G | R | cc | ee | ii | PB |
| 33. | G | R | ff | mm | nn | PB |
| 34. | H | I | O | *Q* | ff | PB |
| 35. | H | cc | hh | qq | rr | PB |
| 36. | I | R | W | cc | hh | PB |
| 37. | I | ee | ii | mm | rr | PB |
| 38. | J | K | jj | kk | pp | PB |
| 39. | J | P | X | Z | *ll* | PB |
| 40. | J | V | bb | gg | ss | PB |
| 41. | K | L | U | X | ss | PB |
| 42. | K | M | N | bb | *ll* | PB |
| 43. | K | V | Y | Z | dd | PB |
| 44. | L | N | Z | gg | pp | PB |
| 45. | L | P | Y | bb | jj | PB |
| 46. | M | P | U | V | pp | PB |
| 47. | M | X | Y | gg | kk | PB |
| 48. | N | P | dd | kk | ss | PB |
| 49. | O | S | W | mm | qq | PB |
| 50. | *Q* | T | W | ii | nn | PB |
| 51. | *Q* | aa | hh | mm | oo | PB |
| 52. | S | T | ee | ff | hh | PB |
| 53. | U | dd | gg | jj | *ll* | PB |



# POWERBALL BALANCED WHEEL® 52147PB

## Wheel 47 Numbers + PB in 60 Games for a 2 of 3 Win

With Powerball

| Numbers Matched | Maximum Wins 5 + 1 | 4 + 1 | 3 + 1 | 2 + 1 | 1 + 1 | 0 + 1 | Minimum Wins 5 + 1 | 4 + 1 | 3 + 1 | 2 + 1 | 1 + 1 | 0 + 1 |
|---|---|---|---|---|---|---|---|---|---|---|---|---|
| 5 + 1 | 1 | 1 | 0 | 3 | 25 | 30 | 0 | 0 | 0 | 4 | 21 | 35 |
| 4 + 1 | - | 2 | 0 | 1 | 22 | 35 | - | 0 | 0 | 2 | 20 | 38 |
| 3 + 1 | - | - | 2 | 2 | 15 | 41 | - | - | 0 | 1 | 15 | 44 |
| 2 + 1 | - | - | - | 4 | 9 | 47 | - | - | - | 0 | 12 | 48 |
| 1 + 1 | - | - | - | - | 9 | 51 | - | - | - | - | 5 | 55 |
| 0 + 1 | - | - | - | - | - | 60 | - | - | - | - | - | 60 |

Without Powerball

| Numbers Matched | Maximum Wins 5 + 0 | 4 + 0 | 3 + 0 | 2 + 0 | 1 + 0 | Minimum Wins 5 + 0 | 4 + 0 | 3 + 0 | 2 + 0 | 1 + 0 |
|---|---|---|---|---|---|---|---|---|---|---|
| 5 + 0 | 1 | 1 | 0 | 3 | 25 | 0 | 0 | 0 | 4 | 21 |
| 4 + 0 | - | 2 | 0 | 1 | 22 | - | 0 | 0 | 2 | 20 |
| 3 + 0 | - | - | 2 | 2 | 15 | - | - | 0 | 1 | 15 |
| 2 + 0 | - | - | - | 4 | 9 | - | - | - | 0 | 12 |
| 1 + 0 | - | - | - | - | 9 | - | - | - | - | 5 |

(Continued Next Page)

**POWERBALL BALANCED WHEEL® 52147PB** (Continued from previous page)

## Your 47 Numbers + PB to Wheel

| A | B | C | D | E | F | G | H | I | J |
|---|---|---|---|---|---|---|---|---|---|
| 8 | 5 | 7 | 7 | 7 | 5 | 5 | 5 | 8 | 7 |
| **K** | **L** | **M** | **N** | **O** | **P** | **Q** | **R** | **S** | **T** |
| 7 | 5 | 5 | 5 | 9 | 5 | 5 | 8 | 5 | 7 |
| **U** | **V** | **W** | **X** | **Y** | **Z** | **aa** | **bb** | **cc** | **dd** |
| 7 | 7 | 5 | 8 | 9 | 7 | 7 | 5 | 7 | 5 |
| **ee** | **ff** | **gg** | **hh** | **ii** | **jj** | **kk** | **ll** | **mm** | **nn** |
| 7 | 7 | 7 | 8 | 5 | 8 | 5 | 7 | 5 | 5 |
| **oo** | **pp** | **qq** | **rr** | **ss** | **tt** | **uu** | **PB** | | |
| 5 | 5 | 5 | 7 | 8 | 5 | 9 | 60 | | |

## The 60 Games to Play

| | | | | | | |
|---|---|---|---|---|---|---|
| 1. | A | C | O | X | ll | PB |
| 2. | A | D | aa | hh | uu | PB |
| 3. | A | E | R | V | uu | PB |
| 4. | A | I | Y | rr | ss | PB |
| 5. | A | J | K | X | cc | PB |
| 6. | A | O | Y | Z | uu | PB |
| 7. | A | T | U | ee | hh | PB |
| 8. | A | ff | gg | jj | uu | PB |
| 9. | B | F | M | bb | dd | PB |
| 10. | B | G | W | qq | tt | PB |
| 11. | B | H | L | ii | kk | PB |
| 12. | B | N | P | S | mm | PB |
| 13. | B | Q | nn | oo | pp | PB |
| 14. | C | D | Z | aa | cc | PB |
| 15. | C | E | K | U | jj | PB |
| 16. | C | I | J | ss | uu | PB |
| 17. | C | J | T | V | ff | PB |
| 18. | C | O | ee | gg | uu | PB |
| 19. | C | R | Y | hh | rr | PB |
| 20. | D | E | X | ff | rr | PB |
| 21. | D | I | K | T | ll | PB |
| 22. | D | J | U | Y | gg | PB |
| 23. | D | K | O | R | aa | PB |
| 24. | D | V | ee | jj | ss | PB |
| 25. | E | I | J | Z | ee | PB |
| 26. | E | O | V | ff | hh | PB |
| 27. | E | T | aa | gg | ss | PB |
| 28. | E | V | Y | cc | ll | PB |
| 29. | F | G | L | mm | oo | PB |
| 30. | F | H | Q | S | W | PB |
| 31. | F | N | ii | pp | qq | PB |
| 32. | F | P | kk | nn | tt | PB |
| 33. | G | H | P | bb | pp | PB |
| 34. | G | M | S | ii | nn | PB |
| 35. | G | N | Q | dd | kk | PB |
| 36. | H | M | N | oo | tt | PB |
| 37. | H | dd | mm | nn | qq | PB |
| 38. | I | O | Y | jj | ss | PB |
| 39. | I | R | cc | ff | ss | PB |
| 40. | I | U | V | X | aa | PB |
| 41. | I | cc | gg | hh | jj | PB |
| 42. | J | O | R | Z | hh | PB |
| 43. | J | aa | jj | ll | rr | PB |
| 44. | K | V | Z | gg | rr | PB |
| 45. | K | X | hh | ss | uu | PB |
| 46. | K | Y | aa | ee | ff | PB |
| 47. | L | M | P | Q | qq | PB |
| 48. | L | N | W | bb | nn | PB |



(Continued Next Page)

**POWERBALL BALANCED WHEEL® 52147PB** (Continued from previous page)

| | | | | | | |
|---|---|---|---|---|---|---|
| 49. | L | S | dd | pp | tt | PB |
| 50. | M | W | kk | mm | pp | PB |
| 51. | O | T | cc | rr | uu | PB |
| 52. | O | U | cc | ee | rr | PB |
| 53. | P | W | dd | ii | oo | PB |
| 54. | *Q* | bb | ii | mm | tt | PB |
| 55. | R | T | X | Y | jj | PB |
| 56. | R | U | hh | *ll* | uu | PB |
| 57. | R | X | ee | gg | *ll* | PB |
| 58. | S | bb | kk | oo | qq | PB |
| 59. | T | X | Y | Z | jj | PB |
| 60. | U | Z | ff | *ll* | ss | PB |



# POWERBALL BALANCED WHEEL® 52155PB

## Wheel 55 Numbers + PB in 86 Games for a 2 of 3 Win

With Powerball

| Numbers Matched | Maximum Wins | | | | | | Minimum Wins | | | | | |
|---|---|---|---|---|---|---|---|---|---|---|---|---|
| | 5 + 1 | 4 + 1 | 3 + 1 | 2 + 1 | 1 + 1 | 0 + 1 | 5 + 1 | 4 + 1 | 3 + 1 | 2 + 1 | 1 + 1 | 0 + 1 |
| 5 + 1 | 1 | 0 | 1 | 6 | 12 | 66 | 0 | 0 | 0 | 4 | 26 | 56 |
| 4 + 1 | - | 1 | 1 | 4 | 22 | 58 | - | 0 | 0 | 2 | 24 | 60 |
| 3 + 1 | - | - | 2 | 3 | 16 | 65 | - | - | 0 | 1 | 18 | 67 |
| 2 + 1 | - | - | - | 7 | 0 | 79 | - | - | - | 0 | 14 | 72 |
| 1 + 1 | - | - | - | - | 10 | 76 | - | - | - | - | 6 | 80 |
| 0 + 1 | - | - | - | - | - | 86 | - | - | - | - | - | 86 |

Without Powerball

| Numbers Matched | Maximum Wins | | | | | Minimum Wins | | | | |
|---|---|---|---|---|---|---|---|---|---|---|
| | 5 + 0 | 4 + 0 | 3 + 0 | 2 + 0 | 1 + 0 | 5 + 0 | 4 + 0 | 3 + 0 | 2 + 0 | 1 + 0 |
| 5 + 0 | 1 | 0 | 1 | 6 | 12 | 0 | 0 | 0 | 4 | 26 |
| 4 + 0 | - | 1 | 1 | 4 | 22 | - | 0 | 0 | 2 | 24 |
| 3 + 0 | - | - | 2 | 3 | 16 | - | - | 0 | 1 | 18 |
| 2 + 0 | - | - | - | 7 | 0 | - | - | - | 0 | 14 |
| 1 + 0 | - | - | - | - | 10 | - | - | - | - | 6 |

## Your 55 Numbers + PB to Wheel

| A | B | C | D | E | F | G | H | I | J |
|---|---|---|---|---|---|---|---|---|---|
| 10 | 10 | 10 | 10 | 10 | 10 | 9 | 9 | 9 | 9 |
| **K** | **L** | **M** | **N** | **O** | **P** | **Q** | **R** | **S** | **T** |
| 9 | 9 | 9 | 9 | 9 | 9 | 9 | 9 | 9 | 9 |
| **U** | **V** | **W** | **X** | **Y** | **Z** | **aa** | **bb** | **cc** | **dd** |
| 9 | 9 | 9 | 9 | 9 | 9 | 9 | 9 | 8 | 8 |
| **ee** | **ff** | **gg** | **hh** | **ii** | **jj** | **kk** | ***ll*** | **mm** | **nn** |
| 8 | 8 | 6 | 6 | 6 | 6 | 6 | 6 | 6 | 6 |
| **oo** | **pp** | **qq** | **rr** | **ss** | **tt** | **uu** | **vv** | **ww** | **xx** |
| 6 | 6 | 6 | 6 | 6 | 7 | 6 | 6 | 6 | 6 |
| **yy** | **zz** | **AA** | **BB** | **CC** | **PB** | | | | |
| 6 | 6 | 6 | 6 | 7 | 86 | | | | |

## The 86 Games to Play

| | | | | | | |
|---|---|---|---|---|---|---|
| 1. | A | B | C | F | U | PB |
| 2. | A | B | L | *Q* | S | PB |
| 3. | A | C | G | X | Z | PB |
| 4. | A | D | E | W | aa | PB |
| 5. | A | E | M | Y | ee | PB |
| 6. | A | H | K | O | U | PB |



(Continued Next Page)

## POWERBALL BALANCED WHEEL® 52155PB (Continued from previous page)

| | | | | | | |
|---|---|---|---|---|---|---|
| 7. | A | I | N | T | cc | PB |
| 8. | A | J | O | W | dd | PB |
| 9. | A | J | P | cc | ff | PB |
| 10. | A | J | R | V | bb | PB |
| 11. | B | C | J | N | Y | PB |
| 12. | B | D | P | X | bb | PB |
| 13. | B | E | N | P | V | PB |
| 14. | B | F | Z | aa | dd | PB |
| 15. | B | G | H | P | S | PB |
| 16. | B | I | K | R | ff | PB |
| 17. | B | L | W | cc | ee | PB |
| 18. | B | M | O | R | T | PB |
| 19. | C | D | E | R | cc | PB |
| 20. | C | E | F | I | S | PB |
| 21. | C | G | V | ee | ff | PB |
| 22. | C | H | *Q* | T | aa | PB |
| 23. | C | K | P | W | Y | PB |
| 24. | C | L | M | O | P | PB |
| 25. | C | L | X | bb | dd | PB |
| 26. | D | E | K | *Q* | dd | PB |
| 27. | D | F | G | M | U | PB |
| 28. | D | H | I | L | ff | PB |
| 29. | D | H | J | N | X | PB |
| 30. | D | K | *Q* | bb | ee | PB |
| 31. | D | O | T | V | Y | PB |
| 32. | D | S | T | Z | bb | PB |
| 33. | E | G | W | Y | bb | PB |
| 34. | E | H | R | W | Y | PB |
| 35. | E | J | L | T | U | PB |
| 36. | E | O | X | Z | ff | PB |
| 37. | F | H | I | O | bb | PB |
| 38. | F | H | J | Z | ee | PB |
| 39. | F | K | L | N | V | PB |
| 40. | F | P | R | U | aa | PB |
| 41. | F | *Q* | T | W | ff | PB |

| | | | | | | |
|---|---|---|---|---|---|---|
| 42. | F | *Q* | X | Y | cc | PB |
| 43. | G | I | J | M | *Q* | PB |
| 44. | G | K | M | T | X | PB |
| 45. | G | L | N | R | dd | PB |
| 46. | G | O | S | aa | cc | PB |
| 47. | H | M | V | cc | dd | PB |
| 48. | I | L | Y | Z | aa | PB |
| 49. | I | P | T | dd | ee | PB |
| 50. | I | U | V | W | X | PB |
| 51. | J | K | S | V | aa | PB |
| 52. | K | U | Z | bb | cc | PB |
| 53. | M | N | S | W | Z | PB |
| 54. | M | N | aa | bb | ff | PB |
| 55. | N | O | *Q* | U | ee | PB |
| 56. | P | *Q* | R | V | Z | PB |
| 57. | R | S | X | aa | ee | PB |
| 58. | S | U | Y | dd | ff | PB |
| 59. | gg | hh | ii | *ll* | zz | PB |
| 60. | gg | hh | ii | tt | CC | PB |
| 61. | gg | jj | mm | pp | ww | PB |
| 62. | gg | kk | uu | xx | yy | PB |
| 63. | gg | nn | oo | vv | AA | PB |
| 64. | gg | qq | rr | ss | BB | PB |
| 65. | hh | jj | kk | qq | AA | PB |
| 66. | hh | mm | nn | uu | BB | PB |
| 67. | hh | oo | rr | ww | yy | PB |
| 68. | hh | pp | ss | vv | xx | PB |
| 69. | ii | jj | oo | ss | uu | PB |
| 70. | ii | kk | mm | rr | vv | PB |
| 71. | ii | nn | pp | qq | yy | PB |
| 72. | ii | ww | xx | AA | BB | PB |
| 73. | jj | *ll* | nn | rr | xx | PB |
| 74. | jj | *ll* | tt | ww | CC | PB |
| 75. | jj | vv | yy | zz | BB | PB |
| 76. | kk | *ll* | oo | pp | BB | PB |



(Continued Next Page)

**POWERBALL BALANCED WHEEL® 52155PB** (Continued from previous page)

| | | | | | | |
|---|---|---|---|---|---|---|
| 77. | kk | nn | oo | tt | CC | PB |
| 78. | kk | nn | ss | ww | zz | PB |
| 79. | ll | mm | ss | yy | AA | PB |
| 80. | ll | qq | uu | vv | ww | PB |
| 81. | mm | oo | qq | xx | zz | PB |
| 82. | mm | ss | tt | xx | CC | PB |
| 83. | pp | rr | tt | BB | CC | PB |
| 84. | pp | rr | uu | zz | AA | PB |
| 85. | qq | tt | uu | vv | CC | PB |
| 86. | tt | yy | zz | AA | CC | PB |



# POWERBALL BALANCED WHEEL® 52156PB

## Wheel 56 Numbers + PB in 91 Games for a 2 of 3 Win

With Powerball

| Numbers Matched | Maximum Wins 5 + 1 | 4 + 1 | 3 + 1 | 2 + 1 | 1 + 1 | 0 + 1 | Minimum Wins 5 + 1 | 4 + 1 | 3 + 1 | 2 + 1 | 1 + 1 | 0 + 1 |
|---|---|---|---|---|---|---|---|---|---|---|---|---|
| 5 + 1 | 1 | 1 | 0 | 4 | 19 | 66 | 0 | 0 | 0 | 4 | 26 | 61 |
| 4 + 1 | - | 2 | 0 | 0 | 21 | 68 | - | 0 | 0 | 2 | 24 | 65 |
| 3 + 1 | - | - | 3 | 5 | 5 | 78 | - | - | 0 | 1 | 18 | 72 |
| 2 + 1 | - | - | - | 8 | 0 | 83 | - | - | - | 0 | 14 | 77 |
| 1 + 1 | - | - | - | - | 10 | 81 | - | - | - | - | 6 | 85 |
| 0 + 1 | - | - | - | - | - | 91 | - | - | - | - | - | 91 |

Without Powerball

| Numbers Matched | Maximum Wins 5 + 0 | 4 + 0 | 3 + 0 | 2 + 0 | 1 + 0 | Minimum Wins 5 + 0 | 4 + 0 | 3 + 0 | 2 + 0 | 1 + 0 |
|---|---|---|---|---|---|---|---|---|---|---|
| 5 + 0 | 1 | 1 | 0 | 4 | 19 | 0 | 0 | 0 | 4 | 26 |
| 4 + 0 | - | 2 | 0 | 0 | 21 | - | 0 | 0 | 2 | 24 |
| 3 + 0 | - | - | 3 | 5 | 5 | - | - | 0 | 1 | 18 |
| 2 + 0 | - | - | - | 8 | 0 | - | - | - | 0 | 14 |
| 1 + 0 | - | - | - | - | 10 | - | - | - | - | 6 |

## Your 56 Numbers + PB to Wheel

| A | B | C | D | E | F | G | H | I | J |
|---|---|---|---|---|---|---|---|---|---|
| 6 | 6 | 6 | 6 | 7 | 6 | 6 | 7 | 7 | 8 |
| **K** | **L** | **M** | **N** | **O** | **P** | **Q** | **R** | **S** | **T** |
| 7 | 7 | 7 | 7 | 7 | 7 | 7 | 6 | 7 | 8 |
| **U** | **V** | **W** | **X** | **Y** | **Z** | **aa** | **bb** | **cc** | **dd** |
| 8 | 8 | 8 | 7 | 7 | 8 | 8 | 8 | 9 | 9 |
| **ee** | **ff** | **gg** | **hh** | **ii** | **jj** | **kk** | **ll** | **mm** | **nn** |
| 9 | 9 | 9 | 9 | 9 | 9 | 9 | 9 | 9 | 9 |
| **oo** | **pp** | **qq** | **rr** | **ss** | **tt** | **uu** | **vv** | **ww** | **xx** |
| 9 | 9 | 9 | 9 | 9 | 9 | 9 | 9 | 9 | 9 |
| **yy** | **zz** | **AA** | **BB** | **CC** | **DD** | **PB** | | | |
| 10 | 10 | 10 | 10 | 10 | 10 | 91 | | | |

## The 91 Games to Play

| | | | | | | |
|---|---|---|---|---|---|---|
| 1. | A | B | G | M | O | PB |
| 2. | A | C | J | P | S | PB |
| 3. | A | D | F | H | R | PB |
| 4. | A | E | I | N | X | PB |
| 5. | A | E | Z | aa | bb | PB |
| 6. | A | K | L | Q | Y | PB |
| 7. | B | C | H | K | X | PB |
| 8. | B | D | N | Q | S | PB |



(Continued Next Page)

## POWERBALL BALANCED WHEEL® 52156PB (Continued from previous page)

| | | | | | | |
|---|---|---|---|---|---|---|
| 9. | B | D | Z | aa | bb | PB |
| 10. | B | E | L | P | R | PB |
| 11. | B | F | I | J | Y | PB |
| 12. | C | D | E | G | Y | PB |
| 13. | C | F | L | N | O | PB |
| 14. | C | I | M | R | aa | PB |
| 15. | C | I | *Q* | Z | bb | PB |
| 16. | D | I | K | O | P | PB |
| 17. | D | J | L | M | X | PB |
| 18. | E | F | K | M | S | PB |
| 19. | E | H | J | O | *Q* | PB |
| 20. | E | H | J | O | S | PB |
| 21. | F | G | P | *Q* | X | PB |
| 22. | F | O | Z | aa | bb | PB |
| 23. | G | H | I | S | aa | PB |
| 24. | G | H | L | Z | bb | PB |
| 25. | G | J | K | N | R | PB |
| 26. | H | M | N | P | Y | PB |
| 27. | I | L | M | *Q* | aa | PB |
| 28. | J | K | N | P | aa | PB |
| 29. | J | R | S | Z | bb | PB |
| 30. | K | M | P | Z | bb | PB |
| 31. | L | S | X | Y | aa | PB |
| 32. | N | X | Y | Z | bb | PB |
| 33. | O | *Q* | R | X | Y | PB |
| 34. | T | U | ee | vv | yy | PB |
| 35. | T | V | ii | tt | zz | PB |
| 36. | T | W | kk | *ll* | ww | PB |
| 37. | T | cc | jj | qq | BB | PB |
| 38. | T | dd | ff | hh | xx | PB |
| 39. | T | ff | mm | ss | DD | PB |
| 40. | T | gg | oo | AA | CC | PB |
| 41. | T | nn | pp | rr | uu | PB |
| 42. | U | V | kk | qq | AA | PB |
| 43. | U | W | oo | uu | xx | PB |
| 44. | U | cc | hh | pp | CC | PB |
| 45. | U | dd | gg | rr | ss | PB |
| 46. | U | ff | tt | ww | BB | PB |
| 47. | U | ii | jj | *ll* | DD | PB |
| 48. | U | *ll* | mm | nn | zz | PB |
| 49. | V | W | gg | jj | vv | PB |
| 50. | V | cc | mm | ss | xx | PB |
| 51. | V | dd | *ll* | ww | AA | PB |
| 52. | V | ee | hh | rr | uu | PB |
| 53. | V | ff | oo | pp | BB | PB |
| 54. | V | nn | yy | CC | DD | PB |
| 55. | W | cc | rr | zz | BB | PB |
| 56. | W | dd | ee | ii | nn | PB |
| 57. | W | ff | mm | CC | DD | PB |
| 58. | W | hh | qq | tt | AA | PB |
| 59. | W | ii | pp | ss | yy | PB |
| 60. | cc | dd | gg | tt | uu | PB |
| 61. | cc | ee | pp | yy | AA | PB |
| 62. | cc | ff | kk | nn | vv | PB |
| 63. | cc | ii | *ll* | oo | rr | PB |
| 64. | cc | ss | uu | ww | DD | PB |
| 65. | dd | ii | mm | vv | BB | PB |
| 66. | dd | jj | pp | qq | DD | PB |
| 67. | dd | kk | vv | zz | CC | PB |
| 68. | dd | oo | qq | yy | zz | PB |
| 69. | ee | ff | gg | *ll* | qq | PB |
| 70. | ee | gg | mm | pp | ww | PB |
| 71. | ee | gg | xx | BB | DD | PB |
| 72. | ee | jj | kk | uu | zz | PB |
| 73. | ee | oo | ss | tt | CC | PB |
| 74. | ff | ii | uu | zz | AA | PB |
| 75. | ff | jj | rr | ww | yy | PB |
| 76. | gg | hh | ii | kk | yy | PB |
| 77. | gg | hh | nn | ww | zz | PB |
| 78. | hh | jj | *ll* | ss | BB | PB |



(Continued Next Page)

**POWERBALL BALANCED WHEEL® 52156PB** (Continued from previous page)

| | | | | | | |
|---|---|---|---|---|---|---|
| 79. | hh | jj | mm | xx | AA | PB |
| 80. | hh | oo | vv | ww | DD | PB |
| 81. | ii | qq | ww | xx | CC | PB |
| 82. | jj | nn | oo | tt | CC | PB |
| 83. | kk | mm | oo | tt | yy | PB |
| 84. | kk | nn | rr | xx | BB | PB |
| 85. | kk | pp | ss | zz | DD | PB |
| 86. | ll | pp | tt | vv | xx | PB |
| 87. | ll | uu | yy | BB | CC | PB |
| 88. | mm | qq | rr | uu | vv | PB |
| 89. | nn | qq | ss | vv | AA | PB |
| 90. | rr | tt | AA | CC | DD | PB |
| 91. | xx | yy | zz | AA | BB | PB |



# POWERBALL BALANCED WHEEL® 52007PB

## Wheel 7 Numbers + PB in 3 Games for a 2 of 2 Win

With Powerball

| Numbers Matched | Maximum Wins | | | | | | Minimum Wins | | | | | |
|---|---|---|---|---|---|---|---|---|---|---|---|---|
| | 5 + 1 | 4 + 1 | 3 + 1 | 2 + 1 | 1 + 1 | 0 + 1 | 5 + 1 | 4 + 1 | 3 + 1 | 2 + 1 | 1 + 1 | 0 + 1 |
| 5 + 1 | 1 | 0 | 2 | 0 | 0 | 0 | 0 | 1 | 2 | 0 | 0 | 0 |
| 4 + 1 | - | 1 | 1 | 1 | 0 | 0 | - | 0 | 2 | 1 | 0 | 0 |
| 3 + 1 | - | - | 2 | 0 | 1 | 0 | - | - | 0 | 3 | 0 | 0 |
| 2 + 1 | - | - | - | 2 | 1 | 0 | - | - | - | 1 | 2 | 0 |
| 1 + 1 | - | - | - | - | 3 | 0 | - | - | - | - | 2 | 1 |
| 0 + 1 | - | - | - | - | - | 3 | - | - | - | - | - | 3 |

Without Powerball

| Numbers Matched | Maximum Wins | | | | | Minimum Wins | | | | |
|---|---|---|---|---|---|---|---|---|---|---|
| | 5 + 0 | 4 + 0 | 3 + 0 | 2 + 0 | 1 + 0 | 5 + 0 | 4 + 0 | 3 + 0 | 2 + 0 | 1 + 0 |
| 5 + 0 | 1 | 0 | 2 | 0 | 0 | 0 | 1 | 2 | 0 | 0 |
| 4 + 0 | - | 1 | 1 | 1 | 0 | - | 0 | 2 | 1 | 0 |
| 3 + 0 | - | - | 2 | 0 | 1 | - | - | 0 | 3 | 0 |
| 2 + 0 | - | - | - | 2 | 1 | - | - | - | 1 | 2 |
| 1 + 0 | - | - | - | - | 3 | - | - | - | - | 2 |

## Your 7 Numbers + PB to Wheel

| A | B | C | D | E | F | G | PB |
|---|---|---|---|---|---|---|---|
| 2 | 2 | 2 | 2 | 2 | 2 | 3 | 3 |

## The 3 Games to Play

| | | | | | | |
|---|---|---|---|---|---|---|
| 1. | A | B | E | F | G | PB |
| 2. | A | C | D | F | G | PB |
| 3. | B | C | D | E | G | PB |



# POWERBALL BALANCED WHEEL® 52008PB

## Wheel 8 Numbers + PB in 4 Games for a 2 of 2 Win

With Powerball

| Numbers Matched | Maximum Wins | | | | | | Minimum Wins | | | | | |
|---|---|---|---|---|---|---|---|---|---|---|---|---|
| | 5 + 1 | 4 + 1 | 3 + 1 | 2 + 1 | 1 + 1 | 0 + 1 | 5 + 1 | 4 + 1 | 3 + 1 | 2 + 1 | 1 + 1 | 0 + 1 |
| 5 + 1 | 1 | 1 | 1 | 1 | 0 | 0 | 0 | 0 | 4 | 0 | 0 | 0 |
| 4 + 1 | - | 2 | 1 | 0 | 1 | 0 | - | 0 | 1 | 3 | 0 | 0 |
| 3 + 1 | - | - | 3 | 0 | 0 | 1 | - | - | 0 | 3 | 1 | 0 |
| 2 + 1 | - | - | - | 3 | 0 | 1 | - | - | - | 1 | 2 | 1 |
| 1 + 1 | - | - | - | - | 3 | 1 | - | - | - | - | 2 | 2 |
| 0 + 1 | - | - | - | - | - | 4 | - | - | - | - | - | 4 |

(Continued Next Page)

## POWERBALL BALANCED WHEEL® 52008PB (Continued from previous page)

Without Powerball

| Numbers Matched | Maximum Wins | | | | | Minimum Wins | | | | |
|---|---|---|---|---|---|---|---|---|---|---|
| | 5 + 0 | 4 + 0 | 3 + 0 | 2 + 0 | 1 + 0 | 5 + 0 | 4 + 0 | 3 + 0 | 2 + 0 | 1 + 0 |
| 5 + 0 | 1 | 1 | 1 | 1 | 0 | 0 | 0 | 4 | 0 | 0 |
| 4 + 0 | - | 2 | 1 | 0 | 1 | - | 0 | 1 | 3 | 0 |
| 3 + 0 | - | - | 3 | 0 | 0 | - | - | 0 | 3 | 1 |
| 2 + 0 | - | - | - | 3 | 0 | - | - | - | 1 | 2 |
| 1 + 0 | - | - | - | - | 3 | - | - | - | - | 2 |

## Your 8 Numbers + PB to Wheel

| A | B | C | D | E | F | G | H | PB |
|---|---|---|---|---|---|---|---|---|
| 2 | 3 | 2 | 2 | 3 | 3 | 2 | 3 | 4 |

## The 4 Games to Play

| | | | | | | |
|---|---|---|---|---|---|---|
| 1. | A | B | E | F | H | PB |
| 2. | A | C | D | G | H | PB |
| 3. | B | C | E | F | H | PB |
| 4. | B | D | E | F | G | PB |



# POWERBALL BALANCED WHEEL® 52009PB

## Wheel 9 Numbers + PB in 5 Games for a 2 of 2 Win

With Powerball

| Numbers Matched | Maximum Wins | | | | | | Minimum Wins | | | | | |
|---|---|---|---|---|---|---|---|---|---|---|---|---|
| | 5 + 1 | 4 + 1 | 3 + 1 | 2 + 1 | 1 + 1 | 0 + 1 | 5 + 1 | 4 + 1 | 3 + 1 | 2 + 1 | 1 + 1 | 0 + 1 |
| 5 + 1 | 1 | 1 | 0 | 2 | 1 | 0 | 0 | 0 | 3 | 2 | 0 | 0 |
| 4 + 1 | - | 2 | 0 | 2 | 0 | 1 | - | 0 | 1 | 3 | 1 | 0 |
| 3 + 1 | - | - | 3 | 0 | 0 | 2 | - | - | 0 | 3 | 1 | 1 |
| 2 + 1 | - | - | - | 3 | 0 | 2 | - | - | - | 1 | 2 | 2 |
| 1 + 1 | - | - | - | - | 3 | 2 | - | - | - | - | 2 | 3 |
| 0 + 1 | - | - | - | - | - | 5 | - | - | - | - | - | 5 |

Without Powerball

| Numbers Matched | Maximum Wins | | | | | Minimum Wins | | | | |
|---|---|---|---|---|---|---|---|---|---|---|
| | 5 + 0 | 4 + 0 | 3 + 0 | 2 + 0 | 1 + 0 | 5 + 0 | 4 + 0 | 3 + 0 | 2 + 0 | 1 + 0 |
| 5 + 0 | 1 | 1 | 0 | 2 | 1 | 0 | 0 | 3 | 2 | 0 |
| 4 + 0 | - | 2 | 0 | 2 | 0 | - | 0 | 1 | 3 | 1 |
| 3 + 0 | - | - | 3 | 0 | 0 | - | - | 0 | 3 | 1 |
| 2 + 0 | - | - | - | 3 | 0 | - | - | - | 1 | 2 |
| 1 + 0 | - | - | - | - | 3 | - | - | - | - | 2 |

## Your 9 Numbers + PB to Wheel

| A | B | C | D | E | F | G | H | I | PB |
|---|---|---|---|---|---|---|---|---|---|
| 3 | 2 | 3 | 3 | 2 | 3 | 3 | 3 | 3 | 5 |

## The 5 Games to Play

| | | | | | | |
|---|---|---|---|---|---|---|
| 1. | A | B | D | H | I | PB |
| 2. | A | C | F | G | H | PB |
| 3. | A | D | E | H | I | PB |
| 4. | B | C | E | F | G | PB |
| 5. | C | D | F | G | I | PB |

# POWERBALL BALANCED WHEEL® 52010PB

## Wheel 10 Numbers + PB in 6 Games for a 2 of 2 Win

With Powerball

| Numbers Matched | Maximum Wins 5 + 1 | 4 + 1 | 3 + 1 | 2 + 1 | 1 + 1 | 0 + 1 | Minimum Wins 5 + 1 | 4 + 1 | 3 + 1 | 2 + 1 | 1 + 1 | 0 + 1 |
|---|---|---|---|---|---|---|---|---|---|---|---|---|
| 5 + 1 | 1 | 0 | 0 | 5 | 0 | 0 | 0 | 0 | 3 | 3 | 0 | 0 |
| 4 + 1 | - | 1 | 0 | 3 | 2 | 0 | - | 0 | 0 | 6 | 0 | 0 |
| 3 + 1 | - | - | 1 | 2 | 2 | 1 | - | - | 0 | 3 | 3 | 0 |
| 2 + 1 | - | - | - | 2 | 2 | 2 | - | - | - | 1 | 4 | 1 |
| 1 + 1 | - | - | - | - | 3 | 3 | - | - | - | - | 3 | 3 |
| 0 + 1 | - | - | - | - | - | 6 | - | - | - | - | - | 6 |

Without Powerball

| Numbers Matched | Maximum Wins 5 + 0 | 4 + 0 | 3 + 0 | 2 + 0 | 1 + 0 | Minimum Wins 5 + 0 | 4 + 0 | 3 + 0 | 2 + 0 | 1 + 0 |
|---|---|---|---|---|---|---|---|---|---|---|
| 5 + 0 | 1 | 0 | 0 | 5 | 0 | 0 | 0 | 3 | 3 | 0 |
| 4 + 0 | - | 1 | 0 | 3 | 2 | - | 0 | 0 | 6 | 0 |
| 3 + 0 | - | - | 1 | 2 | 2 | - | - | 0 | 3 | 3 |
| 2 + 0 | - | - | - | 2 | 2 | - | - | - | 1 | 4 |
| 1 + 0 | - | - | - | - | 3 | - | - | - | - | 3 |

## Your 10 Numbers + PB to Wheel

| A | B | C | D | E | F | G | H | I | J | PB |
|---|---|---|---|---|---|---|---|---|---|---|
| 3 | 3 | 3 | 3 | 3 | 3 | 3 | 3 | 3 | 3 | 6 |

## The 6 Games to Play

| | | | | | | |
|---|---|---|---|---|---|---|
| 1. | A | B | C | I | J | PB |
| 2. | A | D | F | G | J | PB |
| 3. | A | E | F | H | I | PB |
| 4. | B | C | F | G | H | PB |
| 5. | B | D | E | H | J | PB |
| 6. | C | D | E | G | I | PB |



# POWERBALL BALANCED WHEEL® 52011PB

## Wheel 11 Numbers + PB in 7 Games for a 2 of 2 Win

With Powerball

| Numbers Matched | Maximum Wins 5 + 1 | 4 + 1 | 3 + 1 | 2 + 1 | 1 + 1 | 0 + 1 | Minimum Wins 5 + 1 | 4 + 1 | 3 + 1 | 2 + 1 | 1 + 1 | 0 + 1 |
|---|---|---|---|---|---|---|---|---|---|---|---|---|
| 5 + 1 | 1 | 0 | 3 | 0 | 3 | 0 | 0 | 0 | 2 | 4 | 1 | 0 |
| 4 + 1 | - | 1 | 2 | 1 | 2 | 1 | - | 0 | 0 | 6 | 0 | 1 |
| 3 + 1 | - | - | 2 | 2 | 1 | 2 | - | - | 0 | 3 | 3 | 1 |
| 2 + 1 | - | - | - | 4 | 0 | 3 | - | - | - | 1 | 4 | 2 |
| 1 + 1 | - | - | - | - | 4 | 3 | - | - | - | - | 3 | 4 |
| 0 + 1 | - | - | - | - | - | 7 | - | - | - | - | - | 7 |

Without Powerball

| Numbers Matched | Maximum Wins 5 + 0 | 4 + 0 | 3 + 0 | 2 + 0 | 1 + 0 | Minimum Wins 5 + 0 | 4 + 0 | 3 + 0 | 2 + 0 | 1 + 0 |
|---|---|---|---|---|---|---|---|---|---|---|
| 5 + 0 | 1 | 0 | 3 | 0 | 3 | 0 | 0 | 2 | 4 | 1 |
| 4 + 0 | - | 1 | 2 | 1 | 2 | - | 0 | 0 | 6 | 0 |
| 3 + 0 | - | - | 2 | 2 | 1 | - | - | 0 | 3 | 3 |
| 2 + 0 | - | - | - | 4 | 0 | - | - | - | 1 | 4 |
| 1 + 0 | - | - | - | - | 4 | - | - | - | - | 3 |

(Continued Next Page)

**POWERBALL BALANCED WHEEL® 52011PB** (Continued from previous page)

## Your 11 Numbers + PB to Wheel

| A | B | C | D | E | F |
|---|---|---|---|---|---|
| 4 | 3 | 3 | 3 | 3 | 3 |

| G | H | I | J | K | PB |
|---|---|---|---|---|---|
| 3 | 3 | 3 | 3 | 4 | 7 |

## The 7 Games to Play

| | | | | | | |
|---|---|---|---|---|---|---|
| 1. | A | B | C | I | K | PB |
| 2. | A | C | E | G | K | PB |
| 3. | A | D | E | J | K | PB |
| 4. | A | F | G | H | K | PB |
| 5. | B | D | G | I | J | PB |
| 6. | B | E | F | H | I | PB |
| 7. | C | D | F | H | J | PB |



# POWERBALL BALANCED WHEEL® 52012PB

## Wheel 12 Numbers + PB in 9 Games for a 2 of 2 Win

With Powerball

| Numbers Matched | Maximum Wins 5 + 1 | 4 + 1 | 3 + 1 | 2 + 1 | 1 + 1 | 0 + 1 | Minimum Wins 5 + 1 | 4 + 1 | 3 + 1 | 2 + 1 | 1 + 1 | 0 + 1 |
|---|---|---|---|---|---|---|---|---|---|---|---|---|
| 5 + 1 | 1 | 1 | 0 | 4 | 3 | 0 | 0 | 0 | 1 | 7 | 1 | 0 |
| 4 + 1 | - | 2 | 0 | 2 | 4 | 1 | - | 0 | 0 | 6 | 1 | 2 |
| 3 + 1 | - | - | 2 | 2 | 2 | 3 | - | - | 0 | 3 | 3 | 3 |
| 2 + 1 | - | - | - | 4 | 0 | 5 | - | - | - | 1 | 4 | 4 |
| 1 + 1 | - | - | - | - | 4 | 5 | - | - | - | - | 3 | 6 |
| 0 + 1 | - | - | - | - | - | 9 | - | - | - | - | - | 9 |

Without Powerball

| Numbers Matched | Maximum Wins 5 + 0 | 4 + 0 | 3 + 0 | 2 + 0 | 1 + 0 | Minimum Wins 5 + 0 | 4 + 0 | 3 + 0 | 2 + 0 | 1 + 0 |
|---|---|---|---|---|---|---|---|---|---|---|
| 5 + 0 | 1 | 1 | 0 | 4 | 3 | 0 | 0 | 1 | 7 | 1 |
| 4 + 0 | - | 2 | 0 | 2 | 4 | - | 0 | 0 | 6 | 1 |
| 3 + 0 | - | - | 2 | 2 | 2 | - | - | 0 | 3 | 3 |
| 2 + 0 | - | - | - | 4 | 0 | - | - | - | 1 | 4 |
| 1 + 0 | - | - | - | - | 4 | - | - | - | - | 3 |

## Your 12 Numbers + PB to Wheel

| A | B | C | D | E | F | G |
|---|---|---|---|---|---|---|
| 4 | 4 | 4 | 4 | 4 | 3 | 4 |

| H | I | J | K | L | PB |
|---|---|---|---|---|---|
| 3 | 4 | 4 | 3 | 4 | 9 |

## The 9 Games to Play

| | | | | | | |
|---|---|---|---|---|---|---|
| 1. | A | B | I | K | L | PB |
| 2. | A | C | G | I | J | PB |
| 3. | A | D | F | I | J | PB |
| 4. | A | E | G | H | I | PB |
| 5. | B | C | F | H | L | PB |
| 6. | B | D | E | G | L | PB |
| 7. | B | D | E | J | L | PB |
| 8. | C | D | H | J | K | PB |
| 9. | C | E | F | G | K | PB |

# POWERBALL BALANCED WHEEL® 52013PB

## Wheel 13 Numbers + PB in 10 Games for a 2 of 2 Win

With Powerball

| Numbers Matched | Maximum Wins 5 + 1 | 4 + 1 | 3 + 1 | 2 + 1 | 1 + 1 | 0 + 1 | Minimum Wins 5 + 1 | 4 + 1 | 3 + 1 | 2 + 1 | 1 + 1 | 0 + 1 |
|---|---|---|---|---|---|---|---|---|---|---|---|---|
| 5 + 1 | 1 | 0 | 2 | 2 | 5 | 0 | 0 | 0 | 1 | 7 | 1 | 1 |
| 4 + 1 | - | 1 | 1 | 3 | 3 | 2 | - | 0 | 0 | 6 | 2 | 2 |
| 3 + 1 | - | - | 2 | 2 | 2 | 4 | - | - | 0 | 3 | 4 | 3 |
| 2 + 1 | - | - | - | 4 | 0 | 6 | - | - | - | 1 | 4 | 5 |
| 1 + 1 | - | - | - | - | 4 | 6 | - | - | - | - | 3 | 7 |
| 0 + 1 | - | - | - | - | - | 10 | - | - | - | - | - | 10 |

Without Powerball

| Numbers Matched | Maximum Wins 5 + 0 | 4 + 0 | 3 + 0 | 2 + 0 | 1 + 0 | Minimum Wins 5 + 0 | 4 + 0 | 3 + 0 | 2 + 0 | 1 + 0 |
|---|---|---|---|---|---|---|---|---|---|---|
| 5 + 0 | 1 | 0 | 2 | 2 | 5 | 0 | 0 | 1 | 7 | 1 |
| 4 + 0 | - | 1 | 1 | 3 | 3 | - | 0 | 0 | 6 | 2 |
| 3 + 0 | - | - | 2 | 2 | 2 | - | - | 0 | 3 | 4 |
| 2 + 0 | - | - | - | 4 | 0 | - | - | - | 1 | 4 |
| 1 + 0 | - | - | - | - | 4 | - | - | - | - | 3 |

## Your 13 Numbers + PB to Wheel

| A | B | C | D | E | F | G |
|---|---|---|---|---|---|---|
| 4 | 4 | 4 | 4 | 3 | 4 | 3 |
| **H** | **I** | **J** | **K** | **L** | **M** | **PB** |
| 4 | 4 | 4 | 4 | 4 | 4 | 10 |

## The 10 Games to Play

| | | | | | | |
|---|---|---|---|---|---|---|
| 1. | A | B | F | K | L | PB |
| 2. | A | C | D | K | M | PB |
| 3. | A | E | G | H | K | PB |
| 4. | A | H | I | J | K | PB |
| 5. | B | C | E | I | L | PB |
| 6. | B | C | G | J | L | PB |
| 7. | B | D | H | L | M | PB |
| 8. | C | F | H | I | J | PB |
| 9. | D | E | F | J | M | PB |
| 10. | D | F | G | I | M | PB |



# POWERBALL BALANCED WHEEL® 52014PB

## Wheel 14 Numbers + PB in 12 Games for a 2 of 2 Win

With Powerball

| Numbers Matched | Maximum Wins 5 + 1 | 4 + 1 | 3 + 1 | 2 + 1 | 1 + 1 | 0 + 1 | Minimum Wins 5 + 1 | 4 + 1 | 3 + 1 | 2 + 1 | 1 + 1 | 0 + 1 |
|---|---|---|---|---|---|---|---|---|---|---|---|---|
| 5 + 1 | 1 | 0 | 2 | 3 | 6 | 0 | 0 | 0 | 0 | 10 | 1 | 1 |
| 4 + 1 | - | 1 | 2 | 1 | 7 | 1 | - | 0 | 0 | 6 | 4 | 2 |
| 3 + 1 | - | - | 2 | 1 | 7 | 2 | - | - | 0 | 3 | 6 | 3 |
| 2 + 1 | - | - | - | 4 | 0 | 8 | - | - | - | 1 | 6 | 5 |
| 1 + 1 | - | - | - | - | 5 | 7 | - | - | - | - | 4 | 8 |
| 0 + 1 | - | - | - | - | - | 12 | - | - | - | - | - | 12 |

(Continued Next Page)

## POWERBALL BALANCED WHEEL® 52014PB (Continued from previous page)

Without Powerball

| Numbers Matched | Maximum Wins 5 + 0 | 4 + 0 | 3 + 0 | 2 + 0 | 1 + 0 | Minimum Wins 5 + 0 | 4 + 0 | 3 + 0 | 2 + 0 | 1 + 0 |
|---|---|---|---|---|---|---|---|---|---|---|
| 5 + 0 | 1 | 0 | 2 | 3 | 6 | 0 | 0 | 0 | 10 | 1 |
| 4 + 0 | - | 1 | 2 | 1 | 7 | - | 0 | 0 | 6 | 4 |
| 3 + 0 | - | - | 2 | 1 | 7 | - | - | 0 | 3 | 6 |
| 2 + 0 | - | - | - | 4 | 0 | - | - | - | 1 | 6 |
| 1 + 0 | - | - | - | - | 5 | - | - | - | - | 4 |

## Your 14 Numbers + PB to Wheel

| A | B | C | D | E | F | G | H |
|---|---|---|---|---|---|---|---|
| 4 | 4 | 4 | 5 | 5 | 5 | 4 | 4 |

| I | J | K | L | M | N | PB |
|---|---|---|---|---|---|---|
| 4 | 4 | 4 | 4 | 5 | 4 | 12 |

## The 12 Games to Play

| | | | | | | |
|---|---|---|---|---|---|---|
| 1. | A | B | F | G | N | PB |
| 2. | A | C | F | L | M | PB |
| 3. | A | D | E | J | M | PB |
| 4. | A | H | I | K | M | PB |
| 5. | B | C | J | K | N | PB |
| 6. | B | D | H | M | N | PB |
| 7. | B | E | I | L | N | PB |
| 8. | C | D | G | I | K | PB |
| 9. | C | E | G | H | M | PB |
| 10. | D | E | F | I | J | PB |
| 11. | D | E | F | K | L | PB |
| 12. | F | G | H | J | L | PB |



# POWERBALL BALANCED WHEEL® 52015PB

## Wheel 15 Numbers + PB in 13 Games for a 2 of 2 Win

With Powerball

| Numbers Matched | Maximum Wins 5 + 1 | 4 + 1 | 3 + 1 | 2 + 1 | 1 + 1 | 0 + 1 | Minimum Wins 5 + 1 | 4 + 1 | 3 + 1 | 2 + 1 | 1 + 1 | 0 + 1 |
|---|---|---|---|---|---|---|---|---|---|---|---|---|
| 5 + 1 | 1 | 0 | 0 | 7 | 5 | 0 | 0 | 0 | 0 | 10 | 1 | 2 |
| 4 + 1 | - | 1 | 0 | 5 | 6 | 1 | - | 0 | 0 | 6 | 4 | 3 |
| 3 + 1 | - | - | 1 | 4 | 3 | 5 | - | - | 0 | 3 | 6 | 4 |
| 2 + 1 | - | - | - | 4 | 2 | 7 | - | - | - | 1 | 6 | 6 |
| 1 + 1 | - | - | - | - | 6 | 7 | - | - | - | - | 4 | 9 |
| 0 + 1 | - | - | - | - | - | 13 | - | - | - | - | - | 13 |

Without Powerball

| Numbers Matched | Maximum Wins 5 + 0 | 4 + 0 | 3 + 0 | 2 + 0 | 1 + 0 | Minimum Wins 5 + 0 | 4 + 0 | 3 + 0 | 2 + 0 | 1 + 0 |
|---|---|---|---|---|---|---|---|---|---|---|
| 5 + 0 | 1 | 0 | 0 | 7 | 5 | 0 | 0 | 0 | 10 | 1 |
| 4 + 0 | - | 1 | 0 | 5 | 6 | - | 0 | 0 | 6 | 4 |
| 3 + 0 | - | - | 1 | 4 | 3 | - | - | 0 | 3 | 6 |
| 2 + 0 | - | - | - | 4 | 2 | - | - | - | 1 | 6 |
| 1 + 0 | - | - | - | - | 6 | - | - | - | - | 4 |

## Your 15 Numbers + PB to Wheel

| A | B | C | D | E | F | G | H |
|---|---|---|---|---|---|---|---|
| 5 | 4 | 4 | 4 | 5 | 4 | 4 | 4 |

| I | J | K | L | M | N | O | PB |
|---|---|---|---|---|---|---|---|
| 5 | 4 | 4 | 4 | 6 | 4 | 4 | 13 |

(Continued Next Page)

**POWERBALL BALANCED WHEEL® 52015PB** (Continued from previous page)

## The 13 Games to Play

| | | | | | | |
|---|---|---|---|---|---|---|
| 1. | A | B | H | L | N | PB |
| 2. | A | C | D | M | N | PB |
| 3. | A | E | J | K | L | PB |
| 4. | A | F | H | I | O | PB |
| 5. | A | G | K | N | O | PB |
| 6. | B | C | J | M | O | PB |
| 7. | B | D | F | K | M | PB |
| 8. | B | E | G | I | M | PB |
| 9. | C | E | H | I | K | PB |
| 10. | C | F | G | L | M | PB |
| 11. | D | E | I | L | O | PB |
| 12. | D | G | H | J | M | PB |
| 13. | E | F | I | J | N | PB |



# POWERBALL BALANCED WHEEL® 52016PB

## Wheel 16 Numbers + PB in 15 Games for a 2 of 2 Win

With Powerball

| Numbers Matched | Maximum Wins 5 + 1 | 4 + 1 | 3 + 1 | 2 + 1 | 1 + 1 | 0 + 1 | Minimum Wins 5 + 1 | 4 + 1 | 3 + 1 | 2 + 1 | 1 + 1 | 0 + 1 |
|---|---|---|---|---|---|---|---|---|---|---|---|---|
| 5 + 1 | 1 | 0 | 1 | 7 | 6 | 0 | 0 | 0 | 0 | 10 | 2 | 3 |
| 4 + 1 | - | 1 | 1 | 4 | 7 | 2 | - | 0 | 0 | 6 | 4 | 5 |
| 3 + 1 | - | - | 2 | 1 | 8 | 4 | - | - | 0 | 3 | 6 | 6 |
| 2 + 1 | - | - | - | 4 | 3 | 8 | - | - | - | 1 | 6 | 8 |
| 1 + 1 | - | - | - | - | 6 | 9 | - | - | - | - | 4 | 11 |
| 0 + 1 | - | - | - | - | - | 15 | - | - | - | - | - | 15 |

Without Powerball

| Numbers Matched | Maximum Wins 5 + 0 | 4 + 0 | 3 + 0 | 2 + 0 | 1 + 0 | Minimum Wins 5 + 0 | 4 + 0 | 3 + 0 | 2 + 0 | 1 + 0 |
|---|---|---|---|---|---|---|---|---|---|---|
| 5 + 0 | 1 | 0 | 1 | 7 | 6 | 0 | 0 | 0 | 10 | 2 |
| 4 + 0 | - | 1 | 1 | 4 | 7 | - | 0 | 0 | 6 | 4 |
| 3 + 0 | - | - | 2 | 1 | 8 | - | - | 0 | 3 | 6 |
| 2 + 0 | - | - | - | 4 | 3 | - | - | - | 1 | 6 |
| 1 + 0 | - | - | - | - | 6 | - | - | - | - | 4 |

## Your 16 Numbers + PB to Wheel

| A | B | C | D | E | F | G | H | I |
|---|---|---|---|---|---|---|---|---|
| 4 | 6 | 5 | 4 | 6 | 4 | 5 | 5 | 4 |

| J | K | L | M | N | O | P | PB |
|---|---|---|---|---|---|---|---|
| 4 | 4 | 4 | 6 | 5 | 4 | 5 | 15 |

## The 15 Games to Play

| | | | | | | |
|---|---|---|---|---|---|---|
| 1. | A | B | E | L | O | PB |
| 2. | A | C | E | G | P | PB |
| 3. | A | D | H | J | N | PB |
| 4. | A | F | I | K | M | PB |
| 5. | B | C | M | N | P | PB |
| 6. | B | D | I | O | P | PB |
| 7. | B | E | G | H | M | PB |
| 8. | B | E | J | K | P | PB |
| 9. | B | F | H | L | P | PB |
| 10. | C | D | E | F | M | PB |
| 11. | C | H | K | M | O | PB |
| 12. | C | I | J | L | M | PB |
| 13. | D | G | K | L | N | PB |
| 14. | E | G | H | I | N | PB |
| 15. | F | G | J | N | O | PB |

# POWERBALL BALANCED WHEEL® 52017PB

## Wheel 17 Numbers + PB in 16 Games for a 2 of 2 Win

With Powerball

| Numbers Matched | Maximum Wins 5 + 1 | 4 + 1 | 3 + 1 | 2 + 1 | 1 + 1 | 0 + 1 | Minimum Wins 5 + 1 | 4 + 1 | 3 + 1 | 2 + 1 | 1 + 1 | 0 + 1 |
|---|---|---|---|---|---|---|---|---|---|---|---|---|
| 5 + 1 | 1 | 1 | 0 | 3 | 11 | 0 | 0 | 0 | 0 | 10 | 3 | 3 |
| 4 + 1 | - | 2 | 0 | 3 | 7 | 4 | - | 0 | 0 | 6 | 4 | 6 |
| 3 + 1 | - | - | 2 | 2 | 6 | 6 | - | - | 0 | 3 | 6 | 7 |
| 2 + 1 | - | - | - | 4 | 2 | 10 | - | - | - | 1 | 6 | 9 |
| 1 + 1 | - | - | - | - | 6 | 10 | - | - | - | - | 4 | 12 |
| 0 + 1 | - | - | - | - | - | 16 | - | - | - | - | - | 16 |

Without Powerball

| Numbers Matched | Maximum Wins 5 + 0 | 4 + 0 | 3 + 0 | 2 + 0 | 1 + 0 | Minimum Wins 5 + 0 | 4 + 0 | 3 + 0 | 2 + 0 | 1 + 0 |
|---|---|---|---|---|---|---|---|---|---|---|
| 5 + 0 | 1 | 1 | 0 | 3 | 11 | 0 | 0 | 0 | 10 | 3 |
| 4 + 0 | - | 2 | 0 | 3 | 7 | - | 0 | 0 | 6 | 4 |
| 3 + 0 | - | - | 2 | 2 | 6 | - | - | 0 | 3 | 6 |
| 2 + 0 | - | - | - | 4 | 2 | - | - | - | 1 | 6 |
| 1 + 0 | - | - | - | - | 6 | - | - | - | - | 4 |

## Your 17 Numbers + PB to Wheel

| A | B | C | D | E | F | G | H | I |
|---|---|---|---|---|---|---|---|---|
| 5 | 5 | 4 | 5 | 5 | 4 | 4 | 4 | 5 |

| J | K | L | M | N | O | P | Q | PB |
|---|---|---|---|---|---|---|---|---|
| 5 | 6 | 4 | 5 | 5 | 5 | 4 | 5 | 16 |

## The 16 Games to Play

| | | | | | | |
|---|---|---|---|---|---|---|
| 1. | A | B | I | M | O | PB |
| 2. | A | C | F | H | O | PB |
| 3. | A | D | E | K | N | PB |
| 4. | A | G | L | O | P | PB |
| 5. | A | I | J | O | Q | PB |
| 6. | B | C | E | G | Q | PB |
| 7. | B | D | H | P | Q | PB |
| 8. | B | F | L | N | Q | PB |
| 9. | B | J | K | M | Q | PB |
| 10. | C | D | J | L | M | PB |
| 11. | C | I | K | N | P | PB |
| 12. | D | E | K | N | O | PB |
| 13. | D | F | G | I | K | PB |
| 14. | E | F | J | M | P | PB |
| 15. | E | H | I | K | L | PB |
| 16. | G | H | J | M | N | PB |



# POWERBALL BALANCED WHEEL® 52018PB

## Wheel 18 Numbers + PB in 19 Games for a 2 of 2 Win

With Powerball

| Numbers Matched | Maximum Wins 5 + 1 | 4 + 1 | 3 + 1 | 2 + 1 | 1 + 1 | 0 + 1 | Minimum Wins 5 + 1 | 4 + 1 | 3 + 1 | 2 + 1 | 1 + 1 | 0 + 1 |
|---|---|---|---|---|---|---|---|---|---|---|---|---|
| 5 + 1 | 1 | 0 | 1 | 6 | 9 | 2 | 0 | 0 | 0 | 10 | 5 | 4 |
| 4 + 1 | - | 1 | 1 | 4 | 8 | 5 | - | 0 | 0 | 6 | 8 | 5 |
| 3 + 1 | - | - | 2 | 1 | 10 | 6 | - | - | 0 | 3 | 9 | 7 |
| 2 + 1 | - | - | - | 4 | 4 | 11 | - | - | - | 1 | 8 | 10 |
| 1 + 1 | - | - | - | - | 7 | 12 | - | - | - | - | 5 | 14 |
| 0 + 1 | - | - | - | - | - | 19 | - | - | - | - | - | 19 |

(Continued Next Page)

## POWERBALL BALANCED WHEEL® 52018PB (Continued from previous page)

Without Powerball

| Numbers Matched | Maximum Wins 5 + 0 | 4 + 0 | 3 + 0 | 2 + 0 | 1 + 0 | Minimum Wins 5 + 0 | 4 + 0 | 3 + 0 | 2 + 0 | 1 + 0 |
|---|---|---|---|---|---|---|---|---|---|---|
| 5 + 0 | 1 | 0 | 1 | 6 | 9 | 0 | 0 | 0 | 10 | 5 |
| 4 + 0 | - | 1 | 1 | 4 | 8 | - | 0 | 0 | 6 | 8 |
| 3 + 0 | - | - | 2 | 1 | 10 | - | - | 0 | 3 | 9 |
| 2 + 0 | - | - | - | 4 | 4 | - | - | - | 1 | 8 |
| 1 + 0 | - | - | - | - | 7 | - | - | - | - | 5 |

## Your 18 Numbers + PB to Wheel

| A | B | C | D | E | F | G | H | I | J |
|---|---|---|---|---|---|---|---|---|---|
| 5 | 6 | 5 | 5 | 5 | 5 | 5 | 5 | 5 | 5 |

| K | L | M | N | O | P | Q | R | PB |
|---|---|---|---|---|---|---|---|---|
| 5 | 7 | 6 | 6 | 5 | 5 | 5 | 5 | 19 |

## The 19 Games to Play

| | | | | | | |
|---|---|---|---|---|---|---|
| 1. | A | B | C | M | *Q* | PB |
| 2. | A | D | F | K | P | PB |
| 3. | A | E | J | L | N | PB |
| 4. | A | G | H | I | O | PB |
| 5. | A | I | P | *Q* | R | PB |
| 6. | B | D | L | M | R | PB |
| 7. | B | E | H | K | R | PB |
| 8. | B | F | G | N | R | PB |
| 9. | B | F | I | J | N | PB |
| 10. | B | M | N | O | P | PB |
| 11. | C | D | J | O | R | PB |
| 12. | C | E | G | L | P | PB |
| 13. | C | F | H | L | M | PB |
| 14. | C | I | K | L | N | PB |
| 15. | D | E | I | L | M | PB |
| 16. | D | G | H | N | *Q* | PB |
| 17. | E | F | L | O | *Q* | PB |
| 18. | G | J | K | M | *Q* | PB |
| 19. | H | J | K | O | P | PB |



# POWERBALL BALANCED WHEEL® 52019PB

## Wheel 19 Numbers + PB in 20 Games for a 2 of 2 Win

With Powerball

| Numbers Matched | Maximum Wins 5 + 1 | 4 + 1 | 3 + 1 | 2 + 1 | 1 + 1 | 0 + 1 | Minimum Wins 5 + 1 | 4 + 1 | 3 + 1 | 2 + 1 | 1 + 1 | 0 + 1 |
|---|---|---|---|---|---|---|---|---|---|---|---|---|
| 5 + 1 | 1 | 0 | 1 | 4 | 11 | 3 | 0 | 0 | 0 | 10 | 5 | 5 |
| 4 + 1 | - | 1 | 1 | 2 | 11 | 5 | - | 0 | 0 | 6 | 8 | 6 |
| 3 + 1 | - | - | 2 | 0 | 11 | 7 | - | - | 0 | 3 | 9 | 8 |
| 2 + 1 | - | - | - | 3 | 5 | 12 | - | - | - | 1 | 8 | 11 |
| 1 + 1 | - | - | - | - | 6 | 14 | - | - | - | - | 5 | 15 |
| 0 + 1 | - | - | - | - | - | 20 | - | - | - | - | - | 20 |

Without Powerball

| Numbers Matched | Maximum Wins 5 + 0 | 4 + 0 | 3 + 0 | 2 + 0 | 1 + 0 | Minimum Wins 5 + 0 | 4 + 0 | 3 + 0 | 2 + 0 | 1 + 0 |
|---|---|---|---|---|---|---|---|---|---|---|
| 5 + 0 | 1 | 0 | 1 | 4 | 11 | 0 | 0 | 0 | 10 | 5 |
| 4 + 0 | - | 1 | 1 | 2 | 11 | - | 0 | 0 | 6 | 8 |
| 3 + 0 | - | - | 2 | 0 | 11 | - | - | 0 | 3 | 9 |
| 2 + 0 | - | - | - | 3 | 5 | - | - | - | 1 | 8 |
| 1 + 0 | - | - | - | - | 6 | - | - | - | - | 5 |

(Continued Next Page)

**POWERBALL BALANCED WHEEL® 52019PB** (Continued from previous page)

## Your 19 Numbers + PB to Wheel

| A | B | C | D | E | F | G | H | I | J |
|---|---|---|---|---|---|---|---|---|---|
| 5 | 6 | 5 | 5 | 6 | 5 | 5 | 5 | 6 | 5 |

| K | L | M | N | O | P | Q | R | S | PB |
|---|---|---|---|---|---|---|---|---|---|
| 5 | 5 | 5 | 5 | 5 | 6 | 5 | 6 | 5 | 20 |

## The 20 Games to Play

| | | | | | | | | | | | | | |
|---|---|---|---|---|---|---|---|---|---|---|---|---|---|
| 1. | A | B | P | Q | R | PB | 11. | C | D | E | Q | S | PB |
| 2. | A | C | H | L | N | PB | 12. | C | D | I | J | L | PB |
| 3. | A | D | F | K | R | PB | 13. | C | G | K | O | R | PB |
| 4. | A | E | G | J | P | PB | 14. | D | G | M | N | P | PB |
| 5. | A | I | M | O | S | PB | 15. | E | F | L | O | P | PB |
| 6. | B | C | F | M | P | PB | 16. | E | H | I | M | R | PB |
| 7. | B | D | H | J | O | PB | 17. | F | G | H | I | Q | PB |
| 8. | B | E | I | K | N | PB | 18. | F | J | N | R | S | PB |
| 9. | B | E | N | O | Q | PB | 19. | H | I | K | P | S | PB |
| 10. | B | G | L | R | S | PB | 20. | J | K | L | M | Q | PB |



# POWERBALL BALANCED WHEEL® 52020PB

## Wheel 20 Numbers + PB in 21 Games for a 2 of 2 Win

With Powerball

| Numbers Matched | Maximum Wins 5 + 1 | 4 + 1 | 3 + 1 | 2 + 1 | 1 + 1 | 0 + 1 | Minimum Wins 5 + 1 | 4 + 1 | 3 + 1 | 2 + 1 | 1 + 1 | 0 + 1 |
|---|---|---|---|---|---|---|---|---|---|---|---|---|
| 5 + 1 | 1 | 0 | 0 | 5 | 15 | 0 | 0 | 0 | 0 | 10 | 5 | 6 |
| 4 + 1 | - | 1 | 0 | 4 | 13 | 3 | - | 0 | 0 | 6 | 8 | 7 |
| 3 + 1 | - | - | 1 | 3 | 11 | 6 | - | - | 0 | 3 | 9 | 9 |
| 2 + 1 | - | - | - | 2 | 10 | 9 | - | - | - | 1 | 8 | 12 |
| 1 + 1 | - | - | - | - | 8 | 13 | - | - | - | - | 5 | 16 |
| 0 + 1 | - | - | - | - | - | 21 | - | - | - | - | - | 21 |

Without Powerball

| Numbers Matched | Maximum Wins 5 + 0 | 4 + 0 | 3 + 0 | 2 + 0 | 1 + 0 | Minimum Wins 5 + 0 | 4 + 0 | 3 + 0 | 2 + 0 | 1 + 0 |
|---|---|---|---|---|---|---|---|---|---|---|
| 5 + 0 | 1 | 0 | 0 | 5 | 15 | 0 | 0 | 0 | 10 | 5 |
| 4 + 0 | - | 1 | 0 | 4 | 13 | - | 0 | 0 | 6 | 8 |
| 3 + 0 | - | - | 1 | 3 | 11 | - | - | 0 | 3 | 9 |
| 2 + 0 | - | - | - | 2 | 10 | - | - | - | 1 | 8 |
| 1 + 0 | - | - | - | - | 8 | - | - | - | - | 5 |

## Your 20 Numbers + PB to Wheel

| A | B | C | D | E | F | G | H | I | J | K |
|---|---|---|---|---|---|---|---|---|---|---|
| 5 | 5 | 5 | 5 | 5 | 5 | 5 | 5 | 5 | 5 | 5 |

| L | M | N | O | P | Q | R | S | T | PB |
|---|---|---|---|---|---|---|---|---|---|
| 5 | 5 | 5 | 8 | 6 | 6 | 5 | 5 | 5 | 21 |

(Continued Next Page)

**POWERBALL BALANCED WHEEL® 52020PB** (Continued from previous page)

## The 21 Games to Play

| | | | | | | |
|---|---|---|---|---|---|---|
| 1. | A | B | J | M | N | PB |
| 2. | A | C | E | O | P | PB |
| 3. | A | D | G | K | O | PB |
| 4. | A | F | H | L | R | PB |
| 5. | A | I | Q | S | T | PB |
| 6. | B | C | D | H | T | PB |
| 7. | B | E | K | L | Q | PB |
| 8. | B | F | O | Q | S | PB |
| 9. | B | G | I | P | R | PB |
| 10. | C | F | G | J | Q | PB |
| 11. | C | I | L | N | O | PB |
| 12. | C | K | M | R | S | PB |
| 13. | D | E | F | I | M | PB |
| 14. | D | J | L | P | S | PB |
| 15. | D | N | P | Q | R | PB |
| 16. | E | G | H | N | S | PB |
| 17. | E | J | O | R | T | PB |
| 18. | F | K | N | P | T | PB |
| 19. | G | L | M | O | T | PB |
| 20. | H | I | J | K | O | PB |
| 21. | H | M | O | P | Q | PB |



# POWERBALL BALANCED WHEEL® 52022PB

## Wheel 22 Numbers + PB in 27 Games for a 2 of 2 Win

With Powerball

| Numbers Matched | Maximum Wins 5 + 1 | 4 + 1 | 3 + 1 | 2 + 1 | 1 + 1 | 0 + 1 | Minimum Wins 5 + 1 | 4 + 1 | 3 + 1 | 2 + 1 | 1 + 1 | 0 + 1 |
|---|---|---|---|---|---|---|---|---|---|---|---|---|
| 5 + 1 | 1 | 1 | 0 | 3 | 18 | 4 | 0 | 0 | 0 | 10 | 10 | 7 |
| 4 + 1 | - | 2 | 0 | 0 | 19 | 6 | - | 0 | 0 | 6 | 12 | 9 |
| 3 + 1 | - | - | 2 | 0 | 15 | 10 | - | - | 0 | 3 | 12 | 12 |
| 2 + 1 | - | - | - | 2 | 10 | 15 | - | - | - | 1 | 10 | 16 |
| 1 + 1 | - | - | - | - | 7 | 20 | - | - | - | - | 6 | 21 |
| 0 + 1 | - | - | - | - | - | 27 | - | - | - | - | - | 27 |

Without Powerball

| Numbers Matched | Maximum Wins 5 + 0 | 4 + 0 | 3 + 0 | 2 + 0 | 1 + 0 | Minimum Wins 5 + 0 | 4 + 0 | 3 + 0 | 2 + 0 | 1 + 0 |
|---|---|---|---|---|---|---|---|---|---|---|
| 5 + 0 | 1 | 1 | 0 | 3 | 18 | 0 | 0 | 0 | 10 | 10 |
| 4 + 0 | - | 2 | 0 | 0 | 19 | - | 0 | 0 | 6 | 12 |
| 3 + 0 | - | - | 2 | 0 | 15 | - | - | 0 | 3 | 12 |
| 2 + 0 | - | - | - | 2 | 10 | - | - | - | 1 | 10 |
| 1 + 0 | - | - | - | - | 7 | - | - | - | - | 6 |

## Your 22 Numbers + PB to Wheel

| A | B | C | D | E | F | G | H |
|---|---|---|---|---|---|---|---|
| 6 | 6 | 6 | 6 | 6 | 6 | 7 | 7 |
| **I** | **J** | **K** | **L** | **M** | **N** | **O** | **P** |
| 6 | 6 | 6 | 6 | 6 | 6 | 7 | 6 |
| **Q** | **R** | **S** | **T** | **U** | **V** | **PB** | |
| 6 | 6 | 6 | 6 | 6 | 6 | 27 | |

## The 27 Games to Play

| | | | | | | |
|---|---|---|---|---|---|---|
| 1. | A | B | C | Q | R | PB |
| 2. | A | D | I | N | O | PB |
| 3. | A | E | G | J | P | PB |
| 4. | A | F | H | K | M | PB |



(Continued Next Page)

**POWERBALL BALANCED WHEEL® 52022PB** (Continued from previous page)

| | | | | | | |
|---|---|---|---|---|---|---|
| 5. | A | K | P | U | V | PB |
| 6. | A | L | S | T | U | PB |
| 7. | B | D | E | K | U | PB |
| 8. | B | F | N | P | S | PB |
| 9. | B | G | H | O | T | PB |
| 10. | B | G | M | R | V | PB |
| 11. | B | I | J | L | M | PB |
| 12. | C | D | M | P | T | PB |
| 13. | C | E | H | L | N | PB |
| 14. | C | E | L | Q | V | PB |
| 15. | C | F | J | O | U | PB |
| 16. | C | G | I | K | S | PB |
| 17. | D | F | G | L | Q | PB |
| 18. | D | H | J | R | S | PB |
| 19. | D | H | J | S | V | PB |
| 20. | E | F | I | R | T | PB |
| 21. | E | M | O | Q | S | PB |
| 22. | F | I | N | O | V | PB |
| 23. | G | H | O | T | V | PB |
| 24. | G | M | N | R | U | PB |
| 25. | H | I | P | Q | U | PB |
| 26. | J | K | N | Q | T | PB |
| 27. | K | L | O | P | R | PB |



# POWERBALL BALANCED WHEEL® 52023PB

## Wheel 23 Numbers + PB in 28 Games for a 2 of 2 Win

With Powerball

| Numbers Matched | Maximum Wins 5 + 1 | 4 + 1 | 3 + 1 | 2 + 1 | 1 + 1 | 0 + 1 | Minimum Wins 5 + 1 | 4 + 1 | 3 + 1 | 2 + 1 | 1 + 1 | 0 + 1 |
|---|---|---|---|---|---|---|---|---|---|---|---|---|
| 5 + 1 | 1 | 0 | 1 | 4 | 16 | 6 | 0 | 0 | 0 | 10 | 10 | 8 |
| 4 + 1 | - | 1 | 1 | 0 | 18 | 8 | - | 0 | 0 | 6 | 12 | 10 |
| 3 + 1 | - | - | 2 | 0 | 12 | 14 | - | - | 0 | 3 | 12 | 13 |
| 2 + 1 | - | - | - | 5 | 4 | 19 | - | - | - | 1 | 10 | 17 |
| 1 + 1 | - | - | - | - | 7 | 21 | - | - | - | - | 6 | 22 |
| 0 + 1 | - | - | - | - | - | 28 | - | - | - | - | - | 28 |

Without Powerball

| Numbers Matched | Maximum Wins 5 + 0 | 4 + 0 | 3 + 0 | 2 + 0 | 1 + 0 | Minimum Wins 5 + 0 | 4 + 0 | 3 + 0 | 2 + 0 | 1 + 0 |
|---|---|---|---|---|---|---|---|---|---|---|
| 5 + 0 | 1 | 0 | 1 | 4 | 16 | 0 | 0 | 0 | 10 | 10 |
| 4 + 0 | - | 1 | 1 | 0 | 18 | - | 0 | 0 | 6 | 12 |
| 3 + 0 | - | - | 2 | 0 | 12 | - | - | 0 | 3 | 12 |
| 2 + 0 | - | - | - | 5 | 4 | - | - | - | 1 | 10 |
| 1 + 0 | - | - | - | - | 7 | - | - | - | - | 6 |

## Your 23 Numbers + PB to Wheel

| A | B | C | D | E | F | G | H |
|---|---|---|---|---|---|---|---|
| 7 | 6 | 6 | 6 | 6 | 6 | 6 | 6 |
| **I** | **J** | **K** | **L** | **M** | **N** | **O** | **P** |
| 6 | 6 | 6 | 6 | 6 | 6 | 6 | 6 |
| **Q** | **R** | **S** | **T** | **U** | **V** | **W** | **PB** |
| 6 | 6 | 7 | 6 | 6 | 6 | 6 | 28 |

## The 28 Games to Play

| | | | | | | |
|---|---|---|---|---|---|---|
| 1. | A | B | H | P | R | PB |
| 2. | A | C | L | N | S | PB |
| 3. | A | D | G | P | S | PB |
| 4. | A | E | I | K | P | PB |



(Continued Next Page)

## POWERBALL BALANCED WHEEL® 52023PB (Continued from previous page)

| | | | | | | |
|---|---|---|---|---|---|---|
| 5. | A | F | Q | S | T | PB |
| 6. | A | J | M | S | V | PB |
| 7. | A | O | S | U | W | PB |
| 8. | B | C | G | O | U | PB |
| 9. | B | D | H | I | S | PB |
| 10. | B | E | F | L | M | PB |
| 11. | B | J | R | T | V | PB |
| 12. | B | K | N | Q | W | PB |
| 13. | C | D | L | N | R | PB |
| 14. | C | E | H | Q | V | PB |
| 15. | C | F | I | J | K | PB |
| 16. | C | M | P | T | W | PB |
| 17. | D | E | J | U | W | PB |
| 18. | D | F | G | Q | T | PB |
| 19. | D | K | M | O | V | PB |
| 20. | E | G | K | R | S | PB |
| 21. | E | I | N | O | T | PB |
| 22. | F | H | O | R | W | PB |
| 23. | F | N | P | U | V | PB |
| 24. | G | H | J | M | N | PB |
| 25. | G | I | L | V | W | PB |
| 26. | H | K | L | T | U | PB |
| 27. | I | M | Q | R | U | PB |
| 28. | J | L | O | P | Q | PB |



# POWERBALL BALANCED WHEEL® 52024PB

## Wheel 24 Numbers + PB in 32 Games for a 2 of 2 Win

With Powerball

| Numbers Matched | Maximum Wins 5 + 1 | 4 + 1 | 3 + 1 | 2 + 1 | 1 + 1 | 0 + 1 | Minimum Wins 5 + 1 | 4 + 1 | 3 + 1 | 2 + 1 | 1 + 1 | 0 + 1 |
|---|---|---|---|---|---|---|---|---|---|---|---|---|
| 5 + 1 | 1 | 0 | 1 | 8 | 13 | 9 | 0 | 0 | 0 | 10 | 10 | 12 |
| 4 + 1 | - | 1 | 1 | 7 | 10 | 13 | - | 0 | 0 | 6 | 12 | 14 |
| 3 + 1 | - | - | 2 | 7 | 5 | 18 | - | - | 0 | 3 | 12 | 17 |
| 2 + 1 | - | - | - | 5 | 7 | 20 | - | - | - | 1 | 10 | 21 |
| 1 + 1 | - | - | - | - | 9 | 23 | - | - | - | - | 6 | 26 |
| 0 + 1 | - | - | - | - | - | 32 | - | - | - | - | - | 32 |

Without Powerball

| Numbers Matched | Maximum Wins 5 + 0 | 4 + 0 | 3 + 0 | 2 + 0 | 1 + 0 | Minimum Wins 5 + 0 | 4 + 0 | 3 + 0 | 2 + 0 | 1 + 0 |
|---|---|---|---|---|---|---|---|---|---|---|
| 5 + 0 | 1 | 0 | 1 | 8 | 13 | 0 | 0 | 0 | 10 | 10 |
| 4 + 0 | - | 1 | 1 | 7 | 10 | - | 0 | 0 | 6 | 12 |
| 3 + 0 | - | - | 2 | 7 | 5 | - | - | 0 | 3 | 12 |
| 2 + 0 | - | - | - | 5 | 7 | - | - | - | 1 | 10 |
| 1 + 0 | - | - | - | - | 9 | - | - | - | - | 6 |

## Your 24 Numbers + PB to Wheel

| A | B | C | D | E | F | G | H | I |
|---|---|---|---|---|---|---|---|---|
| 6 | 6 | 7 | 8 | 7 | 6 | 7 | 8 | 9 |
| **J** | **K** | **L** | **M** | **N** | **O** | **P** | **Q** | **R** |
| 7 | 6 | 6 | 7 | 6 | 6 | 6 | 6 | 6 |
| **S** | **T** | **U** | **V** | **W** | **X** | **PB** | | |
| 6 | 6 | 7 | 6 | 7 | 8 | 32 | | |

## The 32 Games to Play

| | | | | | | |
|---|---|---|---|---|---|---|
| 1. | A | B | D | N | Q | PB |
| 2. | A | C | J | L | T | PB |
| 3. | A | E | F | M | R | PB |
| 4. | A | G | O | P | S | PB |



(Continued Next Page)

## POWERBALL BALANCED WHEEL® 52024PB (Continued from previous page)

| | | | | | | | | | | | | | |
|---|---|---|---|---|---|---|---|---|---|---|---|---|---|
| 5. | A | H | I | S | X | PB | 19. | D | F | L | P | U | PB |
| 6. | A | K | U | V | W | PB | 20. | D | G | H | I | W | PB |
| 7. | B | C | F | K | S | PB | 21. | D | I | R | V | X | PB |
| 8. | B | E | H | I | T | PB | 22. | D | M | S | T | W | PB |
| 9. | B | G | L | R | W | PB | 23. | E | H | I | N | P | PB |
| 10. | B | J | M | P | V | PB | 24. | E | L | Q | S | V | PB |
| 11. | B | O | T | U | X | PB | 25. | F | G | N | T | V | PB |
| 12. | C | D | I | J | M | PB | 26. | F | H | J | Q | X | PB |
| 13. | C | E | I | U | X | PB | 27. | F | I | O | Q | W | PB |
| 14. | C | G | M | Q | U | PB | 28. | G | H | M | U | X | PB |
| 15. | C | H | O | R | V | PB | 29. | H | I | K | L | X | PB |
| 16. | C | N | P | W | X | PB | 30. | J | N | R | S | U | PB |
| 17. | D | E | G | J | K | PB | 31. | K | L | M | N | O | PB |
| 18. | D | E | J | O | W | PB | 32. | K | P | Q | R | T | PB |



# POWERBALL BALANCED WHEEL® 52025PB

## Wheel 25 Numbers + PB in 36 Games for a 2 of 2 Win

With Powerball

| Numbers Matched | Maximum Wins 5 + 1 | 4 + 1 | 3 + 1 | 2 + 1 | 1 + 1 | 0 + 1 | Minimum Wins 5 + 1 | 4 + 1 | 3 + 1 | 2 + 1 | 1 + 1 | 0 + 1 |
|---|---|---|---|---|---|---|---|---|---|---|---|---|
| 5 + 1 | 1 | 1 | 0 | 2 | 24 | 8 | 0 | 0 | 0 | 10 | 13 | 13 |
| 4 + 1 | - | 2 | 0 | 1 | 19 | 14 | - | 0 | 0 | 6 | 14 | 16 |
| 3 + 1 | - | - | 2 | 6 | 7 | 21 | - | - | 0 | 3 | 13 | 20 |
| 2 + 1 | - | - | - | 8 | 0 | 28 | - | - | - | 1 | 10 | 25 |
| 1 + 1 | - | - | - | - | 9 | 27 | - | - | - | - | 6 | 30 |
| 0 + 1 | - | - | - | - | - | 36 | - | - | - | - | - | 36 |

Without Powerball

| Numbers Matched | Maximum Wins 5 + 0 | 4 + 0 | 3 + 0 | 2 + 0 | 1 + 0 | Minimum Wins 5 + 0 | 4 + 0 | 3 + 0 | 2 + 0 | 1 + 0 |
|---|---|---|---|---|---|---|---|---|---|---|
| 5 + 0 | 1 | 1 | 0 | 2 | 24 | 0 | 0 | 0 | 10 | 13 |
| 4 + 0 | - | 2 | 0 | 1 | 19 | - | 0 | 0 | 6 | 14 |
| 3 + 0 | - | - | 2 | 6 | 7 | - | - | 0 | 3 | 13 |
| 2 + 0 | - | - | - | 8 | 0 | - | - | - | 1 | 10 |
| 1 + 0 | - | - | - | - | 9 | - | - | - | - | 6 |

## Your 25 Numbers + PB to Wheel

| A | B | C | D | E | F | G | H | I |
|---|---|---|---|---|---|---|---|---|
| 8 | 7 | 7 | 7 | 7 | 7 | 7 | 8 | 7 |
| **J** | **K** | **L** | **M** | **N** | **O** | **P** | **Q** | **R** |
| 8 | 7 | 6 | 7 | 7 | 7 | 7 | 8 | 7 |
| **S** | **T** | **U** | **V** | **W** | **X** | **Y** | **PB** | |
| 7 | 8 | 7 | 7 | 9 | 7 | 6 | 36 | |

(Continued Next Page)

**POWERBALL BALANCED WHEEL® 52025PB** (Continued from previous page)

## The 36 Games to Play

| | | | | | | |
|---|---|---|---|---|---|---|
| 1. | A | B | C | Q | T | PB |
| 2. | A | D | I | P | T | PB |
| 3. | A | E | T | U | W | PB |
| 4. | A | F | L | M | T | PB |
| 5. | A | G | H | S | T | PB |
| 6. | A | J | T | W | Y | PB |
| 7. | A | K | N | O | T | PB |
| 8. | A | R | T | V | X | PB |
| 9. | B | C | I | Q | V | PB |
| 10. | B | D | G | O | R | PB |
| 11. | B | E | K | S | Y | PB |
| 12. | B | F | H | M | W | PB |
| 13. | B | H | J | L | W | PB |
| 14. | B | N | P | U | X | PB |
| 15. | C | D | K | M | X | PB |
| 16. | C | E | G | L | N | PB |
| 17. | C | F | O | P | S | PB |
| 18. | C | H | R | U | Y | PB |
| 19. | C | J | R | S | W | PB |
| 20. | D | E | H | I | P | PB |
| 21. | D | F | N | Q | Y | PB |
| 22. | D | J | N | Q | W | PB |
| 23. | D | L | S | U | V | PB |
| 24. | E | F | R | V | X | PB |
| 25. | E | J | M | Q | U | PB |
| 26. | E | M | O | Q | U | PB |
| 27. | F | G | I | J | W | PB |
| 28. | F | G | I | K | U | PB |
| 29. | G | H | Q | S | X | PB |
| 30. | G | M | P | V | Y | PB |
| 31. | H | J | P | W | X | PB |
| 32. | H | K | N | O | V | PB |
| 33. | I | L | O | X | Y | PB |
| 34. | I | M | N | R | S | PB |
| 35. | J | K | O | V | W | PB |
| 36. | K | L | P | Q | R | PB |



# POWERBALL BALANCED WHEEL® 52026PB

## Wheel 26 Numbers + PB in 39 Games for a 2 of 2 Win

With Powerball

| Numbers Matched | Maximum Wins | | | | | | Minimum Wins | | | | | |
|---|---|---|---|---|---|---|---|---|---|---|---|---|
| | 5 + 1 | 4 + 1 | 3 + 1 | 2 + 1 | 1 + 1 | 0 + 1 | 5 + 1 | 4 + 1 | 3 + 1 | 2 + 1 | 1 + 1 | 0 + 1 |
| 5 + 1 | 1 | 1 | 0 | 3 | 25 | 9 | 0 | 0 | 0 | 10 | 15 | 14 |
| 4 + 1 | - | 2 | 0 | 1 | 22 | 14 | - | 0 | 0 | 6 | 16 | 17 |
| 3 + 1 | - | - | 2 | 2 | 15 | 20 | - | - | 0 | 3 | 15 | 21 |
| 2 + 1 | - | - | - | 4 | 9 | 26 | - | - | - | 1 | 12 | 26 |
| 1 + 1 | - | - | - | - | 9 | 30 | - | - | - | - | 7 | 32 |
| 0 + 1 | - | - | - | - | - | 39 | - | - | - | - | - | 39 |

Without Powerball

| Numbers Matched | Maximum Wins | | | | | Minimum Wins | | | | |
|---|---|---|---|---|---|---|---|---|---|---|
| | 5 + 0 | 4 + 0 | 3 + 0 | 2 + 0 | 1 + 0 | 5 + 0 | 4 + 0 | 3 + 0 | 2 + 0 | 1 + 0 |
| 5 + 0 | 1 | 1 | 0 | 3 | 25 | 0 | 0 | 0 | 10 | 15 |
| 4 + 0 | - | 2 | 0 | 1 | 22 | - | 0 | 0 | 6 | 16 |
| 3 + 0 | - | - | 2 | 2 | 15 | - | - | 0 | 3 | 15 |
| 2 + 0 | - | - | - | 4 | 9 | - | - | - | 1 | 12 |
| 1 + 0 | - | - | - | - | 9 | - | - | - | - | 7 |

(Continued Next Page)

## POWERBALL BALANCED WHEEL® 52026PB (Continued from previous page)

# Your 26 Numbers + PB to Wheel

| A | B | C | D | E | F | G | H | I |
|---|---|---|---|---|---|---|---|---|
| 7 | 9 | 8 | 9 | 7 | 7 | 7 | 7 | 9 |
| **J** | **K** | **L** | **M** | **N** | **O** | **P** | **Q** | **R** |
| 7 | 7 | 7 | 7 | 8 | 7 | 8 | 7 | 8 |
| **S** | **T** | **U** | **V** | **W** | **X** | **Y** | **Z** | **PB** |
| 7 | 7 | 8 | 7 | 7 | 8 | 7 | 8 | 39 |

# The 39 Games to Play

| | | | | | | |
|---|---|---|---|---|---|---|
| 1. | A | B | C | F | Z | PB |
| 2. | A | D | J | L | Q | PB |
| 3. | A | E | I | M | O | PB |
| 4. | A | F | V | X | Y | PB |
| 5. | A | G | N | S | U | PB |
| 6. | A | H | K | P | T | PB |
| 7. | A | L | R | W | Z | PB |
| 8. | B | C | G | H | R | PB |
| 9. | B | D | I | R | Y | PB |
| 10. | B | D | J | Q | W | PB |
| 11. | B | D | K | L | M | PB |
| 12. | B | E | R | S | Z | PB |
| 13. | B | K | O | U | X | PB |
| 14. | B | M | P | R | V | PB |
| 15. | B | N | T | X | Z | PB |
| 16. | C | D | E | S | T | PB |
| 17. | C | D | O | Y | Z | PB |
| 18. | C | F | L | M | N | PB |
| 19. | C | I | K | Q | Z | PB |
| 20. | C | I | N | P | W | PB |
| 21. | C | J | U | V | X | PB |
| 22. | D | F | K | N | R | PB |
| 23. | D | G | H | V | Z | PB |
| 24. | D | I | P | U | X | PB |
| 25. | E | F | T | U | W | PB |
| 26. | E | G | L | P | X | PB |
| 27. | E | H | N | Q | V | PB |
| 28. | E | J | K | S | Y | PB |
| 29. | F | G | H | I | J | PB |
| 30. | F | O | P | Q | S | PB |
| 31. | G | K | O | V | W | PB |
| 32. | G | M | Q | T | Y | PB |
| 33. | H | L | O | U | Y | PB |
| 34. | H | M | S | W | X | PB |
| 35. | I | L | S | T | V | PB |
| 36. | I | N | P | W | Y | PB |
| 37. | I | Q | R | U | X | PB |
| 38. | J | M | P | U | Z | PB |
| 39. | J | N | O | R | T | PB |

# POWERBALL BALANCED WHEEL® 52027PB

## Wheel 27 Numbers + PB in 42 Games for a 2 of 2 Win

With Powerball

| Numbers Matched | Maximum Wins 5 + 1 | 4 + 1 | 3 + 1 | 2 + 1 | 1 + 1 | 0 + 1 | Minimum Wins 5 + 1 | 4 + 1 | 3 + 1 | 2 + 1 | 1 + 1 | 0 + 1 |
|---|---|---|---|---|---|---|---|---|---|---|---|---|
| 5 + 1 | 1 | 0 | 1 | 5 | 22 | 13 | 0 | 0 | 0 | 10 | 15 | 17 |
| 4 + 1 | - | 1 | 1 | 5 | 16 | 19 | - | 0 | 0 | 6 | 16 | 20 |
| 3 + 1 | - | - | 2 | 3 | 13 | 24 | - | - | 0 | 3 | 15 | 24 |
| 2 + 1 | - | - | - | 4 | 9 | 29 | - | - | - | 1 | 12 | 29 |
| 1 + 1 | - | - | - | - | 9 | 33 | - | - | - | - | 7 | 35 |
| 0 + 1 | - | - | - | - | - | 42 | - | - | - | - | - | 42 |

Without Powerball

| Numbers Matched | Maximum Wins 5 + 0 | 4 + 0 | 3 + 0 | 2 + 0 | 1 + 0 | Minimum Wins 5 + 0 | 4 + 0 | 3 + 0 | 2 + 0 | 1 + 0 |
|---|---|---|---|---|---|---|---|---|---|---|
| 5 + 0 | 1 | 0 | 1 | 5 | 22 | 0 | 0 | 0 | 10 | 15 |
| 4 + 0 | - | 1 | 1 | 5 | 16 | - | 0 | 0 | 6 | 16 |
| 3 + 0 | - | - | 2 | 3 | 13 | - | - | 0 | 3 | 15 |
| 2 + 0 | - | - | - | 4 | 9 | - | - | - | 1 | 12 |
| 1 + 0 | - | - | - | - | 9 | - | - | - | - | 7 |

## Your 27 Numbers + PB to Wheel

| A | B | C | D | E | F | G | H | I | J |
|---|---|---|---|---|---|---|---|---|---|
| 7 | 7 | 9 | 8 | 9 | 8 | 7 | 7 | 8 | 8 |
| **K** | **L** | **M** | **N** | **O** | **P** | **Q** | **R** | **S** | **T** |
| 7 | 8 | 7 | 7 | 9 | 8 | 8 | 8 | 8 | 8 |
| **U** | **V** | **W** | **X** | **Y** | **Z** | **aa** | **PB** | | |
| 8 | 8 | 8 | 8 | 7 | 7 | 8 | 42 | | |

## The 42 Games to Play

| | | | | | | |
|---|---|---|---|---|---|---|
| 1. | A | B | D | T | Y | PB |
| 2. | A | C | T | U | W | PB |
| 3. | A | E | Q | R | aa | PB |
| 4. | A | F | H | M | X | PB |
| 5. | A | G | I | J | S | PB |
| 6. | A | K | P | W | Z | PB |
| 7. | A | L | N | O | V | PB |
| 8. | B | C | M | R | U | PB |
| 9. | B | E | M | Q | aa | PB |
| 10. | B | F | G | O | P | PB |
| 11. | B | H | I | V | W | PB |
| 12. | B | J | K | N | X | PB |
| 13. | B | L | M | S | Z | PB |
| 14. | C | D | G | W | X | PB |
| 15. | C | D | O | R | T | PB |
| 16. | C | E | H | N | Z | PB |
| 17. | C | F | K | L | aa | PB |
| 18. | C | I | O | P | S | PB |
| 19. | C | J | P | Q | V | PB |
| 20. | C | S | V | X | Y | PB |
| 21. | D | E | J | K | O | PB |
| 22. | D | F | L | U | V | PB |
| 23. | D | H | O | S | aa | PB |
| 24. | D | I | M | N | P | PB |
| 25. | D | O | Q | X | Z | PB |
| 26. | E | F | R | S | W | PB |
| 27. | E | G | L | Q | W | PB |
| 28. | E | I | T | X | aa | PB |
| 29. | E | L | R | V | X | PB |
| 30. | E | P | U | Y | aa | PB |
| 31. | F | I | L | Q | Y | PB |
| 32. | F | J | V | Z | aa | PB |



(Continued Next Page)

## POWERBALL BALANCED WHEEL® 52027PB (Continued from previous page)

| | | | | | | |
|---|---|---|---|---|---|---|
| 33. | F | N | *Q* | S | T | PB |
| 34. | G | H | R | Y | Z | PB |
| 35. | G | K | M | T | V | PB |
| 36. | G | N | U | W | aa | PB |
| 37. | H | J | L | P | T | PB |
| 38. | H | K | *Q* | S | U | PB |
| 39. | I | K | N | R | Y | PB |
| 40. | I | O | T | U | Z | PB |
| 41. | J | M | O | W | Y | PB |
| 42. | J | P | R | U | X | PB |



# POWERBALL BALANCED WHEEL® 52028PB
## Wheel 28 Numbers + PB in 45 Games for a 2 of 2 Win

With Powerball

| Numbers Matched | Maximum Wins 5 + 1 | 4 + 1 | 3 + 1 | 2 + 1 | 1 + 1 | 0 + 1 | Minimum Wins 5 + 1 | 4 + 1 | 3 + 1 | 2 + 1 | 1 + 1 | 0 + 1 |
|---|---|---|---|---|---|---|---|---|---|---|---|---|
| 5 + 1 | 1 | 0 | 1 | 4 | 25 | 14 | 0 | 0 | 0 | 10 | 20 | 15 |
| 4 + 1 | - | 1 | 1 | 3 | 20 | 20 | - | 0 | 0 | 6 | 20 | 19 |
| 3 + 1 | - | - | 2 | 2 | 15 | 26 | - | - | 0 | 3 | 18 | 24 |
| 2 + 1 | - | - | - | 4 | 8 | 33 | - | - | - | 1 | 14 | 30 |
| 1 + 1 | - | - | - | - | 9 | 36 | - | - | - | - | 8 | 37 |
| 0 + 1 | - | - | - | - | - | 45 | - | - | - | - | - | 45 |

Without Powerball

| Numbers Matched | Maximum Wins 5 + 0 | 4 + 0 | 3 + 0 | 2 + 0 | 1 + 0 | Minimum Wins 5 + 0 | 4 + 0 | 3 + 0 | 2 + 0 | 1 + 0 |
|---|---|---|---|---|---|---|---|---|---|---|
| 5 + 0 | 1 | 0 | 1 | 4 | 25 | 0 | 0 | 0 | 10 | 20 |
| 4 + 0 | - | 1 | 1 | 3 | 20 | - | 0 | 0 | 6 | 20 |
| 3 + 0 | - | - | 2 | 2 | 15 | - | - | 0 | 3 | 18 |
| 2 + 0 | - | - | - | 4 | 8 | - | - | - | 1 | 14 |
| 1 + 0 | - | - | - | - | 9 | - | - | - | - | 8 |

## Your 28 Numbers + PB to Wheel

| A | B | C | D | E | F | G | H | I | J |
|---|---|---|---|---|---|---|---|---|---|
| 8 | 8 | 8 | 8 | 8 | 8 | 8 | 8 | 8 | 8 |
| **K** | **L** | **M** | **N** | **O** | **P** | **Q** | **R** | **S** | **T** |
| 8 | 8 | 8 | 8 | 8 | 8 | 8 | 9 | 8 | 8 |
| **U** | **V** | **W** | **X** | **Y** | **Z** | **aa** | **bb** | **PB** | |
| 8 | 8 | 8 | 8 | 8 | 8 | 8 | 8 | 45 | |

## The 45 Games to Play

| | | | | | | |
|---|---|---|---|---|---|---|
| 1. | A | B | L | N | *Q* | PB |
| 2. | A | C | E | O | Z | PB |
| 3. | A | D | F | H | X | PB |
| 4. | A | G | J | M | R | PB |
| 5. | A | I | K | O | P | PB |
| 6. | A | O | S | T | bb | PB |
| 7. | A | O | U | V | aa | PB |
| 8. | A | P | W | Y | Z | PB |
| 9. | B | C | U | W | bb | PB |
| 10. | B | D | K | X | aa | PB |
| 11. | B | E | M | S | X | PB |
| 12. | B | F | J | P | T | PB |
| 13. | B | G | H | O | Y | PB |
| 14. | B | I | V | X | Z | PB |
| 15. | B | J | R | U | X | PB |
| 16. | C | D | N | P | aa | PB |
| 17. | C | E | H | I | *Q* | PB |
| 18. | C | F | G | L | U | PB |



(Continued Next Page)

## POWERBALL BALANCED WHEEL® 52028PB (Continued from previous page)

| | | | | | | |
|---|---|---|---|---|---|---|
| 19. | C | F | M | V | Z | PB |
| 20. | C | J | K | R | S | PB |
| 21. | C | N | T | X | Y | PB |
| 22. | D | E | G | L | T | PB |
| 23. | D | I | N | O | R | PB |
| 24. | D | J | Q | V | Y | PB |
| 25. | D | K | M | W | bb | PB |
| 26. | D | L | S | U | Z | PB |
| 27. | E | F | K | N | W | PB |
| 28. | E | F | R | V | bb | PB |
| 29. | E | G | I | J | aa | PB |
| 30. | E | P | S | U | Y | PB |
| 31. | F | I | S | aa | bb | PB |
| 32. | F | M | O | Q | Y | PB |
| 33. | G | K | T | V | Z | PB |
| 34. | G | N | S | V | W | PB |
| 35. | G | P | Q | X | bb | PB |
| 36. | H | J | N | Z | bb | PB |
| 37. | H | K | Q | S | U | PB |
| 38. | H | L | M | P | V | PB |
| 39. | H | Q | R | T | W | PB |
| 40. | H | Q | R | Z | aa | PB |
| 41. | I | L | W | Y | aa | PB |
| 42. | I | M | N | T | U | PB |
| 43. | J | L | O | W | X | PB |
| 44. | K | L | R | Y | bb | PB |
| 45. | M | P | R | T | aa | PB |



# POWERBALL BALANCED WHEEL® 52029PB

## Wheel 29 Numbers + PB in 48 Games for a 2 of 2 Win

With Powerball

| Numbers Matched | Maximum Wins 5 + 1 | 4 + 1 | 3 + 1 | 2 + 1 | 1 + 1 | 0 + 1 | Minimum Wins 5 + 1 | 4 + 1 | 3 + 1 | 2 + 1 | 1 + 1 | 0 + 1 |
|---|---|---|---|---|---|---|---|---|---|---|---|---|
| 5 + 1 | 1 | 0 | 1 | 6 | 23 | 17 | 0 | 0 | 0 | 10 | 20 | 18 |
| 4 + 1 | - | 1 | 1 | 5 | 18 | 23 | - | 0 | 0 | 6 | 20 | 22 |
| 3 + 1 | - | - | 2 | 1 | 18 | 27 | - | - | 0 | 3 | 18 | 27 |
| 2 + 1 | - | - | - | 4 | 9 | 35 | - | - | - | 1 | 14 | 33 |
| 1 + 1 | - | - | - | - | 9 | 39 | - | - | - | - | 8 | 40 |
| 0 + 1 | - | - | - | - | - | 48 | - | - | - | - | - | 48 |

Without Powerball

| Numbers Matched | Maximum Wins 5 + 0 | 4 + 0 | 3 + 0 | 2 + 0 | 1 + 0 | Minimum Wins 5 + 0 | 4 + 0 | 3 + 0 | 2 + 0 | 1 + 0 |
|---|---|---|---|---|---|---|---|---|---|---|
| 5 + 0 | 1 | 0 | 1 | 6 | 23 | 0 | 0 | 0 | 10 | 20 |
| 4 + 0 | - | 1 | 1 | 5 | 18 | - | 0 | 0 | 6 | 20 |
| 3 + 0 | - | - | 2 | 1 | 18 | - | - | 0 | 3 | 18 |
| 2 + 0 | - | - | - | 4 | 9 | - | - | - | 1 | 14 |
| 1 + 0 | - | - | - | - | 9 | - | - | - | - | 8 |

## Your 29 Numbers + PB to Wheel

| A | B | C | D | E | F | G | H | I | J |
|---|---|---|---|---|---|---|---|---|---|
| 8 | 8 | 9 | 9 | 8 | 8 | 8 | 8 | 8 | 9 |
| **K** | **L** | **M** | **N** | **O** | **P** | **Q** | **R** | **S** | **T** |
| 9 | 9 | 8 | 8 | 8 | 8 | 8 | 8 | 8 | 8 |
| **U** | **V** | **W** | **X** | **Y** | **Z** | **aa** | **bb** | **cc** | **PB** |
| 9 | 8 | 8 | 9 | 8 | 8 | 8 | 8 | 9 | 48 |

(Continued Next Page)

## POWERBALL BALANCED WHEEL® 52029PB (Continued from previous page)

# The 48 Games to Play

| | | | | | | |
|---|---|---|---|---|---|---|
| 1. | A | B | M | V | W | PB |
| 2. | A | C | F | L | X | PB |
| 3. | A | D | R | U | bb | PB |
| 4. | A | E | N | S | aa | PB |
| 5. | A | G | Z | bb | cc | PB |
| 6. | A | H | I | O | *Q* | PB |
| 7. | A | J | K | L | T | PB |
| 8. | A | P | T | V | Y | PB |
| 9. | B | C | I | K | U | PB |
| 10. | B | D | E | T | W | PB |
| 11. | B | F | H | U | Y | PB |
| 12. | B | G | *Q* | S | X | PB |
| 13. | B | J | O | P | bb | PB |
| 14. | B | K | N | W | Z | PB |
| 15. | B | L | R | aa | cc | PB |
| 16. | C | D | E | U | V | PB |
| 17. | C | E | H | P | Z | PB |
| 18. | C | G | M | V | cc | PB |
| 19. | C | J | S | W | Y | PB |
| 20. | C | N | O | *Q* | R | PB |
| 21. | C | N | U | X | aa | PB |
| 22. | C | R | S | T | bb | PB |
| 23. | D | F | J | M | *Q* | PB |
| 24. | D | G | I | Y | aa | PB |
| 25. | D | H | K | P | S | PB |
| 26. | D | J | N | Y | cc | PB |
| 27. | D | L | S | V | Z | PB |
| 28. | D | O | X | Y | cc | PB |
| 29. | E | F | M | O | S | PB |
| 30. | E | G | J | K | cc | PB |
| 31. | E | I | R | W | X | PB |
| 32. | E | L | *Q* | Y | bb | PB |
| 33. | F | G | K | P | R | PB |
| 34. | F | I | N | V | bb | PB |
| 35. | F | J | T | Z | aa | PB |
| 36. | F | P | *Q* | W | cc | PB |
| 37. | G | H | N | T | cc | PB |
| 38. | G | L | O | U | W | PB |
| 39. | H | J | R | V | X | PB |
| 40. | H | K | L | X | bb | PB |
| 41. | H | M | W | aa | bb | PB |
| 42. | I | J | S | U | cc | PB |
| 43. | I | L | P | X | aa | PB |
| 44. | I | M | T | X | Z | PB |
| 45. | K | M | R | Y | Z | PB |
| 46. | K | O | *Q* | V | aa | PB |
| 47. | L | M | N | P | U | PB |
| 48. | O | *Q* | T | U | Z | PB |



# POWERBALL BALANCED WHEEL® 52030PB

## Wheel 30 Numbers + PB in 51 Games for a 2 of 2 Win

With Powerball

| Numbers Matched | Maximum Wins | | | | | | Minimum Wins | | | | | |
|---|---|---|---|---|---|---|---|---|---|---|---|---|
| | 5 + 1 | 4 + 1 | 3 + 1 | 2 + 1 | 1 + 1 | 0 + 1 | 5 + 1 | 4 + 1 | 3 + 1 | 2 + 1 | 1 + 1 | 0 + 1 |
| 5 + 1 | 1 | 0 | 1 | 5 | 28 | 16 | 0 | 0 | 0 | 10 | 20 | 21 |
| 4 + 1 | - | 1 | 1 | 3 | 24 | 22 | - | 0 | 0 | 6 | 20 | 25 |
| 3 + 1 | - | - | 2 | 0 | 22 | 27 | - | - | 0 | 3 | 18 | 30 |
| 2 + 1 | - | - | - | 4 | 10 | 37 | - | - | - | 1 | 14 | 36 |
| 1 + 1 | - | - | - | - | 10 | 41 | - | - | - | - | 8 | 43 |
| 0 + 1 | - | - | - | - | - | 51 | - | - | - | - | - | 51 |

(Continued Next Page)

## POWERBALL BALANCED WHEEL® 52030PB

(Continued from previous page)

Without Powerball

| Numbers Matched | Maximum Wins 5 + 0 | 4 + 0 | 3 + 0 | 2 + 0 | 1 + 0 | Minimum Wins 5 + 0 | 4 + 0 | 3 + 0 | 2 + 0 | 1 + 0 |
|---|---|---|---|---|---|---|---|---|---|---|
| 5 + 0 | 1 | 0 | 1 | 5 | 28 | 0 | 0 | 0 | 10 | 20 |
| 4 + 0 | - | 1 | 1 | 3 | 24 | - | 0 | 0 | 6 | 20 |
| 3 + 0 | - | - | 2 | 0 | 22 | - | - | 0 | 3 | 18 |
| 2 + 0 | - | - | - | 4 | 10 | - | - | - | 1 | 14 |
| 1 + 0 | - | - | - | - | 10 | - | - | - | - | 8 |

## Your 30 Numbers + PB to Wheel

| A | B | C | D | E | F | G | H | I | J | K |
|---|---|---|---|---|---|---|---|---|---|---|
| 8 | 8 | 8 | 8 | 9 | 9 | 9 | 9 | 8 | 9 | 9 |
| **L** | **M** | **N** | **O** | **P** | **Q** | **R** | **S** | **T** | **U** | **V** |
| 8 | 9 | 9 | 9 | 8 | 10 | 8 | 9 | 8 | 9 | 8 |
| **W** | **X** | **Y** | **Z** | **aa** | **bb** | **cc** | **dd** | **PB** | | |
| 8 | 8 | 8 | 8 | 8 | 9 | 9 | 8 | 51 | | |

## The 51 Games to Play

| | | | | | | |
|---|---|---|---|---|---|---|
| 1. | A | B | J | M | Y | PB |
| 2. | A | C | H | R | X | PB |
| 3. | A | D | O | Q | W | PB |
| 4. | A | E | G | Z | bb | PB |
| 5. | A | F | U | aa | cc | PB |
| 6. | A | H | L | N | cc | PB |
| 7. | A | I | M | P | V | PB |
| 8. | A | K | S | T | dd | PB |
| 9. | B | C | J | K | cc | PB |
| 10. | B | D | G | J | V | PB |
| 11. | B | E | H | J | dd | PB |
| 12. | B | F | O | R | T | PB |
| 13. | B | I | N | U | bb | PB |
| 14. | B | L | S | W | aa | PB |
| 15. | B | P | Q | X | Z | PB |
| 16. | C | D | L | M | N | PB |
| 17. | C | E | S | W | X | PB |
| 18. | C | F | Q | V | bb | PB |
| 19. | C | G | U | aa | dd | PB |
| 20. | C | I | O | T | Z | PB |
| 21. | C | P | U | Y | bb | PB |
| 22. | D | E | U | X | aa | PB |
| 23. | D | F | H | I | S | PB |
| 24. | D | F | K | M | Z | PB |
| 25. | D | G | R | T | Y | PB |
| 26. | D | P | bb | cc | dd | PB |
| 27. | E | F | N | R | cc | PB |
| 28. | E | I | L | Q | dd | PB |
| 29. | E | K | O | V | X | PB |
| 30. | E | M | P | T | aa | PB |
| 31. | E | S | V | Y | cc | PB |
| 32. | F | G | L | O | P | PB |
| 33. | F | J | P | R | W | PB |
| 34. | F | N | X | Y | dd | PB |
| 35. | G | H | K | M | Q | PB |
| 36. | G | H | Q | S | bb | PB |
| 37. | G | I | M | X | cc | PB |
| 38. | G | N | W | Z | cc | PB |
| 39. | H | K | N | P | S | PB |
| 40. | H | O | Y | Z | aa | PB |
| 41. | H | T | U | V | W | PB |
| 42. | I | J | K | W | Y | PB |
| 43. | I | K | R | aa | bb | PB |
| 44. | J | L | T | X | bb | PB |
| 45. | J | N | Q | V | aa | PB |
| 46. | J | O | S | U | Z | PB |



(Continued Next Page)

**POWERBALL BALANCED WHEEL® 52030PB** (Continued from previous page)

| | | | | | | |
|---|---|---|---|---|---|---|
| 47. | K | L | Q | U | Y | PB |
| 48. | L | R | V | Z | dd | PB |
| 49. | M | O | W | bb | dd | PB |
| 50. | M | Q | R | S | U | PB |
| 51. | N | O | Q | T | cc | PB |



# POWERBALL BALANCED WHEEL® 52031PB

## Wheel 31 Numbers + PB in 55 Games for a 2 of 2 Win

With Powerball

| Numbers Matched | Maximum Wins 5 + 1 | 4 + 1 | 3 + 1 | 2 + 1 | 1 + 1 | 0 + 1 | Minimum Wins 5 + 1 | 4 + 1 | 3 + 1 | 2 + 1 | 1 + 1 | 0 + 1 |
|---|---|---|---|---|---|---|---|---|---|---|---|---|
| 5 + 1 | 1 | 0 | 1 | 5 | 29 | 19 | 0 | 0 | 0 | 10 | 20 | 25 |
| 4 + 1 | - | 1 | 1 | 2 | 27 | 24 | - | 0 | 0 | 6 | 20 | 29 |
| 3 + 1 | - | - | 2 | 1 | 21 | 31 | - | - | 0 | 3 | 18 | 34 |
| 2 + 1 | - | - | - | 4 | 12 | 39 | - | - | - | 1 | 14 | 40 |
| 1 + 1 | - | - | - | - | 10 | 45 | - | - | - | - | 8 | 47 |
| 0 + 1 | - | - | - | - | - | 55 | - | - | - | - | - | 55 |

Without Powerball

| Numbers Matched | Maximum Wins 5 + 0 | 4 + 0 | 3 + 0 | 2 + 0 | 1 + 0 | Minimum Wins 5 + 0 | 4 + 0 | 3 + 0 | 2 + 0 | 1 + 0 |
|---|---|---|---|---|---|---|---|---|---|---|
| 5 + 0 | 1 | 0 | 1 | 5 | 29 | 0 | 0 | 0 | 10 | 20 |
| 4 + 0 | - | 1 | 1 | 2 | 27 | - | 0 | 0 | 6 | 20 |
| 3 + 0 | - | - | 2 | 1 | 21 | - | - | 0 | 3 | 18 |
| 2 + 0 | - | - | - | 4 | 12 | - | - | - | 1 | 14 |
| 1 + 0 | - | - | - | - | 10 | - | - | - | - | 8 |

## Your 31 Numbers + PB to Wheel

| A | B | C | D | E | F | G | H | I | J | K |
|---|---|---|---|---|---|---|---|---|---|---|
| 9 | 9 | 8 | 9 | 9 | 10 | 8 | 8 | 9 | 8 | 8 |
| **L** | **M** | **N** | **O** | **P** | **Q** | **R** | **S** | **T** | **U** | **V** |
| 8 | 9 | 10 | 10 | 9 | 9 | 9 | 9 | 9 | 9 | 9 |
| **W** | **X** | **Y** | **Z** | **aa** | **bb** | **cc** | **dd** | **ee** | **PB** | |
| 9 | 8 | 8 | 9 | 9 | 9 | 10 | 9 | 9 | 55 | |

## The 55 Games to Play

| | | | | | | |
|---|---|---|---|---|---|---|
| 1. | A | B | K | M | aa | PB |
| 2. | A | C | O | P | R | PB |
| 3. | A | D | G | V | bb | PB |
| 4. | A | D | I | L | Z | PB |
| 5. | A | E | F | V | Y | PB |
| 6. | A | H | P | X | cc | PB |
| 7. | A | J | L | Q | S | PB |
| 8. | A | N | U | W | aa | PB |
| 9. | A | T | U | dd | ee | PB |
| 10. | B | C | Q | Y | bb | PB |
| 11. | B | D | N | T | W | PB |
| 12. | B | E | G | P | Z | PB |
| 13. | B | F | I | O | dd | PB |
| 14. | B | H | I | S | bb | PB |
| 15. | B | J | N | O | ee | PB |
| 16. | B | L | X | bb | dd | PB |
| 17. | B | R | U | V | cc | PB |
| 18. | C | D | E | K | ee | PB |
| 19. | C | F | M | N | cc | PB |
| 20. | C | G | I | M | T | PB |
| 21. | C | H | L | O | U | PB |
| 22. | C | J | V | X | aa | PB |



(Continued Next Page)

**POWERBALL BALANCED WHEEL® 52031PB** (Continued from previous page)

| | | | | | | |
|---|---|---|---|---|---|---|
| 23. | C | S | W | Z | dd | PB |
| 24. | D | F | T | aa | cc | PB |
| 25. | D | H | M | *Q* | T | PB |
| 26. | D | I | J | P | S | PB |
| 27. | D | O | Y | cc | dd | PB |
| 28. | D | R | U | X | bb | PB |
| 29. | E | H | J | R | dd | PB |
| 30. | E | I | K | O | X | PB |
| 31. | E | I | N | *Q* | V | PB |
| 32. | E | L | P | V | W | PB |
| 33. | E | M | S | U | cc | PB |
| 34. | E | P | T | aa | bb | PB |
| 35. | F | G | J | U | W | PB |
| 36. | F | H | K | W | Y | PB |
| 37. | F | L | aa | cc | ee | PB |
| 38. | F | N | P | R | Y | PB |
| 39. | F | N | *Q* | W | X | PB |
| 40. | F | N | S | Z | bb | PB |
| 41. | G | H | N | aa | dd | PB |
| 42. | G | K | L | N | R | PB |
| 43. | G | O | *Q* | Z | cc | PB |
| 44. | G | S | X | Y | ee | PB |
| 45. | H | *Q* | V | Z | ee | PB |
| 46. | I | R | W | cc | ee | PB |
| 47. | I | U | Y | Z | aa | PB |
| 48. | J | K | Z | bb | cc | PB |
| 49. | J | L | M | T | Y | PB |
| 50. | K | O | S | T | V | PB |
| 51. | K | P | *Q* | U | dd | PB |
| 52. | M | O | W | bb | ee | PB |
| 53. | M | P | V | dd | ee | PB |
| 54. | M | R | T | X | Z | PB |
| 55. | O | *Q* | R | S | aa | PB |



# POWERBALL BALANCED WHEEL® 52032PB

## Wheel 32 Numbers + PB in 58 Games for a 2 of 2 Win

With Powerball

| Numbers Matched | Maximum Wins | | | | | | Minimum Wins | | | | | |
|---|---|---|---|---|---|---|---|---|---|---|---|---|
| | 5 + 1 | 4 + 1 | 3 + 1 | 2 + 1 | 1 + 1 | 0 + 1 | 5 + 1 | 4 + 1 | 3 + 1 | 2 + 1 | 1 + 1 | 0 + 1 |
| 5 + 1 | 1 | 0 | 1 | 4 | 30 | 22 | 0 | 0 | 0 | 10 | 21 | 27 |
| 4 + 1 | - | 1 | 1 | 4 | 22 | 30 | - | 0 | 0 | 6 | 20 | 32 |
| 3 + 1 | - | - | 2 | 3 | 16 | 37 | - | - | 0 | 3 | 18 | 37 |
| 2 + 1 | - | - | - | 3 | 14 | 41 | - | - | - | 1 | 14 | 43 |
| 1 + 1 | - | - | - | - | 10 | 48 | - | - | - | - | 8 | 50 |
| 0 + 1 | - | - | - | - | - | 58 | - | - | - | - | - | 58 |

Without Powerball

| Numbers Matched | Maximum Wins | | | | | Minimum Wins | | | | |
|---|---|---|---|---|---|---|---|---|---|---|
| | 5 + 0 | 4 + 0 | 3 + 0 | 2 + 0 | 1 + 0 | 5 + 0 | 4 + 0 | 3 + 0 | 2 + 0 | 1 + 0 |
| 5 + 0 | 1 | 0 | 1 | 4 | 30 | 0 | 0 | 0 | 10 | 21 |
| 4 + 0 | - | 1 | 1 | 4 | 22 | - | 0 | 0 | 6 | 20 |
| 3 + 0 | - | - | 2 | 3 | 16 | - | - | 0 | 3 | 18 |
| 2 + 0 | - | - | - | 3 | 14 | - | - | - | 1 | 14 |
| 1 + 0 | - | - | - | - | 10 | - | - | - | - | 8 |

(Continued Next Page)

**POWERBALL BALANCED WHEEL® 52032PB** (Continued from previous page)

## Your 32 Numbers + PB to Wheel

| A | B | C | D | E | F | G | H | I | J | K |
|---|---|---|---|---|---|---|---|---|---|---|
| 9 | 9 | 8 | 9 | 10 | 9 | 9 | 9 | 9 | 9 | 9 |
| **L** | **M** | **N** | **O** | **P** | **Q** | **R** | **S** | **T** | **U** | **V** |
| 9 | 10 | 9 | 9 | 9 | 10 | 8 | 10 | 10 | 9 | 9 |
| **W** | **X** | **Y** | **Z** | **aa** | **bb** | **cc** | **dd** | **ee** | **ff** | **PB** |
| 8 | 8 | 9 | 9 | 9 | 10 | 9 | 9 | 9 | 9 | 58 |

## The 58 Games to Play

| | | | | | | |
|---|---|---|---|---|---|---|
| 1. | A | B | H | P | Y | PB |
| 2. | A | C | I | aa | bb | PB |
| 3. | A | D | N | O | ff | PB |
| 4. | A | E | J | X | ee | PB |
| 5. | A | F | *Q* | Z | dd | PB |
| 6. | A | G | U | V | W | PB |
| 7. | A | I | K | *Q* | T | PB |
| 8. | A | J | S | bb | ff | PB |
| 9. | A | L | M | R | cc | PB |
| 10. | B | C | D | R | Z | PB |
| 11. | B | E | K | T | dd | PB |
| 12. | B | F | G | O | V | PB |
| 13. | B | F | I | S | U | PB |
| 14. | B | J | K | L | U | PB |
| 15. | B | M | O | aa | dd | PB |
| 16. | B | N | *Q* | cc | ee | PB |
| 17. | B | W | X | bb | ff | PB |
| 18. | C | E | L | O | *Q* | PB |
| 19. | C | F | S | Y | ee | PB |
| 20. | C | G | H | X | cc | PB |
| 21. | C | J | M | T | V | PB |
| 22. | C | K | N | P | W | PB |
| 23. | C | U | aa | dd | ff | PB |
| 24. | D | E | S | W | cc | PB |
| 25. | D | F | L | P | ff | PB |
| 26. | D | G | J | Y | dd | PB |
| 27. | D | H | M | *Q* | ff | PB |
| 28. | D | I | V | X | dd | PB |
| 29. | D | K | aa | bb | ee | PB |
| 30. | D | N | T | U | ee | PB |
| 31. | E | F | H | N | aa | PB |
| 32. | E | G | M | P | bb | PB |
| 33. | E | I | Y | cc | ff | PB |
| 34. | E | *Q* | R | U | bb | PB |
| 35. | E | *Q* | S | V | Y | PB |
| 36. | E | U | Y | Z | cc | PB |
| 37. | F | J | M | W | Z | PB |
| 38. | F | K | R | S | X | PB |
| 39. | F | T | bb | cc | dd | PB |
| 40. | G | I | J | N | *Q* | PB |
| 41. | G | K | T | Z | ff | PB |
| 42. | G | L | S | T | aa | PB |
| 43. | G | R | V | ee | ff | PB |
| 44. | H | I | J | O | R | PB |
| 45. | H | K | M | U | V | PB |
| 46. | H | L | W | dd | ee | PB |
| 47. | H | M | S | T | bb | PB |
| 48. | H | O | S | Z | ee | PB |
| 49. | I | L | O | *Q* | W | PB |
| 50. | I | M | P | Z | ee | PB |
| 51. | J | P | V | aa | cc | PB |
| 52. | K | O | Y | bb | cc | PB |
| 53. | L | M | N | X | Y | PB |
| 54. | L | N | V | Z | bb | PB |
| 55. | N | P | R | S | dd | PB |
| 56. | O | P | T | U | X | PB |



(Continued Next Page)

**POWERBALL BALANCED WHEEL® 52032PB** (Continued from previous page)

| | | | | | | |
|---|---|---|---|---|---|---|
| 57. | P | Q | X | Z | aa | PB |
| 58. | R | T | W | Y | aa | PB |



# POWERBALL BALANCED WHEEL® 52033PB

## Wheel 33 Numbers + PB in 62 Games for a 2 of 2 Win

With Powerball

| Numbers Matched | Maximum Wins 5 + 1 | 4 + 1 | 3 + 1 | 2 + 1 | 1 + 1 | 0 + 1 | Minimum Wins 5 + 1 | 4 + 1 | 3 + 1 | 2 + 1 | 1 + 1 | 0 + 1 |
|---|---|---|---|---|---|---|---|---|---|---|---|---|
| 5 + 1 | 1 | 0 | 1 | 6 | 30 | 24 | 0 | 0 | 0 | 10 | 24 | 28 |
| 4 + 1 | - | 1 | 1 | 4 | 25 | 31 | - | 0 | 0 | 6 | 23 | 33 |
| 3 + 1 | - | - | 2 | 2 | 20 | 38 | - | - | 0 | 3 | 20 | 39 |
| 2 + 1 | - | - | - | 4 | 12 | 46 | - | - | - | 1 | 15 | 46 |
| 1 + 1 | - | - | - | - | 11 | 51 | - | - | - | - | 8 | 54 |
| 0 + 1 | - | - | - | - | - | 62 | - | - | - | - | - | 62 |

Without Powerball

| Numbers Matched | Maximum Wins 5 + 0 | 4 + 0 | 3 + 0 | 2 + 0 | 1 + 0 | Minimum Wins 5 + 0 | 4 + 0 | 3 + 0 | 2 + 0 | 1 + 0 |
|---|---|---|---|---|---|---|---|---|---|---|
| 5 + 0 | 1 | 0 | 1 | 6 | 30 | 0 | 0 | 0 | 10 | 24 |
| 4 + 0 | - | 1 | 1 | 4 | 25 | - | 0 | 0 | 6 | 23 |
| 3 + 0 | - | - | 2 | 2 | 20 | - | - | 0 | 3 | 20 |
| 2 + 0 | - | - | - | 4 | 12 | - | - | - | 1 | 15 |
| 1 + 0 | - | - | - | - | 11 | - | - | - | - | 8 |

## Your 33 Numbers + PB to Wheel

| A | B | C | D | E | F | G | H | I |
|---|---|---|---|---|---|---|---|---|
| 9 | 10 | 8 | 10 | 9 | 9 | 9 | 10 | 9 |
| **J** | **K** | **L** | **M** | **N** | **O** | **P** | **Q** | **R** |
| 10 | 10 | 9 | 10 | 10 | 9 | 10 | 9 | 10 |
| **S** | **T** | **U** | **V** | **W** | **X** | **Y** | **Z** | **aa** |
| 9 | 9 | 9 | 9 | 10 | 9 | 9 | 9 | 11 |
| **bb** | **cc** | **dd** | **ee** | **ff** | **gg** | **PB** | | |
| 9 | 9 | 10 | 9 | 10 | 9 | 62 | | |

## The 62 Games to Play

| | | | | | | |
|---|---|---|---|---|---|---|
| 1. | A | B | Z | bb | dd | PB |
| 2. | A | C | U | V | W | PB |
| 3. | A | D | E | T | X | PB |
| 4. | A | E | H | O | R | PB |
| 5. | A | E | ee | ff | gg | PB |
| 6. | A | F | I | N | S | PB |
| 7. | A | G | M | P | cc | PB |
| 8. | A | J | V | aa | cc | PB |
| 9. | A | K | L | Q | Y | PB |
| 10. | B | C | aa | ff | gg | PB |
| 11. | B | D | G | N | T | PB |
| 12. | B | E | J | S | Y | PB |
| 13. | B | F | H | M | ee | PB |
| 14. | B | F | L | V | X | PB |
| 15. | B | H | K | M | dd | PB |
| 16. | B | I | U | cc | dd | PB |
| 17. | B | O | P | Q | W | PB |
| 18. | B | Q | R | dd | gg | PB |
| 19. | C | D | H | L | Z | PB |
| 20. | C | E | I | M | Q | PB |
| 21. | C | F | J | N | R | PB |
| 22. | C | G | K | O | S | PB |



(Continued Next Page)

## POWERBALL BALANCED WHEEL® 52033PB (Continued from previous page)

| | | | | | | |
|---|---|---|---|---|---|---|
| 23. | C | P | T | bb | cc | PB |
| 24. | C | X | Y | dd | ee | PB |
| 25. | D | E | F | P | dd | PB |
| 26. | D | I | O | V | Y | PB |
| 27. | D | J | U | W | gg | PB |
| 28. | D | K | Q | cc | ff | PB |
| 29. | D | M | P | S | aa | PB |
| 30. | D | O | aa | bb | ee | PB |
| 31. | D | R | S | U | ee | PB |
| 32. | E | G | L | W | aa | PB |
| 33. | E | K | U | V | bb | PB |
| 34. | E | N | O | Z | cc | PB |
| 35. | F | G | Q | U | Z | PB |
| 36. | F | I | O | T | gg | PB |
| 37. | F | K | Y | aa | ff | PB |
| 38. | F | W | Y | bb | cc | PB |
| 39. | G | H | I | J | bb | PB |
| 40. | G | N | W | dd | ee | PB |
| 41. | G | R | V | Y | gg | PB |
| 42. | G | R | X | Z | ff | PB |
| 43. | H | K | N | W | X | PB |
| 44. | H | N | P | U | Y | PB |
| 45. | H | N | P | V | ff | PB |
| 46. | H | N | Q | T | aa | PB |
| 47. | H | S | X | cc | gg | PB |
| 48. | I | J | K | Z | ee | PB |
| 49. | I | J | L | P | X | PB |
| 50. | I | R | W | aa | ff | PB |
| 51. | J | L | O | dd | ff | PB |
| 52. | J | M | R | bb | ff | PB |
| 53. | J | Q | T | V | ee | PB |
| 54. | K | P | Z | aa | gg | PB |
| 55. | K | R | T | aa | dd | PB |
| 56. | L | M | N | bb | gg | PB |
| 57. | L | P | R | cc | ee | PB |
| 58. | L | S | T | U | ff | PB |
| 59. | M | O | U | X | aa | PB |
| 60. | M | S | V | Z | dd | PB |
| 61. | M | T | W | Y | Z | PB |
| 62. | Q | S | W | X | bb | PB |



# POWERBALL BALANCED WHEEL® 52034PB

## Wheel 34 Numbers + PB in 67 Games for a 2 of 2 Win

With Powerball

| Numbers Matched | Maximum Wins 5 + 1 | 4 + 1 | 3 + 1 | 2 + 1 | 1 + 1 | 0 + 1 | Minimum Wins 5 + 1 | 4 + 1 | 3 + 1 | 2 + 1 | 1 + 1 | 0 + 1 |
|---|---|---|---|---|---|---|---|---|---|---|---|---|
| 5 + 1 | 1 | 0 | 1 | 7 | 30 | 28 | 0 | 0 | 0 | 10 | 25 | 32 |
| 4 + 1 | - | 1 | 1 | 5 | 25 | 35 | - | 0 | 0 | 6 | 24 | 37 |
| 3 + 1 | - | - | 2 | 4 | 18 | 43 | - | - | 0 | 3 | 21 | 43 |
| 2 + 1 | - | - | - | 5 | 12 | 50 | - | - | - | 1 | 16 | 50 |
| 1 + 1 | - | - | - | - | 11 | 56 | - | - | - | - | 9 | 58 |
| 0 + 1 | - | - | - | - | - | 67 | - | - | - | - | - | 67 |

Without Powerball

| Numbers Matched | Maximum Wins 5 + 0 | 4 + 0 | 3 + 0 | 2 + 0 | 1 + 0 | Minimum Wins 5 + 0 | 4 + 0 | 3 + 0 | 2 + 0 | 1 + 0 |
|---|---|---|---|---|---|---|---|---|---|---|
| 5 + 0 | 1 | 0 | 1 | 7 | 30 | 0 | 0 | 0 | 10 | 25 |
| 4 + 0 | - | 1 | 1 | 5 | 25 | - | 0 | 0 | 6 | 24 |
| 3 + 0 | - | - | 2 | 4 | 18 | - | - | 0 | 3 | 21 |
| 2 + 0 | - | - | - | 5 | 12 | - | - | - | 1 | 16 |
| 1 + 0 | - | - | - | - | 11 | - | - | - | - | 9 |

(Continued Next Page)

**POWERBALL BALANCED WHEEL® 52034PB** (Continued from previous page)

## Your 34 Numbers + PB to Wheel

| A | B | C | D | E | F | G | H | I |
|---|---|---|---|---|---|---|---|---|
| 10 | 10 | 10 | 10 | 10 | 10 | 10 | 10 | 10 |
| **J** | **K** | **L** | **M** | **N** | **O** | **P** | **Q** | **R** |
| 11 | 11 | 9 | 10 | 9 | 10 | 10 | 10 | 10 |
| **S** | **T** | **U** | **V** | **W** | **X** | **Y** | **Z** | **aa** |
| 10 | 9 | 9 | 10 | 10 | 11 | 10 | 9 | 9 |
| **bb** | **cc** | **dd** | **ee** | **ff** | **gg** | **hh** | **PB** | |
| 10 | 10 | 10 | 10 | 9 | 10 | 9 | 67 | |

## The 67 Games to Play

| | | | | | | |
|---|---|---|---|---|---|---|
| 1. | A | B | K | X | Z | PB |
| 2. | A | C | Q | T | Y | PB |
| 3. | A | D | M | N | R | PB |
| 4. | A | E | aa | bb | gg | PB |
| 5. | A | F | O | ff | gg | PB |
| 6. | A | G | I | P | cc | PB |
| 7. | A | G | J | U | bb | PB |
| 8. | A | H | S | W | ee | PB |
| 9. | A | L | cc | dd | gg | PB |
| 10. | A | V | cc | dd | hh | PB |
| 11. | B | C | J | W | hh | PB |
| 12. | B | D | O | U | Y | PB |
| 13. | B | E | H | M | T | PB |
| 14. | B | F | R | bb | ee | PB |
| 15. | B | G | R | Y | cc | PB |
| 16. | B | H | aa | dd | ff | PB |
| 17. | B | I | K | M | S | PB |
| 18. | B | K | V | X | gg | PB |
| 19. | B | L | N | P | Q | PB |
| 20. | C | D | F | L | U | PB |
| 21. | C | D | M | P | V | PB |
| 22. | C | E | F | G | dd | PB |
| 23. | C | H | U | X | cc | PB |
| 24. | C | I | Z | aa | ee | PB |
| 25. | C | K | O | X | bb | PB |
| 26. | C | N | bb | cc | ff | PB |
| 27. | C | R | S | gg | hh | PB |
| 28. | D | E | G | S | ff | PB |
| 29. | D | F | H | K | Q | PB |
| 30. | D | G | X | aa | hh | PB |
| 31. | D | I | J | O | W | PB |
| 32. | D | T | Z | bb | dd | PB |
| 33. | D | T | cc | ee | gg | PB |
| 34. | E | F | I | U | V | PB |
| 35. | E | F | P | Q | X | PB |
| 36. | E | G | L | M | ee | PB |
| 37. | E | H | J | Y | gg | PB |
| 38. | E | K | R | W | cc | PB |
| 39. | E | N | O | Z | hh | PB |
| 40. | F | J | S | Z | cc | PB |
| 41. | F | M | Y | bb | hh | PB |
| 42. | F | N | T | W | aa | PB |
| 43. | G | H | N | O | V | PB |
| 44. | G | K | L | O | T | PB |
| 45. | G | Q | W | Z | gg | PB |
| 46. | H | I | L | P | hh | PB |
| 47. | H | I | Q | S | bb | PB |
| 48. | H | L | R | Z | ff | PB |
| 49. | I | J | N | dd | gg | PB |
| 50. | I | Q | Y | ee | ff | PB |
| 51. | I | R | S | T | X | PB |
| 52. | J | K | P | R | aa | PB |



(Continued Next Page)

**POWERBALL BALANCED WHEEL® 52034PB** (Continued from previous page)

| | | | | | | |
|---|---|---|---|---|---|---|
| 53. | J | L | W | X | bb | PB |
| 54. | J | M | W | X | ff | PB |
| 55. | J | P | T | V | ff | PB |
| 56. | J | Q | V | ee | hh | PB |
| 57. | K | M | X | dd | ee | PB |
| 58. | K | N | X | Y | dd | PB |
| 59. | K | T | U | ff | hh | PB |
| 60. | L | S | V | Y | aa | PB |

| | | | | | | |
|---|---|---|---|---|---|---|
| 61. | M | O | Q | aa | cc | PB |
| 62. | M | P | U | Z | gg | PB |
| 63. | N | S | U | aa | ee | PB |
| 64. | O | P | S | dd | ee | PB |
| 65. | O | R | V | Y | Z | PB |
| 66. | P | V | W | Y | bb | PB |
| 67. | Q | R | U | W | dd | PB |



# POWERBALL BALANCED WHEEL® 52035PB

## Wheel 35 Numbers + PB in 71 Games for a 2 of 2 Win

With Powerball

| Numbers Matched | Maximum Wins 5 + 1 | 4 + 1 | 3 + 1 | 2 + 1 | 1 + 1 | 0 + 1 | Minimum Wins 5 + 1 | 4 + 1 | 3 + 1 | 2 + 1 | 1 + 1 | 0 + 1 |
|---|---|---|---|---|---|---|---|---|---|---|---|---|
| 5 + 1 | 1 | 0 | 0 | 9 | 29 | 32 | 0 | 0 | 0 | 10 | 27 | 34 |
| 4 + 1 | - | 1 | 0 | 6 | 26 | 38 | - | 0 | 0 | 6 | 25 | 40 |
| 3 + 1 | - | - | 1 | 5 | 18 | 47 | - | - | 0 | 3 | 21 | 47 |
| 2 + 1 | - | - | - | 3 | 17 | 51 | - | - | - | 1 | 16 | 54 |
| 1 + 1 | - | - | - | - | 12 | 59 | - | - | - | - | 9 | 62 |
| 0 + 1 | - | - | - | - | - | 71 | - | - | - | - | - | 71 |

Without Powerball

| Numbers Matched | Maximum Wins 5 + 0 | 4 + 0 | 3 + 0 | 2 + 0 | 1 + 0 | Minimum Wins 5 + 0 | 4 + 0 | 3 + 0 | 2 + 0 | 1 + 0 |
|---|---|---|---|---|---|---|---|---|---|---|
| 5 + 0 | 1 | 0 | 0 | 9 | 29 | 0 | 0 | 0 | 10 | 27 |
| 4 + 0 | - | 1 | 0 | 6 | 26 | - | 0 | 0 | 6 | 25 |
| 3 + 0 | - | - | 1 | 5 | 18 | - | - | 0 | 3 | 21 |
| 2 + 0 | - | - | - | 3 | 17 | - | - | - | 1 | 16 |
| 1 + 0 | - | - | - | - | 12 | - | - | - | - | 9 |

## Your 35 Numbers + PB to Wheel

| A | B | C | D | E | F | G | H | I |
|---|---|---|---|---|---|---|---|---|
| 10 | 10 | 11 | 10 | 10 | 10 | 11 | 11 | 9 |
| **J** | **K** | **L** | **M** | **N** | **O** | **P** | **Q** | **R** |
| 10 | 10 | 10 | 10 | 10 | 10 | 10 | 10 | 10 |
| **S** | **T** | **U** | **V** | **W** | **X** | **Y** | **Z** | **aa** |
| 9 | 10 | 10 | 11 | 10 | 10 | 10 | 10 | 10 |
| **bb** | **cc** | **dd** | **ee** | **ff** | **gg** | **hh** | **ii** | **PB** |
| 10 | 12 | 11 | 11 | 10 | 9 | 10 | 10 | 71 |

## The 71 Games to Play

| | | | | | | |
|---|---|---|---|---|---|---|
| 1. | A | B | G | Y | dd | PB |
| 2. | A | C | I | S | V | PB |
| 3. | A | D | N | ee | hh | PB |
| 4. | A | E | J | M | gg | PB |

| | | | | | | |
|---|---|---|---|---|---|---|
| 5. | A | F | K | O | U | PB |
| 6. | A | H | Q | R | W | PB |
| 7. | A | L | X | ee | ff | PB |
| 8. | A | O | bb | cc | ff | PB |



(Continued Next Page)

**POWERBALL BALANCED WHEEL® 52035PB** (Continued from previous page)

| | | | | | | |
|---|---|---|---|---|---|---|
| 9. | A | P | T | dd | hh | PB |
| 10. | A | Z | aa | hh | ii | PB |
| 11. | B | C | M | *Q* | ff | PB |
| 12. | B | D | H | aa | cc | PB |
| 13. | B | D | J | K | Z | PB |
| 14. | B | E | L | O | hh | PB |
| 15. | B | E | P | ee | ii | PB |
| 16. | B | F | L | N | gg | PB |
| 17. | B | I | K | R | T | PB |
| 18. | B | S | X | Z | ee | PB |
| 19. | B | U | V | W | bb | PB |
| 20. | C | D | E | W | ee | PB |
| 21. | C | F | V | cc | hh | PB |
| 22. | C | G | J | X | hh | PB |
| 23. | C | G | K | L | Z | PB |
| 24. | C | G | P | U | aa | PB |
| 25. | C | H | O | ee | gg | PB |
| 26. | C | N | R | U | ii | PB |
| 27. | C | N | T | aa | ff | PB |
| 28. | C | Y | bb | dd | hh | PB |
| 29. | D | F | H | S | bb | PB |
| 30. | D | G | L | *Q* | U | PB |
| 31. | D | I | dd | ff | gg | PB |
| 32. | D | L | M | P | V | PB |
| 33. | D | L | R | Y | aa | PB |
| 34. | D | O | T | X | ii | PB |
| 35. | E | F | H | Z | ff | PB |
| 36. | E | G | I | T | bb | PB |
| 37. | E | H | U | X | cc | PB |
| 38. | E | K | *Q* | X | Y | PB |
| 39. | E | N | S | V | aa | PB |
| 40. | E | R | U | dd | ee | PB |

| | | | | | | |
|---|---|---|---|---|---|---|
| 41. | F | G | R | V | X | PB |
| 42. | F | I | Y | cc | ee | PB |
| 43. | F | J | N | W | aa | PB |
| 44. | F | M | P | R | Z | PB |
| 45. | F | *Q* | T | dd | ii | PB |
| 46. | G | H | V | ff | ii | PB |
| 47. | G | M | N | cc | ee | PB |
| 48. | G | O | S | V | dd | PB |
| 49. | G | P | W | X | gg | PB |
| 50. | H | I | M | U | hh | PB |
| 51. | H | J | L | bb | dd | PB |
| 52. | H | K | N | P | Y | PB |
| 53. | H | M | O | T | W | PB |
| 54. | I | J | L | W | ii | PB |
| 55. | I | N | X | Z | bb | PB |
| 56. | I | O | P | *Q* | aa | PB |
| 57. | J | M | bb | cc | ii | PB |
| 58. | J | O | R | Y | ff | PB |
| 59. | J | P | S | U | ff | PB |
| 60. | J | *Q* | T | V | ee | PB |
| 61. | K | M | S | Y | ii | PB |
| 62. | K | V | cc | gg | ii | PB |
| 63. | K | W | dd | ff | hh | PB |
| 64. | K | aa | bb | ee | gg | PB |
| 65. | L | S | T | W | cc | PB |
| 66. | M | X | aa | cc | dd | PB |
| 67. | N | O | *Q* | Z | dd | PB |
| 68. | P | *Q* | R | bb | cc | PB |
| 69. | *Q* | R | S | gg | hh | PB |
| 70. | T | U | Y | Z | gg | PB |
| 71. | V | W | Y | Z | cc | PB |

# POWERBALL BALANCED WHEEL® 52036PB

## Wheel 36 Numbers + PB in 75 Games for a 2 of 2 Win

With Powerball

| Numbers Matched | Maximum Wins | | | | | | Minimum Wins | | | | | |
|---|---|---|---|---|---|---|---|---|---|---|---|---|
| | 5 + 1 | 4 + 1 | 3 + 1 | 2 + 1 | 1 + 1 | 0 + 1 | 5 + 1 | 4 + 1 | 3 + 1 | 2 + 1 | 1 + 1 | 0 + 1 |
| 5 + 1 | 1 | 0 | 1 | 3 | 39 | 31 | 0 | 0 | 0 | 10 | 28 | 37 |
| 4 + 1 | - | 1 | 1 | 3 | 30 | 40 | - | 0 | 0 | 6 | 26 | 43 |
| 3 + 1 | - | - | 2 | 0 | 27 | 46 | - | - | 0 | 3 | 22 | 50 |
| 2 + 1 | - | - | - | 4 | 14 | 57 | - | - | - | 1 | 16 | 58 |
| 1 + 1 | - | - | - | - | 12 | 63 | - | - | - | - | 9 | 66 |
| 0 + 1 | - | - | - | - | - | 75 | - | - | - | - | - | 75 |

Without Powerball

| Numbers Matched | Maximum Wins | | | | | Minimum Wins | | | | |
|---|---|---|---|---|---|---|---|---|---|---|
| | 5 + 0 | 4 + 0 | 3 + 0 | 2 + 0 | 1 + 0 | 5 + 0 | 4 + 0 | 3 + 0 | 2 + 0 | 1 + 0 |
| 5 + 0 | 1 | 0 | 1 | 3 | 39 | 0 | 0 | 0 | 10 | 28 |
| 4 + 0 | - | 1 | 1 | 3 | 30 | - | 0 | 0 | 6 | 26 |
| 3 + 0 | - | - | 2 | 0 | 27 | - | - | 0 | 3 | 22 |
| 2 + 0 | - | - | - | 4 | 14 | - | - | - | 1 | 16 |
| 1 + 0 | - | - | - | - | 12 | - | - | - | - | 9 |

## Your 36 Numbers + PB to Wheel

| A | B | C | D | E | F | G | H | I | J |
|---|---|---|---|---|---|---|---|---|---|
| 11 | 11 | 11 | 11 | 10 | 10 | 11 | 10 | 10 | 10 |
| **K** | **L** | **M** | **N** | **O** | **P** | **Q** | **R** | **S** | **T** |
| 9 | 11 | 11 | 10 | 12 | 10 | 11 | 11 | 10 | 10 |
| **U** | **V** | **W** | **X** | **Y** | **Z** | **aa** | **bb** | **cc** | **dd** |
| 10 | 9 | 10 | 11 | 10 | 10 | 11 | 10 | 10 | 12 |
| **ee** | **ff** | **gg** | **hh** | **ii** | **jj** | **PB** | | | |
| 10 | 10 | 11 | 10 | 11 | 10 | 75 | | | |

## The 75 Games to Play

| | | | | | | |
|---|---|---|---|---|---|---|
| 1. | A | B | R | X | ee | PB |
| 2. | A | C | D | V | gg | PB |
| 3. | A | C | L | cc | jj | PB |
| 4. | A | D | N | T | W | PB |
| 5. | A | E | I | P | aa | PB |
| 6. | A | F | P | Q | S | PB |
| 7. | A | G | H | L | dd | PB |
| 8. | A | J | K | Y | ff | PB |
| 9. | A | J | V | hh | jj | PB |
| 10. | A | M | O | Z | dd | PB |
| 11. | A | U | Y | bb | ii | PB |
| 12. | B | C | O | Y | bb | PB |
| 13. | B | D | G | S | gg | PB |
| 14. | B | E | N | O | Q | PB |
| 15. | B | F | Z | ii | jj | PB |
| 16. | B | H | V | Y | aa | PB |
| 17. | B | I | O | ff | hh | PB |
| 18. | B | J | L | M | R | PB |
| 19. | B | K | P | Q | W | PB |
| 20. | B | T | cc | gg | hh | PB |
| 21. | B | U | aa | dd | jj | PB |
| 22. | C | D | K | M | aa | PB |
| 23. | C | E | R | W | bb | PB |
| 24. | C | F | I | T | dd | PB |
| 25. | C | G | L | Q | X | PB |
| 26. | C | G | R | S | ii | PB |
| 27. | C | H | P | ee | ii | PB |
| 28. | C | I | J | N | Z | PB |



(Continued Next Page)

## POWERBALL BALANCED WHEEL® 52036PB (Continued from previous page)

| | | | | | | |
|---|---|---|---|---|---|---|
| 29. | C | U | W | ff | hh | PB |
| 30. | D | E | M | hh | ii | PB |
| 31. | D | F | Y | dd | hh | PB |
| 32. | D | H | Z | cc | ff | PB |
| 33. | D | I | L | ee | hh | PB |
| 34. | D | J | Q | U | gg | PB |
| 35. | D | L | O | P | R | PB |
| 36. | D | M | X | bb | jj | PB |
| 37. | E | F | N | ee | ff | PB |
| 38. | E | G | J | Y | cc | PB |
| 39. | E | H | K | T | jj | PB |
| 40. | E | L | S | U | X | PB |
| 41. | E | N | V | dd | ii | PB |
| 42. | E | O | T | Z | gg | PB |
| 43. | F | G | K | L | V | PB |
| 44. | F | G | M | O | U | PB |
| 45. | F | H | R | bb | cc | PB |
| 46. | F | J | O | aa | ii | PB |
| 47. | F | W | X | dd | gg | PB |
| 48. | G | I | M | W | jj | PB |
| 49. | G | L | T | ff | ii | PB |
| 50. | G | N | P | bb | hh | PB |
| 51. | G | U | Z | aa | ee | PB |
| 52. | H | I | X | Y | gg | PB |
| 53. | H | J | O | S | W | PB |
| 54. | H | M | N | U | cc | PB |
| 55. | H | Q | X | aa | hh | PB |
| 56. | I | K | U | bb | dd | PB |
| 57. | I | M | S | V | cc | PB |
| 58. | I | Q | R | gg | ii | PB |
| 59. | J | P | X | cc | dd | PB |
| 60. | J | S | T | bb | ee | PB |
| 61. | K | N | X | dd | ii | PB |
| 62. | K | O | cc | ee | gg | PB |
| 63. | K | R | S | Z | hh | PB |
| 64. | L | N | aa | bb | gg | PB |
| 65. | L | P | W | Y | Z | PB |
| 66. | M | P | ff | gg | jj | PB |
| 67. | M | Q | T | Y | ee | PB |
| 68. | N | R | S | Y | jj | PB |
| 69. | O | Q | dd | ee | jj | PB |
| 70. | O | V | W | X | ee | PB |
| 71. | P | R | T | U | V | PB |
| 72. | Q | V | Z | bb | ff | PB |
| 73. | Q | W | aa | cc | ii | PB |
| 74. | R | S | aa | dd | ff | PB |
| 75. | T | X | Z | aa | ff | PB |



# POWERBALL BALANCED WHEEL® 52037PB

## Wheel 37 Numbers + PB in 78 Games for a 2 of 2 Win

With Powerball

| Numbers Matched | Maximum Wins 5 + 1 | 4 + 1 | 3 + 1 | 2 + 1 | 1 + 1 | 0 + 1 | Minimum Wins 5 + 1 | 4 + 1 | 3 + 1 | 2 + 1 | 1 + 1 | 0 + 1 |
|---|---|---|---|---|---|---|---|---|---|---|---|---|
| 5 + 1 | 1 | 0 | 1 | 3 | 41 | 32 | 0 | 0 | 0 | 10 | 27 | 41 |
| 4 + 1 | - | 1 | 1 | 3 | 31 | 42 | - | 0 | 0 | 6 | 25 | 47 |
| 3 + 1 | - | - | 2 | 2 | 24 | 50 | - | - | 0 | 3 | 21 | 54 |
| 2 + 1 | - | - | - | 4 | 15 | 59 | - | - | - | 1 | 16 | 61 |
| 1 + 1 | - | - | - | - | 12 | 66 | - | - | - | - | 9 | 69 |
| 0 + 1 | - | - | - | - | - | 78 | - | - | - | - | - | 78 |

(Continued Next Page)

## POWERBALL BALANCED WHEEL® 52037PB (Continued from previous page)

Without Powerball

| Numbers Matched | Maximum Wins 5 + 0 | 4 + 0 | 3 + 0 | 2 + 0 | 1 + 0 | Minimum Wins 5 + 0 | 4 + 0 | 3 + 0 | 2 + 0 | 1 + 0 |
|---|---|---|---|---|---|---|---|---|---|---|
| 5 + 0 | 1 | 0 | 1 | 3 | 41 | 0 | 0 | 0 | 10 | 27 |
| 4 + 0 | - | 1 | 1 | 3 | 31 | - | 0 | 0 | 6 | 25 |
| 3 + 0 | - | - | 2 | 2 | 24 | - | - | 0 | 3 | 21 |
| 2 + 0 | - | - | - | 4 | 15 | - | - | - | 1 | 16 |
| 1 + 0 | - | - | - | - | 12 | - | - | - | - | 9 |

## Your 37 Numbers + PB to Wheel

| A | B | C | D | E | F | G | H | I | J |
|---|---|---|---|---|---|---|---|---|---|
| 10 | 11 | 11 | 10 | 11 | 12 | 11 | 10 | 10 | 11 |
| **K** | **L** | **M** | **N** | **O** | **P** | **Q** | **R** | **S** | **T** |
| 11 | 10 | 11 | 11 | 11 | 12 | 10 | 10 | 12 | 11 |
| **U** | **V** | **W** | **X** | **Y** | **Z** | **aa** | **bb** | **cc** | **dd** |
| 11 | 10 | 10 | 10 | 10 | 9 | 9 | 11 | 12 | 10 |
| **ee** | **ff** | **gg** | **hh** | **ii** | **jj** | **kk** | ***PB*** | | |
| 10 | 9 | 11 | 10 | 10 | 10 | 12 | 78 | | |

## The 78 Games to Play

| | | | | | | |
|---|---|---|---|---|---|---|
| 1. | A | B | D | S | X | PB |
| 2. | A | C | T | W | cc | PB |
| 3. | A | E | G | U | aa | PB |
| 4. | A | F | L | M | Z | PB |
| 5. | A | F | Q | R | kk | PB |
| 6. | A | F | V | bb | jj | PB |
| 7. | A | H | J | Y | ee | PB |
| 8. | A | H | K | N | dd | PB |
| 9. | A | I | K | P | hh | PB |
| 10. | A | O | ff | gg | ii | PB |
| 11. | B | C | E | L | cc | PB |
| 12. | B | F | M | N | ii | PB |
| 13. | B | G | W | cc | jj | PB |
| 14. | B | H | T | bb | hh | PB |
| 15. | B | I | P | cc | dd | PB |
| 16. | B | J | M | O | V | PB |
| 17. | B | K | R | U | Y | PB |
| 18. | B | K | Z | cc | gg | PB |
| 19. | B | L | Q | aa | ee | PB |
| 20. | B | V | Y | ff | kk | PB |
| 21. | C | D | G | Q | gg | PB |
| 22. | C | E | dd | ff | jj | PB |
| 23. | C | F | H | U | X | PB |
| 24. | C | G | I | N | O | PB |
| 25. | C | G | N | S | Y | PB |
| 26. | C | J | U | V | hh | PB |
| 27. | C | K | M | P | X | PB |
| 28. | C | K | aa | bb | ii | PB |
| 29. | C | R | Z | ee | kk | PB |
| 30. | D | E | F | K | W | PB |
| 31. | D | H | O | P | R | PB |
| 32. | D | I | U | Z | ff | PB |
| 33. | D | J | M | bb | kk | PB |
| 34. | D | L | dd | hh | kk | PB |
| 35. | D | N | T | V | aa | PB |
| 36. | D | R | bb | cc | ii | PB |
| 37. | D | Y | ee | gg | jj | PB |
| 38. | E | F | O | P | T | PB |
| 39. | E | H | I | M | Q | PB |
| 40. | E | J | N | P | Z | PB |
| 41. | E | L | R | S | T | PB |
| 42. | E | P | S | bb | gg | PB |



(Continued Next Page)

**POWERBALL BALANCED WHEEL® 52037PB** (Continued from previous page)

| | | | | | | | | | | | | | |
|---|---|---|---|---|---|---|---|---|---|---|---|---|---|
| 43. | E | V | X | cc | kk | PB | 61. | J | K | *Q* | T | ff | PB |
| 44. | E | Y | ee | hh | ii | PB | 62. | J | S | T | U | jj | PB |
| 45. | F | G | M | bb | ff | PB | 63. | J | W | X | cc | ii | PB |
| 46. | F | G | *Q* | hh | kk | PB | 64. | K | L | N | O | jj | PB |
| 47. | F | I | L | Y | bb | PB | 65. | K | O | S | dd | kk | PB |
| 48. | F | J | aa | dd | gg | PB | 66. | L | P | X | ff | hh | PB |
| 49. | F | M | S | cc | ee | PB | 67. | M | N | U | gg | kk | PB |
| 50. | G | H | T | Z | jj | PB | 68. | M | R | aa | hh | jj | PB |
| 51. | G | J | L | U | ii | PB | 69. | M | T | W | Y | dd | PB |
| 52. | G | K | P | V | ee | PB | 70. | N | O | cc | gg | hh | PB |
| 53. | G | R | X | dd | gg | PB | 71. | N | *Q* | X | bb | jj | PB |
| 54. | H | L | V | W | gg | PB | 72. | N | R | W | ee | ff | PB |
| 55. | H | S | T | ii | kk | PB | 73. | O | *Q* | S | U | W | PB |
| 56. | H | S | aa | cc | ff | PB | 74. | O | U | bb | dd | ee | PB |
| 57. | I | J | R | S | V | PB | 75. | O | X | Y | Z | aa | PB |
| 58. | I | P | W | aa | kk | PB | 76. | P | *Q* | U | Y | cc | PB |
| 59. | I | P | ii | jj | kk | PB | 77. | *Q* | V | Z | dd | ii | PB |
| 60. | I | T | X | ee | gg | PB | 78. | S | W | Z | bb | hh | PB |



# POWERBALL BALANCED WHEEL® 52038PB

## Wheel 38 Numbers + PB in 83 Games for a 2 of 2 Win

With Powerball

| Numbers Matched | Maximum Wins | | | | | | Minimum Wins | | | | | |
|---|---|---|---|---|---|---|---|---|---|---|---|---|
| | 5 + 1 | 4 + 1 | 3 + 1 | 2 + 1 | 1 + 1 | 0 + 1 | 5 + 1 | 4 + 1 | 3 + 1 | 2 + 1 | 1 + 1 | 0 + 1 |
| 5 + 1 | 1 | 0 | 1 | 7 | 37 | 37 | 0 | 0 | 0 | 10 | 30 | 43 |
| 4 + 1 | - | 1 | 1 | 7 | 28 | 46 | - | 0 | 0 | 6 | 28 | 49 |
| 3 + 1 | - | - | 2 | 5 | 22 | 54 | - | - | 0 | 3 | 24 | 56 |
| 2 + 1 | - | - | - | 5 | 16 | 62 | - | - | - | 1 | 18 | 64 |
| 1 + 1 | - | - | - | - | 13 | 70 | - | - | - | - | 10 | 73 |
| 0 + 1 | - | - | - | - | - | 83 | - | - | - | - | - | 83 |

Without Powerball

| Numbers Matched | Maximum Wins | | | | | Minimum Wins | | | | |
|---|---|---|---|---|---|---|---|---|---|---|
| | 5 + 0 | 4 + 0 | 3 + 0 | 2 + 0 | 1 + 0 | 5 + 0 | 4 + 0 | 3 + 0 | 2 + 0 | 1 + 0 |
| 5 + 0 | 1 | 0 | 1 | 7 | 37 | 0 | 0 | 0 | 10 | 30 |
| 4 + 0 | - | 1 | 1 | 7 | 28 | - | 0 | 0 | 6 | 28 |
| 3 + 0 | - | - | 2 | 5 | 22 | - | - | 0 | 3 | 24 |
| 2 + 0 | - | - | - | 5 | 16 | - | - | - | 1 | 18 |
| 1 + 0 | - | - | - | - | 13 | - | - | - | - | 10 |

(Continued Next Page)

**POWERBALL BALANCED WHEEL® 52038PB** (Continued from previous page)

## Your 38 Numbers + PB to Wheel

| A | B | C | D | E | F | G | H | I | J |
|---|---|---|---|---|---|---|---|---|---|
| 11 | 13 | 11 | 11 | 12 | 11 | 11 | 13 | 11 | 11 |
| **K** | **L** | **M** | **N** | **O** | **P** | **Q** | **R** | **S** | **T** |
| 10 | 11 | 11 | 11 | 10 | 12 | 11 | 11 | 10 | 10 |
| **U** | **V** | **W** | **X** | **Y** | **Z** | **aa** | **bb** | **cc** | **dd** |
| 10 | 11 | 12 | 11 | 11 | 11 | 11 | 10 | 10 | 11 |
| **ee** | **ff** | **gg** | **hh** | **ii** | **jj** | **kk** | **ll** | **PB** | |
| 13 | 10 | 10 | 11 | 10 | 11 | 10 | 10 | 83 | |

## The 83 Games to Play

| | | | | | | | | | | | | |
|---|---|---|---|---|---|---|---|---|---|---|---|---|
| 1. | A | B | N | Z | ee | PB | 27. | C | G | V | cc | hh | PB |
| 2. | A | C | O | P | Y | PB | 28. | C | H | I | K | V | PB |
| 3. | A | C | S | U | X | PB | 29. | C | M | Z | kk | ll | PB |
| 4. | A | D | I | ee | ii | PB | 30. | C | Q | T | ee | jj | PB |
| 5. | A | E | M | ff | jj | PB | 31. | C | aa | dd | ff | kk | PB |
| 6. | A | F | H | J | hh | PB | 32. | D | E | O | hh | kk | PB |
| 7. | A | G | K | L | Z | PB | 33. | D | E | T | X | ll | PB |
| 8. | A | L | N | R | ll | PB | 34. | D | G | M | Y | bb | PB |
| 9. | A | L | T | aa | cc | PB | 35. | D | H | J | S | cc | PB |
| 10. | A | Q | W | gg | kk | PB | 36. | D | K | U | W | jj | PB |
| 11. | A | V | bb | dd | gg | PB | 37. | D | L | P | Q | V | PB |
| 12. | B | C | E | bb | ee | PB | 38. | D | Z | aa | bb | jj | PB |
| 13. | B | D | H | dd | ff | PB | 39. | E | F | R | aa | ii | PB |
| 14. | B | E | G | P | V | PB | 40. | E | H | Q | W | Z | PB |
| 15. | B | E | cc | ee | gg | PB | 41. | E | I | Y | dd | hh | PB |
| 16. | B | F | K | O | ee | PB | 42. | E | K | M | N | S | PB |
| 17. | B | H | O | W | ll | PB | 43. | E | U | V | aa | ee | PB |
| 18. | B | I | L | X | kk | PB | 44. | F | G | ee | hh | ll | PB |
| 19. | B | J | K | ee | kk | PB | 45. | F | I | L | M | P | PB |
| 20. | B | J | M | Q | aa | PB | 46. | F | M | T | V | W | PB |
| 21. | B | P | hh | ii | jj | PB | 47. | F | Q | R | S | ff | PB |
| 22. | B | R | U | Y | aa | PB | 48. | F | R | dd | ee | jj | PB |
| 23. | B | S | T | Z | dd | PB | 49. | F | U | bb | cc | kk | PB |
| 24. | C | D | F | N | W | PB | 50. | F | X | Y | Z | gg | PB |
| 25. | C | D | H | R | gg | PB | 51. | G | H | P | S | ee | PB |
| 26. | C | E | J | L | ii | PB | 52. | G | I | J | N | gg | PB |



(Continued Next Page)

**POWERBALL BALANCED WHEEL® 52038PB** (Continued from previous page)

| | | | | | | |
|---|---|---|---|---|---|---|
| 53. | G | O | *Q* | X | aa | PB |
| 54. | G | O | U | ff | ii | PB |
| 55. | G | P | R | T | kk | PB |
| 56. | G | W | X | dd | jj | PB |
| 57. | H | I | M | *Q* | U | PB |
| 58. | H | I | S | W | aa | PB |
| 59. | H | J | L | X | jj | PB |
| 60. | H | K | T | Y | ii | PB |
| 61. | H | N | bb | ii | kk | PB |
| 62. | I | O | R | V | Z | PB |
| 63. | I | T | X | bb | ff | PB |
| 64. | I | Y | cc | jj | *ll* | PB |
| 65. | J | M | O | cc | dd | PB |
| 66. | J | P | R | W | bb | PB |
| 67. | J | T | U | Z | hh | PB |
| 68. | J | V | Y | ff | *ll* | PB |
| 69. | K | P | R | X | cc | PB |
| 70. | K | *Q* | bb | dd | *ll* | PB |
| 71. | K | aa | ff | gg | hh | PB |
| 72. | L | O | S | bb | hh | PB |
| 73. | L | P | U | dd | gg | PB |
| 74. | L | W | Y | ee | ff | PB |
| 75. | M | R | X | ee | hh | PB |
| 76. | M | S | gg | ii | *ll* | PB |
| 77. | N | O | T | gg | jj | PB |
| 78. | N | P | U | aa | *ll* | PB |
| 79. | N | P | Z | cc | ff | PB |
| 80. | N | *Q* | W | Y | hh | PB |
| 81. | N | V | X | dd | ii | PB |
| 82. | *Q* | W | Z | cc | ii | PB |
| 83. | S | V | Y | jj | kk | PB |



# POWERBALL BALANCED WHEEL® 52039PB

## Wheel 39 Numbers + PB in 88 Games for a 2 of 2 Win

With Powerball

| Numbers Matched | Maximum Wins 5 + 1 | 4 + 1 | 3 + 1 | 2 + 1 | 1 + 1 | 0 + 1 | Minimum Wins 5 + 1 | 4 + 1 | 3 + 1 | 2 + 1 | 1 + 1 | 0 + 1 |
|---|---|---|---|---|---|---|---|---|---|---|---|---|
| 5 + 1 | 1 | 0 | 1 | 6 | 39 | 41 | 0 | 0 | 0 | 10 | 30 | 48 |
| 4 + 1 | - | 1 | 1 | 5 | 31 | 50 | - | 0 | 0 | 6 | 28 | 54 |
| 3 + 1 | - | - | 2 | 1 | 28 | 57 | - | - | 0 | 3 | 24 | 61 |
| 2 + 1 | - | - | - | 4 | 17 | 67 | - | - | - | 1 | 18 | 69 |
| 1 + 1 | - | - | - | - | 13 | 75 | - | - | - | - | 10 | 78 |
| 0 + 1 | - | - | - | - | - | 88 | - | - | - | - | - | 88 |

Without Powerball

| Numbers Matched | Maximum Wins 5 + 0 | 4 + 0 | 3 + 0 | 2 + 0 | 1 + 0 | Minimum Wins 5 + 0 | 4 + 0 | 3 + 0 | 2 + 0 | 1 + 0 |
|---|---|---|---|---|---|---|---|---|---|---|
| 5 + 0 | 1 | 0 | 1 | 6 | 39 | 0 | 0 | 0 | 10 | 30 |
| 4 + 0 | - | 1 | 1 | 5 | 31 | - | 0 | 0 | 6 | 28 |
| 3 + 0 | - | - | 2 | 1 | 28 | - | - | 0 | 3 | 24 |
| 2 + 0 | - | - | - | 4 | 17 | - | - | - | 1 | 18 |
| 1 + 0 | - | - | - | - | 13 | - | - | - | - | 10 |

(Continued Next Page)

**POWERBALL BALANCED WHEEL® 52039PB** (Continued from previous page)

## Your 39 Numbers + PB to Wheel

| A | B | C | D | E | F | G | H | I | J |
|---|---|---|---|---|---|---|---|---|---|
| 11 | 11 | 10 | 11 | 11 | 13 | 12 | 12 | 12 | 11 |
| K | L | M | N | O | P | Q | R | S | T |
| 11 | 11 | 11 | 12 | 12 | 12 | 13 | 10 | 11 | 10 |
| U | V | W | X | Y | Z | aa | bb | cc | dd |
| 12 | 12 | 11 | 10 | 11 | 12 | 11 | 11 | 11 | 11 |
| ee | ff | gg | hh | ii | jj | kk | ll | mm | PB |
| 11 | 11 | 12 | 10 | 12 | 11 | 11 | 12 | 11 | 88 |

## The 88 Games to Play

| | | | | | | |
|---|---|---|---|---|---|---|
| 1. | A | B | W | X | jj | PB |
| 2. | A | C | T | Y | ff | PB |
| 3. | A | D | K | O | bb | PB |
| 4. | A | E | J | ff | hh | PB |
| 5. | A | F | I | M | ll | PB |
| 6. | A | G | L | Z | aa | PB |
| 7. | A | G | S | ee | ii | PB |
| 8. | A | H | M | R | mm | PB |
| 9. | A | L | N | U | cc | PB |
| 10. | A | L | P | V | ii | PB |
| 11. | A | Q | dd | gg | kk | PB |
| 12. | B | C | L | gg | kk | PB |
| 13. | B | D | M | S | V | PB |
| 14. | B | E | P | jj | mm | PB |
| 15. | B | F | N | R | V | PB |
| 16. | B | G | H | J | dd | PB |
| 17. | B | I | aa | bb | ee | PB |
| 18. | B | K | M | T | hh | PB |
| 19. | B | M | P | Y | cc | PB |
| 20. | B | O | P | Z | ff | PB |
| 21. | B | Q | U | ii | ll | PB |
| 22. | C | D | U | ii | mm | PB |
| 23. | C | E | V | W | aa | PB |
| 24. | C | F | P | S | bb | PB |
| 25. | C | G | I | X | cc | PB |
| 26. | C | H | K | O | dd | PB |
| 27. | C | J | M | N | Q | PB |
| 28. | C | R | Z | ee | jj | PB |
| 29. | C | Z | hh | jj | ll | PB |
| 30. | D | E | H | Y | aa | PB |
| 31. | D | F | X | gg | ll | PB |
| 32. | D | G | T | V | Z | PB |
| 33. | D | I | J | R | ll | PB |
| 34. | D | L | Q | ee | hh | PB |
| 35. | D | L | bb | cc | jj | PB |
| 36. | D | N | P | W | kk | PB |
| 37. | D | S | U | dd | ff | PB |
| 38. | E | F | T | gg | ii | PB |
| 39. | E | G | O | S | ll | PB |
| 40. | E | I | N | dd | hh | PB |
| 41. | E | K | L | X | mm | PB |
| 42. | E | K | P | R | U | PB |
| 43. | E | M | Z | bb | kk | PB |
| 44. | E | Q | cc | ee | gg | PB |
| 45. | F | G | M | dd | jj | PB |
| 46. | F | H | U | X | Z | PB |
| 47. | F | I | L | M | W | PB |
| 48. | F | J | K | Q | aa | PB |
| 49. | F | J | ff | gg | jj | PB |
| 50. | F | K | Y | ee | ll | PB |
| 51. | F | O | kk | ll | mm | PB |
| 52. | F | Q | S | cc | hh | PB |



(Continued Next Page)

## POWERBALL BALANCED WHEEL® 52039PB (Continued from previous page)

| | | | | | | |
|---|---|---|---|---|---|---|
| 53. | G | I | K | ff | kk | PB |
| 54. | G | J | P | W | Y | PB |
| 55. | G | N | bb | gg | mm | PB |
| 56. | G | O | *Q* | U | jj | PB |
| 57. | G | R | Y | gg | hh | PB |
| 58. | H | I | K | V | jj | PB |
| 59. | H | I | P | *Q* | gg | PB |
| 60. | H | L | R | S | ff | PB |
| 61. | H | N | V | ee | *ll* | PB |
| 62. | H | T | W | cc | *ll* | PB |
| 63. | H | U | V | Y | kk | PB |
| 64. | H | U | bb | hh | ii | PB |
| 65. | I | N | S | T | X | PB |
| 66. | I | O | U | W | ee | PB |
| 67. | I | Y | Z | ii | mm | PB |
| 68. | J | L | O | T | U | PB |
| 69. | J | S | aa | cc | mm | PB |
| 70. | J | V | X | bb | dd | PB |
| 71. | J | Z | ee | ii | kk | PB |
| 72. | K | N | O | cc | ii | PB |
| 73. | K | S | W | Z | gg | PB |
| 74. | L | Y | bb | dd | *ll* | PB |
| 75. | M | O | U | aa | gg | PB |
| 76. | M | X | ee | ff | ii | PB |
| 77. | N | P | aa | ff | *ll* | PB |
| 78. | N | *Q* | V | Z | gg | PB |
| 79. | N | S | Y | jj | kk | PB |
| 80. | O | *Q* | R | X | Y | PB |
| 81. | O | V | W | hh | mm | PB |
| 82. | P | T | dd | ee | mm | PB |
| 83. | P | X | aa | hh | kk | PB |
| 84. | *Q* | T | aa | ii | jj | PB |
| 85. | *Q* | W | bb | ff | mm | PB |
| 86. | R | T | bb | cc | kk | PB |
| 87. | R | W | aa | dd | ii | PB |
| 88. | V | Z | cc | dd | ff | PB |



# POWERBALL BALANCED WHEEL® 52040PB

## Wheel 40 Numbers + PB in 92 Games for a 2 of 2 Win

With Powerball

| Numbers Matched | Maximum Wins 5 + 1 | 4 + 1 | 3 + 1 | 2 + 1 | 1 + 1 | 0 + 1 | Minimum Wins 5 + 1 | 4 + 1 | 3 + 1 | 2 + 1 | 1 + 1 | 0 + 1 |
|---|---|---|---|---|---|---|---|---|---|---|---|---|
| 5 + 1 | 1 | 1 | 0 | 3 | 46 | 41 | 0 | 0 | 0 | 10 | 35 | 47 |
| 4 + 1 | - | 2 | 0 | 1 | 39 | 50 | - | 0 | 0 | 6 | 32 | 54 |
| 3 + 1 | - | - | 2 | 3 | 25 | 62 | - | - | 0 | 3 | 27 | 62 |
| 2 + 1 | - | - | - | 4 | 17 | 71 | - | - | - | 1 | 20 | 71 |
| 1 + 1 | - | - | - | - | 13 | 79 | - | - | - | - | 11 | 81 |
| 0 + 1 | - | - | - | - | - | 92 | - | - | - | - | - | 92 |

Without Powerball

| Numbers Matched | Maximum Wins 5 + 0 | 4 + 0 | 3 + 0 | 2 + 0 | 1 + 0 | Minimum Wins 5 + 0 | 4 + 0 | 3 + 0 | 2 + 0 | 1 + 0 |
|---|---|---|---|---|---|---|---|---|---|---|
| 5 + 0 | 1 | 1 | 0 | 3 | 46 | 0 | 0 | 0 | 10 | 35 |
| 4 + 0 | - | 2 | 0 | 1 | 39 | - | 0 | 0 | 6 | 32 |
| 3 + 0 | - | - | 2 | 3 | 25 | - | - | 0 | 3 | 27 |
| 2 + 0 | - | - | - | 4 | 17 | - | - | - | 1 | 20 |
| 1 + 0 | - | - | - | - | 13 | - | - | - | - | 11 |

(Continued Next Page)

**POWERBALL BALANCED WHEEL® 52040PB** (Continued from previous page)

## Your 40 Numbers + PB to Wheel

| A | B | C | D | E | F | G | H | I | J | K |
|---|---|---|---|---|---|---|---|---|---|---|
| 11 | 13 | 11 | 12 | 13 | 12 | 11 | 11 | 11 | 11 | 12 |
| **L** | **M** | **N** | **O** | **P** | **Q** | **R** | **S** | **T** | **U** | **V** |
| 11 | 11 | 11 | 11 | 11 | 11 | 11 | 11 | 12 | 11 | 11 |
| **W** | **X** | **Y** | **Z** | **aa** | **bb** | **cc** | **dd** | **ee** | **ff** | **gg** |
| 11 | 12 | 11 | 12 | 12 | 11 | 12 | 12 | 12 | 11 | 13 |
| **hh** | **ii** | **jj** | **kk** | ***ll*** | **mm** | **nn** | **PB** | | | |
| 12 | 12 | 12 | 11 | 11 | 12 | 11 | 92 | | | |

## The 92 Games to Play

| | | | | | | |
|---|---|---|---|---|---|---|
| 1. | A | B | K | *Q* | Z | PB |
| 2. | A | C | cc | dd | gg | PB |
| 3. | A | D | F | V | X | PB |
| 4. | A | E | ii | *ll* | mm | PB |
| 5. | A | G | L | P | S | PB |
| 6. | A | H | N | U | ff | PB |
| 7. | A | I | Y | ee | jj | PB |
| 8. | A | J | W | aa | ee | PB |
| 9. | A | M | R | aa | nn | PB |
| 10. | A | M | gg | hh | jj | PB |
| 11. | A | O | T | bb | kk | PB |
| 12. | B | C | M | bb | *ll* | PB |
| 13. | B | D | L | W | Z | PB |
| 14. | B | E | Z | dd | hh | PB |
| 15. | B | F | H | K | jj | PB |
| 16. | B | F | O | ee | ii | PB |
| 17. | B | G | X | aa | bb | PB |
| 18. | B | I | P | U | kk | PB |
| 19. | B | J | V | gg | ii | PB |
| 20. | B | N | R | dd | mm | PB |
| 21. | B | N | T | hh | ii | PB |
| 22. | B | S | Z | ff | hh | PB |
| 23. | B | Y | cc | mm | nn | PB |
| 24. | C | D | J | *Q* | kk | PB |
| 25. | C | E | I | S | V | PB |
| 26. | C | F | N | T | aa | PB |
| 27. | C | G | O | dd | ff | PB |
| 28. | C | H | O | U | Z | PB |
| 29. | C | K | L | R | Y | PB |
| 30. | C | K | X | ee | ii | PB |
| 31. | C | P | hh | jj | mm | PB |
| 32. | C | V | W | ff | nn | PB |
| 33. | D | E | M | P | T | PB |
| 34. | D | E | O | gg | nn | PB |
| 35. | D | E | *Q* | Y | bb | PB |
| 36. | D | G | R | ii | kk | PB |
| 37. | D | H | T | X | ee | PB |
| 38. | D | I | ff | *ll* | mm | PB |
| 39. | D | K | N | S | nn | PB |
| 40. | D | R | U | X | hh | PB |
| 41. | D | aa | cc | dd | jj | PB |
| 42. | E | F | R | W | gg | PB |
| 43. | E | F | W | gg | mm | PB |
| 44. | E | G | ee | hh | kk | PB |
| 45. | E | H | I | J | R | PB |
| 46. | E | K | U | aa | *ll* | PB |
| 47. | E | L | X | ff | jj | PB |
| 48. | E | N | R | Z | cc | PB |
| 49. | F | G | H | *Q* | S | PB |
| 50. | F | I | L | cc | hh | PB |
| 51. | F | J | ff | kk | *ll* | PB |
| 52. | F | M | Z | ee | nn | PB |



(Continued Next Page)

## POWERBALL BALANCED WHEEL® 52040PB (Continued from previous page)

| | | | | | | |
|---|---|---|---|---|---|---|
| 53. | F | P | U | Y | dd | PB |
| 54. | F | Z | bb | cc | ii | PB |
| 55. | G | I | *Q* | jj | nn | PB |
| 56. | G | J | M | N | Y | PB |
| 57. | G | K | V | cc | mm | PB |
| 58. | G | P | Z | gg | *ll* | PB |
| 59. | G | T | U | W | jj | PB |
| 60. | H | J | aa | ii | jj | PB |
| 61. | H | L | M | kk | mm | PB |
| 62. | H | P | V | W | bb | PB |
| 63. | H | Y | hh | *ll* | nn | PB |
| 64. | H | cc | dd | ee | gg | PB |
| 65. | I | K | M | O | X | PB |
| 66. | I | N | bb | gg | jj | PB |
| 67. | I | T | Z | aa | mm | PB |
| 68. | I | W | dd | ii | *ll* | PB |
| 69. | J | K | T | bb | hh | PB |
| 70. | J | L | U | ii | nn | PB |
| 71. | J | O | P | cc | mm | PB |
| 72. | J | S | X | Z | dd | PB |
| 73. | K | O | W | X | Y | PB |
| 74. | K | P | *Q* | aa | ff | PB |
| 75. | K | aa | dd | gg | kk | PB |
| 76. | L | N | V | ee | *ll* | PB |
| 77. | L | O | V | aa | hh | PB |
| 78. | L | *Q* | X | gg | mm | PB |
| 79. | L | T | bb | dd | nn | PB |
| 80. | M | *Q* | U | V | dd | PB |
| 81. | M | S | W | cc | kk | PB |
| 82. | M | S | Y | ff | ii | PB |
| 83. | N | O | *Q* | W | hh | PB |
| 84. | N | P | X | kk | nn | PB |
| 85. | O | R | S | jj | *ll* | PB |
| 86. | P | *Q* | R | ee | ii | PB |
| 87. | *Q* | T | X | cc | *ll* | PB |
| 88. | R | T | V | bb | ff | PB |
| 89. | S | T | Y | aa | gg | PB |
| 90. | S | U | bb | ee | mm | PB |
| 91. | U | cc | ee | ff | gg | PB |
| 92. | V | Y | Z | jj | kk | PB |



# POWERBALL BALANCED WHEEL® 52042PB

## Wheel 42 Numbers + PB in 102 Games for a 2 of 2 Win

With Powerball

| Numbers Matched | Maximum Wins | | | | | | Minimum Wins | | | | | |
|---|---|---|---|---|---|---|---|---|---|---|---|---|
| | 5 + 1 | 4 + 1 | 3 + 1 | 2 + 1 | 1 + 1 | 0 + 1 | 5 + 1 | 4 + 1 | 3 + 1 | 2 + 1 | 1 + 1 | 0 + 1 |
| 5 + 1 | 1 | 0 | 2 | 3 | 47 | 49 | 0 | 0 | 0 | 10 | 35 | 57 |
| 4 + 1 | - | 1 | 2 | 0 | 41 | 58 | - | 0 | 0 | 6 | 32 | 64 |
| 3 + 1 | - | - | 2 | 1 | 30 | 69 | - | - | 0 | 3 | 27 | 72 |
| 2 + 1 | - | - | - | 4 | 18 | 80 | - | - | - | 1 | 20 | 81 |
| 1 + 1 | - | - | - | - | 14 | 88 | - | - | - | - | 11 | 91 |
| 0 + 1 | - | - | - | - | - | 102 | - | - | - | - | - | 102 |

Without Powerball

| Numbers Matched | Maximum Wins | | | | | Minimum Wins | | | | |
|---|---|---|---|---|---|---|---|---|---|---|
| | 5 + 0 | 4 + 0 | 3 + 0 | 2 + 0 | 1 + 0 | 5 + 0 | 4 + 0 | 3 + 0 | 2 + 0 | 1 + 0 |
| 5 + 0 | 1 | 0 | 2 | 3 | 47 | 0 | 0 | 0 | 10 | 35 |
| 4 + 0 | - | 1 | 2 | 0 | 41 | - | 0 | 0 | 6 | 32 |
| 3 + 0 | - | - | 2 | 1 | 30 | - | - | 0 | 3 | 27 |
| 2 + 0 | - | - | - | 4 | 18 | - | - | - | 1 | 20 |
| 1 + 0 | - | - | - | - | 14 | - | - | - | - | 11 |

(Continued Next Page)

**POWERBALL BALANCED WHEEL® 52042PB** (Continued from previous page)

## Your 42 Numbers + PB to Wheel

| A | B | C | D | E | F | G | H | I | J | K |
|---|---|---|---|---|---|---|---|---|---|---|
| 12 | 12 | 13 | 12 | 12 | 12 | 13 | 13 | 12 | 14 | 12 |
| **L** | **M** | **N** | **O** | **P** | **Q** | **R** | **S** | **T** | **U** | **V** |
| 12 | 11 | 14 | 12 | 12 | 12 | 11 | 12 | 12 | 11 | 13 |
| **W** | **X** | **Y** | **Z** | **aa** | **bb** | **cc** | **dd** | **ee** | **ff** | **gg** |
| 12 | 12 | 13 | 12 | 12 | 11 | 13 | 12 | 12 | 12 | 12 |
| **hh** | **ii** | **jj** | **kk** | ***ll*** | **mm** | **nn** | **oo** | **pp** | **PB** | |
| 12 | 11 | 12 | 11 | 12 | 13 | 12 | 13 | 12 | 102 | |

## The 102 Games to Play

| | | | | | | |
|---|---|---|---|---|---|---|
| 1. | A | B | ee | gg | oo | PB |
| 2. | A | C | M | U | ff | PB |
| 3. | A | D | J | S | bb | PB |
| 4. | A | E | M | T | ee | PB |
| 5. | A | F | Y | hh | ii | PB |
| 6. | A | G | I | *Q* | mm | PB |
| 7. | A | H | T | dd | pp | PB |
| 8. | A | I | V | Z | mm | PB |
| 9. | A | K | aa | ii | jj | PB |
| 10. | A | L | N | P | kk | PB |
| 11. | A | O | R | *ll* | nn | PB |
| 12. | A | W | X | cc | oo | PB |
| 13. | B | C | E | V | pp | PB |
| 14. | B | D | H | O | oo | PB |
| 15. | B | F | K | M | X | PB |
| 16. | B | G | R | W | ff | PB |
| 17. | B | I | L | S | U | PB |
| 18. | B | J | N | Z | *ll* | PB |
| 19. | B | J | P | Y | mm | PB |
| 20. | B | *Q* | hh | jj | *ll* | PB |
| 21. | B | T | W | aa | cc | PB |
| 22. | B | bb | cc | ii | nn | PB |
| 23. | B | dd | kk | oo | pp | PB |
| 24. | C | D | W | hh | mm | PB |
| 25. | C | E | I | P | Z | PB |
| 26. | C | F | O | dd | ff | PB |
| 27. | C | G | H | K | aa | PB |
| 28. | C | J | L | jj | nn | PB |
| 29. | C | K | N | *Q* | pp | PB |
| 30. | C | N | S | ee | kk | PB |
| 31. | C | O | V | X | Y | PB |
| 32. | C | P | R | cc | hh | PB |
| 33. | C | T | ii | *ll* | oo | PB |
| 34. | C | Z | aa | bb | gg | PB |
| 35. | D | E | L | N | aa | PB |
| 36. | D | E | jj | kk | *ll* | PB |
| 37. | D | F | I | T | gg | PB |
| 38. | D | G | R | ii | pp | PB |
| 39. | D | H | J | V | nn | PB |
| 40. | D | J | X | dd | gg | PB |
| 41. | D | K | U | Y | cc | PB |
| 42. | D | L | M | P | oo | PB |
| 43. | D | *Q* | Z | ee | ff | PB |
| 44. | E | F | O | bb | pp | PB |
| 45. | E | G | X | dd | nn | PB |
| 46. | E | H | J | K | Y | PB |
| 47. | E | *Q* | W | gg | ii | PB |
| 48. | E | R | S | T | U | PB |
| 49. | E | S | Z | cc | hh | PB |
| 50. | E | bb | ff | mm | oo | PB |
| 51. | F | G | J | N | gg | PB |
| 52. | F | H | W | cc | kk | PB |

(Continued Next Page)

## POWERBALL BALANCED WHEEL® 52042PB (Continued from previous page)

| | | | | | | |
|---|---|---|---|---|---|---|
| 53. | F | L | R | X | mm | PB |
| 54. | F | P | *Q* | aa | nn | PB |
| 55. | F | S | V | *ll* | oo | PB |
| 56. | F | U | W | Z | nn | PB |
| 57. | F | X | ee | hh | jj | PB |
| 58. | G | H | L | Z | *ll* | PB |
| 59. | G | H | U | bb | ee | PB |
| 60. | G | M | O | *Q* | cc | PB |
| 61. | G | N | U | dd | jj | PB |
| 62. | G | O | P | S | Y | PB |
| 63. | G | *Q* | cc | mm | oo | PB |
| 64. | G | T | V | hh | kk | PB |
| 65. | H | I | N | X | ff | PB |
| 66. | H | M | R | gg | jj | PB |
| 67. | H | P | U | V | ii | PB |
| 68. | H | *Q* | S | V | X | PB |
| 69. | H | W | hh | mm | pp | PB |
| 70. | I | J | R | ee | ii | PB |
| 71. | I | K | kk | nn | oo | PB |
| 72. | I | M | W | Y | *ll* | PB |
| 73. | I | O | aa | dd | hh | PB |
| 74. | I | P | jj | mm | pp | PB |
| 75. | I | bb | cc | dd | *ll* | PB |
| 76. | J | K | O | S | W | PB |
| 77. | J | L | cc | ff | pp | PB |

| | | | | | | |
|---|---|---|---|---|---|---|
| 78. | J | M | V | aa | kk | PB |
| 79. | J | *Q* | U | hh | oo | PB |
| 80. | J | T | cc | gg | jj | PB |
| 81. | K | L | ff | gg | hh | PB |
| 82. | K | P | T | X | bb | PB |
| 83. | K | R | V | Z | dd | PB |
| 84. | K | aa | ee | *ll* | mm | PB |
| 85. | L | N | O | ee | ii | PB |
| 86. | L | *Q* | T | Y | dd | PB |
| 87. | L | V | W | bb | jj | PB |
| 88. | M | N | bb | hh | nn | PB |
| 89. | M | S | dd | ii | mm | PB |
| 90. | M | Y | Z | ee | pp | PB |
| 91. | N | P | W | dd | ee | PB |
| 92. | N | R | Y | aa | oo | PB |
| 93. | N | T | ff | mm | nn | PB |
| 94. | N | V | cc | ee | nn | PB |
| 95. | O | T | Z | jj | oo | PB |
| 96. | O | U | gg | kk | mm | PB |
| 97. | P | V | ff | gg | *ll* | PB |
| 98. | *Q* | R | Y | bb | kk | PB |
| 99. | S | Y | aa | ff | jj | PB |
| 100. | S | Y | gg | nn | pp | PB |
| 101. | U | X | aa | *ll* | pp | PB |
| 102. | X | Z | ff | ii | kk | PB |



# POWERBALL BALANCED WHEEL® 52045PB

## Wheel 45 Numbers + PB in 116 Games for a 2 of 2 Win

With Powerball

| Numbers Matched | Maximum Wins 5 + 1 | 4 + 1 | 3 + 1 | 2 + 1 | 1 + 1 | 0 + 1 | Minimum Wins 5 + 1 | 4 + 1 | 3 + 1 | 2 + 1 | 1 + 1 | 0 + 1 |
|---|---|---|---|---|---|---|---|---|---|---|---|---|
| 5 + 1 | 1 | 0 | 2 | 6 | 46 | 61 | 0 | 0 | 0 | 10 | 40 | 66 |
| 4 + 1 | - | 1 | 1 | 5 | 38 | 71 | - | 0 | 0 | 6 | 36 | 74 |
| 3 + 1 | - | - | 2 | 2 | 31 | 81 | - | - | 0 | 3 | 30 | 83 |
| 2 + 1 | - | - | - | 4 | 19 | 93 | - | - | - | 1 | 22 | 93 |
| 1 + 1 | - | - | - | - | 15 | 101 | - | - | - | - | 12 | 104 |
| 0 + 1 | - | - | - | - | - | 116 | - | - | - | - | - | 116 |

(Continued Next Page)

## POWERBALL BALANCED WHEEL® 52045PB (Continued from previous page)

Without Powerball

| Numbers Matched | Maximum Wins | | | | | Minimum Wins | | | | |
|---|---|---|---|---|---|---|---|---|---|---|
| | 5 + 0 | 4 + 0 | 3 + 0 | 2 + 0 | 1 + 0 | 5 + 0 | 4 + 0 | 3 + 0 | 2 + 0 | 1 + 0 |
| 5 + 0 | 1 | 0 | 2 | 6 | 46 | 0 | 0 | 0 | 10 | 40 |
| 4 + 0 | - | 1 | 1 | 5 | 38 | - | 0 | 0 | 6 | 36 |
| 3 + 0 | - | - | 2 | 2 | 31 | - | - | 0 | 3 | 30 |
| 2 + 0 | - | - | - | 4 | 19 | - | - | - | 1 | 22 |
| 1 + 0 | - | - | - | - | 15 | - | - | - | - | 12 |

# Your 45 Numbers + PB to Wheel

| A | B | C | D | E | F | G | H | I | J |
|---|---|---|---|---|---|---|---|---|---|
| 13 | 14 | 13 | 13 | 13 | 14 | 13 | 13 | 12 | 13 |
| **K** | **L** | **M** | **N** | **O** | **P** | **Q** | **R** | **S** | **T** |
| 13 | 12 | 12 | 13 | 12 | 13 | 13 | 12 | 13 | 12 |
| **U** | **V** | **W** | **X** | **Y** | **Z** | **aa** | **bb** | **cc** | **dd** |
| 15 | 12 | 14 | 14 | 13 | 12 | 13 | 12 | 12 | 13 |
| **ee** | **ff** | **gg** | **hh** | **ii** | **jj** | **kk** | **ll** | **mm** | **nn** |
| 12 | 13 | 12 | 12 | 13 | 13 | 14 | 13 | 13 | 13 |
| **oo** | **pp** | **qq** | **rr** | **ss** | **PB** | | | | |
| 13 | 13 | 13 | 14 | 13 | 116 | | | | |

# The 116 Games to Play

| | | | | | | |
|---|---|---|---|---|---|---|
| 1. | A | B | J | ff | nn | PB |
| 2. | A | C | S | T | qq | PB |
| 3. | A | D | aa | jj | mm | PB |
| 4. | A | E | G | H | ii | PB |
| 5. | A | E | Q | R | rr | PB |
| 6. | A | F | L | X | Z | PB |
| 7. | A | F | gg | qq | ss | PB |
| 8. | A | H | I | W | cc | PB |
| 9. | A | K | O | kk | oo | PB |
| 10. | A | M | U | Y | ll | PB |
| 11. | A | N | U | V | ee | PB |
| 12. | A | P | bb | dd | rr | PB |
| 13. | A | Q | hh | ii | pp | PB |
| 14. | B | C | P | Z | rr | PB |
| 15. | B | D | E | ee | gg | PB |
| 16. | B | D | G | R | oo | PB |
| 17. | B | F | Q | kk | pp | PB |
| 18. | B | F | T | mm | nn | PB |
| 19. | B | H | X | ll | qq | PB |
| 20. | B | I | R | gg | hh | PB |
| 21. | B | K | L | S | bb | PB |
| 22. | B | L | aa | ii | ss | PB |
| 23. | B | M | V | dd | pp | PB |
| 24. | B | N | O | cc | jj | PB |
| 25. | B | P | W | kk | rr | PB |
| 26. | B | U | W | Y | kk | PB |
| 27. | C | D | ee | ll | nn | PB |
| 28. | C | E | hh | jj | ll | PB |
| 29. | C | F | I | N | X | PB |
| 30. | C | G | L | Q | dd | PB |
| 31. | C | H | J | ii | mm | PB |
| 32. | C | K | M | R | W | PB |
| 33. | C | N | V | Y | ff | PB |
| 34. | C | N | bb | dd | ll | PB |
| 35. | C | O | cc | gg | pp | PB |
| 36. | C | Q | U | aa | kk | PB |
| 37. | C | S | ee | oo | ss | PB |
| 38. | D | E | L | P | V | PB |



(Continued Next Page)

## POWERBALL BALANCED WHEEL® 52045PB (Continued from previous page)

| | | | | | | |
|---|---|---|---|---|---|---|
| 39. | D | F | S | dd | hh | PB |
| 40. | D | H | O | *Q* | X | PB |
| 41. | D | I | M | ff | ii | PB |
| 42. | D | J | cc | kk | qq | PB |
| 43. | D | K | N | ii | nn | PB |
| 44. | D | T | Y | oo | rr | PB |
| 45. | D | U | bb | pp | qq | PB |
| 46. | D | W | Z | jj | ss | PB |
| 47. | E | F | Y | ff | qq | PB |
| 48. | E | G | N | S | U | PB |
| 49. | E | I | dd | nn | qq | PB |
| 50. | E | J | bb | kk | mm | PB |
| 51. | E | K | Z | cc | oo | PB |
| 52. | E | M | O | mm | ss | PB |
| 53. | E | O | T | W | *ll* | PB |
| 54. | E | X | aa | *ll* | pp | PB |
| 55. | F | G | O | bb | ee | PB |
| 56. | F | G | ii | *ll* | rr | PB |
| 57. | F | H | K | P | U | PB |
| 58. | F | J | V | aa | oo | PB |
| 59. | F | J | W | jj | pp | PB |
| 60. | F | M | T | cc | rr | PB |
| 61. | F | P | R | jj | mm | PB |
| 62. | G | I | V | kk | ss | PB |
| 63. | G | J | T | hh | ss | PB |
| 64. | G | K | Y | mm | pp | PB |
| 65. | G | L | W | jj | qq | PB |
| 66. | G | M | Z | aa | qq | PB |
| 67. | G | P | cc | ff | *ll* | PB |
| 68. | G | X | gg | nn | ss | PB |
| 69. | H | I | T | Z | bb | PB |
| 70. | H | L | M | kk | nn | PB |
| 71. | H | N | aa | hh | oo | PB |
| 72. | H | R | S | V | *ll* | PB |
| 73. | H | U | Z | ee | pp | PB |

| | | | | | | |
|---|---|---|---|---|---|---|
| 74. | H | Y | dd | ff | ss | PB |
| 75. | H | ff | gg | jj | rr | PB |
| 76. | I | J | O | U | dd | PB |
| 77. | I | K | aa | ee | rr | PB |
| 78. | I | L | *ll* | mm | oo | PB |
| 79. | I | P | pp | rr | ss | PB |
| 80. | I | *Q* | S | Y | jj | PB |
| 81. | J | K | *Q* | *ll* | ss | PB |
| 82. | J | L | U | gg | rr | PB |
| 83. | J | M | N | P | S | PB |
| 84. | J | R | Y | Z | dd | PB |
| 85. | J | X | ee | ff | mm | PB |
| 86. | K | O | P | hh | qq | PB |
| 87. | K | T | V | X | gg | PB |
| 88. | K | T | aa | dd | ff | PB |
| 89. | K | V | jj | oo | qq | PB |
| 90. | L | N | R | T | pp | PB |
| 91. | L | O | W | aa | ff | PB |
| 92. | L | Y | cc | ee | hh | PB |
| 93. | M | *Q* | bb | gg | oo | PB |
| 94. | M | U | X | hh | mm | PB |
| 95. | M | dd | ee | jj | kk | PB |
| 96. | N | *Q* | mm | qq | rr | PB |
| 97. | N | U | W | nn | ss | PB |
| 98. | N | Z | gg | kk | *ll* | PB |
| 99. | O | R | V | nn | rr | PB |
| 100. | O | S | Y | Z | ii | PB |
| 101. | P | *Q* | T | W | ee | PB |
| 102. | P | W | X | nn | oo | PB |
| 103. | P | Y | aa | gg | ii | PB |
| 104. | *Q* | V | Z | cc | mm | PB |
| 105. | *Q* | Z | ff | hh | nn | PB |
| 106. | R | U | bb | cc | ss | PB |
| 107. | R | X | ee | ii | qq | PB |
| 108. | R | aa | bb | ff | kk | PB |



(Continued Next Page)

**POWERBALL BALANCED WHEEL® 52045PB** (Continued from previous page)

| | | | | | | |
|---|---|---|---|---|---|---|
| 109. | S | U | ff | oo | pp | PB |
| 110. | S | W | dd | gg | mm | PB |
| 111. | S | X | hh | kk | rr | PB |
| 112. | S | aa | cc | nn | pp | PB |
| 113. | T | U | ii | jj | kk | PB |
| 114. | V | W | bb | hh | ii | PB |
| 115. | X | Y | bb | jj | nn | PB |
| 116. | X | cc | dd | ii | oo | PB |



# POWERBALL BALANCED WHEEL® 52047PB

## Wheel 47 Numbers + PB in 126 Games for a 2 of 2 Win

With Powerball

| Numbers Matched | Maximum Wins 5 + 1 | 4 + 1 | 3 + 1 | 2 + 1 | 1 + 1 | 0 + 1 | Minimum Wins 5 + 1 | 4 + 1 | 3 + 1 | 2 + 1 | 1 + 1 | 0 + 1 |
|---|---|---|---|---|---|---|---|---|---|---|---|---|
| 5 + 1 | 1 | 0 | 1 | 3 | 55 | 66 | 0 | 0 | 0 | 10 | 43 | 73 |
| 4 + 1 | - | 1 | 1 | 2 | 44 | 78 | - | 0 | 0 | 6 | 38 | 82 |
| 3 + 1 | - | - | 2 | 0 | 36 | 88 | - | - | 0 | 3 | 31 | 92 |
| 2 + 1 | - | - | - | 3 | 23 | 100 | - | - | - | 1 | 22 | 103 |
| 1 + 1 | - | - | - | - | 15 | 111 | - | - | - | - | 12 | 114 |
| 0 + 1 | - | - | - | - | - | 126 | - | - | - | - | - | 126 |

Without Powerball

| Numbers Matched | Maximum Wins 5 + 0 | 4 + 0 | 3 + 0 | 2 + 0 | 1 + 0 | Minimum Wins 5 + 0 | 4 + 0 | 3 + 0 | 2 + 0 | 1 + 0 |
|---|---|---|---|---|---|---|---|---|---|---|
| 5 + 0 | 1 | 0 | 1 | 3 | 55 | 0 | 0 | 0 | 10 | 43 |
| 4 + 0 | - | 1 | 1 | 2 | 44 | - | 0 | 0 | 6 | 38 |
| 3 + 0 | - | - | 2 | 0 | 36 | - | - | 0 | 3 | 31 |
| 2 + 0 | - | - | - | 3 | 23 | - | - | - | 1 | 22 |
| 1 + 0 | - | - | - | - | 15 | - | - | - | - | 12 |

## Your 47 Numbers + PB to Wheel

| A | B | C | D | E | F | G | H | I | J |
|---|---|---|---|---|---|---|---|---|---|
| 12 | 13 | 14 | 15 | 13 | 14 | 13 | 13 | 14 | 13 |
| **K** | **L** | **M** | **N** | **O** | **P** | **Q** | **R** | **S** | **T** |
| 13 | 14 | 13 | 13 | 14 | 13 | 13 | 13 | 13 | 13 |
| **U** | **V** | **W** | **X** | **Y** | **Z** | **aa** | **bb** | **cc** | **dd** |
| 13 | 14 | 14 | 13 | 13 | 13 | 13 | 13 | 15 | 13 |
| **ee** | **ff** | **gg** | **hh** | **ii** | **jj** | **kk** | ***ll*** | **mm** | **nn** |
| 14 | 14 | 13 | 13 | 13 | 13 | 14 | 14 | 15 | 14 |
| **oo** | **pp** | **qq** | **rr** | **ss** | **tt** | **uu** | **PB** | | |
| 13 | 14 | 13 | 14 | 14 | 12 | 13 | 126 | | |

## The 126 Games to Play

| | | | | | | |
|---|---|---|---|---|---|---|
| 1. | A | B | D | U | *ll* | PB |
| 2. | A | C | N | S | dd | PB |
| 3. | A | E | R | S | nn | PB |
| 4. | A | F | L | V | gg | PB |
| 5. | A | G | M | O | jj | PB |
| 6. | A | H | pp | qq | ss | PB |
| 7. | A | I | K | mm | rr | PB |
| 8. | A | J | W | ee | uu | PB |
| 9. | A | P | *Q* | cc | hh | PB |
| 10. | A | T | X | oo | tt | PB |
| 11. | A | Y | aa | bb | kk | PB |
| 12. | A | Z | ff | ii | ss | PB |
| 13. | B | C | T | W | ee | PB |
| 14. | B | E | L | W | Y | PB |



(Continued Next Page)

**POWERBALL BALANCED WHEEL® 52047PB** (Continued from previous page)

| | | | | | | |
|---|---|---|---|---|---|---|
| 15. | B | F | P | ff | mm | PB |
| 16. | B | G | H | cc | nn | PB |
| 17. | B | I | S | X | Z | PB |
| 18. | B | J | K | ii | qq | PB |
| 19. | B | M | S | V | rr | PB |
| 20. | B | N | gg | oo | uu | PB |
| 21. | B | O | aa | hh | ss | PB |
| 22. | B | *Q* | dd | kk | rr | PB |
| 23. | B | R | bb | mm | tt | PB |
| 24. | B | T | Y | jj | pp | PB |
| 25. | C | D | bb | hh | ii | PB |
| 26. | C | E | F | U | ss | PB |
| 27. | C | E | G | ff | mm | PB |
| 28. | C | F | L | nn | pp | PB |
| 29. | C | H | O | *Q* | uu | PB |
| 30. | C | I | Z | aa | gg | PB |
| 31. | C | J | T | V | dd | PB |
| 32. | C | K | X | Y | rr | PB |
| 33. | C | M | ee | kk | oo | PB |
| 34. | C | P | W | kk | *ll* | PB |
| 35. | C | R | V | mm | qq | PB |
| 36. | C | V | cc | jj | tt | PB |
| 37. | D | E | J | X | cc | PB |
| 38. | D | F | L | *Q* | *ll* | PB |
| 39. | D | G | *Q* | T | Z | PB |
| 40. | D | G | Y | qq | tt | PB |
| 41. | D | H | K | S | kk | PB |
| 42. | D | I | L | V | ss | PB |
| 43. | D | I | P | qq | uu | PB |
| 44. | D | L | aa | ff | uu | PB |
| 45. | D | M | N | V | ii | PB |
| 46. | D | O | gg | jj | rr | PB |
| 47. | D | R | Z | *ll* | nn | PB |
| 48. | D | W | Z | jj | oo | PB |
| 49. | D | dd | ee | mm | pp | PB |

| | | | | | | |
|---|---|---|---|---|---|---|
| 50. | E | H | M | P | bb | PB |
| 51. | E | I | R | hh | kk | PB |
| 52. | E | I | cc | dd | oo | PB |
| 53. | E | K | *Q* | V | ee | PB |
| 54. | E | N | O | *ll* | ss | PB |
| 55. | E | *Q* | gg | ii | tt | PB |
| 56. | E | T | aa | jj | qq | PB |
| 57. | E | Z | pp | rr | uu | PB |
| 58. | F | G | X | ii | uu | PB |
| 59. | F | H | I | J | jj | PB |
| 60. | F | K | *ll* | oo | qq | PB |
| 61. | F | M | O | T | cc | PB |
| 62. | F | M | Y | Z | cc | PB |
| 63. | F | N | aa | kk | tt | PB |
| 64. | F | *Q* | R | ff | oo | PB |
| 65. | F | S | bb | ee | *ll* | PB |
| 66. | F | W | dd | hh | rr | PB |
| 67. | G | I | N | bb | pp | PB |
| 68. | G | J | O | S | W | PB |
| 69. | G | K | P | gg | ss | PB |
| 70. | G | L | X | dd | kk | PB |
| 71. | G | R | aa | ee | rr | PB |
| 72. | G | U | ee | hh | pp | PB |
| 73. | G | V | hh | *ll* | oo | PB |
| 74. | H | J | Y | ff | hh | PB |
| 75. | H | L | mm | oo | rr | PB |
| 76. | H | N | Z | ee | gg | PB |
| 77. | H | O | U | ee | tt | PB |
| 78. | H | R | dd | ii | jj | PB |
| 79. | H | T | *ll* | mm | uu | PB |
| 80. | H | V | W | X | aa | PB |
| 81. | I | J | M | R | gg | PB |
| 82. | I | O | ff | mm | nn | PB |
| 83. | I | *Q* | W | pp | tt | PB |
| 84. | I | T | U | ii | rr | PB |



(Continued Next Page)

## POWERBALL BALANCED WHEEL® 52047PB (Continued from previous page)

| | | | | | | |
|---|---|---|---|---|---|---|
| 85. | I | Y | ee | ii | ll | PB |
| 86. | J | L | M | N | U | PB |
| 87. | J | P | ll | rr | tt | PB |
| 88. | J | Q | aa | mm | nn | PB |
| 89. | J | V | Z | kk | pp | PB |
| 90. | J | bb | oo | rr | ss | PB |
| 91. | K | L | Z | hh | tt | PB |
| 92. | K | M | W | ff | pp | PB |
| 93. | K | N | hh | jj | uu | PB |
| 94. | K | O | R | X | pp | PB |
| 95. | K | T | bb | cc | nn | PB |
| 96. | K | U | aa | cc | dd | PB |
| 97. | L | N | P | R | T | PB |
| 98. | L | O | S | ii | oo | PB |
| 99. | L | bb | jj | kk | mm | PB |
| 100. | L | cc | ee | qq | rr | PB |
| 101. | M | Q | aa | ll | ss | PB |
| 102. | M | X | hh | mm | qq | PB |
| 103. | M | dd | nn | tt | uu | PB |
| 104. | N | Q | X | Y | bb | PB |
| 105. | N | W | cc | ii | mm | PB |
| 106. | N | ff | nn | qq | rr | PB |
| 107. | O | P | V | Y | nn | PB |
| 108. | O | Z | bb | dd | qq | PB |
| 109. | O | hh | ii | kk | nn | PB |
| 110. | P | S | U | Z | mm | PB |
| 111. | P | U | X | ee | ff | PB |
| 112. | P | aa | ii | oo | pp | PB |
| 113. | P | dd | ff | jj | ll | PB |
| 114. | Q | S | U | jj | qq | PB |
| 115. | R | U | Y | nn | oo | PB |
| 116. | R | W | cc | ss | uu | PB |
| 117. | S | T | gg | hh | pp | PB |
| 118. | S | V | ff | ss | tt | PB |
| 119. | S | Y | aa | cc | uu | PB |
| 120. | T | cc | ff | kk | ss | PB |
| 121. | U | V | bb | kk | uu | PB |
| 122. | U | W | bb | ff | gg | PB |
| 123. | W | gg | kk | nn | qq | PB |
| 124. | X | cc | gg | ll | pp | PB |
| 125. | X | ee | jj | nn | ss | PB |
| 126. | Y | dd | gg | mm | ss | PB |



# POWERBALL BALANCED WHEEL® 52055PB

## Wheel 55 Numbers + PB in 172 Games for a 2 of 2 Win

With Powerball

| Numbers Matched | Maximum Wins | | | | | | Minimum Wins | | | | | |
|---|---|---|---|---|---|---|---|---|---|---|---|---|
| | 5 + 1 | 4 + 1 | 3 + 1 | 2 + 1 | 1 + 1 | 0 + 1 | 5 + 1 | 4 + 1 | 3 + 1 | 2 + 1 | 1 + 1 | 0 + 1 |
| 5 + 1 | 1 | 0 | 1 | 5 | 62 | 103 | 0 | 0 | 0 | 10 | 54 | 108 |
| 4 + 1 | - | 1 | 1 | 3 | 54 | 113 | - | 0 | 0 | 6 | 47 | 119 |
| 3 + 1 | - | - | 2 | 1 | 39 | 130 | - | - | 0 | 3 | 38 | 131 |
| 2 + 1 | - | - | - | 4 | 25 | 143 | - | - | - | 1 | 27 | 144 |
| 1 + 1 | - | - | - | - | 17 | 155 | - | - | - | - | 14 | 158 |
| 0 + 1 | - | - | - | - | - | 172 | - | - | - | - | - | 172 |

Without Powerball

| Numbers Matched | Maximum Wins | | | | | Minimum Wins | | | | |
|---|---|---|---|---|---|---|---|---|---|---|
| | 5 + 0 | 4 + 0 | 3 + 0 | 2 + 0 | 1 + 0 | 5 + 0 | 4 + 0 | 3 + 0 | 2 + 0 | 1 + 0 |
| 5 + 0 | 1 | 0 | 1 | 5 | 62 | 0 | 0 | 0 | 10 | 54 |
| 4 + 0 | - | 1 | 1 | 3 | 54 | - | 0 | 0 | 6 | 47 |
| 3 + 0 | - | - | 2 | 1 | 39 | - | - | 0 | 3 | 38 |
| 2 + 0 | - | - | - | 4 | 25 | - | - | - | 1 | 27 |
| 1 + 0 | - | - | - | - | 17 | - | - | - | - | 14 |

(Continued Next Page)

**POWERBALL BALANCED WHEEL® 52055PB** (Continued from previous page)

## Your 55 Numbers + PB to Wheel

| A | B | C | D | E | F | G | H | I | J |
|---|---|---|---|---|---|---|---|---|---|
| 17 | 15 | 16 | 17 | 15 | 17 | 16 | 15 | 16 | 17 |
| **K** | **L** | **M** | **N** | **O** | **P** | **Q** | **R** | **S** | **T** |
| 16 | 17 | 16 | 15 | 17 | 15 | 16 | 16 | 16 | 15 |
| **U** | **V** | **W** | **X** | **Y** | **Z** | **aa** | **bb** | **cc** | **dd** |
| 16 | 15 | 16 | 15 | 15 | 16 | 15 | 15 | 15 | 16 |
| **ee** | **ff** | **gg** | **hh** | **ii** | **jj** | **kk** | ***ll*** | **mm** | **nn** |
| 16 | 17 | 15 | 16 | 15 | 15 | 16 | 15 | 15 | 15 |
| **oo** | **pp** | **qq** | **rr** | **ss** | **tt** | **uu** | **vv** | **ww** | **xx** |
| 15 | 15 | 15 | 16 | 16 | 17 | 16 | 15 | 14 | 15 |
| **yy** | **zz** | **AA** | **BB** | **CC** | **PB** | | | | |
| 15 | 15 | 16 | 15 | 16 | 172 | | | | |

## The 172 Games to Play

| | | | | | | |
|---|---|---|---|---|---|---|
| 1. | A | B | D | Y | kk | PB |
| 2. | A | C | H | K | AA | PB |
| 3. | A | C | M | W | pp | PB |
| 4. | A | D | J | S | mm | PB |
| 5. | A | E | O | Z | yy | PB |
| 6. | A | F | V | Z | *ll* | PB |
| 7. | A | G | I | vv | ww | PB |
| 8. | A | G | L | oo | yy | PB |
| 9. | A | K | *Q* | T | U | PB |
| 10. | A | M | mm | tt | uu | PB |
| 11. | A | N | R | jj | qq | PB |
| 12. | A | O | nn | rr | BB | PB |
| 13. | A | P | dd | ff | hh | PB |
| 14. | A | S | U | V | ee | PB |
| 15. | A | X | gg | ii | CC | PB |
| 16. | A | aa | bb | cc | zz | PB |
| 17. | A | aa | gg | ss | xx | PB |
| 18. | B | C | O | P | oo | PB |
| 19. | B | D | L | gg | zz | PB |
| 20. | B | E | V | cc | vv | PB |
| 21. | B | F | I | tt | xx | PB |
| 22. | B | G | S | aa | qq | PB |
| 23. | B | G | hh | rr | uu | PB |
| 24. | B | H | W | ff | yy | PB |
| 25. | B | J | *Q* | dd | nn | PB |
| 26. | B | K | R | yy | CC | PB |
| 27. | B | M | T | ss | ww | PB |
| 28. | B | N | U | X | ii | PB |
| 29. | B | P | *Q* | bb | jj | PB |
| 30. | B | *Q* | *ll* | AA | BB | PB |
| 31. | B | Z | ee | mm | pp | PB |
| 32. | C | D | dd | mm | ww | PB |
| 33. | C | E | *Q* | xx | CC | PB |
| 34. | C | F | J | kk | yy | PB |
| 35. | C | F | L | Y | zz | PB |
| 36. | C | F | T | ee | ff | PB |
| 37. | C | G | V | ss | tt | PB |
| 38. | C | I | L | dd | ii | PB |
| 39. | C | N | *Q* | S | Z | PB |
| 40. | C | R | U | jj | CC | PB |
| 41. | C | S | cc | hh | nn | PB |
| 42. | C | U | bb | uu | BB | PB |
| 43. | C | X | aa | dd | vv | PB |
| 44. | C | gg | *ll* | qq | rr | PB |



(Continued Next Page)

## POWERBALL BALANCED WHEEL® 52055PB (Continued from previous page)

| | | | | | | |
|---|---|---|---|---|---|---|
| 45. | D | E | O | aa | uu | PB |
| 46. | D | F | hh | ii | vv | PB |
| 47. | D | G | K | Z | hh | PB |
| 48. | D | H | *Q* | X | ee | PB |
| 49. | D | I | M | U | *ll* | PB |
| 50. | D | J | bb | ff | AA | PB |
| 51. | D | K | W | qq | BB | PB |
| 52. | D | L | V | W | CC | PB |
| 53. | D | L | ee | rr | ss | PB |
| 54. | D | N | *ll* | oo | pp | PB |
| 55. | D | P | T | jj | yy | PB |
| 56. | D | R | cc | nn | xx | PB |
| 57. | D | W | bb | tt | AA | PB |
| 58. | E | F | jj | kk | ss | PB |
| 59. | E | G | Y | pp | AA | PB |
| 60. | E | H | M | dd | rr | PB |
| 61. | E | I | U | qq | zz | PB |
| 62. | E | J | hh | *ll* | tt | PB |
| 63. | E | K | P | nn | ss | PB |
| 64. | E | L | ff | mm | BB | PB |
| 65. | E | N | T | bb | uu | PB |
| 66. | E | R | ee | ii | uu | PB |
| 67. | E | S | W | ff | gg | PB |
| 68. | E | X | nn | oo | ww | PB |
| 69. | F | G | R | BB | CC | PB |
| 70. | F | H | mm | qq | tt | PB |
| 71. | F | K | O | *Q* | tt | PB |
| 72. | F | K | O | X | pp | PB |
| 73. | F | M | ff | jj | nn | PB |
| 74. | F | N | P | aa | rr | PB |
| 75. | F | P | S | kk | uu | PB |
| 76. | F | U | kk | ww | AA | PB |
| 77. | F | W | cc | dd | oo | PB |
| 78. | F | bb | dd | ee | gg | PB |
| 79. | G | H | J | P | U | PB |
| 80. | G | M | X | bb | ff | PB |
| 81. | G | N | gg | nn | tt | PB |
| 82. | G | O | W | ee | kk | PB |
| 83. | G | *Q* | ii | ss | zz | PB |
| 84. | G | R | dd | *ll* | ss | PB |
| 85. | G | T | cc | *ll* | mm | PB |
| 86. | G | W | Z | jj | xx | PB |
| 87. | H | I | hh | kk | pp | PB |
| 88. | H | L | M | *Q* | R | PB |
| 89. | H | N | ss | xx | BB | PB |
| 90. | H | O | jj | *ll* | ww | PB |
| 91. | H | S | T | Y | CC | PB |
| 92. | H | V | bb | ii | nn | PB |
| 93. | H | Z | aa | oo | tt | PB |
| 94. | H | cc | jj | oo | zz | PB |
| 95. | H | gg | uu | vv | AA | PB |
| 96. | I | J | V | oo | uu | PB |
| 97. | I | J | W | X | Y | PB |
| 98. | I | K | S | jj | uu | PB |
| 99. | I | M | N | aa | CC | PB |
| 100. | I | M | P | ee | AA | PB |
| 101. | I | M | cc | yy | BB | PB |
| 102. | I | O | R | bb | hh | PB |
| 103. | I | *Q* | mm | rr | vv | PB |
| 104. | I | R | T | Z | gg | PB |
| 105. | I | Y | ff | nn | ss | PB |
| 106. | J | K | U | cc | gg | PB |
| 107. | J | L | N | jj | vv | PB |
| 108. | J | M | ee | qq | xx | PB |
| 109. | J | N | ss | yy | AA | PB |
| 110. | J | O | R | Y | ii | PB |
| 111. | J | R | aa | ff | kk | PB |
| 112. | J | T | pp | rr | zz | PB |
| 113. | J | Z | ii | ww | BB | PB |
| 114. | J | ee | *ll* | nn | CC | PB |



(Continued Next Page)

**POWERBALL BALANCED WHEEL® 52055PB** (Continued from previous page)

| | | | | | | | | | | | | | |
|---|---|---|---|---|---|---|---|---|---|---|---|---|---|
| 115. | K | L | aa | ee | ww | PB | 144. | *Q* | Y | cc | uu | AA | PB |
| 116. | K | M | V | ii | kk | PB | 145. | *Q* | ff | pp | rr | ww | PB |
| 117. | K | N | Y | dd | kk | PB | 146. | R | V | W | rr | ww | PB |
| 118. | K | R | X | mm | zz | PB | 147. | S | U | dd | pp | xx | PB |
| 119. | K | U | bb | oo | rr | PB | 148. | S | V | aa | pp | BB | PB |
| 120. | K | ff | *ll* | vv | xx | PB | 149. | S | X | *ll* | ss | uu | PB |
| 121. | L | O | U | ff | tt | PB | 150. | S | Y | bb | qq | ww | PB |
| 122. | L | P | T | X | BB | PB | 151. | S | ii | rr | tt | yy | PB |
| 123. | L | P | Z | cc | qq | PB | 152. | T | ff | ii | oo | xx | PB |
| 124. | L | R | S | oo | AA | PB | 153. | T | kk | nn | qq | vv | PB |
| 125. | L | T | hh | tt | BB | PB | 154. | U | W | Z | ss | vv | PB |
| 126. | L | W | nn | pp | uu | PB | 155. | U | aa | mm | nn | yy | PB |
| 127. | L | bb | kk | *ll* | xx | PB | 156. | V | gg | jj | pp | BB | PB |
| 128. | M | O | S | vv | zz | PB | 157. | X | Y | jj | rr | tt | PB |
| 129. | M | *Q* | gg | kk | oo | PB | 158. | X | Z | cc | kk | rr | PB |
| 130. | M | U | Y | Z | hh | PB | 159. | X | hh | rr | xx | AA | PB |
| 131. | N | O | W | gg | mm | PB | 160. | Y | aa | gg | *ll* | yy | PB |
| 132. | N | V | ff | hh | zz | PB | 161. | Y | ee | oo | vv | BB | PB |
| 133. | N | cc | ee | tt | ww | PB | 162. | Z | bb | kk | mm | CC | PB |
| 134. | O | T | V | dd | AA | PB | 163. | Z | dd | ff | qq | uu | PB |
| 135. | O | cc | ff | ss | CC | PB | 164. | Z | ee | nn | zz | AA | PB |
| 136. | O | oo | xx | zz | CC | PB | 165. | aa | ii | jj | mm | AA | PB |
| 137. | O | qq | rr | AA | CC | PB | 166. | bb | pp | ss | vv | yy | PB |
| 138. | P | R | pp | tt | vv | PB | 167. | cc | ii | pp | qq | CC | PB |
| 139. | P | V | Y | mm | xx | PB | 168. | dd | ee | hh | jj | yy | PB |
| 140. | P | W | ii | *ll* | zz | PB | 169. | dd | kk | tt | zz | BB | PB |
| 141. | P | gg | hh | ww | CC | PB | 170. | dd | tt | uu | vv | CC | PB |
| 142. | *Q* | T | W | aa | hh | PB | 171. | hh | mm | oo | qq | ss | PB |
| 143. | *Q* | V | X | qq | yy | PB | 172. | uu | ww | xx | yy | zz | PB |

# POWERBALL BALANCED WHEEL® 52056PB

## Wheel 56 Numbers + PB in 178 Games for a 2 of 2 Win

With Powerball

| Numbers Matched | Maximum Wins | | | | | | Minimum Wins | | | | | |
|---|---|---|---|---|---|---|---|---|---|---|---|---|
| | 5 + 1 | 4 + 1 | 3 + 1 | 2 + 1 | 1 + 1 | 0 + 1 | 5 + 1 | 4 + 1 | 3 + 1 | 2 + 1 | 1 + 1 | 0 + 1 |
| 5 + 1 | 1 | 0 | 1 | 7 | 61 | 108 | 0 | 0 | 0 | 10 | 55 | 113 |
| 4 + 1 | - | 1 | 1 | 5 | 48 | 123 | - | 0 | 0 | 6 | 48 | 124 |
| 3 + 1 | - | - | 2 | 1 | 42 | 133 | - | - | 0 | 3 | 39 | 136 |
| 2 + 1 | - | - | - | 5 | 24 | 149 | - | - | - | 1 | 28 | 149 |
| 1 + 1 | - | - | - | - | 17 | 161 | - | - | - | - | 15 | 163 |
| 0 + 1 | - | - | - | - | - | 178 | - | - | - | - | - | 178 |

Without Powerball

| Numbers Matched | Maximum Wins | | | | | Minimum Wins | | | | |
|---|---|---|---|---|---|---|---|---|---|---|
| | 5 + 0 | 4 + 0 | 3 + 0 | 2 + 0 | 1 + 0 | 5 + 0 | 4 + 0 | 3 + 0 | 2 + 0 | 1 + 0 |
| 5 + 0 | 1 | 0 | 1 | 7 | 61 | 0 | 0 | 0 | 10 | 55 |
| 4 + 0 | - | 1 | 1 | 5 | 48 | - | 0 | 0 | 6 | 48 |
| 3 + 0 | - | - | 2 | 1 | 42 | - | - | 0 | 3 | 39 |
| 2 + 0 | - | - | - | 5 | 24 | - | - | - | 1 | 28 |
| 1 + 0 | - | - | - | - | 17 | - | - | - | - | 15 |

## Your 56 Numbers + PB to Wheel

| A | B | C | D | E | F | G | H | I | J |
|---|---|---|---|---|---|---|---|---|---|
| 17 | 17 | 17 | 17 | 17 | 16 | 17 | 17 | 15 | 17 |
| **K** | **L** | **M** | **N** | **O** | **P** | **Q** | **R** | **S** | **T** |
| 16 | 16 | 16 | 17 | 15 | 16 | 16 | 15 | 16 | 16 |
| **U** | **V** | **W** | **X** | **Y** | **Z** | **aa** | **bb** | **cc** | **dd** |
| 16 | 17 | 16 | 16 | 16 | 16 | 15 | 15 | 16 | 16 |
| **ee** | **ff** | **gg** | **hh** | **ii** | **jj** | **kk** | ***ll*** | **mm** | **nn** |
| 16 | 17 | 16 | 16 | 16 | 17 | 16 | 16 | 16 | 16 |
| **oo** | **pp** | **qq** | **rr** | **ss** | **tt** | **uu** | **vv** | **ww** | **xx** |
| 16 | 16 | 15 | 15 | 15 | 15 | 15 | 15 | 15 | 15 |
| **yy** | **zz** | **AA** | **BB** | **CC** | **DD** | **PB** | | | |
| 15 | 15 | 15 | 16 | 15 | 15 | 178 | | | |

## The 178 Games to Play

| | | | | | | |
|---|---|---|---|---|---|---|
| 1. | A | B | T | *ll* | mm | PB |
| 2. | A | C | J | *ll* | rr | PB |
| 3. | A | C | ee | vv | CC | PB |
| 4. | A | D | tt | yy | BB | PB |
| 5. | A | E | Z | aa | nn | PB |
| 6. | A | F | N | P | *Q* | PB |
| 7. | A | G | M | T | U | PB |
| 8. | A | G | X | qq | zz | PB |
| 9. | A | H | I | L | hh | PB |
| 10. | A | K | V | nn | oo | PB |
| 11. | A | O | Y | ff | jj | PB |
| 12. | A | O | ii | kk | nn | PB |
| 13. | A | P | bb | pp | DD | PB |
| 14. | A | R | dd | uu | CC | PB |
| 15. | A | S | V | gg | ww | PB |
| 16. | A | T | W | xx | AA | PB |
| 17. | A | cc | dd | ee | ss | PB |
| 18. | B | C | G | O | S | PB |
| 19. | B | C | W | aa | yy | PB |
| 20. | B | D | gg | pp | uu | PB |
| 21. | B | E | K | L | dd | PB |
| 22. | B | E | hh | tt | CC | PB |



(Continued Next Page)

## POWERBALL BALANCED WHEEL® 52056PB (Continued from previous page)

| | | | | | | |
|---|---|---|---|---|---|---|
| 23. | B | F | G | H | bb | PB |
| 24. | B | G | R | rr | DD | PB |
| 25. | B | G | ss | ww | AA | PB |
| 26. | B | I | Z | ii | oo | PB |
| 27. | B | J | N | S | X | PB |
| 28. | B | K | M | P | X | PB |
| 29. | B | N | nn | qq | CC | PB |
| 30. | B | *Q* | kk | vv | zz | PB |
| 31. | B | S | V | cc | BB | PB |
| 32. | B | U | ff | jj | xx | PB |
| 33. | B | Y | cc | ee | mm | PB |
| 34. | C | D | F | K | S | PB |
| 35. | C | D | I | Y | DD | PB |
| 36. | C | D | N | V | zz | PB |
| 37. | C | E | N | ff | ww | PB |
| 38. | C | H | R | T | tt | PB |
| 39. | C | H | U | mm | BB | PB |
| 40. | C | L | P | ii | uu | PB |
| 41. | C | M | gg | qq | ss | PB |
| 42. | C | *Q* | S | kk | oo | PB |
| 43. | C | X | Y | Z | bb | PB |
| 44. | C | cc | nn | pp | AA | PB |
| 45. | C | dd | hh | xx | BB | PB |
| 46. | C | dd | jj | oo | DD | PB |
| 47. | D | E | F | ee | zz | PB |
| 48. | D | G | V | Z | xx | PB |
| 49. | D | G | dd | mm | vv | PB |
| 50. | D | H | *Q* | qq | AA | PB |
| 51. | D | J | M | Z | CC | PB |
| 52. | D | K | O | W | cc | PB |
| 53. | D | L | Z | kk | mm | PB |
| 54. | D | P | Y | hh | ss | PB |
| 55. | D | R | U | ii | ww | PB |
| 56. | D | T | ff | oo | rr | PB |
| 57. | D | V | aa | bb | *ll* | PB |
| 58. | D | X | hh | jj | nn | PB |
| 59. | E | G | I | J | V | PB |
| 60. | E | G | *Q* | gg | BB | PB |
| 61. | E | G | kk | pp | BB | PB |
| 62. | E | H | P | S | CC | PB |
| 63. | E | M | N | W | xx | PB |
| 64. | E | O | X | ss | DD | PB |
| 65. | E | R | V | Y | yy | PB |
| 66. | E | T | X | cc | ii | PB |
| 67. | E | U | X | dd | AA | PB |
| 68. | E | bb | ff | oo | vv | PB |
| 69. | E | jj | *ll* | qq | uu | PB |
| 70. | E | jj | mm | rr | ss | PB |
| 71. | F | I | qq | ww | xx | PB |
| 72. | F | J | L | W | jj | PB |
| 73. | F | K | pp | vv | BB | PB |
| 74. | F | M | bb | hh | AA | PB |
| 75. | F | N | aa | dd | rr | PB |
| 76. | F | O | *Q* | R | mm | PB |
| 77. | F | T | ff | uu | DD | PB |
| 78. | F | U | Z | ss | tt | PB |
| 79. | F | U | gg | kk | *ll* | PB |
| 80. | F | V | cc | ff | jj | PB |
| 81. | F | X | ff | nn | yy | PB |
| 82. | F | Y | ii | oo | CC | PB |
| 83. | G | K | N | jj | tt | PB |
| 84. | G | L | aa | ff | CC | PB |
| 85. | G | N | ee | oo | uu | PB |
| 86. | G | P | cc | ww | yy | PB |
| 87. | G | W | hh | ii | pp | PB |
| 88. | G | Y | dd | *ll* | nn | PB |
| 89. | H | J | K | V | ee | PB |
| 90. | H | K | *ll* | ss | yy | PB |
| 91. | H | M | kk | nn | DD | PB |
| 92. | H | N | *Q* | Y | Z | PB |



(Continued Next Page)

## POWERBALL BALANCED WHEEL® 52056PB (Continued from previous page)

| | | | | | | |
|---|---|---|---|---|---|---|
| 93. | H | O | T | aa | ww | PB |
| 94. | H | P | U | W | oo | PB |
| 95. | H | R | X | kk | xx | PB |
| 96. | H | Z | rr | uu | yy | PB |
| 97. | H | cc | dd | gg | kk | PB |
| 98. | H | ff | mm | pp | zz | PB |
| 99. | H | ii | jj | vv | yy | PB |
| 100. | I | J | *Q* | X | aa | PB |
| 101. | I | K | uu | xx | zz | PB |
| 102. | I | M | aa | mm | oo | PB |
| 103. | I | N | R | nn | BB | PB |
| 104. | I | O | P | dd | gg | PB |
| 105. | I | S | T | ee | jj | PB |
| 106. | I | U | bb | cc | CC | PB |
| 107. | I | W | *ll* | tt | DD | PB |
| 108. | I | ff | kk | pp | ss | PB |
| 109. | I | rr | vv | yy | AA | PB |
| 110. | J | N | X | gg | mm | PB |
| 111. | J | O | bb | uu | BB | PB |
| 112. | J | P | T | kk | rr | PB |
| 113. | J | R | S | bb | ss | PB |
| 114. | J | R | U | zz | AA | PB |
| 115. | J | S | nn | vv | xx | PB |
| 116. | J | Y | hh | pp | ww | PB |
| 117. | J | cc | dd | ff | tt | PB |
| 118. | J | ee | xx | yy | DD | PB |
| 119. | J | ii | oo | qq | tt | PB |
| 120. | K | *Q* | T | bb | nn | PB |
| 121. | K | R | Z | ff | hh | PB |
| 122. | K | U | Y | hh | mm | PB |
| 123. | K | aa | gg | ii | DD | PB |
| 124. | K | bb | qq | rr | ww | PB |
| 125. | K | kk | uu | AA | CC | PB |
| 126. | L | M | S | Y | uu | PB |
| 127. | L | M | pp | tt | yy | PB |

| | | | | | | |
|---|---|---|---|---|---|---|
| 128. | L | N | T | hh | DD | PB |
| 129. | L | O | U | pp | qq | PB |
| 130. | L | *Q* | bb | ee | tt | PB |
| 131. | L | *Q* | cc | rr | xx | PB |
| 132. | L | R | W | *ll* | vv | PB |
| 133. | L | V | ii | ss | zz | PB |
| 134. | L | X | oo | AA | BB | PB |
| 135. | L | ee | gg | nn | ww | PB |
| 136. | M | N | O | V | vv | PB |
| 137. | M | *Q* | dd | ii | ww | PB |
| 138. | M | R | cc | gg | oo | PB |
| 139. | M | ee | ii | rr | BB | PB |
| 140. | M | ff | gg | jj | AA | PB |
| 141. | M | *ll* | oo | ww | zz | PB |
| 142. | N | U | bb | kk | yy | PB |
| 143. | N | cc | ii | *ll* | AA | PB |
| 144. | N | oo | pp | ss | xx | PB |
| 145. | O | P | *ll* | xx | CC | PB |
| 146. | O | *Q* | hh | oo | yy | PB |
| 147. | O | Z | aa | ee | AA | PB |
| 148. | O | nn | rr | tt | zz | PB |
| 149. | P | R | aa | jj | qq | PB |
| 150. | P | U | ee | nn | vv | PB |
| 151. | P | V | mm | tt | AA | PB |
| 152. | P | Z | *ll* | zz | BB | PB |
| 153. | P | ff | jj | qq | BB | PB |
| 154. | *Q* | U | V | uu | DD | PB |
| 155. | *Q* | W | ee | ff | *ll* | PB |
| 156. | *Q* | jj | pp | ss | CC | PB |
| 157. | R | X | ee | *ll* | pp | PB |
| 158. | S | U | aa | pp | rr | PB |
| 159. | S | W | Z | gg | tt | PB |
| 160. | S | Y | zz | AA | DD | PB |
| 161. | S | dd | mm | qq | yy | PB |
| 162. | S | ff | hh | ii | *ll* | PB |



(Continued Next Page)

**POWERBALL BALANCED WHEEL® 52056PB** (Continued from previous page)

| | | | | | | | | | | | | | |
|---|---|---|---|---|---|---|---|---|---|---|---|---|---|
| 163. | T | V | Z | dd | pp | PB | 171. | W | mm | nn | ss | uu | PB |
| 164. | T | W | Y | qq | BB | PB | 172. | X | tt | uu | vv | ww | PB |
| 165. | T | aa | ss | vv | BB | PB | 173. | Y | aa | kk | tt | xx | PB |
| 166. | T | gg | yy | zz | CC | PB | 174. | Y | gg | hh | rr | vv | PB |
| 167. | V | W | X | rr | CC | PB | 175. | Z | cc | qq | vv | DD | PB |
| 168. | V | ee | hh | kk | qq | PB | 176. | aa | cc | hh | uu | zz | PB |
| 169. | W | Z | jj | kk | ww | PB | 177. | bb | gg | ii | mm | xx | PB |
| 170. | W | bb | dd | jj | zz | PB | 178. | mm | ww | BB | CC | DD | PB |



# POWERBALL BALANCED WHEEL® 53210PB

## Wheel 10 Numbers + PB in 2 Games for a 3 of 5 Win

With Powerball

| Numbers Matched | Maximum Wins 5 + 1 | 4 + 1 | 3 + 1 | 2 + 1 | 1 + 1 | 0 + 1 | Minimum Wins 5 + 1 | 4 + 1 | 3 + 1 | 2 + 1 | 1 + 1 | 0 + 1 |
|---|---|---|---|---|---|---|---|---|---|---|---|---|
| 5 + 1 | 1 | 0 | 0 | 0 | 0 | 1 | 0 | 0 | 1 | 1 | 0 | 0 |
| 4 + 1 | - | 1 | 0 | 0 | 0 | 1 | - | 0 | 0 | 2 | 0 | 0 |
| 3 + 1 | - | - | 1 | 0 | 0 | 1 | - | - | 0 | 1 | 1 | 0 |
| 2 + 1 | - | - | - | 1 | 0 | 1 | - | - | - | 0 | 2 | 0 |
| 1 + 1 | - | - | - | - | 1 | 1 | - | - | - | - | 1 | 1 |
| 0 + 1 | - | - | - | - | - | 2 | - | - | - | - | - | 2 |

Without Powerball

| Numbers Matched | Maximum Wins 5 + 0 | 4 + 0 | 3 + 0 | 2 + 0 | 1 + 0 | Minimum Wins 5 + 0 | 4 + 0 | 3 + 0 | 2 + 0 | 1 + 0 |
|---|---|---|---|---|---|---|---|---|---|---|
| 5 + 0 | 1 | 0 | 0 | 0 | 0 | 0 | 0 | 1 | 1 | 0 |
| 4 + 0 | - | 1 | 0 | 0 | 0 | - | 0 | 0 | 2 | 0 |
| 3 + 0 | - | - | 1 | 0 | 0 | - | - | 0 | 1 | 1 |
| 2 + 0 | - | - | - | 1 | 0 | - | - | - | 0 | 2 |
| 1 + 0 | - | - | - | - | 1 | - | - | - | - | 1 |

## Your 10 Numbers + PB to Wheel

| A | B | C | D | E | F | G | H | I | J | PB |
|---|---|---|---|---|---|---|---|---|---|---|
| 1 | 1 | 1 | 1 | 1 | 1 | 1 | 1 | 1 | 1 | 2 |

## The 2 Games to Play

| | | | | | | | | | | | | | |
|---|---|---|---|---|---|---|---|---|---|---|---|---|---|
| 1. | A | B | F | I | J | PB | 2. | C | D | E | G | H | PB |



# POWERBALL BALANCED WHEEL® 53211PB

## Wheel 11 Numbers + PB in 5 Games for a 3 of 5 Win

With Powerball

| Numbers Matched | Maximum Wins 5 + 1 | 4 + 1 | 3 + 1 | 2 + 1 | 1 + 1 | 0 + 1 | Minimum Wins 5 + 1 | 4 + 1 | 3 + 1 | 2 + 1 | 1 + 1 | 0 + 1 |
|---|---|---|---|---|---|---|---|---|---|---|---|---|
| 5 + 1 | 1 | 2 | 0 | 1 | 0 | 1 | 0 | 0 | 1 | 2 | 2 | 0 |
| 4 + 1 | - | 2 | 1 | 0 | 1 | 1 | - | 0 | 0 | 3 | 2 | 0 |
| 3 + 1 | - | - | 3 | 0 | 0 | 2 | - | - | 0 | 1 | 3 | 1 |
| 2 + 1 | - | - | - | 3 | 0 | 2 | - | - | - | 0 | 4 | 1 |
| 1 + 1 | - | - | - | - | 3 | 2 | - | - | - | - | 1 | 4 |
| 0 + 1 | - | - | - | - | - | 5 | - | - | - | - | - | 5 |

(Continued Next Page)

## POWERBALL BALANCED WHEEL® 53211PB (Continued from previous page)

Without Powerball

| Numbers Matched | Maximum Wins 5 + 0 | 4 + 0 | 3 + 0 | 2 + 0 | 1 + 0 | Minimum Wins 5 + 0 | 4 + 0 | 3 + 0 | 2 + 0 | 1 + 0 |
|---|---|---|---|---|---|---|---|---|---|---|
| 5 + 0 | 1 | 2 | 0 | 1 | 0 | 0 | 0 | 1 | 2 | 2 |
| 4 + 0 | - | 2 | 1 | 0 | 1 | - | 0 | 0 | 3 | 2 |
| 3 + 0 | - | - | 3 | 0 | 0 | - | - | 0 | 1 | 3 |
| 2 + 0 | - | - | - | 3 | 0 | - | - | - | 0 | 4 |
| 1 + 0 | - | - | - | - | 3 | - | - | - | - | 1 |

## Your 11 Numbers + PB to Wheel

| A | B | C | D | E | F |
|---|---|---|---|---|---|
| 2 | 3 | 1 | 2 | 3 | 3 |

| G | H | I | J | K | PB |
|---|---|---|---|---|---|
| 3 | 3 | 3 | 1 | 1 | 5 |

## The 5 Games to Play

| | | | | | | |
|---|---|---|---|---|---|---|
| 1. | A | C | D | J | K | PB |
| 2. | A | D | G | H | I | PB |
| 3. | B | E | F | G | H | PB |
| 4. | B | E | F | G | I | PB |
| 5. | B | E | F | H | I | PB |



# POWERBALL BALANCED WHEEL® 53212PB

## Wheel 12 Numbers + PB in 6 Games for a 3 of 5 Win

With Powerball

| Numbers Matched | Maximum Wins 5 + 1 | 4 + 1 | 3 + 1 | 2 + 1 | 1 + 1 | 0 + 1 | Minimum Wins 5 + 1 | 4 + 1 | 3 + 1 | 2 + 1 | 1 + 1 | 0 + 1 |
|---|---|---|---|---|---|---|---|---|---|---|---|---|
| 5 + 1 | 1 | 1 | 1 | 0 | 3 | 0 | 0 | 0 | 1 | 3 | 2 | 0 |
| 4 + 1 | - | 2 | 1 | 0 | 1 | 2 | - | 0 | 0 | 3 | 3 | 0 |
| 3 + 1 | - | - | 3 | 0 | 0 | 3 | - | - | 0 | 1 | 5 | 0 |
| 2 + 1 | - | - | - | 3 | 0 | 3 | - | - | - | 0 | 4 | 2 |
| 1 + 1 | - | - | - | - | 3 | 3 | - | - | - | - | 2 | 4 |
| 0 + 1 | - | - | - | - | - | 6 | - | - | - | - | - | 6 |

Without Powerball

| Numbers Matched | Maximum Wins 5 + 0 | 4 + 0 | 3 + 0 | 2 + 0 | 1 + 0 | Minimum Wins 5 + 0 | 4 + 0 | 3 + 0 | 2 + 0 | 1 + 0 |
|---|---|---|---|---|---|---|---|---|---|---|
| 5 + 0 | 1 | 1 | 1 | 0 | 3 | 0 | 0 | 1 | 3 | 2 |
| 4 + 0 | - | 2 | 1 | 0 | 1 | - | 0 | 0 | 3 | 3 |
| 3 + 0 | - | - | 3 | 0 | 0 | - | - | 0 | 1 | 5 |
| 2 + 0 | - | - | - | 3 | 0 | - | - | - | 0 | 4 |
| 1 + 0 | - | - | - | - | 3 | - | - | - | - | 2 |

## Your 12 Numbers + PB to Wheel

| A | B | C | D | E | F | G |
|---|---|---|---|---|---|---|
| 3 | 2 | 2 | 3 | 2 | 3 | 2 |

| H | I | J | K | L | PB |
|---|---|---|---|---|---|
| 3 | 3 | 2 | 2 | 3 | 6 |

## The 6 Games to Play

| | | | | | | |
|---|---|---|---|---|---|---|
| 1. | A | C | G | J | K | PB |
| 2. | A | D | F | H | L | PB |
| 3. | A | D | H | I | L | PB |
| 4. | B | D | E | H | L | PB |
| 5. | B | F | G | I | J | PB |
| 6. | C | E | F | I | K | PB |

# POWERBALL BALANCED WHEEL® 53213PB

## Wheel 13 Numbers + PB in 9 Games for a 3 of 5 Win

With Powerball

| Numbers Matched | Maximum Wins 5 + 1 | 4 + 1 | 3 + 1 | 2 + 1 | 1 + 1 | 0 + 1 | Minimum Wins 5 + 1 | 4 + 1 | 3 + 1 | 2 + 1 | 1 + 1 | 0 + 1 |
|---|---|---|---|---|---|---|---|---|---|---|---|---|
| 5 + 1 | 1 | 1 | 1 | 2 | 4 | 0 | 0 | 0 | 1 | 5 | 3 | 0 |
| 4 + 1 | - | 2 | 1 | 2 | 2 | 2 | - | 0 | 0 | 4 | 5 | 0 |
| 3 + 1 | - | - | 3 | 1 | 2 | 3 | - | - | 0 | 1 | 8 | 0 |
| 2 + 1 | - | - | - | 4 | 1 | 4 | - | - | - | 0 | 6 | 3 |
| 1 + 1 | - | - | - | - | 5 | 4 | - | - | - | - | 3 | 6 |
| 0 + 1 | - | - | - | - | - | 9 | - | - | - | - | - | 9 |

Without Powerball

| Numbers Matched | Maximum Wins 5 + 0 | 4 + 0 | 3 + 0 | 2 + 0 | 1 + 0 | Minimum Wins 5 + 0 | 4 + 0 | 3 + 0 | 2 + 0 | 1 + 0 |
|---|---|---|---|---|---|---|---|---|---|---|
| 5 + 0 | 1 | 1 | 1 | 2 | 4 | 0 | 0 | 1 | 5 | 3 |
| 4 + 0 | - | 2 | 1 | 2 | 2 | - | 0 | 0 | 4 | 5 |
| 3 + 0 | - | - | 3 | 1 | 2 | - | - | 0 | 1 | 8 |
| 2 + 0 | - | - | - | 4 | 1 | - | - | - | 0 | 6 |
| 1 + 0 | - | - | - | - | 5 | - | - | - | - | 3 |

## Your 13 Numbers + PB to Wheel

| A | B | C | D | E | F | G |
|---|---|---|---|---|---|---|
| 4 | 4 | 4 | 3 | 3 | 3 | 3 |
| **H** | **I** | **J** | **K** | **L** | **M** | **PB** |
| 3 | 3 | 3 | 3 | 4 | 5 | 9 |

## The 9 Games to Play

| | | | | | | |
|---|---|---|---|---|---|---|
| 1. | A | B | D | L | M | PB |
| 2. | A | B | G | K | M | PB |
| 3. | A | C | E | L | M | PB |
| 4. | A | C | H | L | M | PB |
| 5. | B | C | F | J | M | PB |
| 6. | B | F | I | J | L | PB |
| 7. | C | D | G | I | K | PB |
| 8. | D | E | F | H | J | PB |
| 9. | E | G | H | I | K | PB |



# POWERBALL BALANCED WHEEL® 53214PB

## Wheel 14 Numbers + PB in 10 Games for a 3 of 5 Win

With Powerball

| Numbers Matched | Maximum Wins 5 + 1 | 4 + 1 | 3 + 1 | 2 + 1 | 1 + 1 | 0 + 1 | Minimum Wins 5 + 1 | 4 + 1 | 3 + 1 | 2 + 1 | 1 + 1 | 0 + 1 |
|---|---|---|---|---|---|---|---|---|---|---|---|---|
| 5 + 1 | 1 | 2 | 2 | 0 | 0 | 5 | 0 | 0 | 1 | 5 | 3 | 1 |
| 4 + 1 | - | 3 | 0 | 2 | 0 | 5 | - | 0 | 0 | 4 | 4 | 2 |
| 3 + 1 | - | - | 3 | 1 | 1 | 5 | - | - | 0 | 2 | 5 | 3 |
| 2 + 1 | - | - | - | 4 | 0 | 6 | - | - | - | 0 | 6 | 4 |
| 1 + 1 | - | - | - | - | 4 | 6 | - | - | - | - | 3 | 7 |
| 0 + 1 | - | - | - | - | - | 10 | - | - | - | - | - | 10 |

(Continued Next Page)

## POWERBALL BALANCED WHEEL® 53214PB (Continued from previous page)

Without Powerball

| Numbers Matched | Maximum Wins 5 + 0 | 4 + 0 | 3 + 0 | 2 + 0 | 1 + 0 | Minimum Wins 5 + 0 | 4 + 0 | 3 + 0 | 2 + 0 | 1 + 0 |
|---|---|---|---|---|---|---|---|---|---|---|
| 5 + 0 | 1 | 2 | 2 | 0 | 0 | 0 | 0 | 1 | 5 | 3 |
| 4 + 0 | - | 3 | 0 | 2 | 0 | - | 0 | 0 | 4 | 4 |
| 3 + 0 | - | - | 3 | 1 | 1 | - | - | 0 | 2 | 5 |
| 2 + 0 | - | - | - | 4 | 0 | - | - | - | 0 | 6 |
| 1 + 0 | - | - | - | - | 4 | - | - | - | - | 3 |

### Your 14 Numbers + PB to Wheel

| A | B | C | D | E | F | G | H |
|---|---|---|---|---|---|---|---|
| 4 | 4 | 4 | 4 | 3 | 3 | 3 | 3 |

| I | J | K | L | M | N | PB |
|---|---|---|---|---|---|---|
| 3 | 3 | 4 | 4 | 4 | 4 | 10 |

### The 10 Games to Play

| | | | | | | |
|---|---|---|---|---|---|---|
| 1. | A | C | H | K | M | PB |
| 2. | A | C | I | K | M | PB |
| 3. | A | C | J | K | M | PB |
| 4. | A | H | I | J | M | PB |
| 5. | B | D | E | L | N | PB |
| 6. | B | D | F | L | N | PB |
| 7. | B | D | G | L | N | PB |
| 8. | B | E | F | G | N | PB |
| 9. | C | H | I | J | K | PB |
| 10. | D | E | F | G | L | PB |



## POWERBALL BALANCED WHEEL® 53215PB

### Wheel 15 Numbers + PB in 13 Games for a 3 of 5 Win

With Powerball

| Numbers Matched | Maximum Wins 5 + 1 | 4 + 1 | 3 + 1 | 2 + 1 | 1 + 1 | 0 + 1 | Minimum Wins 5 + 1 | 4 + 1 | 3 + 1 | 2 + 1 | 1 + 1 | 0 + 1 |
|---|---|---|---|---|---|---|---|---|---|---|---|---|
| 5 + 1 | 1 | 1 | 0 | 6 | 3 | 2 | 0 | 0 | 1 | 5 | 7 | 0 |
| 4 + 1 | - | 2 | 0 | 6 | 0 | 5 | - | 0 | 0 | 4 | 9 | 0 |
| 3 + 1 | - | - | 2 | 3 | 3 | 5 | - | - | 0 | 2 | 7 | 4 |
| 2 + 1 | - | - | - | 5 | 0 | 8 | - | - | - | 0 | 8 | 5 |
| 1 + 1 | - | - | - | - | 5 | 8 | - | - | - | - | 3 | 10 |
| 0 + 1 | - | - | - | - | - | 13 | - | - | - | - | - | 13 |

Without Powerball

| Numbers Matched | Maximum Wins 5 + 0 | 4 + 0 | 3 + 0 | 2 + 0 | 1 + 0 | Minimum Wins 5 + 0 | 4 + 0 | 3 + 0 | 2 + 0 | 1 + 0 |
|---|---|---|---|---|---|---|---|---|---|---|
| 5 + 0 | 1 | 1 | 0 | 6 | 3 | 0 | 0 | 1 | 5 | 7 |
| 4 + 0 | - | 2 | 0 | 6 | 0 | - | 0 | 0 | 4 | 9 |
| 3 + 0 | - | - | 2 | 3 | 3 | - | - | 0 | 2 | 7 |
| 2 + 0 | - | - | - | 5 | 0 | - | - | - | 0 | 8 |
| 1 + 0 | - | - | - | - | 5 | - | - | - | - | 3 |

### Your 15 Numbers + PB to Wheel

| A | B | C | D | E | F | G | H |
|---|---|---|---|---|---|---|---|
| 5 | 5 | 4 | 4 | 5 | 4 | 4 | 4 |

| I | J | K | L | M | N | O | PB |
|---|---|---|---|---|---|---|---|
| 4 | 4 | 4 | 3 | 5 | 5 | 5 | 13 |

### The 13 Games to Play

| | | | | | | |
|---|---|---|---|---|---|---|
| 1. | A | B | C | N | O | PB |
| 2. | A | B | K | N | O | PB |



(Continued Next Page)

**POWERBALL BALANCED WHEEL® 53215PB** (Continued from previous page)

| | | | | | | |
|---|---|---|---|---|---|---|
| 3. | A | D | E | M | O | PB |
| 4. | A | E | J | M | O | PB |
| 5. | A | G | I | L | O | PB |
| 6. | B | E | G | I | N | PB |
| 7. | B | F | H | L | N | PB |
| 8. | B | G | I | M | N | PB |
| 9. | C | D | J | K | L | PB |
| 10. | C | E | F | K | M | PB |
| 11. | C | E | H | K | M | PB |
| 12. | D | F | G | H | J | PB |
| 13. | D | F | H | I | J | PB |



# POWERBALL BALANCED WHEEL® 53216PB

## Wheel 16 Numbers + PB in 16 Games for a 3 of 5 Win

With Powerball

| Numbers Matched | Maximum Wins 5 + 1 | 4 + 1 | 3 + 1 | 2 + 1 | 1 + 1 | 0 + 1 | Minimum Wins 5 + 1 | 4 + 1 | 3 + 1 | 2 + 1 | 1 + 1 | 0 + 1 |
|---|---|---|---|---|---|---|---|---|---|---|---|---|
| 5 + 1 | 1 | 0 | 6 | 1 | 0 | 8 | 0 | 0 | 1 | 7 | 8 | 0 |
| 4 + 1 | - | 1 | 3 | 3 | 1 | 8 | - | 0 | 0 | 4 | 12 | 0 |
| 3 + 1 | - | - | 2 | 3 | 3 | 8 | - | - | 0 | 2 | 11 | 3 |
| 2 + 1 | - | - | - | 3 | 4 | 9 | - | - | - | 0 | 10 | 6 |
| 1 + 1 | - | - | - | - | 5 | 11 | - | - | - | - | 5 | 11 |
| 0 + 1 | - | - | - | - | - | 16 | - | - | - | - | - | 16 |

Without Powerball

| Numbers Matched | Maximum Wins 5 + 0 | 4 + 0 | 3 + 0 | 2 + 0 | 1 + 0 | Minimum Wins 5 + 0 | 4 + 0 | 3 + 0 | 2 + 0 | 1 + 0 |
|---|---|---|---|---|---|---|---|---|---|---|
| 5 + 0 | 1 | 0 | 6 | 1 | 0 | 0 | 0 | 1 | 7 | 8 |
| 4 + 0 | - | 1 | 3 | 3 | 1 | - | 0 | 0 | 4 | 12 |
| 3 + 0 | - | - | 2 | 3 | 3 | - | - | 0 | 2 | 11 |
| 2 + 0 | - | - | - | 3 | 4 | - | - | - | 0 | 10 |
| 1 + 0 | - | - | - | - | 5 | - | - | - | - | 5 |

## Your 16 Numbers + PB to Wheel

| A | B | C | D | E | F | G | H | I |
|---|---|---|---|---|---|---|---|---|
| 5 | 5 | 5 | 5 | 5 | 5 | 5 | 5 | 5 |

| J | K | L | M | N | O | P | PB |
|---|---|---|---|---|---|---|---|
| 5 | 5 | 5 | 5 | 5 | 5 | 5 | 16 |

## The 16 Games to Play

| | | | | | | |
|---|---|---|---|---|---|---|
| 1. | A | B | E | K | P | PB |
| 2. | A | B | F | L | N | PB |
| 3. | A | E | F | L | P | PB |
| 4. | A | E | K | L | N | PB |
| 5. | A | F | K | N | P | PB |
| 6. | B | E | F | K | N | PB |
| 7. | B | E | L | N | P | PB |
| 8. | B | F | K | L | P | PB |
| 9. | C | D | G | H | O | PB |
| 10. | C | D | I | J | M | PB |
| 11. | C | G | H | I | M | PB |
| 12. | C | G | I | J | O | PB |
| 13. | C | H | J | M | O | PB |
| 14. | D | G | H | J | M | PB |
| 15. | D | G | I | M | O | PB |
| 16. | D | H | I | J | O | PB |

# POWERBALL BALANCED WHEEL® 53217PB

## Wheel 17 Numbers + PB in 20 Games for a 3 of 5 Win

With Powerball

| Numbers Matched | Maximum Wins 5 + 1 | 4 + 1 | 3 + 1 | 2 + 1 | 1 + 1 | 0 + 1 | Minimum Wins 5 + 1 | 4 + 1 | 3 + 1 | 2 + 1 | 1 + 1 | 0 + 1 |
|---|---|---|---|---|---|---|---|---|---|---|---|---|
| 5 + 1 | 1 | 1 | 4 | 2 | 0 | 12 | 0 | 0 | 1 | 8 | 8 | 3 |
| 4 + 1 | - | 2 | 2 | 2 | 2 | 12 | - | 0 | 0 | 5 | 12 | 3 |
| 3 + 1 | - | - | 3 | 3 | 6 | 8 | - | - | 0 | 2 | 12 | 6 |
| 2 + 1 | - | - | - | 5 | 4 | 11 | - | - | - | 0 | 11 | 9 |
| 1 + 1 | - | - | - | - | 7 | 13 | - | - | - | - | 5 | 15 |
| 0 + 1 | - | - | - | - | - | 20 | - | - | - | - | - | 20 |

Without Powerball

| Numbers Matched | Maximum Wins 5 + 0 | 4 + 0 | 3 + 0 | 2 + 0 | 1 + 0 | Minimum Wins 5 + 0 | 4 + 0 | 3 + 0 | 2 + 0 | 1 + 0 |
|---|---|---|---|---|---|---|---|---|---|---|
| 5 + 0 | 1 | 1 | 4 | 2 | 0 | 0 | 0 | 1 | 8 | 8 |
| 4 + 0 | - | 2 | 2 | 2 | 2 | - | 0 | 0 | 5 | 12 |
| 3 + 0 | - | - | 3 | 3 | 6 | - | - | 0 | 2 | 12 |
| 2 + 0 | - | - | - | 5 | 4 | - | - | - | 0 | 11 |
| 1 + 0 | - | - | - | - | 7 | - | - | - | - | 5 |

## Your 17 Numbers + PB to Wheel

| A | B | C | D | E | F | G | H | I |
|---|---|---|---|---|---|---|---|---|
| 5 | 5 | 5 | 5 | 6 | 6 | 6 | 7 | 7 |
| **J** | **K** | **L** | **M** | **N** | **O** | **P** | **Q** | **PB** |
| 7 | 7 | 7 | 7 | 5 | 5 | 5 | 5 | 20 |

## The 20 Games to Play

| | | | | | | |
|---|---|---|---|---|---|---|
| 1. | A | B | C | P | Q | PB |
| 2. | A | B | D | N | O | PB |
| 3. | A | C | D | O | Q | PB |
| 4. | A | C | N | P | Q | PB |
| 5. | A | D | O | P | Q | PB |
| 6. | B | C | D | N | P | PB |
| 7. | B | C | N | O | P | PB |
| 8. | B | D | N | O | Q | PB |
| 9. | E | F | G | H | J | PB |
| 10. | E | F | G | I | M | PB |
| 11. | E | F | G | K | L | PB |
| 12. | E | H | I | J | L | PB |
| 13. | E | H | K | L | M | PB |
| 14. | E | I | J | K | M | PB |
| 15. | F | H | I | L | M | PB |
| 16. | F | H | J | K | M | PB |
| 17. | F | I | J | K | L | PB |
| 18. | G | H | I | J | M | PB |
| 19. | G | H | I | K | L | PB |
| 20. | G | J | K | L | M | PB |

# POWERBALL BALANCED WHEEL® 53218PB

## Wheel 18 Numbers + PB in 24 Games for a 3 of 5 Win

With Powerball

| Numbers Matched | Maximum Wins | | | | | | Minimum Wins | | | | | |
|---|---|---|---|---|---|---|---|---|---|---|---|---|
| | 5 + 1 | 4 + 1 | 3 + 1 | 2 + 1 | 1 + 1 | 0 + 1 | 5 + 1 | 4 + 1 | 3 + 1 | 2 + 1 | 1 + 1 | 0 + 1 |
| 5 + 1 | 1 | 1 | 6 | 3 | 1 | 12 | 0 | 0 | 1 | 9 | 10 | 4 |
| 4 + 1 | - | 2 | 3 | 4 | 3 | 12 | - | 0 | 0 | 6 | 12 | 6 |
| 3 + 1 | - | - | 3 | 4 | 4 | 13 | - | - | 0 | 3 | 12 | 9 |
| 2 + 1 | - | - | - | 6 | 2 | 16 | - | - | - | 0 | 12 | 12 |
| 1 + 1 | - | - | - | - | 7 | 17 | - | - | - | - | 6 | 18 |
| 0 + 1 | - | - | - | - | - | 24 | - | - | - | - | - | 24 |

Without Powerball

| Numbers Matched | Maximum Wins | | | | | Minimum Wins | | | | |
|---|---|---|---|---|---|---|---|---|---|---|
| | 5 + 0 | 4 + 0 | 3 + 0 | 2 + 0 | 1 + 0 | 5 + 0 | 4 + 0 | 3 + 0 | 2 + 0 | 1 + 0 |
| 5 + 0 | 1 | 1 | 6 | 3 | 1 | 0 | 0 | 1 | 9 | 10 |
| 4 + 0 | - | 2 | 3 | 4 | 3 | - | 0 | 0 | 6 | 12 |
| 3 + 0 | - | - | 3 | 4 | 4 | - | - | 0 | 3 | 12 |
| 2 + 0 | - | - | - | 6 | 2 | - | - | - | 0 | 12 |
| 1 + 0 | - | - | - | - | 7 | - | - | - | - | 6 |

## Your 18 Numbers + PB to Wheel

| A | B | C | D | E | F | G | H | I | J |
|---|---|---|---|---|---|---|---|---|---|
| 6 | 6 | 7 | 6 | 7 | 7 | 7 | 6 | 7 | 7 |

| K | L | M | N | O | P | Q | R | PB |
|---|---|---|---|---|---|---|---|---|
| 7 | 7 | 7 | 7 | 7 | 7 | 6 | 6 | 24 |

## The 24 Games to Play

| | | | | | | |
|---|---|---|---|---|---|---|
| 1. | A | D | F | M | Q | PB |
| 2. | A | D | G | L | O | PB |
| 3. | A | D | I | L | Q | PB |
| 4. | A | F | G | I | O | PB |
| 5. | A | F | I | L | M | PB |
| 6. | A | G | M | O | Q | PB |
| 7. | B | C | E | J | P | PB |
| 8. | B | C | H | J | R | PB |
| 9. | B | C | J | K | N | PB |
| 10. | B | E | H | P | R | PB |
| 11. | B | E | K | N | P | PB |
| 12. | B | H | K | N | R | PB |
| 13. | C | E | H | J | K | PB |
| 14. | C | E | N | P | R | PB |
| 15. | C | H | K | N | P | PB |
| 16. | C | J | K | P | R | PB |
| 17. | D | F | G | L | M | PB |
| 18. | D | F | I | M | O | PB |
| 19. | D | G | I | O | Q | PB |
| 20. | E | H | J | N | P | PB |
| 21. | E | J | K | N | R | PB |
| 22. | F | G | L | O | Q | PB |
| 23. | F | I | L | M | Q | PB |
| 24. | G | I | L | M | O | PB |

# POWERBALL BALANCED WHEEL® 53219PB

## Wheel 19 Numbers + PB in 28 Games for a 3 of 5 Win

With Powerball

| Numbers Matched | Maximum Wins | | | | | | Minimum Wins | | | | | |
|---|---|---|---|---|---|---|---|---|---|---|---|---|
| | 5 + 1 | 4 + 1 | 3 + 1 | 2 + 1 | 1 + 1 | 0 + 1 | 5 + 1 | 4 + 1 | 3 + 1 | 2 + 1 | 1 + 1 | 0 + 1 |
| 5 + 1 | 1 | 0 | 6 | 10 | 3 | 8 | 0 | 0 | 1 | 8 | 14 | 5 |
| 4 + 1 | - | 1 | 4 | 6 | 8 | 9 | - | 0 | 0 | 5 | 18 | 5 |
| 3 + 1 | - | - | 4 | 0 | 16 | 8 | - | - | 0 | 2 | 15 | 11 |
| 2 + 1 | - | - | - | 4 | 11 | 13 | - | - | - | 0 | 14 | 14 |
| 1 + 1 | - | - | - | - | 10 | 18 | - | - | - | - | 5 | 23 |
| 0 + 1 | - | - | - | - | - | 28 | - | - | - | - | - | 28 |

Without Powerball

| Numbers Matched | Maximum Wins | | | | | Minimum Wins | | | | |
|---|---|---|---|---|---|---|---|---|---|---|
| | 5 + 0 | 4 + 0 | 3 + 0 | 2 + 0 | 1 + 0 | 5 + 0 | 4 + 0 | 3 + 0 | 2 + 0 | 1 + 0 |
| 5 + 0 | 1 | 0 | 6 | 10 | 3 | 0 | 0 | 1 | 8 | 14 |
| 4 + 0 | - | 1 | 4 | 6 | 8 | - | 0 | 0 | 5 | 18 |
| 3 + 0 | - | - | 4 | 0 | 16 | - | - | 0 | 2 | 15 |
| 2 + 0 | - | - | - | 4 | 11 | - | - | - | 0 | 14 |
| 1 + 0 | - | - | - | - | 10 | - | - | - | - | 5 |

## Your 19 Numbers + PB to Wheel

| A | B | C | D | E | F | G | H | I | J |
|---|---|---|---|---|---|---|---|---|---|
| 5 | 10 | 5 | 9 | 9 | 5 | 5 | 9 | 9 | 5 |

| K | L | M | N | O | P | Q | R | S | PB |
|---|---|---|---|---|---|---|---|---|---|
| 9 | 9 | 9 | 5 | 9 | 9 | 5 | 9 | 5 | 28 |

## The 28 Games to Play

| | | | | | | |
|---|---|---|---|---|---|---|
| 1. | A | C | F | G | S | PB |
| 2. | A | C | F | N | Q | PB |
| 3. | A | C | G | J | Q | PB |
| 4. | A | F | G | J | N | PB |
| 5. | A | J | N | Q | S | PB |
| 6. | B | D | E | I | P | PB |
| 7. | B | D | H | I | K | PB |
| 8. | B | D | I | L | O | PB |
| 9. | B | D | I | M | R | PB |
| 10. | B | E | H | K | P | PB |
| 11. | B | E | L | O | P | PB |
| 12. | B | E | M | P | R | PB |
| 13. | B | H | K | L | O | PB |
| 14. | B | H | K | M | R | PB |
| 15. | B | L | M | O | R | PB |
| 16. | C | F | J | N | S | PB |
| 17. | C | G | N | Q | S | PB |
| 18. | D | E | H | L | R | PB |
| 19. | D | E | K | M | O | PB |
| 20. | D | H | M | O | P | PB |
| 21. | D | K | L | M | P | PB |
| 22. | D | K | O | P | R | PB |
| 23. | E | H | I | L | M | PB |
| 24. | E | H | I | O | R | PB |
| 25. | E | I | K | L | R | PB |
| 26. | F | G | J | Q | S | PB |
| 27. | H | I | L | P | R | PB |
| 28. | I | K | M | O | P | PB |

# POWERBALL BALANCED WHEEL® 53220PB

## Wheel 20 Numbers + PB in 32 Games for a 3 of 5 Win

With Powerball

| Numbers Matched | Maximum Wins 5 + 1 | 4 + 1 | 3 + 1 | 2 + 1 | 1 + 1 | 0 + 1 | Minimum Wins 5 + 1 | 4 + 1 | 3 + 1 | 2 + 1 | 1 + 1 | 0 + 1 |
|---|---|---|---|---|---|---|---|---|---|---|---|---|
| 5 + 1 | 1 | 1 | 5 | 5 | 0 | 20 | 0 | 0 | 1 | 9 | 16 | 6 |
| 4 + 1 | - | 2 | 2 | 6 | 2 | 20 | - | 0 | 0 | 6 | 18 | 8 |
| 3 + 1 | - | - | 4 | 0 | 16 | 12 | - | - | 0 | 3 | 15 | 14 |
| 2 + 1 | - | - | - | 5 | 4 | 23 | - | - | - | 0 | 15 | 17 |
| 1 + 1 | - | - | - | - | 10 | 22 | - | - | - | - | 6 | 26 |
| 0 + 1 | - | - | - | - | - | 32 | - | - | - | - | - | 32 |

Without Powerball

| Numbers Matched | Maximum Wins 5 + 0 | 4 + 0 | 3 + 0 | 2 + 0 | 1 + 0 | Minimum Wins 5 + 0 | 4 + 0 | 3 + 0 | 2 + 0 | 1 + 0 |
|---|---|---|---|---|---|---|---|---|---|---|
| 5 + 0 | 1 | 1 | 5 | 5 | 0 | 0 | 0 | 1 | 9 | 16 |
| 4 + 0 | - | 2 | 2 | 6 | 2 | - | 0 | 0 | 6 | 18 |
| 3 + 0 | - | - | 4 | 0 | 16 | - | - | 0 | 3 | 15 |
| 2 + 0 | - | - | - | 5 | 4 | - | - | - | 0 | 15 |
| 1 + 0 | - | - | - | - | 10 | - | - | - | - | 6 |

## Your 20 Numbers + PB to Wheel

| A | B | C | D | E | F | G | H | I | J | K |
|---|---|---|---|---|---|---|---|---|---|---|
| 7 | 6 | 6 | 7 | 10 | 9 | 9 | 9 | 9 | 9 | 9 |

| L | M | N | O | P | Q | R | S | T | PB |
|---|---|---|---|---|---|---|---|---|---|
| 6 | 9 | 9 | 9 | 9 | 7 | 7 | 7 | 7 | 32 |

## The 32 Games to Play

| | | | | | | |
|---|---|---|---|---|---|---|
| 1. | A | B | C | L | T | PB |
| 2. | A | B | D | Q | R | PB |
| 3. | A | B | Q | S | T | PB |
| 4. | A | C | D | Q | R | PB |
| 5. | A | C | R | S | T | PB |
| 6. | A | D | L | S | T | PB |
| 7. | A | L | Q | R | S | PB |
| 8. | B | C | D | L | R | PB |
| 9. | B | C | L | Q | S | PB |
| 10. | B | D | R | S | T | PB |
| 11. | C | D | Q | S | T | PB |
| 12. | D | L | Q | R | T | PB |
| 13. | E | F | G | N | O | PB |
| 14. | E | F | H | J | N | PB |
| 15. | E | F | I | M | N | PB |
| 16. | E | F | K | N | P | PB |
| 17. | E | G | H | J | O | PB |
| 18. | E | G | I | M | O | PB |
| 19. | E | G | K | O | P | PB |
| 20. | E | H | I | J | M | PB |
| 21. | E | H | J | K | P | PB |
| 22. | E | I | K | M | P | PB |
| 23. | F | G | H | I | K | PB |
| 24. | F | G | H | M | P | PB |
| 25. | F | G | J | K | M | PB |
| 26. | F | H | K | M | O | PB |
| 27. | F | I | J | O | P | PB |
| 28. | G | H | K | M | N | PB |
| 29. | G | I | J | N | P | PB |
| 30. | H | I | N | O | P | PB |
| 31. | I | J | K | N | O | PB |
| 32. | J | M | N | O | P | PB |

# POWERBALL BALANCED WHEEL® 53221PB

## Wheel 21 Numbers + PB in 37 Games for a 3 of 5 Win

With Powerball

| Numbers Matched | Maximum Wins 5 + 1 | 4 + 1 | 3 + 1 | 2 + 1 | 1 + 1 | 0 + 1 | Minimum Wins 5 + 1 | 4 + 1 | 3 + 1 | 2 + 1 | 1 + 1 | 0 + 1 |
|---|---|---|---|---|---|---|---|---|---|---|---|---|
| 5 + 1 | 1 | 2 | 4 | 8 | 2 | 20 | 0 | 0 | 1 | 9 | 21 | 6 |
| 4 + 1 | - | 2 | 3 | 6 | 6 | 20 | - | 0 | 0 | 6 | 22 | 9 |
| 3 + 1 | - | - | 4 | 2 | 10 | 21 | - | - | 0 | 3 | 19 | 15 |
| 2 + 1 | - | - | - | 6 | 6 | 25 | - | - | - | 0 | 17 | 20 |
| 1 + 1 | - | - | - | - | 10 | 27 | - | - | - | - | 8 | 29 |
| 0 + 1 | - | - | - | - | - | 37 | - | - | - | - | - | 37 |

Without Powerball

| Numbers Matched | Maximum Wins 5 + 0 | 4 + 0 | 3 + 0 | 2 + 0 | 1 + 0 | Minimum Wins 5 + 0 | 4 + 0 | 3 + 0 | 2 + 0 | 1 + 0 |
|---|---|---|---|---|---|---|---|---|---|---|
| 5 + 0 | 1 | 2 | 4 | 8 | 2 | 0 | 0 | 1 | 9 | 21 |
| 4 + 0 | - | 2 | 3 | 6 | 6 | - | 0 | 0 | 6 | 22 |
| 3 + 0 | - | - | 4 | 2 | 10 | - | - | 0 | 3 | 19 |
| 2 + 0 | - | - | - | 6 | 6 | - | - | - | 0 | 17 |
| 1 + 0 | - | - | - | - | 10 | - | - | - | - | 8 |

## Your 21 Numbers + PB to Wheel

| A | B | C | D | E | F | G | H | I | J | K |
|---|---|---|---|---|---|---|---|---|---|---|
| 9 | 8 | 9 | 9 | 9 | 9 | 9 | 9 | 8 | 8 | 9 |

| L | M | N | O | P | Q | R | S | T | U | PB |
|---|---|---|---|---|---|---|---|---|---|---|
| 9 | 8 | 9 | 9 | 9 | 10 | 9 | 9 | 8 | 9 | 37 |

## The 37 Games to Play

| | | | | | | |
|---|---|---|---|---|---|---|
| 1. | A | B | F | M | T | PB |
| 2. | A | B | H | J | R | PB |
| 3. | A | B | I | R | S | PB |
| 4. | A | F | H | I | S | PB |
| 5. | A | F | J | R | S | PB |
| 6. | A | H | J | M | R | PB |
| 7. | A | H | M | R | T | PB |
| 8. | A | I | J | R | T | PB |
| 9. | A | I | M | S | T | PB |
| 10. | B | F | H | I | T | PB |
| 11. | B | F | J | M | S | PB |
| 12. | B | F | R | S | T | PB |
| 13. | B | H | M | R | S | PB |
| 14. | B | I | J | M | T | PB |
| 15. | C | D | E | L | U | PB |
| 16. | C | D | G | K | N | PB |
| 17. | C | D | O | P | Q | PB |
| 18. | C | E | G | P | U | PB |
| 19. | C | E | K | L | P | PB |
| 20. | C | E | N | O | Q | PB |
| 21. | C | G | L | O | Q | PB |
| 22. | C | K | O | Q | U | PB |
| 23. | C | L | N | P | U | PB |
| 24. | D | E | G | K | O | PB |
| 25. | D | E | N | P | Q | PB |
| 26. | D | G | L | P | Q | PB |
| 27. | D | G | N | O | U | PB |
| 28. | D | K | L | N | O | PB |
| 29. | D | K | P | Q | U | PB |
| 30. | E | G | L | N | Q | PB |
| 31. | E | K | N | Q | U | PB |
| 32. | E | L | O | P | U | PB |
| 33. | F | H | I | J | S | PB |
| 34. | F | H | I | M | R | PB |
| 35. | F | H | J | S | T | PB |
| 36. | G | K | L | Q | U | PB |



(Continued Next Page)

**POWERBALL BALANCED WHEEL® 53221PB** (Continued from previous page)

| | | | | | | |
|---|---|---|---|---|---|---|
| 37. | G | K | N | O | P | PB |



# POWERBALL BALANCED WHEEL® 53222PB

## Wheel 22 Numbers + PB in 40 Games for a 3 of 5 Win

With Powerball

| Numbers Matched | Maximum Wins 5 + 1 | 4 + 1 | 3 + 1 | 2 + 1 | 1 + 1 | 0 + 1 | Minimum Wins 5 + 1 | 4 + 1 | 3 + 1 | 2 + 1 | 1 + 1 | 0 + 1 |
|---|---|---|---|---|---|---|---|---|---|---|---|---|
| 5 + 1 | 1 | 0 | 6 | 10 | 3 | 20 | 0 | 0 | 1 | 10 | 22 | 7 |
| 4 + 1 | - | 1 | 4 | 6 | 8 | 21 | - | 0 | 0 | 6 | 24 | 10 |
| 3 + 1 | - | - | 4 | 0 | 16 | 20 | - | - | 0 | 3 | 21 | 16 |
| 2 + 1 | - | - | - | 4 | 11 | 25 | - | - | - | 0 | 18 | 22 |
| 1 + 1 | - | - | - | - | 10 | 30 | - | - | - | - | 9 | 31 |
| 0 + 1 | - | - | - | - | - | 40 | - | - | - | - | - | 40 |

Without Powerball

| Numbers Matched | Maximum Wins 5 + 0 | 4 + 0 | 3 + 0 | 2 + 0 | 1 + 0 | Minimum Wins 5 + 0 | 4 + 0 | 3 + 0 | 2 + 0 | 1 + 0 |
|---|---|---|---|---|---|---|---|---|---|---|
| 5 + 0 | 1 | 0 | 6 | 10 | 3 | 0 | 0 | 1 | 10 | 22 |
| 4 + 0 | - | 1 | 4 | 6 | 8 | - | 0 | 0 | 6 | 24 |
| 3 + 0 | - | - | 4 | 0 | 16 | - | - | 0 | 3 | 21 |
| 2 + 0 | - | - | - | 4 | 11 | - | - | - | 0 | 18 |
| 1 + 0 | - | - | - | - | 10 | - | - | - | - | 9 |

## Your 22 Numbers + PB to Wheel

| A | B | C | D | E | F | G | H |
|---|---|---|---|---|---|---|---|
| 9 | 9 | 9 | 9 | 9 | 9 | 9 | 9 |
| **I** | **J** | **K** | **L** | **M** | **N** | **O** | **P** |
| 9 | 9 | 10 | 10 | 9 | 9 | 9 | 9 |
| **Q** | **R** | **S** | **T** | **U** | **V** | **PB** | |
| 9 | 9 | 9 | 9 | 9 | 9 | 40 | |

## The 40 Games to Play

| | | | | | | |
|---|---|---|---|---|---|---|
| 1. | A | B | F | O | S | PB |
| 2. | A | B | I | J | S | PB |
| 3. | A | B | I | O | P | PB |
| 4. | A | B | L | M | V | PB |
| 5. | A | F | I | L | V | PB |
| 6. | A | F | J | M | P | PB |
| 7. | A | I | M | O | S | PB |
| 8. | A | J | L | O | V | PB |
| 9. | A | L | P | S | V | PB |
| 10. | B | F | I | L | M | PB |
| 11. | B | F | J | P | V | PB |
| 12. | B | I | O | S | V | PB |
| 13. | B | J | L | M | O | PB |
| 14. | B | L | M | P | S | PB |
| 15. | C | D | E | K | T | PB |
| 16. | C | D | G | K | Q | PB |
| 17. | C | D | H | K | R | PB |
| 18. | C | D | K | N | U | PB |
| 19. | C | E | G | H | U | PB |
| 20. | C | E | N | Q | R | PB |
| 21. | C | G | H | N | T | PB |
| 22. | C | G | R | T | U | PB |
| 23. | C | H | Q | T | U | PB |
| 24. | D | E | G | N | R | PB |
| 25. | D | E | H | N | Q | PB |
| 26. | D | E | Q | R | U | PB |



(Continued Next Page)

## POWERBALL BALANCED WHEEL® 53222PB (Continued from previous page)

| | | | | | | |
|---|---|---|---|---|---|---|
| 27. | D | G | H | T | U | PB |
| 28. | D | N | Q | R | T | PB |
| 29. | E | G | K | Q | T | PB |
| 30. | E | H | K | R | T | PB |
| 31. | E | K | N | T | U | PB |
| 32. | F | I | J | L | O | PB |
| 33. | F | I | L | P | S | PB |
| 34. | F | J | M | S | V | PB |
| 35. | F | M | O | P | V | PB |
| 36. | G | H | K | Q | R | PB |
| 37. | G | K | N | Q | U | PB |
| 38. | H | K | N | R | U | PB |
| 39. | I | J | M | P | V | PB |
| 40. | J | L | O | P | S | PB |



# POWERBALL BALANCED WHEEL® 53224PB

## Wheel 24 Numbers + PB in 54 Games for a 3 of 5 Win

With Powerball

| Numbers Matched | Maximum Wins 5 + 1 | 4 + 1 | 3 + 1 | 2 + 1 | 1 + 1 | 0 + 1 | Minimum Wins 5 + 1 | 4 + 1 | 3 + 1 | 2 + 1 | 1 + 1 | 0 + 1 |
|---|---|---|---|---|---|---|---|---|---|---|---|---|
| 5 + 1 | 1 | 0 | 8 | 16 | 5 | 24 | 0 | 0 | 1 | 11 | 28 | 14 |
| 4 + 1 | - | 1 | 4 | 12 | 13 | 24 | - | 0 | 0 | 7 | 30 | 17 |
| 3 + 1 | - | - | 5 | 0 | 25 | 24 | - | - | 0 | 3 | 25 | 26 |
| 2 + 1 | - | - | - | 7 | 12 | 35 | - | - | - | 0 | 22 | 32 |
| 1 + 1 | - | - | - | - | 14 | 40 | - | - | - | - | 9 | 45 |
| 0 + 1 | - | - | - | - | - | 54 | - | - | - | - | - | 54 |

Without Powerball

| Numbers Matched | Maximum Wins 5 + 0 | 4 + 0 | 3 + 0 | 2 + 0 | 1 + 0 | Minimum Wins 5 + 0 | 4 + 0 | 3 + 0 | 2 + 0 | 1 + 0 |
|---|---|---|---|---|---|---|---|---|---|---|
| 5 + 0 | 1 | 0 | 8 | 16 | 5 | 0 | 0 | 1 | 11 | 28 |
| 4 + 0 | - | 1 | 4 | 12 | 13 | - | 0 | 0 | 7 | 30 |
| 3 + 0 | - | - | 5 | 0 | 25 | - | - | 0 | 3 | 25 |
| 2 + 0 | - | - | - | 7 | 12 | - | - | - | 0 | 22 |
| 1 + 0 | - | - | - | - | 14 | - | - | - | - | 9 |

## Your 24 Numbers + PB to Wheel

| A | B | C | D | E | F | G | H | I |
|---|---|---|---|---|---|---|---|---|
| 9 | 13 | 13 | 9 | 13 | 9 | 13 | 13 | 13 |
| **J** | **K** | **L** | **M** | **N** | **O** | **P** | **Q** | **R** |
| 9 | 9 | 13 | 9 | 9 | 13 | 13 | 13 | 13 |
| **S** | **T** | **U** | **V** | **W** | **X** | **PB** | | |
| 10 | 9 | 13 | 9 | 14 | 9 | 54 | | |

## The 54 Games to Play

| | | | | | | |
|---|---|---|---|---|---|---|
| 1. | A | D | F | J | T | PB |
| 2. | A | D | F | M | V | PB |
| 3. | A | D | J | M | N | PB |
| 4. | A | D | K | S | X | PB |
| 5. | A | F | J | M | X | PB |
| 6. | A | F | K | N | S | PB |
| 7. | A | J | K | S | V | PB |
| 8. | A | K | M | S | T | PB |
| 9. | A | N | T | V | X | PB |
| 10. | B | C | E | U | W | PB |
| 11. | B | C | G | O | Q | PB |
| 12. | B | C | H | O | R | PB |
| 13. | B | C | I | L | P | PB |
| 14. | B | E | G | R | U | PB |



(Continued Next Page)

## POWERBALL BALANCED WHEEL® 53224PB (Continued from previous page)

| | | | | | | |
|---|---|---|---|---|---|---|
| 15. | B | E | H | *Q* | U | PB |
| 16. | B | E | I | P | U | PB |
| 17. | B | E | L | O | U | PB |
| 18. | B | G | H | I | P | PB |
| 19. | B | G | L | *Q* | W | PB |
| 20. | B | H | L | R | W | PB |
| 21. | B | I | O | P | W | PB |
| 22. | B | I | P | *Q* | R | PB |
| 23. | C | E | G | I | *Q* | PB |
| 24. | C | E | H | I | R | PB |
| 25. | C | E | L | O | P | PB |
| 26. | C | G | H | U | W | PB |
| 27. | C | G | L | P | R | PB |
| 28. | C | H | L | P | *Q* | PB |
| 29. | C | I | O | U | W | PB |
| 30. | C | L | P | U | W | PB |
| 31. | C | *Q* | R | U | W | PB |
| 32. | D | F | J | K | M | PB |
| 33. | D | F | N | S | X | PB |
| 34. | D | J | S | V | X | PB |
| 35. | D | K | N | T | V | PB |
| 36. | D | M | S | T | X | PB |
| 37. | E | G | H | L | O | PB |
| 38. | E | G | P | *Q* | W | PB |
| 39. | E | H | P | R | W | PB |
| 40. | E | I | L | O | W | PB |
| 41. | E | L | O | *Q* | R | PB |
| 42. | F | J | N | S | V | PB |
| 43. | F | K | T | V | X | PB |
| 44. | F | M | N | S | T | PB |
| 45. | G | H | *Q* | R | W | PB |
| 46. | G | I | L | *Q* | U | PB |
| 47. | G | I | O | R | W | PB |
| 48. | G | O | P | *Q* | U | PB |
| 49. | H | I | L | R | U | PB |
| 50. | H | I | O | *Q* | W | PB |
| 51. | H | O | P | R | U | PB |
| 52. | J | K | N | T | X | PB |
| 53. | J | M | S | T | V | PB |
| 54. | K | M | N | V | X | PB |



# POWERBALL BALANCED WHEEL® 53225PB

## Wheel 25 Numbers + PB in 63 Games for a 3 of 5 Win

With Powerball

| Numbers Matched | Maximum Wins | | | | | | Minimum Wins | | | | | |
|---|---|---|---|---|---|---|---|---|---|---|---|---|
| | 5 + 1 | 4 + 1 | 3 + 1 | 2 + 1 | 1 + 1 | 0 + 1 | 5 + 1 | 4 + 1 | 3 + 1 | 2 + 1 | 1 + 1 | 0 + 1 |
| 5 + 1 | 1 | 1 | 7 | 12 | 8 | 34 | 0 | 0 | 1 | 13 | 32 | 17 |
| 4 + 1 | - | 2 | 3 | 9 | 15 | 34 | - | 0 | 0 | 8 | 33 | 22 |
| 3 + 1 | - | - | 5 | 1 | 20 | 37 | - | - | 0 | 4 | 28 | 31 |
| 2 + 1 | - | - | - | 7 | 12 | 44 | - | - | - | 0 | 24 | 39 |
| 1 + 1 | - | - | - | - | 14 | 49 | - | - | - | - | 11 | 52 |
| 0 + 1 | - | - | - | - | - | 63 | - | - | - | - | - | 63 |

Without Powerball

| Numbers Matched | Maximum Wins | | | | | Minimum Wins | | | | |
|---|---|---|---|---|---|---|---|---|---|---|
| | 5 + 0 | 4 + 0 | 3 + 0 | 2 + 0 | 1 + 0 | 5 + 0 | 4 + 0 | 3 + 0 | 2 + 0 | 1 + 0 |
| 5 + 0 | 1 | 1 | 7 | 12 | 8 | 0 | 0 | 1 | 13 | 32 |
| 4 + 0 | - | 2 | 3 | 9 | 15 | - | 0 | 0 | 8 | 33 |
| 3 + 0 | - | - | 5 | 1 | 20 | - | - | 0 | 4 | 28 |
| 2 + 0 | - | - | - | 7 | 12 | - | - | - | 0 | 24 |
| 1 + 0 | - | - | - | - | 14 | - | - | - | - | 11 |

(Continued Next Page)

**POWERBALL BALANCED WHEEL® 53225PB** (Continued from previous page)

## Your 25 Numbers + PB to Wheel

| A | B | C | D | E | F | G | H | I |
|---|---|---|---|---|---|---|---|---|
| 13 | 12 | 12 | 13 | 13 | 13 | 11 | 13 | 12 |
| **J** | **K** | **L** | **M** | **N** | **O** | **P** | **Q** | **R** |
| 13 | 12 | 13 | 12 | 13 | 13 | 12 | 13 | 12 |
| **S** | **T** | **U** | **V** | **W** | **X** | **Y** | **PB** | |
| 13 | 13 | 13 | 14 | 12 | 13 | 12 | 63 | |

## The 63 Games to Play

| | | | | | | | | | | | | | |
|---|---|---|---|---|---|---|---|---|---|---|---|---|---|
| 1. | A | D | E | L | X | PB | 29. | C | I | K | R | W | PB |
| 2. | A | D | F | U | V | PB | 30. | C | I | M | O | R | PB |
| 3. | A | D | H | S | T | PB | 31. | C | K | O | *Q* | Y | PB |
| 4. | A | D | J | N | T | PB | 32. | C | M | *Q* | W | Y | PB |
| 5. | A | E | F | N | T | PB | 33. | C | P | *Q* | R | Y | PB |
| 6. | A | E | H | J | U | PB | 34. | D | E | F | V | X | PB |
| 7. | A | E | S | T | V | PB | 35. | D | E | H | J | X | PB |
| 8. | A | F | H | T | X | PB | 36. | D | E | N | S | X | PB |
| 9. | A | F | J | L | S | PB | 37. | D | E | T | U | X | PB |
| 10. | A | H | L | N | V | PB | 38. | D | F | H | N | V | PB |
| 11. | A | J | T | V | X | PB | 39. | D | F | J | S | V | PB |
| 12. | A | L | T | U | V | PB | 40. | D | F | L | T | V | PB |
| 13. | A | N | S | U | X | PB | 41. | D | H | L | S | U | PB |
| 14. | B | C | G | M | R | PB | 42. | D | J | L | N | U | PB |
| 15. | B | C | I | *Q* | Y | PB | 43. | E | F | H | J | S | PB |
| 16. | B | C | K | M | P | PB | 44. | E | F | L | N | U | PB |
| 17. | B | C | O | P | W | PB | 45. | E | H | J | L | T | PB |
| 18. | B | G | I | O | *Q* | PB | 46. | E | H | J | N | V | PB |
| 19. | B | G | K | M | W | PB | 47. | E | L | S | U | V | PB |
| 20. | B | G | K | P | Y | PB | 48. | F | H | L | U | X | PB |
| 21. | B | I | K | O | *Q* | PB | 49. | F | J | N | S | X | PB |
| 22. | B | I | M | *Q* | W | PB | 50. | F | J | S | T | U | PB |
| 23. | B | I | P | *Q* | R | PB | 51. | G | I | M | R | Y | PB |
| 24. | B | K | R | W | Y | PB | 52. | G | K | O | P | R | PB |
| 25. | B | M | O | R | Y | PB | 53. | G | M | O | P | *Q* | PB |
| 26. | C | G | I | K | *Q* | PB | 54. | G | *Q* | R | W | Y | PB |
| 27. | C | G | I | P | W | PB | 55. | H | N | S | V | X | PB |
| 28. | C | G | O | W | Y | PB | 56. | H | N | T | U | V | PB |



(Continued Next Page)

**POWERBALL BALANCED WHEEL® 53225PB** (Continued from previous page)

| | | | | | | |
|---|---|---|---|---|---|---|
| 57. | I | K | M | P | Y | PB |
| 58. | I | O | P | W | Y | PB |
| 59. | J | L | U | V | X | PB |
| 60. | K | M | O | Q | R | PB |

| | | | | | | |
|---|---|---|---|---|---|---|
| 61. | K | O | P | Q | W | PB |
| 62. | L | N | S | T | X | PB |
| 63. | M | O | P | R | W | PB |



# POWERBALL BALANCED WHEEL® 53227PB

## Wheel 27 Numbers + PB in 77 Games for a 3 of 5 Win

With Powerball

| Numbers Matched | Maximum Wins 5 + 1 | 4 + 1 | 3 + 1 | 2 + 1 | 1 + 1 | 0 + 1 | Minimum Wins 5 + 1 | 4 + 1 | 3 + 1 | 2 + 1 | 1 + 1 | 0 + 1 |
|---|---|---|---|---|---|---|---|---|---|---|---|---|
| 5 + 1 | 1 | 2 | 8 | 16 | 14 | 36 | 0 | 0 | 1 | 13 | 36 | 27 |
| 4 + 1 | - | 2 | 5 | 12 | 20 | 38 | - | 0 | 0 | 8 | 36 | 33 |
| 3 + 1 | - | - | 6 | 1 | 30 | 40 | - | - | 0 | 4 | 31 | 42 |
| 2 + 1 | - | - | - | 7 | 20 | 50 | - | - | - | 0 | 26 | 51 |
| 1 + 1 | - | - | - | - | 17 | 60 | - | - | - | - | 13 | 64 |
| 0 + 1 | - | - | - | - | - | 77 | - | - | - | - | - | 77 |

Without Powerball

| Numbers Matched | Maximum Wins 5 + 0 | 4 + 0 | 3 + 0 | 2 + 0 | 1 + 0 | Minimum Wins 5 + 0 | 4 + 0 | 3 + 0 | 2 + 0 | 1 + 0 |
|---|---|---|---|---|---|---|---|---|---|---|
| 5 + 0 | 1 | 2 | 8 | 16 | 14 | 0 | 0 | 1 | 13 | 36 |
| 4 + 0 | - | 2 | 5 | 12 | 20 | - | 0 | 0 | 8 | 36 |
| 3 + 0 | - | - | 6 | 1 | 30 | - | - | 0 | 4 | 31 |
| 2 + 0 | - | - | - | 7 | 20 | - | - | - | 0 | 26 |
| 1 + 0 | - | - | - | - | 17 | - | - | - | - | 13 |

## Your 27 Numbers + PB to Wheel

| A | B | C | D | E | F | G | H | I | J |
|---|---|---|---|---|---|---|---|---|---|
| 16 | 13 | 15 | 15 | 13 | 13 | 15 | 17 | 13 | 13 |
| **K** | **L** | **M** | **N** | **O** | **P** | **Q** | **R** | **S** | **T** |
| 13 | 13 | 13 | 17 | 13 | 15 | 17 | 13 | 16 | 13 |
| **U** | **V** | **W** | **X** | **Y** | **Z** | **aa** | **PB** | | |
| 15 | 13 | 16 | 13 | 13 | 14 | 15 | 77 | | |

## The 77 Games to Play

| | | | | | | |
|---|---|---|---|---|---|---|
| 1. | A | C | D | H | aa | PB |
| 2. | A | C | G | S | W | PB |
| 3. | A | C | K | R | U | PB |
| 4. | A | C | N | P | Q | PB |
| 5. | A | D | G | P | aa | PB |
| 6. | A | D | H | K | aa | PB |
| 7. | A | D | N | Q | R | PB |
| 8. | A | D | S | U | W | PB |
| 9. | A | G | H | P | R | PB |
| 10. | A | G | H | P | U | PB |



| | | | | | | |
|---|---|---|---|---|---|---|
| 11. | A | G | K | N | Q | PB |
| 12. | A | H | N | Q | S | PB |
| 13. | A | H | N | Q | W | PB |
| 14. | A | K | P | S | W | PB |
| 15. | A | N | Q | U | aa | PB |
| 16. | A | R | S | W | aa | PB |
| 17. | B | E | F | M | O | PB |
| 18. | B | E | I | J | Z | PB |
| 19. | B | E | I | L | T | PB |
| 20. | B | E | V | X | Y | PB |

(Continued Next Page)

## POWERBALL BALANCED WHEEL® 53227PB

(Continued from previous page)

| | | | | | | |
|---|---|---|---|---|---|---|
| 21. | B | F | I | T | X | PB |
| 22. | B | F | I | V | Z | PB |
| 23. | B | F | J | L | Y | PB |
| 24. | B | I | J | M | X | PB |
| 25. | B | I | L | M | V | PB |
| 26. | B | I | O | Y | Z | PB |
| 27. | B | J | O | T | V | PB |
| 28. | B | L | O | X | Z | PB |
| 29. | B | M | T | Y | Z | PB |
| 30. | C | D | G | N | U | PB |
| 31. | C | D | K | N | W | PB |
| 32. | C | D | N | W | aa | PB |
| 33. | C | D | P | R | W | PB |
| 34. | C | D | Q | S | aa | PB |
| 35. | C | G | H | K | P | PB |
| 36. | C | G | Q | R | aa | PB |
| 37. | C | H | N | R | S | PB |
| 38. | C | H | Q | U | W | PB |
| 39. | C | K | Q | S | aa | PB |
| 40. | C | P | S | U | aa | PB |
| 41. | D | G | H | Q | W | PB |
| 42. | D | G | K | R | S | PB |
| 43. | D | H | N | P | S | PB |
| 44. | D | H | R | U | aa | PB |
| 45. | D | K | P | Q | U | PB |
| 46. | E | F | I | M | Y | PB |
| 47. | E | F | J | L | M | PB |
| 48. | E | F | M | T | Z | PB |
| 49. | E | F | M | V | X | PB |
| 50. | E | I | O | V | X | PB |
| 51. | E | J | O | Y | Z | PB |
| 52. | E | J | T | V | X | PB |
| 53. | E | L | O | T | Y | PB |
| 54. | E | L | V | X | Z | PB |
| 55. | F | I | J | L | O | PB |
| 56. | F | J | L | T | V | PB |
| 57. | F | J | L | X | Z | PB |
| 58. | F | O | T | X | Y | PB |
| 59. | F | O | V | Y | Z | PB |
| 60. | G | H | N | S | aa | PB |
| 61. | G | K | U | W | aa | PB |
| 62. | G | N | P | U | W | PB |
| 63. | G | N | R | U | W | PB |
| 64. | G | P | Q | S | U | PB |
| 65. | H | K | N | S | U | PB |
| 66. | H | K | Q | R | W | PB |
| 67. | H | N | Q | S | W | PB |
| 68. | H | P | Q | W | aa | PB |
| 69. | I | J | T | V | Y | PB |
| 70. | I | L | X | Y | Z | PB |
| 71. | I | M | O | T | Z | PB |
| 72. | J | M | O | X | Y | PB |
| 73. | J | M | T | V | Z | PB |
| 74. | K | N | P | R | aa | PB |
| 75. | L | M | O | V | Y | PB |
| 76. | L | M | T | X | Z | PB |
| 77. | P | Q | R | S | U | PB |

# POWERBALL BALANCED WHEEL® 53228PB

## Wheel 28 Numbers + PB in 86 Games for a 3 of 5 Win

With Powerball

| Numbers Matched | Maximum Wins 5 + 1 | 4 + 1 | 3 + 1 | 2 + 1 | 1 + 1 | 0 + 1 | Minimum Wins 5 + 1 | 4 + 1 | 3 + 1 | 2 + 1 | 1 + 1 | 0 + 1 |
|---|---|---|---|---|---|---|---|---|---|---|---|---|
| 5 + 1 | 1 | 2 | 8 | 16 | 14 | 45 | 0 | 0 | 1 | 13 | 38 | 34 |
| 4 + 1 | - | 2 | 5 | 12 | 20 | 47 | - | 0 | 0 | 8 | 36 | 42 |
| 3 + 1 | - | - | 6 | 1 | 30 | 49 | - | - | 0 | 4 | 31 | 51 |
| 2 + 1 | - | - | - | 7 | 20 | 59 | - | - | - | 0 | 26 | 60 |
| 1 + 1 | - | - | - | - | 17 | 69 | - | - | - | - | 13 | 73 |
| 0 + 1 | - | - | - | - | - | 86 | - | - | - | - | - | 86 |

Without Powerball

| Numbers Matched | Maximum Wins 5 + 0 | 4 + 0 | 3 + 0 | 2 + 0 | 1 + 0 | Minimum Wins 5 + 0 | 4 + 0 | 3 + 0 | 2 + 0 | 1 + 0 |
|---|---|---|---|---|---|---|---|---|---|---|
| 5 + 0 | 1 | 2 | 8 | 16 | 14 | 0 | 0 | 1 | 13 | 38 |
| 4 + 0 | - | 2 | 5 | 12 | 20 | - | 0 | 0 | 8 | 36 |
| 3 + 0 | - | - | 6 | 1 | 30 | - | - | 0 | 4 | 31 |
| 2 + 0 | - | - | - | 7 | 20 | - | - | - | 0 | 26 |
| 1 + 0 | - | - | - | - | 17 | - | - | - | - | 13 |

## Your 28 Numbers + PB to Wheel

| A | B | C | D | E | F | G | H | I | J |
|---|---|---|---|---|---|---|---|---|---|
| 15 | 13 | 13 | 13 | 13 | 15 | 17 | 17 | 17 | 17 |
| **K** | **L** | **M** | **N** | **O** | **P** | **Q** | **R** | **S** | **T** |
| 17 | 17 | 16 | 16 | 16 | 16 | 16 | 16 | 15 | 15 |
| **U** | **V** | **W** | **X** | **Y** | **Z** | **aa** | **bb** | **PB** | |
| 15 | 15 | 15 | 15 | 15 | 15 | 15 | 15 | 86 | |

## The 86 Games to Play

| | | | | | | |
|---|---|---|---|---|---|---|
| 1. | A | C | D | L | X | PB |
| 2. | A | C | F | R | bb | PB |
| 3. | A | C | I | M | aa | PB |
| 4. | A | C | K | P | Y | PB |
| 5. | A | D | F | I | aa | PB |
| 6. | A | D | K | Y | bb | PB |
| 7. | A | D | M | P | R | PB |
| 8. | A | F | K | L | M | PB |
| 9. | A | F | P | X | Y | PB |
| 10. | A | I | K | R | X | PB |
| 11. | A | I | L | P | bb | PB |
| 12. | A | I | M | Y | aa | PB |
| 13. | A | K | P | Y | aa | PB |
| 14. | A | L | R | Y | aa | PB |
| 15. | A | M | X | aa | bb | PB |
| 16. | B | E | G | T | W | PB |
| 17. | B | E | H | J | Q | PB |
| 18. | B | E | N | U | V | PB |
| 19. | B | E | O | S | Z | PB |
| 20. | B | G | H | N | S | PB |
| 21. | B | G | J | O | V | PB |
| 22. | B | G | Q | U | Z | PB |
| 23. | B | H | O | U | W | PB |
| 24. | B | H | T | V | Z | PB |
| 25. | B | J | N | W | Z | PB |
| 26. | B | J | S | T | U | PB |
| 27. | B | N | O | Q | T | PB |
| 28. | B | Q | S | V | W | PB |
| 29. | C | D | F | M | Y | PB |
| 30. | C | D | I | K | R | PB |
| 31. | C | D | P | aa | bb | PB |
| 32. | C | F | I | L | P | PB |



(Continued Next Page)

## POWERBALL BALANCED WHEEL® 53228PB (Continued from previous page)

| | | | | | | |
|---|---|---|---|---|---|---|
| 33. | C | F | K | X | aa | PB |
| 34. | C | I | X | Y | bb | PB |
| 35. | C | K | L | M | bb | PB |
| 36. | C | L | R | Y | aa | PB |
| 37. | C | M | P | R | X | PB |
| 38. | D | F | K | P | X | PB |
| 39. | D | F | L | R | bb | PB |
| 40. | D | I | L | P | Y | PB |
| 41. | D | I | M | X | bb | PB |
| 42. | D | K | L | M | aa | PB |
| 43. | D | R | X | Y | aa | PB |
| 44. | E | G | H | N | Z | PB |
| 45. | E | G | J | O | U | PB |
| 46. | E | G | Q | S | V | PB |
| 47. | E | H | O | T | V | PB |
| 48. | E | H | S | U | W | PB |
| 49. | E | J | N | S | T | PB |
| 50. | E | J | V | W | Z | PB |
| 51. | E | N | O | Q | W | PB |
| 52. | E | Q | T | U | Z | PB |
| 53. | F | I | K | R | Y | PB |
| 54. | F | I | M | X | bb | PB |
| 55. | F | K | P | X | bb | PB |
| 56. | F | L | R | X | bb | PB |
| 57. | F | L | Y | aa | bb | PB |
| 58. | F | M | P | R | aa | PB |
| 59. | G | H | J | N | O | PB |
| 60. | G | H | J | N | Q | PB |
| 61. | G | H | J | O | Q | PB |
| 62. | G | H | N | T | U | PB |
| 63. | G | H | N | V | W | PB |
| 64. | G | J | O | S | W | PB |
| 65. | G | J | O | T | Z | PB |
| 66. | G | Q | S | T | V | PB |
| 67. | G | Q | U | W | Z | PB |
| 68. | G | S | U | V | Z | PB |
| 69. | H | J | Q | S | Z | PB |
| 70. | H | J | Q | T | W | PB |
| 71. | H | J | Q | U | V | PB |
| 72. | H | O | S | T | V | PB |
| 73. | H | O | U | W | Z | PB |
| 74. | I | K | L | M | P | PB |
| 75. | I | K | L | M | R | PB |
| 76. | I | K | L | P | R | PB |
| 77. | I | K | R | aa | bb | PB |
| 78. | I | L | P | X | aa | PB |
| 79. | J | N | S | T | V | PB |
| 80. | J | N | U | W | Z | PB |
| 81. | K | L | M | X | Y | PB |
| 82. | M | P | R | Y | bb | PB |
| 83. | N | O | Q | S | U | PB |
| 84. | N | O | Q | V | Z | PB |
| 85. | N | S | T | W | Z | PB |
| 86. | O | T | U | V | W | PB |



# POWERBALL BALANCED WHEEL® 53230PB

## Wheel 30 Numbers + PB in 102 Games for a 3 of 5 Win

With Powerball

| Numbers Matched | Maximum Wins 5 + 1 | 4 + 1 | 3 + 1 | 2 + 1 | 1 + 1 | 0 + 1 | Minimum Wins 5 + 1 | 4 + 1 | 3 + 1 | 2 + 1 | 1 + 1 | 0 + 1 |
|---|---|---|---|---|---|---|---|---|---|---|---|---|
| 5 + 1 | 1 | 0 | 8 | 16 | 5 | 72 | 0 | 0 | 1 | 14 | 48 | 39 |
| 4 + 1 | - | 1 | 4 | 12 | 13 | 72 | - | 0 | 0 | 9 | 48 | 45 |
| 3 + 1 | - | - | 5 | 0 | 25 | 72 | - | - | 0 | 4 | 38 | 60 |
| 2 + 1 | - | - | - | 7 | 12 | 83 | - | - | - | 0 | 33 | 69 |
| 1 + 1 | - | - | - | - | 20 | 82 | - | - | - | - | 13 | 89 |
| 0 + 1 | - | - | - | - | - | 102 | - | - | - | - | - | 102 |

(Continued Next Page)

## POWERBALL BALANCED WHEEL® 53230PB (Continued from previous page)

Without Powerball

| Numbers Matched | Maximum Wins 5 + 0 | 4 + 0 | 3 + 0 | 2 + 0 | 1 + 0 | Minimum Wins 5 + 0 | 4 + 0 | 3 + 0 | 2 + 0 | 1 + 0 |
|---|---|---|---|---|---|---|---|---|---|---|
| 5 + 0 | 1 | 0 | 8 | 16 | 5 | 0 | 0 | 1 | 14 | 48 |
| 4 + 0 | - | 1 | 4 | 12 | 13 | - | 0 | 0 | 9 | 48 |
| 3 + 0 | - | - | 5 | 0 | 25 | - | - | 0 | 4 | 38 |
| 2 + 0 | - | - | - | 7 | 12 | - | - | - | 0 | 33 |
| 1 + 0 | - | - | - | - | 20 | - | - | - | - | 13 |

## Your 30 Numbers + PB to Wheel

| A | B | C | D | E | F | G | H | I | J | K |
|---|---|---|---|---|---|---|---|---|---|---|
| 13 | 13 | 13 | 13 | 13 | 14 | 20 | 20 | 20 | 20 | 20 |
| **L** | **M** | **N** | **O** | **P** | **Q** | **R** | **S** | **T** | **U** | **V** |
| 20 | 20 | 20 | 20 | 20 | 20 | 20 | 20 | 20 | 20 | 20 |
| **W** | **X** | **Y** | **Z** | **aa** | **bb** | **cc** | **dd** | **PB** | | |
| 20 | 13 | 13 | 13 | 13 | 13 | 13 | 13 | 102 | | |

## The 102 Games to Play

| | | | | | | |
|---|---|---|---|---|---|---|
| 1. | A | B | C | cc | dd | PB |
| 2. | A | B | D | E | bb | PB |
| 3. | A | B | F | Y | Z | PB |
| 4. | A | B | X | Y | aa | PB |
| 5. | A | C | D | Z | aa | PB |
| 6. | A | C | E | F | X | PB |
| 7. | A | C | F | Y | bb | PB |
| 8. | A | D | F | Y | cc | PB |
| 9. | A | D | X | Y | dd | PB |
| 10. | A | E | Y | Z | dd | PB |
| 11. | A | E | Y | aa | cc | PB |
| 12. | A | F | aa | bb | dd | PB |
| 13. | A | X | Z | bb | cc | PB |
| 14. | B | C | D | E | Y | PB |
| 15. | B | C | F | Z | bb | PB |
| 16. | B | C | X | aa | bb | PB |
| 17. | B | D | E | F | X | PB |
| 18. | B | D | E | Z | aa | PB |
| 19. | B | D | E | cc | dd | PB |
| 20. | B | F | aa | cc | dd | PB |
| 21. | B | X | Z | cc | dd | PB |
| 22. | B | Y | bb | cc | dd | PB |
| 23. | C | D | F | bb | cc | PB |
| 24. | C | D | X | bb | dd | PB |
| 25. | C | E | Z | bb | dd | PB |
| 26. | C | E | aa | bb | cc | PB |
| 27. | C | F | Y | aa | dd | PB |
| 28. | C | X | Y | Z | cc | PB |
| 29. | D | F | Z | aa | dd | PB |
| 30. | D | X | Z | aa | cc | PB |
| 31. | D | Y | Z | aa | bb | PB |
| 32. | E | F | X | Y | bb | PB |
| 33. | E | F | X | Z | cc | PB |
| 34. | E | F | X | aa | dd | PB |
| 35. | G | H | I | J | S | PB |
| 36. | G | H | K | N | W | PB |
| 37. | G | H | L | M | V | PB |
| 38. | G | H | O | P | Q | PB |
| 39. | G | H | R | T | U | PB |
| 40. | G | I | K | O | T | PB |
| 41. | G | I | L | U | W | PB |
| 42. | G | I | M | N | Q | PB |
| 43. | G | I | P | R | V | PB |
| 44. | G | J | K | L | P | PB |
| 45. | G | J | M | O | U | PB |
| 46. | G | J | N | T | V | PB |



(Continued Next Page)

## POWERBALL BALANCED WHEEL® 53230PB (Continued from previous page)

| | | | | | | |
|---|---|---|---|---|---|---|
| 47. | G | J | *Q* | R | W | PB |
| 48. | G | K | M | R | S | PB |
| 49. | G | K | *Q* | U | V | PB |
| 50. | G | L | N | O | R | PB |
| 51. | G | L | *Q* | S | T | PB |
| 52. | G | M | P | T | W | PB |
| 53. | G | N | P | S | U | PB |
| 54. | G | O | S | V | W | PB |
| 55. | H | I | K | L | R | PB |
| 56. | H | I | M | P | U | PB |
| 57. | H | I | N | O | V | PB |
| 58. | H | I | *Q* | T | W | PB |
| 59. | H | J | K | M | *Q* | PB |
| 60. | H | J | L | O | T | PB |
| 61. | H | J | N | P | R | PB |
| 62. | H | J | U | V | W | PB |
| 63. | H | K | O | S | U | PB |
| 64. | H | K | P | T | V | PB |
| 65. | H | L | N | *Q* | U | PB |
| 66. | H | L | P | S | W | PB |
| 67. | H | M | N | S | T | PB |
| 68. | H | M | O | R | W | PB |
| 69. | H | *Q* | R | S | V | PB |
| 70. | I | J | K | N | U | PB |
| 71. | I | J | L | *Q* | V | PB |
| 72. | I | J | M | R | T | PB |
| 73. | I | J | O | P | W | PB |
| 74. | I | K | M | V | W | PB |

| | | | | | | |
|---|---|---|---|---|---|---|
| 75. | I | K | P | *Q* | S | PB |
| 76. | I | L | M | O | S | PB |
| 77. | I | L | N | P | T | PB |
| 78. | I | N | R | S | W | PB |
| 79. | I | O | *Q* | R | U | PB |
| 80. | I | S | T | U | V | PB |
| 81. | J | K | O | R | V | PB |
| 82. | J | K | S | T | W | PB |
| 83. | J | L | M | N | W | PB |
| 84. | J | L | R | S | U | PB |
| 85. | J | M | P | S | V | PB |
| 86. | J | N | O | *Q* | S | PB |
| 87. | J | P | *Q* | T | U | PB |
| 88. | K | L | M | T | U | PB |
| 89. | K | L | N | S | V | PB |
| 90. | K | L | O | *Q* | W | PB |
| 91. | K | M | N | O | P | PB |
| 92. | K | N | *Q* | R | T | PB |
| 93. | K | P | R | U | W | PB |
| 94. | L | M | P | *Q* | R | PB |
| 95. | L | O | P | U | V | PB |
| 96. | L | R | T | V | W | PB |
| 97. | M | N | R | U | V | PB |
| 98. | M | O | *Q* | T | V | PB |
| 99. | M | *Q* | S | U | W | PB |
| 100. | N | O | T | U | W | PB |
| 101. | N | P | *Q* | V | W | PB |
| 102. | O | P | R | S | T | PB |

# POWERBALL BALANCED WHEEL® 53231PB

## Wheel 31 Numbers + PB in 111 Games for a 3 of 5 Win

With Powerball

| Numbers Matched | Maximum Wins | | | | | | Minimum Wins | | | | | |
|---|---|---|---|---|---|---|---|---|---|---|---|---|
| | 5 + 1 | 4 + 1 | 3 + 1 | 2 + 1 | 1 + 1 | 0 + 1 | 5 + 1 | 4 + 1 | 3 + 1 | 2 + 1 | 1 + 1 | 0 + 1 |
| 5 + 1 | 1 | 2 | 8 | 16 | 14 | 70 | 0 | 0 | 1 | 14 | 50 | 46 |
| 4 + 1 | - | 2 | 5 | 12 | 20 | 72 | - | 0 | 0 | 9 | 48 | 54 |
| 3 + 1 | - | - | 6 | 1 | 30 | 74 | - | - | 0 | 4 | 38 | 69 |
| 2 + 1 | - | - | - | 7 | 20 | 84 | - | - | - | 0 | 33 | 78 |
| 1 + 1 | - | - | - | - | 20 | 91 | - | - | - | - | 13 | 98 |
| 0 + 1 | - | - | - | - | - | 111 | - | - | - | - | - | 111 |

Without Powerball

| Numbers Matched | Maximum Wins | | | | | Minimum Wins | | | | |
|---|---|---|---|---|---|---|---|---|---|---|
| | 5 + 0 | 4 + 0 | 3 + 0 | 2 + 0 | 1 + 0 | 5 + 0 | 4 + 0 | 3 + 0 | 2 + 0 | 1 + 0 |
| 5 + 0 | 1 | 2 | 8 | 16 | 14 | 0 | 0 | 1 | 14 | 50 |
| 4 + 0 | - | 2 | 5 | 12 | 20 | - | 0 | 0 | 9 | 48 |
| 3 + 0 | - | - | 6 | 1 | 30 | - | - | 0 | 4 | 38 |
| 2 + 0 | - | - | - | 7 | 20 | - | - | - | 0 | 33 |
| 1 + 0 | - | - | - | - | 20 | - | - | - | - | 13 |

## Your 31 Numbers + PB to Wheel

| A | B | C | D | E | F | G | H | I | J | K |
|---|---|---|---|---|---|---|---|---|---|---|
| 20 | 16 | 15 | 17 | 17 | 15 | 13 | 16 | 13 | 15 | 20 |
| **L** | **M** | **N** | **O** | **P** | **Q** | **R** | **S** | **T** | **U** | **V** |
| 20 | 20 | 20 | 20 | 20 | 20 | 20 | 15 | 20 | 20 | 20 |
| **W** | **X** | **Y** | **Z** | **aa** | **bb** | **cc** | **dd** | **ee** | **PB** | |
| 20 | 20 | 20 | 20 | 20 | 15 | 15 | 17 | 16 | 111 | |

## The 111 Games to Play

| | | | | | | |
|---|---|---|---|---|---|---|
| 1. | A | K | L | Q | aa | PB |
| 2. | A | K | M | P | W | PB |
| 3. | A | K | N | T | Y | PB |
| 4. | A | K | O | R | V | PB |
| 5. | A | K | U | X | Z | PB |
| 6. | A | L | M | N | Z | PB |
| 7. | A | L | O | U | W | PB |
| 8. | A | L | P | R | T | PB |
| 9. | A | L | V | X | Y | PB |
| 10. | A | M | O | Q | Y | PB |
| 11. | A | M | R | X | aa | PB |
| 12. | A | M | T | U | V | PB |
| 13. | A | N | O | P | X | PB |
| 14. | A | N | Q | R | U | PB |
| 15. | A | N | V | W | aa | PB |
| 16. | A | O | T | Z | aa | PB |
| 17. | A | P | Q | V | Z | PB |
| 18. | A | P | U | Y | aa | PB |
| 19. | A | Q | T | W | X | PB |
| 20. | A | R | W | Y | Z | PB |
| 21. | B | C | D | I | cc | PB |
| 22. | B | C | D | J | cc | PB |
| 23. | B | C | E | S | dd | PB |
| 24. | B | C | F | bb | cc | PB |
| 25. | B | C | G | H | ee | PB |
| 26. | B | D | E | H | dd | PB |
| 27. | B | D | E | dd | ee | PB |
| 28. | B | D | F | G | bb | PB |
| 29. | B | D | F | S | bb | PB |
| 30. | B | E | F | I | dd | PB |
| 31. | B | E | G | cc | dd | PB |
| 32. | B | E | J | bb | dd | PB |



(Continued Next Page)

## POWERBALL BALANCED WHEEL® 53231PB (Continued from previous page)

| | | | | | | |
|---|---|---|---|---|---|---|
| 33. | B | F | H | J | ee | PB |
| 34. | B | G | I | J | S | PB |
| 35. | B | H | I | bb | ee | PB |
| 36. | B | H | S | cc | ee | PB |
| 37. | C | D | E | F | ee | PB |
| 38. | C | D | G | S | cc | PB |
| 39. | C | D | H | bb | dd | PB |
| 40. | C | E | G | I | bb | PB |
| 41. | C | E | H | J | cc | PB |
| 42. | C | F | G | J | dd | PB |
| 43. | C | F | H | I | S | PB |
| 44. | C | I | J | dd | ee | PB |
| 45. | C | J | S | bb | ee | PB |
| 46. | C | J | cc | dd | ee | PB |
| 47. | D | E | G | J | ee | PB |
| 48. | D | E | H | dd | ee | PB |
| 49. | D | E | I | S | ee | PB |
| 50. | D | E | bb | cc | ee | PB |
| 51. | D | F | H | cc | dd | PB |
| 52. | D | F | I | J | bb | PB |
| 53. | D | G | H | I | dd | PB |
| 54. | D | H | J | S | dd | PB |
| 55. | E | F | G | H | S | PB |
| 56. | E | F | H | S | bb | PB |
| 57. | E | F | J | S | cc | PB |
| 58. | E | H | I | J | cc | PB |
| 59. | F | G | I | cc | ee | PB |
| 60. | F | S | bb | dd | ee | PB |
| 61. | G | H | J | bb | cc | PB |
| 62. | G | S | bb | dd | ee | PB |
| 63. | I | S | bb | cc | dd | PB |
| 64. | K | L | M | U | Y | PB |
| 65. | K | L | N | R | X | PB |
| 66. | K | L | O | P | Z | PB |
| 67. | K | L | T | V | W | PB |
| 68. | K | M | N | O | aa | PB |
| 69. | K | M | *Q* | V | X | PB |
| 70. | K | M | R | T | Z | PB |
| 71. | K | N | P | U | V | PB |
| 72. | K | N | *Q* | W | Z | PB |
| 73. | K | O | *Q* | T | U | PB |
| 74. | K | O | W | X | Y | PB |
| 75. | K | P | *Q* | R | Y | PB |
| 76. | K | P | T | X | aa | PB |
| 77. | K | R | U | W | aa | PB |
| 78. | K | V | Y | Z | aa | PB |
| 79. | L | M | O | T | X | PB |
| 80. | L | M | P | V | aa | PB |
| 81. | L | M | *Q* | R | W | PB |
| 82. | L | N | O | *Q* | V | PB |
| 83. | L | N | P | W | Y | PB |
| 84. | L | N | T | U | aa | PB |
| 85. | L | O | R | Y | aa | PB |
| 86. | L | P | *Q* | U | X | PB |
| 87. | L | *Q* | T | Y | Z | PB |
| 88. | L | R | U | V | Z | PB |
| 89. | L | W | X | Z | aa | PB |
| 90. | M | N | P | *Q* | T | PB |
| 91. | M | N | R | V | Y | PB |
| 92. | M | N | U | W | X | PB |
| 93. | M | O | P | R | U | PB |
| 94. | M | O | V | W | Z | PB |
| 95. | M | P | X | Y | Z | PB |
| 96. | M | *Q* | U | Z | aa | PB |
| 97. | M | T | W | Y | aa | PB |
| 98. | N | O | R | T | W | PB |
| 99. | N | O | U | Y | Z | PB |
| 100. | N | P | R | Z | aa | PB |
| 101. | N | *Q* | X | Y | aa | PB |
| 102. | N | T | V | X | Z | PB |



(Continued Next Page)

**POWERBALL BALANCED WHEEL® 53231PB** (Continued from previous page)

| | | | | | | |
|---|---|---|---|---|---|---|
| 103. | O | P | Q | W | aa | PB |
| 104. | O | P | T | V | Y | PB |
| 105. | O | Q | R | X | Z | PB |
| 106. | O | U | V | X | aa | PB |
| 107. | P | R | V | W | X | PB |
| 108. | P | T | U | W | Z | PB |
| 109. | Q | R | T | V | aa | PB |
| 110. | Q | U | V | W | Y | PB |
| 111. | R | T | U | X | Y | PB |



# POWERBALL BALANCED WHEEL® 53232PB

## Wheel 32 Numbers + PB in 125 Games for a 3 of 5 Win

With Powerball

| Numbers Matched | Maximum Wins 5 + 1 | 4 + 1 | 3 + 1 | 2 + 1 | 1 + 1 | 0 + 1 | Minimum Wins 5 + 1 | 4 + 1 | 3 + 1 | 2 + 1 | 1 + 1 | 0 + 1 |
|---|---|---|---|---|---|---|---|---|---|---|---|---|
| 5 + 1 | 1 | 0 | 10 | 18 | 24 | 72 | 0 | 0 | 1 | 17 | 60 | 47 |
| 4 + 1 | - | 1 | 6 | 12 | 30 | 76 | - | 0 | 0 | 10 | 58 | 57 |
| 3 + 1 | - | - | 6 | 2 | 35 | 82 | - | - | 0 | 5 | 48 | 72 |
| 2 + 1 | - | - | - | 7 | 24 | 94 | - | - | - | 0 | 39 | 86 |
| 1 + 1 | - | - | - | - | 20 | 105 | - | - | - | - | 19 | 106 |
| 0 + 1 | - | - | - | - | - | 125 | - | - | - | - | - | 125 |

Without Powerball

| Numbers Matched | Maximum Wins 5 + 0 | 4 + 0 | 3 + 0 | 2 + 0 | 1 + 0 | Minimum Wins 5 + 0 | 4 + 0 | 3 + 0 | 2 + 0 | 1 + 0 |
|---|---|---|---|---|---|---|---|---|---|---|
| 5 + 0 | 1 | 0 | 10 | 18 | 24 | 0 | 0 | 1 | 17 | 60 |
| 4 + 0 | - | 1 | 6 | 12 | 30 | - | 0 | 0 | 10 | 58 |
| 3 + 0 | - | - | 6 | 2 | 35 | - | - | 0 | 5 | 48 |
| 2 + 0 | - | - | - | 7 | 24 | - | - | - | 0 | 39 |
| 1 + 0 | - | - | - | - | 20 | - | - | - | - | 19 |

## Your 32 Numbers + PB to Wheel

| A | B | C | D | E | F | G | H | I | J | K |
|---|---|---|---|---|---|---|---|---|---|---|
| 20 | 19 | 20 | 19 | 19 | 20 | 19 | 20 | 20 | 19 | 19 |
| **L** | **M** | **N** | **O** | **P** | **Q** | **R** | **S** | **T** | **U** | **V** |
| 20 | 20 | 19 | 20 | 20 | 19 | 19 | 20 | 20 | 19 | 19 |
| **W** | **X** | **Y** | **Z** | **aa** | **bb** | **cc** | **dd** | **ee** | **ff** | **PB** |
| 20 | 20 | 19 | 20 | 19 | 19 | 20 | 20 | 20 | 19 | 125 |

## The 125 Games to Play

| | | | | | | |
|---|---|---|---|---|---|---|
| 1. | A | C | F | O | W | PB |
| 2. | A | C | H | L | cc | PB |
| 3. | A | C | I | P | ee | PB |
| 4. | A | C | M | S | T | PB |
| 5. | A | C | X | Z | dd | PB |
| 6. | A | F | H | P | S | PB |
| 7. | A | F | I | T | dd | PB |
| 8. | A | F | L | X | ee | PB |
| 9. | A | F | M | Z | cc | PB |
| 10. | A | H | I | O | Z | PB |
| 11. | A | H | M | dd | ee | PB |
| 12. | A | H | T | W | X | PB |
| 13. | A | I | L | M | W | PB |
| 14. | A | I | S | X | cc | PB |
| 15. | A | L | O | S | dd | PB |
| 16. | A | L | P | T | Z | PB |
| 17. | A | M | O | P | X | PB |
| 18. | A | O | T | cc | ee | PB |



(Continued Next Page)

## POWERBALL BALANCED WHEEL® 53232PB (Continued from previous page)

| | | | | | | |
|---|---|---|---|---|---|---|
| 19. | A | P | W | cc | dd | PB |
| 20. | A | S | W | Z | ee | PB |
| 21. | B | D | E | R | V | PB |
| 22. | B | D | G | N | Y | PB |
| 23. | B | D | J | K | ff | PB |
| 24. | B | D | Q | Y | aa | PB |
| 25. | B | D | R | U | bb | PB |
| 26. | B | E | G | J | V | PB |
| 27. | B | E | K | Q | V | PB |
| 28. | B | E | K | R | Y | PB |
| 29. | B | E | N | V | ff | PB |
| 30. | B | E | U | V | bb | PB |
| 31. | B | E | V | Y | aa | PB |
| 32. | B | G | K | N | aa | PB |
| 33. | B | G | N | Q | R | PB |
| 34. | B | G | U | bb | ff | PB |
| 35. | B | J | N | U | bb | PB |
| 36. | B | J | Q | Y | ff | PB |
| 37. | B | J | R | aa | ff | PB |
| 38. | B | K | U | aa | bb | PB |
| 39. | B | Q | U | Y | bb | PB |
| 40. | C | F | H | Z | ee | PB |
| 41. | C | F | I | L | S | PB |
| 42. | C | F | M | P | dd | PB |
| 43. | C | F | T | X | cc | PB |
| 44. | C | H | I | M | X | PB |
| 45. | C | H | O | P | T | PB |
| 46. | C | H | S | W | dd | PB |
| 47. | C | I | O | cc | dd | PB |
| 48. | C | I | T | W | Z | PB |
| 49. | C | L | M | O | Z | PB |
| 50. | C | L | P | W | X | PB |
| 51. | C | L | T | dd | ee | PB |
| 52. | C | M | W | cc | ee | PB |
| 53. | C | O | S | X | ee | PB |
| 54. | C | P | S | Z | cc | PB |
| 55. | D | E | G | K | U | PB |
| 56. | D | E | J | Y | bb | PB |
| 57. | D | E | K | N | ff | PB |
| 58. | D | E | Q | V | aa | PB |
| 59. | D | G | J | V | Y | PB |
| 60. | D | G | K | R | Y | PB |
| 61. | D | G | Q | aa | ff | PB |
| 62. | D | G | R | bb | ff | PB |
| 63. | D | J | N | Q | aa | PB |
| 64. | D | J | N | R | U | PB |
| 65. | D | K | N | V | bb | PB |
| 66. | D | K | Q | aa | bb | PB |
| 67. | D | Q | R | U | aa | PB |
| 68. | D | U | V | Y | ff | PB |
| 69. | E | G | N | bb | ff | PB |
| 70. | E | G | Q | U | Y | PB |
| 71. | E | G | R | U | aa | PB |
| 72. | E | J | K | aa | bb | PB |
| 73. | E | J | N | U | ff | PB |
| 74. | E | J | Q | R | bb | PB |
| 75. | E | N | Q | R | ff | PB |
| 76. | E | N | Y | aa | ff | PB |
| 77. | F | H | I | W | cc | PB |
| 78. | F | H | L | M | T | PB |
| 79. | F | H | O | X | dd | PB |
| 80. | F | I | M | O | ee | PB |
| 81. | F | I | P | X | Z | PB |
| 82. | F | L | O | P | cc | PB |
| 83. | F | L | W | Z | dd | PB |
| 84. | F | M | S | W | X | PB |
| 85. | F | O | S | T | Z | PB |
| 86. | F | P | T | W | ee | PB |
| 87. | F | S | cc | dd | ee | PB |
| 88. | G | J | K | Q | V | PB |



(Continued Next Page)

**POWERBALL BALANCED WHEEL® 53232PB** (Continued from previous page)

| | | | | | | |
|---|---|---|---|---|---|---|
| 89. | G | J | N | U | V | PB |
| 90. | G | J | R | V | aa | PB |
| 91. | G | J | V | bb | ff | PB |
| 92. | G | K | *Q* | bb | ff | PB |
| 93. | G | Y | aa | bb | ff | PB |
| 94. | H | I | L | P | dd | PB |
| 95. | H | I | S | T | ee | PB |
| 96. | H | L | O | W | ee | PB |
| 97. | H | L | S | X | Z | PB |
| 98. | H | M | O | S | cc | PB |
| 99. | H | M | P | W | Z | PB |
| 100. | H | P | X | cc | ee | PB |
| 101. | H | T | Z | cc | dd | PB |
| 102. | I | L | O | T | X | PB |
| 103. | I | L | Z | cc | ee | PB |
| 104. | I | M | P | T | cc | PB |
| 105. | I | M | S | Z | dd | PB |
| 106. | I | O | P | S | W | PB |
| 107. | I | W | X | dd | ee | PB |
| 108. | J | K | N | *Q* | U | PB |
| 109. | J | K | *Q* | R | Y | PB |
| 110. | J | N | U | Y | aa | PB |
| 111. | K | N | R | U | Y | PB |
| 112. | K | R | V | Y | aa | PB |
| 113. | K | R | Y | bb | ff | PB |
| 114. | K | U | V | aa | ff | PB |
| 115. | L | M | P | S | ee | PB |
| 116. | L | M | X | cc | dd | PB |
| 117. | L | S | T | W | cc | PB |
| 118. | M | O | T | W | dd | PB |
| 119. | M | T | X | Z | ee | PB |
| 120. | N | *Q* | V | Y | bb | PB |
| 121. | N | R | V | aa | bb | PB |
| 122. | O | P | Z | dd | ee | PB |
| 123. | O | W | X | Z | cc | PB |
| 124. | P | S | T | X | dd | PB |
| 125. | *Q* | R | U | V | ff | PB |



# POWERBALL BALANCED WHEEL® 53234PB

## Wheel 34 Numbers + PB in 136 Games for a 3 of 5 Win

With Powerball

| Numbers Matched | Maximum Wins | | | | | | Minimum Wins | | | | | |
|---|---|---|---|---|---|---|---|---|---|---|---|---|
| | 5 + 1 | 4 + 1 | 3 + 1 | 2 + 1 | 1 + 1 | 0 + 1 | 5 + 1 | 4 + 1 | 3 + 1 | 2 + 1 | 1 + 1 | 0 + 1 |
| 5 + 1 | 1 | 0 | 0 | 40 | 15 | 80 | 0 | 0 | 1 | 17 | 63 | 55 |
| 4 + 1 | - | 1 | 0 | 24 | 28 | 83 | - | 0 | 0 | 10 | 60 | 66 |
| 3 + 1 | - | - | 1 | 12 | 33 | 90 | - | - | 0 | 5 | 50 | 81 |
| 2 + 1 | - | - | - | 5 | 30 | 101 | - | - | - | 0 | 40 | 96 |
| 1 + 1 | - | - | - | - | 20 | 116 | - | - | - | - | 20 | 116 |
| 0 + 1 | - | - | - | - | - | 136 | - | - | - | - | - | 136 |

Without Powerball

| Numbers Matched | Maximum Wins | | | | | Minimum Wins | | | | |
|---|---|---|---|---|---|---|---|---|---|---|
| | 5 + 0 | 4 + 0 | 3 + 0 | 2 + 0 | 1 + 0 | 5 + 0 | 4 + 0 | 3 + 0 | 2 + 0 | 1 + 0 |
| 5 + 0 | 1 | 0 | 0 | 40 | 15 | 0 | 0 | 1 | 17 | 63 |
| 4 + 0 | - | 1 | 0 | 24 | 28 | - | 0 | 0 | 10 | 60 |
| 3 + 0 | - | - | 1 | 12 | 33 | - | - | 0 | 5 | 50 |
| 2 + 0 | - | - | - | 5 | 30 | - | - | - | 0 | 40 |
| 1 + 0 | - | - | - | - | 20 | - | - | - | - | 20 |

(Continued Next Page)

**POWERBALL BALANCED WHEEL® 53234PB** (Continued from previous page)

## Your 34 Numbers + PB to Wheel

| A | B | C | D | E | F | G | H | I |
|---|---|---|---|---|---|---|---|---|
| 20 | 20 | 20 | 20 | 20 | 20 | 20 | 20 | 20 |
| **J** | **K** | **L** | **M** | **N** | **O** | **P** | **Q** | **R** |
| 20 | 20 | 20 | 20 | 20 | 20 | 20 | 20 | 20 |
| **S** | **T** | **U** | **V** | **W** | **X** | **Y** | **Z** | **aa** |
| 20 | 20 | 20 | 20 | 20 | 20 | 20 | 20 | 20 |
| **bb** | **cc** | **dd** | **ee** | **ff** | **gg** | **hh** | **PB** | |
| 20 | 20 | 20 | 20 | 20 | 20 | 20 | 136 | |

## The 136 Games to Play

| | | | | | | |
|---|---|---|---|---|---|---|
| 1. | A | D | E | N | ff | PB |
| 2. | A | D | F | V | ee | PB |
| 3. | A | D | J | S | T | PB |
| 4. | A | D | K | aa | hh | PB |
| 5. | A | D | L | R | W | PB |
| 6. | A | E | F | J | hh | PB |
| 7. | A | E | K | R | S | PB |
| 8. | A | E | L | V | aa | PB |
| 9. | A | E | T | W | ee | PB |
| 10. | A | F | K | N | W | PB |
| 11. | A | F | L | S | ff | PB |
| 12. | A | F | R | T | aa | PB |
| 13. | A | J | K | L | ee | PB |
| 14. | A | J | N | R | V | PB |
| 15. | A | J | W | aa | ff | PB |
| 16. | A | K | T | V | ff | PB |
| 17. | A | L | N | T | hh | PB |
| 18. | A | N | S | aa | ee | PB |
| 19. | A | R | ee | ff | hh | PB |
| 20. | A | S | V | W | hh | PB |
| 21. | B | C | G | X | bb | PB |
| 22. | B | C | H | *Q* | Z | PB |
| 23. | B | C | I | cc | gg | PB |
| 24. | B | C | M | Y | dd | PB |
| 25. | B | C | O | P | U | PB |
| 26. | B | G | H | O | gg | PB |
| 27. | B | G | I | M | *Q* | PB |
| 28. | B | G | P | Y | cc | PB |
| 29. | B | G | U | Z | dd | PB |
| 30. | B | H | I | U | Y | PB |
| 31. | B | H | M | P | X | PB |
| 32. | B | H | bb | cc | dd | PB |
| 33. | B | I | O | X | dd | PB |
| 34. | B | I | P | Z | bb | PB |
| 35. | B | M | O | Z | cc | PB |
| 36. | B | M | U | bb | gg | PB |
| 37. | B | O | *Q* | Y | bb | PB |
| 38. | B | P | *Q* | dd | gg | PB |
| 39. | B | *Q* | U | X | cc | PB |
| 40. | B | X | Y | Z | gg | PB |
| 41. | C | G | H | I | dd | PB |
| 42. | C | G | M | P | Z | PB |
| 43. | C | G | O | *Q* | cc | PB |
| 44. | C | G | U | Y | gg | PB |
| 45. | C | H | M | U | cc | PB |
| 46. | C | H | O | X | Y | PB |
| 47. | C | H | P | bb | gg | PB |
| 48. | C | I | M | O | bb | PB |
| 49. | C | I | P | *Q* | Y | PB |
| 50. | C | I | U | X | Z | PB |
| 51. | C | M | *Q* | X | gg | PB |
| 52. | C | O | Z | dd | gg | PB |



(Continued Next Page)

**POWERBALL BALANCED WHEEL® 53234PB** (Continued from previous page)

| | | | | | | |
|---|---|---|---|---|---|---|
| 53. | C | P | X | cc | dd | PB |
| 54. | C | *Q* | U | bb | dd | PB |
| 55. | C | Y | Z | bb | cc | PB |
| 56. | D | E | F | S | W | PB |
| 57. | D | E | J | aa | ee | PB |
| 58. | D | E | K | L | T | PB |
| 59. | D | E | R | V | hh | PB |
| 60. | D | F | J | K | R | PB |
| 61. | D | F | L | N | aa | PB |
| 62. | D | F | T | ff | hh | PB |
| 63. | D | J | L | V | ff | PB |
| 64. | D | J | N | W | hh | PB |
| 65. | D | K | N | S | V | PB |
| 66. | D | K | W | ee | ff | PB |
| 67. | D | L | S | ee | hh | PB |
| 68. | D | N | R | T | ee | PB |
| 69. | D | R | S | aa | ff | PB |
| 70. | D | T | V | W | aa | PB |
| 71. | E | F | K | aa | ff | PB |
| 72. | E | F | L | R | ee | PB |
| 73. | E | F | N | T | V | PB |
| 74. | E | J | K | V | W | PB |
| 75. | E | J | L | N | S | PB |
| 76. | E | J | R | T | ff | PB |
| 77. | E | K | N | ee | hh | PB |
| 78. | E | L | W | ff | hh | PB |
| 79. | E | N | R | W | aa | PB |
| 80. | E | S | T | aa | hh | PB |
| 81. | E | S | V | ee | ff | PB |
| 82. | F | J | L | T | W | PB |
| 83. | F | J | N | ee | ff | PB |
| 84. | F | J | S | V | aa | PB |
| 85. | F | K | L | V | hh | PB |
| 86. | F | K | S | T | ee | PB |
| 87. | F | N | R | S | hh | PB |

| | | | | | | |
|---|---|---|---|---|---|---|
| 88. | F | R | V | W | ff | PB |
| 89. | F | W | aa | ee | hh | PB |
| 90. | G | H | M | Y | bb | PB |
| 91. | G | H | P | *Q* | U | PB |
| 92. | G | H | X | Z | cc | PB |
| 93. | G | I | O | Y | Z | PB |
| 94. | G | I | P | X | gg | PB |
| 95. | G | I | U | bb | cc | PB |
| 96. | G | M | O | U | X | PB |
| 97. | G | M | cc | dd | gg | PB |
| 98. | G | O | P | bb | dd | PB |
| 99. | G | *Q* | X | Y | dd | PB |
| 100. | G | *Q* | Z | bb | gg | PB |
| 101. | H | I | M | Z | gg | PB |
| 102. | H | I | O | P | cc | PB |
| 103. | H | I | *Q* | X | bb | PB |
| 104. | H | M | O | *Q* | dd | PB |
| 105. | H | O | U | Z | bb | PB |
| 106. | H | P | Y | Z | dd | PB |
| 107. | H | *Q* | Y | cc | gg | PB |
| 108. | H | U | X | dd | gg | PB |
| 109. | I | M | P | U | dd | PB |
| 110. | I | M | X | Y | cc | PB |
| 111. | I | O | *Q* | U | gg | PB |
| 112. | I | *Q* | Z | cc | dd | PB |
| 113. | I | Y | bb | dd | gg | PB |
| 114. | J | K | N | T | aa | PB |
| 115. | J | K | S | ff | hh | PB |
| 116. | J | L | R | aa | hh | PB |
| 117. | J | R | S | W | ee | PB |
| 118. | J | T | V | ee | hh | PB |
| 119. | K | L | N | R | ff | PB |
| 120. | K | L | S | W | aa | PB |
| 121. | K | R | T | W | hh | PB |
| 122. | K | R | V | aa | ee | PB |



(Continued Next Page)

## POWERBALL BALANCED WHEEL® 53234PB (Continued from previous page)

| | | | | | | |
|---|---|---|---|---|---|---|
| 123. | L | N | V | W | ee | PB |
| 124. | L | R | S | T | V | PB |
| 125. | L | T | aa | ee | ff | PB |
| 126. | M | O | P | Y | gg | PB |
| 127. | M | P | Q | bb | cc | PB |
| 128. | M | Q | U | Y | Z | PB |
| 129. | M | X | Z | bb | dd | PB |
| 130. | N | S | T | W | ff | PB |
| 131. | N | V | aa | ff | hh | PB |
| 132. | O | P | Q | X | Z | PB |
| 133. | O | U | Y | cc | dd | PB |
| 134. | O | X | bb | cc | gg | PB |
| 135. | P | U | X | Y | bb | PB |
| 136. | P | U | Z | cc | gg | PB |



# POWERBALL BALANCED WHEEL® 53236PB

## Wheel 36 Numbers + PB in 176 Games for a 3 of 5 Win

With Powerball

| Numbers Matched | Maximum Wins | | | | | | Minimum Wins | | | | | |
|---|---|---|---|---|---|---|---|---|---|---|---|---|
| | 5 + 1 | 4 + 1 | 3 + 1 | 2 + 1 | 1 + 1 | 0 + 1 | 5 + 1 | 4 + 1 | 3 + 1 | 2 + 1 | 1 + 1 | 0 + 1 |
| 5 + 1 | 1 | 2 | 13 | 22 | 52 | 86 | 0 | 0 | 1 | 18 | 77 | 80 |
| 4 + 1 | - | 3 | 12 | 5 | 62 | 94 | - | 0 | 0 | 11 | 74 | 91 |
| 3 + 1 | - | - | 9 | 7 | 50 | 110 | - | - | 0 | 5 | 58 | 113 |
| 2 + 1 | - | - | - | 15 | 32 | 129 | - | - | - | 0 | 48 | 128 |
| 1 + 1 | - | - | - | - | 31 | 145 | - | - | - | - | 20 | 156 |
| 0 + 1 | - | - | - | - | - | 176 | - | - | - | - | - | 176 |

Without Powerball

| Numbers Matched | Maximum Wins | | | | | Minimum Wins | | | | |
|---|---|---|---|---|---|---|---|---|---|---|
| | 5 + 0 | 4 + 0 | 3 + 0 | 2 + 0 | 1 + 0 | 5 + 0 | 4 + 0 | 3 + 0 | 2 + 0 | 1 + 0 |
| 5 + 0 | 1 | 2 | 13 | 22 | 52 | 0 | 0 | 1 | 18 | 77 |
| 4 + 0 | - | 3 | 12 | 5 | 62 | - | 0 | 0 | 11 | 74 |
| 3 + 0 | - | - | 9 | 7 | 50 | - | - | 0 | 5 | 58 |
| 2 + 0 | - | - | - | 15 | 32 | - | - | - | 0 | 48 |
| 1 + 0 | - | - | - | - | 31 | - | - | - | - | 20 |

## Your 36 Numbers + PB to Wheel

| A | B | C | D | E | F | G | H | I | J |
|---|---|---|---|---|---|---|---|---|---|
| 20 | 20 | 20 | 31 | 28 | 28 | 28 | 28 | 28 | 20 |
| **K** | **L** | **M** | **N** | **O** | **P** | **Q** | **R** | **S** | **T** |
| 20 | 28 | 20 | 20 | 29 | 28 | 20 | 31 | 20 | 28 |
| **U** | **V** | **W** | **X** | **Y** | **Z** | **aa** | **bb** | **cc** | **dd** |
| 28 | 20 | 28 | 20 | 20 | 28 | 28 | 28 | 20 | 20 |
| **ee** | **ff** | **gg** | **hh** | **ii** | **jj** | **PB** | | | |
| 29 | 20 | 28 | 20 | 28 | 20 | 176 | | | |

## The 176 Games to Play

| | | | | | | |
|---|---|---|---|---|---|---|
| 1. | A | B | C | V | cc | PB |
| 2. | A | B | J | Y | dd | PB |
| 3. | A | B | K | S | jj | PB |
| 4. | A | B | M | Q | ff | PB |
| 5. | A | B | N | X | hh | PB |
| 6. | A | C | J | K | X | PB |
| 7. | A | C | M | N | jj | PB |
| 8. | A | C | Q | S | Y | PB |
| 9. | A | C | dd | ff | hh | PB |
| 10. | A | J | M | S | hh | PB |



(Continued Next Page)

**POWERBALL BALANCED WHEEL® 53236PB** (Continued from previous page)

| | | | | | | |
|---|---|---|---|---|---|---|
| 11. | A | J | N | Q | cc | PB |
| 12. | A | J | V | ff | jj | PB |
| 13. | A | K | M | cc | dd | PB |
| 14. | A | K | N | Y | ff | PB |
| 15. | A | K | Q | V | hh | PB |
| 16. | A | M | V | X | Y | PB |
| 17. | A | N | S | V | dd | PB |
| 18. | A | Q | X | dd | jj | PB |
| 19. | A | S | X | cc | ff | PB |
| 20. | A | Y | cc | hh | jj | PB |
| 21. | B | C | J | N | ff | PB |
| 22. | B | C | K | M | Y | PB |
| 23. | B | C | Q | hh | jj | PB |
| 24. | B | C | S | X | dd | PB |
| 25. | B | J | K | cc | hh | PB |
| 26. | B | J | M | X | jj | PB |
| 27. | B | J | Q | S | V | PB |
| 28. | B | K | N | Q | dd | PB |
| 29. | B | K | V | X | ff | PB |
| 30. | B | M | N | S | cc | PB |
| 31. | B | M | V | dd | hh | PB |
| 32. | B | N | V | Y | jj | PB |
| 33. | B | Q | X | Y | cc | PB |
| 34. | B | S | Y | ff | hh | PB |
| 35. | B | cc | dd | ff | jj | PB |
| 36. | C | J | M | Q | dd | PB |
| 37. | C | J | S | cc | jj | PB |
| 38. | C | J | V | Y | hh | PB |
| 39. | C | K | N | S | hh | PB |
| 40. | C | K | Q | cc | ff | PB |
| 41. | C | K | V | dd | jj | PB |
| 42. | C | M | S | V | ff | PB |
| 43. | C | M | X | cc | hh | PB |
| 44. | C | N | Q | V | X | PB |
| 45. | C | N | Y | cc | dd | PB |

| | | | | | | |
|---|---|---|---|---|---|---|
| 46. | C | X | Y | ff | jj | PB |
| 47. | D | E | F | G | ii | PB |
| 48. | D | E | H | U | bb | PB |
| 49. | D | E | I | W | aa | PB |
| 50. | D | E | L | P | Z | PB |
| 51. | D | E | O | R | gg | PB |
| 52. | D | E | R | T | ee | PB |
| 53. | D | F | H | W | gg | PB |
| 54. | D | F | I | Z | bb | PB |
| 55. | D | F | L | T | U | PB |
| 56. | D | F | O | P | R | PB |
| 57. | D | F | R | aa | ee | PB |
| 58. | D | G | H | L | aa | PB |
| 59. | D | G | I | R | ee | PB |
| 60. | D | G | L | W | bb | PB |
| 61. | D | G | O | R | Z | PB |
| 62. | D | G | P | U | W | PB |
| 63. | D | G | T | bb | gg | PB |
| 64. | D | H | I | P | T | PB |
| 65. | D | H | O | R | ii | PB |
| 66. | D | H | R | Z | ee | PB |
| 67. | D | I | L | gg | ii | PB |
| 68. | D | I | O | R | U | PB |
| 69. | D | L | O | R | ee | PB |
| 70. | D | O | R | T | aa | PB |
| 71. | D | O | R | W | ee | PB |
| 72. | D | O | R | bb | ee | PB |
| 73. | D | P | R | ee | gg | PB |
| 74. | D | P | aa | bb | ii | PB |
| 75. | D | R | U | ee | ii | PB |
| 76. | D | T | W | Z | ii | PB |
| 77. | D | U | Z | aa | gg | PB |
| 78. | E | F | G | R | ii | PB |
| 79. | E | F | G | W | ii | PB |
| 80. | E | F | H | I | ee | PB |



(Continued Next Page)

## POWERBALL BALANCED WHEEL® 53236PB (Continued from previous page)

| | | | | | | | | | | | | | |
|---|---|---|---|---|---|---|---|---|---|---|---|---|---|
| 81. | E | F | L | aa | gg | PB | 116. | G | H | I | bb | ii | PB |
| 82. | E | F | O | U | Z | PB | 117. | G | H | O | U | ee | PB |
| 83. | E | F | P | T | bb | PB | 118. | G | H | R | W | aa | PB |
| 84. | E | G | H | P | gg | PB | 119. | G | I | P | Z | aa | PB |
| 85. | E | G | I | L | O | PB | 120. | G | I | T | W | ee | PB |
| 86. | E | G | T | U | aa | PB | 121. | G | L | R | T | gg | PB |
| 87. | E | G | Z | bb | ee | PB | 122. | G | L | U | Z | ii | PB |
| 88. | E | H | L | R | U | PB | 123. | G | O | P | T | ii | PB |
| 89. | E | H | O | T | W | PB | 124. | G | O | W | Z | gg | PB |
| 90. | E | H | Z | aa | ii | PB | 125. | G | P | R | U | bb | PB |
| 91. | E | I | P | U | ii | PB | 126. | G | aa | ee | gg | ii | PB |
| 92. | E | I | R | aa | bb | PB | 127. | H | I | L | P | T | PB |
| 93. | E | I | T | Z | gg | PB | 128. | H | I | L | W | bb | PB |
| 94. | E | L | T | ee | ii | PB | 129. | H | I | O | aa | gg | PB |
| 95. | E | L | W | bb | gg | PB | 130. | H | I | P | R | T | PB |
| 96. | E | O | P | aa | ee | PB | 131. | H | I | U | W | Z | PB |
| 97. | E | O | bb | gg | ii | PB | 132. | H | L | Z | ee | gg | PB |
| 98. | E | P | R | W | Z | PB | 133. | H | O | P | Z | bb | PB |
| 99. | E | U | W | ee | gg | PB | 134. | H | P | W | ee | ii | PB |
| 100. | F | G | H | T | Z | PB | 135. | H | T | U | gg | ii | PB |
| 101. | F | G | I | U | gg | PB | 136. | H | T | aa | bb | ee | PB |
| 102. | F | G | L | P | ee | PB | 137. | I | L | U | aa | ee | PB |
| 103. | F | G | O | aa | bb | PB | 138. | I | O | T | U | bb | PB |
| 104. | F | H | L | O | ii | PB | 139. | I | O | Z | ee | ii | PB |
| 105. | F | H | P | U | aa | PB | 140. | I | P | bb | ee | gg | PB |
| 106. | F | H | R | bb | gg | PB | 141. | I | R | W | gg | ii | PB |
| 107. | F | I | L | R | Z | PB | 142. | J | K | M | N | V | PB |
| 108. | F | I | O | P | W | PB | 143. | J | K | Q | Y | jj | PB |
| 109. | F | I | T | aa | ii | PB | 144. | J | K | S | dd | ff | PB |
| 110. | F | L | T | W | bb | PB | 145. | J | M | Y | cc | ff | PB |
| 111. | F | O | T | ee | gg | PB | 146. | J | N | S | X | Y | PB |
| 112. | F | P | Z | gg | ii | PB | 147. | J | N | dd | hh | jj | PB |
| 113. | F | R | T | U | W | PB | 148. | J | Q | X | ff | hh | PB |
| 114. | F | U | bb | ee | ii | PB | 149. | J | V | X | cc | dd | PB |
| 115. | F | W | Z | aa | ee | PB | 150. | K | M | Q | S | X | PB |



(Continued Next Page)

## POWERBALL BALANCED WHEEL® 53236PB (Continued from previous page)

| | | | | | | | | | | | | | |
|---|---|---|---|---|---|---|---|---|---|---|---|---|---|
| 151. | K | M | ff | hh | jj | PB | 164. | M | *Q* | V | cc | jj | PB |
| 152. | K | N | X | cc | jj | PB | 165. | M | S | Y | dd | jj | PB |
| 153. | K | S | V | Y | cc | PB | 166. | N | *Q* | S | ff | jj | PB |
| 154. | K | X | Y | dd | hh | PB | 167. | N | V | cc | ff | hh | PB |
| 155. | L | O | P | U | gg | PB | 168. | O | U | W | aa | ii | PB |
| 156. | L | O | R | W | bb | PB | 169. | P | T | U | Z | ee | PB |
| 157. | L | O | T | Z | aa | PB | 170. | P | T | W | aa | gg | PB |
| 158. | L | P | R | aa | ii | PB | 171. | *Q* | S | cc | dd | hh | PB |
| 159. | L | P | W | Z | bb | PB | 172. | *Q* | V | Y | dd | ff | PB |
| 160. | L | U | W | aa | bb | PB | 173. | R | T | Z | bb | ii | PB |
| 161. | L | W | bb | ee | ii | PB | 174. | R | U | Z | aa | gg | PB |
| 162. | M | N | *Q* | Y | hh | PB | 175. | S | V | X | hh | jj | PB |
| 163. | M | N | X | dd | ff | PB | 176. | U | Z | aa | bb | gg | PB |



# POWERBALL BALANCED WHEEL® 53239PB

## Wheel 39 Numbers + PB in 241 Games for a 3 of 5 Win

With Powerball

| Numbers Matched | Maximum Wins 5 + 1 | 4 + 1 | 3 + 1 | 2 + 1 | 1 + 1 | 0 + 1 | Minimum Wins 5 + 1 | 4 + 1 | 3 + 1 | 2 + 1 | 1 + 1 | 0 + 1 |
|---|---|---|---|---|---|---|---|---|---|---|---|---|
| 5 + 1 | 1 | 2 | 13 | 22 | 52 | 151 | 0 | 0 | 1 | 21 | 105 | 114 |
| 4 + 1 | - | 3 | 12 | 5 | 62 | 159 | - | 0 | 0 | 12 | 98 | 131 |
| 3 + 1 | - | - | 9 | 7 | 50 | 175 | - | - | 0 | 6 | 77 | 158 |
| 2 + 1 | - | - | - | 15 | 32 | 194 | - | - | - | 0 | 61 | 180 |
| 1 + 1 | - | - | - | - | 38 | 203 | - | - | - | - | 28 | 213 |
| 0 + 1 | - | - | - | - | - | 241 | - | - | - | - | - | 241 |

Without Powerball

| Numbers Matched | Maximum Wins 5 + 0 | 4 + 0 | 3 + 0 | 2 + 0 | 1 + 0 | Minimum Wins 5 + 0 | 4 + 0 | 3 + 0 | 2 + 0 | 1 + 0 |
|---|---|---|---|---|---|---|---|---|---|---|
| 5 + 0 | 1 | 2 | 13 | 22 | 52 | 0 | 0 | 1 | 21 | 105 |
| 4 + 0 | - | 3 | 12 | 5 | 62 | - | 0 | 0 | 12 | 98 |
| 3 + 0 | - | - | 9 | 7 | 50 | - | - | 0 | 6 | 77 |
| 2 + 0 | - | - | - | 15 | 32 | - | - | - | 0 | 61 |
| 1 + 0 | - | - | - | - | 38 | - | - | - | - | 28 |

## Your 39 Numbers + PB to Wheel

| A | B | C | D | E | F | G | H | I | J |
|---|---|---|---|---|---|---|---|---|---|
| 29 | 28 | 33 | 33 | 28 | 28 | 28 | 31 | 28 | 28 |
| **K** | **L** | **M** | **N** | **O** | **P** | **Q** | **R** | **S** | **T** |
| 33 | 33 | 38 | 33 | 33 | 33 | 28 | 28 | 33 | 28 |
| **U** | **V** | **W** | **X** | **Y** | **Z** | **aa** | **bb** | **cc** | **dd** |
| 33 | 33 | 33 | 33 | 31 | 33 | 28 | 33 | 28 | 29 |
| **ee** | **ff** | **gg** | **hh** | **ii** | **jj** | **kk** | ***ll*** | **mm** | **PB** |
| 33 | 33 | 28 | 33 | 33 | 28 | 28 | 28 | 33 | 241 |

(Continued Next Page)

## POWERBALL BALANCED WHEEL® 53239PB (Continued from previous page)

# The 241 Games to Play

| | | | | | | |
|---|---|---|---|---|---|---|
| 1. | A | B | E | R | jj | PB |
| 2. | A | B | F | aa | *ll* | PB |
| 3. | A | B | G | gg | kk | PB |
| 4. | A | B | H | Y | cc | PB |
| 5. | A | B | I | *Q* | cc | PB |
| 6. | A | B | J | T | dd | PB |
| 7. | A | E | F | J | gg | PB |
| 8. | A | E | G | T | cc | PB |
| 9. | A | E | H | Y | *ll* | PB |
| 10. | A | E | I | kk | *ll* | PB |
| 11. | A | E | *Q* | aa | dd | PB |
| 12. | A | F | G | *Q* | jj | PB |
| 13. | A | F | H | J | Y | PB |
| 14. | A | F | I | R | T | PB |
| 15. | A | F | cc | dd | kk | PB |
| 16. | A | G | H | *Q* | Y | PB |
| 17. | A | G | I | J | aa | PB |
| 18. | A | G | R | dd | *ll* | PB |
| 19. | A | H | I | Y | dd | PB |
| 20. | A | H | R | Y | aa | PB |
| 21. | A | H | T | Y | kk | PB |
| 22. | A | H | Y | dd | gg | PB |
| 23. | A | H | Y | dd | jj | PB |
| 24. | A | I | aa | gg | jj | PB |
| 25. | A | J | *Q* | R | kk | PB |
| 26. | A | J | cc | jj | *ll* | PB |
| 27. | A | *Q* | T | gg | *ll* | PB |
| 28. | A | R | aa | cc | gg | PB |
| 29. | A | T | aa | jj | kk | PB |
| 30. | B | E | F | G | dd | PB |
| 31. | B | E | H | T | gg | PB |
| 32. | B | E | I | T | Y | PB |
| 33. | B | E | J | *Q* | *ll* | PB |
| 34. | B | E | aa | cc | kk | PB |
| 35. | B | F | H | *Q* | R | PB |
| 36. | B | F | I | J | kk | PB |
| 37. | B | F | *Q* | R | Y | PB |
| 38. | B | F | *Q* | R | gg | PB |
| 39. | B | F | T | cc | jj | PB |
| 40. | B | G | H | I | *ll* | PB |
| 41. | B | G | J | R | cc | PB |
| 42. | B | G | *Q* | T | aa | PB |
| 43. | B | G | Y | jj | *ll* | PB |
| 44. | B | H | J | aa | jj | PB |
| 45. | B | H | Y | dd | kk | PB |
| 46. | B | I | R | aa | dd | PB |
| 47. | B | I | R | gg | jj | PB |
| 48. | B | J | Y | aa | gg | PB |
| 49. | B | *Q* | dd | jj | kk | PB |
| 50. | B | R | T | kk | *ll* | PB |
| 51. | B | cc | dd | gg | *ll* | PB |
| 52. | C | D | K | U | hh | PB |
| 53. | C | D | L | W | ee | PB |
| 54. | C | D | M | V | bb | PB |
| 55. | C | D | M | X | ii | PB |
| 56. | C | D | N | O | Z | PB |
| 57. | C | D | P | S | ii | PB |
| 58. | C | D | P | ff | mm | PB |
| 59. | C | K | L | M | S | PB |
| 60. | C | K | N | X | bb | PB |
| 61. | C | K | O | bb | mm | PB |
| 62. | C | K | P | Z | bb | PB |
| 63. | C | K | U | ee | ff | PB |
| 64. | C | K | V | W | ii | PB |
| 65. | C | L | N | hh | ii | PB |
| 66. | C | L | O | X | ee | PB |
| 67. | C | L | P | U | V | PB |
| 68. | C | L | Z | ii | mm | PB |



(Continued Next Page)

**POWERBALL BALANCED WHEEL® 53239PB** (Continued from previous page)

| | | | | | | |
|---|---|---|---|---|---|---|
| 69. | C | L | bb | ff | ii | PB |
| 70. | C | M | N | ee | mm | PB |
| 71. | C | M | O | P | hh | PB |
| 72. | C | M | S | W | mm | PB |
| 73. | C | M | S | X | ff | PB |
| 74. | C | M | U | X | Z | PB |
| 75. | C | N | O | S | U | PB |
| 76. | C | N | O | V | ff | PB |
| 77. | C | N | P | W | X | PB |
| 78. | C | O | P | ee | ii | PB |
| 79. | C | O | U | W | mm | PB |
| 80. | C | S | V | Z | ee | PB |
| 81. | C | S | bb | ee | hh | PB |
| 82. | C | U | W | bb | ii | PB |
| 83. | C | V | X | hh | mm | PB |
| 84. | C | W | Z | ff | hh | PB |
| 85. | D | K | L | bb | hh | PB |
| 86. | D | K | M | X | mm | PB |
| 87. | D | K | N | V | ii | PB |
| 88. | D | K | O | ff | hh | PB |
| 89. | D | K | P | V | ee | PB |
| 90. | D | K | S | W | Z | PB |
| 91. | D | L | M | P | Z | PB |
| 92. | D | L | N | S | mm | PB |
| 93. | D | L | O | U | ii | PB |
| 94. | D | L | V | X | ff | PB |
| 95. | D | M | N | W | ff | PB |
| 96. | D | M | N | ee | hh | PB |
| 97. | D | M | O | X | ee | PB |
| 98. | D | M | S | U | ee | PB |
| 99. | D | N | P | U | bb | PB |
| 100. | D | N | X | Z | hh | PB |
| 101. | D | O | P | W | bb | PB |
| 102. | D | O | S | V | mm | PB |
| 103. | D | P | S | X | bb | PB |
| 104. | D | P | V | Z | hh | PB |
| 105. | D | S | ff | hh | ii | PB |
| 106. | D | U | V | W | X | PB |
| 107. | D | U | Z | ff | mm | PB |
| 108. | D | W | hh | ii | mm | PB |
| 109. | D | Z | bb | ee | ii | PB |
| 110. | D | bb | ee | ff | mm | PB |
| 111. | E | F | H | I | aa | PB |
| 112. | E | F | *Q* | T | kk | PB |
| 113. | E | F | R | cc | *ll* | PB |
| 114. | E | F | Y | aa | jj | PB |
| 115. | E | G | H | J | kk | PB |
| 116. | E | G | I | *Q* | R | PB |
| 117. | E | G | I | gg | jj | PB |
| 118. | E | G | J | Y | kk | PB |
| 119. | E | G | J | jj | kk | PB |
| 120. | E | G | aa | gg | *ll* | PB |
| 121. | E | H | *Q* | cc | jj | PB |
| 122. | E | H | R | Y | dd | PB |
| 123. | E | I | J | cc | dd | PB |
| 124. | E | J | R | T | aa | PB |
| 125. | E | *Q* | Y | cc | gg | PB |
| 126. | E | R | dd | gg | kk | PB |
| 127. | E | T | dd | jj | *ll* | PB |
| 128. | F | G | H | cc | gg | PB |
| 129. | F | G | I | Y | cc | PB |
| 130. | F | G | J | T | *ll* | PB |
| 131. | F | G | R | aa | kk | PB |
| 132. | F | H | T | Y | dd | PB |
| 133. | F | H | jj | kk | *ll* | PB |
| 134. | F | I | *Q* | dd | *ll* | PB |
| 135. | F | I | T | gg | jj | PB |
| 136. | F | J | *Q* | aa | cc | PB |
| 137. | F | J | R | dd | jj | PB |
| 138. | F | T | aa | dd | gg | PB |



(Continued Next Page)

## POWERBALL BALANCED WHEEL® 53239PB

(Continued from previous page)

| | | | | | | |
|---|---|---|---|---|---|---|
| 139. | F | Y | gg | kk | *ll* | PB |
| 140. | G | H | R | T | jj | PB |
| 141. | G | H | Y | aa | dd | PB |
| 142. | G | I | T | dd | kk | PB |
| 143. | G | J | *Q* | dd | gg | PB |
| 144. | G | *Q* | cc | kk | *ll* | PB |
| 145. | G | R | T | Y | gg | PB |
| 146. | G | aa | cc | dd | jj | PB |
| 147. | H | I | J | *Q* | T | PB |
| 148. | H | I | R | cc | kk | PB |
| 149. | H | I | dd | gg | jj | PB |
| 150. | H | J | R | gg | *ll* | PB |
| 151. | H | J | Y | cc | dd | PB |
| 152. | H | *Q* | Y | dd | *ll* | PB |
| 153. | H | *Q* | aa | gg | kk | PB |
| 154. | H | T | aa | cc | *ll* | PB |
| 155. | I | J | *Q* | gg | jj | PB |
| 156. | I | J | R | Y | *ll* | PB |
| 157. | I | *Q* | Y | aa | kk | PB |
| 158. | I | T | aa | cc | *ll* | PB |
| 159. | I | Y | gg | jj | *ll* | PB |
| 160. | I | cc | gg | jj | kk | PB |
| 161. | J | *Q* | T | Y | jj | PB |
| 162. | J | T | cc | gg | kk | PB |
| 163. | J | aa | dd | kk | *ll* | PB |
| 164. | K | L | M | Z | ee | PB |
| 165. | K | L | N | ff | mm | PB |
| 166. | K | L | O | V | ii | PB |
| 167. | K | L | P | bb | ee | PB |
| 168. | K | L | U | W | X | PB |
| 169. | K | M | N | U | Z | PB |
| 170. | K | M | O | P | U | PB |
| 171. | K | M | U | V | mm | PB |
| 172. | K | M | W | bb | ff | PB |
| 173. | K | M | Z | hh | ii | PB |

| | | | | | | |
|---|---|---|---|---|---|---|
| 174. | K | N | O | W | ee | PB |
| 175. | K | N | P | S | hh | PB |
| 176. | K | O | S | X | Z | PB |
| 177. | K | P | W | hh | mm | PB |
| 178. | K | P | X | ff | ii | PB |
| 179. | K | S | U | bb | ii | PB |
| 180. | K | S | V | bb | ff | PB |
| 181. | K | S | ee | ii | mm | PB |
| 182. | K | V | X | ee | hh | PB |
| 183. | K | V | Z | ff | mm | PB |
| 184. | L | M | N | V | bb | PB |
| 185. | L | M | O | Z | ff | PB |
| 186. | L | M | P | W | ii | PB |
| 187. | L | M | P | X | hh | PB |
| 188. | L | M | U | hh | mm | PB |
| 189. | L | N | O | P | mm | PB |
| 190. | L | N | O | X | hh | PB |
| 191. | L | N | U | W | Z | PB |
| 192. | L | N | U | bb | ee | PB |
| 193. | L | O | S | W | bb | PB |
| 194. | L | P | S | U | ff | PB |
| 195. | L | S | V | Z | hh | PB |
| 196. | L | S | X | ee | ii | PB |
| 197. | L | V | W | ee | mm | PB |
| 198. | L | W | ee | ff | hh | PB |
| 199. | L | X | Z | bb | mm | PB |
| 200. | M | N | O | bb | ii | PB |
| 201. | M | N | P | V | ee | PB |
| 202. | M | N | S | V | X | PB |
| 203. | M | O | S | hh | ii | PB |
| 204. | M | O | V | W | hh | PB |
| 205. | M | O | ff | ii | mm | PB |
| 206. | M | P | S | Z | mm | PB |
| 207. | M | P | bb | ff | hh | PB |
| 208. | M | S | U | bb | mm | PB |



(Continued Next Page)

**POWERBALL BALANCED WHEEL® 53239PB** (Continued from previous page)

| | | | | | | |
|---|---|---|---|---|---|---|
| 209. | M | U | W | ff | ii | PB |
| 210. | M | V | W | Z | bb | PB |
| 211. | M | V | ee | ff | ii | PB |
| 212. | M | W | X | bb | ee | PB |
| 213. | N | P | Z | ff | ii | PB |
| 214. | N | S | W | ee | ii | PB |
| 215. | N | S | Z | bb | ff | PB |
| 216. | N | U | V | ff | hh | PB |
| 217. | N | U | X | ii | mm | PB |
| 218. | N | V | W | Z | mm | PB |
| 219. | N | W | bb | hh | mm | PB |
| 220. | N | X | Z | ee | ff | PB |
| 221. | O | P | S | ee | ff | PB |
| 222. | O | P | V | X | Z | PB |
| 223. | O | U | V | bb | ee | PB |
| 224. | O | U | X | bb | ff | PB |
| 225. | O | U | Z | bb | hh | PB |
| 226. | O | W | X | Z | ii | PB |
| 227. | O | W | X | ff | mm | PB |
| 228. | O | Z | ee | hh | mm | PB |
| 229. | P | S | V | W | ff | PB |
| 230. | P | U | W | Z | ee | PB |
| 231. | P | U | X | ee | mm | PB |
| 232. | P | U | ee | hh | ii | PB |
| 233. | P | V | bb | ii | mm | PB |
| 234. | *Q* | R | T | cc | dd | PB |
| 235. | *Q* | R | aa | jj | *ll* | PB |
| 236. | R | Y | cc | jj | kk | PB |
| 237. | S | U | V | Z | ii | PB |
| 238. | S | U | W | X | hh | PB |
| 239. | S | X | ff | hh | mm | PB |
| 240. | T | Y | aa | cc | *ll* | PB |
| 241. | V | X | bb | hh | ii | PB |



# POWERBALL BALANCED WHEEL® 53245PB

## Wheel 45 Numbers + PB in 359 Games for a 3 of 5 Win

With Powerball

| Numbers Matched | Maximum Wins 5 + 1 | 4 + 1 | 3 + 1 | 2 + 1 | 1 + 1 | 0 + 1 | Minimum Wins 5 + 1 | 4 + 1 | 3 + 1 | 2 + 1 | 1 + 1 | 0 + 1 |
|---|---|---|---|---|---|---|---|---|---|---|---|---|
| 5 + 1 | 1 | 1 | 5 | 49 | 75 | 228 | 0 | 0 | 1 | 25 | 144 | 189 |
| 4 + 1 | - | 2 | 2 | 31 | 82 | 242 | - | 0 | 0 | 14 | 130 | 215 |
| 3 + 1 | - | - | 10 | 0 | 105 | 244 | - | - | 0 | 7 | 104 | 248 |
| 2 + 1 | - | - | - | 10 | 75 | 274 | - | - | - | 0 | 79 | 280 |
| 1 + 1 | - | - | - | - | 55 | 304 | - | - | - | - | 39 | 320 |
| 0 + 1 | - | - | - | - | - | 359 | - | - | - | - | - | 359 |

Without Powerball

| Numbers Matched | Maximum Wins 5 + 0 | 4 + 0 | 3 + 0 | 2 + 0 | 1 + 0 | Minimum Wins 5 + 0 | 4 + 0 | 3 + 0 | 2 + 0 | 1 + 0 |
|---|---|---|---|---|---|---|---|---|---|---|
| 5 + 0 | 1 | 1 | 5 | 49 | 75 | 0 | 0 | 1 | 25 | 144 |
| 4 + 0 | - | 2 | 2 | 31 | 82 | - | 0 | 0 | 14 | 130 |
| 3 + 0 | - | - | 10 | 0 | 105 | - | - | 0 | 7 | 104 |
| 2 + 0 | - | - | - | 10 | 75 | - | - | - | 0 | 79 |
| 1 + 0 | - | - | - | - | 55 | - | - | - | - | 39 |

(Continued Next Page)

**POWERBALL BALANCED WHEEL® 53245PB** (Continued from previous page)

## Your 45 Numbers + PB to Wheel

| A | B | C | D | E | F | G | H | I | J |
|---|---|---|---|---|---|---|---|---|---|
| 39 | 40 | 40 | 39 | 39 | 40 | 39 | 39 | 39 | 39 |
| **K** | **L** | **M** | **N** | **O** | **P** | **Q** | **R** | **S** | **T** |
| 40 | 40 | 40 | 40 | 40 | 39 | 40 | 39 | 39 | 39 |
| **U** | **V** | **W** | **X** | **Y** | **Z** | **aa** | **bb** | **cc** | **dd** |
| 39 | 40 | 40 | 40 | 40 | 40 | 39 | 39 | 39 | 40 |
| **ee** | **ff** | **gg** | **hh** | **ii** | **jj** | **kk** | ***ll*** | **mm** | **nn** |
| 40 | 39 | 40 | 40 | 40 | 39 | 55 | 40 | 40 | 40 |
| **oo** | **pp** | **qq** | **rr** | **ss** | **PB** | | | | |
| 39 | 39 | 40 | 39 | 40 | 359 | | | | |

## The 359 Games to Play

| | | | | | | |
|---|---|---|---|---|---|---|
| 1. | A | D | E | T | pp | PB |
| 2. | A | D | G | I | ss | PB |
| 3. | A | D | H | P | oo | PB |
| 4. | A | D | J | jj | rr | PB |
| 5. | A | D | P | T | cc | PB |
| 6. | A | D | R | U | ss | PB |
| 7. | A | D | R | bb | ff | PB |
| 8. | A | D | S | aa | ee | PB |
| 9. | A | E | G | U | cc | PB |
| 10. | A | E | H | S | ss | PB |
| 11. | A | E | I | J | bb | PB |
| 12. | A | E | P | R | jj | PB |
| 13. | A | E | U | ee | ff | PB |
| 14. | A | E | aa | oo | rr | PB |
| 15. | A | G | H | bb | pp | PB |
| 16. | A | G | J | S | T | PB |
| 17. | A | G | P | aa | ff | PB |
| 18. | A | G | R | ee | rr | PB |
| 19. | A | G | U | jj | oo | PB |
| 20. | A | H | I | U | rr | PB |
| 21. | A | H | J | R | aa | PB |
| 22. | A | H | T | ee | jj | PB |
| 23. | A | H | cc | ee | ff | PB |
| 24. | A | I | J | aa | ee | PB |
| 25. | A | I | P | ee | pp | PB |
| 26. | A | I | R | T | oo | PB |
| 27. | A | I | S | ff | jj | PB |
| 28. | A | I | cc | pp | rr | PB |
| 29. | A | J | P | U | ss | PB |
| 30. | A | J | bb | cc | jj | PB |
| 31. | A | J | ff | oo | pp | PB |
| 32. | A | P | S | bb | rr | PB |
| 33. | A | R | S | U | pp | PB |
| 34. | A | R | cc | rr | ss | PB |
| 35. | A | S | aa | cc | oo | PB |
| 36. | A | T | U | aa | bb | PB |
| 37. | A | T | ff | rr | ss | PB |
| 38. | A | aa | jj | pp | ss | PB |
| 39. | A | bb | ee | oo | ss | PB |
| 40. | B | C | F | hh | nn | PB |
| 41. | B | C | K | M | dd | PB |
| 42. | B | C | L | *Q* | qq | PB |
| 43. | B | C | N | O | Z | PB |
| 44. | B | C | V | W | Y | PB |
| 45. | B | C | X | ii | *ll* | PB |
| 46. | B | C | gg | kk | mm | PB |
| 47. | B | F | K | Z | mm | PB |
| 48. | B | F | L | N | Y | PB |



(Continued Next Page)

## POWERBALL BALANCED WHEEL® 53245PB (Continued from previous page)

| | | | | | | |
|---|---|---|---|---|---|---|
| 49. | B | F | M | V | qq | PB |
| 50. | B | F | O | *Q* | ii | PB |
| 51. | B | F | W | dd | *ll* | PB |
| 52. | B | F | X | gg | kk | PB |
| 53. | B | K | L | W | nn | PB |
| 54. | B | K | N | X | qq | PB |
| 55. | B | K | O | V | *ll* | PB |
| 56. | B | K | *Q* | gg | kk | PB |
| 57. | B | K | Y | hh | ii | PB |
| 58. | B | L | M | hh | *ll* | PB |
| 59. | B | L | O | gg | kk | PB |
| 60. | B | L | V | X | mm | PB |
| 61. | B | L | Z | dd | ii | PB |
| 62. | B | M | N | *Q* | W | PB |
| 63. | B | M | O | mm | nn | PB |
| 64. | B | M | X | Y | Z | PB |
| 65. | B | M | gg | ii | kk | PB |
| 66. | B | N | V | ii | nn | PB |
| 67. | B | N | dd | hh | mm | PB |
| 68. | B | N | gg | kk | *ll* | PB |
| 69. | B | O | W | X | hh | PB |
| 70. | B | O | Y | dd | qq | PB |
| 71. | B | *Q* | V | Z | hh | PB |
| 72. | B | *Q* | X | dd | nn | PB |
| 73. | B | *Q* | Y | *ll* | mm | PB |
| 74. | B | V | dd | gg | kk | PB |
| 75. | B | W | Z | gg | kk | PB |
| 76. | B | W | ii | mm | qq | PB |
| 77. | B | Y | gg | kk | nn | PB |
| 78. | B | Z | *ll* | nn | qq | PB |
| 79. | B | gg | hh | kk | qq | PB |
| 80. | C | F | K | L | *ll* | PB |
| 81. | C | F | M | *Q* | Y | PB |
| 82. | C | F | N | W | qq | PB |
| 83. | C | F | O | dd | gg | PB |
| 84. | C | F | V | Z | ii | PB |
| 85. | C | F | X | kk | mm | PB |
| 86. | C | K | N | gg | nn | PB |
| 87. | C | K | O | W | ii | PB |
| 88. | C | K | *Q* | kk | mm | PB |
| 89. | C | K | V | X | hh | PB |
| 90. | C | K | Y | Z | qq | PB |
| 91. | C | L | M | N | V | PB |
| 92. | C | L | O | kk | mm | PB |
| 93. | C | L | W | dd | hh | PB |
| 94. | C | L | X | Z | nn | PB |
| 95. | C | L | Y | gg | ii | PB |
| 96. | C | M | O | X | qq | PB |
| 97. | C | M | W | *ll* | nn | PB |
| 98. | C | M | Z | gg | hh | PB |
| 99. | C | M | ii | kk | mm | PB |
| 100. | C | N | *Q* | hh | ii | PB |
| 101. | C | N | X | Y | dd | PB |
| 102. | C | N | kk | *ll* | mm | PB |
| 103. | C | O | *Q* | V | nn | PB |
| 104. | C | O | Y | hh | *ll* | PB |
| 105. | C | *Q* | W | X | gg | PB |
| 106. | C | *Q* | Z | dd | *ll* | PB |
| 107. | C | V | dd | kk | mm | PB |
| 108. | C | V | gg | *ll* | qq | PB |
| 109. | C | W | Z | kk | mm | PB |
| 110. | C | Y | kk | mm | nn | PB |
| 111. | C | dd | ii | nn | qq | PB |
| 112. | C | hh | kk | mm | qq | PB |
| 113. | D | E | G | P | U | PB |
| 114. | D | E | H | R | rr | PB |
| 115. | D | E | I | ff | oo | PB |
| 116. | D | E | J | P | aa | PB |
| 117. | D | E | S | U | oo | PB |
| 118. | D | E | S | bb | cc | PB |



(Continued Next Page)

## POWERBALL BALANCED WHEEL® 53245PB (Continued from previous page)

| | | | | | | |
|---|---|---|---|---|---|---|
| 119. | D | E | ee | jj | ss | PB |
| 120. | D | G | H | J | cc | PB |
| 121. | D | G | P | R | S | PB |
| 122. | D | G | T | ff | jj | PB |
| 123. | D | G | aa | bb | rr | PB |
| 124. | D | G | ee | oo | pp | PB |
| 125. | D | H | I | bb | ee | PB |
| 126. | D | H | S | jj | pp | PB |
| 127. | D | H | T | aa | ss | PB |
| 128. | D | H | U | bb | ff | PB |
| 129. | D | I | J | R | pp | PB |
| 130. | D | I | P | cc | jj | PB |
| 131. | D | I | S | T | rr | PB |
| 132. | D | I | U | aa | cc | PB |
| 133. | D | I | aa | bb | jj | PB |
| 134. | D | J | S | ff | ss | PB |
| 135. | D | J | T | bb | oo | PB |
| 136. | D | J | U | ee | jj | PB |
| 137. | D | P | bb | pp | ss | PB |
| 138. | D | P | ee | ff | rr | PB |
| 139. | D | R | T | cc | ee | PB |
| 140. | D | R | aa | jj | oo | PB |
| 141. | D | T | U | pp | rr | PB |
| 142. | D | aa | cc | ff | pp | PB |
| 143. | D | cc | oo | rr | ss | PB |
| 144. | E | G | H | bb | jj | PB |
| 145. | E | G | I | S | aa | PB |
| 146. | E | G | J | T | ee | PB |
| 147. | E | G | R | ff | ss | PB |
| 148. | E | G | oo | pp | rr | PB |
| 149. | E | H | I | T | cc | PB |
| 150. | E | H | J | jj | oo | PB |
| 151. | E | H | P | T | ff | PB |
| 152. | E | H | P | U | bb | PB |
| 153. | E | H | aa | ee | pp | PB |

| | | | | | | |
|---|---|---|---|---|---|---|
| 154. | E | I | P | rr | ss | PB |
| 155. | E | I | R | S | ee | PB |
| 156. | E | I | U | jj | pp | PB |
| 157. | E | J | R | T | ff | PB |
| 158. | E | J | S | U | rr | PB |
| 159. | E | J | cc | pp | ss | PB |
| 160. | E | P | S | ff | pp | PB |
| 161. | E | P | cc | ee | oo | PB |
| 162. | E | R | U | aa | cc | PB |
| 163. | E | R | bb | oo | pp | PB |
| 164. | E | S | T | aa | jj | PB |
| 165. | E | T | U | oo | ss | PB |
| 166. | E | T | bb | ee | rr | PB |
| 167. | E | aa | bb | ff | ss | PB |
| 168. | E | cc | ff | jj | rr | PB |
| 169. | F | K | M | W | hh | PB |
| 170. | F | K | N | dd | ii | PB |
| 171. | F | K | O | nn | qq | PB |
| 172. | F | K | *Q* | X | kk | PB |
| 173. | F | K | V | Y | gg | PB |
| 174. | F | L | M | dd | nn | PB |
| 175. | F | L | O | X | kk | PB |
| 176. | F | L | *Q* | V | W | PB |
| 177. | F | L | Z | gg | qq | PB |
| 178. | F | L | hh | ii | mm | PB |
| 179. | F | M | N | gg | mm | PB |
| 180. | F | M | O | Z | *ll* | PB |
| 181. | F | M | X | ii | kk | PB |
| 182. | F | N | O | V | hh | PB |
| 183. | F | N | *Q* | Z | nn | PB |
| 184. | F | N | X | kk | *ll* | PB |
| 185. | F | O | W | Y | mm | PB |
| 186. | F | *Q* | dd | mm | qq | PB |
| 187. | F | *Q* | gg | hh | *ll* | PB |
| 188. | F | V | X | dd | kk | PB |



(Continued Next Page)

## POWERBALL BALANCED WHEEL® 53245PB (Continued from previous page)

| | | | | | | |
|---|---|---|---|---|---|---|
| 189. | F | V | *ll* | mm | nn | PB |
| 190. | F | W | X | Z | kk | PB |
| 191. | F | W | gg | ii | nn | PB |
| 192. | F | X | Y | kk | nn | PB |
| 193. | F | X | hh | kk | qq | PB |
| 194. | F | Y | Z | dd | hh | PB |
| 195. | F | Y | ii | *ll* | qq | PB |
| 196. | G | H | I | R | jj | PB |
| 197. | G | H | P | ee | ss | PB |
| 198. | G | H | S | U | aa | PB |
| 199. | G | H | S | ff | ss | PB |
| 200. | G | H | T | oo | rr | PB |
| 201. | G | I | J | ff | rr | PB |
| 202. | G | I | P | bb | oo | PB |
| 203. | G | I | S | cc | pp | PB |
| 204. | G | I | T | U | ee | PB |
| 205. | G | J | P | jj | pp | PB |
| 206. | G | J | R | U | bb | PB |
| 207. | G | J | aa | oo | ss | PB |
| 208. | G | P | S | T | oo | PB |
| 209. | G | P | U | cc | rr | PB |
| 210. | G | R | T | aa | pp | PB |
| 211. | G | R | cc | ff | oo | PB |
| 212. | G | S | bb | ee | ff | PB |
| 213. | G | S | jj | rr | ss | PB |
| 214. | G | T | bb | cc | ss | PB |
| 215. | G | U | ff | pp | ss | PB |
| 216. | G | aa | cc | ee | jj | PB |
| 217. | H | I | J | P | S | PB |
| 218. | H | I | aa | ff | oo | PB |
| 219. | H | I | oo | pp | ss | PB |
| 220. | H | J | T | U | pp | PB |
| 221. | H | J | bb | rr | ss | PB |
| 222. | H | J | ee | ff | jj | PB |
| 223. | H | P | R | cc | pp | PB |

| | | | | | | |
|---|---|---|---|---|---|---|
| 224. | H | P | aa | jj | rr | PB |
| 225. | H | R | S | T | bb | PB |
| 226. | H | R | S | oo | ss | PB |
| 227. | H | R | U | ee | oo | PB |
| 228. | H | R | ff | pp | rr | PB |
| 229. | H | S | cc | ee | rr | PB |
| 230. | H | U | cc | jj | ss | PB |
| 231. | H | aa | bb | cc | oo | PB |
| 232. | I | J | S | ee | oo | PB |
| 233. | I | J | T | jj | ss | PB |
| 234. | I | J | U | cc | oo | PB |
| 235. | I | P | R | U | ff | PB |
| 236. | I | P | T | aa | rr | PB |
| 237. | I | R | aa | pp | ss | PB |
| 238. | I | R | bb | cc | rr | PB |
| 239. | I | S | U | bb | ss | PB |
| 240. | I | T | bb | ff | pp | PB |
| 241. | I | cc | ee | ff | ss | PB |
| 242. | I | ee | jj | oo | rr | PB |
| 243. | J | P | R | oo | rr | PB |
| 244. | J | P | T | cc | ee | PB |
| 245. | J | P | bb | cc | ff | PB |
| 246. | J | R | S | cc | jj | PB |
| 247. | J | R | bb | ee | ss | PB |
| 248. | J | S | aa | bb | pp | PB |
| 249. | J | T | aa | cc | rr | PB |
| 250. | J | U | aa | ff | jj | PB |
| 251. | J | ee | pp | rr | ss | PB |
| 252. | K | L | M | X | gg | PB |
| 253. | K | L | N | Z | hh | PB |
| 254. | K | L | O | *Q* | kk | PB |
| 255. | K | L | V | ii | qq | PB |
| 256. | K | L | Y | dd | mm | PB |
| 257. | K | M | N | O | Y | PB |
| 258. | K | M | *Q* | ii | kk | PB |



(Continued Next Page)

**POWERBALL BALANCED WHEEL® 53245PB** (Continued from previous page)

| | | | | | | |
|---|---|---|---|---|---|---|
| 259. | K | M | V | Z | nn | PB |
| 260. | K | M | *ll* | mm | qq | PB |
| 261. | K | N | *Q* | kk | *ll* | PB |
| 262. | K | N | V | W | mm | PB |
| 263. | K | O | X | Z | dd | PB |
| 264. | K | O | gg | hh | mm | PB |
| 265. | K | *Q* | V | dd | kk | PB |
| 266. | K | *Q* | W | Z | kk | PB |
| 267. | K | *Q* | Y | kk | nn | PB |
| 268. | K | *Q* | hh | kk | qq | PB |
| 269. | K | W | X | Y | *ll* | PB |
| 270. | K | W | dd | gg | qq | PB |
| 271. | K | X | ii | mm | nn | PB |
| 272. | K | Z | gg | ii | *ll* | PB |
| 273. | K | dd | hh | *ll* | nn | PB |
| 274. | L | M | O | ii | kk | PB |
| 275. | L | M | *Q* | Z | mm | PB |
| 276. | L | M | W | Y | qq | PB |
| 277. | L | N | O | kk | *ll* | PB |
| 278. | L | N | *Q* | dd | gg | PB |
| 279. | L | N | W | X | ii | PB |
| 280. | L | N | mm | nn | qq | PB |
| 281. | L | O | V | dd | kk | PB |
| 282. | L | O | W | Z | kk | PB |
| 283. | L | O | Y | kk | nn | PB |
| 284. | L | O | hh | kk | qq | PB |
| 285. | L | *Q* | X | Y | hh | PB |
| 286. | L | *Q* | ii | *ll* | nn | PB |
| 287. | L | V | Y | Z | *ll* | PB |
| 288. | L | V | gg | hh | nn | PB |
| 289. | L | W | gg | *ll* | mm | PB |
| 290. | L | X | dd | *ll* | qq | PB |
| 291. | M | N | X | hh | nn | PB |
| 292. | M | N | Z | dd | qq | PB |
| 293. | M | N | ii | kk | *ll* | PB |

| | | | | | | |
|---|---|---|---|---|---|---|
| 294. | M | O | *Q* | dd | hh | PB |
| 295. | M | O | V | W | gg | PB |
| 296. | M | *Q* | V | X | *ll* | PB |
| 297. | M | *Q* | gg | nn | qq | PB |
| 298. | M | V | Y | hh | mm | PB |
| 299. | M | V | dd | ii | kk | PB |
| 300. | M | W | X | dd | mm | PB |
| 301. | M | W | Z | ii | kk | PB |
| 302. | M | Y | dd | gg | *ll* | PB |
| 303. | M | Y | ii | kk | nn | PB |
| 304. | M | hh | ii | kk | qq | PB |
| 305. | N | O | *Q* | X | mm | PB |
| 306. | N | O | W | dd | nn | PB |
| 307. | N | O | gg | ii | qq | PB |
| 308. | N | *Q* | V | Y | qq | PB |
| 309. | N | V | X | Z | gg | PB |
| 310. | N | V | dd | kk | *ll* | PB |
| 311. | N | W | Y | gg | hh | PB |
| 312. | N | W | Z | kk | *ll* | PB |
| 313. | N | Y | Z | ii | mm | PB |
| 314. | N | Y | kk | *ll* | nn | PB |
| 315. | N | hh | kk | *ll* | qq | PB |
| 316. | O | *Q* | W | *ll* | qq | PB |
| 317. | O | *Q* | Y | Z | gg | PB |
| 318. | O | V | X | Y | ii | PB |
| 319. | O | V | Z | mm | qq | PB |
| 320. | O | X | gg | *ll* | nn | PB |
| 321. | O | Z | hh | ii | nn | PB |
| 322. | O | dd | ii | *ll* | mm | PB |
| 323. | P | R | T | pp | ss | PB |
| 324. | P | R | aa | bb | ee | PB |
| 325. | P | S | U | ee | jj | PB |
| 326. | P | S | aa | cc | ss | PB |
| 327. | P | T | U | bb | jj | PB |
| 328. | P | U | aa | oo | pp | PB |



(Continued Next Page)

**POWERBALL BALANCED WHEEL® 53245PB** (Continued from previous page)

| | | | | | | |
|---|---|---|---|---|---|---|
| 329. | P | bb | jj | pp | rr | PB |
| 330. | P | ff | jj | oo | ss | PB |
| 331. | Q | V | gg | ii | mm | PB |
| 332. | Q | W | Y | dd | ii | PB |
| 333. | Q | W | hh | mm | nn | PB |
| 334. | Q | X | Z | ii | qq | PB |
| 335. | R | S | aa | ff | rr | PB |
| 336. | R | T | U | jj | rr | PB |
| 337. | R | bb | ee | jj | ss | PB |
| 338. | R | ee | ff | jj | pp | PB |
| 339. | S | T | U | cc | ff | PB |
| 340. | S | T | ee | pp | ss | PB |
| 341. | S | aa | oo | pp | rr | PB |
| 342. | S | bb | ff | jj | oo | PB |
| 343. | T | aa | ee | ff | oo | PB |
| 344. | T | cc | jj | oo | pp | PB |
| 345. | U | aa | ee | rr | ss | PB |
| 346. | U | bb | cc | ee | pp | PB |
| 347. | U | bb | ff | oo | rr | PB |
| 348. | V | W | X | nn | qq | PB |
| 349. | V | W | Z | dd | kk | PB |
| 350. | V | W | hh | ii | ll | PB |
| 351. | V | Y | dd | kk | nn | PB |
| 352. | V | dd | hh | kk | qq | PB |
| 353. | W | Y | Z | kk | nn | PB |
| 354. | W | Z | hh | kk | qq | PB |
| 355. | X | Y | gg | mm | qq | PB |
| 356. | X | Z | hh | ll | mm | PB |
| 357. | X | dd | gg | hh | ii | PB |
| 358. | Y | hh | kk | nn | qq | PB |
| 359. | Z | dd | gg | mm | nn | PB |



# POWERBALL BALANCED WHEEL® 53109PB

## Wheel 9 Numbers + PB in 5 Games for a 3 of 4 Win

With Powerball

| Numbers Matched | Maximum Wins 5 + 1 | 4 + 1 | 3 + 1 | 2 + 1 | 1 + 1 | 0 + 1 | Minimum Wins 5 + 1 | 4 + 1 | 3 + 1 | 2 + 1 | 1 + 1 | 0 + 1 |
|---|---|---|---|---|---|---|---|---|---|---|---|---|
| 5 + 1 | 1 | 0 | 2 | 2 | 0 | 0 | 0 | 0 | 3 | 2 | 0 | 0 |
| 4 + 1 | - | 1 | 2 | 1 | 0 | 1 | - | 0 | 1 | 3 | 1 | 0 |
| 3 + 1 | - | - | 2 | 1 | 1 | 1 | - | - | 0 | 2 | 3 | 0 |
| 2 + 1 | - | - | - | 3 | 0 | 2 | - | - | - | 0 | 5 | 0 |
| 1 + 1 | - | - | - | - | 3 | 2 | - | - | - | - | 2 | 3 |
| 0 + 1 | - | - | - | - | - | 5 | - | - | - | - | - | 5 |

Without Powerball

| Numbers Matched | Maximum Wins 5 + 0 | 4 + 0 | 3 + 0 | 2 + 0 | 1 + 0 | Minimum Wins 5 + 0 | 4 + 0 | 3 + 0 | 2 + 0 | 1 + 0 |
|---|---|---|---|---|---|---|---|---|---|---|
| 5 + 0 | 1 | 0 | 2 | 2 | 0 | 0 | 0 | 3 | 2 | 0 |
| 4 + 0 | - | 1 | 2 | 1 | 0 | - | 0 | 1 | 3 | 1 |
| 3 + 0 | - | - | 2 | 1 | 1 | - | - | 0 | 2 | 3 |
| 2 + 0 | - | - | - | 3 | 0 | - | - | - | 0 | 5 |
| 1 + 0 | - | - | - | - | 3 | - | - | - | - | 2 |

## Your 9 Numbers + PB to Wheel

| A | B | C | D | E | F | G | H | I | PB |
|---|---|---|---|---|---|---|---|---|---|
| 3 | 3 | 2 | 3 | 3 | 3 | 2 | 3 | 3 | 5 |

## The 5 Games to Play

| | | | | | | |
|---|---|---|---|---|---|---|
| 1. | A | B | C | H | I | PB |
| 2. | A | D | E | F | H | PB |
| 3. | A | D | F | G | I | PB |
| 4. | B | C | E | G | H | PB |



(Continued Next Page)

**POWERBALL BALANCED WHEEL® 53109PB** (Continued from previous page)

| | | | | | | |
|---|---|---|---|---|---|---|
| 5. | B | D | E | F | I | PB |



# POWERBALL BALANCED WHEEL® 53110PB

## Wheel 10 Numbers + PB in 7 Games for a 3 of 4 Win

With Powerball

| Numbers Matched | Maximum Wins | | | | | | Minimum Wins | | | | | |
|---|---|---|---|---|---|---|---|---|---|---|---|---|
| | 5 + 1 | 4 + 1 | 3 + 1 | 2 + 1 | 1 + 1 | 0 + 1 | 5 + 1 | 4 + 1 | 3 + 1 | 2 + 1 | 1 + 1 | 0 + 1 |
| 5 + 1 | 1 | 1 | 1 | 4 | 0 | 0 | 0 | 0 | 3 | 3 | 1 | 0 |
| 4 + 1 | - | 2 | 0 | 3 | 2 | 0 | - | 0 | 1 | 4 | 1 | 1 |
| 3 + 1 | - | - | 2 | 3 | 0 | 2 | - | - | 0 | 3 | 3 | 1 |
| 2 + 1 | - | - | - | 4 | 0 | 3 | - | - | - | 0 | 7 | 0 |
| 1 + 1 | - | - | - | - | 4 | 3 | - | - | - | - | 3 | 4 |
| 0 + 1 | - | - | - | - | - | 7 | - | - | - | - | - | 7 |

Without Powerball

| Numbers Matched | Maximum Wins | | | | | Minimum Wins | | | | |
|---|---|---|---|---|---|---|---|---|---|---|
| | 5 + 0 | 4 + 0 | 3 + 0 | 2 + 0 | 1 + 0 | 5 + 0 | 4 + 0 | 3 + 0 | 2 + 0 | 1 + 0 |
| 5 + 0 | 1 | 1 | 1 | 4 | 0 | 0 | 0 | 3 | 3 | 1 |
| 4 + 0 | - | 2 | 0 | 3 | 2 | - | 0 | 1 | 4 | 1 |
| 3 + 0 | - | - | 2 | 3 | 0 | - | - | 0 | 3 | 3 |
| 2 + 0 | - | - | - | 4 | 0 | - | - | - | 0 | 7 |
| 1 + 0 | - | - | - | - | 4 | - | - | - | - | 3 |

## Your 10 Numbers + PB to Wheel

| A | B | C | D | E | F | G | H | I | J | PB |
|---|---|---|---|---|---|---|---|---|---|---|
| 16 (3) | 23 (4) | 34 (4) | 41 (4) | 11 (3) | 19 (3) | 27 (3) | 14 (3) | 44 (4) | 37 (4) | 20 (7) |

## The 7 Games to Play

| | | | | | | |
|---|---|---|---|---|---|---|
| 1. | A 16 | C 34 | F 19 | H 14 | I 44 | PB 20 |
| 2. | A 16 | D 41 | E 11 | F 19 | J 37 | PB 20 |
| 3. | A 16 | D 41 | F 19 | G 27 | J 37 | PB 20 |
| 4. | B 23 | C 34 | D 41 | H 14 | J 37 | PB 20 |
| 5. | B 23 | C 34 | D 41 | I 44 | J 37 | PB 20 |
| 6. | B 23 | C 34 | E 11 | G 27 | I 44 | PB 20 |
| 7. | B 23 | E 11 | G 27 | H 14 | I 44 | PB 20 |



# POWERBALL BALANCED WHEEL® 53111PB

## Wheel 11 Numbers + PB in 10 Games for a 3 of 4 Win

With Powerball

| Numbers Matched | Maximum Wins | | | | | | Minimum Wins | | | | | |
|---|---|---|---|---|---|---|---|---|---|---|---|---|
| | 5 + 1 | 4 + 1 | 3 + 1 | 2 + 1 | 1 + 1 | 0 + 1 | 5 + 1 | 4 + 1 | 3 + 1 | 2 + 1 | 1 + 1 | 0 + 1 |
| 5 + 1 | 1 | 0 | 4 | 4 | 1 | 0 | 0 | 0 | 3 | 5 | 1 | 1 |
| 4 + 1 | - | 1 | 3 | 3 | 2 | 1 | - | 0 | 1 | 5 | 3 | 1 |
| 3 + 1 | - | - | 3 | 1 | 2 | 4 | - | - | 0 | 3 | 7 | 0 |
| 2 + 1 | - | - | - | 4 | 3 | 3 | - | - | - | 0 | 9 | 1 |
| 1 + 1 | - | - | - | - | 6 | 4 | - | - | - | - | 4 | 6 |
| 0 + 1 | - | - | - | - | - | 10 | - | - | - | - | - | 10 |

(Continued Next Page)

## POWERBALL BALANCED WHEEL® 53111PB (Continued from previous page)

Without Powerball

| Numbers Matched | Maximum Wins 5 + 0 | 4 + 0 | 3 + 0 | 2 + 0 | 1 + 0 | Minimum Wins 5 + 0 | 4 + 0 | 3 + 0 | 2 + 0 | 1 + 0 |
|---|---|---|---|---|---|---|---|---|---|---|
| 5 + 0 | 1 | 0 | 4 | 4 | 1 | 0 | 0 | 3 | 5 | 1 |
| 4 + 0 | - | 1 | 3 | 3 | 2 | - | 0 | 1 | 5 | 3 |
| 3 + 0 | - | - | 3 | 1 | 2 | - | - | 0 | 3 | 7 |
| 2 + 0 | - | - | - | 4 | 3 | - | - | - | 0 | 9 |
| 1 + 0 | - | - | - | - | 6 | - | - | - | - | 4 |

### Your 11 Numbers + PB to Wheel

| A | B | C | D | E | F |
|---|---|---|---|---|---|
| 6 | 18 | 20 | 23 | 26 | 29 |
| 4 | 5 | 5 | 5 | 5 | 4 |

| G | H | I | J | K | PB |
|---|---|---|---|---|---|
| 35 | 37 | 48 | 51 | 52 | |
| 4 | 4 | 4 | 4 | 6 | 10 |

### The 10 Games to Play

| | | | | | | |
|---|---|---|---|---|---|---|
| 1. | A 6 | C 20 | D 23 | J 51 | K 52 | PB 12 |
| 2. | A 6 | D 23 | E 26 | G 35 | H 37 | PB Q |
| 3. | A 6 | D 23 | F 29 | H 37 | J 51 | PB 12 |
| 4. | A 6 | D 23 | H 37 | I 48 | K 52 | PB Q |
| 5. | B 18 | C 20 | D 23 | E 26 | K 52 | PB 12 |
| 6. | B 18 | C 20 | F 29 | G 35 | I 48 | PB 4 |
| 7. | B 18 | C 20 | H 37 | J 51 | K 52 | PB 12 |
| 8. | B 18 | E 26 | F 29 | G 35 | K 52 | PB |
| 9. | B 18 | E 26 | G 35 | I 48 | J 51 | PB 12 |
| 10. | C 20 | E 26 | F 29 | I 48 | K 52 | PB 4 |



## POWERBALL BALANCED WHEEL® 53112PB

### Wheel 12 Numbers + PB in 12 Games for a 3 of 4 Win

With Powerball

| Numbers Matched | Maximum Wins 5 + 1 | 4 + 1 | 3 + 1 | 2 + 1 | 1 + 1 | 0 + 1 | Minimum Wins 5 + 1 | 4 + 1 | 3 + 1 | 2 + 1 | 1 + 1 | 0 + 1 |
|---|---|---|---|---|---|---|---|---|---|---|---|---|
| 5 + 1 | 1 | 0 | 0 | 9 | 2 | 0 | 0 | 0 | 3 | 7 | 2 | 0 |
| 4 + 1 | - | 1 | 0 | 6 | 4 | 1 | - | 0 | 1 | 6 | 5 | 0 |
| 3 + 1 | - | - | 1 | 3 | 6 | 2 | - | - | 0 | 4 | 7 | 1 |
| 2 + 1 | - | - | - | 2 | 6 | 4 | - | - | - | 1 | 8 | 3 |
| 1 + 1 | - | - | - | - | 5 | 7 | - | - | - | - | 5 | 7 |
| 0 + 1 | - | - | - | - | - | 12 | - | - | - | - | - | 12 |

Without Powerball

| Numbers Matched | Maximum Wins 5 + 0 | 4 + 0 | 3 + 0 | 2 + 0 | 1 + 0 | Minimum Wins 5 + 0 | 4 + 0 | 3 + 0 | 2 + 0 | 1 + 0 |
|---|---|---|---|---|---|---|---|---|---|---|
| 5 + 0 | 1 | 0 | 0 | 9 | 2 | 0 | 0 | 3 | 7 | 2 |
| 4 + 0 | - | 1 | 0 | 6 | 4 | - | 0 | 1 | 6 | 5 |
| 3 + 0 | - | - | 1 | 3 | 6 | - | - | 0 | 4 | 7 |
| 2 + 0 | - | - | - | 2 | 6 | - | - | - | 1 | 8 |
| 1 + 0 | - | - | - | - | 5 | - | - | - | - | 5 |

### Your 12 Numbers + PB to Wheel

| A | B | C | D | E | F | G |
|---|---|---|---|---|---|---|
| 5 | 5 | 5 | 5 | 5 | 5 | 5 |

| H | I | J | K | L | PB |
|---|---|---|---|---|---|
| 5 | 5 | 5 | 5 | 5 | 12 |

### The 12 Games to Play

| | | | | | | |
|---|---|---|---|---|---|---|
| 1. | A | B | D | I | K | PB |
| 2. | A | C | F | G | L | PB |



(Continued Next Page)

## POWERBALL BALANCED WHEEL® 53112PB (Continued from previous page)

| | | | | | | | | | | | | |
|---|---|---|---|---|---|---|---|---|---|---|---|---|
| 3. | A | D | G | H | J | PB | 8. | B | D | F | H | L | PB |
| 4. | A | E | F | I | J | PB | 9. | B | F | G | J | K | PB |
| 5. | A | E | H | K | L | PB | 10. | C | D | E | J | K | PB |
| 6. | B | C | E | G | H | PB | 11. | C | F | H | I | K | PB |
| 7. | B | C | I | J | L | PB | 12. | D | E | G | I | L | PB |



# POWERBALL BALANCED WHEEL® 53113PB

## Wheel 13 Numbers + PB in 18 Games for a 3 of 4 Win

With Powerball

| Numbers Matched | Maximum Wins 5 + 1 | 4 + 1 | 3 + 1 | 2 + 1 | 1 + 1 | 0 + 1 | Minimum Wins 5 + 1 | 4 + 1 | 3 + 1 | 2 + 1 | 1 + 1 | 0 + 1 |
|---|---|---|---|---|---|---|---|---|---|---|---|---|
| 5 + 1 | 1 | 1 | 2 | 5 | 9 | 0 | 0 | 0 | 3 | 10 | 5 | 0 |
| 4 + 1 | - | 2 | 0 | 7 | 6 | 3 | - | 0 | 1 | 8 | 8 | 1 |
| 3 + 1 | - | - | 2 | 4 | 7 | 5 | - | - | 0 | 5 | 10 | 3 |
| 2 + 1 | - | - | - | 4 | 6 | 8 | - | - | - | 1 | 12 | 5 |
| 1 + 1 | - | - | - | - | 7 | 11 | - | - | - | - | 6 | 12 |
| 0 + 1 | - | - | - | - | - | 18 | - | - | - | - | - | 18 |

Without Powerball

| Numbers Matched | Maximum Wins 5 + 0 | 4 + 0 | 3 + 0 | 2 + 0 | 1 + 0 | Minimum Wins 5 + 0 | 4 + 0 | 3 + 0 | 2 + 0 | 1 + 0 |
|---|---|---|---|---|---|---|---|---|---|---|
| 5 + 0 | 1 | 1 | 2 | 5 | 9 | 0 | 0 | 3 | 10 | 5 |
| 4 + 0 | - | 2 | 0 | 7 | 6 | - | 0 | 1 | 8 | 8 |
| 3 + 0 | - | - | 2 | 4 | 7 | - | - | 0 | 5 | 10 |
| 2 + 0 | - | - | - | 4 | 6 | - | - | - | 1 | 12 |
| 1 + 0 | - | - | - | - | 7 | - | - | - | - | 6 |

## Your 13 Numbers + PB to Wheel

| A | B | C | D | E | F | G |
|---|---|---|---|---|---|---|
| 7 | 7 | 7 | 7 | 7 | 7 | 6 |
| **H** | **I** | **J** | **K** | **L** | **M** | **PB** |
| 7 | 7 | 7 | 7 | 7 | 7 | 18 |

## The 18 Games to Play

| | | | | | | | | | | | | |
|---|---|---|---|---|---|---|---|---|---|---|---|---|
| 1. | A | B | C | I | M | PB | 10. | B | D | E | H | K | PB |
| 2. | A | C | G | J | L | PB | 11. | B | E | J | L | M | PB |
| 3. | A | C | H | K | L | PB | 12. | B | F | G | I | K | PB |
| 4. | A | D | F | L | M | PB | 13. | B | F | I | K | L | PB |
| 5. | A | D | H | I | J | PB | 14. | C | D | E | I | L | PB |
| 6. | A | E | F | J | K | PB | 15. | C | D | J | K | M | PB |
| 7. | A | G | H | L | M | PB | 16. | C | G | H | J | M | PB |
| 8. | B | C | F | H | J | PB | 17. | D | E | F | G | K | PB |
| 9. | B | D | E | G | I | PB | 18. | E | F | H | I | M | PB |

# POWERBALL BALANCED WHEEL® 53114PB

## Wheel 14 Numbers + PB in 23 Games for a 3 of 4 Win

With Powerball

| Numbers Matched | Maximum Wins 5 + 1 | 4 + 1 | 3 + 1 | 2 + 1 | 1 + 1 | 0 + 1 | Minimum Wins 5 + 1 | 4 + 1 | 3 + 1 | 2 + 1 | 1 + 1 | 0 + 1 |
|---|---|---|---|---|---|---|---|---|---|---|---|---|
| 5 + 1 | 1 | 2 | 2 | 9 | 8 | 1 | 0 | 0 | 3 | 11 | 7 | 2 |
| 4 + 1 | - | 3 | 0 | 10 | 6 | 4 | - | 0 | 1 | 8 | 11 | 3 |
| 3 + 1 | - | - | 3 | 8 | 5 | 7 | - | - | 0 | 5 | 12 | 6 |
| 2 + 1 | - | - | - | 11 | 0 | 12 | - | - | - | 1 | 13 | 9 |
| 1 + 1 | - | - | - | - | 11 | 12 | - | - | - | - | 7 | 16 |
| 0 + 1 | - | - | - | - | - | 23 | - | - | - | - | - | 23 |

Without Powerball

| Numbers Matched | Maximum Wins 5 + 0 | 4 + 0 | 3 + 0 | 2 + 0 | 1 + 0 | Minimum Wins 5 + 0 | 4 + 0 | 3 + 0 | 2 + 0 | 1 + 0 |
|---|---|---|---|---|---|---|---|---|---|---|
| 5 + 0 | 1 | 2 | 2 | 9 | 8 | 0 | 0 | 3 | 11 | 7 |
| 4 + 0 | - | 3 | 0 | 10 | 6 | - | 0 | 1 | 8 | 11 |
| 3 + 0 | - | - | 3 | 8 | 5 | - | - | 0 | 5 | 12 |
| 2 + 0 | - | - | - | 11 | 0 | - | - | - | 1 | 13 |
| 1 + 0 | - | - | - | - | 11 | - | - | - | - | 7 |

## Your 14 Numbers + PB to Wheel

| A | B | C | D | E | F | G | H |
|---|---|---|---|---|---|---|---|
| 11 | 8 | 8 | 7 | 8 | 8 | 8 | 8 |

| I | J | K | L | M | N | PB |
|---|---|---|---|---|---|---|
| 8 | 7 | 8 | 8 | 11 | 7 | 23 |

## The 23 Games to Play

| | | | | | | |
|---|---|---|---|---|---|---|
| 1. | A | B | D | I | M | PB |
| 2. | A | B | I | J | M | PB |
| 3. | A | B | I | M | N | PB |
| 4. | A | C | E | G | M | PB |
| 5. | A | C | F | H | M | PB |
| 6. | A | C | K | L | M | PB |
| 7. | A | D | J | M | N | PB |
| 8. | A | E | F | K | M | PB |
| 9. | A | E | H | L | M | PB |
| 10. | A | F | G | L | M | PB |
| 11. | A | G | H | K | M | PB |
| 12. | B | C | G | H | J | PB |
| 13. | B | C | I | K | L | PB |
| 14. | B | D | E | H | I | PB |
| 15. | B | D | J | K | N | PB |
| 16. | B | E | F | L | N | PB |
| 17. | C | D | F | J | L | PB |
| 18. | C | E | H | K | N | PB |
| 19. | C | F | G | I | N | PB |
| 20. | D | E | F | G | K | PB |
| 21. | D | G | H | L | N | PB |
| 22. | E | G | I | J | L | PB |
| 23. | F | H | I | J | K | PB |

# POWERBALL BALANCED WHEEL® 53115PB

## Wheel 15 Numbers + PB in 28 Games for a 3 of 4 Win

With Powerball

| Numbers Matched | Maximum Wins | | | | | | Minimum Wins | | | | | |
|---|---|---|---|---|---|---|---|---|---|---|---|---|
| | 5 + 1 | 4 + 1 | 3 + 1 | 2 + 1 | 1 + 1 | 0 + 1 | 5 + 1 | 4 + 1 | 3 + 1 | 2 + 1 | 1 + 1 | 0 + 1 |
| 5 + 1 | 1 | 1 | 3 | 12 | 9 | 2 | 0 | 0 | 3 | 11 | 13 | 1 |
| 4 + 1 | - | 2 | 1 | 7 | 15 | 3 | - | 0 | 1 | 8 | 15 | 4 |
| 3 + 1 | - | - | 3 | 3 | 15 | 7 | - | - | 0 | 5 | 15 | 8 |
| 2 + 1 | - | - | - | 6 | 8 | 14 | - | - | - | 1 | 15 | 12 |
| 1 + 1 | - | - | - | - | 11 | 17 | - | - | - | - | 8 | 20 |
| 0 + 1 | - | - | - | - | - | 28 | - | - | - | - | - | 28 |

Without Powerball

| Numbers Matched | Maximum Wins | | | | | Minimum Wins | | | | |
|---|---|---|---|---|---|---|---|---|---|---|
| | 5 + 0 | 4 + 0 | 3 + 0 | 2 + 0 | 1 + 0 | 5 + 0 | 4 + 0 | 3 + 0 | 2 + 0 | 1 + 0 |
| 5 + 0 | 1 | 1 | 3 | 12 | 9 | 0 | 0 | 3 | 11 | 13 |
| 4 + 0 | - | 2 | 1 | 7 | 15 | - | 0 | 1 | 8 | 15 |
| 3 + 0 | - | - | 3 | 3 | 15 | - | - | 0 | 5 | 15 |
| 2 + 0 | - | - | - | 6 | 8 | - | - | - | 1 | 15 |
| 1 + 0 | - | - | - | - | 11 | - | - | - | - | 8 |

## Your 15 Numbers + PB to Wheel

| A | B | C | D | E | F | G | H |
|---|---|---|---|---|---|---|---|
| 11 | 8 | 10 | 8 | 9 | 9 | 10 | 9 |
| **I** | **J** | **K** | **L** | **M** | **N** | **O** | **PB** |
| 9 | 9 | 9 | 9 | 10 | 11 | 9 | 28 |

## The 28 Games to Play

| | | | | | | |
|---|---|---|---|---|---|---|
| 1. | A | B | D | I | K | PB |
| 2. | A | B | E | G | L | PB |
| 3. | A | C | F | N | O | PB |
| 4. | A | C | H | L | O | PB |
| 5. | A | C | J | K | M | PB |
| 6. | A | D | E | N | O | PB |
| 7. | A | E | H | I | L | PB |
| 8. | A | F | K | M | N | PB |
| 9. | A | G | J | L | M | PB |
| 10. | A | G | L | M | N | PB |
| 11. | A | J | K | L | N | PB |
| 12. | B | C | G | K | O | PB |
| 13. | B | C | K | L | N | PB |
| 14. | B | D | H | J | M | PB |
| 15. | B | E | F | M | N | PB |
| 16. | B | F | H | J | N | PB |
| 17. | B | I | J | M | O | PB |
| 18. | C | D | E | F | J | PB |
| 19. | C | D | G | M | O | PB |
| 20. | C | E | G | H | I | PB |
| 21. | C | F | G | I | J | PB |
| 22. | C | F | H | M | N | PB |
| 23. | D | F | G | H | K | PB |
| 24. | D | F | I | L | O | PB |
| 25. | D | G | H | I | N | PB |
| 26. | E | G | I | N | O | PB |
| 27. | E | H | J | K | O | PB |
| 28. | E | I | K | L | M | PB |

# POWERBALL BALANCED WHEEL® 53116PB

## Wheel 16 Numbers + PB in 37 Games for a 3 of 4 Win

With Powerball

| Numbers Matched | Maximum Wins 5 + 1 | 4 + 1 | 3 + 1 | 2 + 1 | 1 + 1 | 0 + 1 | Minimum Wins 5 + 1 | 4 + 1 | 3 + 1 | 2 + 1 | 1 + 1 | 0 + 1 |
|---|---|---|---|---|---|---|---|---|---|---|---|---|
| 5 + 1 | 1 | 2 | 2 | 13 | 15 | 4 | 0 | 0 | 3 | 15 | 14 | 5 |
| 4 + 1 | - | 3 | 0 | 12 | 14 | 8 | - | 0 | 1 | 10 | 19 | 7 |
| 3 + 1 | - | - | 3 | 11 | 11 | 12 | - | - | 0 | 6 | 19 | 12 |
| 2 + 1 | - | - | - | 14 | 0 | 23 | - | - | - | 1 | 19 | 17 |
| 1 + 1 | - | - | - | - | 14 | 23 | - | - | - | - | 10 | 27 |
| 0 + 1 | - | - | - | - | - | 37 | - | - | - | - | - | 37 |

Without Powerball

| Numbers Matched | Maximum Wins 5 + 0 | 4 + 0 | 3 + 0 | 2 + 0 | 1 + 0 | Minimum Wins 5 + 0 | 4 + 0 | 3 + 0 | 2 + 0 | 1 + 0 |
|---|---|---|---|---|---|---|---|---|---|---|
| 5 + 0 | 1 | 2 | 2 | 13 | 15 | 0 | 0 | 3 | 15 | 14 |
| 4 + 0 | - | 3 | 0 | 12 | 14 | - | 0 | 1 | 10 | 19 |
| 3 + 0 | - | - | 3 | 11 | 11 | - | - | 0 | 6 | 19 |
| 2 + 0 | - | - | - | 14 | 0 | - | - | - | 1 | 19 |
| 1 + 0 | - | - | - | - | 14 | - | - | - | - | 10 |

## Your 16 Numbers + PB to Wheel

| A | B | C | D | E | F | G | H | I |
|---|---|---|---|---|---|---|---|---|
| 14 | 10 | 10 | 11 | 11 | 14 | 11 | 11 | 11 |

| J | K | L | M | N | O | P | PB |
|---|---|---|---|---|---|---|---|
| 11 | 11 | 11 | 11 | 14 | 14 | 10 | 37 |

## The 37 Games to Play

| | | | | | | |
|---|---|---|---|---|---|---|
| 1. | A | B | D | J | N | PB |
| 2. | A | B | L | M | N | PB |
| 3. | A | B | N | O | P | PB |
| 4. | A | C | E | K | N | PB |
| 5. | A | C | F | H | N | PB |
| 6. | A | C | G | I | N | PB |
| 7. | A | D | L | N | O | PB |
| 8. | A | D | M | N | P | PB |
| 9. | A | E | F | I | N | PB |
| 10. | A | E | G | H | N | PB |
| 11. | A | F | G | K | N | PB |
| 12. | A | H | I | K | N | PB |
| 13. | A | J | L | N | P | PB |
| 14. | A | J | M | N | O | PB |
| 15. | B | C | F | O | P | PB |
| 16. | B | C | G | I | J | PB |
| 17. | B | C | K | L | P | PB |
| 18. | B | D | J | M | P | PB |
| 19. | B | E | F | L | O | PB |
| 20. | B | E | H | I | L | PB |
| 21. | B | G | H | K | M | PB |
| 22. | C | D | E | G | M | PB |
| 23. | C | D | H | I | K | PB |
| 24. | C | E | F | L | O | PB |
| 25. | C | H | J | L | M | PB |
| 26. | D | E | J | K | L | PB |
| 27. | D | F | G | H | O | PB |
| 28. | D | F | I | M | O | PB |
| 29. | D | F | J | K | O | PB |
| 30. | D | G | I | L | P | PB |
| 31. | E | F | L | O | P | PB |
| 32. | E | G | H | J | P | PB |
| 33. | E | I | K | M | P | PB |
| 34. | F | G | I | K | O | PB |
| 35. | F | G | J | M | O | PB |
| 36. | F | H | I | J | O | PB |



(Continued Next Page)

**POWERBALL BALANCED WHEEL® 53116PB** (Continued from previous page)

| | | | | | | |
|---|---|---|---|---|---|---|
| 37. | F | H | K | M | O | PB |



# POWERBALL BALANCED WHEEL® 53117PB

## Wheel 17 Numbers + PB in 46 Games for a 3 of 4 Win

With Powerball

| Numbers Matched | Maximum Wins | | | | | | Minimum Wins | | | | | |
|---|---|---|---|---|---|---|---|---|---|---|---|---|
| | 5 + 1 | 4 + 1 | 3 + 1 | 2 + 1 | 1 + 1 | 0 + 1 | 5 + 1 | 4 + 1 | 3 + 1 | 2 + 1 | 1 + 1 | 0 + 1 |
| 5 + 1 | 1 | 11 | 0 | 0 | 14 | 20 | 0 | 0 | 3 | 19 | 18 | 6 |
| 4 + 1 | - | 12 | 0 | 0 | 0 | 34 | - | 0 | 1 | 11 | 28 | 6 |
| 3 + 1 | - | - | 12 | 0 | 0 | 34 | - | - | 0 | 5 | 29 | 12 |
| 2 + 1 | - | - | - | 12 | 0 | 34 | - | - | - | 0 | 25 | 21 |
| 1 + 1 | - | - | - | - | 15 | 31 | - | - | - | - | 12 | 34 |
| 0 + 1 | - | - | - | - | - | 46 | - | - | - | - | - | 46 |

Without Powerball

| Numbers Matched | Maximum Wins | | | | | Minimum Wins | | | | |
|---|---|---|---|---|---|---|---|---|---|---|
| | 5 + 0 | 4 + 0 | 3 + 0 | 2 + 0 | 1 + 0 | 5 + 0 | 4 + 0 | 3 + 0 | 2 + 0 | 1 + 0 |
| 5 + 0 | 1 | 11 | 0 | 0 | 14 | 0 | 0 | 3 | 19 | 18 |
| 4 + 0 | - | 12 | 0 | 0 | 0 | - | 0 | 1 | 11 | 28 |
| 3 + 0 | - | - | 12 | 0 | 0 | - | - | 0 | 5 | 29 |
| 2 + 0 | - | - | - | 12 | 0 | - | - | - | 0 | 25 |
| 1 + 0 | - | - | - | - | 15 | - | - | - | - | 12 |

## Your 17 Numbers + PB to Wheel

| A | B | C | D | E | F | G | H | I |
|---|---|---|---|---|---|---|---|---|
| 12 | 12 | 14 | 14 | 14 | 13 | 14 | 14 | 14 |

| J | K | L | M | N | O | P | Q | PB |
|---|---|---|---|---|---|---|---|---|
| 14 | 14 | 14 | 12 | 14 | 12 | 14 | 15 | 46 |

## The 46 Games to Play

| | | | | | | |
|---|---|---|---|---|---|---|
| 1. | A | B | C | M | O | PB |
| 2. | A | B | D | M | O | PB |
| 3. | A | B | E | M | O | PB |
| 4. | A | B | G | M | O | PB |
| 5. | A | B | H | M | O | PB |
| 6. | A | B | I | M | O | PB |
| 7. | A | B | J | M | O | PB |
| 8. | A | B | K | M | O | PB |
| 9. | A | B | L | M | O | PB |
| 10. | A | B | M | N | O | PB |
| 11. | A | B | M | O | P | PB |
| 12. | A | B | M | O | Q | PB |
| 13. | C | D | E | P | Q | PB |
| 14. | C | D | F | I | K | PB |
| 15. | C | D | G | L | N | PB |
| 16. | C | D | H | J | L | PB |
| 17. | C | E | F | I | P | PB |
| 18. | C | E | G | H | P | PB |
| 19. | C | E | J | N | P | PB |
| 20. | C | E | K | L | P | PB |
| 21. | C | F | G | I | J | PB |
| 22. | C | F | H | I | N | PB |
| 23. | C | F | I | L | Q | PB |
| 24. | C | G | K | N | Q | PB |
| 25. | C | H | J | K | Q | PB |
| 26. | D | E | F | G | N | PB |
| 27. | D | E | F | H | J | PB |
| 28. | D | E | I | K | L | PB |
| 29. | D | F | L | P | Q | PB |
| 30. | D | G | H | I | K | PB |



(Continued Next Page)

## POWERBALL BALANCED WHEEL® 53117PB (Continued from previous page)

| | | | | | | |
|---|---|---|---|---|---|---|
| 31. | D | G | J | P | Q | PB |
| 32. | D | H | N | P | Q | PB |
| 33. | D | I | J | K | N | PB |
| 34. | D | I | K | P | Q | PB |
| 35. | E | F | K | L | Q | PB |
| 36. | E | G | I | N | Q | PB |
| 37. | E | G | J | K | L | PB |
| 38. | E | H | I | J | Q | PB |
| 39. | E | H | K | L | N | PB |
| 40. | F | G | H | L | Q | PB |
| 41. | F | G | K | N | P | PB |
| 42. | F | H | J | K | P | PB |
| 43. | F | J | L | N | Q | PB |
| 44. | G | H | J | N | Q | PB |
| 45. | G | I | L | N | P | PB |
| 46. | H | I | J | L | P | PB |



# POWERBALL BALANCED WHEEL® 53118PB

## Wheel 18 Numbers + PB in 56 Games for a 3 of 4 Win

With Powerball

| Numbers Matched | Maximum Wins | | | | | | Minimum Wins | | | | | |
|---|---|---|---|---|---|---|---|---|---|---|---|---|
| | 5 + 1 | 4 + 1 | 3 + 1 | 2 + 1 | 1 + 1 | 0 + 1 | 5 + 1 | 4 + 1 | 3 + 1 | 2 + 1 | 1 + 1 | 0 + 1 |
| 5 + 1 | 1 | 2 | 2 | 19 | 19 | 13 | 0 | 0 | 3 | 20 | 22 | 11 |
| 4 + 1 | - | 3 | 0 | 18 | 14 | 21 | - | 0 | 1 | 13 | 28 | 14 |
| 3 + 1 | - | - | 4 | 15 | 11 | 26 | - | - | 0 | 7 | 29 | 20 |
| 2 + 1 | - | - | - | 19 | 0 | 37 | - | - | - | 1 | 27 | 28 |
| 1 + 1 | - | - | - | - | 19 | 37 | - | - | - | - | 14 | 42 |
| 0 + 1 | - | - | - | - | - | 56 | - | - | - | - | - | 56 |

Without Powerball

| Numbers Matched | Maximum Wins | | | | | Minimum Wins | | | | |
|---|---|---|---|---|---|---|---|---|---|---|
| | 5 + 0 | 4 + 0 | 3 + 0 | 2 + 0 | 1 + 0 | 5 + 0 | 4 + 0 | 3 + 0 | 2 + 0 | 1 + 0 |
| 5 + 0 | 1 | 2 | 2 | 19 | 19 | 0 | 0 | 3 | 20 | 22 |
| 4 + 0 | - | 3 | 0 | 18 | 14 | - | 0 | 1 | 13 | 28 |
| 3 + 0 | - | - | 4 | 15 | 11 | - | - | 0 | 7 | 29 |
| 2 + 0 | - | - | - | 19 | 0 | - | - | - | 1 | 27 |
| 1 + 0 | - | - | - | - | 19 | - | - | - | - | 14 |

## Your 18 Numbers + PB to Wheel

| A | B | C | D | E | F | G | H | I | J |
|---|---|---|---|---|---|---|---|---|---|
| 17 | 19 | 15 | 17 | 15 | 14 | 15 | 17 | 15 | 15 |

| K | L | M | N | O | P | Q | R | PB |
|---|---|---|---|---|---|---|---|---|
| 14 | 14 | 14 | 14 | 15 | 14 | 19 | 17 | 56 |

## The 56 Games to Play

| | | | | | | |
|---|---|---|---|---|---|---|
| 1. | A | B | D | K | Q | PB |
| 2. | A | B | H | N | Q | PB |
| 3. | A | B | M | Q | R | PB |
| 4. | A | C | E | G | R | PB |
| 5. | A | C | I | M | R | PB |
| 6. | A | C | J | O | R | PB |
| 7. | A | D | F | H | P | PB |
| 8. | A | D | H | J | M | PB |
| 9. | A | D | H | N | O | PB |
| 10. | A | E | I | O | R | PB |
| 11. | A | E | J | M | R | PB |
| 12. | A | F | K | N | R | PB |
| 13. | A | F | L | P | R | PB |
| 14. | A | G | I | J | R | PB |
| 15. | A | G | M | O | R | PB |
| 16. | A | K | L | N | R | PB |



(Continued Next Page)

## POWERBALL BALANCED WHEEL® 53118PB (Continued from previous page)

| | | | | | | |
|---|---|---|---|---|---|---|
| 17. | A | K | N | P | R | PB |
| 18. | B | C | E | I | *Q* | PB |
| 19. | B | C | F | J | *Q* | PB |
| 20. | B | C | G | L | *Q* | PB |
| 21. | B | C | O | P | *Q* | PB |
| 22. | B | D | H | M | *Q* | PB |
| 23. | B | D | N | *Q* | R | PB |
| 24. | B | E | F | L | *Q* | PB |
| 25. | B | E | G | O | *Q* | PB |
| 26. | B | E | J | P | *Q* | PB |
| 27. | B | F | G | P | *Q* | PB |
| 28. | B | F | I | O | *Q* | PB |
| 29. | B | G | I | J | *Q* | PB |
| 30. | B | H | K | *Q* | R | PB |
| 31. | B | I | L | P | *Q* | PB |
| 32. | B | J | L | O | *Q* | PB |
| 33. | B | K | M | N | *Q* | PB |
| 34. | C | D | E | H | L | PB |
| 35. | C | D | G | H | I | PB |
| 36. | C | D | H | K | R | PB |
| 37. | C | E | F | L | M | PB |
| 38. | C | E | N | O | P | PB |
| 39. | C | F | I | K | N | PB |
| 40. | C | G | I | L | O | PB |
| 41. | C | G | J | K | P | PB |
| 42. | D | E | G | H | R | PB |
| 43. | D | E | H | I | K | PB |
| 44. | D | F | H | J | N | PB |
| 45. | D | F | H | M | O | PB |
| 46. | D | G | H | K | L | PB |
| 47. | D | H | I | L | R | PB |
| 48. | D | H | J | O | P | PB |
| 49. | D | H | M | N | P | PB |
| 50. | E | F | G | I | J | PB |
| 51. | E | I | K | M | P | PB |
| 52. | E | J | K | L | O | PB |
| 53. | F | G | L | N | P | PB |
| 54. | F | J | M | O | P | PB |
| 55. | G | K | M | N | O | PB |
| 56. | I | J | L | M | N | PB |



# POWERBALL BALANCED WHEEL® 53119PB

## Wheel 19 Numbers + PB in 66 Games for a 3 of 4 Win

With Powerball

| Numbers Matched | Maximum Wins | | | | | | Minimum Wins | | | | | |
|---|---|---|---|---|---|---|---|---|---|---|---|---|
| | 5 + 1 | 4 + 1 | 3 + 1 | 2 + 1 | 1 + 1 | 0 + 1 | 5 + 1 | 4 + 1 | 3 + 1 | 2 + 1 | 1 + 1 | 0 + 1 |
| 5 + 1 | 1 | 7 | 4 | 6 | 27 | 21 | 0 | 0 | 3 | 21 | 34 | 8 |
| 4 + 1 | - | 8 | 2 | 8 | 14 | 34 | - | 0 | 1 | 13 | 38 | 14 |
| 3 + 1 | - | - | 9 | 4 | 16 | 37 | - | - | 0 | 6 | 39 | 21 |
| 2 + 1 | - | - | - | 16 | 7 | 43 | - | - | - | 1 | 31 | 34 |
| 1 + 1 | - | - | - | - | 20 | 46 | - | - | - | - | 16 | 50 |
| 0 + 1 | - | - | - | - | - | 66 | - | - | - | - | - | 66 |

Without Powerball

| Numbers Matched | Maximum Wins | | | | | Minimum Wins | | | | |
|---|---|---|---|---|---|---|---|---|---|---|
| | 5 + 0 | 4 + 0 | 3 + 0 | 2 + 0 | 1 + 0 | 5 + 0 | 4 + 0 | 3 + 0 | 2 + 0 | 1 + 0 |
| 5 + 0 | 1 | 7 | 4 | 6 | 27 | 0 | 0 | 3 | 21 | 34 |
| 4 + 0 | - | 8 | 2 | 8 | 14 | - | 0 | 1 | 13 | 38 |
| 3 + 0 | - | - | 9 | 4 | 16 | - | - | 0 | 6 | 39 |
| 2 + 0 | - | - | - | 16 | 7 | - | - | - | 1 | 31 |
| 1 + 0 | - | - | - | - | 20 | - | - | - | - | 16 |

(Continued Next Page)

**POWERBALL BALANCED WHEEL® 53119PB** (Continued from previous page)

## Your 19 Numbers + PB to Wheel

| A | B | C | D | E | F | G | H | I | J |
|---|---|---|---|---|---|---|---|---|---|
| 20 | 19 | 17 | 18 | 17 | 17 | 19 | 17 | 18 | 17 |
| **K** | **L** | **M** | **N** | **O** | **P** | **Q** | **R** | **S** | **PB** |
| 17 | 17 | 18 | 17 | 17 | 17 | 16 | 16 | 16 | 66 |

## The 66 Games to Play

| | | | | | | |
|---|---|---|---|---|---|---|
| 1. | A | B | C | F | Q | PB |
| 2. | A | B | C | H | K | PB |
| 3. | A | B | C | J | R | PB |
| 4. | A | B | C | L | S | PB |
| 5. | A | B | D | F | K | PB |
| 6. | A | B | E | G | O | PB |
| 7. | A | B | E | H | Q | PB |
| 8. | A | B | E | J | K | PB |
| 9. | A | B | E | L | M | PB |
| 10. | A | B | E | N | P | PB |
| 11. | A | B | F | G | N | PB |
| 12. | A | B | F | J | L | PB |
| 13. | A | B | F | O | P | PB |
| 14. | A | B | G | H | P | PB |
| 15. | A | B | H | N | O | PB |
| 16. | A | B | H | R | S | PB |
| 17. | A | C | D | G | I | PB |
| 18. | A | C | F | I | M | PB |
| 19. | A | D | E | H | I | PB |
| 20. | A | G | J | M | N | PB |
| 21. | B | C | D | E | I | PB |
| 22. | B | C | D | H | M | PB |
| 23. | B | F | H | I | M | PB |
| 24. | C | E | F | G | M | PB |
| 25. | C | E | F | H | J | PB |
| 26. | C | E | F | H | L | PB |
| 27. | C | E | F | H | N | PB |
| 28. | C | E | F | H | O | PB |
| 29. | C | E | F | H | P | PB |
| 30. | C | E | F | H | Q | PB |
| 31. | C | E | F | H | R | PB |
| 32. | C | E | F | H | S | PB |
| 33. | D | G | I | J | R | PB |
| 34. | D | G | J | Q | S | PB |
| 35. | D | G | K | N | P | PB |
| 36. | D | G | L | M | O | PB |
| 37. | D | I | K | P | Q | PB |
| 38. | D | I | L | O | S | PB |
| 39. | D | I | M | N | R | PB |
| 40. | D | J | K | M | P | PB |
| 41. | D | J | L | N | O | PB |
| 42. | D | K | L | O | P | PB |
| 43. | D | K | P | R | S | PB |
| 44. | D | L | O | Q | R | PB |
| 45. | D | M | N | Q | S | PB |
| 46. | E | F | G | H | K | PB |
| 47. | G | I | J | L | P | PB |
| 48. | G | I | K | M | Q | PB |
| 49. | G | I | N | O | S | PB |
| 50. | G | J | K | L | S | PB |
| 51. | G | J | K | O | R | PB |
| 52. | G | J | O | P | Q | PB |
| 53. | G | L | N | Q | R | PB |
| 54. | G | M | P | R | S | PB |
| 55. | I | J | K | N | Q | PB |
| 56. | I | J | M | O | S | PB |
| 57. | I | K | L | Q | R | PB |
| 58. | I | K | O | Q | S | PB |



(Continued Next Page)

**POWERBALL BALANCED WHEEL® 53119PB** (Continued from previous page)

| | | | | | | | | | | | | | |
|---|---|---|---|---|---|---|---|---|---|---|---|---|---|
| 59. | I | L | M | N | P | PB | 63. | K | L | M | N | S | PB |
| 60. | I | O | P | R | S | PB | 64. | K | M | N | O | R | PB |
| 61. | J | L | M | Q | R | PB | 65. | L | P | Q | R | S | PB |
| 62. | J | N | P | R | S | PB | 66. | M | N | O | P | Q | PB |



# POWERBALL BALANCED WHEEL® 53120PB

## Wheel 20 Numbers + PB in 76 Games for a 3 of 4 Win

With Powerball

| Numbers Matched | Maximum Wins | | | | | | Minimum Wins | | | | | |
|---|---|---|---|---|---|---|---|---|---|---|---|---|
| | 5 + 1 | 4 + 1 | 3 + 1 | 2 + 1 | 1 + 1 | 0 + 1 | 5 + 1 | 4 + 1 | 3 + 1 | 2 + 1 | 1 + 1 | 0 + 1 |
| 5 + 1 | 1 | 0 | 7 | 5 | 30 | 33 | 0 | 0 | 3 | 18 | 33 | 22 |
| 4 + 1 | - | 1 | 7 | 0 | 20 | 48 | - | 0 | 1 | 12 | 30 | 33 |
| 3 + 1 | - | - | 8 | 0 | 0 | 68 | - | - | 0 | 6 | 37 | 33 |
| 2 + 1 | - | - | - | 8 | 0 | 68 | - | - | - | 0 | 28 | 48 |
| 1 + 1 | - | - | - | - | 21 | 55 | - | - | - | - | 8 | 68 |
| 0 + 1 | - | - | - | - | - | 76 | - | - | - | - | - | 76 |

Without Powerball

| Numbers Matched | Maximum Wins | | | | | Minimum Wins | | | | |
|---|---|---|---|---|---|---|---|---|---|---|
| | 5 + 0 | 4 + 0 | 3 + 0 | 2 + 0 | 1 + 0 | 5 + 0 | 4 + 0 | 3 + 0 | 2 + 0 | 1 + 0 |
| 5 + 0 | 1 | 0 | 7 | 5 | 30 | 0 | 0 | 3 | 18 | 33 |
| 4 + 0 | - | 1 | 7 | 0 | 20 | - | 0 | 1 | 12 | 30 |
| 3 + 0 | - | - | 8 | 0 | 0 | - | - | 0 | 6 | 37 |
| 2 + 0 | - | - | - | 8 | 0 | - | - | - | 0 | 28 |
| 1 + 0 | - | - | - | - | 21 | - | - | - | - | 8 |

## Your 20 Numbers + PB to Wheel

| A | B | C | D | E | F | G | H | I | J | K |
|---|---|---|---|---|---|---|---|---|---|---|
| 8 | 21 | 21 | 21 | 21 | 21 | 21 | 21 | 21 | 21 | 21 |

| L | M | N | O | P | Q | R | S | T | PB |
|---|---|---|---|---|---|---|---|---|---|
| 21 | 21 | 21 | 21 | 21 | 20 | 8 | 8 | 21 | 76 |

## The 76 Games to Play

| | | | | | | | | | | | | | |
|---|---|---|---|---|---|---|---|---|---|---|---|---|---|
| 1. | A | B | F | R | S | PB | 13. | B | C | I | O | P | PB |
| 2. | A | C | M | R | S | PB | 14. | B | D | F | M | O | PB |
| 3. | A | D | J | R | S | PB | 15. | B | D | G | H | P | PB |
| 4. | A | E | O | R | S | PB | 16. | B | D | I | K | N | PB |
| 5. | A | G | L | R | S | PB | 17. | B | D | J | L | T | PB |
| 6. | A | H | I | R | S | PB | 18. | B | E | F | J | P | PB |
| 7. | A | K | P | R | S | PB | 19. | B | E | G | K | M | PB |
| 8. | A | N | R | S | T | PB | 20. | B | E | H | I | L | PB |
| 9. | B | C | D | E | Q | PB | 21. | B | E | N | O | T | PB |
| 10. | B | C | F | K | L | PB | 22. | B | F | G | I | T | PB |
| 11. | B | C | G | J | N | PB | 23. | B | F | H | N | Q | PB |
| 12. | B | C | H | M | T | PB | 24. | B | G | L | O | Q | PB |



(Continued Next Page)

## POWERBALL BALANCED WHEEL® 53120PB (Continued from previous page)

| | | | | | | |
|---|---|---|---|---|---|---|
| 25. | B | H | J | K | O | PB |
| 26. | B | I | J | M | Q | PB |
| 27. | B | K | P | Q | T | PB |
| 28. | B | L | M | N | P | PB |
| 29. | C | D | F | N | T | PB |
| 30. | C | D | G | I | M | PB |
| 31. | C | D | H | L | O | PB |
| 32. | C | D | J | K | P | PB |
| 33. | C | E | F | G | O | PB |
| 34. | C | E | H | N | P | PB |
| 35. | C | E | I | K | T | PB |
| 36. | C | E | J | L | M | PB |
| 37. | C | F | H | I | J | PB |
| 38. | C | F | M | P | Q | PB |
| 39. | C | G | H | K | Q | PB |
| 40. | C | G | L | P | T | PB |
| 41. | C | I | L | N | Q | PB |
| 42. | C | J | O | Q | T | PB |
| 43. | C | K | M | N | O | PB |
| 44. | D | E | F | H | K | PB |
| 45. | D | E | G | L | N | PB |
| 46. | D | E | I | J | O | PB |
| 47. | D | E | M | P | T | PB |
| 48. | D | F | G | J | Q | PB |
| 49. | D | F | I | L | P | PB |
| 50. | D | G | K | O | T | PB |
| 51. | D | H | I | Q | T | PB |
| 52. | D | H | J | M | N | PB |
| 53. | D | K | L | M | Q | PB |
| 54. | D | N | O | P | Q | PB |
| 55. | E | F | I | M | N | PB |
| 56. | E | F | L | Q | T | PB |
| 57. | E | G | H | J | T | PB |
| 58. | E | G | I | P | Q | PB |
| 59. | E | H | M | O | Q | PB |
| 60. | E | J | K | N | Q | PB |
| 61. | E | K | L | O | P | PB |
| 62. | F | G | H | L | M | PB |
| 63. | F | G | K | N | P | PB |
| 64. | F | H | O | P | T | PB |
| 65. | F | I | K | O | Q | PB |
| 66. | F | J | K | M | T | PB |
| 67. | F | J | L | N | O | PB |
| 68. | G | H | I | N | O | PB |
| 69. | G | I | J | K | L | PB |
| 70. | G | J | M | O | P | PB |
| 71. | G | M | N | Q | T | PB |
| 72. | H | I | K | M | P | PB |
| 73. | H | J | L | P | Q | PB |
| 74. | H | K | L | N | T | PB |
| 75. | I | J | N | P | T | PB |
| 76. | I | L | M | O | T | PB |



# POWERBALL BALANCED WHEEL® 53121PB

## Wheel 21 Numbers + PB in 84 Games for a 3 of 4 Win

With Powerball

| Numbers Matched | Maximum Wins 5 + 1 | 4 + 1 | 3 + 1 | 2 + 1 | 1 + 1 | 0 + 1 | Minimum Wins 5 + 1 | 4 + 1 | 3 + 1 | 2 + 1 | 1 + 1 | 0 + 1 |
|---|---|---|---|---|---|---|---|---|---|---|---|---|
| 5 + 1 | 1 | 10 | 2 | 3 | 20 | 48 | 0 | 0 | 3 | 24 | 35 | 22 |
| 4 + 1 | - | 11 | 2 | 3 | 0 | 68 | - | 0 | 1 | 14 | 47 | 22 |
| 3 + 1 | - | - | 13 | 0 | 3 | 68 | - | - | 0 | 6 | 45 | 33 |
| 2 + 1 | - | - | - | 13 | 2 | 69 | - | - | - | 0 | 36 | 48 |
| 1 + 1 | - | - | - | - | 23 | 61 | - | - | - | - | 14 | 70 |
| 0 + 1 | - | - | - | - | - | 84 | - | - | - | - | - | 84 |

(Continued Next Page)

## POWERBALL BALANCED WHEEL® 53121PB (Continued from previous page)

Without Powerball

| Numbers Matched | Maximum Wins 5 + 0 | 4 + 0 | 3 + 0 | 2 + 0 | 1 + 0 | Minimum Wins 5 + 0 | 4 + 0 | 3 + 0 | 2 + 0 | 1 + 0 |
|---|---|---|---|---|---|---|---|---|---|---|
| 5 + 0 | 1 | 10 | 2 | 3 | 20 | 0 | 0 | 3 | 24 | 35 |
| 4 + 0 | - | 11 | 2 | 3 | 0 | - | 0 | 1 | 14 | 47 |
| 3 + 0 | - | - | 13 | 0 | 3 | - | - | 0 | 6 | 45 |
| 2 + 0 | - | - | - | 13 | 2 | - | - | - | 0 | 36 |
| 1 + 0 | - | - | - | - | 23 | - | - | - | - | 14 |

## Your 21 Numbers + PB to Wheel

| A | B | C | D | E | F | G | H | I | J | K |
|---|---|---|---|---|---|---|---|---|---|---|
| 14 | 14 | 21 | 21 | 21 | 21 | 21 | 21 | 21 | 21 | 21 |

| L | M | N | O | P | Q | R | S | T | U | PB |
|---|---|---|---|---|---|---|---|---|---|---|
| 23 | 21 | 22 | 22 | 22 | 22 | 22 | 21 | 14 | 14 | 84 |

## The 84 Games to Play

| | | | | | |
|---|---|---|---|---|---|
| 1. | A | B | C | T | U | PB |
| 2. | A | B | D | T | U | PB |
| 3. | A | B | E | T | U | PB |
| 4. | A | B | F | T | U | PB |
| 5. | A | B | G | T | U | PB |
| 6. | A | B | H | T | U | PB |
| 7. | A | B | I | T | U | PB |
| 8. | A | B | J | T | U | PB |
| 9. | A | B | K | T | U | PB |
| 10. | A | B | M | T | U | PB |
| 11. | A | B | P | Q | R | PB |
| 12. | A | B | S | T | U | PB |
| 13. | A | L | R | T | U | PB |
| 14. | A | P | Q | T | U | PB |
| 15. | B | L | N | O | T | PB |
| 16. | B | L | N | O | U | PB |
| 17. | C | D | E | F | S | PB |
| 18. | C | D | G | O | Q | PB |
| 19. | C | D | H | L | P | PB |
| 20. | C | D | I | K | M | PB |
| 21. | C | D | J | N | R | PB |
| 22. | C | E | G | L | N | PB |
| 23. | C | E | H | M | R | PB |
| 24. | C | E | I | J | Q | PB |
| 25. | C | E | K | O | P | PB |
| 26. | C | F | G | K | R | PB |
| 27. | C | F | H | J | O | PB |
| 28. | C | F | I | N | P | PB |
| 29. | C | F | L | M | Q | PB |
| 30. | C | G | H | I | S | PB |
| 31. | C | G | J | M | P | PB |
| 32. | C | H | K | N | Q | PB |
| 33. | C | I | L | O | R | PB |
| 34. | C | J | K | L | S | PB |
| 35. | C | M | N | O | S | PB |
| 36. | C | P | Q | R | S | PB |
| 37. | D | E | G | H | K | PB |
| 38. | D | E | I | P | R | PB |
| 39. | D | E | J | L | O | PB |
| 40. | D | E | M | N | Q | PB |
| 41. | D | F | G | I | J | PB |
| 42. | D | F | H | Q | R | PB |
| 43. | D | F | K | L | N | PB |
| 44. | D | F | M | O | P | PB |
| 45. | D | G | L | M | R | PB |
| 46. | D | G | N | P | S | PB |
| 47. | D | H | I | N | O | PB |
| 48. | D | H | J | M | S | PB |
| 49. | D | I | L | Q | S | PB |
| 50. | D | J | K | P | Q | PB |



(Continued Next Page)

**POWERBALL BALANCED WHEEL® 53121PB** (Continued from previous page)

| | | | | | | |
|---|---|---|---|---|---|---|
| 51. | D | K | O | R | S | PB |
| 52. | E | F | G | P | *Q* | PB |
| 53. | E | F | H | I | L | PB |
| 54. | E | F | J | K | M | PB |
| 55. | E | F | N | O | R | PB |
| 56. | E | G | I | M | O | PB |
| 57. | E | G | J | R | S | PB |
| 58. | E | H | J | N | P | PB |
| 59. | E | H | O | *Q* | S | PB |
| 60. | E | I | K | N | S | PB |
| 61. | E | K | L | *Q* | R | PB |
| 62. | E | L | M | P | S | PB |
| 63. | F | G | H | M | N | PB |
| 64. | F | G | L | O | S | PB |
| 65. | F | H | K | P | S | PB |
| 66. | F | I | K | O | *Q* | PB |
| 67. | F | I | M | R | S | PB |
| 68. | F | J | L | P | R | PB |
| 69. | F | J | N | *Q* | S | PB |
| 70. | G | H | J | L | *Q* | PB |
| 71. | G | H | O | P | R | PB |
| 72. | G | I | K | L | P | PB |
| 73. | G | I | N | *Q* | R | PB |
| 74. | G | J | K | N | O | PB |
| 75. | G | K | M | *Q* | S | PB |
| 76. | H | I | J | K | R | PB |
| 77. | H | I | M | P | *Q* | PB |
| 78. | H | K | L | M | O | PB |
| 79. | H | L | N | R | S | PB |
| 80. | I | J | L | M | N | PB |
| 81. | I | J | O | P | S | PB |
| 82. | J | M | O | *Q* | R | PB |
| 83. | K | M | N | P | R | PB |
| 84. | L | N | O | P | *Q* | PB |



# POWERBALL BALANCED WHEEL® 53122PB

## Wheel 22 Numbers + PB in 98 Games for a 3 of 4 Win

With Powerball

| Numbers Matched | Maximum Wins 5 + 1 | 4 + 1 | 3 + 1 | 2 + 1 | 1 + 1 | 0 + 1 | Minimum Wins 5 + 1 | 4 + 1 | 3 + 1 | 2 + 1 | 1 + 1 | 0 + 1 |
|---|---|---|---|---|---|---|---|---|---|---|---|---|
| 5 + 1 | 1 | 2 | 7 | 12 | 43 | 33 | 0 | 0 | 3 | 21 | 52 | 22 |
| 4 + 1 | - | 3 | 0 | 16 | 41 | 38 | - | 0 | 1 | 14 | 49 | 34 |
| 3 + 1 | - | - | 7 | 9 | 14 | 68 | - | - | 0 | 7 | 48 | 43 |
| 2 + 1 | - | - | - | 13 | 11 | 74 | - | - | - | 0 | 40 | 58 |
| 1 + 1 | - | - | - | - | 24 | 74 | - | - | - | - | 16 | 82 |
| 0 + 1 | - | - | - | - | - | 98 | - | - | - | - | - | 98 |

Without Powerball

| Numbers Matched | Maximum Wins 5 + 0 | 4 + 0 | 3 + 0 | 2 + 0 | 1 + 0 | Minimum Wins 5 + 0 | 4 + 0 | 3 + 0 | 2 + 0 | 1 + 0 |
|---|---|---|---|---|---|---|---|---|---|---|
| 5 + 0 | 1 | 2 | 7 | 12 | 43 | 0 | 0 | 3 | 21 | 52 |
| 4 + 0 | - | 3 | 0 | 16 | 41 | - | 0 | 1 | 14 | 49 |
| 3 + 0 | - | - | 7 | 9 | 14 | - | - | 0 | 7 | 48 |
| 2 + 0 | - | - | - | 13 | 11 | - | - | - | 0 | 40 |
| 1 + 0 | - | - | - | - | 24 | - | - | - | - | 16 |

(Continued Next Page)

**POWERBALL BALANCED WHEEL® 53122PB** (Continued from previous page)

## Your 22 Numbers + PB to Wheel

| A | B | C | D | E | F | G | H |
|---|---|---|---|---|---|---|---|
| 18 | 18 | 23 | 23 | 23 | 23 | 24 | 24 |
| **I** | **J** | **K** | **L** | **M** | **N** | **O** | **P** |
| 24 | 24 | 24 | 24 | 24 | 24 | 24 | 24 |
| **Q** | **R** | **S** | **T** | **U** | **V** | **PB** | |
| 24 | 24 | 19 | 16 | 17 | 22 | 98 | |

## The 98 Games to Play

| | | | | | | |
|---|---|---|---|---|---|---|
| 1. | A | B | E | T | U | PB |
| 2. | A | B | F | T | U | PB |
| 3. | A | B | G | N | S | PB |
| 4. | A | B | H | J | U | PB |
| 5. | A | B | I | K | U | PB |
| 6. | A | B | L | P | U | PB |
| 7. | A | B | M | O | S | PB |
| 8. | A | B | Q | R | S | PB |
| 9. | A | E | F | S | T | PB |
| 10. | A | G | N | S | T | PB |
| 11. | A | G | N | S | U | PB |
| 12. | A | H | J | S | T | PB |
| 13. | A | I | K | S | T | PB |
| 14. | A | L | P | S | T | PB |
| 15. | A | M | O | S | T | PB |
| 16. | A | M | O | S | U | PB |
| 17. | A | Q | R | S | T | PB |
| 18. | A | Q | R | S | U | PB |
| 19. | B | C | D | T | V | PB |
| 20. | B | C | E | F | S | PB |
| 21. | B | D | H | J | S | PB |
| 22. | B | G | N | T | U | PB |
| 23. | B | I | K | S | U | PB |
| 24. | B | I | K | T | U | PB |
| 25. | B | L | P | S | U | PB |
| 26. | B | L | P | T | U | PB |
| 27. | B | M | O | T | U | PB |
| 28. | B | Q | R | T | U | PB |
| 29. | C | D | E | J | Q | PB |
| 30. | C | D | F | H | R | PB |
| 31. | C | D | G | O | V | PB |
| 32. | C | D | I | N | P | PB |
| 33. | C | D | K | L | M | PB |
| 34. | C | D | S | U | V | PB |
| 35. | C | E | F | M | P | PB |
| 36. | C | E | G | H | N | PB |
| 37. | C | E | I | K | V | PB |
| 38. | C | E | L | O | R | PB |
| 39. | C | F | G | K | Q | PB |
| 40. | C | F | I | J | O | PB |
| 41. | C | F | L | N | V | PB |
| 42. | C | G | I | M | R | PB |
| 43. | C | G | J | L | P | PB |
| 44. | C | H | I | L | Q | PB |
| 45. | C | H | J | M | V | PB |
| 46. | C | H | K | O | P | PB |
| 47. | C | J | K | N | R | PB |
| 48. | C | M | N | O | Q | PB |
| 49. | C | P | Q | R | V | PB |
| 50. | D | E | F | K | O | PB |
| 51. | D | E | G | I | L | PB |
| 52. | D | E | H | P | V | PB |
| 53. | D | E | M | N | R | PB |
| 54. | D | F | G | J | N | PB |
| 55. | D | F | I | M | V | PB |
| 56. | D | F | L | P | Q | PB |

(Continued Next Page)

## POWERBALL BALANCED WHEEL® 53122PB (Continued from previous page)

| | | | | | | |
|---|---|---|---|---|---|---|
| 57. | D | G | H | M | Q | PB |
| 58. | D | G | K | P | R | PB |
| 59. | D | H | I | J | K | PB |
| 60. | D | H | L | N | O | PB |
| 61. | D | I | O | Q | R | PB |
| 62. | D | J | L | R | V | PB |
| 63. | D | J | M | O | P | PB |
| 64. | D | K | N | Q | V | PB |
| 65. | E | F | G | R | V | PB |
| 66. | E | F | H | J | L | PB |
| 67. | E | F | I | N | Q | PB |
| 68. | E | G | J | K | M | PB |
| 69. | E | G | O | P | Q | PB |
| 70. | E | H | I | M | O | PB |
| 71. | E | H | K | Q | R | PB |
| 72. | E | I | J | P | R | PB |
| 73. | E | J | N | O | V | PB |
| 74. | E | K | L | N | P | PB |
| 75. | E | L | M | Q | V | PB |
| 76. | F | G | H | I | P | PB |
| 77. | F | G | L | M | O | PB |
| 78. | F | H | K | M | N | PB |
| 79. | F | H | O | Q | V | PB |
| 80. | F | I | K | L | R | PB |
| 81. | F | J | K | P | V | PB |
| 82. | F | J | M | Q | R | PB |
| 83. | F | N | O | P | R | PB |
| 84. | G | H | J | O | R | PB |
| 85. | G | H | K | L | V | PB |
| 86. | G | I | J | Q | V | PB |
| 87. | G | I | K | N | O | PB |
| 88. | G | L | N | Q | R | PB |
| 89. | G | M | N | P | V | PB |
| 90. | H | I | N | R | V | PB |
| 91. | H | J | N | P | Q | PB |
| 92. | H | J | S | T | U | PB |
| 93. | H | L | M | P | R | PB |
| 94. | I | J | L | M | N | PB |
| 95. | I | K | M | P | Q | PB |
| 96. | I | L | O | P | V | PB |
| 97. | J | K | L | O | Q | PB |
| 98. | K | M | O | R | V | PB |



# POWERBALL BALANCED WHEEL® 53124PB

## Wheel 24 Numbers + PB in 129 Games for a 3 of 4 Win

With Powerball

| Numbers | Maximum Wins | | | | | | Minimum Wins | | | | | |
|---|---|---|---|---|---|---|---|---|---|---|---|---|
| Matched | 5 + 1 | 4 + 1 | 3 + 1 | 2 + 1 | 1 + 1 | 0 + 1 | 5 + 1 | 4 + 1 | 3 + 1 | 2 + 1 | 1 + 1 | 0 + 1 |
| 5 + 1 | 1 | 1 | 8 | 30 | 39 | 50 | 0 | 0 | 3 | 29 | 63 | 34 |
| 4 + 1 | - | 2 | 7 | 25 | 25 | 70 | - | 0 | 1 | 19 | 63 | 46 |
| 3 + 1 | - | - | 5 | 13 | 37 | 74 | - | - | 0 | 9 | 60 | 60 |
| 2 + 1 | - | - | - | 11 | 30 | 88 | - | - | - | 1 | 51 | 77 |
| 1 + 1 | - | - | - | - | 30 | 99 | - | - | - | - | 25 | 104 |
| 0 + 1 | - | - | - | - | - | 129 | - | - | - | - | - | 129 |

Without Powerball

| Numbers | Maximum Wins | | | | | Minimum Wins | | | | |
|---|---|---|---|---|---|---|---|---|---|---|
| Matched | 5 + 0 | 4 + 0 | 3 + 0 | 2 + 0 | 1 + 0 | 5 + 0 | 4 + 0 | 3 + 0 | 2 + 0 | 1 + 0 |
| 5 + 0 | 1 | 1 | 8 | 30 | 39 | 0 | 0 | 3 | 29 | 63 |
| 4 + 0 | - | 2 | 7 | 25 | 25 | - | 0 | 1 | 19 | 63 |
| 3 + 0 | - | - | 5 | 13 | 37 | - | - | 0 | 9 | 60 |
| 2 + 0 | - | - | - | 11 | 30 | - | - | - | 1 | 51 |
| 1 + 0 | - | - | - | - | 30 | - | - | - | - | 25 |

(Continued Next Page)

**POWERBALL BALANCED WHEEL® 53124PB** (Continued from previous page)

## Your 24 Numbers + PB to Wheel

| A | B | C | D | E | F | G | H | I |
|---|---|---|---|---|---|---|---|---|
| 27 | 26 | 27 | 27 | 27 | 27 | 27 | 27 | 27 |
| **J** | **K** | **L** | **M** | **N** | **O** | **P** | **Q** | **R** |
| 26 | 26 | 26 | 27 | 25 | 26 | 25 | 26 | 30 |
| **S** | **T** | **U** | **V** | **W** | **X** | **PB** | | |
| 29 | 28 | 28 | 27 | 27 | 27 | 129 | | |

## The 129 Games to Play

| | | | | | | |
|---|---|---|---|---|---|---|
| 1. | A | B | H | I | Q | PB |
| 2. | A | B | H | K | P | PB |
| 3. | A | B | H | N | O | PB |
| 4. | A | C | D | V | X | PB |
| 5. | A | C | E | M | S | PB |
| 6. | A | C | F | H | W | PB |
| 7. | A | C | G | L | U | PB |
| 8. | A | C | J | R | T | PB |
| 9. | A | D | E | F | U | PB |
| 10. | A | D | G | R | W | PB |
| 11. | A | D | H | J | S | PB |
| 12. | A | D | L | M | T | PB |
| 13. | A | E | G | J | V | PB |
| 14. | A | E | H | L | R | PB |
| 15. | A | E | T | W | X | PB |
| 16. | A | F | G | S | T | PB |
| 17. | A | F | J | L | X | PB |
| 18. | A | F | M | R | V | PB |
| 19. | A | G | H | M | X | PB |
| 20. | A | H | N | P | Q | PB |
| 21. | A | H | T | U | V | PB |
| 22. | A | I | K | N | W | PB |
| 23. | A | I | O | P | T | PB |
| 24. | A | J | M | U | W | PB |
| 25. | A | K | O | Q | X | PB |
| 26. | A | L | S | V | W | PB |
| 27. | A | R | S | U | X | PB |
| 28. | B | C | G | I | O | PB |
| 29. | B | C | K | N | R | PB |
| 30. | B | C | P | Q | T | PB |
| 31. | B | D | I | P | S | PB |
| 32. | B | D | K | N | U | PB |
| 33. | B | D | O | Q | R | PB |
| 34. | B | E | F | I | N | PB |
| 35. | B | E | I | L | X | PB |
| 36. | B | E | J | K | Q | PB |
| 37. | B | E | N | P | R | PB |
| 38. | B | F | I | K | T | PB |
| 39. | B | F | J | N | P | PB |
| 40. | B | F | Q | S | X | PB |
| 41. | B | G | K | P | W | PB |
| 42. | B | G | N | Q | W | PB |
| 43. | B | I | J | Q | R | PB |
| 44. | B | I | N | O | W | PB |
| 45. | B | I | N | U | V | PB |
| 46. | B | K | L | O | V | PB |
| 47. | B | K | Q | R | U | PB |
| 48. | B | M | O | P | X | PB |
| 49. | B | N | O | S | T | PB |
| 50. | B | O | P | S | U | PB |
| 51. | C | D | E | J | W | PB |
| 52. | C | D | F | L | S | PB |
| 53. | C | D | G | H | T | PB |
| 54. | C | D | M | R | U | PB |
| 55. | C | E | F | G | R | PB |
| 56. | C | E | H | U | X | PB |



(Continued Next Page)

**POWERBALL BALANCED WHEEL® 53124PB** (Continued from previous page)

| | | | | | | |
|---|---|---|---|---|---|---|
| 57. | C | E | L | T | V | PB |
| 58. | C | F | J | U | V | PB |
| 59. | C | F | M | T | X | PB |
| 60. | C | G | J | S | X | PB |
| 61. | C | G | M | V | W | PB |
| 62. | C | H | J | L | M | PB |
| 63. | C | H | R | S | V | PB |
| 64. | C | I | K | L | *Q* | PB |
| 65. | C | I | N | P | T | PB |
| 66. | C | K | O | P | R | PB |
| 67. | C | L | R | W | X | PB |
| 68. | C | N | O | *Q* | V | PB |
| 69. | C | S | T | U | W | PB |
| 70. | D | E | G | L | X | PB |
| 71. | D | E | H | M | V | PB |
| 72. | D | E | R | S | T | PB |
| 73. | D | F | G | J | M | PB |
| 74. | D | F | H | R | X | PB |
| 75. | D | F | T | V | W | PB |
| 76. | D | G | N | O | P | PB |
| 77. | D | G | S | U | V | PB |
| 78. | D | H | L | U | W | PB |
| 79. | D | I | K | O | V | PB |
| 80. | D | I | N | *Q* | T | PB |
| 81. | D | J | L | R | V | PB |
| 82. | D | J | T | U | X | PB |
| 83. | D | K | P | *Q* | S | PB |
| 84. | D | M | S | W | X | PB |
| 85. | E | F | H | J | T | PB |
| 86. | E | F | L | M | W | PB |
| 87. | E | F | S | V | X | PB |
| 88. | E | G | H | S | W | PB |
| 89. | E | G | M | T | U | PB |
| 90. | E | I | P | *Q* | R | PB |
| 91. | E | J | L | S | U | PB |

| | | | | | | |
|---|---|---|---|---|---|---|
| 92. | E | J | M | R | X | PB |
| 93. | E | K | O | P | T | PB |
| 94. | E | N | O | *Q* | R | PB |
| 95. | E | R | U | V | W | PB |
| 96. | F | G | H | L | V | PB |
| 97. | F | G | U | W | X | PB |
| 98. | F | H | M | S | U | PB |
| 99. | F | I | K | O | P | PB |
| 100. | F | I | M | *Q* | U | PB |
| 101. | F | J | R | S | W | PB |
| 102. | F | L | R | T | U | PB |
| 103. | F | N | O | *Q* | U | PB |
| 104. | G | H | I | K | N | PB |
| 105. | G | H | J | R | U | PB |
| 106. | G | H | K | O | *Q* | PB |
| 107. | G | I | P | *Q* | W | PB |
| 108. | G | J | L | T | W | PB |
| 109. | G | L | M | R | S | PB |
| 110. | G | R | T | V | X | PB |
| 111. | H | I | O | P | R | PB |
| 112. | H | J | V | W | X | PB |
| 113. | H | L | S | T | X | PB |
| 114. | H | M | R | T | W | PB |
| 115. | I | J | K | N | X | PB |
| 116. | I | J | O | P | W | PB |
| 117. | I | K | M | O | S | PB |
| 118. | I | K | O | P | U | PB |
| 119. | I | K | *Q* | V | X | PB |
| 120. | I | M | N | R | S | PB |
| 121. | J | L | N | O | *Q* | PB |
| 122. | J | M | S | T | V | PB |
| 123. | K | L | M | N | P | PB |
| 124. | K | M | O | *Q* | T | PB |
| 125. | K | N | P | S | V | PB |
| 126. | K | O | *Q* | S | W | PB |



(Continued Next Page)

**POWERBALL BALANCED WHEEL® 53124PB** (Continued from previous page)

| | | | | | | |
|---|---|---|---|---|---|---|
| 127. | L | M | P | Q | V | PB |
| 128. | L | M | U | V | X | PB |
| 129. | N | P | Q | U | X | PB |



# POWERBALL BALANCED WHEEL® 53006PB

## Wheel 6 Numbers + PB in 4 Games for a 3 of 3 Win

With Powerball

| Numbers Matched | Maximum Wins 5 + 1 | 4 + 1 | 3 + 1 | 2 + 1 | 1 + 1 | 0 + 1 | Minimum Wins 5 + 1 | 4 + 1 | 3 + 1 | 2 + 1 | 1 + 1 | 0 + 1 |
|---|---|---|---|---|---|---|---|---|---|---|---|---|
| 5 + 1 | 1 | 3 | 0 | 0 | 0 | 0 | 0 | 4 | 0 | 0 | 0 | 0 |
| 4 + 1 | - | 2 | 2 | 0 | 0 | 0 | - | 0 | 4 | 0 | 0 | 0 |
| 3 + 1 | - | - | 3 | 1 | 0 | 0 | - | - | 1 | 3 | 0 | 0 |
| 2 + 1 | - | - | - | 4 | 0 | 0 | - | - | - | 2 | 2 | 0 |
| 1 + 1 | - | - | - | - | 4 | 0 | - | - | - | - | 3 | 1 |
| 0 + 1 | - | - | - | - | - | 4 | - | - | - | - | - | 4 |

Without Powerball

| Numbers Matched | Maximum Wins 5 + 0 | 4 + 0 | 3 + 0 | 2 + 0 | 1 + 0 | Minimum Wins 5 + 0 | 4 + 0 | 3 + 0 | 2 + 0 | 1 + 0 |
|---|---|---|---|---|---|---|---|---|---|---|
| 5 + 0 | 1 | 3 | 0 | 0 | 0 | 0 | 4 | 0 | 0 | 0 |
| 4 + 0 | - | 2 | 2 | 0 | 0 | - | 0 | 4 | 0 | 0 |
| 3 + 0 | - | - | 3 | 1 | 0 | - | - | 1 | 3 | 0 |
| 2 + 0 | - | - | - | 4 | 0 | - | - | - | 2 | 2 |
| 1 + 0 | - | - | - | - | 4 | - | - | - | - | 3 |

## Your 6 Numbers + PB to Wheel

| A | B | C | D | E | F | PB |
|---|---|---|---|---|---|---|
| 4 | 3 | 3 | 3 | 3 | 4 | 4 |

## The 4 Games to Play

| | | | | | | |
|---|---|---|---|---|---|---|
| 1. | A | B | C | D | F | PB |
| 2. | A | B | C | E | F | PB |
| 3. | A | B | D | E | F | PB |
| 4. | A | C | D | E | F | PB |



# POWERBALL BALANCED WHEEL® 53007PB

## Wheel 7 Numbers + PB in 5 Games for a 3 of 3 Win

With Powerball

| Numbers Matched | Maximum Wins 5 + 1 | 4 + 1 | 3 + 1 | 2 + 1 | 1 + 1 | 0 + 1 | Minimum Wins 5 + 1 | 4 + 1 | 3 + 1 | 2 + 1 | 1 + 1 | 0 + 1 |
|---|---|---|---|---|---|---|---|---|---|---|---|---|
| 5 + 1 | 1 | 2 | 2 | 0 | 0 | 0 | 0 | 2 | 3 | 0 | 0 | 0 |
| 4 + 1 | - | 3 | 0 | 2 | 0 | 0 | - | 0 | 4 | 1 | 0 | 0 |
| 3 + 1 | - | - | 3 | 1 | 1 | 0 | - | - | 1 | 3 | 1 | 0 |
| 2 + 1 | - | - | - | 4 | 0 | 1 | - | - | - | 2 | 2 | 1 |
| 1 + 1 | - | - | - | - | 4 | 1 | - | - | - | - | 3 | 2 |
| 0 + 1 | - | - | - | - | - | 5 | - | - | - | - | - | 5 |

Without Powerball

| Numbers Matched | Maximum Wins 5 + 0 | 4 + 0 | 3 + 0 | 2 + 0 | 1 + 0 | Minimum Wins 5 + 0 | 4 + 0 | 3 + 0 | 2 + 0 | 1 + 0 |
|---|---|---|---|---|---|---|---|---|---|---|
| 5 + 0 | 1 | 2 | 2 | 0 | 0 | 0 | 2 | 3 | 0 | 0 |
| 4 + 0 | - | 3 | 0 | 2 | 0 | - | 0 | 4 | 1 | 0 |
| 3 + 0 | - | - | 3 | 1 | 1 | - | - | 1 | 3 | 1 |
| 2 + 0 | - | - | - | 4 | 0 | - | - | - | 2 | 2 |
| 1 + 0 | - | - | - | - | 4 | - | - | - | - | 3 |

(Continued Next Page)

**POWERBALL BALANCED WHEEL® 53007PB** (Continued from previous page)

## Your 7 Numbers + PB to Wheel

| A | B | C | D | E | F | G | PB |
|---|---|---|---|---|---|---|---|
| 4 | 4 | 3 | 3 | 3 | 4 | 4 | 5 |

## The 5 Games to Play

| # | | | | | | |
|---|---|---|---|---|---|---|
| 1. | A | B | C | F | G | PB |
| 2. | A | B | D | F | G | PB |
| 3. | A | B | E | F | G | PB |
| 4. | A | C | D | E | G | PB |
| 5. | B | C | D | E | F | PB |



# POWERBALL BALANCED WHEEL® 53008PB

## Wheel 8 Numbers + PB in 8 Games for a 3 of 3 Win

With Powerball

| Numbers Matched | Maximum Wins 5 + 1 | 4 + 1 | 3 + 1 | 2 + 1 | 1 + 1 | 0 + 1 | Minimum Wins 5 + 1 | 4 + 1 | 3 + 1 | 2 + 1 | 1 + 1 | 0 + 1 |
|---|---|---|---|---|---|---|---|---|---|---|---|---|
| 5 + 1 | 1 | 0 | 6 | 1 | 0 | 0 | 0 | 2 | 5 | 1 | 0 | 0 |
| 4 + 1 | - | 1 | 3 | 3 | 1 | 0 | - | 0 | 4 | 4 | 0 | 0 |
| 3 + 1 | - | - | 2 | 3 | 3 | 0 | - | - | 1 | 5 | 2 | 0 |
| 2 + 1 | - | - | - | 3 | 4 | 1 | - | - | - | 2 | 6 | 0 |
| 1 + 1 | - | - | - | - | 5 | 3 | - | - | - | - | 5 | 3 |
| 0 + 1 | - | - | - | - | - | 8 | - | - | - | - | - | 8 |

Without Powerball

| Numbers Matched | Maximum Wins 5 + 0 | 4 + 0 | 3 + 0 | 2 + 0 | 1 + 0 | Minimum Wins 5 + 0 | 4 + 0 | 3 + 0 | 2 + 0 | 1 + 0 |
|---|---|---|---|---|---|---|---|---|---|---|
| 5 + 0 | 1 | 0 | 6 | 1 | 0 | 0 | 2 | 5 | 1 | 0 |
| 4 + 0 | - | 1 | 3 | 3 | 1 | - | 0 | 4 | 4 | 0 |
| 3 + 0 | - | - | 2 | 3 | 3 | - | - | 1 | 5 | 2 |
| 2 + 0 | - | - | - | 3 | 4 | - | - | - | 2 | 6 |
| 1 + 0 | - | - | - | - | 5 | - | - | - | - | 5 |

## Your 8 Numbers + PB to Wheel

| A | B | C | D | E | F | G | H | PB |
|---|---|---|---|---|---|---|---|---|
| 5 | 5 | 5 | 5 | 5 | 5 | 5 | 5 | 8 |

## The 8 Games to Play

| # | | | | | | |
|---|---|---|---|---|---|---|
| 1. | A | B | C | F | H | PB |
| 2. | A | B | D | E | H | PB |
| 3. | A | B | E | F | G | PB |
| 4. | A | C | D | E | G | PB |
| 5. | A | D | F | G | H | PB |
| 6. | B | C | D | F | G | PB |
| 7. | B | C | E | G | H | PB |
| 8. | C | D | E | F | H | PB |

# POWERBALL BALANCED WHEEL® 53009PB

## Wheel 9 Numbers + PB in 12 Games for a 3 of 3 Win

With Powerball

| Numbers Matched | Maximum Wins | | | | | | Minimum Wins | | | | | |
|---|---|---|---|---|---|---|---|---|---|---|---|---|
| | 5 + 1 | 4 + 1 | 3 + 1 | 2 + 1 | 1 + 1 | 0 + 1 | 5 + 1 | 4 + 1 | 3 + 1 | 2 + 1 | 1 + 1 | 0 + 1 |
| 5 + 1 | 1 | 1 | 5 | 5 | 0 | 0 | 0 | 0 | 10 | 1 | 1 | 0 |
| 4 + 1 | - | 2 | 2 | 6 | 2 | 0 | - | 0 | 4 | 6 | 2 | 0 |
| 3 + 1 | - | - | 3 | 4 | 4 | 1 | - | - | 1 | 6 | 4 | 1 |
| 2 + 1 | - | - | - | 5 | 4 | 3 | - | - | - | 3 | 6 | 3 |
| 1 + 1 | - | - | - | - | 7 | 5 | - | - | - | - | 6 | 6 |
| 0 + 1 | - | - | - | - | - | 12 | - | - | - | - | - | 12 |

Without Powerball

| Numbers Matched | Maximum Wins | | | | | Minimum Wins | | | | |
|---|---|---|---|---|---|---|---|---|---|---|
| | 5 + 0 | 4 + 0 | 3 + 0 | 2 + 0 | 1 + 0 | 5 + 0 | 4 + 0 | 3 + 0 | 2 + 0 | 1 + 0 |
| 5 + 0 | 1 | 1 | 5 | 5 | 0 | 0 | 0 | 10 | 1 | 1 |
| 4 + 0 | - | 2 | 2 | 6 | 2 | - | 0 | 4 | 6 | 2 |
| 3 + 0 | - | - | 3 | 4 | 4 | - | - | 1 | 6 | 4 |
| 2 + 0 | - | - | - | 5 | 4 | - | - | - | 3 | 6 |
| 1 + 0 | - | - | - | - | 7 | - | - | - | - | 6 |

## Your 9 Numbers + PB to Wheel

| A | B | C | D | E | F | G | H | I | PB |
|---|---|---|---|---|---|---|---|---|---|
| 7 | 7 | 7 | 6 | 6 | 7 | 6 | 7 | 7 | 12 |

## The 12 Games to Play

| | | | | | | |
|---|---|---|---|---|---|---|
| 1. | A | B | C | G | I | PB |
| 2. | A | B | D | F | H | PB |
| 3. | A | B | E | F | H | PB |
| 4. | A | C | D | H | I | PB |
| 5. | A | C | E | F | I | PB |
| 6. | A | D | E | G | H | PB |
| 7. | A | F | G | H | I | PB |
| 8. | B | C | D | F | I | PB |
| 9. | B | C | E | H | I | PB |
| 10. | B | C | F | G | H | PB |
| 11. | B | D | E | G | I | PB |
| 12. | C | D | E | F | G | PB |



# POWERBALL BALANCED WHEEL® 53010PB

## Wheel 10 Numbers + PB in 17 Games for a 3 of 3 Win

With Powerball

| Numbers Matched | Maximum Wins | | | | | | Minimum Wins | | | | | |
|---|---|---|---|---|---|---|---|---|---|---|---|---|
| | 5 + 1 | 4 + 1 | 3 + 1 | 2 + 1 | 1 + 1 | 0 + 1 | 5 + 1 | 4 + 1 | 3 + 1 | 2 + 1 | 1 + 1 | 0 + 1 |
| 5 + 1 | 1 | 2 | 4 | 8 | 2 | 0 | 0 | 0 | 10 | 5 | 2 | 0 |
| 4 + 1 | - | 2 | 3 | 6 | 6 | 0 | - | 0 | 4 | 8 | 5 | 0 |
| 3 + 1 | - | - | 4 | 2 | 10 | 1 | - | - | 1 | 6 | 9 | 1 |
| 2 + 1 | - | - | - | 6 | 6 | 5 | - | - | - | 3 | 10 | 4 |
| 1 + 1 | - | - | - | - | 9 | 8 | - | - | - | - | 8 | 9 |
| 0 + 1 | - | - | - | - | - | 17 | - | - | - | - | - | 17 |

Without Powerball

| Numbers Matched | Maximum Wins | | | | | Minimum Wins | | | | |
|---|---|---|---|---|---|---|---|---|---|---|
| | 5 + 0 | 4 + 0 | 3 + 0 | 2 + 0 | 1 + 0 | 5 + 0 | 4 + 0 | 3 + 0 | 2 + 0 | 1 + 0 |
| 5 + 0 | 1 | 2 | 4 | 8 | 2 | 0 | 0 | 10 | 5 | 2 |
| 4 + 0 | - | 2 | 3 | 6 | 6 | - | 0 | 4 | 8 | 5 |
| 3 + 0 | - | - | 4 | 2 | 10 | - | - | 1 | 6 | 9 |
| 2 + 0 | - | - | - | 6 | 6 | - | - | - | 3 | 10 |
| 1 + 0 | - | - | - | - | 9 | - | - | - | - | 8 |

(Continued Next Page)

**POWERBALL BALANCED WHEEL® 53010PB** (Continued from previous page)

## Your 10 Numbers + PB to Wheel

| A | B | C | D | E | F | G | H | I | J | PB |
|---|---|---|---|---|---|---|---|---|---|---|
| 9 | 9 | 8 | 9 | 8 | 8 | 9 | 8 | 9 | 8 | 17 |

## The 17 Games to Play

| | | | | | | |
|---|---|---|---|---|---|---|
| 1. | A | B | C | G | H | PB |
| 2. | A | B | D | E | H | PB |
| 3. | A | B | F | H | I | PB |
| 4. | A | B | G | I | J | PB |
| 5. | A | C | D | E | I | PB |
| 6. | A | C | F | I | J | PB |
| 7. | A | D | E | F | G | PB |
| 8. | A | D | E | I | J | PB |
| 9. | A | D | H | I | J | PB |
| 10. | B | C | D | G | J | PB |
| 11. | B | C | E | F | I | PB |
| 12. | B | D | F | G | I | PB |
| 13. | B | D | F | G | J | PB |
| 14. | B | E | G | H | J | PB |
| 15. | C | D | F | G | H | PB |
| 16. | C | E | F | H | J | PB |
| 17. | C | E | G | H | I | PB |



# POWERBALL BALANCED WHEEL® 53011PB

## Wheel 11 Numbers + PB in 20 Games for a 3 of 3 Win

With Powerball

| Numbers Matched | Maximum Wins | | | | | | Minimum Wins | | | | | |
|---|---|---|---|---|---|---|---|---|---|---|---|---|
| | 5 + 1 | 4 + 1 | 3 + 1 | 2 + 1 | 1 + 1 | 0 + 1 | 5 + 1 | 4 + 1 | 3 + 1 | 2 + 1 | 1 + 1 | 0 + 1 |
| 5 + 1 | 1 | 0 | 6 | 10 | 3 | 0 | 0 | 0 | 10 | 6 | 4 | 0 |
| 4 + 1 | - | 1 | 4 | 6 | 8 | 1 | - | 0 | 4 | 8 | 8 | 0 |
| 3 + 1 | - | - | 4 | 0 | 16 | 0 | - | - | 1 | 7 | 10 | 2 |
| 2 + 1 | - | - | - | 4 | 11 | 5 | - | - | - | 3 | 12 | 5 |
| 1 + 1 | - | - | - | - | 10 | 10 | - | - | - | - | 9 | 11 |
| 0 + 1 | - | - | - | - | - | 20 | - | - | - | - | - | 20 |

Without Powerball

| Numbers Matched | Maximum Wins | | | | | Minimum Wins | | | | |
|---|---|---|---|---|---|---|---|---|---|---|
| | 5 + 0 | 4 + 0 | 3 + 0 | 2 + 0 | 1 + 0 | 5 + 0 | 4 + 0 | 3 + 0 | 2 + 0 | 1 + 0 |
| 5 + 0 | 1 | 0 | 6 | 10 | 3 | 0 | 0 | 10 | 6 | 4 |
| 4 + 0 | - | 1 | 4 | 6 | 8 | - | 0 | 4 | 8 | 8 |
| 3 + 0 | - | - | 4 | 0 | 16 | - | - | 1 | 7 | 10 |
| 2 + 0 | - | - | - | 4 | 11 | - | - | - | 3 | 12 |
| 1 + 0 | - | - | - | - | 10 | - | - | - | - | 9 |

## Your 11 Numbers + PB to Wheel

| A | B | C | D | E | F |
|---|---|---|---|---|---|
| 9 | 9 | 9 | 9 | 10 | 9 |

| G | H | I | J | K | PB |
|---|---|---|---|---|---|
| 9 | 9 | 9 | 9 | 9 | 20 |

## The 20 Games to Play

| | | | | | | |
|---|---|---|---|---|---|---|
| 1. | A | B | C | H | J | PB |
| 2. | A | B | D | G | K | PB |
| 3. | A | B | E | F | I | PB |
| 4. | A | C | D | F | J | PB |
| 5. | A | C | E | G | I | PB |
| 6. | A | C | F | H | K | PB |



(Continued Next Page)

**POWERBALL BALANCED WHEEL® 53011PB** (Continued from previous page)

| | | | | | | |
|---|---|---|---|---|---|---|
| 7. | A | D | E | H | I | PB |
| 8. | A | E | I | J | K | PB |
| 9. | A | F | G | H | J | PB |
| 10. | B | C | D | I | K | PB |
| 11. | B | C | E | F | G | PB |
| 12. | B | D | E | F | H | PB |
| 13. | B | D | G | I | J | PB |
| 14. | B | E | F | J | K | PB |
| 15. | B | G | H | I | K | PB |
| 16. | C | D | E | G | H | PB |
| 17. | C | E | G | J | K | PB |
| 18. | C | F | H | I | J | PB |
| 19. | D | E | H | J | K | PB |
| 20. | D | F | G | I | K | PB |



# POWERBALL BALANCED WHEEL® 53012PB

## Wheel 12 Numbers + PB in 29 Games for a 3 of 3 Win

With Powerball

| Numbers Matched | Maximum Wins 5 + 1 | 4 + 1 | 3 + 1 | 2 + 1 | 1 + 1 | 0 + 1 | Minimum Wins 5 + 1 | 4 + 1 | 3 + 1 | 2 + 1 | 1 + 1 | 0 + 1 |
|---|---|---|---|---|---|---|---|---|---|---|---|---|
| 5 + 1 | 1 | 1 | 7 | 12 | 8 | 0 | 0 | 0 | 10 | 11 | 7 | 1 |
| 4 + 1 | - | 2 | 3 | 9 | 15 | 0 | - | 0 | 4 | 12 | 11 | 2 |
| 3 + 1 | - | - | 5 | 1 | 20 | 3 | - | - | 1 | 9 | 14 | 5 |
| 2 + 1 | - | - | - | 6 | 14 | 9 | - | - | - | 4 | 15 | 10 |
| 1 + 1 | - | - | - | - | 13 | 16 | - | - | - | - | 11 | 18 |
| 0 + 1 | - | - | - | - | - | 29 | - | - | - | - | - | 29 |

Without Powerball

| Numbers Matched | Maximum Wins 5 + 0 | 4 + 0 | 3 + 0 | 2 + 0 | 1 + 0 | Minimum Wins 5 + 0 | 4 + 0 | 3 + 0 | 2 + 0 | 1 + 0 |
|---|---|---|---|---|---|---|---|---|---|---|
| 5 + 0 | 1 | 1 | 7 | 12 | 8 | 0 | 0 | 10 | 11 | 7 |
| 4 + 0 | - | 2 | 3 | 9 | 15 | - | 0 | 4 | 12 | 11 |
| 3 + 0 | - | - | 5 | 1 | 20 | - | - | 1 | 9 | 14 |
| 2 + 0 | - | - | - | 6 | 14 | - | - | - | 4 | 15 |
| 1 + 0 | - | - | - | - | 13 | - | - | - | - | 11 |

## Your 12 Numbers + PB to Wheel

| A | B | C | D | E | F | G |
|---|---|---|---|---|---|---|
| 12 | 12 | 12 | 11 | 12 | 13 | 13 |

| H | I | J | K | L | PB |
|---|---|---|---|---|---|
| 12 | 12 | 12 | 12 | 12 | 29 |

## The 29 Games to Play

| | | | | | | |
|---|---|---|---|---|---|---|
| 1. | A | B | C | H | K | PB |
| 2. | A | B | D | I | K | PB |
| 3. | A | B | E | H | J | PB |
| 4. | A | B | F | G | L | PB |
| 5. | A | C | D | K | L | PB |
| 6. | A | C | E | I | L | PB |
| 7. | A | C | F | G | J | PB |
| 8. | A | D | E | G | J | PB |
| 9. | A | D | F | H | L | PB |
| 10. | A | E | F | G | K | PB |
| 11. | A | F | G | H | I | PB |
| 12. | A | I | J | K | L | PB |
| 13. | B | C | D | F | J | PB |
| 14. | B | C | D | G | H | PB |
| 15. | B | C | E | F | L | PB |
| 16. | B | C | G | I | J | PB |
| 17. | B | D | E | J | L | PB |
| 18. | B | E | G | I | K | PB |



(Continued Next Page)

**POWERBALL BALANCED WHEEL® 53012PB** (Continued from previous page)

| | | | | | | |
|---|---|---|---|---|---|---|
| 19. | B | F | H | I | L | PB |
| 20. | B | F | J | K | L | PB |
| 21. | C | D | E | H | I | PB |
| 22. | C | E | G | J | K | PB |
| 23. | C | F | H | I | K | PB |
| 24. | C | G | H | J | L | PB |
| 25. | D | E | F | G | K | PB |
| 26. | D | F | G | I | L | PB |
| 27. | D | H | I | J | K | PB |
| 28. | E | F | H | I | J | PB |
| 29. | E | G | H | K | L | PB |



# POWERBALL BALANCED WHEEL® 53013PB

## Wheel 13 Numbers + PB in 34 Games for a 3 of 3 Win

With Powerball

| Numbers Matched | Maximum Wins 5 + 1 | 4 + 1 | 3 + 1 | 2 + 1 | 1 + 1 | 0 + 1 | Minimum Wins 5 + 1 | 4 + 1 | 3 + 1 | 2 + 1 | 1 + 1 | 0 + 1 |
|---|---|---|---|---|---|---|---|---|---|---|---|---|
| 5 + 1 | 1 | 0 | 8 | 16 | 5 | 4 | 0 | 0 | 10 | 11 | 13 | 0 |
| 4 + 1 | - | 1 | 4 | 12 | 13 | 4 | - | 0 | 4 | 12 | 16 | 2 |
| 3 + 1 | - | - | 5 | 0 | 25 | 4 | - | - | 1 | 9 | 18 | 6 |
| 2 + 1 | - | - | - | 7 | 12 | 15 | - | - | - | 4 | 18 | 12 |
| 1 + 1 | - | - | - | - | 14 | 20 | - | - | - | - | 13 | 21 |
| 0 + 1 | - | - | - | - | - | 34 | - | - | - | - | - | 34 |

Without Powerball

| Numbers Matched | Maximum Wins 5 + 0 | 4 + 0 | 3 + 0 | 2 + 0 | 1 + 0 | Minimum Wins 5 + 0 | 4 + 0 | 3 + 0 | 2 + 0 | 1 + 0 |
|---|---|---|---|---|---|---|---|---|---|---|
| 5 + 0 | 1 | 0 | 8 | 16 | 5 | 0 | 0 | 10 | 11 | 13 |
| 4 + 0 | - | 1 | 4 | 12 | 13 | - | 0 | 4 | 12 | 16 |
| 3 + 0 | - | - | 5 | 0 | 25 | - | - | 1 | 9 | 18 |
| 2 + 0 | - | - | - | 7 | 12 | - | - | - | 4 | 18 |
| 1 + 0 | - | - | - | - | 14 | - | - | - | - | 13 |

## Your 13 Numbers + PB to Wheel

| A | B | C | D | E | F | G |
|---|---|---|---|---|---|---|
| 13 | 13 | 13 | 13 | 13 | 13 | 13 |
| **H** | **I** | **J** | **K** | **L** | **M** | **PB** |
| 14 | 13 | 13 | 13 | 13 | 13 | 34 |

## The 34 Games to Play

| | | | | | | |
|---|---|---|---|---|---|---|
| 1. | A | B | C | E | M | PB |
| 2. | A | B | D | G | L | PB |
| 3. | A | B | F | H | L | PB |
| 4. | A | B | I | J | K | PB |
| 5. | A | C | D | F | M | PB |
| 6. | A | C | G | H | M | PB |
| 7. | A | C | I | L | M | PB |
| 8. | A | C | J | K | M | PB |
| 9. | A | D | E | G | I | PB |
| 10. | A | D | H | J | K | PB |
| 11. | A | E | F | H | I | PB |
| 12. | A | E | J | K | L | PB |
| 13. | A | F | G | J | K | PB |
| 14. | B | C | D | F | I | PB |
| 15. | B | C | G | K | L | PB |
| 16. | B | C | H | J | L | PB |
| 17. | B | D | E | H | K | PB |
| 18. | B | D | J | L | M | PB |
| 19. | B | E | F | G | J | PB |
| 20. | B | E | H | I | L | PB |



(Continued Next Page)

**POWERBALL BALANCED WHEEL® 53013PB** (Continued from previous page)

| | | | | | | |
|---|---|---|---|---|---|---|
| 21. | B | F | K | L | M | PB |
| 22. | B | G | H | I | M | PB |
| 23. | C | D | E | F | L | PB |
| 24. | C | D | F | G | J | PB |
| 25. | C | D | F | H | K | PB |
| 26. | C | E | G | I | K | PB |
| 27. | C | E | H | I | J | PB |
| 28. | D | E | I | J | M | PB |
| 29. | D | G | H | K | M | PB |
| 30. | D | H | I | K | L | PB |
| 31. | E | F | I | K | M | PB |
| 32. | E | G | H | L | M | PB |
| 33. | F | G | H | J | M | PB |
| 34. | F | G | I | J | L | PB |



# POWERBALL BALANCED WHEEL® 53014PB

## Wheel 14 Numbers + PB in 43 Games for a 3 of 3 Win

With Powerball

| Numbers Matched | Maximum Wins 5 + 1 | 4 + 1 | 3 + 1 | 2 + 1 | 1 + 1 | 0 + 1 | Minimum Wins 5 + 1 | 4 + 1 | 3 + 1 | 2 + 1 | 1 + 1 | 0 + 1 |
|---|---|---|---|---|---|---|---|---|---|---|---|---|
| 5 + 1 | 1 | 2 | 8 | 16 | 14 | 2 | 0 | 0 | 10 | 12 | 18 | 3 |
| 4 + 1 | - | 2 | 5 | 12 | 20 | 4 | - | 0 | 4 | 12 | 20 | 7 |
| 3 + 1 | - | - | 6 | 1 | 30 | 6 | - | - | 1 | 9 | 20 | 13 |
| 2 + 1 | - | - | - | 7 | 20 | 16 | - | - | - | 4 | 18 | 21 |
| 1 + 1 | - | - | - | - | 17 | 26 | - | - | - | - | 13 | 30 |
| 0 + 1 | - | - | - | - | - | 43 | - | - | - | - | - | 43 |

Without Powerball

| Numbers Matched | Maximum Wins 5 + 0 | 4 + 0 | 3 + 0 | 2 + 0 | 1 + 0 | Minimum Wins 5 + 0 | 4 + 0 | 3 + 0 | 2 + 0 | 1 + 0 |
|---|---|---|---|---|---|---|---|---|---|---|
| 5 + 0 | 1 | 2 | 8 | 16 | 14 | 0 | 0 | 10 | 12 | 18 |
| 4 + 0 | - | 2 | 5 | 12 | 20 | - | 0 | 4 | 12 | 20 |
| 3 + 0 | - | - | 6 | 1 | 30 | - | - | 1 | 9 | 20 |
| 2 + 0 | - | - | - | 7 | 20 | - | - | - | 4 | 18 |
| 1 + 0 | - | - | - | - | 17 | - | - | - | - | 13 |

## Your 14 Numbers + PB to Wheel

| A | B | C | D | E | F | G | H |
|---|---|---|---|---|---|---|---|
| 15 | 17 | 17 | 15 | 16 | 15 | 16 | 15 |

| I | J | K | L | M | N | PB |
|---|---|---|---|---|---|---|
| 17 | 15 | 13 | 16 | 13 | 15 | 43 |

## The 43 Games to Play

| | | | | | | |
|---|---|---|---|---|---|---|
| 1. | A | B | C | J | L | PB |
| 2. | A | B | D | F | M | PB |
| 3. | A | B | E | H | N | PB |
| 4. | A | B | G | I | K | PB |
| 5. | A | C | D | H | K | PB |
| 6. | A | C | E | F | I | PB |
| 7. | A | C | G | H | M | PB |
| 8. | A | C | G | H | N | PB |
| 9. | A | D | E | G | L | PB |
| 10. | A | D | I | J | N | PB |
| 11. | A | E | J | K | M | PB |
| 12. | A | F | G | H | J | PB |
| 13. | A | F | K | L | N | PB |
| 14. | A | H | I | L | N | PB |
| 15. | A | I | L | M | N | PB |
| 16. | B | C | D | L | N | PB |
| 17. | B | C | E | G | I | PB |
| 18. | B | C | E | I | L | PB |



(Continued Next Page)

## POWERBALL BALANCED WHEEL® 53014PB (Continued from previous page)

| | | | | | | |
|---|---|---|---|---|---|---|
| 19. | B | C | F | H | L | PB |
| 20. | B | C | G | I | L | PB |
| 21. | B | C | K | L | M | PB |
| 22. | B | D | E | F | J | PB |
| 23. | B | D | E | F | K | PB |
| 24. | B | D | G | H | I | PB |
| 25. | B | E | H | M | N | PB |
| 26. | B | F | G | I | N | PB |
| 27. | B | G | I | J | M | PB |
| 28. | B | H | J | K | N | PB |
| 29. | C | D | E | I | M | PB |
| 30. | C | D | F | G | J | PB |
| 31. | C | E | H | I | J | PB |
| 32. | C | E | I | K | N | PB |
| 33. | C | F | G | J | K | PB |
| 34. | C | F | J | M | N | PB |
| 35. | D | E | F | H | N | PB |
| 36. | D | F | I | J | L | PB |
| 37. | D | G | K | M | N | PB |
| 38. | D | H | J | L | M | PB |
| 39. | D | I | J | K | L | PB |
| 40. | E | F | G | L | M | PB |
| 41. | E | G | H | K | L | PB |
| 42. | E | G | J | L | N | PB |
| 43. | F | H | I | K | M | PB |



# POWERBALL BALANCED WHEEL® 53015PB

## Wheel 15 Numbers + PB in 57 Games for a 3 of 3 Win

With Powerball

| Numbers Matched | Maximum Wins 5 + 1 | 4 + 1 | 3 + 1 | 2 + 1 | 1 + 1 | 0 + 1 | Minimum Wins 5 + 1 | 4 + 1 | 3 + 1 | 2 + 1 | 1 + 1 | 0 + 1 |
|---|---|---|---|---|---|---|---|---|---|---|---|---|
| 5 + 1 | 1 | 0 | 10 | 18 | 24 | 4 | 0 | 0 | 10 | 22 | 21 | 4 |
| 4 + 1 | - | 1 | 6 | 12 | 30 | 8 | - | 0 | 4 | 19 | 26 | 8 |
| 3 + 1 | - | - | 6 | 2 | 35 | 14 | - | - | 1 | 12 | 30 | 14 |
| 2 + 1 | - | - | - | 7 | 24 | 26 | - | - | - | 5 | 28 | 24 |
| 1 + 1 | - | - | - | - | 19 | 38 | - | - | - | - | 19 | 38 |
| 0 + 1 | - | - | - | - | - | 57 | - | - | - | - | - | 57 |

Without Powerball

| Numbers Matched | Maximum Wins 5 + 0 | 4 + 0 | 3 + 0 | 2 + 0 | 1 + 0 | Minimum Wins 5 + 0 | 4 + 0 | 3 + 0 | 2 + 0 | 1 + 0 |
|---|---|---|---|---|---|---|---|---|---|---|
| 5 + 0 | 1 | 0 | 10 | 18 | 24 | 0 | 0 | 10 | 22 | 21 |
| 4 + 0 | - | 1 | 6 | 12 | 30 | - | 0 | 4 | 19 | 26 |
| 3 + 0 | - | - | 6 | 2 | 35 | - | - | 1 | 12 | 30 |
| 2 + 0 | - | - | - | 7 | 24 | - | - | - | 5 | 28 |
| 1 + 0 | - | - | - | - | 19 | - | - | - | - | 19 |

## Your 15 Numbers + PB to Wheel

| A | B | C | D | E | F | G | H |
|---|---|---|---|---|---|---|---|
| 19 | 19 | 19 | 19 | 19 | 19 | 19 | 19 |
| **I** | **J** | **K** | **L** | **M** | **N** | **O** | **PB** |
| 19 | 19 | 19 | 19 | 19 | 19 | 19 | 57 |

## The 57 Games to Play

| | | | | | | |
|---|---|---|---|---|---|---|
| 1. | A | B | C | H | N | PB |
| 2. | A | B | D | K | L | PB |
| 3. | A | B | E | I | J | PB |
| 4. | A | B | E | M | O | PB |
| 5. | A | B | F | G | L | PB |
| 6. | A | C | D | K | N | PB |



(Continued Next Page)

## POWERBALL BALANCED WHEEL® 53015PB (Continued from previous page)

| | | | | | | |
|---|---|---|---|---|---|---|
| 7. | A | C | E | F | O | PB |
| 8. | A | C | E | H | L | PB |
| 9. | A | C | G | H | I | PB |
| 10. | A | C | J | L | M | PB |
| 11. | A | D | E | K | M | PB |
| 12. | A | D | F | I | K | PB |
| 13. | A | D | G | J | K | PB |
| 14. | A | D | H | K | O | PB |
| 15. | A | E | G | M | N | PB |
| 16. | A | F | H | I | M | PB |
| 17. | A | F | J | L | N | PB |
| 18. | A | G | H | J | O | PB |
| 19. | A | I | L | N | O | PB |
| 20. | B | C | D | E | N | PB |
| 21. | B | C | F | J | N | PB |
| 22. | B | C | G | I | N | PB |
| 23. | B | C | K | L | N | PB |
| 24. | B | C | M | N | O | PB |
| 25. | B | D | F | G | H | PB |
| 26. | B | D | H | M | O | PB |
| 27. | B | D | I | J | L | PB |
| 28. | B | E | F | G | K | PB |
| 29. | B | E | H | L | N | PB |
| 30. | B | F | I | M | O | PB |
| 31. | B | G | J | M | O | PB |
| 32. | B | H | I | J | K | PB |
| 33. | B | K | L | M | O | PB |
| 34. | C | D | F | L | O | PB |
| 35. | C | D | G | I | L | PB |
| 36. | C | D | H | J | M | PB |
| 37. | C | E | G | I | K | PB |
| 38. | C | E | J | K | M | PB |
| 39. | C | F | G | I | M | PB |
| 40. | C | F | H | K | O | PB |
| 41. | C | G | I | J | O | PB |
| 42. | D | E | F | I | M | PB |
| 43. | D | E | F | J | N | PB |
| 44. | D | E | G | J | O | PB |
| 45. | D | E | H | I | L | PB |
| 46. | D | G | L | M | N | PB |
| 47. | D | H | I | N | O | PB |
| 48. | E | F | H | L | M | PB |
| 49. | E | G | H | K | L | PB |
| 50. | E | H | J | L | O | PB |
| 51. | E | I | K | N | O | PB |
| 52. | F | G | J | N | O | PB |
| 53. | F | H | J | K | N | PB |
| 54. | F | I | J | M | N | PB |
| 55. | F | I | K | L | M | PB |
| 56. | G | H | K | M | N | PB |
| 57. | G | J | K | L | O | PB |



# POWERBALL BALANCED WHEEL® 53016PB

## Wheel 16 Numbers + PB in 65 Games for a 3 of 3 Win

With Powerball

| Numbers Matched | Maximum Wins | | | | | | Minimum Wins | | | | | |
|---|---|---|---|---|---|---|---|---|---|---|---|---|
| | 5 + 1 | 4 + 1 | 3 + 1 | 2 + 1 | 1 + 1 | 0 + 1 | 5 + 1 | 4 + 1 | 3 + 1 | 2 + 1 | 1 + 1 | 0 + 1 |
| 5 + 1 | 1 | 1 | 9 | 20 | 27 | 7 | 0 | 0 | 10 | 20 | 30 | 5 |
| 4 + 1 | - | 2 | 5 | 13 | 34 | 11 | - | 0 | 4 | 18 | 32 | 11 |
| 3 + 1 | - | - | 7 | 0 | 41 | 17 | - | - | 1 | 12 | 33 | 19 |
| 2 + 1 | - | - | - | 7 | 29 | 29 | - | - | - | 5 | 30 | 30 |
| 1 + 1 | - | - | - | - | 22 | 43 | - | - | - | - | 20 | 45 |
| 0 + 1 | - | - | - | - | - | 65 | - | - | - | - | - | 65 |

(Continued Next Page)

## POWERBALL BALANCED WHEEL® 53016PB (Continued from previous page)

Without Powerball

| Numbers Matched | Maximum Wins 5 + 0 | 4 + 0 | 3 + 0 | 2 + 0 | 1 + 0 | Minimum Wins 5 + 0 | 4 + 0 | 3 + 0 | 2 + 0 | 1 + 0 |
|---|---|---|---|---|---|---|---|---|---|---|
| 5 + 0 | 1 | 1 | 9 | 20 | 27 | 0 | 0 | 10 | 20 | 30 |
| 4 + 0 | - | 2 | 5 | 13 | 34 | - | 0 | 4 | 18 | 32 |
| 3 + 0 | - | - | 7 | 0 | 41 | - | - | 1 | 12 | 33 |
| 2 + 0 | - | - | - | 7 | 29 | - | - | - | 5 | 30 |
| 1 + 0 | - | - | - | - | 22 | - | - | - | - | 20 |

## Your 16 Numbers + PB to Wheel

| A | B | C | D | E | F | G | H | I |
|---|---|---|---|---|---|---|---|---|
| 20 | 21 | 20 | 21 | 22 | 20 | 20 | 20 | 20 |

| J | K | L | M | N | O | P | PB |
|---|---|---|---|---|---|---|---|
| 20 | 20 | 21 | 20 | 20 | 20 | 20 | 65 |

## The 65 Games to Play

| | | | | | |
|---|---|---|---|---|---|
| 1. A | B | C | I | L | PB |
| 2. A | B | D | H | P | PB |
| 3. A | B | E | K | O | PB |
| 4. A | B | F | J | M | PB |
| 5. A | B | G | J | N | PB |
| 6. A | C | D | H | N | PB |
| 7. A | C | E | J | L | PB |
| 8. A | C | F | G | O | PB |
| 9. A | C | K | M | P | PB |
| 10. A | D | E | H | I | PB |
| 11. A | D | F | H | L | PB |
| 12. A | D | G | H | M | PB |
| 13. A | D | H | J | K | PB |
| 14. A | D | H | L | O | PB |
| 15. A | E | F | N | P | PB |
| 16. A | E | G | I | M | PB |
| 17. A | F | I | K | N | PB |
| 18. A | G | K | L | P | PB |
| 19. A | I | J | O | P | PB |
| 20. A | L | M | N | O | PB |
| 21. B | C | D | G | K | PB |
| 22. B | C | E | I | J | PB |
| 23. B | C | E | J | O | PB |
| 24. B | C | F | H | M | PB |
| 25. B | C | N | O | P | PB |
| 26. B | D | E | F | M | PB |
| 27. B | D | I | K | N | PB |
| 28. B | D | J | L | O | PB |
| 29. B | E | F | M | O | PB |
| 30. B | E | G | L | P | PB |
| 31. B | E | H | L | N | PB |
| 32. B | F | G | M | N | PB |
| 33. B | F | I | M | P | PB |
| 34. B | F | K | L | M | PB |
| 35. B | G | H | I | O | PB |
| 36. B | H | J | K | P | PB |
| 37. C | D | E | J | P | PB |
| 38. C | D | F | L | N | PB |
| 39. C | D | I | M | O | PB |
| 40. C | E | F | J | K | PB |
| 41. C | E | G | H | J | PB |
| 42. C | E | J | M | N | PB |
| 43. C | F | H | I | P | PB |
| 44. C | G | I | K | N | PB |
| 45. C | G | L | M | P | PB |
| 46. C | H | K | L | O | PB |
| 47. D | E | G | N | O | PB |
| 48. D | E | K | L | M | PB |
| 49. D | F | G | I | J | PB |
| 50. D | F | K | O | P | PB |



(Continued Next Page)

**POWERBALL BALANCED WHEEL® 53016PB** (Continued from previous page)

| | | | | | | |
|---|---|---|---|---|---|---|
| 51. | D | G | I | L | P | PB |
| 52. | D | G | L | O | P | PB |
| 53. | D | J | M | N | P | PB |
| 54. | E | F | G | H | K | PB |
| 55. | E | F | I | L | O | PB |
| 56. | E | H | M | O | P | PB |
| 57. | E | I | K | N | O | PB |
| 58. | E | I | K | N | P | PB |
| 59. | F | G | J | L | P | PB |
| 60. | F | H | J | N | O | PB |
| 61. | G | H | L | N | P | PB |
| 62. | G | J | K | M | O | PB |
| 63. | H | I | J | L | M | PB |
| 64. | H | I | K | M | N | PB |
| 65. | I | J | K | L | N | PB |



# POWERBALL BALANCED WHEEL® 53017PB

## Wheel 17 Numbers + PB in 68 Games for a 3 of 3 Win

With Powerball

| Numbers Matched | Maximum Wins 5 + 1 | 4 + 1 | 3 + 1 | 2 + 1 | 1 + 1 | 0 + 1 | Minimum Wins 5 + 1 | 4 + 1 | 3 + 1 | 2 + 1 | 1 + 1 | 0 + 1 |
|---|---|---|---|---|---|---|---|---|---|---|---|---|
| 5 + 1 | 1 | 0 | 0 | 40 | 15 | 12 | 0 | 0 | 10 | 20 | 30 | 8 |
| 4 + 1 | - | 1 | 0 | 24 | 28 | 15 | - | 0 | 4 | 18 | 32 | 14 |
| 3 + 1 | - | - | 1 | 12 | 33 | 22 | - | - | 1 | 12 | 33 | 22 |
| 2 + 1 | - | - | - | 5 | 30 | 33 | - | - | - | 5 | 30 | 33 |
| 1 + 1 | - | - | - | - | 20 | 48 | - | - | - | - | 20 | 48 |
| 0 + 1 | - | - | - | - | - | 68 | - | - | - | - | - | 68 |

Without Powerball

| Numbers Matched | Maximum Wins 5 + 0 | 4 + 0 | 3 + 0 | 2 + 0 | 1 + 0 | Minimum Wins 5 + 0 | 4 + 0 | 3 + 0 | 2 + 0 | 1 + 0 |
|---|---|---|---|---|---|---|---|---|---|---|
| 5 + 0 | 1 | 0 | 0 | 40 | 15 | 0 | 0 | 10 | 20 | 30 |
| 4 + 0 | - | 1 | 0 | 24 | 28 | - | 0 | 4 | 18 | 32 |
| 3 + 0 | - | - | 1 | 12 | 33 | - | - | 1 | 12 | 33 |
| 2 + 0 | - | - | - | 5 | 30 | - | - | - | 5 | 30 |
| 1 + 0 | - | - | - | - | 20 | - | - | - | - | 20 |

## Your 17 Numbers + PB to Wheel

| A | B | C | D | E | F | G | H | I |
|---|---|---|---|---|---|---|---|---|
| 20 | 20 | 20 | 20 | 20 | 20 | 20 | 20 | 20 |
| **J** | **K** | **L** | **M** | **N** | **O** | **P** | **Q** | **PB** |
| 20 | 20 | 20 | 20 | 20 | 20 | 20 | 20 | 68 |

## The 68 Games to Play

| | | | | | | |
|---|---|---|---|---|---|---|
| 1. | A | B | C | K | O | PB |
| 2. | A | B | D | H | N | PB |
| 3. | A | B | E | F | P | PB |
| 4. | A | B | G | J | Q | PB |
| 5. | A | B | I | L | M | PB |
| 6. | A | C | D | E | Q | PB |
| 7. | A | C | F | J | M | PB |
| 8. | A | C | G | L | N | PB |
| 9. | A | C | H | I | P | PB |
| 10. | A | D | F | K | L | PB |
| 11. | A | D | G | M | P | PB |
| 12. | A | D | I | J | O | PB |
| 13. | A | E | G | I | K | PB |
| 14. | A | E | H | J | L | PB |
| 15. | A | E | M | N | O | PB |
| 16. | A | F | G | H | O | PB |



(Continued Next Page)

## POWERBALL BALANCED WHEEL® 53017PB (Continued from previous page)

| | | | | | | |
|---|---|---|---|---|---|---|
| 17. | A | F | I | N | Q | PB |
| 18. | A | H | K | M | Q | PB |
| 19. | A | J | K | N | P | PB |
| 20. | A | L | O | P | Q | PB |
| 21. | B | C | D | J | P | PB |
| 22. | B | C | E | I | N | PB |
| 23. | B | C | F | L | Q | PB |
| 24. | B | C | G | H | M | PB |
| 25. | B | D | E | G | L | PB |
| 26. | B | D | F | M | O | PB |
| 27. | B | D | I | K | Q | PB |
| 28. | B | E | H | O | Q | PB |
| 29. | B | E | J | K | M | PB |
| 30. | B | F | G | K | N | PB |
| 31. | B | F | H | I | J | PB |
| 32. | B | G | I | O | P | PB |
| 33. | B | H | K | L | P | PB |
| 34. | B | J | L | N | O | PB |
| 35. | B | M | N | P | Q | PB |
| 36. | C | D | F | G | I | PB |
| 37. | C | D | H | L | O | PB |
| 38. | C | D | K | M | N | PB |
| 39. | C | E | F | H | K | PB |
| 40. | C | E | G | J | O | PB |
| 41. | C | E | L | M | P | PB |
| 42. | C | F | N | O | P | PB |
| 43. | C | G | K | P | Q | PB |
| 44. | C | H | J | N | Q | PB |
| 45. | C | I | J | K | L | PB |
| 46. | C | I | M | O | Q | PB |
| 47. | D | E | F | J | N | PB |
| 48. | D | E | H | I | M | PB |
| 49. | D | E | K | O | P | PB |
| 50. | D | F | H | P | Q | PB |
| 51. | D | G | H | J | K | PB |
| 52. | D | G | N | O | Q | PB |
| 53. | D | I | L | N | P | PB |
| 54. | D | J | L | M | Q | PB |
| 55. | E | F | G | M | Q | PB |
| 56. | E | F | I | L | O | PB |
| 57. | E | G | H | N | P | PB |
| 58. | E | I | J | P | Q | PB |
| 59. | E | K | L | N | Q | PB |
| 60. | F | G | J | L | P | PB |
| 61. | F | H | L | M | N | PB |
| 62. | F | I | K | M | P | PB |
| 63. | F | J | K | O | Q | PB |
| 64. | G | H | I | L | Q | PB |
| 65. | G | I | J | M | N | PB |
| 66. | G | K | L | M | O | PB |
| 67. | H | I | K | N | O | PB |
| 68. | H | J | M | O | P | PB |



# POWERBALL BALANCED WHEEL® 53018PB

## Wheel 18 Numbers + PB in 94 Games for a 3 of 3 Win

With Powerball

| Numbers Matched | Maximum Wins | | | | | | Minimum Wins | | | | | |
|---|---|---|---|---|---|---|---|---|---|---|---|---|
| | 5 + 1 | 4 + 1 | 3 + 1 | 2 + 1 | 1 + 1 | 0 + 1 | 5 + 1 | 4 + 1 | 3 + 1 | 2 + 1 | 1 + 1 | 0 + 1 |
| 5 + 1 | 1 | 2 | 4 | 34 | 39 | 14 | 0 | 0 | 10 | 30 | 40 | 14 |
| 4 + 1 | - | 2 | 2 | 24 | 44 | 22 | - | 0 | 4 | 24 | 44 | 22 |
| 3 + 1 | - | - | 3 | 13 | 45 | 33 | - | - | 1 | 15 | 45 | 33 |
| 2 + 1 | - | - | - | 8 | 38 | 48 | - | - | - | 6 | 40 | 48 |
| 1 + 1 | - | - | - | - | 27 | 67 | - | - | - | - | 26 | 68 |
| 0 + 1 | - | - | - | - | - | 94 | - | - | - | - | - | 94 |

(Continued Next Page)

## POWERBALL BALANCED WHEEL® 53018PB (Continued from previous page)

Without Powerball

| Numbers Matched | Maximum Wins 5 + 0 | 4 + 0 | 3 + 0 | 2 + 0 | 1 + 0 | Minimum Wins 5 + 0 | 4 + 0 | 3 + 0 | 2 + 0 | 1 + 0 |
|---|---|---|---|---|---|---|---|---|---|---|
| 5 + 0 | 1 | 2 | 4 | 34 | 39 | 0 | 0 | 10 | 30 | 40 |
| 4 + 0 | - | 2 | 2 | 24 | 44 | - | 0 | 4 | 24 | 44 |
| 3 + 0 | - | - | 3 | 13 | 45 | - | - | 1 | 15 | 45 |
| 2 + 0 | - | - | - | 8 | 38 | - | - | - | 6 | 40 |
| 1 + 0 | - | - | - | - | 27 | - | - | - | - | 26 |

## Your 18 Numbers + PB to Wheel

| A | B | C | D | E | F | G | H | I | J |
|---|---|---|---|---|---|---|---|---|---|
| 26 | 26 | 27 | 27 | 26 | 26 | 26 | 26 | 26 | 26 |

| K | L | M | N | O | P | Q | R | PB |
|---|---|---|---|---|---|---|---|---|
| 26 | 26 | 26 | 26 | 26 | 26 | 26 | 26 | 94 |

## The 94 Games to Play

| | | | | | | |
|---|---|---|---|---|---|---|
| 1. | A | B | C | D | Q | PB |
| 2. | A | B | C | G | P | PB |
| 3. | A | B | D | L | R | PB |
| 4. | A | B | E | I | J | PB |
| 5. | A | B | F | H | O | PB |
| 6. | A | B | K | M | N | PB |
| 7. | A | C | D | I | N | PB |
| 8. | A | C | E | H | M | PB |
| 9. | A | C | F | K | L | PB |
| 10. | A | C | J | O | R | PB |
| 11. | A | D | E | F | P | PB |
| 12. | A | D | G | M | O | PB |
| 13. | A | D | H | J | K | PB |
| 14. | A | E | G | K | R | PB |
| 15. | A | E | L | N | O | PB |
| 16. | A | E | L | N | Q | PB |
| 17. | A | F | G | J | N | PB |
| 18. | A | F | H | K | Q | PB |
| 19. | A | F | I | M | R | PB |
| 20. | A | G | H | I | L | PB |
| 21. | A | G | I | P | Q | PB |
| 22. | A | H | N | P | R | PB |
| 23. | A | I | K | O | P | PB |
| 24. | A | I | N | Q | R | PB |
| 25. | A | J | L | M | P | PB |
| 26. | A | J | M | O | Q | PB |
| 27. | B | C | D | E | O | PB |
| 28. | B | C | D | Q | R | PB |
| 29. | B | C | F | J | M | PB |
| 30. | B | C | H | L | N | PB |
| 31. | B | C | I | K | R | PB |
| 32. | B | D | F | G | K | PB |
| 33. | B | D | H | I | M | PB |
| 34. | B | D | J | N | P | PB |
| 35. | B | E | F | N | R | PB |
| 36. | B | E | G | L | M | PB |
| 37. | B | E | H | K | P | PB |
| 38. | B | E | H | O | Q | PB |
| 39. | B | F | I | L | P | PB |
| 40. | B | F | M | P | Q | PB |
| 41. | B | G | H | J | R | PB |
| 42. | B | G | I | N | O | PB |
| 43. | B | G | J | L | Q | PB |
| 44. | B | I | K | N | Q | PB |
| 45. | B | J | K | L | O | PB |
| 46. | B | M | O | P | R | PB |
| 47. | C | D | F | H | R | PB |
| 48. | C | D | G | J | L | PB |
| 49. | C | D | K | M | P | PB |
| 50. | C | D | P | Q | R | PB |



(Continued Next Page)

## POWERBALL BALANCED WHEEL® 53018PB (Continued from previous page)

| | | | | | | |
|---|---|---|---|---|---|---|
| 51. | C | E | F | G | I | PB |
| 52. | C | E | F | G | *Q* | PB |
| 53. | C | E | J | K | N | PB |
| 54. | C | E | L | P | R | PB |
| 55. | C | F | N | O | P | PB |
| 56. | C | G | H | K | O | PB |
| 57. | C | G | M | N | R | PB |
| 58. | C | H | I | J | P | PB |
| 59. | C | H | I | J | *Q* | PB |
| 60. | C | I | L | M | O | PB |
| 61. | C | K | L | M | *Q* | PB |
| 62. | C | N | O | P | *Q* | PB |
| 63. | D | E | G | H | N | PB |
| 64. | D | E | I | K | L | PB |
| 65. | D | E | I | M | *Q* | PB |
| 66. | D | E | J | M | R | PB |
| 67. | D | F | I | J | O | PB |
| 68. | D | F | J | N | *Q* | PB |
| 69. | D | F | L | M | N | PB |
| 70. | D | G | I | P | R | PB |
| 71. | D | G | K | O | *Q* | PB |
| 72. | D | H | L | O | P | PB |
| 73. | D | H | L | P | *Q* | PB |
| 74. | D | K | N | O | R | PB |
| 75. | E | F | H | J | L | PB |
| 76. | E | F | K | M | O | PB |
| 77. | E | G | J | O | P | PB |
| 78. | E | H | I | O | R | PB |
| 79. | E | H | O | *Q* | R | PB |
| 80. | E | I | M | N | P | PB |
| 81. | E | J | K | P | *Q* | PB |
| 82. | F | G | H | M | P | PB |
| 83. | F | G | L | O | R | PB |
| 84. | F | H | I | K | N | PB |
| 85. | F | I | L | O | *Q* | PB |
| 86. | F | J | K | P | R | PB |
| 87. | F | K | L | *Q* | R | PB |
| 88. | G | H | M | N | *Q* | PB |
| 89. | G | I | J | K | M | PB |
| 90. | G | J | M | *Q* | R | PB |
| 91. | G | K | L | N | P | PB |
| 92. | H | J | M | N | O | PB |
| 93. | H | K | L | M | R | PB |
| 94. | I | J | L | N | R | PB |



# POWERBALL BALANCED WHEEL® 53019PB

## Wheel 19 Numbers + PB in 108 Games for a 3 of 3 Win

With Powerball

| Numbers Matched | Maximum Wins | | | | | | Minimum Wins | | | | | |
|---|---|---|---|---|---|---|---|---|---|---|---|---|
| | 5 + 1 | 4 + 1 | 3 + 1 | 2 + 1 | 1 + 1 | 0 + 1 | 5 + 1 | 4 + 1 | 3 + 1 | 2 + 1 | 1 + 1 | 0 + 1 |
| 5 + 1 | 1 | 2 | 13 | 22 | 52 | 18 | 0 | 0 | 10 | 30 | 51 | 17 |
| 4 + 1 | - | 3 | 12 | 5 | 62 | 26 | - | 0 | 4 | 24 | 52 | 28 |
| 3 + 1 | - | - | 9 | 7 | 50 | 42 | - | - | 1 | 15 | 51 | 41 |
| 2 + 1 | - | - | - | 15 | 32 | 61 | - | - | - | 6 | 44 | 58 |
| 1 + 1 | - | - | - | - | 31 | 77 | - | - | - | - | 28 | 80 |
| 0 + 1 | - | - | - | - | - | 108 | - | - | - | - | - | 108 |

(Continued Next Page)

## POWERBALL BALANCED WHEEL® 53019PB (Continued from previous page)

Without Powerball

| Numbers Matched | Maximum Wins 5 + 0 | 4 + 0 | 3 + 0 | 2 + 0 | 1 + 0 | Minimum Wins 5 + 0 | 4 + 0 | 3 + 0 | 2 + 0 | 1 + 0 |
|---|---|---|---|---|---|---|---|---|---|---|
| 5 + 0 | 1 | 2 | 13 | 22 | 52 | 0 | 0 | 10 | 30 | 51 |
| 4 + 0 | - | 3 | 12 | 5 | 62 | - | 0 | 4 | 24 | 52 |
| 3 + 0 | - | - | 9 | 7 | 50 | - | - | 1 | 15 | 51 |
| 2 + 0 | - | - | - | 15 | 32 | - | - | - | 6 | 44 |
| 1 + 0 | - | - | - | - | 31 | - | - | - | - | 28 |

# Your 19 Numbers + PB to Wheel

| A | B | C | D | E | F | G | H | I | J |
|---|---|---|---|---|---|---|---|---|---|
| 28 | 28 | 28 | 28 | 31 | 28 | 29 | 28 | 31 | 28 |

| K | L | M | N | O | P | Q | R | S | PB |
|---|---|---|---|---|---|---|---|---|---|
| 28 | 28 | 29 | 28 | 28 | 28 | 28 | 28 | 28 | 108 |

# The 108 Games to Play

| | | | | | | |
|---|---|---|---|---|---|---|
| 1. | A | B | C | I | Q | PB |
| 2. | A | B | D | J | L | PB |
| 3. | A | B | E | Q | R | PB |
| 4. | A | B | F | N | O | PB |
| 5. | A | B | G | M | S | PB |
| 6. | A | B | H | K | P | PB |
| 7. | A | C | D | E | P | PB |
| 8. | A | C | F | H | S | PB |
| 9. | A | C | G | L | N | PB |
| 10. | A | C | J | K | M | PB |
| 11. | A | C | O | R | S | PB |
| 12. | A | D | F | M | Q | PB |
| 13. | A | D | G | H | R | PB |
| 14. | A | D | I | O | P | PB |
| 15. | A | D | K | N | S | PB |
| 16. | A | E | F | K | L | PB |
| 17. | A | E | G | H | I | PB |
| 18. | A | E | I | M | N | PB |
| 19. | A | E | J | O | S | PB |
| 20. | A | F | G | J | P | PB |
| 21. | A | F | I | K | L | PB |
| 22. | A | F | K | L | R | PB |
| 23. | A | G | K | O | Q | PB |
| 24. | A | H | J | N | Q | PB |
| 25. | A | H | L | M | O | PB |
| 26. | A | I | J | R | S | PB |
| 27. | A | L | P | Q | S | PB |
| 28. | A | M | N | P | R | PB |
| 29. | B | C | D | H | M | PB |
| 30. | B | C | E | L | S | PB |
| 31. | B | C | F | G | K | PB |
| 32. | B | C | H | O | R | PB |
| 33. | B | C | J | N | P | PB |
| 34. | B | D | E | K | O | PB |
| 35. | B | D | F | P | S | PB |
| 36. | B | D | G | N | Q | PB |
| 37. | B | D | I | K | R | PB |
| 38. | B | E | F | G | I | PB |
| 39. | B | E | H | I | M | PB |
| 40. | B | E | J | N | P | PB |
| 41. | B | F | H | L | Q | PB |
| 42. | B | F | J | M | R | PB |
| 43. | B | G | H | J | O | PB |
| 44. | B | G | L | P | R | PB |
| 45. | B | H | N | R | S | PB |
| 46. | B | I | J | N | P | PB |
| 47. | B | I | L | O | S | PB |
| 48. | B | J | K | Q | S | PB |
| 49. | B | K | L | M | N | PB |
| 50. | B | M | O | P | Q | PB |



(Continued Next Page)

## POWERBALL BALANCED WHEEL® 53019PB (Continued from previous page)

| | | | | | | |
|---|---|---|---|---|---|---|
| 51. | C | D | F | I | N | PB |
| 52. | C | D | G | J | S | PB |
| 53. | C | D | G | O | R | PB |
| 54. | C | D | K | L | Q | PB |
| 55. | C | E | F | J | Q | PB |
| 56. | C | E | G | I | M | PB |
| 57. | C | E | H | K | N | PB |
| 58. | C | E | M | O | R | PB |
| 59. | C | F | L | M | P | PB |
| 60. | C | F | O | P | R | PB |
| 61. | C | G | H | P | Q | PB |
| 62. | C | H | I | J | L | PB |
| 63. | C | I | K | P | S | PB |
| 64. | C | I | O | Q | R | PB |
| 65. | C | J | N | O | R | PB |
| 66. | C | K | L | O | R | PB |
| 67. | C | M | N | Q | S | PB |
| 68. | D | E | F | N | R | PB |
| 69. | D | E | G | I | J | PB |
| 70. | D | E | H | Q | S | PB |
| 71. | D | E | I | L | M | PB |
| 72. | D | F | G | L | O | PB |
| 73. | D | F | H | J | K | PB |
| 74. | D | G | K | M | P | PB |
| 75. | D | H | I | Q | S | PB |
| 76. | D | H | L | N | P | PB |
| 77. | D | H | O | Q | S | PB |
| 78. | D | J | M | N | O | PB |
| 79. | D | J | P | Q | R | PB |
| 80. | D | L | M | R | S | PB |
| 81. | E | F | H | O | P | PB |
| 82. | E | F | I | M | S | PB |
| 83. | E | G | I | K | Q | PB |
| 84. | E | G | I | L | P | PB |
| 85. | E | G | I | M | O | PB |
| 86. | E | G | I | M | R | PB |
| 87. | E | G | I | N | S | PB |
| 88. | E | H | J | L | R | PB |
| 89. | E | I | J | K | M | PB |
| 90. | E | I | M | P | Q | PB |
| 91. | E | K | P | R | S | PB |
| 92. | E | L | N | O | Q | PB |
| 93. | F | G | H | M | N | PB |
| 94. | F | G | Q | R | S | PB |
| 95. | F | H | I | P | R | PB |
| 96. | F | I | J | O | Q | PB |
| 97. | F | J | L | N | S | PB |
| 98. | F | K | M | O | S | PB |
| 99. | F | K | N | P | Q | PB |
| 100. | G | H | K | L | S | PB |
| 101. | G | J | K | N | R | PB |
| 102. | G | J | L | M | Q | PB |
| 103. | G | N | O | P | S | PB |
| 104. | H | I | K | N | O | PB |
| 105. | H | J | M | P | S | PB |
| 106. | H | K | M | Q | R | PB |
| 107. | I | L | N | Q | R | PB |
| 108. | J | K | L | O | P | PB |

# POWERBALL BALANCED WHEEL® 53020PB

## Wheel 20 Numbers + PB in 133 Games for a 3 of 3 Win

With Powerball

| Numbers Matched | Maximum Wins | | | | | | Minimum Wins | | | | | |
|---|---|---|---|---|---|---|---|---|---|---|---|---|
| | 5 + 1 | 4 + 1 | 3 + 1 | 2 + 1 | 1 + 1 | 0 + 1 | 5 + 1 | 4 + 1 | 3 + 1 | 2 + 1 | 1 + 1 | 0 + 1 |
| 5 + 1 | 1 | 0 | 6 | 46 | 55 | 25 | 0 | 0 | 10 | 35 | 65 | 23 |
| 4 + 1 | - | 1 | 5 | 24 | 70 | 33 | - | 0 | 4 | 26 | 68 | 35 |
| 3 + 1 | - | - | 3 | 14 | 67 | 49 | - | - | 1 | 16 | 64 | 52 |
| 2 + 1 | - | - | - | 8 | 55 | 70 | - | - | - | 6 | 54 | 73 |
| 1 + 1 | - | - | - | - | 38 | 95 | - | - | - | - | 33 | 100 |
| 0 + 1 | - | - | - | - | - | 133 | - | - | - | - | - | 133 |

Without Powerball

| Numbers Matched | Maximum Wins | | | | | Minimum Wins | | | | |
|---|---|---|---|---|---|---|---|---|---|---|
| | 5 + 0 | 4 + 0 | 3 + 0 | 2 + 0 | 1 + 0 | 5 + 0 | 4 + 0 | 3 + 0 | 2 + 0 | 1 + 0 |
| 5 + 0 | 1 | 0 | 6 | 46 | 55 | 0 | 0 | 10 | 35 | 65 |
| 4 + 0 | - | 1 | 5 | 24 | 70 | - | 0 | 4 | 26 | 68 |
| 3 + 0 | - | - | 3 | 14 | 67 | - | - | 1 | 16 | 64 |
| 2 + 0 | - | - | - | 8 | 55 | - | - | - | 6 | 54 |
| 1 + 0 | - | - | - | - | 38 | - | - | - | - | 33 |

## Your 20 Numbers + PB to Wheel

| A | B | C | D | E | F | G | H | I | J | K |
|---|---|---|---|---|---|---|---|---|---|---|
| 33 | 33 | 33 | 33 | 33 | 33 | 33 | 33 | 33 | 38 | 33 |

| L | M | N | O | P | Q | R | S | T | PB |
|---|---|---|---|---|---|---|---|---|---|
| 33 | 33 | 33 | 33 | 33 | 33 | 33 | 33 | 33 | 133 |

## The 133 Games to Play

| | | | | | | |
|---|---|---|---|---|---|---|
| 1. | A | B | C | M | S | PB |
| 2. | A | B | D | L | O | PB |
| 3. | A | B | E | H | T | PB |
| 4. | A | B | F | J | K | PB |
| 5. | A | B | G | N | R | PB |
| 6. | A | B | I | P | Q | PB |
| 7. | A | C | D | K | L | PB |
| 8. | A | C | E | I | O | PB |
| 9. | A | C | F | G | Q | PB |
| 10. | A | C | H | J | N | PB |
| 11. | A | C | P | R | T | PB |
| 12. | A | D | E | G | Q | PB |
| 13. | A | D | F | I | R | PB |
| 14. | A | D | H | N | P | PB |
| 15. | A | D | H | R | S | PB |
| 16. | A | D | J | M | T | PB |
| 17. | A | E | F | M | N | PB |
| 18. | A | E | J | L | S | PB |
| 19. | A | E | K | P | R | PB |
| 20. | A | F | H | O | T | PB |
| 21. | A | F | J | P | S | PB |
| 22. | A | F | L | N | P | PB |
| 23. | A | G | H | I | M | PB |
| 24. | A | G | H | L | T | PB |
| 25. | A | G | I | K | P | PB |
| 26. | A | G | J | O | S | PB |
| 27. | A | H | K | M | Q | PB |
| 28. | A | I | J | L | M | PB |
| 29. | A | I | N | S | T | PB |
| 30. | A | J | L | Q | R | PB |
| 31. | A | K | N | O | Q | PB |
| 32. | A | K | Q | S | T | PB |
| 33. | A | M | O | P | R | PB |
| 34. | B | C | D | Q | S | PB |
| 35. | B | C | E | G | T | PB |
| 36. | B | C | F | N | O | PB |



(Continued Next Page)

## POWERBALL BALANCED WHEEL® 53020PB (Continued from previous page)

| | | | | | | |
|---|---|---|---|---|---|---|
| 37. | B | C | H | I | J | PB |
| 38. | B | C | K | P | S | PB |
| 39. | B | C | L | O | R | PB |
| 40. | B | D | E | J | P | PB |
| 41. | B | D | F | N | *Q* | PB |
| 42. | B | D | G | H | K | PB |
| 43. | B | D | I | M | R | PB |
| 44. | B | D | J | N | T | PB |
| 45. | B | E | F | R | S | PB |
| 46. | B | E | I | L | N | PB |
| 47. | B | E | K | L | *Q* | PB |
| 48. | B | E | M | O | *Q* | PB |
| 49. | B | F | G | I | S | PB |
| 50. | B | F | H | L | M | PB |
| 51. | B | F | P | *Q* | T | PB |
| 52. | B | G | J | M | *Q* | PB |
| 53. | B | G | L | O | P | PB |
| 54. | B | H | N | O | S | PB |
| 55. | B | H | P | *Q* | R | PB |
| 56. | B | I | J | K | O | PB |
| 57. | B | I | M | O | T | PB |
| 58. | B | J | K | R | T | PB |
| 59. | B | J | L | S | T | PB |
| 60. | B | K | M | N | P | PB |
| 61. | C | D | E | I | R | PB |
| 62. | C | D | F | J | T | PB |
| 63. | C | D | G | N | P | PB |
| 64. | C | D | H | M | O | PB |
| 65. | C | E | F | H | *Q* | PB |
| 66. | C | E | F | L | P | PB |
| 67. | C | E | J | K | N | PB |
| 68. | C | E | L | M | S | PB |
| 69. | C | F | I | M | P | PB |
| 70. | C | F | K | *Q* | R | PB |
| 71. | C | F | O | S | T | PB |
| 72. | C | G | H | K | O | PB |
| 73. | C | G | I | L | S | PB |
| 74. | C | G | J | M | R | PB |
| 75. | C | H | J | L | P | PB |
| 76. | C | H | R | S | T | PB |
| 77. | C | I | K | M | T | PB |
| 78. | C | I | M | N | *Q* | PB |
| 79. | C | J | N | R | S | PB |
| 80. | C | J | O | P | *Q* | PB |
| 81. | C | L | N | *Q* | T | PB |
| 82. | D | E | F | K | M | PB |
| 83. | D | E | H | L | N | PB |
| 84. | D | E | O | S | T | PB |
| 85. | D | F | G | J | L | PB |
| 86. | D | F | H | J | S | PB |
| 87. | D | F | K | O | P | PB |
| 88. | D | G | I | N | O | PB |
| 89. | D | G | K | R | T | PB |
| 90. | D | G | M | N | S | PB |
| 91. | D | H | I | *Q* | T | PB |
| 92. | D | I | J | K | S | PB |
| 93. | D | I | L | P | T | PB |
| 94. | D | J | O | *Q* | R | PB |
| 95. | D | K | N | *Q* | R | PB |
| 96. | D | L | M | P | *Q* | PB |
| 97. | D | L | P | R | S | PB |
| 98. | E | F | G | M | O | PB |
| 99. | E | F | I | J | T | PB |
| 100. | E | G | H | K | S | PB |
| 101. | E | G | I | J | P | PB |
| 102. | E | G | L | N | R | PB |
| 103. | E | H | I | M | S | PB |
| 104. | E | H | J | M | P | PB |
| 105. | E | H | J | O | R | PB |
| 106. | E | I | J | K | *Q* | PB |



(Continued Next Page)

## POWERBALL BALANCED WHEEL® 53020PB (Continued from previous page)

| | | | | | | |
|---|---|---|---|---|---|---|
| 107. | E | K | L | O | T | PB |
| 108. | E | M | Q | R | T | PB |
| 109. | E | N | O | P | T | PB |
| 110. | E | N | P | Q | S | PB |
| 111. | F | G | H | P | R | PB |
| 112. | F | G | K | N | T | PB |
| 113. | F | H | I | K | N | PB |
| 114. | F | I | L | O | Q | PB |
| 115. | F | J | M | Q | S | PB |
| 116. | F | J | N | O | R | PB |
| 117. | F | K | L | N | S | PB |
| 118. | F | L | M | R | T | PB |
| 119. | G | H | J | N | Q | PB |
| 120. | G | I | O | R | T | PB |
| 121. | G | I | Q | R | S | PB |
| 122. | G | J | K | L | M | PB |
| 123. | G | J | O | Q | T | PB |
| 124. | G | K | L | P | Q | PB |
| 125. | G | M | P | S | T | PB |
| 126. | H | I | K | L | R | PB |
| 127. | H | I | O | P | S | PB |
| 128. | H | J | K | P | T | PB |
| 129. | H | L | O | Q | S | PB |
| 130. | H | M | N | R | T | PB |
| 131. | I | J | N | P | R | PB |
| 132. | J | L | M | N | O | PB |
| 133. | K | M | O | R | S | PB |



# POWERBALL BALANCED WHEEL® 54107PB

## Wheel 7 Numbers + PB in 3 Games for a 4 of 5 Win

With Powerball

| Numbers Matched | Maximum Wins | | | | | | Minimum Wins | | | | | |
|---|---|---|---|---|---|---|---|---|---|---|---|---|
| | 5 + 1 | 4 + 1 | 3 + 1 | 2 + 1 | 1 + 1 | 0 + 1 | 5 + 1 | 4 + 1 | 3 + 1 | 2 + 1 | 1 + 1 | 0 + 1 |
| 5 + 1 | 1 | 0 | 2 | 0 | 0 | 0 | 0 | 1 | 2 | 0 | 0 | 0 |
| 4 + 1 | - | 1 | 1 | 1 | 0 | 0 | - | 0 | 2 | 1 | 0 | 0 |
| 3 + 1 | - | - | 2 | 0 | 1 | 0 | - | - | 0 | 3 | 0 | 0 |
| 2 + 1 | - | - | - | 2 | 1 | 0 | - | - | - | 1 | 2 | 0 |
| 1 + 1 | - | - | - | - | 3 | 0 | - | - | - | - | 2 | 1 |
| 0 + 1 | - | - | - | - | - | 3 | - | - | - | - | - | 3 |

Without Powerball

| Numbers Matched | Maximum Wins | | | | | Minimum Wins | | | | |
|---|---|---|---|---|---|---|---|---|---|---|
| | 5 + 0 | 4 + 0 | 3 + 0 | 2 + 0 | 1 + 0 | 5 + 0 | 4 + 0 | 3 + 0 | 2 + 0 | 1 + 0 |
| 5 + 0 | 1 | 0 | 2 | 0 | 0 | 0 | 1 | 2 | 0 | 0 |
| 4 + 0 | - | 1 | 1 | 1 | 0 | - | 0 | 2 | 1 | 0 |
| 3 + 0 | - | - | 2 | 0 | 1 | - | - | 0 | 3 | 0 |
| 2 + 0 | - | - | - | 2 | 1 | - | - | - | 1 | 2 |
| 1 + 0 | - | - | - | - | 3 | - | - | - | - | 2 |

## Your 7 Numbers + PB to Wheel

| A | B | C | D | E | F | G | PB |
|---|---|---|---|---|---|---|---|
| 2 | 2 | 2 | 3 | 2 | 2 | 2 | 3 |

## The 3 Games to Play

| | | | | | | |
|---|---|---|---|---|---|---|
| 1. | A | B | D | F | G | PB |
| 2. | A | C | D | E | G | PB |
| 3. | B | C | D | E | F | PB |

# POWERBALL BALANCED WHEEL® 54108PB

## Wheel 8 Numbers + PB in 5 Games for a 4 of 5 Win

With Powerball

| Numbers Matched | Maximum Wins 5 + 1 | 4 + 1 | 3 + 1 | 2 + 1 | 1 + 1 | 0 + 1 | Minimum Wins 5 + 1 | 4 + 1 | 3 + 1 | 2 + 1 | 1 + 1 | 0 + 1 |
|---|---|---|---|---|---|---|---|---|---|---|---|---|
| 5 + 1 | 1 | 2 | 1 | 1 | 0 | 0 | 0 | 1 | 2 | 2 | 0 | 0 |
| 4 + 1 | - | 2 | 2 | 0 | 1 | 0 | - | 0 | 2 | 2 | 1 | 0 |
| 3 + 1 | - | - | 4 | 0 | 0 | 1 | - | - | 0 | 4 | 1 | 0 |
| 2 + 1 | - | - | - | 4 | 0 | 1 | - | - | - | 1 | 3 | 1 |
| 1 + 1 | - | - | - | - | 4 | 1 | - | - | - | - | 2 | 3 |
| 0 + 1 | - | - | - | - | - | 5 | - | - | - | - | - | 5 |

Without Powerball

| Numbers Matched | Maximum Wins 5 + 0 | 4 + 0 | 3 + 0 | 2 + 0 | 1 + 0 | Minimum Wins 5 + 0 | 4 + 0 | 3 + 0 | 2 + 0 | 1 + 0 |
|---|---|---|---|---|---|---|---|---|---|---|
| 5 + 0 | 1 | 2 | 1 | 1 | 0 | 0 | 1 | 2 | 2 | 0 |
| 4 + 0 | - | 2 | 2 | 0 | 1 | - | 0 | 2 | 2 | 1 |
| 3 + 0 | - | - | 4 | 0 | 0 | - | - | 0 | 4 | 1 |
| 2 + 0 | - | - | - | 4 | 0 | - | - | - | 1 | 3 |
| 1 + 0 | - | - | - | - | 4 | - | - | - | - | 2 |

## Your 8 Numbers + PB to Wheel

| A | B | C | D | E | F | G | H | PB |
|---|---|---|---|---|---|---|---|---|
| 4 | 2 | 3 | 4 | 3 | 3 | 2 | 4 | 5 |

## The 5 Games to Play

| | | | | | | |
|---|---|---|---|---|---|---|
| 1. | A | B | D | G | H | PB |
| 2. | A | C | D | E | H | PB |
| 3. | A | C | D | F | H | PB |
| 4. | A | D | E | F | H | PB |
| 5. | B | C | E | F | G | PB |



# POWERBALL BALANCED WHEEL® 54109PB

## Wheel 9 Numbers + PB in 9 Games for a 4 of 5 Win

With Powerball

| Numbers Matched | Maximum Wins 5 + 1 | 4 + 1 | 3 + 1 | 2 + 1 | 1 + 1 | 0 + 1 | Minimum Wins 5 + 1 | 4 + 1 | 3 + 1 | 2 + 1 | 1 + 1 | 0 + 1 |
|---|---|---|---|---|---|---|---|---|---|---|---|---|
| 5 + 1 | 1 | 1 | 2 | 5 | 0 | 0 | 0 | 1 | 5 | 3 | 0 | 0 |
| 4 + 1 | - | 2 | 1 | 3 | 3 | 0 | - | 0 | 3 | 5 | 1 | 0 |
| 3 + 1 | - | - | 3 | 1 | 4 | 1 | - | - | 0 | 6 | 3 | 0 |
| 2 + 1 | - | - | - | 4 | 2 | 3 | - | - | - | 2 | 6 | 1 |
| 1 + 1 | - | - | - | - | 5 | 4 | - | - | - | - | 5 | 4 |
| 0 + 1 | - | - | - | - | - | 9 | - | - | - | - | - | 9 |

Without Powerball

| Numbers Matched | Maximum Wins 5 + 0 | 4 + 0 | 3 + 0 | 2 + 0 | 1 + 0 | Minimum Wins 5 + 0 | 4 + 0 | 3 + 0 | 2 + 0 | 1 + 0 |
|---|---|---|---|---|---|---|---|---|---|---|
| 5 + 0 | 1 | 1 | 2 | 5 | 0 | 0 | 1 | 5 | 3 | 0 |
| 4 + 0 | - | 2 | 1 | 3 | 3 | - | 0 | 3 | 5 | 1 |
| 3 + 0 | - | - | 3 | 1 | 4 | - | - | 0 | 6 | 3 |
| 2 + 0 | - | - | - | 4 | 2 | - | - | - | 2 | 6 |
| 1 + 0 | - | - | - | - | 5 | - | - | - | - | 5 |

## Your 9 Numbers + PB to Wheel

| A | B | C | D | E | F | G | H | I | PB |
|---|---|---|---|---|---|---|---|---|---|
| 5 | 5 | 5 | 5 | 5 | 5 | 5 | 5 | 5 | 9 |

(Continued Next Page)

**POWERBALL BALANCED WHEEL® 54109PB** (Continued from previous page)

## The 9 Games to Play

| | | | | | | |
|---|---|---|---|---|---|---|
| 1. | A | B | D | F | I | PB |
| 2. | A | B | E | F | H | PB |
| 3. | A | C | D | G | H | PB |
| 4. | A | C | E | F | G | PB |
| 5. | A | E | F | H | I | PB |
| 6. | B | C | D | E | I | PB |
| 7. | B | C | G | H | I | PB |
| 8. | B | D | E | G | I | PB |
| 9. | C | D | F | G | H | PB |



# POWERBALL BALANCED WHEEL® 54110PB

## Wheel 10 Numbers + PB in 14 Games for a 4 of 5 Win

With Powerball

| Numbers Matched | Maximum Wins 5 + 1 | 4 + 1 | 3 + 1 | 2 + 1 | 1 + 1 | 0 + 1 | Minimum Wins 5 + 1 | 4 + 1 | 3 + 1 | 2 + 1 | 1 + 1 | 0 + 1 |
|---|---|---|---|---|---|---|---|---|---|---|---|---|
| 5 + 1 | 1 | 0 | 6 | 6 | 0 | 1 | 0 | 1 | 6 | 6 | 1 | 0 |
| 4 + 1 | - | 1 | 4 | 4 | 4 | 1 | - | 0 | 3 | 8 | 3 | 0 |
| 3 + 1 | - | - | 3 | 4 | 4 | 3 | - | - | 0 | 7 | 7 | 0 |
| 2 + 1 | - | - | - | 7 | 0 | 7 | - | - | - | 0 | 14 | 0 |
| 1 + 1 | - | - | - | - | 7 | 7 | - | - | - | - | 7 | 7 |
| 0 + 1 | - | - | - | - | - | 14 | - | - | - | - | - | 14 |

Without Powerball

| Numbers Matched | Maximum Wins 5 + 0 | 4 + 0 | 3 + 0 | 2 + 0 | 1 + 0 | Minimum Wins 5 + 0 | 4 + 0 | 3 + 0 | 2 + 0 | 1 + 0 |
|---|---|---|---|---|---|---|---|---|---|---|
| 5 + 0 | 1 | 0 | 6 | 6 | 0 | 0 | 1 | 6 | 6 | 1 |
| 4 + 0 | - | 1 | 4 | 4 | 4 | - | 0 | 3 | 8 | 3 |
| 3 + 0 | - | - | 3 | 4 | 4 | - | - | 0 | 7 | 7 |
| 2 + 0 | - | - | - | 7 | 0 | - | - | - | 0 | 14 |
| 1 + 0 | - | - | - | - | 7 | - | - | - | - | 7 |

## Your 10 Numbers + PB to Wheel

| A | B | C | D | E | F | G | H | I | J | PB |
|---|---|---|---|---|---|---|---|---|---|---|
| 7 | 7 | 7 | 7 | 7 | 7 | 7 | 7 | 7 | 7 | 14 |

## The 14 Games to Play

| | | | | | | |
|---|---|---|---|---|---|---|
| 1. | A | C | D | G | J | PB |
| 2. | A | C | E | F | J | PB |
| 3. | A | C | H | I | J | PB |
| 4. | A | D | E | H | J | PB |
| 5. | A | D | F | I | J | PB |
| 6. | A | E | G | I | J | PB |
| 7. | A | F | G | H | J | PB |
| 8. | B | C | D | E | I | PB |
| 9. | B | C | D | F | H | PB |
| 10. | B | C | E | G | H | PB |
| 11. | B | C | F | G | I | PB |
| 12. | B | D | E | F | G | PB |
| 13. | B | D | G | H | I | PB |
| 14. | B | E | F | H | I | PB |

# POWERBALL BALANCED WHEEL® 54111PB

## Wheel 11 Numbers + PB in 26 Games for a 4 of 5 Win

With Powerball

| Numbers Matched | Maximum Wins 5 + 1 | 4 + 1 | 3 + 1 | 2 + 1 | 1 + 1 | 0 + 1 | Minimum Wins 5 + 1 | 4 + 1 | 3 + 1 | 2 + 1 | 1 + 1 | 0 + 1 |
|---|---|---|---|---|---|---|---|---|---|---|---|---|
| 5 + 1 | 1 | 0 | 10 | 10 | 5 | 0 | 0 | 1 | 10 | 10 | 4 | 1 |
| 4 + 1 | - | 1 | 4 | 12 | 8 | 1 | - | 0 | 5 | 12 | 7 | 2 |
| 3 + 1 | - | - | 4 | 0 | 22 | 0 | - | - | 1 | 10 | 11 | 4 |
| 2 + 1 | - | - | - | 5 | 14 | 7 | - | - | - | 4 | 14 | 8 |
| 1 + 1 | - | - | - | - | 12 | 14 | - | - | - | - | 10 | 16 |
| 0 + 1 | - | - | - | - | - | 26 | - | - | - | - | - | 26 |

Without Powerball

| Numbers Matched | Maximum Wins 5 + 0 | 4 + 0 | 3 + 0 | 2 + 0 | 1 + 0 | Minimum Wins 5 + 0 | 4 + 0 | 3 + 0 | 2 + 0 | 1 + 0 |
|---|---|---|---|---|---|---|---|---|---|---|
| 5 + 0 | 1 | 0 | 10 | 10 | 5 | 0 | 1 | 10 | 10 | 4 |
| 4 + 0 | - | 1 | 4 | 12 | 8 | - | 0 | 5 | 12 | 7 |
| 3 + 0 | - | - | 4 | 0 | 22 | - | - | 1 | 10 | 11 |
| 2 + 0 | - | - | - | 5 | 14 | - | - | - | 4 | 14 |
| 1 + 0 | - | - | - | - | 12 | - | - | - | - | 10 |

## Your 11 Numbers + PB to Wheel

| A | B | C | D | E | F |
|---|---|---|---|---|---|
| 12 | 12 | 12 | 12 | 10 | 12 |
| **G** | **H** | **I** | **J** | **K** | **PB** |
| 12 | 12 | 12 | 12 | 12 | 26 |

## The 26 Games to Play

| | | | | | | |
|---|---|---|---|---|---|---|
| 1. | A | B | C | E | K | PB |
| 2. | A | B | D | E | J | PB |
| 3. | A | B | E | F | G | PB |
| 4. | A | B | E | H | I | PB |
| 5. | A | C | D | F | H | PB |
| 6. | A | C | D | G | I | PB |
| 7. | A | C | F | I | J | PB |
| 8. | A | C | G | H | J | PB |
| 9. | A | D | F | I | K | PB |
| 10. | A | D | G | H | K | PB |
| 11. | A | F | H | J | K | PB |
| 12. | A | G | I | J | K | PB |
| 13. | B | C | D | F | I | PB |
| 14. | B | C | D | G | H | PB |
| 15. | B | C | F | H | J | PB |
| 16. | B | C | G | I | J | PB |
| 17. | B | D | F | H | K | PB |
| 18. | B | D | G | I | K | PB |
| 19. | B | F | I | J | K | PB |
| 20. | B | G | H | J | K | PB |
| 21. | C | D | E | J | K | PB |
| 22. | C | E | F | G | K | PB |
| 23. | C | E | H | I | K | PB |
| 24. | D | E | F | G | J | PB |
| 25. | D | E | H | I | J | PB |
| 26. | E | F | G | H | I | PB |

# POWERBALL BALANCED WHEEL® 54112PB

## Wheel 12 Numbers + PB in 37 Games for a 4 of 5 Win

With Powerball

| Numbers Matched | Maximum Wins | | | | | | Minimum Wins | | | | | |
|---|---|---|---|---|---|---|---|---|---|---|---|---|
| | 5 + 1 | 4 + 1 | 3 + 1 | 2 + 1 | 1 + 1 | 0 + 1 | 5 + 1 | 4 + 1 | 3 + 1 | 2 + 1 | 1 + 1 | 0 + 1 |
| 5 + 1 | 1 | 2 | 7 | 19 | 7 | 1 | 0 | 1 | 8 | 19 | 9 | 0 |
| 4 + 1 | - | 2 | 3 | 16 | 14 | 2 | - | 0 | 4 | 17 | 14 | 2 |
| 3 + 1 | - | - | 3 | 13 | 14 | 7 | - | - | 1 | 11 | 19 | 6 |
| 2 + 1 | - | - | - | 8 | 17 | 12 | - | - | - | 4 | 21 | 12 |
| 1 + 1 | - | - | - | - | 17 | 20 | - | - | - | - | 14 | 23 |
| 0 + 1 | - | - | - | - | - | 37 | - | - | - | - | - | 37 |

Without Powerball

| Numbers Matched | Maximum Wins | | | | | Minimum Wins | | | | |
|---|---|---|---|---|---|---|---|---|---|---|
| | 5 + 0 | 4 + 0 | 3 + 0 | 2 + 0 | 1 + 0 | 5 + 0 | 4 + 0 | 3 + 0 | 2 + 0 | 1 + 0 |
| 5 + 0 | 1 | 2 | 7 | 19 | 7 | 0 | 1 | 8 | 19 | 9 |
| 4 + 0 | - | 2 | 3 | 16 | 14 | - | 0 | 4 | 17 | 14 |
| 3 + 0 | - | - | 3 | 13 | 14 | - | - | 1 | 11 | 19 |
| 2 + 0 | - | - | - | 8 | 17 | - | - | - | 4 | 21 |
| 1 + 0 | - | - | - | - | 17 | - | - | - | - | 14 |

## Your 12 Numbers + PB to Wheel

| A | B | C | D | E | F | G |
|---|---|---|---|---|---|---|
| 15 | 16 | 15 | 17 | 15 | 15 | 15 |

| H | I | J | K | L | PB |
|---|---|---|---|---|---|
| 14 | 15 | 16 | 16 | 16 | 37 |

## The 37 Games to Play

| | | | | | | |
|---|---|---|---|---|---|---|
| 1. | A | B | C | G | I | PB |
| 2. | A | B | D | G | J | PB |
| 3. | A | B | D | I | L | PB |
| 4. | A | B | D | J | K | PB |
| 5. | A | B | E | F | I | PB |
| 6. | A | B | F | H | L | PB |
| 7. | A | C | D | F | H | PB |
| 8. | A | C | E | H | J | PB |
| 9. | A | C | E | K | L | PB |
| 10. | A | C | F | I | K | PB |
| 11. | A | D | E | G | K | PB |
| 12. | A | E | H | I | K | PB |
| 13. | A | F | G | J | L | PB |
| 14. | A | G | H | K | L | PB |
| 15. | A | H | I | J | L | PB |
| 16. | B | C | D | E | K | PB |
| 17. | B | C | D | G | L | PB |
| 18. | B | C | F | J | L | PB |
| 19. | B | C | H | I | K | PB |
| 20. | B | D | E | H | L | PB |
| 21. | B | D | F | G | K | PB |
| 22. | B | D | F | I | J | PB |
| 23. | B | E | G | H | J | PB |
| 24. | B | E | G | I | L | PB |
| 25. | B | E | J | K | L | PB |
| 26. | C | D | E | I | J | PB |
| 27. | C | D | G | J | L | PB |
| 28. | C | D | H | J | K | PB |
| 29. | C | E | F | G | H | PB |
| 30. | C | F | H | I | L | PB |
| 31. | C | G | I | J | K | PB |
| 32. | D | E | F | J | L | PB |
| 33. | D | F | G | H | I | PB |
| 34. | D | F | G | K | L | PB |
| 35. | D | F | I | K | L | PB |
| 36. | E | F | H | J | K | PB |



(Continued Next Page)

**POWERBALL BALANCED WHEEL® 54112PB** (Continued from previous page)

| | | | | | | |
|---|---|---|---|---|---|---|
| 37. | E | G | I | J | K | PB |



# POWERBALL BALANCED WHEEL® 54113PB

## Wheel 13 Numbers + PB in 58 Games for a 4 of 5 Win

With Powerball

| Numbers Matched | Maximum Wins 5 + 1 | 4 + 1 | 3 + 1 | 2 + 1 | 1 + 1 | 0 + 1 | Minimum Wins 5 + 1 | 4 + 1 | 3 + 1 | 2 + 1 | 1 + 1 | 0 + 1 |
|---|---|---|---|---|---|---|---|---|---|---|---|---|
| 5 + 1 | 1 | 3 | 7 | 34 | 10 | 3 | 0 | 1 | 9 | 34 | 10 | 4 |
| 4 + 1 | - | 2 | 5 | 23 | 23 | 5 | - | 0 | 5 | 23 | 24 | 6 |
| 3 + 1 | - | - | 4 | 14 | 30 | 10 | - | - | 1 | 16 | 28 | 13 |
| 2 + 1 | - | - | - | 9 | 30 | 19 | - | - | - | 6 | 30 | 22 |
| 1 + 1 | - | - | - | - | 24 | 34 | - | - | - | - | 21 | 37 |
| 0 + 1 | - | - | - | - | - | 58 | - | - | - | - | - | 58 |

Without Powerball

| Numbers Matched | Maximum Wins 5 + 0 | 4 + 0 | 3 + 0 | 2 + 0 | 1 + 0 | Minimum Wins 5 + 0 | 4 + 0 | 3 + 0 | 2 + 0 | 1 + 0 |
|---|---|---|---|---|---|---|---|---|---|---|
| 5 + 0 | 1 | 3 | 7 | 34 | 10 | 0 | 1 | 9 | 34 | 10 |
| 4 + 0 | - | 2 | 5 | 23 | 23 | - | 0 | 5 | 23 | 24 |
| 3 + 0 | - | - | 4 | 14 | 30 | - | - | 1 | 16 | 28 |
| 2 + 0 | - | - | - | 9 | 30 | - | - | - | 6 | 30 |
| 1 + 0 | - | - | - | - | 24 | - | - | - | - | 21 |

## Your 13 Numbers + PB to Wheel

| A | B | C | D | E | F | G |
|---|---|---|---|---|---|---|
| 22 | 22 | 21 | 24 | 21 | 23 | 24 |
| **H** | **I** | **J** | **K** | **L** | **M** | **PB** |
| 23 | 22 | 21 | 24 | 21 | 22 | 58 |

## The 58 Games to Play

| | | | | | | |
|---|---|---|---|---|---|---|
| 1. | A | B | C | G | L | PB |
| 2. | A | B | C | H | I | PB |
| 3. | A | B | D | H | K | PB |
| 4. | A | B | D | I | M | PB |
| 5. | A | B | E | F | M | PB |
| 6. | A | B | E | G | H | PB |
| 7. | A | B | G | J | K | PB |
| 8. | A | C | D | F | J | PB |
| 9. | A | C | D | K | L | PB |
| 10. | A | C | E | K | M | PB |
| 11. | A | C | G | H | I | PB |
| 12. | A | C | I | K | M | PB |
| 13. | A | D | E | G | K | PB |
| 14. | A | D | E | H | J | PB |
| 15. | A | D | F | I | M | PB |
| 16. | A | D | G | H | J | PB |
| 17. | A | E | F | I | L | PB |
| 18. | A | E | I | J | L | PB |
| 19. | A | F | G | I | M | PB |
| 20. | A | F | H | K | L | PB |
| 21. | A | G | J | L | M | PB |
| 22. | A | H | J | L | M | PB |
| 23. | B | C | D | E | I | PB |
| 24. | B | C | D | H | M | PB |
| 25. | B | C | E | J | M | PB |
| 26. | B | C | F | G | K | PB |
| 27. | B | C | G | I | J | PB |
| 28. | B | D | E | J | L | PB |
| 29. | B | D | F | G | I | PB |
| 30. | B | D | F | G | L | PB |



(Continued Next Page)

## POWERBALL BALANCED WHEEL® 54113PB (Continued from previous page)

| | | | | | | |
|---|---|---|---|---|---|---|
| 31. | B | D | J | K | M | PB |
| 32. | B | E | F | I | K | PB |
| 33. | B | E | H | K | L | PB |
| 34. | B | F | G | J | L | PB |
| 35. | B | F | H | I | J | PB |
| 36. | B | G | H | K | M | PB |
| 37. | B | I | K | L | M | PB |
| 38. | C | D | E | F | H | PB |
| 39. | C | D | G | K | M | PB |
| 40. | C | D | J | K | L | PB |
| 41. | C | E | F | G | J | PB |
| 42. | C | E | F | H | L | PB |
| 43. | C | F | H | K | M | PB |
| 44. | C | F | I | L | M | PB |
| 45. | C | G | H | J | L | PB |
| 46. | C | H | I | J | K | PB |
| 47. | D | E | G | L | M | PB |
| 48. | D | E | H | I | K | PB |
| 49. | D | F | H | L | M | PB |
| 50. | D | F | I | J | K | PB |
| 51. | D | F | J | K | L | PB |
| 52. | D | G | H | I | L | PB |
| 53. | D | G | I | J | M | PB |
| 54. | E | F | G | H | K | PB |
| 55. | E | F | J | K | M | PB |
| 56. | E | G | H | I | M | PB |
| 57. | E | G | I | K | L | PB |
| 58. | F | G | H | K | M | PB |



# POWERBALL BALANCED WHEEL® 54114PB

## Wheel 14 Numbers + PB in 76 Games for a 4 of 5 Win

With Powerball

| Numbers Matched | Maximum Wins | | | | | | Minimum Wins | | | | | |
|---|---|---|---|---|---|---|---|---|---|---|---|---|
| | 5 + 1 | 4 + 1 | 3 + 1 | 2 + 1 | 1 + 1 | 0 + 1 | 5 + 1 | 4 + 1 | 3 + 1 | 2 + 1 | 1 + 1 | 0 + 1 |
| 5 + 1 | 1 | 4 | 11 | 33 | 21 | 6 | 0 | 1 | 11 | 35 | 25 | 4 |
| 4 + 1 | - | 4 | 6 | 27 | 27 | 12 | - | 0 | 5 | 28 | 35 | 8 |
| 3 + 1 | - | - | 8 | 19 | 26 | 23 | - | - | 1 | 18 | 38 | 19 |
| 2 + 1 | - | - | - | 15 | 28 | 33 | - | - | - | 6 | 43 | 27 |
| 1 + 1 | - | - | - | - | 30 | 46 | - | - | - | - | 25 | 51 |
| 0 + 1 | - | - | - | - | - | 76 | - | - | - | - | - | 76 |

Without Powerball

| Numbers Matched | Maximum Wins | | | | | Minimum Wins | | | | |
|---|---|---|---|---|---|---|---|---|---|---|
| | 5 + 0 | 4 + 0 | 3 + 0 | 2 + 0 | 1 + 0 | 5 + 0 | 4 + 0 | 3 + 0 | 2 + 0 | 1 + 0 |
| 5 + 0 | 1 | 4 | 11 | 33 | 21 | 0 | 1 | 11 | 35 | 25 |
| 4 + 0 | - | 4 | 6 | 27 | 27 | - | 0 | 5 | 28 | 35 |
| 3 + 0 | - | - | 8 | 19 | 26 | - | - | 1 | 18 | 38 |
| 2 + 0 | - | - | - | 15 | 28 | - | - | - | 6 | 43 |
| 1 + 0 | - | - | - | - | 30 | - | - | - | - | 25 |

## Your 14 Numbers + PB to Wheel

| A | B | C | D | E | F | G | H |
|---|---|---|---|---|---|---|---|
| 26 | 29 | 26 | 25 | 30 | 28 | 30 | 26 |

| I | J | K | L | M | N | PB |
|---|---|---|---|---|---|---|
| 27 | 29 | 26 | 26 | 26 | 26 | 76 |

## The 76 Games to Play

| | | | | | | |
|---|---|---|---|---|---|---|
| 1. | A | B | C | G | L | PB |
| 2. | A | B | D | F | N | PB |
| 3. | A | B | E | F | L | PB |
| 4. | A | B | E | J | N | PB |



(Continued Next Page)

## POWERBALL BALANCED WHEEL® 54114PB (Continued from previous page)

| | | | | | | | | | | | | | |
|---|---|---|---|---|---|---|---|---|---|---|---|---|---|
| 5. | A | B | G | H | N | PB | 40. | B | F | G | J | K | PB |
| 6. | A | B | G | I | J | PB | 41. | B | F | H | I | K | PB |
| 7. | A | B | G | J | M | PB | 42. | B | G | H | L | M | PB |
| 8. | A | B | J | K | L | PB | 43. | B | G | I | J | L | PB |
| 9. | A | C | D | E | M | PB | 44. | B | G | I | J | M | PB |
| 10. | A | C | E | K | L | PB | 45. | B | G | I | J | N | PB |
| 11. | A | C | F | J | L | PB | 46. | B | G | J | L | N | PB |
| 12. | A | C | F | K | M | PB | 47. | B | J | K | M | N | PB |
| 13. | A | C | H | I | M | PB | 48. | C | D | E | L | N | PB |
| 14. | A | C | I | K | N | PB | 49. | C | D | F | G | I | PB |
| 15. | A | D | E | G | N | PB | 50. | C | D | G | H | K | PB |
| 16. | A | D | F | H | M | PB | 51. | C | D | G | J | K | PB |
| 17. | A | D | H | I | L | PB | 52. | C | E | F | G | H | PB |
| 18. | A | D | H | J | N | PB | 53. | C | E | G | I | K | PB |
| 19. | A | D | I | K | M | PB | 54. | C | E | H | I | J | PB |
| 20. | A | E | F | H | N | PB | 55. | C | E | K | M | N | PB |
| 21. | A | E | F | I | M | PB | 56. | C | F | J | M | N | PB |
| 22. | A | E | G | J | L | PB | 57. | C | F | K | L | N | PB |
| 23. | A | E | H | K | M | PB | 58. | C | G | H | J | K | PB |
| 24. | A | F | G | J | N | PB | 59. | C | H | I | L | N | PB |
| 25. | A | F | G | K | L | PB | 60. | C | I | K | L | M | PB |
| 26. | A | I | L | M | N | PB | 61. | D | E | F | I | J | PB |
| 27. | B | C | D | H | K | PB | 62. | D | E | F | J | K | PB |
| 28. | B | C | D | I | J | PB | 63. | D | E | G | L | M | PB |
| 29. | B | C | E | F | I | PB | 64. | D | F | G | H | I | PB |
| 30. | B | C | E | G | H | PB | 65. | D | F | H | L | N | PB |
| 31. | B | C | F | H | J | PB | 66. | D | H | I | M | N | PB |
| 32. | B | C | G | M | N | PB | 67. | D | H | J | L | M | PB |
| 33. | B | D | E | G | J | PB | 68. | D | I | K | L | N | PB |
| 34. | B | D | E | G | K | PB | 69. | E | F | H | L | M | PB |
| 35. | B | D | E | H | I | PB | 70. | E | F | I | L | N | PB |
| 36. | B | D | F | L | M | PB | 71. | E | G | H | I | K | PB |
| 37. | B | E | F | M | N | PB | 72. | E | G | J | M | N | PB |
| 38. | B | E | I | J | K | PB | 73. | E | H | K | L | N | PB |
| 39. | B | E | J | L | M | PB | 74. | F | G | J | L | M | PB |



(Continued Next Page)

**POWERBALL BALANCED WHEEL® 54114PB** (Continued from previous page)

| | | | | | | | | | | | | | |
|---|---|---|---|---|---|---|---|---|---|---|---|---|---|
| 75. | F | G | K | M | N | PB | 76. | F | H | I | J | K | PB |



# POWERBALL BALANCED WHEEL® 54115PB

## Wheel 15 Numbers + PB in 118 Games for a 4 of 5 Win

With Powerball

| Numbers Matched | Maximum Wins | | | | | | Minimum Wins | | | | | |
|---|---|---|---|---|---|---|---|---|---|---|---|---|
| | 5 + 1 | 4 + 1 | 3 + 1 | 2 + 1 | 1 + 1 | 0 + 1 | 5 + 1 | 4 + 1 | 3 + 1 | 2 + 1 | 1 + 1 | 0 + 1 |
| 5 + 1 | 1 | 4 | 18 | 42 | 43 | 10 | 0 | 1 | 13 | 55 | 38 | 11 |
| 4 + 1 | - | 4 | 8 | 38 | 48 | 20 | - | 0 | 6 | 38 | 58 | 16 |
| 3 + 1 | - | - | 9 | 25 | 47 | 37 | - | - | 1 | 24 | 63 | 30 |
| 2 + 1 | - | - | - | 18 | 47 | 53 | - | - | - | 8 | 62 | 48 |
| 1 + 1 | - | - | - | - | 43 | 75 | - | - | - | - | 36 | 82 |
| 0 + 1 | - | - | - | - | - | 118 | - | - | - | - | - | 118 |

Without Powerball

| Numbers Matched | Maximum Wins | | | | | Minimum Wins | | | | |
|---|---|---|---|---|---|---|---|---|---|---|
| | 5 + 0 | 4 + 0 | 3 + 0 | 2 + 0 | 1 + 0 | 5 + 0 | 4 + 0 | 3 + 0 | 2 + 0 | 1 + 0 |
| 5 + 0 | 1 | 4 | 18 | 42 | 43 | 0 | 1 | 13 | 55 | 38 |
| 4 + 0 | - | 4 | 8 | 38 | 48 | - | 0 | 6 | 38 | 58 |
| 3 + 0 | - | - | 9 | 25 | 47 | - | - | 1 | 24 | 63 |
| 2 + 0 | - | - | - | 18 | 47 | - | - | - | 8 | 62 |
| 1 + 0 | - | - | - | - | 43 | - | - | - | - | 36 |

## Your 15 Numbers + PB to Wheel

| A | B | C | D | E | F | G | H |
|---|---|---|---|---|---|---|---|
| 38 | 38 | 41 | 36 | 38 | 38 | 38 | 38 |

| I | J | K | L | M | N | O | PB |
|---|---|---|---|---|---|---|---|
| 43 | 38 | 42 | 40 | 39 | 43 | 40 | 118 |

## The 118 Games to Play

| | | | | | | |
|---|---|---|---|---|---|---|
| 1. | A | B | C | G | O | PB |
| 2. | A | B | D | J | K | PB |
| 3. | A | B | D | J | L | PB |
| 4. | A | B | E | F | L | PB |
| 5. | A | B | E | K | L | PB |
| 6. | A | B | F | H | I | PB |
| 7. | A | B | F | J | M | PB |
| 8. | A | B | G | I | J | PB |
| 9. | A | B | G | M | N | PB |
| 10. | A | B | H | K | O | PB |
| 11. | A | B | I | K | N | PB |
| 12. | A | C | D | F | O | PB |
| 13. | A | C | D | K | M | PB |
| 14. | A | C | E | H | J | PB |
| 15. | A | C | E | I | N | PB |
| 16. | A | C | F | K | M | PB |
| 17. | A | C | G | I | K | PB |
| 18. | A | C | H | L | M | PB |
| 19. | A | C | I | L | O | PB |
| 20. | A | C | K | L | N | PB |
| 21. | A | D | E | F | K | PB |
| 22. | A | D | E | G | L | PB |
| 23. | A | D | F | I | J | PB |
| 24. | A | D | F | M | N | PB |
| 25. | A | D | G | H | I | PB |
| 26. | A | D | G | J | M | PB |
| 27. | A | E | H | J | N | PB |
| 28. | A | E | I | M | O | PB |
| 29. | A | E | J | K | M | PB |
| 30. | A | E | J | N | O | PB |



(Continued Next Page)

## POWERBALL BALANCED WHEEL® 54115PB (Continued from previous page)

| | | | | | | |
|---|---|---|---|---|---|---|
| 31. | A | F | G | J | L | PB |
| 32. | A | F | J | K | L | PB |
| 33. | A | G | H | I | K | PB |
| 34. | A | G | K | N | O | PB |
| 35. | A | H | I | L | N | PB |
| 36. | A | H | J | N | O | PB |
| 37. | A | H | L | M | O | PB |
| 38. | A | I | J | L | N | PB |
| 39. | B | C | D | E | M | PB |
| 40. | B | C | D | H | N | PB |
| 41. | B | C | D | I | O | PB |
| 42. | B | C | E | K | M | PB |
| 43. | B | C | F | K | L | PB |
| 44. | B | C | F | N | O | PB |
| 45. | B | C | G | I | M | PB |
| 46. | B | C | G | J | N | PB |
| 47. | B | C | H | I | K | PB |
| 48. | B | C | L | N | O | PB |
| 49. | B | D | E | H | O | PB |
| 50. | B | D | E | I | N | PB |
| 51. | B | D | F | G | K | PB |
| 52. | B | D | F | G | L | PB |
| 53. | B | D | H | I | M | PB |
| 54. | B | D | M | N | O | PB |
| 55. | B | E | F | H | M | PB |
| 56. | B | E | F | I | J | PB |
| 57. | B | E | G | H | L | PB |
| 58. | B | E | J | K | N | PB |
| 59. | B | F | H | J | L | PB |
| 60. | B | F | I | K | O | PB |
| 61. | B | F | I | L | M | PB |
| 62. | B | G | I | N | O | PB |
| 63. | B | G | J | M | O | PB |
| 64. | B | I | K | L | M | PB |
| 65. | B | J | K | L | N | PB |
| 66. | C | D | F | I | M | PB |
| 67. | C | D | F | J | N | PB |
| 68. | C | D | G | N | O | PB |
| 69. | C | D | H | K | L | PB |
| 70. | C | D | L | N | O | PB |
| 71. | C | E | F | G | M | PB |
| 72. | C | E | G | K | N | PB |
| 73. | C | E | H | I | L | PB |
| 74. | C | E | H | J | K | PB |
| 75. | C | E | J | L | O | PB |
| 76. | C | E | K | N | O | PB |
| 77. | C | F | G | H | N | PB |
| 78. | C | F | G | I | O | PB |
| 79. | C | F | L | N | O | PB |
| 80. | C | G | J | K | O | PB |
| 81. | C | G | L | N | O | PB |
| 82. | C | H | I | J | N | PB |
| 83. | C | H | J | M | O | PB |
| 84. | C | I | J | L | M | PB |
| 85. | C | I | K | N | O | PB |
| 86. | C | J | M | N | O | PB |
| 87. | D | E | F | H | L | PB |
| 88. | D | E | G | H | M | PB |
| 89. | D | E | G | I | J | PB |
| 90. | D | E | I | K | L | PB |
| 91. | D | F | I | N | O | PB |
| 92. | D | F | J | M | O | PB |
| 93. | D | F | K | M | N | PB |
| 94. | D | G | H | J | L | PB |
| 95. | D | G | H | K | N | PB |
| 96. | D | G | I | L | M | PB |
| 97. | D | I | J | K | O | PB |
| 98. | D | K | L | M | O | PB |
| 99. | E | F | G | H | O | PB |
| 100. | E | F | G | I | K | PB |



(Continued Next Page)

## POWERBALL BALANCED WHEEL® 54115PB (Continued from previous page)

| | | | | | | |
|---|---|---|---|---|---|---|
| 101. | E | F | G | I | N | PB |
| 102. | E | F | H | K | O | PB |
| 103. | E | F | H | L | M | PB |
| 104. | E | G | K | L | O | PB |
| 105. | E | H | L | M | N | PB |
| 106. | E | I | K | N | O | PB |
| 107. | E | I | L | M | O | PB |
| 108. | E | J | L | M | N | PB |
| 109. | F | G | H | I | M | PB |
| 110. | F | G | M | N | O | PB |
| 111. | F | H | I | J | K | PB |
| 112. | F | H | K | L | N | PB |
| 113. | G | H | J | K | M | PB |
| 114. | G | I | K | L | M | PB |
| 115. | G | J | K | N | O | PB |
| 116. | H | I | J | L | O | PB |
| 117. | H | I | J | M | N | PB |
| 118. | H | I | K | M | N | PB |



# POWERBALL BALANCED WHEEL® 54116PB

## Wheel 16 Numbers + PB in 159 Games for a 4 of 5 Win

With Powerball

| Numbers Matched | Maximum Wins 5 + 1 | 4 + 1 | 3 + 1 | 2 + 1 | 1 + 1 | 0 + 1 | Minimum Wins 5 + 1 | 4 + 1 | 3 + 1 | 2 + 1 | 1 + 1 | 0 + 1 |
|---|---|---|---|---|---|---|---|---|---|---|---|---|
| 5 + 1 | 1 | 3 | 29 | 44 | 46 | 36 | 0 | 1 | 15 | 66 | 61 | 16 |
| 4 + 1 | - | 4 | 4 | 58 | 55 | 38 | - | 0 | 6 | 51 | 73 | 29 |
| 3 + 1 | - | - | 8 | 40 | 48 | 63 | - | - | 0 | 31 | 83 | 45 |
| 2 + 1 | - | - | - | 22 | 58 | 79 | - | - | - | 9 | 77 | 73 |
| 1 + 1 | - | - | - | - | 52 | 107 | - | - | - | - | 47 | 112 |
| 0 + 1 | - | - | - | - | - | 159 | - | - | - | - | - | 159 |

Without Powerball

| Numbers Matched | Maximum Wins 5 + 0 | 4 + 0 | 3 + 0 | 2 + 0 | 1 + 0 | Minimum Wins 5 + 0 | 4 + 0 | 3 + 0 | 2 + 0 | 1 + 0 |
|---|---|---|---|---|---|---|---|---|---|---|
| 5 + 0 | 1 | 3 | 29 | 44 | 46 | 0 | 1 | 15 | 66 | 61 |
| 4 + 0 | - | 4 | 4 | 58 | 55 | - | 0 | 6 | 51 | 73 |
| 3 + 0 | - | - | 8 | 40 | 48 | - | - | 0 | 31 | 83 |
| 2 + 0 | - | - | - | 22 | 58 | - | - | - | 9 | 77 |
| 1 + 0 | - | - | - | - | 52 | - | - | - | - | 47 |

## Your 16 Numbers + PB to Wheel

| A | B | C | D | E | F | G | H | I |
|---|---|---|---|---|---|---|---|---|
| 50 | 47 | 52 | 52 | 52 | 48 | 52 | 52 | 48 |

| J | K | L | M | N | O | P | PB |
|---|---|---|---|---|---|---|---|
| 48 | 52 | 47 | 50 | 48 | 47 | 50 | 159 |

## The 159 Games to Play

| | | | | | | |
|---|---|---|---|---|---|---|
| 1. | A | B | E | F | J | PB |
| 2. | A | B | E | F | O | PB |
| 3. | A | B | E | I | N | PB |
| 4. | A | B | E | L | M | PB |
| 5. | A | B | F | I | M | PB |
| 6. | A | B | F | L | N | PB |
| 7. | A | B | I | J | L | PB |
| 8. | A | B | I | L | O | PB |
| 9. | A | B | J | M | O | PB |
| 10. | A | B | M | N | O | PB |
| 11. | A | C | D | E | P | PB |
| 12. | A | C | D | G | K | PB |
| 13. | A | C | D | H | M | PB |
| 14. | A | C | D | J | N | PB |



(Continued Next Page)

## POWERBALL BALANCED WHEEL® 54116PB (Continued from previous page)

| | | | | | | |
|---|---|---|---|---|---|---|
| 15. | A | C | E | G | H | PB |
| 16. | A | C | E | J | M | PB |
| 17. | A | C | E | K | N | PB |
| 18. | A | C | G | J | P | PB |
| 19. | A | C | G | M | N | PB |
| 20. | A | C | H | J | K | PB |
| 21. | A | C | H | N | P | PB |
| 22. | A | C | K | M | P | PB |
| 23. | A | D | E | G | J | PB |
| 24. | A | D | E | H | K | PB |
| 25. | A | D | E | M | N | PB |
| 26. | A | D | G | H | N | PB |
| 27. | A | D | G | M | P | PB |
| 28. | A | D | H | J | P | PB |
| 29. | A | D | J | K | M | PB |
| 30. | A | D | K | N | P | PB |
| 31. | A | E | F | I | J | PB |
| 32. | A | E | F | L | M | PB |
| 33. | A | E | F | N | O | PB |
| 34. | A | E | G | K | M | PB |
| 35. | A | E | G | N | P | PB |
| 36. | A | E | H | J | N | PB |
| 37. | A | E | H | M | P | PB |
| 38. | A | E | I | J | O | PB |
| 39. | A | E | I | L | M | PB |
| 40. | A | E | J | K | P | PB |
| 41. | A | E | L | M | O | PB |
| 42. | A | F | I | L | N | PB |
| 43. | A | F | I | M | O | PB |
| 44. | A | F | J | L | O | PB |
| 45. | A | G | H | J | M | PB |
| 46. | A | G | H | K | P | PB |
| 47. | A | G | J | K | N | PB |
| 48. | A | H | K | M | N | PB |
| 49. | A | I | L | N | O | PB |

| | | | | | | |
|---|---|---|---|---|---|---|
| 50. | A | J | M | N | P | PB |
| 51. | B | C | D | F | L | PB |
| 52. | B | C | D | H | I | PB |
| 53. | B | C | D | K | O | PB |
| 54. | B | C | F | G | H | PB |
| 55. | B | C | F | I | K | PB |
| 56. | B | C | F | O | P | PB |
| 57. | B | C | G | I | O | PB |
| 58. | B | C | G | K | L | PB |
| 59. | B | C | H | L | O | PB |
| 60. | B | C | I | L | P | PB |
| 61. | B | D | F | G | K | PB |
| 62. | B | D | F | H | P | PB |
| 63. | B | D | G | H | O | PB |
| 64. | B | D | G | I | L | PB |
| 65. | B | D | H | K | L | PB |
| 66. | B | D | I | K | P | PB |
| 67. | B | D | L | O | P | PB |
| 68. | B | E | F | I | L | PB |
| 69. | B | E | F | M | N | PB |
| 70. | B | E | I | J | M | PB |
| 71. | B | E | I | M | O | PB |
| 72. | B | E | J | L | O | PB |
| 73. | B | E | L | N | O | PB |
| 74. | B | F | G | I | P | PB |
| 75. | B | F | H | K | O | PB |
| 76. | B | F | I | J | N | PB |
| 77. | B | F | I | J | O | PB |
| 78. | B | F | I | N | O | PB |
| 79. | B | F | J | L | M | PB |
| 80. | B | F | K | L | P | PB |
| 81. | B | F | L | M | O | PB |
| 82. | B | G | H | I | K | PB |
| 83. | B | G | H | L | P | PB |
| 84. | B | G | K | O | P | PB |



(Continued Next Page)

## POWERBALL BALANCED WHEEL® 54116PB (Continued from previous page)

| | | | | | | |
|---|---|---|---|---|---|---|
| 85. | B | H | I | O | P | PB |
| 86. | B | I | L | M | N | PB |
| 87. | B | J | L | N | O | PB |
| 88. | C | D | E | G | N | PB |
| 89. | C | D | E | H | J | PB |
| 90. | C | D | E | K | M | PB |
| 91. | C | D | F | G | I | PB |
| 92. | C | D | F | H | O | PB |
| 93. | C | D | G | H | P | PB |
| 94. | C | D | G | J | M | PB |
| 95. | C | D | G | L | O | PB |
| 96. | C | D | H | K | N | PB |
| 97. | C | D | I | K | L | PB |
| 98. | C | D | I | O | P | PB |
| 99. | C | D | J | K | P | PB |
| 100. | C | D | M | N | P | PB |
| 101. | C | E | G | J | K | PB |
| 102. | C | E | G | M | P | PB |
| 103. | C | E | H | K | P | PB |
| 104. | C | E | H | M | N | PB |
| 105. | C | E | J | N | P | PB |
| 106. | C | F | G | K | O | PB |
| 107. | C | F | G | L | P | PB |
| 108. | C | F | H | I | P | PB |
| 109. | C | F | H | K | L | PB |
| 110. | C | G | H | I | L | PB |
| 111. | C | G | H | J | N | PB |
| 112. | C | G | H | K | M | PB |
| 113. | C | G | K | N | P | PB |
| 114. | C | H | I | K | O | PB |
| 115. | C | H | J | M | P | PB |
| 116. | C | J | K | M | N | PB |
| 117. | C | K | L | O | P | PB |
| 118. | D | E | G | H | M | PB |
| 119. | D | E | G | K | P | PB |
| 120. | D | E | H | N | P | PB |
| 121. | D | E | J | K | N | PB |
| 122. | D | E | J | M | P | PB |
| 123. | D | F | G | H | L | PB |
| 124. | D | F | G | O | P | PB |
| 125. | D | F | H | I | K | PB |
| 126. | D | F | I | L | P | PB |
| 127. | D | F | K | L | O | PB |
| 128. | D | G | H | J | K | PB |
| 129. | D | G | I | K | O | PB |
| 130. | D | G | J | N | P | PB |
| 131. | D | G | K | M | N | PB |
| 132. | D | H | I | L | O | PB |
| 133. | D | H | J | M | N | PB |
| 134. | D | H | K | M | P | PB |
| 135. | E | F | I | L | O | PB |
| 136. | E | F | I | M | N | PB |
| 137. | E | F | J | L | N | PB |
| 138. | E | F | J | M | O | PB |
| 139. | E | G | H | J | P | PB |
| 140. | E | G | H | K | N | PB |
| 141. | E | G | J | M | N | PB |
| 142. | E | H | J | K | M | PB |
| 143. | E | I | J | L | N | PB |
| 144. | E | I | M | N | O | PB |
| 145. | E | K | M | N | P | PB |
| 146. | F | G | H | I | O | PB |
| 147. | F | G | I | K | L | PB |
| 148. | F | H | L | O | P | PB |
| 149. | F | I | J | L | M | PB |
| 150. | F | I | J | N | O | PB |
| 151. | F | I | K | O | P | PB |
| 152. | F | L | M | N | O | PB |
| 153. | G | H | K | L | O | PB |
| 154. | G | H | M | N | P | PB |



(Continued Next Page)

**POWERBALL BALANCED WHEEL® 54116PB** (Continued from previous page)

| | | | | | | |
|---|---|---|---|---|---|---|
| 155. | G | I | L | O | P | PB |
| 156. | G | J | K | M | P | PB |
| 157. | H | I | K | L | P | PB |
| 158. | H | J | K | N | P | PB |
| 159. | I | J | L | M | O | PB |



# POWERBALL BALANCED WHEEL® 54006PB

## Wheel 6 Numbers + PB in 5 Games for a 4 of 4 Win

With Powerball

| Numbers Matched | Maximum Wins 5 + 1 | 4 + 1 | 3 + 1 | 2 + 1 | 1 + 1 | 0 + 1 | Minimum Wins 5 + 1 | 4 + 1 | 3 + 1 | 2 + 1 | 1 + 1 | 0 + 1 |
|---|---|---|---|---|---|---|---|---|---|---|---|---|
| 5 + 1 | 1 | 4 | 0 | 0 | 0 | 0 | 0 | 5 | 0 | 0 | 0 | 0 |
| 4 + 1 | - | 2 | 3 | 0 | 0 | 0 | - | 1 | 4 | 0 | 0 | 0 |
| 3 + 1 | - | - | 3 | 2 | 0 | 0 | - | - | 2 | 3 | 0 | 0 |
| 2 + 1 | - | - | - | 4 | 1 | 0 | - | - | - | 3 | 2 | 0 |
| 1 + 1 | - | - | - | - | 5 | 0 | - | - | - | - | 4 | 1 |
| 0 + 1 | - | - | - | - | - | 5 | - | - | - | - | - | 5 |

Without Powerball

| Numbers Matched | Maximum Wins 5 + 0 | 4 + 0 | 3 + 0 | 2 + 0 | 1 + 0 | Minimum Wins 5 + 0 | 4 + 0 | 3 + 0 | 2 + 0 | 1 + 0 |
|---|---|---|---|---|---|---|---|---|---|---|
| 5 + 0 | 1 | 4 | 0 | 0 | 0 | 0 | 5 | 0 | 0 | 0 |
| 4 + 0 | - | 2 | 3 | 0 | 0 | - | 1 | 4 | 0 | 0 |
| 3 + 0 | - | - | 3 | 2 | 0 | - | - | 2 | 3 | 0 |
| 2 + 0 | - | - | - | 4 | 1 | - | - | - | 3 | 2 |
| 1 + 0 | - | - | - | - | 5 | - | - | - | - | 4 |

## Your 6 Numbers + PB to Wheel

| A | B | C | D | E | F | PB |
|---|---|---|---|---|---|---|
| 4 | 4 | 4 | 4 | 4 | 5 | 5 |

## The 5 Games to Play

| | | | | | | |
|---|---|---|---|---|---|---|
| 1. | A | B | C | D | F | PB |
| 2. | A | B | C | E | F | PB |
| 3. | A | B | D | E | F | PB |
| 4. | A | C | D | E | F | PB |
| 5. | B | C | D | E | F | PB |



# POWERBALL BALANCED WHEEL® 54007PB

## Wheel 7 Numbers + PB in 9 Games for a 4 of 4 Win

With Powerball

| Numbers Matched | Maximum Wins 5 + 1 | 4 + 1 | 3 + 1 | 2 + 1 | 1 + 1 | 0 + 1 | Minimum Wins 5 + 1 | 4 + 1 | 3 + 1 | 2 + 1 | 1 + 1 | 0 + 1 |
|---|---|---|---|---|---|---|---|---|---|---|---|---|
| 5 + 1 | 1 | 4 | 4 | 0 | 0 | 0 | 0 | 5 | 4 | 0 | 0 | 0 |
| 4 + 1 | - | 3 | 3 | 3 | 0 | 0 | - | 1 | 5 | 3 | 0 | 0 |
| 3 + 1 | - | - | 6 | 0 | 3 | 0 | - | - | 2 | 6 | 1 | 0 |
| 2 + 1 | - | - | - | 6 | 2 | 1 | - | - | - | 4 | 4 | 1 |
| 1 + 1 | - | - | - | - | 7 | 2 | - | - | - | - | 6 | 3 |
| 0 + 1 | - | - | - | - | - | 9 | - | - | - | - | - | 9 |

(Continued Next Page)

## POWERBALL BALANCED WHEEL® 54007PB (Continued from previous page)

Without Powerball

| Numbers Matched | Maximum Wins | | | | | Minimum Wins | | | | |
|---|---|---|---|---|---|---|---|---|---|---|
| | 5 + 0 | 4 + 0 | 3 + 0 | 2 + 0 | 1 + 0 | 5 + 0 | 4 + 0 | 3 + 0 | 2 + 0 | 1 + 0 |
| 5 + 0 | 1 | 4 | 4 | 0 | 0 | 0 | 5 | 4 | 0 | 0 |
| 4 + 0 | - | 3 | 3 | 3 | 0 | - | 1 | 5 | 3 | 0 |
| 3 + 0 | - | - | 6 | 0 | 3 | - | - | 2 | 6 | 1 |
| 2 + 0 | - | - | - | 6 | 2 | - | - | - | 4 | 4 |
| 1 + 0 | - | - | - | - | 7 | - | - | - | - | 6 |

### Your 7 Numbers + PB to Wheel

| A | B | C | D | E | F | G | PB |
|---|---|---|---|---|---|---|---|
| 7 | 6 | 6 | 7 | 6 | 6 | 7 | 9 |

### The 9 Games to Play

| | | | | | | |
|---|---|---|---|---|---|---|
| 1. | A | B | C | D | G | PB |
| 2. | A | B | C | E | F | PB |
| 3. | A | B | D | E | G | PB |
| 4. | A | B | D | F | G | PB |
| 5. | A | C | D | E | G | PB |
| 6. | A | C | D | F | G | PB |
| 7. | A | D | E | F | G | PB |
| 8. | B | C | D | E | F | PB |
| 9. | B | C | E | F | G | PB |



## POWERBALL BALANCED WHEEL® 54008PB

### Wheel 8 Numbers + PB in 20 Games for a 4 of 4 Win

With Powerball

| Numbers Matched | Maximum Wins | | | | | | Minimum Wins | | | | | |
|---|---|---|---|---|---|---|---|---|---|---|---|---|
| | 5 + 1 | 4 + 1 | 3 + 1 | 2 + 1 | 1 + 1 | 0 + 1 | 5 + 1 | 4 + 1 | 3 + 1 | 2 + 1 | 1 + 1 | 0 + 1 |
| 5 + 1 | 1 | 6 | 8 | 5 | 0 | 0 | 0 | 5 | 12 | 3 | 0 | 0 |
| 4 + 1 | - | 4 | 4 | 11 | 1 | 0 | - | 1 | 8 | 10 | 1 | 0 |
| 3 + 1 | - | - | 7 | 5 | 8 | 0 | - | - | 3 | 10 | 7 | 0 |
| 2 + 1 | - | - | - | 10 | 6 | 4 | - | - | - | 6 | 12 | 2 |
| 1 + 1 | - | - | - | - | 13 | 7 | - | - | - | - | 12 | 8 |
| 0 + 1 | - | - | - | - | - | 20 | - | - | - | - | - | 20 |

Without Powerball

| Numbers Matched | Maximum Wins | | | | | Minimum Wins | | | | |
|---|---|---|---|---|---|---|---|---|---|---|
| | 5 + 0 | 4 + 0 | 3 + 0 | 2 + 0 | 1 + 0 | 5 + 0 | 4 + 0 | 3 + 0 | 2 + 0 | 1 + 0 |
| 5 + 0 | 1 | 6 | 8 | 5 | 0 | 0 | 5 | 12 | 3 | 0 |
| 4 + 0 | - | 4 | 4 | 11 | 1 | - | 1 | 8 | 10 | 1 |
| 3 + 0 | - | - | 7 | 5 | 8 | - | - | 3 | 10 | 7 |
| 2 + 0 | - | - | - | 10 | 6 | - | - | - | 6 | 12 |
| 1 + 0 | - | - | - | - | 13 | - | - | - | - | 12 |

### Your 8 Numbers + PB to Wheel

| A | B | C | D | E | F | G | H | PB |
|---|---|---|---|---|---|---|---|---|
| 12 | 13 | 13 | 12 | 13 | 12 | 12 | 13 | 20 |

### The 20 Games to Play

| | | | | | | |
|---|---|---|---|---|---|---|
| 1. | A | B | C | D | H | PB |
| 2. | A | B | C | E | H | PB |
| 3. | A | B | C | F | H | PB |
| 4. | A | B | C | G | H | PB |
| 5. | A | B | D | E | H | PB |
| 6. | A | B | D | F | G | PB |
| 7. | A | B | E | F | G | PB |
| 8. | A | C | D | E | F | PB |
| 9. | A | C | D | E | G | PB |
| 10. | A | C | E | F | G | PB |



(Continued Next Page)

## POWERBALL BALANCED WHEEL® 54008PB (Continued from previous page)

| | | | | | | |
|---|---|---|---|---|---|---|
| 11. | A | D | F | G | H | PB |
| 12. | A | E | F | G | H | PB |
| 13. | B | C | D | E | G | PB |
| 14. | B | C | D | F | H | PB |
| 15. | B | C | E | F | H | PB |
| 16. | B | C | F | G | H | PB |
| 17. | B | D | E | F | H | PB |
| 18. | B | D | E | G | H | PB |
| 19. | C | D | E | F | G | PB |
| 20. | C | D | E | G | H | PB |



# POWERBALL BALANCED WHEEL® 54009PB

## Wheel 9 Numbers + PB in 30 Games for a 4 of 4 Win

With Powerball

| Numbers Matched | Maximum Wins 5 + 1 | 4 + 1 | 3 + 1 | 2 + 1 | 1 + 1 | 0 + 1 | Minimum Wins 5 + 1 | 4 + 1 | 3 + 1 | 2 + 1 | 1 + 1 | 0 + 1 |
|---|---|---|---|---|---|---|---|---|---|---|---|---|
| 5 + 1 | 1 | 6 | 14 | 8 | 1 | 0 | 0 | 5 | 11 | 13 | 1 | 0 |
| 4 + 1 | - | 5 | 0 | 24 | 0 | 1 | - | 1 | 8 | 14 | 6 | 1 |
| 3 + 1 | - | - | 7 | 12 | 9 | 2 | - | - | 3 | 12 | 12 | 3 |
| 2 + 1 | - | - | - | 11 | 14 | 5 | - | - | - | 7 | 14 | 9 |
| 1 + 1 | - | - | - | - | 18 | 12 | - | - | - | - | 14 | 16 |
| 0 + 1 | - | - | - | - | - | 30 | - | - | - | - | - | 30 |

Without Powerball

| Numbers Matched | Maximum Wins 5 + 0 | 4 + 0 | 3 + 0 | 2 + 0 | 1 + 0 | Minimum Wins 5 + 0 | 4 + 0 | 3 + 0 | 2 + 0 | 1 + 0 |
|---|---|---|---|---|---|---|---|---|---|---|
| 5 + 0 | 1 | 6 | 14 | 8 | 1 | 0 | 5 | 11 | 13 | 1 |
| 4 + 0 | - | 5 | 0 | 24 | 0 | - | 1 | 8 | 14 | 6 |
| 3 + 0 | - | - | 7 | 12 | 9 | - | - | 3 | 12 | 12 |
| 2 + 0 | - | - | - | 11 | 14 | - | - | - | 7 | 14 |
| 1 + 0 | - | - | - | - | 18 | - | - | - | - | 14 |

## Your 9 Numbers + PB to Wheel

| A | B | C | D | E | F | G | H | I | PB |
|---|---|---|---|---|---|---|---|---|---|
| 17 | 18 | 17 | 17 | 14 | 14 | 18 | 18 | 17 | 30 |

## The 30 Games to Play

| | | | | | | |
|---|---|---|---|---|---|---|
| 1. | A | B | C | D | I | PB |
| 2. | A | B | C | E | H | PB |
| 3. | A | B | C | F | H | PB |
| 4. | A | B | C | G | H | PB |
| 5. | A | B | D | E | G | PB |
| 6. | A | B | D | F | G | PB |
| 7. | A | B | D | G | H | PB |
| 8. | A | B | E | F | I | PB |
| 9. | A | B | G | H | I | PB |
| 10. | A | C | D | E | I | PB |
| 11. | A | C | D | F | I | PB |
| 12. | A | C | D | G | I | PB |
| 13. | A | C | D | H | I | PB |
| 14. | A | C | E | F | G | PB |
| 15. | A | D | E | F | H | PB |
| 16. | A | E | G | H | I | PB |
| 17. | A | F | G | H | I | PB |
| 18. | B | C | D | E | F | PB |
| 19. | B | C | D | G | H | PB |
| 20. | B | C | E | G | I | PB |
| 21. | B | C | F | G | I | PB |
| 22. | B | C | G | H | I | PB |
| 23. | B | D | E | H | I | PB |
| 24. | B | D | F | H | I | PB |
| 25. | B | D | G | H | I | PB |
| 26. | B | E | F | G | H | PB |



(Continued Next Page)

**POWERBALL BALANCED WHEEL® 54009PB** (Continued from previous page)

| | | | | | | |
|---|---|---|---|---|---|---|
| 27. | C | D | E | G | H | PB |
| 28. | C | D | F | G | H | PB |
| 29. | C | E | F | H | I | PB |
| 30. | D | E | F | G | I | PB |



# POWERBALL BALANCED WHEEL® 54010PB

## Wheel 10 Numbers + PB in 51 Games for a 4 of 4 Win

With Powerball

| Numbers Matched | Maximum Wins 5 + 1 | 4 + 1 | 3 + 1 | 2 + 1 | 1 + 1 | 0 + 1 | Minimum Wins 5 + 1 | 4 + 1 | 3 + 1 | 2 + 1 | 1 + 1 | 0 + 1 |
|---|---|---|---|---|---|---|---|---|---|---|---|---|
| 5 + 1 | 1 | 5 | 20 | 21 | 3 | 1 | 0 | 5 | 20 | 20 | 5 | 1 |
| 4 + 1 | - | 6 | 0 | 40 | 1 | 4 | - | 1 | 12 | 24 | 12 | 2 |
| 3 + 1 | - | - | 6 | 20 | 21 | 4 | - | - | 4 | 21 | 21 | 5 |
| 2 + 1 | - | - | - | 14 | 25 | 12 | - | - | - | 11 | 28 | 12 |
| 1 + 1 | - | - | - | - | 27 | 24 | - | - | - | - | 25 | 26 |
| 0 + 1 | - | - | - | - | - | 51 | - | - | - | - | - | 51 |

Without Powerball

| Numbers Matched | Maximum Wins 5 + 0 | 4 + 0 | 3 + 0 | 2 + 0 | 1 + 0 | Minimum Wins 5 + 0 | 4 + 0 | 3 + 0 | 2 + 0 | 1 + 0 |
|---|---|---|---|---|---|---|---|---|---|---|
| 5 + 0 | 1 | 5 | 20 | 21 | 3 | 0 | 5 | 20 | 20 | 5 |
| 4 + 0 | - | 6 | 0 | 40 | 1 | - | 1 | 12 | 24 | 12 |
| 3 + 0 | - | - | 6 | 20 | 21 | - | - | 4 | 21 | 21 |
| 2 + 0 | - | - | - | 14 | 25 | - | - | - | 11 | 28 |
| 1 + 0 | - | - | - | - | 27 | - | - | - | - | 25 |

## Your 10 Numbers + PB to Wheel

| A | B | C | D | E | F | G | H | I | J | PB |
|---|---|---|---|---|---|---|---|---|---|---|
| 27 | 26 | 26 | 25 | 25 | 25 | 25 | 25 | 25 | 26 | 51 |

## The 51 Games to Play

| | | | | | | |
|---|---|---|---|---|---|---|
| 1. | A | B | C | D | J | PB |
| 2. | A | B | C | E | J | PB |
| 3. | A | B | C | F | J | PB |
| 4. | A | B | C | G | J | PB |
| 5. | A | B | C | H | J | PB |
| 6. | A | B | C | I | J | PB |
| 7. | A | B | D | E | I | PB |
| 8. | A | B | D | F | H | PB |
| 9. | A | B | D | G | H | PB |
| 10. | A | B | E | F | G | PB |
| 11. | A | B | E | H | I | PB |
| 12. | A | B | F | G | I | PB |
| 13. | A | C | D | E | H | PB |
| 14. | A | C | D | F | G | PB |
| 15. | A | C | D | F | I | PB |
| 16. | A | C | E | F | H | PB |
| 17. | A | C | E | G | I | PB |
| 18. | A | C | G | H | I | PB |
| 19. | A | D | E | F | J | PB |
| 20. | A | D | E | G | J | PB |
| 21. | A | D | G | I | J | PB |
| 22. | A | D | H | I | J | PB |
| 23. | A | E | F | G | H | PB |
| 24. | A | E | F | I | J | PB |
| 25. | A | E | G | H | J | PB |
| 26. | A | F | G | H | J | PB |
| 27. | A | F | H | I | J | PB |
| 28. | B | C | D | E | F | PB |
| 29. | B | C | D | E | G | PB |
| 30. | B | C | D | G | I | PB |
| 31. | B | C | D | H | I | PB |
| 32. | B | C | E | F | I | PB |



(Continued Next Page)

## POWERBALL BALANCED WHEEL® 54010PB

(Continued from previous page)

| | | | | | | |
|---|---|---|---|---|---|---|
| 33. | B | C | E | G | H | PB |
| 34. | B | C | F | G | H | PB |
| 35. | B | C | F | H | I | PB |
| 36. | B | D | E | H | J | PB |
| 37. | B | D | F | G | J | PB |
| 38. | B | D | F | I | J | PB |
| 39. | B | E | F | H | J | PB |
| 40. | B | E | G | I | J | PB |
| 41. | B | G | H | I | J | PB |
| 42. | C | D | E | I | J | PB |
| 43. | C | D | F | H | J | PB |
| 44. | C | D | G | H | J | PB |
| 45. | C | E | F | G | J | PB |
| 46. | C | E | H | I | J | PB |
| 47. | C | F | G | I | J | PB |
| 48. | D | E | F | G | I | PB |
| 49. | D | E | F | H | I | PB |
| 50. | D | E | G | H | I | PB |
| 51. | D | F | G | H | I | PB |



# POWERBALL BALANCED WHEEL® 54011PB

## Wheel 11 Numbers + PB in 66 Games for a 4 of 4 Win

With Powerball

| Numbers Matched | Maximum Wins | | | | | | Minimum Wins | | | | | |
|---|---|---|---|---|---|---|---|---|---|---|---|---|
| | 5 + 1 | 4 + 1 | 3 + 1 | 2 + 1 | 1 + 1 | 0 + 1 | 5 + 1 | 4 + 1 | 3 + 1 | 2 + 1 | 1 + 1 | 0 + 1 |
| 5 + 1 | 1 | 0 | 30 | 20 | 15 | 0 | 0 | 5 | 20 | 30 | 10 | 1 |
| 4 + 1 | - | 1 | 12 | 30 | 20 | 3 | - | 1 | 12 | 30 | 20 | 3 |
| 3 + 1 | - | - | 4 | 24 | 30 | 8 | - | - | 4 | 24 | 30 | 8 |
| 2 + 1 | - | - | - | 12 | 36 | 18 | - | - | - | 12 | 36 | 18 |
| 1 + 1 | - | - | - | - | 30 | 36 | - | - | - | - | 30 | 36 |
| 0 + 1 | - | - | - | - | - | 66 | - | - | - | - | - | 66 |

Without Powerball

| Numbers Matched | Maximum Wins | | | | | Minimum Wins | | | | |
|---|---|---|---|---|---|---|---|---|---|---|
| | 5 + 0 | 4 + 0 | 3 + 0 | 2 + 0 | 1 + 0 | 5 + 0 | 4 + 0 | 3 + 0 | 2 + 0 | 1 + 0 |
| 5 + 0 | 1 | 0 | 30 | 20 | 15 | 0 | 5 | 20 | 30 | 10 |
| 4 + 0 | - | 1 | 12 | 30 | 20 | - | 1 | 12 | 30 | 20 |
| 3 + 0 | - | - | 4 | 24 | 30 | - | - | 4 | 24 | 30 |
| 2 + 0 | - | - | - | 12 | 36 | - | - | - | 12 | 36 |
| 1 + 0 | - | - | - | - | 30 | - | - | - | - | 30 |

## Your 11 Numbers + PB to Wheel

| A | B | C | D | E | F |
|---|---|---|---|---|---|
| 30 | 30 | 30 | 30 | 30 | 30 |
| **G** | **H** | **I** | **J** | **K** | **PB** |
| 30 | 30 | 30 | 30 | 30 | 66 |

## The 66 Games to Play

| | | | | | | |
|---|---|---|---|---|---|---|
| 1. | A | B | C | D | K | PB |
| 2. | A | B | C | E | I | PB |
| 3. | A | B | C | F | G | PB |
| 4. | A | B | C | H | J | PB |
| 5. | A | B | D | E | G | PB |
| 6. | A | B | D | F | H | PB |
| 7. | A | B | D | I | J | PB |
| 8. | A | B | E | F | J | PB |
| 9. | A | B | E | H | K | PB |
| 10. | A | B | F | I | K | PB |
| 11. | A | B | G | H | I | PB |
| 12. | A | B | G | J | K | PB |



(Continued Next Page)

## POWERBALL BALANCED WHEEL® 54011PB (Continued from previous page)

| | | | | | | |
|---|---|---|---|---|---|---|
| 13. | A | C | D | E | H | PB |
| 14. | A | C | D | F | J | PB |
| 15. | A | C | D | G | I | PB |
| 16. | A | C | E | F | K | PB |
| 17. | A | C | E | G | J | PB |
| 18. | A | C | F | H | I | PB |
| 19. | A | C | G | H | K | PB |
| 20. | A | C | I | J | K | PB |
| 21. | A | D | E | F | I | PB |
| 22. | A | D | E | J | K | PB |
| 23. | A | D | F | G | K | PB |
| 24. | A | D | G | H | J | PB |
| 25. | A | D | H | I | K | PB |
| 26. | A | E | F | G | H | PB |
| 27. | A | E | G | I | K | PB |
| 28. | A | E | H | I | J | PB |
| 29. | A | F | G | I | J | PB |
| 30. | A | F | H | J | K | PB |
| 31. | B | C | D | E | F | PB |
| 32. | B | C | D | G | J | PB |
| 33. | B | C | D | H | I | PB |
| 34. | B | C | E | G | H | PB |
| 35. | B | C | E | J | K | PB |
| 36. | B | C | F | H | K | PB |
| 37. | B | C | F | I | J | PB |
| 38. | B | C | G | I | K | PB |
| 39. | B | D | E | H | J | PB |
| 40. | B | D | E | I | K | PB |
| 41. | B | D | F | G | I | PB |
| 42. | B | D | F | J | K | PB |
| 43. | B | D | G | H | K | PB |
| 44. | B | E | F | G | K | PB |
| 45. | B | E | F | H | I | PB |
| 46. | B | E | G | I | J | PB |
| 47. | B | F | G | H | J | PB |
| 48. | B | H | I | J | K | PB |
| 49. | C | D | E | G | K | PB |
| 50. | C | D | E | I | J | PB |
| 51. | C | D | F | G | H | PB |
| 52. | C | D | F | I | K | PB |
| 53. | C | D | H | J | K | PB |
| 54. | C | E | F | G | I | PB |
| 55. | C | E | F | H | J | PB |
| 56. | C | E | H | I | K | PB |
| 57. | C | F | G | J | K | PB |
| 58. | C | G | H | I | J | PB |
| 59. | D | E | F | G | J | PB |
| 60. | D | E | F | H | K | PB |
| 61. | D | E | G | H | I | PB |
| 62. | D | F | H | I | J | PB |
| 63. | D | G | I | J | K | PB |
| 64. | E | F | I | J | K | PB |
| 65. | E | G | H | J | K | PB |
| 66. | F | G | H | I | K | PB |



# POWERBALL BALANCED WHEEL® 54012PB

## Wheel 12 Numbers + PB in 113 Games for a 4 of 4 Win

With Powerball

| Numbers Matched | Maximum Wins | | | | | | Minimum Wins | | | | | |
|---|---|---|---|---|---|---|---|---|---|---|---|---|
| | 5 + 1 | 4 + 1 | 3 + 1 | 2 + 1 | 1 + 1 | 0 + 1 | 5 + 1 | 4 + 1 | 3 + 1 | 2 + 1 | 1 + 1 | 0 + 1 |
| 5 + 1 | 1 | 4 | 30 | 50 | 25 | 3 | 0 | 5 | 30 | 50 | 25 | 3 |
| 4 + 1 | - | 2 | 15 | 48 | 40 | 8 | - | 1 | 16 | 48 | 40 | 8 |
| 3 + 1 | - | - | 6 | 35 | 54 | 18 | - | - | 5 | 36 | 54 | 18 |
| 2 + 1 | - | - | - | 18 | 59 | 36 | - | - | - | 17 | 60 | 36 |
| 1 + 1 | - | - | - | - | 48 | 65 | - | - | - | - | 47 | 66 |
| 0 + 1 | - | - | - | - | - | 113 | - | - | - | - | - | 113 |

(Continued Next Page)

## POWERBALL BALANCED WHEEL® 54012PB (Continued from previous page)

Without Powerball

| Numbers Matched | Maximum Wins 5 + 0 | 4 + 0 | 3 + 0 | 2 + 0 | 1 + 0 | Minimum Wins 5 + 0 | 4 + 0 | 3 + 0 | 2 + 0 | 1 + 0 |
|---|---|---|---|---|---|---|---|---|---|---|
| 5 + 0 | 1 | 4 | 30 | 50 | 25 | 0 | 5 | 30 | 50 | 25 |
| 4 + 0 | - | 2 | 15 | 48 | 40 | - | 1 | 16 | 48 | 40 |
| 3 + 0 | - | - | 6 | 35 | 54 | - | - | 5 | 36 | 54 |
| 2 + 0 | - | - | - | 18 | 59 | - | - | - | 17 | 60 |
| 1 + 0 | - | - | - | - | 48 | - | - | - | - | 47 |

# Your 12 Numbers + PB to Wheel

| A | B | C | D | E | F | G |
|---|---|---|---|---|---|---|
| 47 | 47 | 47 | 47 | 47 | 47 | 47 |

| H | I | J | K | L | PB |
|---|---|---|---|---|---|
| 48 | 47 | 47 | 47 | 47 | 113 |

# The 113 Games to Play

| | | | | | | | | | | | | | |
|---|---|---|---|---|---|---|---|---|---|---|---|---|---|
| 1. | A | B | C | D | K | PB | 26. | A | C | G | J | L | PB |
| 2. | A | B | C | E | J | PB | 27. | A | C | H | I | J | PB |
| 3. | A | B | C | F | I | PB | 28. | A | C | H | J | K | PB |
| 4. | A | B | C | F | L | PB | 29. | A | C | I | K | L | PB |
| 5. | A | B | C | G | H | PB | 30. | A | D | E | F | K | PB |
| 6. | A | B | D | E | L | PB | 31. | A | D | E | H | J | PB |
| 7. | A | B | D | F | H | PB | 32. | A | D | F | G | I | PB |
| 8. | A | B | D | G | J | PB | 33. | A | D | F | G | L | PB |
| 9. | A | B | D | I | L | PB | 34. | A | D | G | H | K | PB |
| 10. | A | B | E | F | G | PB | 35. | A | D | H | I | K | PB |
| 11. | A | B | E | H | K | PB | 36. | A | D | I | J | K | PB |
| 12. | A | B | E | I | K | PB | 37. | A | D | J | K | L | PB |
| 13. | A | B | F | J | K | PB | 38. | A | E | F | H | I | PB |
| 14. | A | B | G | I | J | PB | 39. | A | E | F | J | L | PB |
| 15. | A | B | G | K | L | PB | 40. | A | E | G | H | L | PB |
| 16. | A | B | H | I | L | PB | 41. | A | E | G | J | K | PB |
| 17. | A | B | H | J | L | PB | 42. | A | E | I | J | L | PB |
| 18. | A | C | D | E | G | PB | 43. | A | F | G | H | J | PB |
| 19. | A | C | D | E | I | PB | 44. | A | F | G | I | L | PB |
| 20. | A | C | D | F | J | PB | 45. | A | F | H | K | L | PB |
| 21. | A | C | D | H | L | PB | 46. | A | F | I | J | K | PB |
| 22. | A | C | E | F | H | PB | 47. | A | G | H | I | K | PB |
| 23. | A | C | E | G | I | PB | 48. | B | C | D | E | F | PB |
| 24. | A | C | E | K | L | PB | 49. | B | C | D | F | I | PB |
| 25. | A | C | F | G | K | PB | 50. | B | C | D | G | L | PB |



(Continued Next Page)

## POWERBALL BALANCED WHEEL® 54012PB (Continued from previous page)

| | | | | | | |
|---|---|---|---|---|---|---|
| 51. | B | C | D | H | J | PB |
| 52. | B | C | E | G | K | PB |
| 53. | B | C | E | H | L | PB |
| 54. | B | C | E | I | J | PB |
| 55. | B | C | F | G | J | PB |
| 56. | B | C | F | H | K | PB |
| 57. | B | C | G | I | L | PB |
| 58. | B | C | H | I | K | PB |
| 59. | B | C | J | K | L | PB |
| 60. | B | D | E | G | H | PB |
| 61. | B | D | E | H | I | PB |
| 62. | B | D | E | J | K | PB |
| 63. | B | D | F | G | K | PB |
| 64. | B | D | F | J | L | PB |
| 65. | B | D | G | I | K | PB |
| 66. | B | D | H | I | J | PB |
| 67. | B | D | H | K | L | PB |
| 68. | B | E | F | H | J | PB |
| 69. | B | E | F | I | L | PB |
| 70. | B | E | F | K | L | PB |
| 71. | B | E | G | H | I | PB |
| 72. | B | E | G | J | L | PB |
| 73. | B | F | G | H | L | PB |
| 74. | B | F | G | I | K | PB |
| 75. | B | F | H | I | J | PB |
| 76. | B | G | H | J | K | PB |
| 77. | B | I | J | K | L | PB |
| 78. | C | D | E | H | K | PB |
| 79. | C | D | E | J | L | PB |
| 80. | C | D | F | G | H | PB |
| 81. | C | D | F | K | L | PB |
| 82. | C | D | G | H | I | PB |
| 83. | C | D | G | J | K | PB |
| 84. | C | D | I | J | L | PB |
| 85. | C | D | I | K | L | PB |
| 86. | C | E | F | G | L | PB |
| 87. | C | E | F | I | K | PB |
| 88. | C | E | F | J | K | PB |
| 89. | C | E | G | H | J | PB |
| 90. | C | E | H | I | L | PB |
| 91. | C | F | G | H | I | PB |
| 92. | C | F | H | J | L | PB |
| 93. | C | F | I | J | L | PB |
| 94. | C | G | H | K | L | PB |
| 95. | C | G | I | J | K | PB |
| 96. | D | E | F | G | J | PB |
| 97. | D | E | F | H | L | PB |
| 98. | D | E | F | I | K | PB |
| 99. | D | E | G | I | L | PB |
| 100. | D | E | G | K | L | PB |
| 101. | D | E | H | I | J | PB |
| 102. | D | F | G | I | J | PB |
| 103. | D | F | H | I | L | PB |
| 104. | D | F | H | J | K | PB |
| 105. | D | G | H | J | L | PB |
| 106. | E | F | G | H | K | PB |
| 107. | E | F | G | I | J | PB |
| 108. | E | G | I | K | L | PB |
| 109. | E | H | I | J | K | PB |
| 110. | E | H | J | K | L | PB |
| 111. | F | G | J | K | L | PB |
| 112. | F | H | I | K | L | PB |
| 113. | G | H | I | J | L | PB |

# POWERBALL BALANCED WHEEL® 54013PB

## Wheel 13 Numbers + PB in 157 Games for a 4 of 4 Win

With Powerball

| Numbers Matched | Maximum Wins 5 + 1 | 4 + 1 | 3 + 1 | 2 + 1 | 1 + 1 | 0 + 1 | Minimum Wins 5 + 1 | 4 + 1 | 3 + 1 | 2 + 1 | 1 + 1 | 0 + 1 |
|---|---|---|---|---|---|---|---|---|---|---|---|---|
| 5 + 1 | 1 | 10 | 28 | 70 | 40 | 8 | 0 | 5 | 30 | 70 | 44 | 8 |
| 4 + 1 | - | 7 | 6 | 76 | 50 | 18 | - | 1 | 16 | 60 | 62 | 18 |
| 3 + 1 | - | - | 10 | 37 | 79 | 31 | - | - | 5 | 42 | 75 | 35 |
| 2 + 1 | - | - | - | 27 | 73 | 57 | - | - | - | 19 | 76 | 62 |
| 1 + 1 | - | - | - | - | 64 | 93 | - | - | - | - | 57 | 100 |
| 0 + 1 | - | - | - | - | - | 157 | - | - | - | - | - | 157 |

Without Powerball

| Numbers Matched | Maximum Wins 5 + 0 | 4 + 0 | 3 + 0 | 2 + 0 | 1 + 0 | Minimum Wins 5 + 0 | 4 + 0 | 3 + 0 | 2 + 0 | 1 + 0 |
|---|---|---|---|---|---|---|---|---|---|---|
| 5 + 0 | 1 | 10 | 28 | 70 | 40 | 0 | 5 | 30 | 70 | 44 |
| 4 + 0 | - | 7 | 6 | 76 | 50 | - | 1 | 16 | 60 | 62 |
| 3 + 0 | - | - | 10 | 37 | 79 | - | - | 5 | 42 | 75 |
| 2 + 0 | - | - | - | 27 | 73 | - | - | - | 19 | 76 |
| 1 + 0 | - | - | - | - | 64 | - | - | - | - | 57 |

## Your 13 Numbers + PB to Wheel

| A | B | C | D | E | F | G |
|---|---|---|---|---|---|---|
| 60 | 63 | 60 | 61 | 64 | 63 | 60 |
| **H** | **I** | **J** | **K** | **L** | **M** | **PB** |
| 59 | 57 | 60 | 60 | 57 | 61 | 157 |

## The 157 Games to Play

| | | | | | | |
|---|---|---|---|---|---|---|
| 1. | A | B | C | D | J | PB |
| 2. | A | B | C | E | I | PB |
| 3. | A | B | C | F | J | PB |
| 4. | A | B | C | G | M | PB |
| 5. | A | B | C | H | J | PB |
| 6. | A | B | C | K | L | PB |
| 7. | A | B | D | E | M | PB |
| 8. | A | B | D | F | H | PB |
| 9. | A | B | D | G | K | PB |
| 10. | A | B | D | I | M | PB |
| 11. | A | B | D | L | M | PB |
| 12. | A | B | E | F | H | PB |
| 13. | A | B | E | G | K | PB |
| 14. | A | B | E | J | L | PB |
| 15. | A | B | F | G | L | PB |
| 16. | A | B | F | H | M | PB |
| 17. | A | B | F | I | K | PB |
| 18. | A | B | G | H | K | PB |
| 19. | A | B | G | I | J | PB |
| 20. | A | B | H | I | L | PB |
| 21. | A | B | J | K | M | PB |
| 22. | A | C | D | E | L | PB |
| 23. | A | C | D | F | G | PB |
| 24. | A | C | D | H | I | PB |
| 25. | A | C | D | K | M | PB |
| 26. | A | C | E | F | M | PB |
| 27. | A | C | E | G | H | PB |
| 28. | A | C | E | J | K | PB |
| 29. | A | C | F | H | K | PB |
| 30. | A | C | F | I | L | PB |
| 31. | A | C | G | I | K | PB |
| 32. | A | C | G | J | L | PB |
| 33. | A | C | H | L | M | PB |
| 34. | A | C | I | J | M | PB |
| 35. | A | D | E | F | M | PB |
| 36. | A | D | E | G | J | PB |



(Continued Next Page)

## POWERBALL BALANCED WHEEL® 54013PB (Continued from previous page)

| | | | | | | |
|---|---|---|---|---|---|---|
| 37. | A | D | E | H | M | PB |
| 38. | A | D | E | I | K | PB |
| 39. | A | D | F | I | J | PB |
| 40. | A | D | F | K | L | PB |
| 41. | A | D | G | H | L | PB |
| 42. | A | D | G | I | M | PB |
| 43. | A | D | H | J | K | PB |
| 44. | A | D | I | L | M | PB |
| 45. | A | D | J | L | M | PB |
| 46. | A | E | F | G | M | PB |
| 47. | A | E | F | I | M | PB |
| 48. | A | E | F | J | M | PB |
| 49. | A | E | F | K | M | PB |
| 50. | A | E | F | L | M | PB |
| 51. | A | E | G | I | L | PB |
| 52. | A | E | H | I | J | PB |
| 53. | A | E | H | K | L | PB |
| 54. | A | F | G | H | I | PB |
| 55. | A | F | G | J | K | PB |
| 56. | A | F | H | J | L | PB |
| 57. | A | G | H | J | M | PB |
| 58. | A | G | K | L | M | PB |
| 59. | A | H | I | K | M | PB |
| 60. | A | I | J | K | L | PB |
| 61. | B | C | D | E | J | PB |
| 62. | B | C | D | F | I | PB |
| 63. | B | C | D | G | L | PB |
| 64. | B | C | D | H | K | PB |
| 65. | B | C | D | J | M | PB |
| 66. | B | C | E | F | G | PB |
| 67. | B | C | E | F | K | PB |
| 68. | B | C | E | H | J | PB |
| 69. | B | C | E | L | M | PB |
| 70. | B | C | F | H | L | PB |
| 71. | B | C | F | J | M | PB |
| 72. | B | C | G | H | I | PB |
| 73. | B | C | G | J | K | PB |
| 74. | B | C | H | J | M | PB |
| 75. | B | C | I | J | L | PB |
| 76. | B | C | I | K | M | PB |
| 77. | B | D | E | F | M | PB |
| 78. | B | D | E | G | I | PB |
| 79. | B | D | E | H | M | PB |
| 80. | B | D | E | K | L | PB |
| 81. | B | D | F | G | K | PB |
| 82. | B | D | F | J | L | PB |
| 83. | B | D | G | H | J | PB |
| 84. | B | D | G | K | M | PB |
| 85. | B | D | H | I | L | PB |
| 86. | B | D | I | J | K | PB |
| 87. | B | E | F | G | J | PB |
| 88. | B | E | F | I | L | PB |
| 89. | B | E | F | J | K | PB |
| 90. | B | E | G | H | L | PB |
| 91. | B | E | G | K | M | PB |
| 92. | B | E | H | I | K | PB |
| 93. | B | E | I | J | M | PB |
| 94. | B | F | G | H | K | PB |
| 95. | B | F | G | I | M | PB |
| 96. | B | F | H | I | J | PB |
| 97. | B | F | K | L | M | PB |
| 98. | B | G | H | K | M | PB |
| 99. | B | G | I | K | L | PB |
| 100. | B | G | J | L | M | PB |
| 101. | B | H | I | L | M | PB |
| 102. | B | H | J | K | L | PB |
| 103. | C | D | E | F | H | PB |
| 104. | C | D | E | G | K | PB |
| 105. | C | D | E | I | M | PB |
| 106. | C | D | F | J | K | PB |



(Continued Next Page)

## POWERBALL BALANCED WHEEL® 54013PB (Continued from previous page)

| | | | | | | |
|---|---|---|---|---|---|---|
| 107. | C | D | F | L | M | PB |
| 108. | C | D | G | H | M | PB |
| 109. | C | D | G | I | J | PB |
| 110. | C | D | H | J | L | PB |
| 111. | C | D | I | K | L | PB |
| 112. | C | E | F | G | I | PB |
| 113. | C | E | F | G | L | PB |
| 114. | C | E | F | I | J | PB |
| 115. | C | E | F | I | K | PB |
| 116. | C | E | G | J | M | PB |
| 117. | C | E | H | I | L | PB |
| 118. | C | E | H | K | M | PB |
| 119. | C | E | J | K | L | PB |
| 120. | C | F | G | H | J | PB |
| 121. | C | F | G | K | M | PB |
| 122. | C | F | H | I | M | PB |
| 123. | C | F | J | K | L | PB |
| 124. | C | G | H | K | L | PB |
| 125. | C | G | I | L | M | PB |
| 126. | C | H | I | J | K | PB |
| 127. | C | J | K | L | M | PB |
| 128. | D | E | F | G | H | PB |
| 129. | D | E | F | H | I | PB |
| 130. | D | E | F | H | J | PB |
| 131. | D | E | F | H | K | PB |
| 132. | D | E | F | H | L | PB |
| 133. | D | E | F | H | M | PB |
| 134. | D | E | G | L | M | PB |
| 135. | D | E | I | J | L | PB |
| 136. | D | E | J | K | M | PB |
| 137. | D | F | G | I | L | PB |
| 138. | D | F | G | J | M | PB |
| 139. | D | F | I | K | M | PB |
| 140. | D | G | H | I | K | PB |
| 141. | D | G | J | K | L | PB |
| 142. | D | H | I | J | M | PB |
| 143. | D | H | K | L | M | PB |
| 144. | E | F | G | J | L | PB |
| 145. | E | F | G | K | L | PB |
| 146. | E | G | H | I | M | PB |
| 147. | E | G | H | J | K | PB |
| 148. | E | G | I | J | K | PB |
| 149. | E | H | J | L | M | PB |
| 150. | E | I | K | L | M | PB |
| 151. | F | G | H | L | M | PB |
| 152. | F | G | I | J | K | PB |
| 153. | F | H | I | K | L | PB |
| 154. | F | H | J | K | M | PB |
| 155. | F | I | J | L | M | PB |
| 156. | G | H | I | J | L | PB |
| 157. | G | I | J | K | M | PB |



# POWERBALL FULL WHEEL 55006PB

## Wheel 6 Numbers + PB in 6 Games for a 5 of 5 Win

With Powerball

| Numbers Matched | Maximum Wins | | | | | | Minimum Wins | | | | | |
|---|---|---|---|---|---|---|---|---|---|---|---|---|
| | 5 + 1 | 4 + 1 | 3 + 1 | 2 + 1 | 1 + 1 | 0 + 1 | 5 + 1 | 4 + 1 | 3 + 1 | 2 + 1 | 1 + 1 | 0 + 1 |
| 5 + 1 | 1 | 5 | 0 | 0 | 0 | 0 | 1 | 5 | 0 | 0 | 0 | 0 |
| 4 + 1 | - | 2 | 4 | 0 | 0 | 0 | - | 2 | 4 | 0 | 0 | 0 |
| 3 + 1 | - | - | 3 | 3 | 0 | 0 | - | - | 3 | 3 | 0 | 0 |
| 2 + 1 | - | - | - | 4 | 2 | 0 | - | - | - | 4 | 2 | 0 |
| 1 + 1 | - | - | - | - | 5 | 1 | - | - | - | - | 5 | 1 |
| 0 + 1 | - | - | - | - | - | 6 | - | - | - | - | - | 6 |

(Continued Next Page)

## POWERBALL FULL WHEEL 55006PB (Continued from previous page)

Without Powerball

| Numbers Matched | Maximum Wins 5 + 0 | 4 + 0 | 3 + 0 | 2 + 0 | 1 + 0 | Minimum Wins 5 + 0 | 4 + 0 | 3 + 0 | 2 + 0 | 1 + 0 |
|---|---|---|---|---|---|---|---|---|---|---|
| 5 + 0 | 1 | 5 | 0 | 0 | 0 | 1 | 5 | 0 | 0 | 0 |
| 4 + 0 | - | 2 | 4 | 0 | 0 | - | 2 | 4 | 0 | 0 |
| 3 + 0 | - | - | 3 | 3 | 0 | - | - | 3 | 3 | 0 |
| 2 + 0 | - | - | - | 4 | 2 | - | - | - | 4 | 2 |
| 1 + 0 | - | - | - | - | 5 | - | - | - | - | 5 |

### Your 6 Numbers + PB to Wheel

| A | B | C | D | E | F | PB |
|---|---|---|---|---|---|---|
| 23 5 | 14 5 | 30 5 | 41 5 | 11 5 | 51 5 | 20 6 |

### The 6 Games to Play

| | | | | | | |
|---|---|---|---|---|---|---|
| 1. | A 23 | B 14 | C 30 | D 41 | E 11 | PB 20 |
| 2. | A 23 | B 14 | C 30 | D 41 | F 51 | PB 20 |
| 3. | A 23 | B 14 | C 30 | E 11 | F 51 | PB 20 |
| 4. | A 23 | B 14 | D 41 | E 11 | F 51 | PB 20 |
| 5. | A 23 | C 30 | D 41 | E 11 | F 51 | PB 20 |
| 6. | B 14 | C 30 | D 41 | E 11 | F 51 | PB 20 |



# POWERBALL FULL WHEEL 55007PB

## Wheel 7 Numbers + PB in 21 Games for a 5 of 5 Win

With Powerball

| Numbers Matched | Maximum Wins 5 + 1 | 4 + 1 | 3 + 1 | 2 + 1 | 1 + 1 | 0 + 1 | Minimum Wins 5 + 1 | 4 + 1 | 3 + 1 | 2 + 1 | 1 + 1 | 0 + 1 |
|---|---|---|---|---|---|---|---|---|---|---|---|---|
| 5 + 1 | 1 | 10 | 10 | 0 | 0 | 0 | 1 | 10 | 10 | 0 | 0 | 0 |
| 4 + 1 | - | 3 | 12 | 6 | 0 | 0 | - | 3 | 12 | 6 | 0 | 0 |
| 3 + 1 | - | - | 6 | 12 | 3 | 0 | - | - | 6 | 12 | 3 | 0 |
| 2 + 1 | - | - | - | 10 | 10 | 1 | - | - | - | 10 | 10 | 1 |
| 1 + 1 | - | - | - | - | 15 | 6 | - | - | - | - | 15 | 6 |
| 0 + 1 | - | - | - | - | - | 21 | - | - | - | - | - | 21 |

Without Powerball

| Numbers Matched | Maximum Wins 5 + 0 | 4 + 0 | 3 + 0 | 2 + 0 | 1 + 0 | Minimum Wins 5 + 0 | 4 + 0 | 3 + 0 | 2 + 0 | 1 + 0 |
|---|---|---|---|---|---|---|---|---|---|---|
| 5 + 0 | 1 | 10 | 10 | 0 | 0 | 1 | 10 | 10 | 0 | 0 |
| 4 + 0 | - | 3 | 12 | 6 | 0 | - | 3 | 12 | 6 | 0 |
| 3 + 0 | - | - | 6 | 12 | 3 | - | - | 6 | 12 | 3 |
| 2 + 0 | - | - | - | 10 | 10 | - | - | - | 10 | 10 |
| 1 + 0 | - | - | - | - | 15 | - | - | - | - | 15 |

### Your 7 Numbers + PB to Wheel

| A | B | C | D | E | F | G | PB |
|---|---|---|---|---|---|---|---|
| 11 15 | 14 15 | 23 15 | 32 15 | 37 15 | 43 15 | 51 15 | 14 21 |

### The 21 Games to Play

| | | | | | | |
|---|---|---|---|---|---|---|
| 1. | A 11 | B | C | D | E | PB 14 |
| 2. | A 11 | B | C | D | F | PB |
| 3. | A 11 | B | C | D | G | PB |
| 4. | A 11 | B | C | E | F | PB |
| 5. | A 11 | B | C | E | G | PB 14 |
| 6. | A 11 | B | C | F | G | PB |
| 7. | A 11 | B | D | E | F | PB |
| 8. | A 11 | B | D | E | G | PB |
| 9. | A | B | D | F | G | PB |
| 10. | A | B | E | F | G | PB 14 |
| 11. | A | C | D | E | F | PB |
| 12. | A | C | D | E | G | PB |
| 13. | A | C | D | F | G | PB |
| 14. | A | C | E | F | G | PB 14 |



(Continued Next Page)

**POWERBALL FULL WHEEL 55007PB** (Continued from previous page)

| | | | | | | |
|---|---|---|---|---|---|---|
| 15. | A | D | E | F | G | PB |
| 16. | B | C | D | E | F | PB |
| 17. | B | C | D | E | G | PB |
| 18. | B | C | D | F | G | PB |
| 19. | B | C | E | F | G | PB |
| 20. | B | D | E | F | G | PB |
| 21. | C | D | E | F | G | PB |



# POWERBALL FULL WHEEL 55008PB

## Wheel 8 Numbers + PB in 56 Games for a 5 of 5 Win

With Powerball

| Numbers Matched | Maximum Wins | | | | | | Minimum Wins | | | | | |
|---|---|---|---|---|---|---|---|---|---|---|---|---|
| | 5 + 1 | 4 + 1 | 3 + 1 | 2 + 1 | 1 + 1 | 0 + 1 | 5 + 1 | 4 + 1 | 3 + 1 | 2 + 1 | 1 + 1 | 0 + 1 |
| 5 + 1 | 1 | 15 | 30 | 10 | 0 | 0 | 1 | 15 | 30 | 10 | 0 | 0 |
| 4 + 1 | - | 4 | 24 | 24 | 4 | 0 | - | 4 | 24 | 24 | 4 | 0 |
| 3 + 1 | - | - | 10 | 30 | 15 | 1 | - | - | 10 | 30 | 15 | 1 |
| 2 + 1 | - | - | - | 20 | 30 | 6 | - | - | - | 20 | 30 | 6 |
| 1 + 1 | - | - | - | - | 35 | 21 | - | - | - | - | 35 | 21 |
| 0 + 1 | - | - | - | - | - | 56 | - | - | - | - | - | 56 |

Without Powerball

| Numbers Matched | Maximum Wins | | | | | Minimum Wins | | | | |
|---|---|---|---|---|---|---|---|---|---|---|
| | 5 + 0 | 4 + 0 | 3 + 0 | 2 + 0 | 1 + 0 | 5 + 0 | 4 + 0 | 3 + 0 | 2 + 0 | 1 + 0 |
| 5 + 0 | 1 | 15 | 30 | 10 | 0 | 1 | 15 | 30 | 10 | 0 |
| 4 + 0 | - | 4 | 24 | 24 | 4 | - | 4 | 24 | 24 | 4 |
| 3 + 0 | - | - | 10 | 30 | 15 | - | - | 10 | 30 | 15 |
| 2 + 0 | - | - | - | 20 | 30 | - | - | - | 20 | 30 |
| 1 + 0 | - | - | - | - | 35 | - | - | - | - | 35 |

## Your 8 Numbers + PB to Wheel

| A | B | C | D | E | F | G | H | PB |
|---|---|---|---|---|---|---|---|---|
| 35 | 35 | 35 | 35 | 35 | 35 | 35 | 35 | 56 |

## The 56 Games to Play

| | | | | | | |
|---|---|---|---|---|---|---|
| 1. | A | B | C | D | E | PB |
| 2. | A | B | C | D | F | PB |
| 3. | A | B | C | D | G | PB |
| 4. | A | B | C | D | H | PB |
| 5. | A | B | C | E | F | PB |
| 6. | A | B | C | E | G | PB |
| 7. | A | B | C | E | H | PB |
| 8. | A | B | C | F | G | PB |
| 9. | A | B | C | F | H | PB |
| 10. | A | B | C | G | H | PB |
| 11. | A | B | D | E | F | PB |
| 12. | A | B | D | E | G | PB |
| 13. | A | B | D | E | H | PB |
| 14. | A | B | D | F | G | PB |
| 15. | A | B | D | F | H | PB |
| 16. | A | B | D | G | H | PB |
| 17. | A | B | E | F | G | PB |
| 18. | A | B | E | F | H | PB |
| 19. | A | B | E | G | H | PB |
| 20. | A | B | F | G | H | PB |
| 21. | A | C | D | E | F | PB |
| 22. | A | C | D | E | G | PB |
| 23. | A | C | D | E | H | PB |
| 24. | A | C | D | F | G | PB |
| 25. | A | C | D | F | H | PB |
| 26. | A | C | D | G | H | PB |
| 27. | A | C | E | F | G | PB |
| 28. | A | C | E | F | H | PB |



(Continued Next Page)

## POWERBALL FULL WHEEL 55008PB (Continued from previous page)

| | | | | | | |
|---|---|---|---|---|---|---|
| 29. | A | C | E | G | H | PB |
| 30. | A | C | F | G | H | PB |
| 31. | A | D | E | F | G | PB |
| 32. | A | D | E | F | H | PB |
| 33. | A | D | E | G | H | PB |
| 34. | A | D | F | G | H | PB |
| 35. | A | E | F | G | H | PB |
| 36. | B | C | D | E | F | PB |
| 37. | B | C | D | E | G | PB |
| 38. | B | C | D | E | H | PB |
| 39. | B | C | D | F | G | PB |
| 40. | B | C | D | F | H | PB |
| 41. | B | C | D | G | H | PB |
| 42. | B | C | E | F | G | PB |
| 43. | B | C | E | F | H | PB |
| 44. | B | C | E | G | H | PB |
| 45. | B | C | F | G | H | PB |
| 46. | B | D | E | F | G | PB |
| 47. | B | D | E | F | H | PB |
| 48. | B | D | E | G | H | PB |
| 49. | B | D | F | G | H | PB |
| 50. | B | E | F | G | H | PB |
| 51. | C | D | E | F | G | PB |
| 52. | C | D | E | F | H | PB |
| 53. | C | D | E | G | H | PB |
| 54. | C | D | F | G | H | PB |
| 55. | C | E | F | G | H | PB |
| 56. | D | E | F | G | H | PB |



# POWERBALL FULL WHEEL 55009PB

## Wheel 9 Numbers + PB in 126 Games for a 5 of 5 Win

With Powerball

| Numbers Matched | Maximum Wins | | | | | | Minimum Wins | | | | | |
|---|---|---|---|---|---|---|---|---|---|---|---|---|
| | 5 + 1 | 4 + 1 | 3 + 1 | 2 + 1 | 1 + 1 | 0 + 1 | 5 + 1 | 4 + 1 | 3 + 1 | 2 + 1 | 1 + 1 | 0 + 1 |
| 5 + 1 | 1 | 20 | 60 | 40 | 5 | 0 | 1 | 20 | 60 | 40 | 5 | 0 |
| 4 + 1 | - | 5 | 40 | 60 | 20 | 1 | - | 5 | 40 | 60 | 20 | 1 |
| 3 + 1 | - | - | 15 | 60 | 45 | 6 | - | - | 15 | 60 | 45 | 6 |
| 2 + 1 | - | - | - | 35 | 70 | 21 | - | - | - | 35 | 70 | 21 |
| 1 + 1 | - | - | - | - | 70 | 56 | - | - | - | - | 70 | 56 |
| 0 + 1 | - | - | - | - | - | 126 | - | - | - | - | - | 126 |

Without Powerball

| Numbers Matched | Maximum Wins | | | | | Minimum Wins | | | | |
|---|---|---|---|---|---|---|---|---|---|---|
| | 5 + 0 | 4 + 0 | 3 + 0 | 2 + 0 | 1 + 0 | 5 + 0 | 4 + 0 | 3 + 0 | 2 + 0 | 1 + 0 |
| 5 + 0 | 1 | 20 | 60 | 40 | 5 | 1 | 20 | 60 | 40 | 5 |
| 4 + 0 | - | 5 | 40 | 60 | 20 | - | 5 | 40 | 60 | 20 |
| 3 + 0 | - | - | 15 | 60 | 45 | - | - | 15 | 60 | 45 |
| 2 + 0 | - | - | - | 35 | 70 | - | - | - | 35 | 70 |
| 1 + 0 | - | - | - | - | 70 | - | - | - | - | 70 |

## Your 9 Numbers + PB to Wheel

| A | B | C | D | E | F | G | H | I | PB |
|---|---|---|---|---|---|---|---|---|---|
| 70 | 70 | 70 | 70 | 70 | 70 | 70 | 70 | 70 | 126 |

## The 126 Games to Play

| | | | | | | |
|---|---|---|---|---|---|---|
| 1. | A | B | C | D | E | PB |
| 2. | A | B | C | D | F | PB |
| 3. | A | B | C | D | G | PB |
| 4. | A | B | C | D | H | PB |
| 5. | A | B | C | D | I | PB |
| 6. | A | B | C | E | F | PB |
| 7. | A | B | C | E | G | PB |
| 8. | A | B | C | E | H | PB |



(Continued Next Page)

## POWERBALL FULL WHEEL 55009PB

(Continued from previous page)

| | | | | | | |
|---|---|---|---|---|---|---|
| 9. | A | B | C | E | I | PB |
| 10. | A | B | C | F | G | PB |
| 11. | A | B | C | F | H | PB |
| 12. | A | B | C | F | I | PB |
| 13. | A | B | C | G | H | PB |
| 14. | A | B | C | G | I | PB |
| 15. | A | B | C | H | I | PB |
| 16. | A | B | D | E | F | PB |
| 17. | A | B | D | E | G | PB |
| 18. | A | B | D | E | H | PB |
| 19. | A | B | D | E | I | PB |
| 20. | A | B | D | F | G | PB |
| 21. | A | B | D | F | H | PB |
| 22. | A | B | D | F | I | PB |
| 23. | A | B | D | G | H | PB |
| 24. | A | B | D | G | I | PB |
| 25. | A | B | D | H | I | PB |
| 26. | A | B | E | F | G | PB |
| 27. | A | B | E | F | H | PB |
| 28. | A | B | E | F | I | PB |
| 29. | A | B | E | G | H | PB |
| 30. | A | B | E | G | I | PB |
| 31. | A | B | E | H | I | PB |
| 32. | A | B | F | G | H | PB |
| 33. | A | B | F | G | I | PB |
| 34. | A | B | F | H | I | PB |
| 35. | A | B | G | H | I | PB |
| 36. | A | C | D | E | F | PB |
| 37. | A | C | D | E | G | PB |
| 38. | A | C | D | E | H | PB |
| 39. | A | C | D | E | I | PB |
| 40. | A | C | D | F | G | PB |
| 41. | A | C | D | F | H | PB |
| 42. | A | C | D | F | I | PB |
| 43. | A | C | D | G | H | PB |
| 44. | A | C | D | G | I | PB |
| 45. | A | C | D | H | I | PB |
| 46. | A | C | E | F | G | PB |
| 47. | A | C | E | F | H | PB |
| 48. | A | C | E | F | I | PB |
| 49. | A | C | E | G | H | PB |
| 50. | A | C | E | G | I | PB |
| 51. | A | C | E | H | I | PB |
| 52. | A | C | F | G | H | PB |
| 53. | A | C | F | G | I | PB |
| 54. | A | C | F | H | I | PB |
| 55. | A | C | G | H | I | PB |
| 56. | A | D | E | F | G | PB |
| 57. | A | D | E | F | H | PB |
| 58. | A | D | E | F | I | PB |
| 59. | A | D | E | G | H | PB |
| 60. | A | D | E | G | I | PB |
| 61. | A | D | E | H | I | PB |
| 62. | A | D | F | G | H | PB |
| 63. | A | D | F | G | I | PB |
| 64. | A | D | F | H | I | PB |
| 65. | A | D | G | H | I | PB |
| 66. | A | E | F | G | H | PB |
| 67. | A | E | F | G | I | PB |
| 68. | A | E | F | H | I | PB |
| 69. | A | E | G | H | I | PB |
| 70. | A | F | G | H | I | PB |
| 71. | B | C | D | E | F | PB |
| 72. | B | C | D | E | G | PB |
| 73. | B | C | D | E | H | PB |
| 74. | B | C | D | E | I | PB |
| 75. | B | C | D | F | G | PB |
| 76. | B | C | D | F | H | PB |
| 77. | B | C | D | F | I | PB |
| 78. | B | C | D | G | H | PB |



(Continued Next Page)

## POWERBALL FULL WHEEL 55009PB (Continued from previous page)

| | | | | | | |
|---|---|---|---|---|---|---|
| 79. | B | C | D | G | I | PB |
| 80. | B | C | D | H | I | PB |
| 81. | B | C | E | F | G | PB |
| 82. | B | C | E | F | H | PB |
| 83. | B | C | E | F | I | PB |
| 84. | B | C | E | G | H | PB |
| 85. | B | C | E | G | I | PB |
| 86. | B | C | E | H | I | PB |
| 87. | B | C | F | G | H | PB |
| 88. | B | C | F | G | I | PB |
| 89. | B | C | F | H | I | PB |
| 90. | B | C | G | H | I | PB |
| 91. | B | D | E | F | G | PB |
| 92. | B | D | E | F | H | PB |
| 93. | B | D | E | F | I | PB |
| 94. | B | D | E | G | H | PB |
| 95. | B | D | E | G | I | PB |
| 96. | B | D | E | H | I | PB |
| 97. | B | D | F | G | H | PB |
| 98. | B | D | F | G | I | PB |
| 99. | B | D | F | H | I | PB |
| 100. | B | D | G | H | I | PB |
| 101. | B | E | F | G | H | PB |
| 102. | B | E | F | G | I | PB |
| 103. | B | E | F | H | I | PB |
| 104. | B | E | G | H | I | PB |
| 105. | B | F | G | H | I | PB |
| 106. | C | D | E | F | G | PB |
| 107. | C | D | E | F | H | PB |
| 108. | C | D | E | F | I | PB |
| 109. | C | D | E | G | H | PB |
| 110. | C | D | E | G | I | PB |
| 111. | C | D | E | H | I | PB |
| 112. | C | D | F | G | H | PB |
| 113. | C | D | F | G | I | PB |
| 114. | C | D | F | H | I | PB |
| 115. | C | D | G | H | I | PB |
| 116. | C | E | F | G | H | PB |
| 117. | C | E | F | G | I | PB |
| 118. | C | E | F | H | I | PB |
| 119. | C | E | G | H | I | PB |
| 120. | C | F | G | H | I | PB |
| 121. | D | E | F | G | H | PB |
| 122. | D | E | F | G | I | PB |
| 123. | D | E | F | H | I | PB |
| 124. | D | E | G | H | I | PB |
| 125. | D | F | G | H | I | PB |
| 126. | E | F | G | H | I | PB |

# INSTANT WHEEL INDEX

( Combinations Required)

| ## | 2/5 | 2/4 | 2/3 | 2/2 | 3/5 | 3/4 | 3/3 | 4/5 | 4/4 | 5/5 | ## |
|---|---|---|---|---|---|---|---|---|---|---|---|
| 6 | – | – | – | – | – | – | 4 | – | 5 | 6 | 6 |
| 7 | – | – | – | 3 | – | – | 5 | 3 | 9 | 21 | 7 |
| 8 | – | – | – | 4 | – | – | 8 | 5 | 20 | 26 | 8 |
| 9 | – | – | – | 5 | – | 5 | 12 | 9 | 30 | 126 | 9 |
| 10 | – | – | – | 6 | 2 | 7 | 17 | 14 | 51 | – | 10 |
| 11 | – | – | – | 7 | 5 | 10 | 20 | 26 | 66 | – | 11 |
| 12 | – | – | 4 | 9 | 6 | 12 | 29 | 37 | 113 | – | 12 |
| 13 | – | – | 5 | 10 | 9 | 18 | 34 | 58 | 157 | – | 13 |
| 14 | – | – | 6 | 12 | 10 | 23 | 43 | 76 | – | – | 14 |
| 15 | – | 3 | 7 | 13 | 13 | 28 | 57 | 118 | – | – | 15 |
| 16 | – | 5 | 8 | 15 | 16 | 37 | 65 | 159 | – | – | 16 |
| 17 | – | 5 | 9 | 16 | 20 | 46 | 68 | – | – | – | 17 |
| 18 | – | 6 | 10 | 19 | 24 | 56 | 94 | – | – | – | 18 |
| 19 | – | 7 | 11 | 20 | 28 | 66 | 108 | – | – | – | 19 |
| 20 | 4 | 8 | 12 | 21 | 32 | 76 | – | – | – | – | 20 |
| 21 | 6 | 9 | 13 | 27 | 37 | 84 | – | – | – | – | 21 |
| 22 | 6 | 10 | 14 | – | 40 | 98 | – | – | – | – | 22 |
| 23 | 7 | 11 | 16 | 28 | – | 114 | – | – | – | – | 23 |
| 24 | 8 | 12 | 17 | 32 | 54 | 129 | – | – | – | – | 24 |
| 25 | 9 | 13 | 19 | 36 | 63 | – | – | – | – | – | 25 |
| 26 | 10 | 14 | 20 | 39 | 68 | – | – | – | – | – | 26 |
| 27 | 11 | 15 | 21 | 42 | 77 | – | – | – | – | – | 27 |
| 28 | 12 | 16 | 23 | 45 | 86 | – | – | – | – | – | 28 |
| 29 | 13 | – | 25 | 48 | – | – | – | – | – | – | 29 |
| 30 | 14 | 18 | 26 | 51 | 102 | – | – | – | – | – | 30 |
| 31 | 15 | 19 | 27 | 55 | 111 | – | – | – | – | – | 31 |
| 32 | 16 | 20 | 28 | 58 | 125 | – | – | – | – | – | 32 |
| 33 | – | – | – | 62 | – | – | – | – | – | – | 33 |
| 34 | 18 | 23 | 31 | 37 | 136 | – | – | – | – | – | 34 |
| 35 | – | – | – | 71 | – | – | – | – | – | – | 35 |
| 36 | 20 | 26 | 34 | 75 | 176 | – | – | – | – | – | 36 |
| 37 | – | – | – | 78 | – | – | – | – | – | – | 37 |
| 38 | – | – | – | 83 | – | – | – | – | – | – | 38 |
| 39 | 23 | 30 | 40 | 88 | 241 | – | – | – | – | – | 39 |
| 40 | – | – | – | 92 | – | – | – | – | – | – | 40 |
| 42 | 26 | 34 | 42 | 102 | – | – | – | – | – | – | 42 |
| 45 | 30 | 38 | 53 | 116 | 359 | – | – | – | – | – | 45 |
| 47 | 33 | 41 | 60 | 126 | – | – | – | – | – | – | 47 |
| 55 | 45 | 52 | 86 | 172 | – | – | – | – | – | – | 55 |
| 56 | 48 | 54 | 91 | 178 | – | – | – | – | – | – | 56 |

## INSTANT WHEEL FINDER™

( Page Numbers )

| ## | 2/5 | 2/4 | 2/3 | 2/2 | 3/5 | 3/4 | 3/3 | 4/5 | 4/4 | 5/5 | ## |
|---|---|---|---|---|---|---|---|---|---|---|---|
| 6 | – | – | – | – | – | – | 226 | – | 257 | 267 | 6 |
| 7 | – | – | – | 115 | – | – | 226 | 244 | 257 | 268 | 7 |
| 8 | – | – | – | 115 | – | – | 227 | 245 | 258 | 269 | 8 |
| 9 | – | – | – | 116 | – | 207 | 228 | 245 | 259 | 270 | 9 |
| 10 | – | – | – | 117 | 167 | 208 | 228 | 246 | 260 | – | 10 |
| 11 | – | – | – | 117 | 167 | 208 | 229 | 247 | 261 | – | 11 |
| 12 | – | – | 85 | 118 | 168 | 209 | 230 | 248 | 262 | – | 12 |
| 13 | – | – | 86 | 119 | 169 | 210 | 231 | 249 | 265 | – | 13 |
| 14 | – | – | 87 | 119 | 169 | 211 | 232 | 250 | – | – | 14 |
| 15 | – | 62 | 87 | 120 | 170 | 212 | 233 | 252 | – | – | 15 |
| 16 | – | 63 | 88 | 121 | 171 | 213 | 234 | 254 | – | – | 16 |
| 17 | – | 63 | 89 | 122 | 172 | 214 | 236 | – | – | – | 17 |
| 18 | – | 64 | 89 | 122 | 173 | 215 | 237 | – | – | – | 18 |
| 19 | – | 65 | 90 | 123 | 174 | 216 | 239 | – | – | – | 19 |
| 20 | 43 | 65 | 91 | 124 | 175 | 218 | 242 | – | – | – | 20 |
| 21 | 43 | 66 | 92 | – | 176 | 219 | – | – | – | – | 21 |
| 22 | 44 | 67 | 92 | 125 | 177 | 221 | – | – | – | – | 22 |
| 23 | 45 | 67 | 93 | 126 | – | – | – | – | – | – | 23 |
| 24 | 45 | 68 | 94 | 127 | 178 | 223 | – | – | – | – | 24 |
| 25 | 46 | 69 | 95 | 128 | 179 | – | – | – | – | – | 25 |
| 26 | 47 | 70 | 96 | 129 | – | – | – | – | – | – | 26 |
| 27 | 48 | 71 | 97 | 131 | 181 | – | – | – | – | – | 27 |
| 28 | 49 | 71 | 98 | 132 | 183 | – | – | – | – | – | 28 |
| 29 | 49 | – | 99 | 133 | – | – | – | – | – | – | 29 |
| 30 | 50 | 72 | 100 | 134 | 184 | – | – | – | – | – | 30 |
| 31 | 51 | 73 | 101 | 136 | 187 | – | – | – | – | – | 31 |
| 32 | 52 | 74 | 102 | 137 | 189 | – | – | – | – | – | 32 |
| 33 | – | – | – | 139 | – | – | – | – | – | – | 33 |
| 34 | 53 | 75 | 103 | 140 | 191 | – | – | – | – | – | 34 |
| 35 | – | – | – | 142 | – | – | – | – | – | – | 35 |
| 36 | 54 | 76 | 104 | 144 | 194 | – | – | – | – | – | 36 |
| 37 | – | – | – | 145 | – | – | – | – | – | – | 37 |
| 38 | – | – | – | 147 | – | – | – | – | – | – | 38 |
| 39 | 55 | 77 | 105 | 149 | 197 | – | – | – | – | – | 39 |
| 40 | – | – | – | 151 | – | – | – | – | – | – | 40 |
| 42 | 56 | 79 | 106 | 153 | – | – | – | – | – | – | 42 |
| 45 | 57 | 80 | 108 | 155 | 201 | – | – | – | – | – | 45 |
| 47 | 58 | 81 | 109 | 125 | – | – | – | – | – | – | 47 |
| 55 | 59 | 82 | 111 | 160 | – | | | | | | 55 |
| 56 | 60 | 84 | 113 | 164 | – | – | – | – | – | – | 56 |

# Budget Wheel Finder® by COST

| Cost | ##'s | Win | Page |
|---|---|---|---|
| 2 | 10 | 3/5 | 167 |
| 3 | 7 | 2/2 | 115 |
| 3 | 7 | 4/5 | 244 |
| 3 | 15 | 2/4 | 62 |
| 4 | 6 | 3/3 | 226 |
| 4 | 8 | 2/2 | 115 |
| 4 | 12 | 2/3 | 85 |
| 4 | 20 | 2/5 | 43 |
| 5 | 6 | 4/4 | 257 |
| 5 | 7 | 3/3 | 226 |
| 5 | 8 | 4/5 | 245 |
| 5 | 9 | 2/2 | 116 |
| 5 | 9 | 3/4 | 207 |
| 5 | 11 | 3/5 | 167 |
| 5 | 13 | 2/3 | 86 |
| 5 | 16 | 2/4 | 63 |
| 5 | 17 | 2/4 | 63 |
| 6 | 6 | 5/5 | 267 |
| 6 | 10 | 2/2 | 117 |
| 6 | 12 | 3/5 | 168 |
| 6 | 14 | 2/3 | 87 |
| 6 | 18 | 2/4 | 64 |
| 6 | 21 | 2/5 | 43 |
| 6 | 22 | 2/5 | 44 |
| 7 | 10 | 3/4 | 208 |
| 7 | 11 | 2/2 | 117 |
| 7 | 15 | 2/3 | 87 |
| 7 | 19 | 2/4 | 65 |
| 7 | 23 | 2/5 | 45 |
| 8 | 8 | 3/3 | 227 |
| 8 | 16 | 2/3 | 88 |
| 8 | 20 | 2/4 | 65 |
| 8 | 24 | 2/5 | 45 |
| 9 | 7 | 4/4 | 257 |
| 9 | 9 | 4/5 | 245 |
| 9 | 12 | 2/2 | 118 |
| 9 | 13 | 3/5 | 169 |
| 9 | 17 | 2/3 | 89 |
| 9 | 21 | 2/4 | 66 |
| 9 | 25 | 2/5 | 46 |
| 10 | 11 | 3/4 | 208 |
| 10 | 13 | 2/2 | 119 |
| 10 | 14 | 3/5 | 169 |
| 10 | 18 | 2/3 | 89 |
| 10 | 22 | 2/4 | 67 |
| 10 | 26 | 2/5 | 47 |
| 11 | 19 | 2/3 | 90 |
| 11 | 23 | 2/4 | 67 |
| 11 | 27 | 2/5 | 48 |
| 12 | 9 | 3/3 | 228 |
| 12 | 12 | 3/4 | 209 |
| 12 | 14 | 2/2 | 119 |
| 12 | 20 | 2/3 | 91 |
| 12 | 24 | 2/4 | 68 |
| 12 | 28 | 2/5 | 49 |
| 13 | 15 | 2/2 | 120 |
| 13 | 15 | 3/5 | 170 |
| 13 | 21 | 2/3 | 92 |
| 13 | 25 | 2/4 | 69 |
| 13 | 29 | 2/5 | 49 |
| 14 | 10 | 4/5 | 246 |
| 14 | 22 | 2/3 | 92 |
| 14 | 26 | 2/4 | 70 |
| 14 | 30 | 2/5 | 50 |
| 15 | 16 | 2/2 | 121 |
| 15 | 27 | 2/4 | 71 |
| 15 | 31 | 2/5 | 51 |
| 16 | 16 | 3/5 | 171 |
| 16 | 17 | 2/2 | 122 |
| 16 | 23 | 2/3 | 93 |
| 16 | 28 | 2/4 | 71 |
| 16 | 32 | 2/5 | 52 |
| 17 | 10 | 3/3 | 228 |
| 17 | 24 | 2/3 | 94 |
| 18 | 13 | 3/4 | 210 |
| 18 | 30 | 2/4 | 72 |
| 18 | 34 | 2/5 | 53 |
| 19 | 18 | 2/2 | 122 |
| 19 | 25 | 2/3 | 95 |
| 19 | 31 | 2/4 | 73 |
| 20 | 8 | 4/4 | 258 |
| 20 | 11 | 3/3 | 229 |
| 20 | 17 | 3/5 | 172 |
| 20 | 19 | 2/2 | 123 |
| 20 | 26 | 2/3 | 96 |
| 20 | 32 | 2/4 | 74 |
| 20 | 36 | 2/5 | 54 |
| 21 | 7 | 5/5 | 268 |
| 21 | 20 | 2/2 | 124 |
| 21 | 27 | 2/3 | 97 |
| 23 | 14 | 3/4 | 211 |
| 23 | 28 | 2/3 | 98 |
| 23 | 34 | 2/4 | 75 |
| 23 | 39 | 2/5 | 55 |
| 24 | 18 | 3/5 | 173 |
| 25 | 29 | 2/3 | 99 |
| 26 | 11 | 4/5 | 247 |
| 26 | 30 | 2/3 | 100 |
| 26 | 36 | 2/4 | 76 |
| 26 | 42 | 2/5 | 56 |
| 27 | 22 | 2/2 | 125 |
| 27 | 31 | 2/3 | 101 |
| 28 | 15 | 3/4 | 212 |
| 28 | 19 | 3/5 | 174 |
| 28 | 23 | 2/2 | 126 |



(Continued Next Page)

# Budget Wheel Finder® by COST

(continued)

| Cost | ##'s | Win | Page |
|---|---|---|---|
| 28 | 32 | 2/3 | 102 |
| 29 | 12 | 3/3 | 230 |
| 30 | 9 | 4/4 | 259 |
| 30 | 39 | 2/4 | 77 |
| 30 | 45 | 2/5 | 57 |
| 31 | 34 | 2/3 | 103 |
| 32 | 20 | 3/5 | 175 |
| 32 | 24 | 2/2 | 127 |
| 33 | 47 | 2/5 | 58 |
| 34 | 13 | 3/3 | 231 |
| 34 | 36 | 2/3 | 104 |
| 34 | 42 | 2/4 | 79 |
| 36 | 25 | 2/2 | 128 |
| 37 | 12 | 4/5 | 248 |
| 37 | 16 | 3/4 | 213 |
| 37 | 21 | 3/5 | 176 |
| 38 | 45 | 2/4 | 80 |
| 39 | 26 | 2/2 | 129 |
| 40 | 22 | 3/5 | 177 |
| 40 | 39 | 2/3 | 105 |
| 41 | 47 | 2/4 | 81 |
| 42 | 27 | 2/2 | 131 |
| 42 | 42 | 2/3 | 106 |
| 43 | 14 | 3/3 | 232 |
| 45 | 28 | 2/2 | 132 |
| 45 | 55 | 2/5 | 59 |
| 46 | 17 | 3/4 | 214 |
| 48 | 29 | 2/2 | 133 |
| 48 | 56 | 2/5 | 60 |
| 51 | 10 | 4/4 | 260 |
| 51 | 30 | 2/2 | 134 |
| 52 | 55 | 2/4 | 82 |

| Cost | ##'s | Win | Page |
|---|---|---|---|
| 53 | 45 | 2/3 | 108 |
| 54 | 24 | 3/5 | 178 |
| 54 | 56 | 2/4 | 84 |
| 55 | 31 | 2/2 | 136 |
| 56 | 8 | 5/5 | 269 |
| 56 | 18 | 3/4 | 215 |
| 57 | 15 | 3/3 | 233 |
| 58 | 13 | 4/5 | 249 |
| 58 | 32 | 2/2 | 137 |
| 60 | 47 | 2/3 | 109 |
| 62 | 33 | 2/2 | 139 |
| 63 | 25 | 3/5 | 179 |
| 65 | 16 | 3/3 | 234 |
| 66 | 11 | 4/4 | 261 |
| 66 | 19 | 3/4 | 216 |
| 67 | 34 | 2/2 | 140 |
| 68 | 17 | 3/3 | 236 |
| 71 | 35 | 2/2 | 142 |
| 75 | 36 | 2/2 | 144 |
| 76 | 14 | 4/5 | 250 |
| 76 | 20 | 3/4 | 218 |
| 77 | 27 | 3/5 | 181 |
| 78 | 37 | 2/2 | 145 |
| 83 | 38 | 2/2 | 147 |
| 84 | 21 | 3/4 | 219 |
| 86 | 28 | 3/5 | 183 |
| 86 | 55 | 2/3 | 111 |
| 88 | 39 | 2/2 | 149 |
| 91 | 56 | 2/3 | 113 |
| 92 | 40 | 2/2 | 151 |
| 94 | 18 | 3/3 | 237 |
| 98 | 22 | 3/4 | 221 |

| Cost | ##'s | Win | Page |
|---|---|---|---|
| 102 | 30 | 3/5 | 184 |
| 102 | 42 | 2/2 | 153 |
| 108 | 19 | 3/3 | 239 |
| 111 | 31 | 3/5 | 187 |
| 113 | 12 | 4/4 | 262 |
| 116 | 45 | 2/2 | 155 |
| 118 | 15 | 4/5 | 252 |
| 125 | 32 | 3/5 | 189 |
| 126 | 9 | 5/5 | 270 |
| 126 | 47 | 2/2 | 158 |
| 129 | 24 | 3/4 | 223 |
| 133 | 20 | 3/3 | 242 |
| 136 | 34 | 3/5 | 191 |
| 157 | 13 | 4/4 | 265 |
| 159 | 16 | 4/5 | 254 |
| 172 | 55 | 2/2 | 160 |
| 176 | 36 | 3/5 | 194 |
| 178 | 56 | 2/2 | 164 |
| 241 | 39 | 3/5 | 197 |
| 359 | 45 | 3/5 | 201 |

# Budget Wheel Finder® by NUMBERS to Wheel

| ##'s | Cost | Win | Page |
|---|---|---|---|
| 6 | 4 | 3/3 | 226 |
| 6 | 5 | 4/4 | 257 |
| 6 | 6 | 5/5 | 267 |
| 7 | 3 | 2/2 | 115 |
| 7 | 3 | 4/5 | 244 |
| 7 | 5 | 3/3 | 226 |
| 7 | 9 | 4/4 | 257 |
| 7 | 21 | 5/5 | 268 |
| 8 | 4 | 2/2 | 115 |
| 8 | 5 | 4/5 | 245 |
| 8 | 8 | 3/3 | 227 |
| 8 | 20 | 4/4 | 258 |
| 8 | 56 | 5/5 | 269 |
| 9 | 5 | 2/2 | 116 |
| 9 | 5 | 3/4 | 207 |
| 9 | 9 | 4/5 | 245 |
| 9 | 12 | 3/3 | 228 |
| 9 | 30 | 4/4 | 259 |
| 9 | 126 | 5/5 | 270 |
| 10 | 2 | 3/5 | 167 |
| 10 | 6 | 2/2 | 117 |
| 10 | 7 | 3/4 | 208 |
| 10 | 14 | 4/5 | 246 |
| 10 | 17 | 3/3 | 228 |
| 10 | 51 | 4/4 | 260 |
| 11 | 5 | 3/5 | 167 |
| 11 | 7 | 2/2 | 117 |
| 11 | 10 | 3/4 | 208 |
| 11 | 20 | 3/3 | 229 |
| 11 | 26 | 4/5 | 247 |
| 11 | 66 | 4/4 | 261 |
| 12 | 4 | 2/3 | 85 |
| 12 | 6 | 3/5 | 168 |

| ##'s | Cost | Win | Page |
|---|---|---|---|
| 12 | 9 | 2/2 | 118 |
| 12 | 12 | 3/4 | 209 |
| 12 | 29 | 3/3 | 230 |
| 12 | 37 | 4/5 | 248 |
| 12 | 113 | 4/4 | 262 |
| 13 | 5 | 2/3 | 86 |
| 13 | 9 | 3/5 | 169 |
| 13 | 10 | 2/2 | 119 |
| 13 | 18 | 3/4 | 210 |
| 13 | 34 | 3/3 | 231 |
| 13 | 58 | 4/5 | 249 |
| 13 | 157 | 4/4 | 265 |
| 14 | 6 | 2/3 | 87 |
| 14 | 10 | 3/5 | 169 |
| 14 | 12 | 2/2 | 119 |
| 14 | 23 | 3/4 | 211 |
| 14 | 43 | 3/3 | 232 |
| 14 | 76 | 4/5 | 250 |
| 15 | 3 | 2/4 | 62 |
| 15 | 7 | 2/3 | 87 |
| 15 | 13 | 2/2 | 120 |
| 15 | 13 | 3/5 | 170 |
| 15 | 28 | 3/4 | 212 |
| 15 | 57 | 3/3 | 233 |
| 15 | 118 | 4/5 | 252 |
| 16 | 5 | 2/4 | 63 |
| 16 | 8 | 2/3 | 88 |
| 16 | 15 | 2/2 | 121 |
| 16 | 16 | 3/5 | 171 |
| 16 | 37 | 3/4 | 213 |
| 16 | 65 | 3/3 | 234 |
| 16 | 159 | 4/5 | 254 |
| 17 | 5 | 2/4 | 63 |

| ##'s | Cost | Win | Page |
|---|---|---|---|
| 17 | 9 | 2/3 | 89 |
| 17 | 16 | 2/2 | 122 |
| 17 | 20 | 3/5 | 172 |
| 17 | 46 | 3/4 | 214 |
| 17 | 68 | 3/3 | 236 |
| 18 | 6 | 2/4 | 64 |
| 18 | 10 | 2/3 | 89 |
| 18 | 19 | 2/2 | 122 |
| 18 | 24 | 3/5 | 173 |
| 18 | 56 | 3/4 | 215 |
| 18 | 94 | 3/3 | 237 |
| 19 | 7 | 2/4 | 65 |
| 19 | 11 | 2/3 | 90 |
| 19 | 20 | 2/2 | 123 |
| 19 | 28 | 3/5 | 174 |
| 19 | 66 | 3/4 | 216 |
| 19 | 108 | 3/3 | 239 |
| 20 | 4 | 2/5 | 43 |
| 20 | 8 | 2/4 | 65 |
| 20 | 12 | 2/3 | 91 |
| 20 | 21 | 2/2 | 124 |
| 20 | 32 | 3/5 | 175 |
| 20 | 76 | 3/4 | 218 |
| 20 | 133 | 3/3 | 242 |
| 21 | 6 | 2/5 | 43 |
| 21 | 9 | 2/4 | 66 |
| 21 | 13 | 2/3 | 92 |
| 21 | 37 | 3/5 | 176 |
| 21 | 84 | 3/4 | 219 |
| 22 | 6 | 2/5 | 44 |
| 22 | 10 | 2/4 | 67 |
| 22 | 14 | 2/3 | 92 |
| 22 | 27 | 2/2 | 125 |

# Budget Wheel Finder® by NUMBERS to Wheel

(Continued)

| ##'s | Cost | Win | Page |
|---|---|---|---|
| 22 | 40 | 3/5 | 177 |
| 22 | 98 | 3/4 | 221 |
| 23 | 7 | 2/5 | 45 |
| 23 | 11 | 2/4 | 67 |
| 23 | 16 | 2/3 | 93 |
| 23 | 28 | 2/2 | 126 |
| 24 | 8 | 2/5 | 45 |
| 24 | 12 | 2/4 | 68 |
| 24 | 17 | 2/3 | 94 |
| 24 | 32 | 2/2 | 127 |
| 24 | 54 | 3/5 | 178 |
| 24 | 129 | 3/4 | 223 |
| 25 | 9 | 2/5 | 46 |
| 25 | 13 | 2/4 | 69 |
| 25 | 19 | 2/3 | 95 |
| 25 | 36 | 2/2 | 128 |
| 25 | 63 | 3/5 | 179 |
| 26 | 10 | 2/5 | 47 |
| 26 | 14 | 2/4 | 70 |
| 26 | 20 | 2/3 | 96 |
| 26 | 39 | 2/2 | 129 |
| 27 | 11 | 2/5 | 48 |
| 27 | 15 | 2/4 | 71 |
| 27 | 21 | 2/3 | 97 |
| 27 | 42 | 2/2 | 131 |
| 27 | 77 | 3/5 | 181 |
| 28 | 12 | 2/5 | 49 |
| 28 | 16 | 2/4 | 71 |
| 28 | 23 | 2/3 | 98 |
| 28 | 45 | 2/2 | 132 |
| 28 | 86 | 3/5 | 183 |
| 29 | 13 | 2/5 | 49 |

| ##'s | Cost | Win | Page |
|---|---|---|---|
| 29 | 25 | 2/3 | 99 |
| 29 | 48 | 2/2 | 133 |
| 30 | 14 | 2/5 | 50 |
| 30 | 18 | 2/4 | 72 |
| 30 | 26 | 2/3 | 100 |
| 30 | 51 | 2/2 | 134 |
| 30 | 102 | 3/5 | 184 |
| 31 | 15 | 2/5 | 51 |
| 31 | 19 | 2/4 | 73 |
| 31 | 27 | 2/3 | 101 |
| 31 | 55 | 2/2 | 136 |
| 31 | 111 | 3/5 | 187 |
| 32 | 16 | 2/5 | 52 |
| 32 | 20 | 2/4 | 74 |
| 32 | 28 | 2/3 | 102 |
| 32 | 58 | 2/2 | 137 |
| 32 | 125 | 3/5 | 189 |
| 33 | 62 | 2/2 | 139 |
| 34 | 18 | 2/5 | 53 |
| 34 | 23 | 2/4 | 75 |
| 34 | 31 | 2/3 | 103 |
| 34 | 67 | 2/2 | 140 |
| 34 | 136 | 3/5 | 191 |
| 35 | 71 | 2/2 | 142 |
| 36 | 20 | 2/5 | 54 |
| 36 | 26 | 2/4 | 76 |
| 36 | 34 | 2/3 | 104 |
| 36 | 75 | 2/2 | 144 |
| 36 | 176 | 3/5 | 194 |
| 37 | 78 | 2/2 | 145 |
| 38 | 83 | 2/2 | 147 |
| 39 | 23 | 2/5 | 55 |

| ##'s | Cost | Win | Page |
|---|---|---|---|
| 39 | 30 | 2/4 | 77 |
| 39 | 40 | 2/3 | 105 |
| 39 | 88 | 2/2 | 149 |
| 39 | 241 | 3/5 | 197 |
| 40 | 92 | 2/2 | 151 |
| 42 | 26 | 2/5 | 56 |
| 42 | 34 | 2/4 | 79 |
| 42 | 42 | 2/3 | 106 |
| 42 | 102 | 2/2 | 153 |
| 45 | 30 | 2/5 | 57 |
| 45 | 38 | 2/4 | 80 |
| 45 | 53 | 2/3 | 108 |
| 45 | 116 | 2/2 | 155 |
| 45 | 359 | 3/5 | 201 |
| 47 | 33 | 2/5 | 58 |
| 47 | 41 | 2/4 | 81 |
| 47 | 60 | 2/3 | 109 |
| 47 | 126 | 2/2 | 158 |
| 55 | 45 | 2/5 | 59 |
| 55 | 52 | 2/4 | 82 |
| 55 | 86 | 2/3 | 111 |
| 55 | 172 | 2/2 | 160 |
| 56 | 48 | 2/5 | 60 |
| 56 | 54 | 2/4 | 84 |
| 56 | 91 | 2/3 | 113 |
| 56 | 178 | 2/2 | 164 |

# Gail Howard's Smart Luck® Order Form
# Lottery Books

- ❑ **LOTTERY MASTER GUIDE** . . . . . . . . . . . . . . . . . . $24.50+Shipping
  Number selection strategies - #1 best selling lottery book
- ❑ **LOTTO HOW TO WHEEL A FORTUNE** . . . . . . . . $19.50+Shipping
  Systems for all pick-6 lotto games
- ❑ **LOTTO WHEEL FIVE TO WIN** . . . . . . . . . . . . . . . . $19.95+Shipping
  Systems for all pick-5 games
- ❑ **LOTTO WINNING WHEELS FOR POWERBALL & MEGA MILLIONS** . . . . . . . . . . $14.95+Shipping

**ALL ORDERS MUST INCLUDE CORRECT SHIPPING:**

Shipping cost for one book: ❑ **$5** within U.S.A., ❑ **$7.50** to Canada, ❑ **$10** to countries that have Global Priority Mail ❑ **$20** to all other countries. Shipping cost for EACH ADDITIONAL book: Within the USA add **$3** each; to Canada add **$4** each; countries with Global Priority Mail add **$5** each; all other countries add **$10** for each additional book.

# Lottery Advantage® Charts

❑ **LOTTERY ADVANTAGE® Charts** cost **$15.00 each set** plus Shipping. Printed set of charts helps pick the best numbers for any specific lotto game of your choice. Tell us both the **Number Field** (such as 6/49) and the **state or country** and **name of the game**. (Example: Florida Lotto, Number Field: 6/53)

Game: ______________________________ Number Field ________

Game: ______________________________ Number Field ________

Game: ______________________________ Number Field ________

An order with one, two or three sets of Lottery Advantage Charts costs the same as shipping one book (see shipping rates above).

**$ ________.___ TOTAL $ ENCLOSED** (ONLY U.S.$ accepted.)

Make Checks or money orders payable to: **SMART LUCK PUBLISHERS**

CREDIT CARD Orders Call: **1-800-692-4245** or **1-850-937-6999**
Or visit us at: **www.smartluck.com**

**SMART LUCK Publishers**
**Dept. B-55, P.O. Box 81770**
**Las Vegas, Nevada 89180-1770 USA**

| | | |
|---|---|---|
| Name: | | |
| Address: | | |
| City: | State: | Zip: |
| Phone: ( ) | | |
| Credit Card #: | | Exp Date: |
| Signature: | | |